Personal Lines Underwriting

Personal Lines Underwriting

G. WILLIAM GLENDENNING, Ph.D., CPCU
Chairperson and Professor
Department of Insurance and Risk
Temple University

ROBERT B. HOLTOM, LL.B., CPCU, AIU
Assistant Vice President
Farmers Insurance Group

Second Edition • 1982

INSURANCE INSTITUTE OF AMERICA
Providence and Sugartown Roads, Malvern, Pennsylvania 19355

Second Printing • June 1988

Library of Congress Catalog Number 77-81989
International Standard Book Number 0-89462-003-7

Printed in the United States of America

Preface

This is the second in a series of four books written specifically for the Insurance Institute of America Associate in Underwriting Program. The first text, *Principles of Property and Liability Underwriting,* for UND 61, describes the principles of underwriting that are common to all property and liability lines. This book, for UND 62, applies those principles to personal lines underwriting. The remaining two books in the series do the same for commercial lines underwriting.

All of these books assume a basic knowledge of the principles and coverages of property and liability insurance. *Personal Lines Underwriting* also assumes a familiarity with the decision-making process and other principles explained in the UND 61 text.

One difficulty in preparing a text on personal lines underwriting is the tremendous differences among the philosophies and procedures followed by various companies. We have attempted to avoid extremes, concentrating on the practices that seem to be generally used. No one company's practices are emphasized, but most companies will find here the basics of their underwriting approaches.

Our aim has been to supply the general techniques used by personal lines underwriting departments. Thus, this book can be a valuable educational tool for underwriters with relatively little experience and, at the same time, can help more experienced underwriters understand the reasons behind many of the techniques in use.

The second edition of this text is primarily an updating of the text in the areas of coverage and figures. It is impossible to have a text that will stay current for the three- or four-year period over which it will be used, so we have made all changes that were necessary as of the time of revision, and will incorporate any other major changes in coverages or underwriting into the Course Guide as these changes develop.

Discussion problems and case studies are often the most effective ways of learning to put into practice the basic approaches discussed here. Such material is included in the UND 62 Course Guide, along with educational objectives, key terms and concepts, review questions, and outlines of the study material.

Students are encouraged to use this text along with the Course Guide as a unit to learn the subjects presented and effectively prepare for the national examination. For actual application in an underwriting context, the guidelines and rules of the company must be used to adapt the general material to a specific situation.

Those not directly involved in the underwriting function may find here the answers to questions concerning the ways in which personal lines underwriters handle risks. This may be valuable information for producers, regulators, and others for whom the underwriting function may be something of a mystery.

The authors wish to express their appreciation to the many individuals and companies who helped in the preparation of this text. We cannot list all of those underwriters, underwriting managers, executives, and educational directors who have contributed critical reviews and assistance in field testing. We do thank all of them.

We would particularly like to express our gratitude to the following persons who reviewed major sections of the first edition of this text: Bernard C. Bengtson, CPCU, Director, Education and Training (now retired), St. Paul Insurance Companies; Robert G. Brakey, CPCU, AIU, Senior Vice President, United Services Automobile Association; Anthony C. DeMotta, CPCU, Assistant Vice President, Marine Office of America Corporation; Edward L. Henninger, Assistant Vice President (now retired), State Farm Mutual Auto Insurance Company; Alan G. R. Morris, CPCU, Director, Insurance Underwriting, Interinsurance Exchange of the Auto Club of So. California; Richard B. Neiley, Jr., CPCU, Vice President—Underwriting, Harleysville Mutual Insurance Company; Margaret M. O'Connell, CPCU, Personal Lines Manager—Operations, Commercial Union Insurance Companies; A. H. Parsons, Vice President (now retired), U. S. Insurance Group; F. E. Schramm, Agency Superintendent (now retired), The Continental Insurance Companies; Robert C. Stites, CPCU, Vice President, State Farm Fire & Casualty Company; and T. George Van Hart, Jr., CPCU, Regional Director Field Management Department, Commercial Insurance Division, Aetna Life & Casualty Company.

In addition, we would like to thank the following persons who reviewed chapters of the first edition in their areas of specialty: Marge P. Adamczak, Commercial Lines Underwriter, Sentry Insurance Group; Raymond F. Begin, CPCU, Secretary, Reliance Insurance Company; Jack L. Carroll, CPCU, CLU, ARM, President, Insurance Consultant's, Inc.; Thomas F. Carroll, Great American Insurance Company; Philip Conlin, Commercial Accounts Unit Manager, Commercial Insurance Department, Aetna Life & Casualty Company; William H. Dean,

Training and Development Manager—Underwriting, Allstate Insurance Company; Richard A. Dempsey, Partner, Risk and Insurance Education; M. H. DeYoung, President, American Association of Insurance Services; Marie Engebretson, Analyst Programmer, Sentry Insurance Group; Joseph P. Fitzmaurice, Assistant Secretary (now retired), The Continental Insurance Companies; Michael D. Gantt, CPCU; David F. Gatton, CPCU, John Deere Insurance Company; Connie Perry Gerlitz, Personal Lines Underwriting Manager, Safeco Insurance Companies; Richard C. Gies, CPCU, CLU, Vice President, Harleysville Mutual Insurance Company; Robert W. Grieb, CPCU, AIU, Executive Vice President, Milwaukee Insurance Group; Michael J. Grob, Second Vice President, CG/Aetna Insurance Company; Larry D. Hall, Regional Underwriting Manager, Nationwide Insurance Company; Donald D. Hansen, CPCU, Vice President, Southeast Region, United Services Automobile Association; Clifford J. Jefferis, CPCU, Staff Vice President, United Services Automobile Association; Patrick V. Mullarkey, CPCU, Commercial Lines Manager, Fireman's Fund Insurance Companies; Harry C. Niemann III, CPCU, Director of Continuing Education, Society of CPCU; Robert Ortciger, Personal Lines Specialist, Grange Mutual Casualty Company; William H. Rodda, CPCU, President, Marine Insurance Handbook, Inc.; Joseph C. Shaughnessy, CPCU, Manager—Personal Insurance Department, Insurance Company of North America; Richard C. Simpson, Secretary, Personal Lines, The Hartford Insurance Group; Robert J. Smith, Assistant Secretary, Personal Lines, The Hartford Insurance Group; Wallace H. Smith, Secretary, Aetna Insurance Company; Clem H. Spalding, CPCU, Vice President, United Services Automobile Association; Hal E. Trimble, Director of Underwriting (now retired), Country Mutual Insurance Company; and William H. Weld, CPCU, CLU, Vice President, Frank B. Hall & Co. of Fairfield/Westchester.

We owe a heavy debt to the contributing authors for their invaluable assistance. They are listed elsewhere and each one deserves our special thanks.

Finally, we want to thank the Institute staff members involved in the textbook project. Without their patience, knowledge, and skill, this book could not have been written and published.

The authors accept full responsibility for all errors and omissions. We welcome readers' criticisms and suggestions so that we can improve future editions.

G. William Glendenning
Robert B. Holtom

Contributing Authors

The Insurance Institute of America and the authors acknowledge, with deep appreciation, the help of the following contributing authors whose manuscripts, written in their areas of expertise, served as the basis of this book:

Robert G. Brakey, CPCU, AIU
Senior Vice President
United Services Automobile Association

Nelson O. Broce, Jr., CPCU
Senior Personal Account Representative
Aetna Life & Casualty Company

James S. Burkart, CPCU, ARM
Assistant Vice President
Collier Cobb & Associates of Alabama, Inc.

David E. A. Carson
President
Middlesex Mutual Assurance Company

Anthony C. DeMotta, CPCU
Assistant Vice President
Marine Office of America Corporation

Leon E. Embry, CPCU
Vice President
Employers Casualty Company

Linton H. Freeman, CPCU
Director, Casualty Underwriting—Retired
Employers Insurance of Texas

Erwin F. Fromm, CPCU
Senior Vice President
Royal Insurance

L. J. Hauss
Manager, Special Accounts
Cravens, Dargan & Company

Peter R. Kensicki, D.B.A., CPCU, CLU
Director of Producer Education
Insurance Institute of America

Thomas M. Mahar, CPCU
Director, Industry Affairs
The Travelers Insurance Company

Dean R. Moffitt, CPCU
Industry Relations Manager
Allstate Insurance Company

Robert B. Morgan
President
Cincinnati Insurance Company

John M. Noel
Vice President
Sentry Assurance International Ltd.

Dennis A. Stimeling, CPCU
Secretary
Insurance Company of North America

Daniel G. St. Onge, CPCU
Assistant Vice President—Underwriting—Retired
Middlesex Mutual Assurance Company

Eric A. Wiening, CPCU, ARM
Assistant Director of Curriculum
Insurance Institute of America

Theodore M. Wood, CPCU, CLU
Zionvillage Insurance Agency, Inc.

James D. Youd, CPCU
President
Attleboro Mutual Fire Insurance Company

Table of Contents

UNDERWRITING OTHER PERSONAL LINES

ADDITIONAL SUBJECTS IN PERSONAL LINES UNDERWRITING

Introduction

CHAPTER 1

The Nature and Significance of Personal Lines Insurance

INTRODUCTION

This course deals with the underwriting of *personal lines insurance*—coverages designed in whole or in part to handle loss exposures arising out of the *nonbusiness* property and activities of individuals and families. Although there are no rigid distinctions as to what is or is not personal lines coverage, there are certain coverages which the industry in general regards as personal in nature. Private passenger auto and homeowners coverages, for example, are considered personal lines. Other coverages such as farmowners, however, might be handled as personal coverage, commercial coverage, or, in the "farm" or other specialty department.

For the purposes of this course, the term "personal lines" includes:

1. private passenger auto insurance, which is referred to as "personal auto insurance";
2. residential coverages for owners or occupants of single-family residences, owners or occupants of dwelling units with a limited number of occupancy units (such as duplexes, three-family houses, etc.), and occupants of multi-unit habitational properties (such as apartments, condominiums, etc.);
3. marine coverages of a nonbusiness nature, including personal floaters and coverages for nonbusiness uses of both watercraft and aircraft; and
4. liability insurance covering hazards arising out of personal activities and farming activities.

Other courses in the Associate in Underwriting Program will deal with exposures to loss arising out of business, governmental, and institutional activities—the so-called "commercial lines" of the property-liability insurance business. However, a few considerations concerning the personal-commercial distinction should be noted herein. First, some coverages regarded as personal lines may involve business activities of insureds. Personal auto coverages, for example, typically protect the insured even though the auto is being used for business purposes at the time of an accident. Second, the distinction between personal lines and commercial lines tends to blur as industry trends change over a period of time. A case in point is the growth in coverage of domestic employees under workers' compensation laws, and the resulting need to write workers' compensation insurance—certainly a commercial line by traditional industry nomenclature—for what previously have been personal lines accounts. Third, "personal" does not necessarily equal "individual." A building contractor doing business as a sole proprietor (rather than in a partnership or as a corporation owner) has numerous insurance needs arising from the existence of the business. All would be met by types of coverages considered to be "commercial" lines, even though the insured is an individual. Fourth, some coverages by design include both personal and commercial exposures. For example, the farmowners program has built into its liability section coverage both for losses arising out of farming activities and for losses arising out of personal (as opposed to farming) activities.

To some extent, *any* division between personal and commercial lines is arbitrary, but a division had to be made for the purposes of this course. The results are defensible, but may involve slight departures from a particular insurer's equally defensible allocation of personal lines on one hand, and commercial or specialty lines on the other.

The term "personal insurance" sometimes is used to denote those types of coverage dealing directly with losses of health or personal earning capacity of the insured or a covered member of the insured's family. Extra expenses, loss of income, or both, resulting from ill health, death, and old age are the subject matter of these coverages; health insurance, life insurance, and annuities are the types of contracts involved.

It sometimes is difficult to distinguish between the broad fields of property-liability coverages and life-health-annuity coverages. A clear overlap exists, for example, between the benefits to the insured under auto no-fault coverage and the benefits under health and (in some cases) life coverages. This course will deal with the former (auto), because it is a part of a property-liability line, but not with the life-health-annuity area, despite the overlap sometimes encountered by the claimant. "Personal lines" in this course does *not* include such "personal insurance" as the life-health-annuity coverages. These are not within the scope of this course, which deals exclusively with property-liability lines.

IMPORTANCE OF PERSONAL LINES INSURANCE

The importance of personal lines coverages can be viewed from the perspective of both the public and insurers. Underwriters should understand *and* appreciate why the products underwritten are important to those who use them and those who provide them.

To the Public

The importance to the public of personal lines insurance can be considered in terms of benefits to insureds and to society as a whole. The benefits cited below can, of course, be supplemented.

Compensation for Loss Most personal lines insureds go for years without incurring an insured loss, but losses do pose a threat to financial well-being. The personal lines insurance contract stands as a buffer between the insured and potentially severe or even ruinous losses.

Should a loss occur, compensation from an insurance contract often is the only prepaid source of liquid assets readily available to an insured. Credit, which is not (typically) free, *might* be available. Loans or gifts from friends or relatives *might* be available. Savings or other assets *might* be available. But to insureds, insurance *is* available as a means of indemnifying for covered losses sustained.

Aid in Obtaining Credit America has a well-developed and widely used credit system. Personal lines insurance coverages can give access to that system to many who could not otherwise qualify.

A creditor (lender) in a secured transaction, such as the granting of a loan to buy a car with the car itself serving as collateral, almost always insists that the borrower arrange for insurance protecting the insurable interest of the creditor. The creditor naturally looks to the reputation, financial position, and income-producing capacity of the borrower as the first line of security for loan repayment. However, if default (failure to pay in accordance with the loan agreement provisions) occurs, the property serving as collateral can be repossessed by the creditor in whole or partial satisfaction of the loan. Obviously, this second line of security is of little use if the collateral has been damaged, destroyed, or stolen. Moreover, loss of the collateral may make the borrower reluctant to repay the outstanding loan balance. Due to their insurable interest, lenders often require as a condition for making the loan that proper insurance protecting the lenders' interests be secured and kept in force by the borrower.

Because of the frequency with which buyers borrow to help purchase autos and residences, the personal auto and residential coverages have become important adjuncts to the credit system. Without these coverages, it is likely that many would-be borrowers could not get certain kinds of credit at all, could get it only in inadequate amounts, or would pay substantially higher rates of interest to lenders. Further, the additional security to lenders tends to encourage putting loanable funds to work, aiding not only the parties to the loan transaction but also manufacturing firms, builders, raw material suppliers, employees of these firms, and the economy as a whole.

Meeting Legal Obligations In many states motorists must, under prescribed conditions, demonstrate in advance the financial ability to respond to damages for which they may be liable because of the operation of an auto. For most motorists, auto liability insurance in appropriate amounts is the only feasible way to demonstrate this ability. In some states employers of household workers are required by law to demonstrate their ability to pay prescribed benefits to or on behalf of their household employees incurring job-related injuries or illnesses. For the vast majority, the only form of security acceptable under the several laws is an insurance policy guaranteeing the payment of the prescribed benefits. Thus, insurance enables individuals to meet obligations imposed on them by a governmental unit.

The three benefits cited above are merely an illustrative list of reasons why personal lines insurance coverages are essential elements in the financial structure of individuals and families in the United States. These major reasons for carrying personal lines insurance also have underwriting implications. Personal lines underwriters are often faced with the challenge of controlling the flow of new business and separating acceptable applicants from the unacceptable ones.

Protecting the insurer against the consequences of adverse selection is the fundamental purpose of underwriting. In personal lines, as opposed to commercial lines, the alternatives to insurance are limited. Unlike large corporations, most consumers would be unwilling or unable to retain or control loss exposures, and personal lines insurance becomes a necessity. The importance of personal lines coverages to applicants should emphasize for underwriters the need to provide some acceptable measure of coverage through modification of rates or coverage.

To the Insurance Industry

Personal lines insurance coverages often are underestimated in their importance to the property-liability insurance industry. Some companies write nothing but commercial lines; others concentrate on commercial lines and write only a minimal book of personal lines business. Many producers handle personal lines only as an accommodation or adjunct to commercial accounts. However, personal lines premium volume accounts for about 46 percent of the total property-liability aggregate premium volume. And there are many more personal lines insureds than commercial insureds. These two factors—economic significance and public contact—demonstrate the importance of personal lines insurance to the property-liability insurance business.

Economic Significance Personal lines net insurance premiums written in 1979 amounted to approximately $40 billion.[1] This measure—premiums written—corresponds with "sales" as a measure in most other business activities.

The Gross National Product, a measure in dollar terms of the total output of goods and services of our economy, reached $2.4 trillion in 1979. Personal lines insurance premiums accounted for about 1.6 cents of every dollar of GNP. Additionally, personal lines insurance premiums account for 2.7 cents out of every dollar spent by households alone.[2] Total property-liability premiums, both personal and commercial, written in 1979 were about $87 billion.[3] (This figure excludes health insurance premiums written by property-liability insurers.)

By a variety of measures, personal lines coverages are of enormous economic importance to the industry as a whole. Unfortunately, that book of business in recent years has not always produced an underwriting profit. These unsatisfactory results cannot, of course, be attributed completely to ineffective performance at the underwriting desk. Many observers feel that inflation (especially increases in auto repair costs and medical costs), rate level inadequacies, and the growing limitations on the free exercise of traditional underwriting prerogatives have been among the major contributors to the recent poor experience. Still, more effective underwriting can help to develop a better book of business—either more profitable or, at least in the short run, less unprofitable. Further, an understanding of the underwriting environment is necessary to anticipating changes in it and to adapting underwriting principles and practices to these changes. This chapter, in particular, and other sections of UND 62 deal largely with the underwriting environment. An awareness of this subject, plus a firm grasp of underwriting concepts and practices, can better equip underwriting personnel to help obtain more profitable personal lines underwriting results.

Public Contact The exact number of personal lines insurance "customers," though unknown, obviously is enormous. Virtually all named insureds and spouses are adults. They vote, pay bills, and reflect their pleasure or displeasure with the products and services they buy and with the industries that provide them. They are a major base for "public opinion" and, while not as organized and cohesive as many other interest groups in our society, they increasingly are able to, and do, express their feelings about insurance to each other and to insurers. The public image of the property-liability insurance business in the broad sense is shaped largely by the experiences of personal lines insurance customers. This does not mean that, for example, an underpriced major class of business can in the long run be liberally underwritten without jeopardizing the best interests of other policyholders and the interests of the insuring public as a whole. It does mean that the underwriting and handling of personal lines—both *what* is done and *how* it is done—can make an important contribution to the public's appraisal of property-liability insurance.

PERSONAL LINES INSURANCE MARKETS AND PRODUCTS

The personal lines insurance market comprises millions of consumers whose insurance needs are met by a great variety of products. This section examines some characteristics of these buyers as opposed to the commercial lines insurance buyers who are dealt with in UND 63 and UND 64. In the process, a number of generalizations will be made which may be subject to exceptions in individual cases.

Characteristics of the Personal Lines Insurance Market

Large Number of Buyers and Sellers The large number of buyers of personal lines insurance products is likely to increase if there is a continuation in the growth of laws making certain types of automobile coverage mandatory. Aside from the number of buyers, a *policy* count would probably show an upward trend because of the growth in less common personal exposures such as boats and recreational vehicles which often are insured under policies separate from the customary auto and residence contracts.

While the timing and size of the flow of submissions certainly varies among firms, branches, departments, and individual underwriting desks, for the business as a whole this enormous volume means a steady demand for its products and a continuing supply of underwriting opportunities. Volume also creates opportunities for division of labor in the risk selection process—structuring the underwriting function so that certain personnel specialize in only a portion (e.g., rating) of the overall underwriting of each individual submission. Volume also contributes to the ability to "underwrite by exception." The similarity of most applications for personal coverages makes it possible and economically feasible to develop boundaries concerning risk characteristics, with intensive underwriting attention given only to those submissions failing to meet all the criteria necessary to fall within the boundaries.

No precise count of companies selling one or more of the personal lines is available, but for 1979 it was reported that 2,867 property-liability companies were chartered in the fifty states.[4] Many of these operate on only a local or regional basis, some restrict their activity to the writing of commercial lines, and less than 1,000 are licensed to transact business in all or most states. Nevertheless, any given buyer is faced with numerous sellers, and the marketplace is therefore competitive. Even the largest writer of personal auto insurance in 1979 commanded less than 18 percent of that market and the ten largest writers combined wrote less than 50 percent.

This large number of sellers, operating in a competitive atmosphere, increases the need for sound underwriting policies and practices. A company which attempts to maintain a price structure comparable to other insurers but which fails to maintain sound underwriting practices will be subject to adverse selection and will probably have a below-average book of business.

Relatively Homogeneous in Exposures and Needs The exposures to loss, and thus the insurance needs, of personal lines insurance buyers are very often similar. Compared to a great many commercial risks, the personal lines market is characterized by a great deal of homogeneity in what can happen to cause loss, the values exposed to loss, and the basic varieties of insurance products needed to handle these exposures to the extent that they are insurable. To the extent that there are significant differences, the enormous number of buyers permits dividing the overall population into large subgroups consisting of members with more in common than the population as a whole. However, even risks presenting identical physical hazards would differ as to moral and/or morale hazards simply because no two individuals have precisely the same set of values, attitudes, habits, and living patterns. Nevertheless, compared to a *hypothetical* group of risks that might include the Empire State Building, the Alaskan pipeline, a manufacturer of swine flu vaccine, and a supertanker, personal lines risks indeed appear to be homogeneous.

This relative homogeneity has several implications for underwriters and the underwriting function. First, the homogeneity can be deceptive because it may tend to create an *appearance* of sameness that masks individual risk differences of extreme importance to the underwriter. Second, homogeneity and a large number of risks fulfill two conditions for the effective operation of the law of large numbers. This simplifies both the prediction of losses (and rating) and the securing of a book of business that provides a valid test of those predictions. A commercial fire underwriter may make from five to ten decisions per day involving new submissions, with the amounts at risk spanning a wide range. One or two "bad" losses could distort experience and create a presumption of inferior performance that is unwarranted because of the limited number and diversity of risks in that underwriter's book. In a comparable period, a personal lines underwriter might make ten times as many decisions, and these decisions involve risks that are *relatively* homogeneous when compared to the commercial fire risks. More credibility can then be attached to the short-run experience of the personal lines underwriter's book than to the other. Substantial deviations from acceptable levels due to chance, not to underwriting effectiveness or the lack of it, are much more probable in the smaller number of *relatively* diverse units in the commercial property book of business.

A third implication, or outgrowth, of homogeneity is product standardization. Similarity in exposures and insurance needs fosters the development of policy forms for a given line that are *essentially* the same among insurers—not identical, certainly, but substantially alike among insurers writing the bulk of personal lines business. This is *not* to say that all insurers charge the same price for the same, or very similar, protection, nor does it ignore other forces encouraging or requiring standardization (e.g., state laws or regulations). The point is that some degree of standardization is inherent in any market where buyer needs are essentially similar.

Lack of Alternatives for Buyers Compared to a large commercial, institutional, or governmental risk, the typical personal lines insurance consumer has less choice among alternative methods for handling loss exposures. At least three factors contribute to this: (1) the consumer's lack of familiarity with "risk management" (the process of identifying and analyzing loss exposures and choosing among alternatives in treating them) and ability to use all alternatives feasibly; (2) a lack of liquidity—cash or assets readily convertible into cash—for financing losses internally; and (3) a greater lack of predictability of experience by the individual or household than for large commercial insureds. A large risk often can generate a body of loss experience enabling it to make reasonable approximations of the future, but so-called "average" experience has little meaning for the individual or household as a guide for today's decisions. The fact that in the long run and *on the average* fire losses will cost a homeowner $40 per year is no help in predicting what will happen over the next twelve months to *that* homeowner. In contrast, a large commercial risk with a number of locations independently exposed to fire can at least to some extent predict what will happen. This predictive ability opens up certain alternative (to full insurance) approaches to handling loss exposures, whereas the personal lines buyer's only *safe* alternative is transfer via insurance if the loss potential is large compared to the person's ability to bear losses. However, in spite of the lack of predictability of a single personal lines insured's experience, the homogeneity of these insureds leads to a high degree of predictability for the insureds as a group.

This lack of alternatives has very deep implications for the underwriting function and the property-liability insurance business. The industry provides a service that is uniformly regarded as an important need, and increasingly as something close to an inalienable right. In personal lines insurance, freedom to accept or reject on the insurer's own terms has narrowed. Evidence of this fact, and the forms that this constriction has taken, will be discussed later in this text.

Relatively Inelastic Demand Economists determine elasticity for a good or service by relating changes in total revenues from sales to changes in unit sales price. If a price increase *reduces* total revenues because many buyers refuse to buy at the higher price, demand is said to be *elastic,* at least between those two (old and new) prices. If a price increase results in increasing total revenues, demand is said to be *inelastic* at that price level. The lack of alternatives in personal lines insurance products means that the buyer has little choice but to continue buying despite price increases. Lower priced substitutes are unavailable.

Characterizing the demand for personal lines insurance as inelastic does not mean that buyers will buy forever at *any* price, no matter how high. There is, in theory, a price level beyond which buyer resistance or incapacity would cause total revenues to *decline* despite the higher price at which each unit is sold. That level, obviously, is a matter of conjecture, but the requirements of states and lending institutions that mandate for many the purchase of auto and residence coverages suggest that the level has not yet been approached. In some states that experienced substantial rate increases, the number of uninsured motorists increased. If auto liability insurance is not mandatory, some persons with limited assets choose to discontinue auto liability insurance when rates are high.

Changes in total revenues do not necessarily equal changes in profitability or even reductions in losses. The subject of demand elasticity involves total revenues and prices. More revenues may not mean a better profit picture. Indeed, if losses and expenses *per dollar of revenue* total more than 100 percent, more revenues mean more dollar losses than if revenues had remained unchanged.

Heavy Regulation of Products and Prices The property-liability insurance business occupies a position of trust in meeting part of a vital human need for economic security, and consequently is heavily regulated, particularly at the state level. Personal lines insurance products and prices are among the most strongly regulated aspects of the industry. In many states the introduction of new, or changes in existing, products and prices is subject to prior approval from state authorities. Since each state operates autonomously, approval in one state does not mean approval in another. Even states not requiring prior approval reserve the right to revoke the use of policy forms or prices subsequent to their introduction.

Several relatively recent developments in the regulatory arena will be discussed more fully in a later section of this chapter.

Relatively Uninformed and Dependent Buyers No such thing as the "average insurance buyer" exists any more than does the "average insurance company." Nevertheless, some generalizations about personal attitudes and interests of at least a large portion of personal lines insurance buyers can be made. The statements that follow are offered in that sense and, as indicated at the outset of this chapter, can be subject to exceptions in individual cases.

Insurance policies are complex documents providing a wide range of protection. Most people have neither the time, the training, nor the inclination to be well versed on what their policies do, do not do, or may require of them. Further, many lack the skills and knowledge needed to identify their own loss exposures and insurance needs. In a way, buyers are dependent upon insurers and their representatives for designing and delivering insurance products and services. Only when it is time to pay a premium or file a claim do many buyers reflect their self-interest.

This is *not* an indictment critical of buyers. This is, however, a realistic appraisal of part of the environment in which the underwriter operates, and should be thought of not as a "problem" but more as a challenge and opportunity for insurers, underwriters, and producers. Careful consideration of unusual loss exposures, adequacy of limits of liability, insurance to value, and ways to reduce hazards, in addition to scheduling valuable property, will benefit insureds and help to meet objectives of insurers.

In a sense, the property-liability insurance business, simply because of its existence in today's society, must take a good deal of responsibility for managing the risks of personal lines insureds.

Obviously, the ability of the personal lines underwriter to anticipate, search out, and verify the needs of the buyer is limited. Costs cannot be ignored, nor can the responsibilities and rights of producers. On the other hand, underwriting often should be more than making a decision, attaching a price, and monitoring results, and the fact that many buyers do not seem to know or care much about their insurance should not blind the underwriter to this.

Commercial insurance buyers range from small sole proprietors to large corporations and governmental units. Some are no better informed or more interested in insurance matters than the bulk of personal lines buyers. However, many employ individuals or staff entire departments for the handling of insurance and related matters. Even if unable to retain staff specialists, the commercial buyer often would have access to helpful advice from attorneys, accountants, safety engineers, and other specialists inside or outside the business. In addition, the commercial buyer on the average is more attuned to the nature and significance of contractual relationships than is the typical personal lines insurance buyer. Finally, the size of the commercial account's insurance premium is more likely to support outlays of time and services by producers and company personnel than will the personal lines premium.

A Market Shown Great Attention by Politicians and Regulators A recent survey indicates that the majority of personal lines auto insurance buyers consider auto insurance premiums to be too high relative to other goods and services.[5] Interest by legislators and regulators in rates, policy forms, availability, and selection criteria and practices of this and other personal insurance lines has been growing. Some underwriters feel that in some cases rates may have been artificially depressed for reasons clearly attached to courting favor with the public. In at least one state, simplification of policy forms has been imposed as a condition precedent to serious consideration of requested rate increases. Broader-based rating classifications have been suggested as a way of spreading the costs of insuring poor (by traditional standards) risks over more premium payers and thus making coverage more "affordable," and hence available, to poor risks. Long-standing and statistically credible underwriting and rating criteria, such as gender in auto insurance, have come under attack.

This text attempts to impose no judgments on the obvious increase in involvement of legislators and regulators in the relationships between buyers and suppliers of insurance. But the personal lines underwriter should know that the increase has been felt most heavily in the personal lines area, and that there are no signs of abatement. With millions of consumers—most of whom are voters—involved, and with a heightened interest in the welfare of the consumer at all levels of government, it seems clear that the personal lines of property-liability insurance will continue to be subject to political attention.

Characteristics of Personal Lines Insurance Products

In the broadest sense, the product sold in the personal lines insurance marketplace is economic security. In the sense in which the term "product" is used here, however, it is synonymous with "insurance policy" or "insurance contract."

Standardized Policies Characteristics discussed in the previous section—homogeneity and large numbers—make the personal lines insurance market ideal for the development and use of standardized policies. The contracts of all insurers writing a particular type of personal lines risk may not be identical, but they often follow a pattern because the needs of buyers are often similar and competition among insurers tends to lead to imitation by a great number of insurers serving the same market.

In some cases (e.g., private passenger auto insurance in some states) the state dictates policy forms. Here, obviously, standardization is complete and extends beyond even the substantial similarity that would otherwise result from competition or voluntary cooperative activities of groups of insurers. In other cases, though complete uniformity is not required, other state mandates set minimum standards (e.g., auto financial responsibility laws) for the scope of protection provided or specify precisely the contents of a portion of the policy (e.g., so-called "no-fault" benefits in auto insurance contracts and the standard fire policy portion of residence insurance contracts).

This uniformity has implications for the underwriter and the underwriting function. First, it imposes some (though *not* necessarily total) order on the apparent maze of competitors' offerings. Second, it places prime importance on competition in price and in service. The effect of *coverage* differences on buyer choice (and in some cases producer choice) tends to be minimized. Third, the answer to coverage questions the underwriter may be called upon to give can be based on a broader body of experience, and perhaps legal precedents, than would be the case in the absence of standardization. Trade association publications, books, and loose-leaf services devoted to insurance law and cases, the standard law reporting services and summaries of existing case law, and other sources can be tapped to aid the underwriter in this area. Fourth, a requirement to use a certain form will save the insurer money that would have been expended in the development of policies and coverages. Finally, standardization gives the underwriter a good idea of what alternatives may be available to the applicant in a particular submission.

High Degree of Packaging In the early 1940s, homeowners policies were unheard of; coverage of the residential theft exposure required a separate policy; and, in most states, it could not be written by the same corporate entity that wrote fire and allied lines insurance on the applicant's personal property. Complete auto insurance protection usually required the issuance of two policies because the coverages involved were, according to state statutes, partly "fire" and partly "casualty."

The passage of multiple-line laws in the late 1940s and early 1950s permitted the combining in a single policy of one insurer all the coverages typically needed in either the auto or property areas. By 1960, packaging had become the norm, combining in a single contract coverages that previously had been available only in separate contracts issued by legally distinct (though perhaps related) insurance companies.

Packaging complicates individual risk underwriting by increasing the number of perils in the average contract. This means that hazard identification is more complex and that more balancing of good and bad points must be done in the making of a single underwriting decision. Underwriting a book of business, on the other hand, gets an assist from packaging in the form of reduced exposure to adverse selection because of the nature of packaging. Handling costs per policy are also reduced, compared to costs that would be incurred in the writing of separate contracts that collectively provide comparable coverage.

A recent development, the so-called "second-stage" package, combines auto and residence coverages and, with some insurers, term life insurance and/or disability income insurance as well. This will be discussed later.

Class Rated With the exception of some personal inland marine policies, some personal umbrella liability policies, and some residential property risks, all personal lines contracts are class rated. This means that risks are assigned to one of a predetermined set of classes. The assignment is based on characteristics of the risk, and an average rate which is applicable to all risks in that class is charged. In contrast, many commercial risks are rated individually and may take a rate (or have a final premium developed) unlike the rate for a seemingly similar risk nearby. Small general liability and workers' compensation risks are class rated, however, and so are a number of small commercial fire risks in an increasing number of states.

UND 61 illustrated both class (manual) and individual risk rate-making techniques. Later work in this course, and in UND 63 and UND 64, will go into more detail.

Class rates substitute workable group equity for individual risk equity. The degree of substitution depends largely on the number and breadth of rating classes in the classification system used and the degree of credibility that can be attached to data in the several classes. Greater refinement in classification tends to sacrifice credibility in some classes and increase the complexity and administrative costs of using a classification system.

For a given class (assuming rate adequacy), the task of the underwriter is to develop a book of business that is average or better than average for the class.

Complex to Buyer An insurance contract is difficult for most buyers to understand. Contracts may contain thousands of words. The terminology used is suited to insurer needs more than to buyer understanding, and provisions in the same document may be inconsistent, perhaps as a result of statutory requirements. Also, many key words are not defined in the contract. Insurance professionals themselves sometimes disagree on the meaning and interpretation of contract provisions, and word meanings themselves are often subject to different interpretations in the courts and elsewhere.

Adding to the complexity, there are some overlaps between some property-liability contracts and other types of insurance. For example, health insurance contracts do not exclude auto injury losses, yet the same losses, or portions thereof, also are covered by the buyer's auto insurance medical payments or no-fault benefits. This overlap further compounds buyers' lack of understanding by blurring the distinctions between the various kinds of insurance.

Product complexity magnifies the difficulty of insurance purchasing and use by even the knowledgeable and interested buyer. Consumers must rely heavily on insurance underwriters and producers for advice so that informed choices can be made. Recently, however, there has been a strong movement toward the use of "readable" policies with larger print, fewer words, easier to understand terms, and an overall less complex format. Even though the persons who read their policies will be better able to understand the policies, many insureds will still rely on someone else to explain the coverages.

Relatively Rigid in Form and Rate To varying degrees, the major personal lines policy forms and the rates applicable to them are firmly fixed. Insurance regulation contributes to this rigidity, requiring in a majority of states that both forms and rates be formally approved prior to use. It is usually necessary to go through regulatory channels before changes can be implemented. In the personal lines in particular, these channels can be very narrow and very slow. In contrast, in commercial lines as a whole there seems to be much more reliance placed by regulators on the workings of the market and the knowledge of commercial insurance buyers.

Another major factor contributing to rigidity in form is the institutional framework within which many insurers operate. The use of "bureau" forms—policy forms usually developed by advisory organizations and voluntarily adopted by companies—results in substantial uniformity in form among many companies. It has already been noted that the nature of personal lines buyers' insurance needs and competition in the marketplace tend to encourage standardization. When that tendency is strengthened by the use of jointly developed forms, the process of change becomes a slower one because of the need to secure support from a sufficient number of companies to make any changes acceptable to the bureau.

Relatively Small Average Unit Premium An industrywide average annual premium per policy for personal lines is probably below $500. It is small compared to commercial lines, where annual premiums over $1,500 are routine and premiums over $10,000 are no longer uncommon. In personal lines, annual premiums as high as $1,500 on a policy are rare except for some individual auto premiums in certain cities and perhaps a small number of residence insurance contracts containing large values in individually scheduled items.

This relatively small average premium means that on the average there are a small number of dollars for coverage of expenses connected with selling, underwriting, and servicing the accounts. The underwriter must decide if it is feasible to obtain the nonroutine underwriting information he or she would like to have before rendering a decision. It costs money to gather additional information, and it takes underwriting time (which is money to the insurer) to decide what is wanted, to request or secure it, and to consider it. If the underwriter knew that a particular submission, if written, would be on the books for years, nonroutine *initial* underwriting expenses would be easier to justify. However, the underwriter cannot make such an assumption.

There are several guidelines which can be applied to this problem of "information efficiency." A risk which is unacceptable on its face will not become more acceptable with additional information, and the underwriter should carefully avoid incurring expenses needlessly in this manner. Also, the underwriter should not be unduly influenced by recent events involving the risk. While past experience should not be ignored, the underwriter should not let isolated or chance events obscure the fact that obtaining information is expensive and personal lines premiums, on the average, do not contain many dollars for that purpose. For example, a recent lightning loss claim under a homeowners policy may not require an extensive investigation of the claim file since it can be considered a chance event which is essentially uncontrollable.

Information efficiency is a key concept in underwriting. It saves expense dollars and helps to avoid the "paralysis of analysis." Before spending time and money to gather additional information, the underwriter should ask, "How will this information affect my decision?" An underwriter who practices information efficiency asks only for information that is *essential* to make a decision and no more. In personal lines, the small average unit premium stresses the need to conserve expense dollars through information efficiency.

BROAD TRENDS AFFECTING THE UNDERWRITING OF PERSONAL LINES

The insurance business functions as a part of a dynamic social and economic system. It is affected by the vicissitudes of the economy and by changes demanded of it by the market it serves and by the legislatures and regulators governing its actions. In the past, there was relatively little regulation by the individual states and therefore there was a great deal of freedom for insurers in making decisions to accept or reject, or retain or cancel, on the basis of their own criteria. More recently, particularly since the mid-1960s, constraints have been placed on the choices available in underwriting and on the criteria that form the basis for underwriting decisions.

In addition, the recent past has seen serious increases in losses from antisocial activities such as arson, vandalism, and other crimes. The dramatic increase in inflation has weakened rating bases tied to past experience and dependent for validity upon reasonable price stability. Also, new insurance products for the family are coming on the market, rate-making discretion is under attack, and regulators are expressing concern about the availability, affordability, readability, and reliability of insurance products. All of these trends have had an effect on personal lines underwriting.

On a more positive note, the number of personal lines insurance buyers is likely to increase in the near future, assuring a sizable market. Improved information systems and the increasing use of the computer will provide underwriters and underwriting managers with more objective data to use in decision making. These technological advances may relieve underwriters of many processing chores and allow more time for contact with producers and insureds.

Limitations on Selectivity

Underwriters are presented with a large amount of information which must be properly analyzed during risk selection. This process of analyzing hazards on individual submissions is the backbone of the underwriting function. In the past, insurers of personal lines risks were fairly free to determine what hazard factors were important and the relative importance of those factors. This freedom is now being increasingly challenged, and underwriters must learn to adjust to new and changing sets of rules governing selection.

Restrictions on Use of Risk Characteristics In evaluating a submission, the underwriter looks at characteristics of the risk. Based on the company's underwriting guidelines and program for the type of risk in question, and his or her own knowledge and experience, the underwriter forms a composite picture of the risk and uses this picture as a guide in decision making. Suppose, however, that the underwriter is suddenly told that there are certain parts of the picture that cannot be used to help reach a decision. The picture would be smaller and incomplete by former standards. Further, the blanked out portions of the picture could pertain to risk characteristics known to be statistically reliable measures of hazard among a large group of risks. Yet, they would be unavailable in developing a composite picture of the submission. For example, it is well established that accident and traffic violation records are good indicators of future loss potential. If this information is denied the underwriter, an important part of the composite risk picture is blanked out and the acceptability and pricing of the risk cannot be adequately determined.

To some extent in the recent past, limitations have been imposed on personal lines underwriting by statute or regulation in a number of states. Factors that the underwriter was formerly free to consider either have been ruled out or their use has been restricted. Age, sex, marital status, occupation, and territory are all factors which have been subject to such regulation.

This trend has been highly erratic, some states being far more active than others in ruling out or modifying the use of traditional underwriting variables. Some states have prohibited rejection of the applicant based *solely* on a particular risk characteristic. For example, some states prohibit the use of marital status or life-style as the basis of rejecting an applicant for auto insurance. It seems to be safe to predict that the regulations placed on the criteria available to underwriters for use in making decisions will continue to increase.

The personal lines of insurance, especially auto insurance, have been much more heavily affected by legislative and administrative activity than have the commercial lines. Subsequent portions of this text will specify many of these changes, but it should be noted that the underwriter must be aware of current restrictions in the geographical areas in which he or she is involved.

Restrictions on Cancellation and Nonrenewal Over time, many insurers experience swings or cycles in loss ratios on the personal lines of insurance. These fluctuations adversely affect many insurers simultaneously. Although unwelcome, these cycles have come to be almost predictable. Insurers may deal with a rising loss ratio by: (1) more restrictive policy contracts, (2) more selective underwriting, (3) increased rate levels, or (4) upgrading a book of business through cancellations and nonrenewals. If the device or combination of devices chosen is effective, experience stabilizes and the unprofitable portion of the cycle is passed.

Unfortunately, the upswing in the cycle sometimes produces undue optimism along with temporary profitability. At times, this has led to intensive competition among insurers, particularly for private passenger auto business. However, the homeowners and pleasure boat lines also have been involved in rate battles. This extreme competition eventually causes a spell of lower rates (or failure to adequately increase rates), higher loss ratios, and more selectivity in the underwriting of new and renewal business—causing the cycle to begin again.

Until the late 1950s and early 1960s, each insurer underwrote much as it pleased, accepting or rejecting risks based on whatever criteria it wanted to establish. In addition, insurers could cancel without providing the insured with the reason for the action. It was inevitable that these facts would come into conflict with the importance of insurance to the public and with the increasing awareness of legislators and regulators to insurance availability and rate levels, thus causing resistance to rate increases. To compound the problem, inflation became almost built-in to the economy and auto insurance loss experience for many insurers deteriorated and remained unsatisfactory for a prolonged period. Efforts to correct the situation for insurers—primarily through greater selectivity and exercise of cancellation rights—increased the problem and, by the mid-1960s, there was substantial agreement that the personal auto insurance market needed more stability than existing practices provided.

In an attempt to impose some order in the marketplace, many independent insurers and the majority of those affiliated with the major industry trade and rating organizations undertook to encourage companies to voluntarily restrict the reasons for canceling a policy. An amendatory endorsement called "amendment of termination provisions" was recommended. It dealt with the timing and bases for cancellation and the notice requirements for nonrenewal.

1. For "underwriting reasons" only within the first sixty days of a new policy and then only by giving ten days written notice, said notice to be mailed prior to the sixtieth day.
2. After sixty days, cancellation is not permitted except for:
   a. nonpayment of premium
   b. suspension or revocation of the driver's license
3. Intention of nonrenewal (termination) must be mailed at least twenty days prior to policy expiration.[6]

Eventually states began to enact laws restricting cancellations, with most laws following the aforementioned endorsement format. It is significant to note that in 1960 there were no laws restricting auto cancellation, while today almost every state has a restrictive law.

The trend in the early 1980s is toward even more restrictive auto insurance cancellation laws possibly coupled with requirements that insurers furnish detailed reasons for any cancellation within the permitted sixty-day underwriting period in most states, or for refusal to renew at the anniversary date. Also, residence insurance coverages are increasingly becoming the subject of similar laws and regulations. These restrictions will be discussed elsewhere in this text.

Residual Markets Another modern phenomenon facing personal lines underwriters is the increasing number of automobile insurance (assigned risk) plans, residual market reinsurance facilities, and joint underwriting associations that force companies to accept a pro rata share of risks uninsurable in the voluntary market within a given state. The nature and operation of these devices vary among states and lines of insurance, but they have one common characteristic—making coverage more available than would be the case if insurers were completely free to determine with whom they wanted to do business.

In general, these involuntary market devices—particularly in the auto insurance field—have not been self-supporting and have required subsidies from other sources of insurer funds, including premiums paid by risks acceptable in the voluntary market. The propriety of such devices and the manner in which they operate depend largely on one's point of view and underlying philosophy of the role of the private insurance mechanism. Regulators and legislators often differ with insurance people on this subject. Regulators seemingly view insurance, particularly the personal lines, more as a basic right than as a privilege within the power of private insurers to grant or withhold.

Participation in involuntary market devices, and thus sharing in their fortunes and misfortunes, is not literally "mandatory" for insurers, but the only available alternative—withdrawal from the state—in most cases has not been regarded as an acceptable alternative.

Changing Perils and Hazards

In the past, personal lines underwriters concerned themselves primarily with underwriting against the risk of loss of a dwelling and its contents by fire or wind, or loss to autos caused by collision or the liability exposure of auto operators. Arson, theft, and vandalism were of minor concern.

Currently, however, the personal lines underwriter needs a broader perspective in evaluating hazards. Package contracts contribute to this need because they have greatly expanded the perils covered. At the same time, losses from theft and vandalism to autos and homes have increased in frequency, particularly in urban areas. Homes are being unoccupied for longer periods of time due to more extended vacations and/or an increase in business travel, thus increasing the probability of theft. The increasing number of two- and three-car families means more autos are left parked in the driveway or on the street, thus making them more susceptible to theft and vandalism losses. Auto thefts have increased dramatically since 1970 so that the theft peril has become a significant consideration in auto underwriting.

Changes in the prevalence of moral hazards are also discernible. If morals decline, fraudulent claims can be expected to increase. Underwriters are concerned about the increase in the crime of arson—the intentional burning of property usually for insurance recovery purposes. Fires of suspicious origin have been increasing dramatically, often, it appears, to remove a mortgage obligation and relieve financial pressures. Many observers today also feel that our more affluent society has brought about an increase in the morale hazard—indifference to loss. With higher average incomes, people seem to feel there is less need to protect and care for property.

These problems create an environment of change in which certain perils and certain hazards take on more meaning because they have more potential for adversely influencing underwriting results. Perhaps twenty years from now the veteran personal lines underwriter will look back and remember the days when the malfunction of solar heating systems was nothing more than an idle curiosity. Social and technological changes inevitably affect insurance practices, coverages, and problems. The underwriting function and underwriting personnel are central to this interaction.

Inflation

The term "inflation" refers to upward price level changes—shifts in the prices of goods and services. Recently, inflation has had a severe debilitating effect on insurance company operating results.

If the rate of change in prices were predictable *and* if insurers could set rates in anticipation of higher prices, the problems posed by inflation would be manageable. Neither of these conditions has been present in recent years, however. Premiums paid in advance have had to finance losses requiring more dollars than anticipated at inception. Further, even if anticipated losses and insurance premiums to cover them could reflect changes in the price level during the period of protection, insurers would be left with the problem of insurance to value in the residence lines because of a lag between value changes and upward changes in amounts of insurance.

The double-digit inflationary spiral of the mid 1970s and early 1980s was particularly harsh on insurers. Moreover, the goods and services that account for a large portion of personal lines insurance loss dollars—home construction costs, auto repair parts and labor charges, hospital room and board charges, physicians' fees—have for a number of years been increasing in price at rates substantially in excess of the rate of increase of prices in general. It appears that inflation will persist, and that its rate will continue to be difficult to predict. This section will analyze the impact of inflation in two related areas—losses and rates, and maintaining insurance to value.

Losses and Rates Personal lines insurance rates are set in advance of the period of protection provided. The rates should be based on past experience adjusted to anticipate changes that are expected to occur during the period for which the rates will be applicable. When the past serves as an inadequate guide, or when expected changes are not or cannot be reflected in rates, underwriting losses are a likely outcome.

Inflation increases loss severity. In recent years the rate of inflation has been steep, particularly for those items toward which a majority of personal lines loss dollars go. Although the Consumer Price Index for 1979 increased 11.3 percent, auto insurance premiums rose only 5.6 percent and property insurance premiums rose 9.7 percent for the same period.[7] It has been impossible for rates to keep pace, particularly in the auto and residence fields and in those states—a majority—requiring prior approval of rate changes. Prior approval, whatever its merits or demerits on other points, conflicts with the need for rate responsiveness in periods of price changes. Rate filings have to be supported with credible and reasonably mature loss data. In periods of substantial inflation, the data become obsolete even before the rates are filed. Trend and development factors can adjust for this obsolescence, but these factors are (1) by definition, estimates supporting the need for higher rates in an inflationary economy; and (2) likely to be the subject of differences of opinion between insurers and rating organizations, on one hand, and regulators subject to a variety of pressures, on the other hand. Regulators may feel that they cannot approve proposed rates in a filing that assumes a continuation of inflation rates witnessed in the recent past. Further aggravating the problem is the frequency with which rate changes must be sought in an inflationary economy. As indicated previously, the personal lines market is politically sensitive, and a regulator might have difficulty approving frequent rate increases based on an assumption that recent high rates of inflation will continue. A granted increase might be a compromise and have insurers still trying to compensate for equally high or even higher rates of inflation in the future.

A recent study has shown that a certain 1980 model auto, with a cost of $6,018 new, would cost over $25,000 to replace if the parts were bought in the normal parts market. Labor costs for auto repairs have skyrocketed. Hospital room and board charges were among the most rapidly increasing cost categories over the past ten years. Construction cost estimates usually include a 1 percent per month increase factor that assumes, for example, that a construction job begun on June 1 will cost 6 percent more than the same job begun the preceding December 1. When insurers are restricted in adjusting rates, the problem of inflation increasing loss costs with resulting rate inadequacy is magnified.

Maintaining Insurance to Value It is axiomatic in the underwriting of residential properties that adequate insurance to value is important in producing satisfactory underwriting results. That is, of course, based upon the fact that the majority of residential losses are partial losses. By encouraging insureds to purchase adequate amounts of insurance relative to the values at risk, rates are more likely to stay at an attractive level to the insurance buyer and loss ratios are more likely to be acceptable to insurers. During periods of substantial inflation, such as the late 1970s and early 1980s, it is extremely difficult to persuade buyers to increase amounts of insurance on residential properties, particularly those built prior to 1970. Homeowners just simply will not believe that their homes may be as much as 40 percent underinsured just because they have not increased the amount of insurance within the last five years. Exhibit 1-1 illustrates the seriousness of the problem. According to the figure, the home purchase subindex of the Consumer Price Index (CPI) increased about 100 percent from 1973 to 1979 and increased almost 60 percent from 1975 to November 1980.

A number of insurance companies are undertaking campaigns to educate the public about the ravages of inflation and to encourage proper insurance to value on the part of each homeowner. Companies are offering optional "inflation guard" endorsements that automatically update the amount of the insurance on a quarterly or annual basis, although this device has limitations as will be pointed out later. In addition, some companies consider the subject so important that they have instituted mandatory insurance-to-value programs.

Changing Subjects of Insurance Coverage

Personal lines underwriters must be capable of adjusting to changes in the nature of the items they are asked to insure. An underwriter of 1920 would have had no difficulty handling horse and wagon rigs, but an underwriter today probably would. And today's underwriter might be baffled by the risks that will exist in the personal lines insurance market in the year 2000.

Today's personal lines underwriting involves not only homes, personal property, and autos, but also boats ranging from simple outboards to oceangoing yachts, all kinds of light aircraft including jets, plus an array of recreational vehicles such as snowmobiles, golf carts, motorbikes, campers, trailers, mobile homes, and motor homes. Extensive travel with an increasing variety and value of personal belongings accompanying the traveler creates exposures to loss for many more items in more situations than was the case even ten years ago. The underwriter must be aware of these exposures and, equally important, he or she must be prepared for change. An underwriter who, around the turn of the century, initiated the writing of auto insurance by adapting a policy form used in the writing of coverage on teams of animals probably did not anticipate the future of auto insurance which now accounts for about 40 percent of the property-liability insurance premium volume.

Another rapidly changing area is that of methods and materials used in residential construction. Modern building methods increasingly involve precut, prefabricated, and modular construction. Modern construction components for new homes are sometimes more flammable, less wind-resistive, and more prone to lightning damage or electrical surge. These factors may modify classification and rating practices, underwriting requirements, or both. Increased emphasis on and acceptance of solar energy in construction of dwellings open up whole new areas of values, hazards, loss projections, and so on. While there

Exhibit 1-1
Home Purchase Subindex of Consumer Price Index*

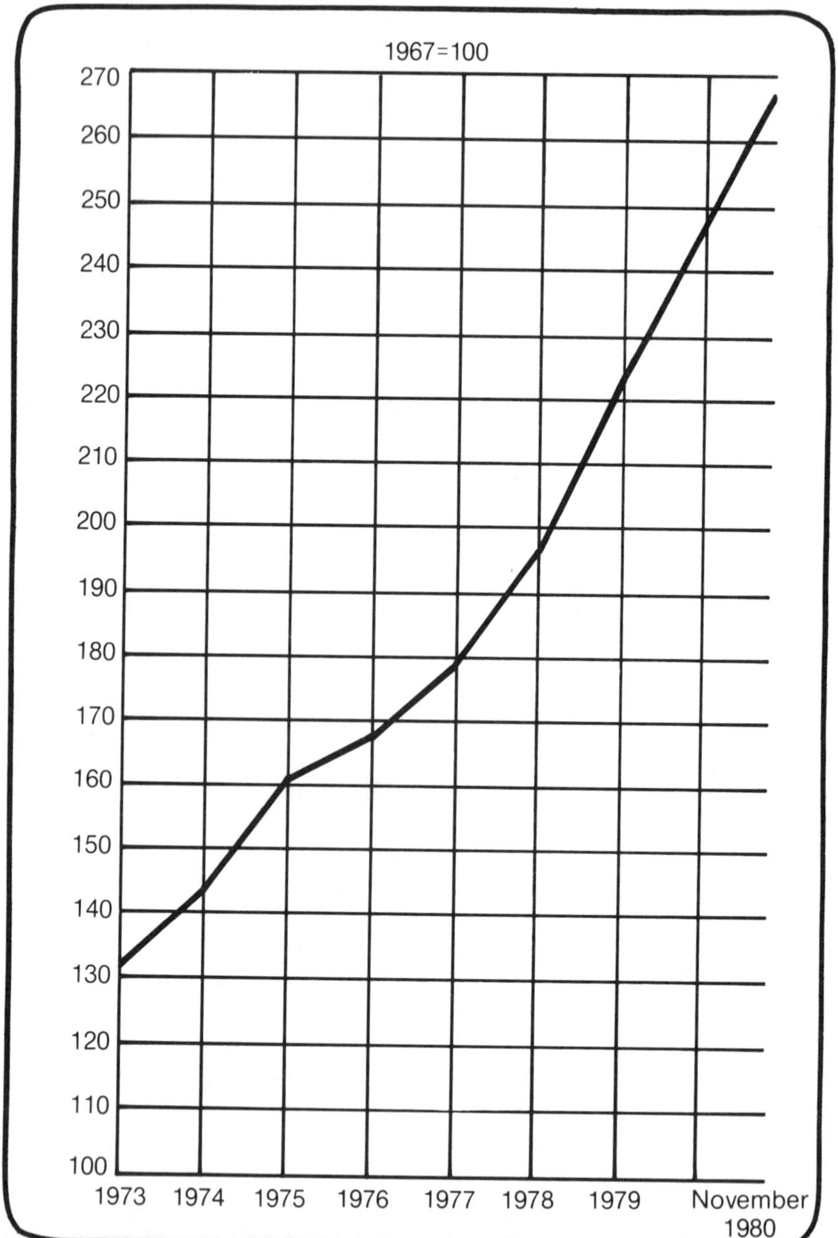

* Adapted from *Economic Report of the President*, U.S. Government Printing Office, 1981.

are no clear-cut guidelines to follow, the underwriting function cannot ignore these challenges.

A final change to be mentioned here deals with dwelling unit forms. "Condominium" and "townhouse" were little-used expressions as recently as 1965. The condominium reflects a unique ownership form of the residential real property of an individual or family. The townhouse reflects a construction format, familiar to many as the rowhouse, having outer side walls that serve the owner of a unit as well as the neighbors on each side. Both of these types of units present the residence underwriter with some considerations different from those associated with the traditional single-family home.

Increased Emphasis on Affordability and the Right to Insurance

The property-liability insurance business increasingly finds itself in a position of conflict between long-accepted practices in selection and rating and the notion that people who need protection from sudden financial loss should be able to have insurance on an affordable basis. This conflict is not new. Indeed, the history of auto insurance plans clearly demonstrates the conflict. These plans have not been self-supporting in providing auto insurance for drivers uninsurable in the voluntary market. Their poor financial performance reflects a reluctance on the part of society to force a segment of the driving population to carry insurance and pay its fair share of losses and expenses. The philosophy underlying these plans has been one of a "right" to insurance coverage. The concept of "fair" or "equitable" prices by traditional insurance rating criteria has been in part replaced by a norm of fairness based on affordability.

The point to be noted is the continuing shift away from insurance as the business of insurance people and toward the right to affordable protection from financial loss, even if that price is less than proportionate to the hazards involved. This trend involves the creation of additional private, public, or mixed markets—such as FAIR plans, the federal crime insurance program, the flood insurance program, windstorm and beach pools—and direct or indirect subsidy from outside the group insured in the particular market.

It is not yet possible for everyone desiring insurance to obtain it at an affordable price. However, the problem of providing insurance at an affordable price is increasingly the concern of persons outside the insurance business who are able to influence whatever legislative decisions are made.

Increased Recognition of Economies of Scale

As used here, the term "economies of scale" refers to the savings in the cost *per unit* (not total costs) brought about by repetition or handling of tasks on a batch basis rather than an individual basis. One auto manufacturer could design a new car, build a factory, buy machinery and equipment, hire and train personnel, buy raw materials, and produce one unit of the new vehicle. Its cost per unit would be the total costs incurred—a rather high unit cost. If it produced a second unit, the cost per unit would be cut almost in half. Five thousand cars later, the cost per unit would be very much lower, and the auto manufacturer would be enjoying economies of scale. In effect, the cost per unit is lowered by "mass production." Where the task(s) to be performed, or the product to be produced, is uniform from performance to performance or unit to unit, and large numbers are involved, the potential for achieving economies of scale is present.

This concept can also be applied to the personal lines of property-liability insurance. The product is relatively standardized, is sold and serviced in large numbers, and involves many activities common to all policies (e.g., issuance, billing). In short, the personal lines insurance field can readily achieve economies of scale. This fact is not new, but the ability to capitalize on it was not exercised to any great extent until the advent of electronic computers and their accessory equipment. The computer caused a revolution in the insurance industry with its combination of speed and reliability, and in the middle and late 1950s many companies began to generate unit cost savings.

Perhaps one of the first mass production methods employed in personal lines insurance was the advent of computer-billed auto policies. Continuous policies were designed which eliminated the need for issuing a new policy each policy period, resulting in obvious cost savings. The information regarding the insured, the coverage, and losses could be permanently stored in the computer, available for call-up at any time. Premium billings are automatic, as are interim updates showing the property covered.

New uses for computers and other equipment for the storage, manipulation, or transmission of data are discovered regularly, particularly in the high-volume personal lines. A later chapter in this text treats this subject in depth.

Another way in which some insurers have seen the potential for economies of scale in the personal lines is through *mass merchandising*—a marketing program directed to members of a group, typically the employees of one employer. These efforts for the most part are not *group* underwriting. Individual risk underwriting is practiced, but economies are sought through simplified sales and servicing activities made possible by dealing with a number of risks under common sponsorship.

Efforts to cut costs or minimize cost increases will continue in the large volume, relatively standardized, personal lines. Insurers recognize the need to maximize the portion of the premium dollar returned to insureds in loss payments and other benefits by reducing the expense portion.

Changes in the Availability and Uses of Information

Another trend of significance to personal lines underwriting is one of increasing constraints on (1) the types of information available for underwriting purposes, and (2) the ways in which underwriting information can be gathered and used. As indicated previously, in a number of states certain risk characteristics traditionally used in making underwriting decisions can no longer be used as underwriting information. In some cases, these risk characteristics may be used for classification and rating, but they may not be used as the basis for a risk-selection decision. Under question today in some states is the propriety of those states providing motor vehicle records to insurance companies. Does this practice invade an individual's privacy by making available information that should (according to the proponents of the change) be a matter strictly between the individual and the state, or is the motor vehicle record "public information" that should be available to any interested party for an appropriate fee? This issue illustrates the public scrutiny to which the underwriting process is subject. It seems certain that this matter—what information the underwriter can use (or get)—will continue to change for some time. There is a great deal of variation among states in the extent to which changes have been made.

Dissatisfaction with outside inspection reports led to the passage of the Fair Credit Reporting Act of 1971, a major piece of federal legislation that has had an impact on the gathering and availability (to the subject of the report) of information collected and retained by private reporting agencies. Since these agencies are a principal source of what the underwriter might refer to as "inspection reports," the new ground rules imposed by the act directly affect insurance companies as well as other users of these agencies. (Much of the information in reports for insurance companies is common to the needs of the other two major users of credit reporting agencies—employers hiring new employees and business firms making loans or extending credit.) The act does little to change the kinds of information that can be gathered and reported by these agencies, but it opens up the process substantially by giving the subject of the report rights involving advance notice of the inspection to be made and access to the information gathered.

THE PERSONAL LINES UNDERWRITING PROCESS

Personal lines underwriting involves people, manuals, policies, calculators, typewriters, buildings, and of course, computers. All of these ingredients are important to the underwriting function, as is the design and use of various systems, procedures, and methods by which the underwriting work flows through the office.

This section will examine broadly the characteristics of personal lines underwriting and review certain aspects of the underwriting process in a personal lines context. In its broadest sense, underwriting refers to the process of hazard recognition and evaluation, risk selection, pricing, and determination of policy terms and conditions.

Of course, this process involves not only the actual acceptance or rejection of risks, but also the development of company underwriting policy and guides, the drafting and implementation of marketing plans, the rating and classification of all risks, the analysis of statistical data, the ordering of needed investigative reports, and finally, the issuing of all new and renewal policies. As its objective, underwriting endeavors to obtain a profitable distribution of risks by line, by class, and by territory, and guards against adverse selection. Essentially, however, underwriting is fundamentally a process of employing people to make decisions. Underwriting should not be confused with equipment, systems, and work procedures that help the underwriter and the underwriting department in their work. Underwriters at Lloyd's 200 years ago did not have the benefit of industrial engineers, systems and computer specialists, rapid communications, or even the battery-powered hand calculators. But they *were* underwriting, and like the decisions of the underwriter today, their decisions were the critical ingredient in the overall underwriting function. Physical surroundings, location, work flow, and the like are not critical elements. The underwriter and the process for making underwriting decisions are the central factors involved.

Characteristics of the Personal Lines Underwriting Process

Relatively Heavy Reliance on Producer for Underwriting Information In order to reach a final decision, the underwriter needs data. Detailed information about the person and/or property to be insured is required.

In personal lines insurance the average policy premium is small and does not contain sufficient expense loading to support extensive efforts to gather and verify information. Therefore, the producer is both the original and primary source of underwriting information, and plays a relatively more important role as an information source in personal lines than in commercial lines. It is the producer's obligation to provide complete and accurate information on an application or daily report and to supply additional information as requested by the underwriter. On a risk not already in force, the producer is expected to give a personal analysis of the risk and perhaps a specific recommendation as to the risk's acceptability.

The producer, then, is a very important element in the underwriting of personal lines risks. Good relationships with producers and their personnel give the underwriter an advantage in developing and maintaining a profitable book of business. The word "good" does not imply a relationship in which the underwriter and the producer always agree. It does mean a relationship in which the underwriter attempts to understand the producer's position, maintains objectivity, knows his or her job, and can support decisions in a clear and reasonable way.

Reliance on Manuals for Classification and Rating Most types of personal lines policies are class rated. Therefore, proper use of manuals in classifying and rating risks is an integral part of processing submissions. This task is not always performed by the underwriter. In many firms, persons subordinate to the underwriter, persons in a separate department, or the producer's office may do the rating. Nevertheless, underwriters must understand the rationale of classifications and class rates, both of which were dealt with fully in UND 61, and they must recognize the importance of relating hazards to rate through proper classification. A misclassified risk is unfair to someone—the applicant if the premium is too high, or the company and (usually) the producer if the premium is too low.

Relatively Small Number of Underwriting Alternatives On large commercial risks an underwriter may use loss control (engineering) principles and techniques to improve a marginal risk and turn it into a clearly acceptable piece of business for the insurer. Or a rating plan may be suggested that will closely relate the cost of insurance to the insured's own loss experience. A very large deductible may be used, or only a portion of the coverage desired may be written.

In personal lines, an underwriter may have relatively few alternatives, but he or she does have some. An auto underwriter, for example, may require a higher collision deductible than that applied for or may require a deductible on comprehensive coverage (sometimes written without a deductible). He or she may require named-peril coverage in place of comprehensive coverage if underwriting information so warrants. The liability limit(s) requested may be refused but the policy issued if lower limits are acceptable to the applicant. The underwriter can refuse to include certain optional coverages such as towing and labor costs. A homeowners underwriter may require that the flue pipe entering the chimney be replaced, that new wiring be installed to provide safe electrical service, that a suitable handrail be placed on the front steps, or that adequate safeguards be installed around the swimming pool. (These assume, of course, that the underwriter has ordered an inspection of the property.)

The principal difference between personal lines and commercial lines underwriting alternatives is that the higher potential commercial lines premium justifies a greater investment in improving and maintaining the quality of a marginal risk. The personal lines underwriter must be very cost conscious in any attempt to work out alternatives to an "accept-or-reject" decision. Personal lines business is a class-rated business that must rely on small dollar profit margins on a large number of risks for profitability, not expensive engineering on individual risks.

Types of Underwriting

Underwriting involves two kinds of selection: *preselection* and *postselection.* Preselection has to do with *new business* going on the books, including the initial underwriting of business already bound by a producer. Postselection deals with *in-force* business—risks that are already on the books—and includes both the review of existing business *mid-term* and the consideration of risks prior to *renewal.* Review and renewal underwriting can be further subdivided into attention to individual policies and attention to a group or book of business identified by some directive of underwriting management (e.g., all personal auto contracts of a particular producer).

New Business Underwriting (Preselection) In underwriting a new risk it is important for the underwriter to see that the underwriting information is complete, that the risk is eligible and acceptable according to company guidelines, and that it is correctly classified and rated. If any conditions are known at inception that could change the risk's desirability in the future (e.g., a fifteen-year-old son as a potential principal operator), then the file should be flagged to bring it up automatically for further consideration at an appropriate point in the future. The underwriter should know enough about the producer and the record of the producer's book of business to properly evaluate the information given by that producer. It may be necessary to check further with the producer on some incomplete or uncertain item. In addition, the underwriter must decide what outside investigative reports, such as a motor vehicle report and/or inspection report, should be ordered and must be prepared to review the file when these reports are received. A prompt decision on acceptance, acceptance with modification, or rejection must be made. The decision must be implemented, and procedures for any special monitoring of the decision should be established.

In-Force Underwriting (Postselection) Most personal lines risks are not static but are constantly changing to at least some extent. In addition, the social, legal, economic, political, and regulatory climate is dynamic. *Monitoring* underwriting decisions is one of the most important activities of underwriting. Good risks may become poor risks due to excessive claim frequency and/or severity. Homes get older and may become less well-maintained. A new high-performance car may replace a standard model. A family may purchase a vacation home on a lake or river or ocean which may be inaccessible at certain times during the year. An insured may open a beauty shop in the home. Company policy may not permit the high limits of liability requested. Underwriting profitability for a particular line may deteriorate to the point that risks once acceptable can no longer be retained. Any one or all of these situations, plus many others, could change the underwriter's original decision to accept into a decision to reject or accept with modification.

Underwriting business already on the books can be looked at in two ways. The first is on an *individual risk* basis which may be prompted on a regular basis (such as at renewal time) or on an irregular basis (such as claims activity). The second is on a *book of business* basis (by territory, by producer, etc.) which is primarily done to identify and solve an underwriting problem.

Individual Policies. Individual policies may be reevaluated, at least in part, for a variety of reasons. The most common points at which this monitoring step may take place are (1) when an endorsement is requested, (2) after a claim, (3) when the risk is about to change, and (4) prior to renewal.

Endorsements. If an underwriter is asked to add a second or third car to be used by a sixteen-year-old student, the risk often will be reevaluated before the issuance of the endorsement adding the second or third car. Should the underwriter issue the endorsement but order motor vehicle reports? Should the youth's car be excluded or written separately? This is in-force underwriting brought about by endorsement. Other requests for changing coverages, changing locations, increasing amounts of insurance, or any number of other changes, are all opportunities to *reunderwrite* so as to continue to have a risk that is acceptable as well as properly classified and rated.

Claims. By far the most common type of in-force underwriting on individual policies takes place after a claim is submitted. While each company has a slightly different set of criteria for in-force underwriting on claims, the following is illustrative:

1. If a claim is severe (over some specified figure, such as $2,500) the file is immediately referred to the underwriter, who may place the file in suspense to watch for future claims of any amount.
2. If there is a frequency of claims (usually two or more in one year), again the file is referred to the underwriter's attention and the underwriting process starts all over again. Because of this new underwriting information, a new decision to accept or reject must be reached. Or, a decision might be made to put the file in suspense until renewal consideration or, if sooner, until another claim of any size or type is submitted or until an endorsement is requested.
3. If, while handling a routine claim, the claims adjuster uncovers adverse data bearing on the risk, the file is referred to the underwriter for proper action based on the new information.

CHANGES IN THE RISK. Some changes in the risk are obvious from policy activity dealing with endorsements and claims. Other changes, however, might be of a kind that are detectable through existing information but do not yet create any policy activity. Some of these are significant enough to warrant advance notice and possibly generate underwriting concern. The existence of a teenager about to reach driving age in a personal auto risk is a good example. It may be that nothing more is done than the triggering of a comprehensive review before renewal. On the other hand, the risk may already be marginal and the rate for the future teenage driver might not be commensurate with the increased exposure, calling for firmer action than simply "reconsideration" prior to renewal.

PRIOR TO RENEWAL. In a sense, all personal lines policies are reunderwritten prior to renewal. While only a small percentage of a company's book of policies may get individual attention at that time, an automatic renewal is, in effect, another decision to accept. The absence of a new decision *is* a decision to write the risk. In most companies, a substantial percentage of personal lines risks move from policy period to policy period in this fashion.

The three factors briefly discussed above indicated a number of circumstances that could result in formal reconsideration of a risk prior to renewal. Numerous other factors could produce the same result—a risk marginal at initial acceptance that has been flagged for obtaining current information on a continuous basis, age of operator or vehicle insured, investigation of amounts of insurance relative to value, rate or classification changes, changes in underwriting policy on particular classes, presence of a particular coverage that has been very unprofitable, and so on. Computer sorting of files, high speed printouts, and file summary reproduction on desk terminals (CRTs) has greatly reduced the labor in isolating policies subject to review.

Companies differ greatly in their approach to renewal underwriting. The goal at this point is to identify that step and some of the reasons it is taken. More detail on the subject, and on monitoring in general, will be presented later in this text.

Review of a Book of Business. A *book* of business means any group of policies with some common denominator. The common denominator used would vary with the purpose of identifying the group. The term "book" could be applied to all in-force business of the company, all private passenger auto business of the company, all business put on the books by an underwriter or by a branch office, all business from one producer, all residence business from one producer or in a particular territory, all business in a particular rating class in a given territory or put on the books by a particular underwriter, and so on. Each grouping can be identified and analyzed for some particular purpose. A company examines its overall book of business and its major subdivisions from time to time to determine operating results, to check for trends, to identify problems, and the like; so do branch and regional offices, underwriting departments, and individual underwriters.

Reviewing various books of business is a routine task of underwriting and general management. It is a control device little different in broad purpose from a manufacturing company's review of its revenues and expenses. It provides information on past company activity and possible future activity, and suggests areas of investigation or change if the organization's results are not being achieved.

Review of an underwriter's book of business, or a subdivision of it (also a "book"), can be triggered by a number of factors—routine control efforts, poor loss ratios, a change in underwriting policy, or a desire to verify classifications, to name some of the more common ones. Review of specific items in the book is known as "group or book review underwriting"—postselection in an organized fashion over a group of policies homogeneous in some way.

To illustrate, consider an underwriter's book of residence insurance in a particular territory. If the book has produced a poor loss ratio over time, hasty action might suggest heavy cancellations or nonrenewals, very selective future underwriting, or perhaps different pricing strategy. Instead, the book might be reviewed to see if the problem(s) can be more narrowly defined. Though overall rate level may be adequate, the book may be overloaded with an underpriced class or with a construction class that has experienced very poor results because of recent unusual weather disturbances in the area. Perhaps loss frequency on older homes is the problem, or perhaps the producers in the territory have not been diligent in securing insurance to value.

The diagnostic procedures can be laid out, information assembled and analyzed, the problem or problems identified, and appropriate underwriting action taken on those policies in the book that appear to be part of the problem. While costly and time consuming in some cases, the process of review may enable the underwriter to take specific underwriting action on a limited number of risks to upgrade the quality of the overall book rather than take some broad action on an indiscriminate basis.

Review underwriting of a book of business is a vital part of the monitoring step in the underwriting process. This step will be discussed in more detail in the discussions of particular lines of business later in this text.

SUMMARY

Personal lines insurance consists of those coverages designed for nonbusiness property and activities of individuals and families. Personal lines insurance is important to the public as compensation for insurable loss, as an aid in obtaining credit, and as a means of meeting legal obligations. The importance of personal lines to the insurance industry is reflected in the large number of insureds and the substantial premium volume.

The personal lines market (as compared to commercial lines) is characterized by a large number of buyers and sellers, the relative similarity of loss exposures, the lack of alternatives to insurance, the relatively inelastic demand, a heavy regulation of products and prices, relatively uninformed buyers, and a politically popular and sensitive market. Personal lines products designed to meet the needs of most insureds are characterized by standardization of policies, a high degree of packaging, and class rating. They also are more rigid in form and rate and involve a smaller average unit premium than most commercial lines products.

A number of trends are affecting the underwriting of personal lines, most of which require monitoring to assure that underwriting policy and philosophy are appropriate. The most important trends are (1) limitations on selectivity; (2) inflation; (3) changes in perils, hazards, and availability and uses of information; and (4) changes in the risks themselves. Of equal importance are the increased recognition of economies of scale, the emphasis on affordability and the right to insurance.

The basic underwriting decision-making process is applicable to personal lines as well as commercial lines. But in personal lines, this process is modified by the smaller number of underwriting alternatives, the use of manuals for rating, and the tendency to rely on the producer as the key source of underwriting information.

Because of the dynamic underwriting environment, monitoring underwriting decisions is becoming increasingly important. Monitoring may be applied to individual risks or to a book of personal lines business.

Chapter Notes

1. *Insurance Facts,* 1980-81 Edition, Insurance Information Institute, p. 18.
2. This calculation was based upon a personal consumption component of GNP of $1.51 trillion.
3. *Insurance Facts,* p. 18.
4. *Insurance Facts,* p. 4
5. *Public Attitude Monitor, 1980, Attitudes of the Public Toward Automobile Insurance,* All Industry Research Advisory Council, March 1981.
6. Duane D. Zellers, "Regulation of Cancellation and Nonrenewals," *CPCU Annals,* June 1973, vol. 26, no. 2, p. 47.
7. *Insurance Facts,* p. 5.

Making Underwriting Decisions: Auto Insurance

CHAPTER 2

Evaluating Hazards

INTRODUCTION

Chapter 2 is the first of four chapters dealing with the underwriting of personal auto insurance. This chapter begins with a brief discussion of the *types* of vehicles that are dealt with in this book. The special underwriting considerations of vehicles that are not private passenger autos (e.g., farm, utility, and recreational vehicles) are included in Chapter 3.

An overview of the scope of the personal auto insurance market and some important data on vehicles, drivers, and accidents, set the stage for the major segment of this chapter—evaluating hazards. Classification, pricing, decision making, and monitoring are covered in the next two chapters.

THE SCOPE OF PERSONAL AUTO INSURANCE

Auto insurers provide protection for damage to, and injury or damage caused by, a wide variety of vehicles ranging from private passenger autos to long-haul trucks and fleets of public passenger-carrying vehicles. In recognition of this diversity, the industry generally divides its policies, rating plans, and underwriting into the two major categories of *personal* and *commercial.*

This course deals only with personal auto risks. However, there are areas of overlap between the two categories both as to vehicle *types* and vehicle *uses.* In some instances, the vehicle type alone determines the category a risk falls into (e.g., a tractor-trailer rig is a commercial vehicle) while in other instances it is the use of the vehicle that decides (e.g., a taxicab, though structurally the same as a personal auto, is classified as a commercial vehicle; on the other hand, a pickup or panel truck owned by an individual or husband and wife may be considered a personal auto, depending upon the use of the vehicle). These and other subtleties of the personal-commercial division will be dealt with in more detail in this chapter.

Types of Vehicles

A wide variety of vehicles may be encountered by the personal auto insurance underwriter. The purpose of this section is to classify and briefly describe these vehicles.

Private Passenger Autos Private passenger autos compose the great bulk of the personal auto insurance market. The personal auto manual of the Insurance Services Office defines a private passenger auto as follows:

1. A private passenger auto is a four wheel motor vehicle, other than a truck type, owned or leased under contract for a continuous period of at least six months, and
    a. not used as a public or livery conveyance for passengers,
    b. not rented to others.
2. A motor vehicle that is a pickup, panel truck, or van, shall be considered a private passenger auto, if:
    a. owned by an individual or by a husband and wife who are residents of the same household, and
    b. not customarily used in the occupation, profession or business of the insured, other than farming or ranching.
3. A motor vehicle owned by a farm family co-partnership, or farm family corporation shall be considered a private passenger auto owned by two or more relatives who are residents of the same household if:
    a. it is principally garaged on a farm or ranch, and
    b. it otherwise meets the definitions in 1. and 2. above.[1]

This definition, or one similar to it, is part of the manual rules of most companies and is used to determine eligibility for personal auto insurance underwriting and rating. The definition is broad enough to include a wide variety of vehicles. For example, dune buggies, hearses, and ambulances, when used as private passenger autos, are within the scope of this definition.

For the most part, private passenger autos are owned by an individual or husband and wife, though other forms of ownership are sometimes encountered.

A private passenger auto may be used for pleasure only, pleasure plus driving to and from work, either or both of the above plus business purposes, or even strictly business purposes. However, most insurers will not consider an auto to be a private passenger auto for insurance purposes if "business use" involves use as a public or livery conveyance (such as a taxi), use in the auto business (such as a dealer or a repair shop), or regular delivery use. These types of use are commercial and generally call for different policy forms and rating plans than those used for private passenger autos.

Farm Vehicles Private passenger autos of farmers are included within the scope of "private passenger autos" as discussed under the preceding heading. Certain trucks used in farming (e.g., pickups, delivery sedans, or panel delivery trucks) are considered personal (as opposed to commercial) risks by most companies. In fact, policy definitions, manual rules, and filings are usually broad enough to include these vehicles under the term "private passenger auto." They are mentioned separately here to reinforce this point. Note, however, that many farm motor vehicles—tractors, larger trucks, special equipment—require separate treatment, though the dividing line between what is and is not handled by the personal lines underwriter varies greatly by company.

Recreational Vehicles Not too many years ago, most underwriters rarely encountered a recreational vehicle submission. Obviously, this situation is quite different today.

Recreational vehicles can be divided into several major categories. Rating plans and underwriting policies and procedures may vary greatly from company to company. A number of companies have designed a special manual and "recreational vehicle" policy for writing some types of these vehicles.

Motor Homes. Probably the most familiar recreational vehicle is the motor home. Motor homes are units in which living quarters are an integral part of the overall vehicle structure. Most are built on a truck chassis, though the finished product bears little resemblance to a truck. Extensive plumbing, electrical, cooking, and air conditioning systems make the motor home unlike either a traditional auto or truck from an underwriting standpoint.

Motor homes are self-propelled vehicular living units. The cost for new units ranges upward from $10,000, with larger and more elaborate units built on a bus chassis costing more than $50,000. At times, underwriters will encounter applications on old school or commercial buses that have been converted into recreational vehicles. Insuring vehicles of this kind involves underwriting considerations drawn from both the personal and commercial sides of the business.

Truck-mounted Campers. The truck-mounted camper unit provides completely sheltered living facilities in rigid structural form, but usually can be removed from the bed or chassis of the pickup truck to which it is attached. Truck-mounted campers are often equipped with stilts for stability when removed from the truck.

Aside from the cost of the truck to which the box-like unit is attached, the cost of truck-mounted campers runs from $2,500 up. Like converted buses, there are some "home-made" campers with which the underwriter may have to contend. Some look like nothing more than a box enclosing the area over the back of a small pickup. Others are more elaborate and, though smaller in interior dimensions than most motor homes, may provide virtually the same range of living accommodations as many motor homes.

Camper Trailers. These are small, compact units designed to be towed by a private passenger car and are sometimes referred to as "pop-up" trailers. They resemble low profile two-wheeled utility trailers when prepared for towing but unfold or crank up onto structures encased in fabric or other soft material to provide sleeping quarters and other modest comforts for temporary living.

House or Travel Trailers. The house or travel trailer (used hereafter) resembles the camper trailer in the sense that it is designed to be towed and has two wheels (or two sets of double wheels) located near the middle of the sides of the unit. However, the travel trailer is usually all metal; of permanently rigid construction; larger, heavier, and more elaborately equipped; often heated and air conditioned; and obviously more suited to longer trips and on-the-road living.

Travel trailers may be as long as thirty feet, and while built as trailers they can be every bit as complete and luxurious as the finest motor homes. Most may be towed by a passenger car, but some have a gooseneck hitch requiring a pickup truck for towing.

Travel trailers should be distinguished from mobile homes because of the different underwriting factors involved. Mobile homes are designed for relatively long or permanent stays in fixed locations as regular residential units with regular utility hookups. They are "trailers" only in the sense that they must be hauled behind a relatively powerful vehicle from location to location. Many travel only once—from dealer to the homesite or rented lot of the buyer—after transit from the manufacturer to the dealer. The underwriting of mobile home coverages is considered in the residence underwriting chapters of this text.

Golf Carts. The golf cart, or golfmobile, is a small low-speed vehicle designed originally for the transportation of golfers on golf courses. Most are powered by an electric battery but some have small gasoline engines.

Many are owned by persons owning property adjacent to or integrated with a golf course. The underwriter of personal auto risks in some states may seldom see an application of this type. However, in some specially designed residential areas (especially in the south and southwest) the golf cart is used as a means of regular transportation and is subject to motor vehicle registration.

Snowmobiles. Snowmobiles have become extremely popular in all areas of the United States offering a reasonably regular snowfall. Priced from about $1,000 up, snowmobiles usually have a single wide track or tread in the back connected to a gasoline engine power source. The steering mechanism is attached to two flexible skis supporting the front of the vehicle. Most are designed to carry one or two people, though a sled may be towed behind. Some states require some form of registration for snowmobiles, which often brings them into the realm of personal auto insurance underwriting. Depending on the state and insurer involved, a snowmobile may be insured under an auto policy or a special recreational vehicle policy.

Midget Automobiles. Small vehicles equipped with lawnmower type gasoline engines, usually having only a single seat for the driver, are known as midget autos or as "go-carts." Most are geared for low speeds but some are capable of speeds of up to sixty mph. Usual sites of operation are parking lots, large open areas, streets, and sidewalks. These vehicles are usually not registered and are often operated by young, unlicensed drivers.

All Terrain Vehicles. These vehicles come in a wide variety of shapes and sizes. A typical ATV seats two people and runs on four oversized tires or, in a few cases, on tracks. It is designed to run over rough ground, through swampy areas, or over sand and snow. The typical ATV is a modification of a standard vehicle, with the major changes involving a shortening of the wheelbase, removal of the standard body, and removal of any frame elements made unnecessary by the other changes. The so-called "dune buggy" is perhaps the most common type of ATV.

Though an ATV is capable of operating on public highways, many states do not permit this unless it is being towed. Some ATVs are amphibious (can operate on land and on water) and present both auto and watercraft exposures.

Minibikes. This type of vehicle is a low-powered, two-wheeled "miniature" motorcycle designed for off-the-road use, often on special trails. Minibikes are geared low for this kind of use and speeds usually do not exceed twenty-five mph. They are usually ridden by one person, often a child not old enough to be licensed to drive, and are often considered a toy more than a means of transportation.

Motorcycles and Mopeds A large segment of personal lines vehicles other than private passenger autos consists of motorcycles. Although occasionally a sidecar and accompanying third wheel are attached, the typical motorcycle is a two-wheeled, gasoline-powered vehicle capable of rapid acceleration, high speeds, and regular road and highway travel. It is larger, faster, and more powerful than the minibike and a close cousin designed for road use, the motorscooter.

Small (relative to their forerunners), mostly Japanese-built motorcycles dominate the United States market today. Many are owned by students and business or professional persons who often use them to ride to and from work because of their economical performance. Others are used largely for recreational purposes on weekends. It is not uncommon to see a motor home with one or two motorcycles (or motorscooters) hitched to the back or side(s). The so-called "trailbike" is a specialized type of motorcycle designed for use on a track or, in some areas, cross country. In some cases, it may be registered for use on the highway.

A recent addition to the ever-growing list of vehicles is the moped. A moped is basically a bicycle equipped with a small motor producing power less than or equal to two brake horsepower that gives the vehicle a top speed of thirty mph. The motor is generally started by pedaling and has an automatic transmission. It is estimated that there were as many as 1 million mopeds on U.S. roadways in 1980 and this could increase to 2.5 million by 1984. The National Highway Traffic Safety Administration estimates that if ridership increases as expected, there may be as many as 1,200 fatalities annually from moped crashes by 1984.[2]

Antique and Classic Automobiles Broadly defined, antique cars are motor vehicles of the private passenger type over twenty-five years of age. In general, antique cars are written at reduced rates if registered as an antique and if use is restricted to exhibitions, parades, or special antique auto club activities, with any on-the-road use being incidental to these types of events. Though otherwise an antique, a thirty-year-old car used for normal driving purposes usually would not be eligible for special rating consideration.

The classic car is more difficult to define. In common with the antique, the available quantities of cars considered classics are usually small, relative to demand for them, but they are not necessarily old. A sign that a "used" car has become a classic is a change from depreciation to appreciation in the market value of cars in good condition. Personal tastes dictate such a change.

Examples of cars now considered classics are the 1955 Ford Thunderbird, the 1965 Ford Mustang, and the ill-fated Ford Edsel of 1957 and 1958. More recently, the 1976 Cadillac convertible, supposedly the last of that type to be manufactured, has already been selling at a premium over initial sale price in the "used" car market.

Replicas of antiques and classics are produced by several specialty manufacturers. These can be assembled on a standard vehicle chassis using a "kit" of parts created to produce a vehicle identical in appearance to the antique or classic.

Utility Autos Utility autos, when used and rated as personal risks, are within the scope of this course. This group includes vehicles such as jeeps, pickup trucks, small vans, and panel trucks. The outdoor recreation boom of recent years has resulted in broader interest in these vehicles. Though more common in our rural areas and western states, they can be found in use as standard family vehicles in all parts of the country.

Today, the pickup truck often is a family's second car. It may be used for driving to and from work most of the year, but on weekends and during vacations a camper unit may be added to make it a recreational vehicle. Current models of pickups (and passenger vans) often have luxurious operator areas, plush carpeting, and stereo radios or tape players—a far cry from the standard truck image. Customized vans are growing in popularity and may have cooking and other facilities for recreational use. Jeeps and jeep-type vehicles can be used for plowing snow, pushing other vehicles, and, along with the pickup, for many chores on farms and ranches.

Trailers In addition to the trailers that are simply towable living accommodations, the personal auto underwriter will encounter a variety of trailers designed for use with a car, light truck, or motor home. These may be specialized in purpose—for boats, horses, farm products, or personal articles needing protection from the elements—or they may be simply utility trailers for hauling cargo or trash.

Electric Cars Recent concern with air pollution and fuel sources has led to increased interest in the development of small passenger autos powered by batteries. The state of technology is not yet well developed and must still overcome limitations on acceleration, speed, and range between battery recharges. Scores of prototypes have been developed, but only two—the Citicar and the Elcar—have been sold in any volume, and that is still comparatively small.

Electric autos probably will grow in popularity with the growth of retirement communities, but the personal auto underwriter may never have to consider one unless a technological breakthrough makes electric power a more acceptable substitute for the internal combustion engine. This text will not deal with electric autos any further except to note that those currently available seem to present a high potential for injury to occupants. Underwriters should treat these vehicles with caution.

The Personal-Commercial Division

There is no consistently applied division between "personal" and "commercial" auto underwriting in the insurance industry. As a result, this chapter and succeeding ones may discuss some types of vehicles that may not be handled as "personal" auto insurance in every company or agency. For some companies, it is convenient to make a split that follows the Insurance Services Office (ISO) personal and commercial rating plans. In other words, if ISO locates rules and rates for a certain type of vehicle in the commercial section of its manual, then a company will categorize it as a commercial line. Other companies may use the nature of the account as the determining factor for classifying a particular risk (and quite probably the underwriting of it) as personal or commercial for internal handling purposes. For example, coverages for an account in which the insured is an individual or husband and wife may be handled by the personal auto underwriter with all others being classed as commercial.

Ownership or use of the vehicle may be the deciding factor. A small truck may still be considered a personal auto risk even though used for certain business activities. For example, a panel truck used by a plumber to carry tools to and from jobs might be considered a personal risk, but a similar vehicle used for wholesale or retail delivery would not. A private passenger type auto owned by a corporation as part of a "fleet" and used by a sales representative for the firm usually is underwritten as a commercial auto, whereas the same vehicle owned by the sales representative or the representative and spouse would get personal auto treatment.

Even recreational vehicles can fall into either category. Snowmobiles and golf carts, for example, would be considered personal if owned and used primarily for recreation by the owner and owner's family, but commercial if held for rental or permissive use by an otherwise commercial account (e.g., a resort hotel).

Vehicle, Driver, and Loss Data

Exhibit 2-1 shows approximately 159,400,000 registered vehicles in the United States in 1979, the vast majority of which are private passenger type autos and station wagons owned by individuals.

The balance of this section focuses on several tables. They contain

Exhibit 2-1
United States Motor Vehicle Registrations—1961-1979 (in billions)*

Year	Total Motor Vehicle Registrations	Yearly Percent Change
1961	76,400	
1962	79,700	+4.3
1963	83,500	+4.8
1964	87,300	+4.6
1965	91,800	+5.2
1966	95,900	+4.5
1967	98,900	+3.1
1968	103,100	+4.2
1969	107,700	+4.5
1970	111,200	+3.2
1971	116,300	+4.6
1972	122,300	+5.2
1973	129,800	+6.1
1974	134,900	+3.9
1975	138,000	+2.3
1976	143,500	+4.0
1977	148,800	+3.7
1978	153,600	+3.2
1979	159,400	+3.8

* Adapted from *Accident Facts 1980 Edition* (Chicago: National Safety Council, 1980), p. 56.

data on a number of variables directly relating to auto insurance and its underwriting.

During 1979 there were 26,699,000 auto accidents resulting in 5,681,000 injuries and an estimated 51,900 deaths. Total economic loss has been estimated at $56 billion.[3]

Exhibit 2-2 shows by state for 1979:

1. the number of motor vehicle traffic deaths,
2. the mileage death rates,
3. the registration death rates, and
4. the population death rates.

Exhibit 2-3 shows deaths and death rates per 100 million vehicle miles over a twenty-nine-year span. While the number of drivers and vehicles has continued to climb, the deaths per 100 million vehicle miles has dropped substantially.

Some of this favorable trend is due to the use of seatbelts and the presence of other safety equipment in cars. Safer highways have also

Exhibit 2-2
Motor Vehicle Deaths Statistics by State—1979*

State	Number of Deaths	Mileage Death Rate[1]	Registration Death Rate[2]	Population Death Rate[3]
Alabama	1,020	3.7	3.5	27.1
Alaska	90	3.1	3.2	22.2
Arizona	1,030	5.1	5.6	42.0
Arkansas	548	3.5	3.6	25.1
California	5,503	3.4	3.3	24.1
Colorado	691	3.4	2.5	24.9
Connecticut	576	2.9	2.5	18.5
Delaware	121	3.1	3.0	20.8
Florida	2,637	3.5	3.6	29.8
Georgia	1,523	3.3	3.9	29.8
Hawaii	205	4.0	3.7	22.4
Idaho	333	4.4	3.9	36.8
Illinois	2,048	3.1	2.7	18.2
Indiana	1,309	3.0	3.2	24.2
Iowa	654	3.1	2.5	22.5
Kansas	520	3.4	2.5	22.0
Kentucky	905	3.2	3.3	25.7
Louisiana	1,187	4.8	4.3	29.5
Maine	241	3.3	3.2	22.0
Maryland	700	2.4	2.4	16.9
Massachusetts	920	2.8	2.4	15.9
Michigan	1,847	2.9	2.7	20.1
Minnesota	881	3.0	3.1	21.7
Mississippi	716	4.3	4.3	29.5
Missouri	1,162	3.4	3.5	23.9
Montana	332	4.9	3.5	42.2
Nebraska	330	2.7	2.6	21.0
Nevada	365	6.3	5.6	52.0
New Hampshire	184	3.0	2.5	20.7
New Jersey	1,141	2.1	2.4	15.6
New Mexico	650	5.6	5.9	52.4
New York	2,377	3.8	2.8	13.5
North Carolina	1,522	3.6	3.3	27.1
North Dakota	127	2.5	2.0	19.3
Ohio	2,281	3.1	2.7	21.3
Oklahoma	869	3.3	3.3	30.0
Oregon	675	3.5	3.3	26.7
Pennsylvania	2,204	3.0	3.1	18.8
Rhode Island	125	1.9	1.8	13.5
South Carolina	900	3.8	4.5	30.7
South Dakota	211	3.8	3.4	30.6

Tennessee	1,236	3.2	4.0	28.2
Texas	4,229	4.1	3.9	31.6
Utah	330	3.5	3.1	24.1
Vermont	163	4.4	4.1	33.1
Virginia	1,014	2.6	2.8	19.5
Washington	1,032	3.5	3.2	26.3
West Virginia	532	4.8	4.2	28.7
Wisconsin	997	3.0	3.3	21.1
Wyoming	244	5.3	5.4	54.2

[1] Motor-vehicle traffic deaths per 100,000,000 vehicle miles.
[2] Motor-vehicle traffic deaths per 10,000 motor vehicles.
[3] Motor-vehicle traffic deaths per 100,000 population.

* Adapted from *Accident Facts 1980 Edition* (Chicago: National Safety Council, 1980), pp. 62, 63.

Exhibit 2-3
Traffic Deaths and Death Rates—1950-1979*

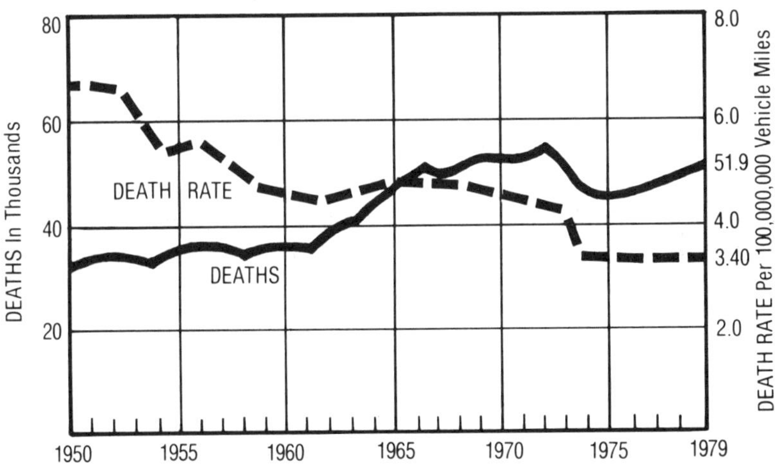

* Adapted from *Accident Facts 1980 Edition* (Chicago: National Safety Council, 1980), p. 59.

been a contributing factor. The energy crisis in 1974 and the accompanying imposition of a national fifty-five mph speed limit caused a further dip in the death rate as well as an absolute decline in the number of highway deaths for a short period. As enforcement of the fifty-five mph speed limit was relaxed in the late seventies, however, the absolute number of deaths again reached 50,000. Exhibit 2-4 shows the number of traffic accidents, deaths, and injuries in the United States during the period from 1955 to 1979.

Exhibit 2-4
Traffic Accidents, Deaths, and Injuries in the United States*

Year	Accidents	Deaths	Injuries
1955	11,516,000	38,426	2,158,000
1960	11,429,000	38,137	3,078,000
1965	14,733,000	49,163	3,982,000
1970	22,116,000	54,633	4,983,000
1975	24,887,000	45,853	4,978,000
1976	25,439,000	47,038	5,269,000
1977	26,716,000	49,510	5,575,000
1978	27,742,000	51,500	5,798,000
1979	26,669,000	51,900	5,681,000

* Adapted from *Insurance Facts*, 1980-81 Edition, (New York: Insurance Information Institute, 1980), p. 53.

Exhibit 2-5 displays passenger auto use by purpose and length of trip. The data are hardly current, but it is doubtful that the passage of time has worked any substantial distortions on the findings of the study.

According to the data in Exhibit 2-5, over half of all auto trips are less than five miles in length, but more total miles are driven on trips in the ten to fifteen mile bracket. Over one-third of all trips and over 40 percent of all miles are devoted to to-and-from work and business related travel. Note also that the average trip distance (one-way) in these two categories is 9.4 miles and 16.1 miles, respectively.

The Personal Auto Insurance Market

The previous section dealt with autos, drivers, and losses in general. But the number of cars and drivers on the highways and the number insured are not the same. This section deals with the latter subject and with the economic significance of auto insurance sales to the property-liability insurance industry.

Insured Cars and Drivers According to the Insurance Information Institute nineteen states require either liability insurance or liability insurance coupled with so-called "no-fault" insurance.[4] As recently as 1970 only three states had such laws. The increase in the number of states requiring insurance has paralleled the initiation and spread of "no-fault" insurance laws. These laws for the most part required certain types of auto insurance. The tendency toward compulsion, imposed on a market growing of its own accord, points toward an

Exhibit 2-5
Auto Use by Purpose and Length of Trip*

Purpose of Travel	Percent of Trips	Distribution Travel (Miles)	Average Distance (Miles-One-Way)	Average Occupants Per Car
Earning a Living:				
To and from Work	31.9%	33.7%	9.4	1.4
Business Related to Work	4.3	7.9	16.1	1.6
Total	36.2	41.6	10.2	1.4
Family Business:				
Medical and Dental	1.8	1.6	8.4	2.1
Shopping	15.2	7.5	4.4	2.0
Other	14.0	10.2	6.5	1.9
Total	31.0	19.3	5.6	2.0
Educational, Civic, or Religion	9.3	4.9	4.7	2.5
Social and Recreational	22.4	33.0	13.1	2.5
All Purposes	100.0%	100.0%	8.9	1.9

Length of Trips

Trip Length (One-Way Miles)	Trips	Vehicle Miles
Under 5	54.1%	11.1%
5— 9	19.6	13.8
10—15	13.8	18.7
16—20	4.3	9.1
21—30	4.0	11.8
31—40	1.6	6.6
41—50	0.8	4.3
51—99	1.0	7.6
100 & Over	0.8	17.0
Total	100.0%	100.0%

*Reprinted from *Nationwide Personal Study (1969)* Reports No. 1 and 7, U.S. Federal Highway Administration.

abundance of personal auto underwriting opportunities for the property-liability insurance industry.

Economic Significance to the Industry In the post-World War II era, there has been an enormous growth in the number of autos and a parallel growth in the number of companies specializing in serving

Exhibit 2-6
Effect of Premium Volume and Loss Experience of Personal Auto on Insurer Results

Premiums earned all lines, 1981	$300,000,000
Losses incurred all lines, 1981	210,000,000
Loss ratio all lines, 1981	70%
Premiums earned personal auto, 1981	$120,000,000
Losses incurred personal auto, 1981	90,000,000
Loss ratio personal auto, 1981	75%

Assume auto losses incurred had been $85,200,000, producing an auto loss ratio of 71 percent and reducing losses incurred all lines to $205,200,000. In this case, the loss ratio for all lines would have been 68.4 percent.

this rapidly growing market. Some of these companies today remain specialty companies serving primarily the personal auto market. Others have branched out into other personal lines, and in some cases to commercial lines as well, but still see personal auto insurance accounting for their largest block of premium income.

During 1979, personal auto insurance written premiums exceeded $29.2 billion. This was 32 percent of total premium writings for the property-liability industry.[5] Personal auto insurance is by far the largest single line of property-liability insurance. When a line represents such a significant portion of overall activity of the industry or of an individual company, results in that line have an enormous effect on industry or company operating results.

Exhibit 2-6 demonstrates this and indirectly demonstrates the importance of sound underwriting. It assumes a company with total earned premiums of $300 million and 40 percent of this volume, or $120 million, in personal auto insurance. The table shows an aggregate loss ratio for all lines and for personal auto and demonstrates what *would* have happened to the aggregate ratio had the auto ratio been four points lower.

Disregarding any effects on the expense ratio, note that a reduction of four points in the personal auto loss ratio would have meant a decline in the company's aggregate loss ratio of 1.6 points. Expressing that reduction in terms of dollars means that incurred losses for the company as a whole would decline by $4,800,000 to $205,200,000. Comparing this figure to the given figure for premiums earned results in an aggregate loss ratio of 68.4 percent, instead of the actual 70 percent.

Exhibit 2-6 does not imply that more effective underwriting of personal auto business is *the* answer to the problem of adverse experience in this line during most recent years. Other forces, such as inflation, rate lags, and increasing statutory restrictions on the exercise of some underwriting options have had a significant impact on underwriting results. Even so, underwriting effectively can help, and is perhaps more important today than in a time of price stability, rate responsiveness, and great underwriting freedom. The field is large in both absolute and relative terms, is growing, is of obvious importance to the industry, and is also a challenge to the underwriter.

INITIAL SELECTION CRITERIA

The underwriter is charged with the responsibility for risk selection. However, to some extent, a rather rough selection is made at the time the particular policy or rating plan is filed with the various state insurance departments through the inclusion of stated objective eligibility criteria. In addition, certain risks may be *eligible* according to the filing but *unacceptable* because of company underwriting policies or guides. This brief section deals with these two variables in the underwriting process for risks in the *voluntary* market. Involuntary (i.e., residual) programs are dealt with in Chapter 5.

Eligibility According to Filing

Rate filings, which are mandatory in most states, are submitted in conjunction with descriptions of risks that will be eligible for coverage under the program and forms to which the filings apply. In some cases, risks specifically *ineligible* are cited. The effect of either approach, inclusive or exclusive, is the same—to clarify and restrict eligibility.

For example, the rules that accompany the personal auto policy stress that it is designed to insure an individual or husband and wife. It is not designed for use by a corporation or partnership to insure their vehicles. Such entities generally are not eligible for the policy. This does not mean that they are not good insurable risks. Rather, it means that the policy is not designed or intended for the exposures represented by most risks in that category. They are usually covered under policies designed for business exposures. Notice, however, that this rule does not restrict the *use* of autos, so with most companies their regular personal auto insurance contracts may be used to insure a private passenger auto used for business purposes so long as the ownership criterion is met. Some farm autos used in the business of farming are eligible.

The rules for the personal auto program of many companies

provide that motorcycles are not eligible. Therefore, such vehicles are written on a more appropriate policy form.

These are but a few examples of ways that insurers exclude certain types of risks from certain policies based solely on the question of whether the risk is essentially personal or business in nature, or by the type of vehicle. In a policy designed for a specific market, the filing may be limited to members of the specific group or market, such as teachers.

Further differentiation is found in special programs adopted by insurers. They may have a *preferred* risk policy or rate filing with certain criteria. Such preferred policies generally are written at less than standard rates, and the company tries to restrict the category of risks eligible for it.

Likewise, there are filings for *standard* rate programs and *substandard* ones. A *substandard* program for auto insurance usually has rates higher than standard along with a system of heavy surcharges for accidents or violations. The risks in such a program are normally those who, for whatever reason, cannot obtain insurance under preferred or standard programs. There is so much variation in the types of programs offered in many states that it is difficult to generalize.

Underwriting Policies and Guides

The discussion above dealt primarily with criteria found in the filing made and approved for a particular auto insurance program. It dealt with the kinds of risks not eligible for the program regardless of other characteristics. While these rules serve the purposes of keeping out those obviously not eligible, there are many other factors which determine whether a specific risk in an eligible category will be written by the company.

No company is willing to insure every auto otherwise eligible according to a particular filing or program. Decisions must be made on individual risks. Short of dealing with individual submissions on their own merits, however, the underwriter (and hopefully, the producer) has preliminary screening done by company underwriting policies and guides that narrow the field of individual underwriting consideration. Certain risks eligible according to filing or program definitions may be unacceptable even for underwriting consideration on an individual basis.

Underwriting policies and guides are not uniform from company to company or from time to time within the same company. They may vary by location, profitability, and the regulatory and economic climate. Some company groups specify that certain classes of risks are to be written in one specific company in the group. Accordingly, underwriting policies and guides will vary considerably between or among the affiliated companies. Virtually any applicant would be acceptable in one of the member companies, and one underwriting responsibility is placing the applicant in the company that charges a premium that reflects the risk's exposure to loss.

The underwriter will work with many selection directives over the years, and should expect them to change as the business and its environment change. No effort will be made here to provide illustrations because practices vary so widely. The point to be made is that each company in effect does some selecting in advance of case-by-case underwriting by specifying certain types of risks that will not be considered under any circumstances even though they may be technically eligible. Effective producer activity spares the underwriter from exposure to many or most of these risks, but their designation as unacceptable or not-to-be-written risks is an important part of the overall underwriting process.

EVALUATING HAZARDS IN PRIVATE PASSENGER AUTO UNDERWRITING

An underwriter is charged with accepting or retaining those risks which, as a group, will prove most compatible with the insurer's underwriting objectives over a period of time. No underwriter can predict with accuracy what will happen to any individual risk in the future, particularly in auto insurance. Successful underwriting involves (1) making decisions in an orderly and logical fashion, and (2) making enough decisions that have good outcomes to outweigh those that have poor outcomes.

Underwriting is not static, nor are risks underwritten static. Bad risks may improve, and good risks may turn sour. A particular class, unprofitable in the past, may now carry a rate commensurate with the exposure and warrant consideration from the underwriter different from that previously afforded. However, despite this volatility, there are certain inviolate maxims in underwriting. One is that the underwriter must be able to identify and evaluate hazards if an underwriting decision is to be made in an orderly and logical way.

The rest of this chapter will discuss hazards and their evaluation in the underwriting of private passenger auto insurance. Other vehicles likely to be encountered by the personal auto underwriter, such as recreational vehicles and motorcycles, will be dealt with in the next chapter. The context of the material in the balance of Chapter 2 is one of *new private passenger auto risks in the voluntary market,* except as otherwise indicated.

Types of Hazards

UND 61 provided a classification system that divided hazards for all types of insurance into three types—physical, moral, and morale. In liability insurance a fourth type of hazard—legal—can be added. This section will define each of these types of hazard and illustrate each in the context of personal auto insurance underwriting.

Physical Hazard Physical hazards are those tangible characteristics of the property or persons insured which affect the likelihood and severity of loss. Some authors restrict this term to apply only to the auto and its use. This text will take a broader view and include the drivers also.

The range covered by the term *physical hazards* is enormous. Weather and geographic conditions, age of applicant and other operators, type and condition of vehicle, annual miles driven, and the use of the vehicle illustrate what this text calls physical hazards. All cannot be measured in numbers, inches, or pounds, but all are there for the eye to see and exist apart from the ethical and psychological makeup of the applicant. Thus, they are independent of the mind and, in that sense, objective.

Moral Hazard Moral hazard is dishonesty. It is less objective and more difficult to detect than physical hazards. In the long run, it will erode underwriting results regardless of the price charged for coverage. Clear evidence of moral hazard should make a risk unacceptable. Thus, it is relatively simple to handle *if* it can be detected.

An insured may deliberately damage a car with an instrument, hoping to simulate hail damage and get a new paint job, or submit false or inflated medical claims under medical payments or no-fault coverage, or try to collect for old damage under a current collision claim.

The problem, of course, is discovering moral hazard before a claim is submitted. In underwriting new business, this is almost impossible for many submissions. For one thing, moral hazard often does not surface without an intervening event. Some people would not think of initiating or feigning a loss to begin with but would have no reservations at all about deliberately inflating an otherwise covered loss.

Morale Hazard Morale hazard is carelessness about, or indifference to, potential loss. It implies no ethical shortcoming of the individual, as does moral hazard, but covers the whole range of other human traits from outright lack of concern about losses to "the little things" that make one less than prudent and careful.

Carelessness in maintaining or operating a vehicle and disregard for traffic laws are examples of morale hazard in auto insurance. Excessive morale hazard may present the underwriter with the so-called "accident on its way to happen."

Legal Hazard Legal hazard can be defined as any characteristic of the legal and regulatory environment that can be used in judging a risk's loss-producing potential. For the most part, there is little the individual underwriter can do about legal hazards, but they often account for major changes in company underwriting policies and guides. Court decisions adverse to the intent of policy language, restrictions on the right to cancel or nonrenew, inability to secure approval of realistic rate levels, and changes in state laws that increase loss exposure (e.g., the striking down of guest statutes as unconstitutional) are examples of legal hazards.

Many legal hazards can be avoided only by not doing business at all. Since this is rarely a viable alternative, the underwriter must live with most of the legal hazards. In the long run, the loss experience in a state, which is a reflection of its legal climate, among other things, should determine the premiums in that state. Thus, the legal hazards should be built into the premiums and recognized by the underwriter as part of the cost of doing business.

Factors in Identifying or Measuring Hazards

Each applicant presents the underwriter with a "bundle of hazards." Literally hundreds of factors can affect an individual risk and its loss producing potential, but they can be classified into two groups: (1) factors concerning the applicant and/or car users, and (2) factors concerning the vehicle and its use. In this section the discussion will concern those factors that are most important in evaluating a personal auto risk, and why they are important. The objective at this point is to list and briefly discuss these factors, not to rank them in order of importance nor to imply that each factor need be carefully considered in every case.

It should be understood that in most cases, none of the factors serve as the sole basis for a decision. Further, often the factors interact. A particular fact about a risk may be little cause for concern by the underwriter when viewed in isolation, but may take on great significance when viewed *in conjunction* with other information about the risk. Sometimes the *combined* effect of information on several factors presents a composite picture far different from that resulting from analyzing a series of isolated facts. For example, the fact that an applicant has been licensed only one year may *not* be considered as an extremely negative underwriting factor by itself. However, if this fact is coupled with the fact that the applicant has had two speeding convictions, the *interaction* of these two factors may be weighed more heavily than each of these would be weighed separately.

The underwriter's job is to evaluate and synthesize all of the information, weighing each factor according to underwriting guides and his or her judgment of the importance of that factor to the specific risk, and then to make a decision. For the individual risk, the decision may be right or wrong. The objective, over a period of time, is to be right on enough occasions.

Part of the problem faced by the underwriter is obtaining the information in the first place. This will be discussed in Chapter 3.

Concerning the Applicant and/or Auto Users

Driving History and Habits. Probably the single most important factor to the underwriter is the driving record of the applicant and others who will drive the auto. While many factors to be discussed subsequently are subjective, the driving record is an objective record of immediate concern.

The driving record is usually composed of three major elements. These are: (1) driving experience (length of time licensed), (2) accidents, and (3) traffic violations.

DRIVING EXPERIENCE. Driving experience is important to the underwriter. The fact that a driver has had no accidents does not mean much if the driver has been licensed for only two weeks. While the underwriter may be willing to insure a newly licensed individual, a risk with some driving experience usually would be preferred. Some insurers charge higher premiums for those licensed only a short time, regardless of the insured's age, in recognition of the increased hazard represented by a new driver.

Two factors influence the underwriter in thinking about an inexperienced driver. First, there is no way to know whether the individual will turn out to be a good or bad driver. Second, inexperienced drivers are often unsure of themselves and may be confused when confronted with a new or unusual situation. Thus, they are more apt to become involved in accidents than a more experienced person.

As with any other category, this does not mean that all inexperienced drivers are poor risks, but it does challenge the underwriter to select the best of the group. Since there is little or no driving record to evaluate, the underwriter must take other factors into consideration. These could include the location and use of the vehicle as they relate to

Exhibit 2-7
Accident Rates by Number of Accidents in a Prior Period*
(Non- concurrent three year period 1972-74; total sample = 113,525)

Number of Accidents (first two years)	Number of Drivers	Relative Increase in Accident Rate Over "0" Accidents Times-as-Many Factor† (third year)	Percent of "Accident-Free" Drivers
0	100.156	1.00	95.84
1	11.899	1.74	93.02
2	1.283	2.93	88.39
3	159	3.61	87.42
4+	28	5.73	75.00

†Correlation coefficient = .061. Times-as-many index represents the relative increase in each group's subsequent accident rate compared to the zero group's subsequent accident mean ($\bar{x}$ = .044).

*Adapted from *The California Driver Fact Book*, State of California, Department of Motor Vehicles, April 1981, Report No. 29, p. 3.

driving hazards in the area, the driving record of the parents, and many of the more subjective factors to be discussed later in this section.

ACCIDENTS. Previous accident experience is a key indicator in identifying and measuring the hazards of a potential auto insurance account. No one knows exactly what will happen in the future. Thus, the past must be used as an indicator of what is likely to happen in the future. It is a curious fact that many people never have an accident, while others seem to be involved frequently. It is this type of history for which the underwriter looks. Certain studies have shown that those who have had recent accidents are more likely to have future accidents than drivers who have had none at all.

Exhibit 2-7 shows the results of one such study, which classified drivers according to the number of accidents during a two-year period. The accident history of these drivers over the following year was also recorded. The results provide strong support for the use of accident history as an underwriting and rating factor.

This exhibit shows that a driver who had four or more accidents in the first two years is 5.73 times more likely to have an accident in the next year than the driver who did not have an accident in the first two years. Drivers who had one, two, or three accidents during the first two years were also more likely to have accidents during the third year than those drivers who had no accidents in the first two years.

Important as past driving history is, it is not an absolute indicator.

The risk could have changed, for better or worse. The new driver who had two or three accidents can mature and become a good risk. Likewise, the driver with a good record could suddenly start having accidents, perhaps because of mental stress and/or excessive drinking brought on by job or domestic problems. It is the task of the underwriter to sort out all of the information and make a judgment based on what he or she thinks the future experience will be.

One of the underwriter's major problems is evaluating the previous accident record. Accidents are generally sorted into the two major categories of *chargeable* (at fault) or *nonchargeable* (not at fault). Many companies use a safe driver or merit rating plan of some type. Under these plans a person is typically given lower premiums if there are no chargeable accidents within the experience period (usually three years), and increased premiums if he or she has had accidents chargeable under the plan. Care must be taken in underwriting, however, because an accident that cannot be surcharged under a merit rating plan is not necessarily considered nonchargeable from an underwriter's point of view. Because of the confusion that can arise from this type of situation, it is important that some typical situations be recognized.

The extreme cases of at-fault and not-at-fault are easy to discern. A person who runs into the rear of another auto stopped at a traffic light or who hits a tree at eighty mph will be considered at fault. The underwriter will consider the driver to have been at fault and will weigh this kind of accident heavily in the evaluation. However, serious as these accidents are, they are not necessarily chargeable under a merit rating plan. For example, many plans do not charge for the accident if there was no bodily injury and if the total property damage was less than $300 (or in some states, if the *paid claim* was less than $300). Thus, a rear-end accident involving only minor damage would not cause additional premium charges even though the driver was totally at fault. The accident involving the individual who hit the tree would be chargeable under most plans. However, some do not charge if there was no bodily injury or property damage liability payment.

At the other extreme is the pure not-at-fault accident. If the insured is legally parked and another party runs into the auto, or if the insured is completely stopped at a traffic light and is struck from behind, the underwriter would consider these as not-at-fault accidents and they would not be chargeable under most merit rating plans.

More troublesome are the accidents occurring between these two extremes. Many accidents happen at intersections, and often there is a question of who had the right of way. Typically, each driver feels in the "right." In fact, in most accidents of this type, both parties contributed to the accident. Under a *comparative negligence* system, the degree of fault must be assessed for claims settlement purposes. But, regardless, the underwriter gives an assessment based on the facts available. On a new application the only information may be from the applicant, but other information may be available and sought by the underwriter if the circumstances justify the costs involved. These kinds of accidents also generate most of the problems and complaints arising out of safe driver or merit rating plans and complicate the administration of the plans.

In reviewing the accident record, the underwriter looks at all accidents, at-fault and not-at-fault. Some individuals seem to have a lot of accidents but are never clearly at-fault. Perhaps they are just unlucky or perhaps they continually expose themselves to situations where they will get involved. Thus, the underwriter first considers total accident involvement and then looks at how many were clearly at-fault or not-at-fault before refining the doubtful ones into one category or the other. The important point is that no accidents are ignored—all are considered in the review.

All companies and underwriters use guidelines of some kind for accident involvement. Some might not insure, as new business, a risk who has had more than one at-fault and one not-at-fault accident in the past three years. Others may permit no at-fault accidents, others two or more. Some will have a limit on not-at-fault as well. Since the underwriter is trying to look into the future, even the insured who is not at fault generates claims, and not all of them can be recovered from the party who was at fault. However, some states do restrict an underwriter from rejecting coverage due to not-at-fault accidents or due to a specified number of at-fault accidents.

Complicating the traditional underwriting approach to accidents is the emergence of no-fault insurance. While the underwriting implications will be discussed further in Chapter 3, the nature of no-fault makes it even more important to carefully review all accidents. Under those no-fault laws limiting subrogation, the insured who always is in the wrong place at the wrong time usually will cost his or her insurer money, not the company insuring the other auto and driver.

What about accident severity? How should the underwriter regard the driver with an otherwise clean record who loses control of an auto on a rainy night, skids into the path of another vehicle, and causes serious injury to passengers in both autos and thousands of dollars in property damage? Should this person be avoided in favor of the driver who has had two speeding violations and two small scrapes over the past three years? Accident severity is usually a matter of chance. The value of property destroyed or the earning power or age of people who are injured or even the number of such injuries are seldom if ever within the control of the driver. Unless the accident is coupled with a

Exhibit 2-8
Number of Convictions vs. Accident Rate—Three-Year Period*

Number of Total Convictions	Relative Increase in Accident Rate Over "0" Convictions (Times-As-Many Factor)	Percent of "Accident Free" Drivers
0	1.00	89.44%
1	1.95	80.09
2	2.70	73.74
3	3.54	66.81
4	3.98	64.44
5	5.17	57.75
6	5.34	55.95
7	6.72	48.12
8	8.11	44.94
9+	9.03	39.56

* Adapted from *The California Driver Fact Book*, State of California, Department of Motor Vehicles, April 1981, Report No. 29, p. 5.

moving violation (reckless driving, for instance), a serious accident in one situation could as easily have been a minor scrape at another time in another place. People who are accident repeaters, on the other hand, are of much more concern. They will cause unprofitable results and, sooner or later, a serious accident will occur.

The accident record should not be viewed in isolation. How does it help to describe the risk's loss potential compared to the group or class of which it is a part? Are the details of the accidents representative of what might be expected in the particular age, auto, use or territorial classification? Or, do they suggest an exposure that deviates markedly from that contemplated by the rate? Questions such as these also are helpful in interpreting a record of traffic convictions.

TRAFFIC VIOLATIONS. Most underwriters consider traffic convictions to be another key indicator of the accident potential of the driver. At least two studies have shown that those drivers with traffic convictions are more apt to have accidents than those with no convictions. Results of one study of this relationship are found in Exhibit 2-8. It shows a direct relationship between the number of traffic convictions and accident rates and an inverse relationship between conviction and accident-free status.

Obviously, these findings do not mean that every driver with a conviction will have an accident. But they do indicate that, as a group, such drivers are more apt to be poorer risks.

Some underwriters view traffic violations more harshly than accidents. An accident can be subject to outside influences—many occur simply because of the design of a road or a lack of road maintenance. Even when conditions are ideal, a collision with another auto is somewhat fortuitous. If the other auto was not there, the accident would not have occurred. Accidents involving pedestrians very frequently are attributable to the pedestrian, such as those involving jay-walking or a child's running out into the street.

Traffic violations, on the other hand, are rarely excusable. A person who is convicted of reckless driving or of driving under the influence of drugs or liquor is not blameless. There is seldom a question of fact in these cases, and the conscious abuse of good driving habits presents a good indication of probable future losses. There will be exceptions, but they are rare, such as the father en route home from a daughter's wedding, or the mother who ignores all traffic regulations in driving a sick child to a doctor's office. But these exceptions will usually reveal themselves through otherwise clean driving records. What about the so-called less serious violations, such as speeding, failure to signal, running a stop sign, failure to yield, and so on? These are not so flagrant and it is probable that most drivers have, at some time, been guilty of at least one of these infractions. A safe driver may be ticketed for violations, but years will separate them. The unsafe driver has more frequent violations, and usually there will be a variety of them—speeding, running stop signs, failure to yield—then perhaps a period of suspension and even attendance at a driver clinic. This could be followed by a period of rehabilitation, and if it continues, the driving record for a three year period will eventually be clean and the underwriter may accept the applicant.

In examining traffic convictions, the underwriter does not weigh all types equally but may mentally divide them into at least three categories. The first, and most serious type of convictions, are those involving driving while under the influence of alcohol or drugs, leaving the scene of an accident, or negligent homicide. In many companies, a driver with any one of these types of convictions within the past three years is not likely to be accepted. In some companies, these more serious convictions over the past six or more years may influence the acceptability of a risk. Also, these violations of the law frequently result in suspension or revocation of license, often for a year or more. From the underwriter's point of view, a driver with a major conviction is not likely to be a good risk. Many merit rating plans surcharge for these convictions even if no accident was involved.

The second group of convictions comprises other moving traffic violations. These include speeding, going through stop lights or stop signs, failing to yield the right of way, and going the wrong way on a one-way street. While most merit rating plans do not charge for these violations, unless there is an accident also, some do. An underwriter is cautious in accepting a risk with traffic convictions of this type, particularly if there are two or more or there seems to be a pattern developing.

The third group of traffic convictions is generally less serious. These involve such violations as no inspection sticker, defective light, or improper equipment. While these are not ignored by the underwriter, they are not given as much weight as moving violations unless there are several of them. However, these convictions do inform the underwriter about the condition and maintenance of the vehicle and the insured's attitude toward safety.

Many people, particularly those who are not underwriters, feel that traffic convictions are not important in determining who is a good risk. They argue that enforcement varies widely and that people in certain areas get convicted because the law enforcement is tighter, not because they are any worse drivers than someone where law enforcement is more relaxed. Also, they argue that who gets stopped is often a matter of chance, such as a situation where ten autos are speeding but only one gets pulled to the side and ticketed.

There is some truth in these statements. In some parts of the country, few traffic tickets are given out; in other places, they are given out frequently. While the underwriter does not accept this argument completely, it is important to be aware of the differences in traffic enforcement within the territories in which the underwriter has a book of business. What may be a routine violation in one place may be unusual or serious somewhere else.

Aside from the statistics about traffic violations and accidents cited earlier, why is the underwriter concerned so much with violations? Basically, the underwriter feels that traffic convictions tell a great deal about the driver and driver habits. The underwriter recognizes that not everyone who speeds gets caught. However, this "bad luck" argument is weakened as the number of violations increases. Most people do not get even one conviction and a relatively small number get three or four. In the underwriter's mind, this is all the more reason why someone with two or three speeding convictions is apt to be a problem. To the underwriter, a person who receives multiple tickets in areas of strict enforcement does not obey the rules despite being aware of the possibility of being caught.

There are some individuals who have numerous traffic convictions and never have an accident. To the underwriter, these are rare exceptions. Drivers who continually speed, run red lights, or fail to yield are almost certain to have more accidents than drivers who drive defensively and carefully. The underwriter usually finds combinations of accidents and convictions and has to weigh the impact of each carefully. He or she looks at the seriousness of the conviction, where it happened, and how long ago. In risks involving several drivers, the underwriter considers whether each driver has convictions or whether they are concentrated in one driver.

Even routine traffic convictions can lead to license suspension or revocation. Many states have some form of point system where each moving violation adds a certain number of points to the record. When the points total a certain number within a time period, the license is suspended. As with traffic enforcement in general, use of license suspensions varies widely among the states. They are so relatively infrequent that the underwriter considers a suspension or revocation to be very serious and will rarely consider a person with a suspension a preferred risk.

As with past accident records, convictions are records of what has happened before, not necessarily what will happen in the future. However, they do give the underwriter solid objective information about the driver seeking insurance. Accident and conviction records must be weighed along with all of the other information at hand.

Age of Operator(s). Age of operator(s) is an important factor in evaluating hazards in a personal auto submission. Classification plans of all insurers reflect hazard differentials by age, as reflected by loss experience stratified by age. However, age as an underwriting variable reaches well beyond rate class differentials.

Young people are physically well equipped for superior driving performance. Their eyesight, reflexes, overall health, and general alertness are well above average. Yet, as a group, they clearly have more than their share of accidents. Lack of emotional maturity and inexperience are the principal reasons. Young drivers are more apt to act in haste and their driving judgment is more apt to be uninformed and influenced by aggressive rather than defensive driving characteristics. The prudent driver, regardless of age, does not "burn rubber," dart in and out of traffic, operate an unsafe car, or engage in horseplay while driving. Though the young have no monopoly on these activities, even the casual observer would agree that they are relatively more prevalent among youthful operators than among operators in general. Further, accidents involving youthful operators often take place at high speed and involve multiple occupants of the vehicle. These factors contribute to both accident frequency and severity. Exhibit 2-9 provides data on 1979 accidents classified by age of driver.

Note that drivers under age twenty-five represented 21.7 percent of all drivers. Compare that percentage to the percentage of drivers in that same age group who were in accidents in 1979. Note that 21.7

Exhibit 2-9
Accidents by Age of Drivers—1979*

Age Group	Number of Drivers	Percent of Total	Drivers in All Accidents	Percent of Total	Drivers in Fatal Accidents	Percent of Total
Under 20	14,000,000	9.8%	5,300,000	17.8%	10,700	16.4%
20-24	17,100,000	11.9	6,000,000	20.2	13,500	20.7
25-29	17,200,000	12.0	4,200,000	14.1	9,100	14.0
30-34	16,400,000	11.5	3,400,000	11.4	7,800	12.0
35-39	13,600,000	9.5	2,100,000	7.1	4,500	6.9
40-44	11,500,000	8.0	1,800,000	6.1	4,400	6.7
45-49	11,300,000	7.9	1,600,000	5.4	3,500	5.4
50-54	11,500,000	8.0	1,300,000	4.4	2,700	4.1
55-59	9,900,000	6.9	1,300,000	4.4	2,500	3.8
60-64	7,300,000	5.1	900,000	3.0	2,200	3.4
65-69	6,300,000	4.4	1,000,000	3.4	1,700	2.6
70-74	4,200,000	3.0	300,000	1.0	1,200	1.8
75 and over	2,800,000	2.0	500,000	1.7	1,400	2.2
Total	143,100,000	100.0%	29,700,000	100.0%	65,200	100.0%

*Adapted from *Insurance Facts*, 1980-81 Edition (New York: Insurance Information Institute, 1980), p. 54.

percent of the drivers had 38 percent of all accidents and 37.1 percent of fatal accidents. Add the next group, the people ages twenty-five to twenty-nine, and note that 33.7 percent of all drivers had 52.1 percent of all accidents and 51.1 percent of fatal accidents. There clearly is an inverse correlation between age and accident frequency at the younger ages. If this raw frequency data were counterbalanced by another underwriting factor, such as substantially more miles driven per year by young drivers on the average, the youthful driver would have a somewhat improved image among underwriters. However, there is no counterbalancing underwriting factor, and even if there were, rates would still have to reflect the experience per car-year and would still be much higher than rates for other age groups.

Youthful operators are a signal suggesting close scrutiny in selection, although age is seldom the sole factor dictating a decision. In fact, some states prohibit underwriting decisions based on age alone. The underwriter looks for signs of immaturity, instability, and inexperience. Age alone indicates the maximum period as a licensed operator. Except for the new or short-time driver, operating record is another obvious measure.

The presence or absence of other signs of immaturity requires some deduction and reasoning. The type(s) and history of employment can help the underwriter, as can information on educational achievement and activity.

Underwriters often encounter youthful drivers as additional operators in existing accounts insuring parents and are heavily influenced by the record of the parents in such cases. While not uniformly so, responsible vehicle operation is contagious. With the newly licensed operator presenting nothing in the way of an operating record, the underwriter is more likely to accept the youthful driver when the parents' record is good. Most underwriters are pessimistic when the parents' record is marred by frequent accidents and/or convictions. While there is no guarantee in the individual case that a youthful driver will emulate parental driving habits and attitudes, there is a tendency for the example set by parents to influence the driving behavior of their children.

While industry experience as a whole dictates a wary attitude toward the youthful driver, the effective underwriter tempers this with an open-mindedness that permits recognition of the young risk with a greater than average degree of responsibility. Good grades in school, successful completion of driver training, a stable employment record, and good experience with the parents of the youthful operator are among the signs of responsibility and maturity.

At the other extreme are elderly drivers. Underwriters are concerned with slowing reflexes, failing eyesight, and the greater possibility of physical impairment which may accompany the aging process. Though the elderly tend to be careful and do not drive as far or as often as younger people, their response time and visual acuity may diminish and cause them to be dangerously cautious.

Underwriters view elderly drivers in a much more favorable light than in the past. Loss experience on the elderly as a group indicates that they are a better class of risks than was once supposed. Exhibit 2-9, cited earlier, shows that both accident frequency and severity rates drop in the age sixty to seventy-four brackets but turn upward above age seventy-four. For most elderly drivers, there is a reduced exposure resulting from their relatively infrequent and short mileage driving. There usually is little apprehension about continuing to insure elderly persons who have "grown old" with the company if the experience has been acceptable and if the underwriter is satisfied that there has been no marked adverse change in health that would affect driving ability.

The elderly new applicant, however, requires careful underwriting. Presumably the applicant was insured elsewhere during the younger years. The underwriter is in a position of possibly accepting a new applicant, insured elsewhere in the past, when it is reasonably certain that driving ability is destined to decline shortly. The underwriter should know what prompted the change in companies. There may be a logical explanation. Perhaps the applicant recently retired and has relocated. In any case, information on driving record and physical condition are necessary in underwriting this class. In some states, again, age alone is neither a valid nor legal basis for making an underwriting decision.

The majority of drivers comprise the group between the youthful and elderly classes. While generally considered the best risks overall because of experience and maturity, this group presents its own peculiarities to the underwriter. For example, many in this group are parents of actual or potential youthful drivers. Thus, the underwriter may want to know the ages of children, even if they are not yet licensed. Applications and renewal information forms of some companies gather that information.

Sex and Marital Status. Sex and marital status have long been factors considered by underwriters. However, the value placed on them has varied considerably by the age of the applicant involved. For example, young female drivers were generally considered to be better than young male drivers. For many years young female drivers paid the same premiums as adult drivers. However, in recent years, young females have paid more than adult drivers in most states, but still considerably less than young males.

In the past, few young females had autos. Today, the differences in use are fewer than they were, and young women have more autonomy and are less dependent on others for transportation. A higher percentage of females, particularly among the young single employed female group, are owners and principal operators of autos. Thus, the importance of separating the sexes in this area may decline. On the other hand, if rate increases for young females are slow to be approved, insurers may be less willing to insure them than the more adequately rated male.

Marital status is recognized in both rating and underwriting, especially at the younger ages. Married male drivers under thirty usually pay less than their single counterparts. This recognizes the fact that, generally, married persons at these ages tend to be more mature and responsible than single persons of the same age, and also that their marital situation tends to result in more time being spent at home.

It is the potential stability of the married state that appeals to underwriters. They would like to think that the people insured today are the same people who will be insured next month and next year. Until recently, underwriters could fairly safely conclude that the married person spends evenings and weekends at home with a family and that the youngsters in that family become safe drivers with the aid of parental guidance and control. Thus, there was a good stable exposure which could be relied on to build a large, profitable book of business.

More recently, the divorce rate has risen dramatically. Further, there has been an increase in young people living together, sometimes as a prelude to marriage and at other times as a casual alliance. In some cases the alliance becomes a marriage in common law.

Of what significance are these changes? The underwriter continues to look for signs of stability or, conversely, instability, and to seek appropriate information on drivers and uses. Can we draw conclusions from marital status or choice of living arrangements? Not statistically, but it is reasonable to conclude that common law marriages of long standing (and each company would have to establish its own time requirement) meet the stability criterion. Conversely, frequent changes of living partners would not. These latter situations make it difficult to accurately identify all drivers who might use the auto regularly. Thus, the underwriter has more difficulty appraising the driving records of all who might be regular operators and the use characteristics of the vehicle than would be the case in a more stable situation. In addition, an insured who is part of a casual alliance may be viewed in a prejudicial manner in litigation in which that person is a defendant.

Applications routinely ask about marital status. The underwriter may want to seek more information in certain situations—for example, when the applicant and another listed operator have different surnames, or the applicant is listed as divorced, separated, or widowed.

Single persons living alone or with parents are a large class of submissions. Any special underwriting consideration for people in this group is dealt with at appropriate places throughout this chapter.

Marital status and sex are two of the underwriting factors about which some states have legislated. In effect most states do not permit the rejection of a risk due to the applicant's sex or marital status. The statutes vary a bit. In some, the rejection is not permitted if an applicant's sex or marital status is the *sole* reason for rejection. In others, sex or marital status cannot be used at all—either alone or in conjunction with other factors—in making an underwriting decision. Additionally, a few states are now trying to prohibit price discrimination on the basis of sex or marital status.

Occupation. The use of occupation as an underwriting variable is based partly on accumulated individual experiences of underwriting personnel and partly on presumptions about habits and characteristics of people in certain occupational groups. Except for specialty insurers who concentrate their writings in certain occupational classes (e.g., school teachers), only a limited number of companies have gathered loss data by occupational group. In some jurisdictions, occupation cannot be considered in underwriting a personal auto risk, and it is not usable as the sole basis for rejection in a number of others.

What does a person's occupation have to do with acceptability as an insured in auto insurance? Information concerning occupation may provide the underwriter with indications of a number of hazard factors, including annual mileage, where and when the auto is parked, the hours during which the auto is frequently driven, the geographic scope of vehicle use, the frequency with which others may use or be in the auto, and the possible use of alcohol or drugs. Care must be exercised, however, to avoid stereotyping the members of any particular occupational class. These classes are not homogeneous. In addition, occupation gives some measure of the insured's ability to pay the premiums. If the applicant is unemployed or in an occupation with very low earnings, the underwriter may sense a constant credit problem. Also, there may be a question as to whether the applicant can afford to keep the auto in good safe mechanical condition.

The principal value of information on occupation is the insight it may provide on the presence of hazards and the resulting potential for loss compared to the average for the class. Occupation *per se* does not produce a good, average, or poor risk. If the experience of an insurer indicates that a particular occupational group warrants close underwriting scrutiny, the cost of allaying fears about individuals in the group can be disproportionately high and far exceed the normal costs of securing underwriting information. The individual risk premium may not carry a general expense allocation sufficient to support such a procedure. Companies differ in attitudes and practices concerning occupational groups. Obviously the underwriter must be familiar with the underwriting policies and guides of his or her company.

One commonly encountered group that can be regarded as occupational in nature is that of "student." With some companies this status has rating implications under certain circumstances. From the point of view of evaluating hazards, however, what does this status tell us about the risk? It may lead the underwriter to wonder about garaging location, where and when the vehicle is driven and parked, frequent multiple occupancy of the vehicle, other operators, the possible use of the vehicle to drive to and from a part-time job, and the like. More information may be required to provide answers to these questions on hazards that derive from this particular occupational status. Again, it is not the status itself that is conclusive, or even significant, but the objective factors to which the particular occupation may serve as a clue.

While use of occupation as an underwriting tool has declined in importance to some degree, it is considered very important as a marketing criterion. If the kind of business you want to insure is composed of people who own two cars and a home, you are unlikely to find many in a group of low-income workers. On the other hand, a group of professional people such as accountants may have a high percentage who meet the standard. Since most companies have a limited number of producers, they try to direct them to the groups who are likely to be the most desirable in terms of company marketing objectives and programs. In this case, occupation still exists as a very important criterion in selecting the group the company wishes to solicit, but in a broad and impersonal way. Also, many companies began as insurers of people in specific occupational categories and continue that emphasis today.

Physical Condition. State licensing and license renewal requirements determine and should monitor the physical capacity of persons to operate a vehicle. Physically impaired persons should be permitted on the road only if adequate safeguards are imposed in the way of corrective devices, vehicle modifications, and use restrictions. But even assuming no discrepancies of this sort (and the underwriter should be sure there are none) physical impairments may, when combined with other factors, present a risk with excessive exposure to loss. On the other hand, the very existence of the impairment may result in substantially lower than average exposure on matters such as vehicle use and mileage.

Education. General education is a factor that, on the surface, has little to do with how good a driver someone is. It is probably more important at the lower or minimum end than at higher levels. The insured should be able to fill out an accident report and help the company in defending a claim.

Another aspect of education has to do with education relating directly to driving. Most insurers offer lower premiums to young drivers who have taken an approved driver training course. Also, credits are given in some areas for defensive driving or other safety-related courses. The feeling is that graduates of such formal courses will be more aware of the hazards they will face on the road and better equipped to deal with them.

Some insurers associate the current quality of educational effort, as reflected in grades, with hazards. This association is reflected in "good student" discounts offered by some companies and by a presumption that equates outstanding academic achievement by young persons with less free (i.e., driving) time and more mature driving habits.

Personal Characteristics. In addition to all the factors mentioned so far, the underwriter also considers many other personal characteristics, to the extent he or she knows about them. Much personal information is subjective and must be used with extreme care. Information on personal habits is very tenuous, and the underwriter must be concerned with the source of the information. For example, information that the applicant is "known to drive fast" must be reviewed skeptically unless it is confirmed by accident or traffic records.

Similarly, information relating to the person's integrity or financial condition is also difficult to evaluate. A person who has filed for bankruptcy may quite properly be considered a poor risk to pay premiums, but information that someone is having financial difficulties or has a poor reputation must be used with care.

The underwriter looks for unusual things in the consideration of a risk. Most people do not have criminal records or even arrests for criminal violations. The underwriter will look very closely at any risk who has an unusual history in terms of a criminal record, use of drugs, mental impairments, or other factors.

Concerning the Vehicle and Its Use

Type of Vehicle. The underwriter is always concerned with the type of vehicle insured. This concern encompasses many different elements.

As indicated earlier, the first concern is about whether the vehicle is eligible for coverage under the filings made for the policy. A dump truck, for example, is not eligible for policies designed to insure private passenger autos.

Beyond eligibility questions, however, the underwriter is interested in other factors. Does the vehicle have a standard engine and equipment or does it have a high horsepower engine and drive system designed for speed? Has it been specially modified, equipped with special shock absorbers, wide tires, or even a roll bar? These kinds of equipment give a strong indication that the vehicle is used for racing, whether formal or informal in nature. When these characteristics are present, the underwriter will be doubly cautious because of concern that there may be considerable high speed or reckless driving habits.

The underwriter may have similar concerns if the vehicle is a sports car. One of the problems here is the determination of what is or is not a sports car. Some cars, such as a Jaguar XKE or Corvette, are fast, expensive, and considered sports cars by almost everyone. On the other hand, a sporty little convertible with a four cylinder engine may or may not present the typical sports car loss exposure.

The underwriter does not consider the type of car alone but looks at the age and record of the driver in the deliberation. Any decision will be based heavily on an evaluation of the character of the driver in conjunction with consideration of the type of auto.

A very expensive or unusual car will also concern the underwriter. Insuring a Rolls Royce is not the same as insuring a $7,000 Chevrolet. One significant difference is that these expensive or unusual cars are prime targets for theft. In some cases, it is very difficult to obtain parts or to find someone who can repair the car. Repairs may be inordinately expensive, and owners may be very demanding in their judgment as to the quality of repair work. These characteristics may bring the underwriter to the decision of insuring the vehicle for liability but not for comprehensive or collision. Another problem with many of these vehicles is that the premiums may not be adequate for the exposures involved.

There has also been concern about insuring subcompact cars, both foreign and domestic. Various studies have indicated that small cars incur more damage than larger ones in similar accidents and cost more to repair. According to the Highway Loss Data Institute (HLDI), the smallest cars have the worst records for personal injuries and among the worst for collision damage.[6] The results of a study of personal injury protection coverage claims for 1977-1979 models by the HLDI is shown in Exhibit 2-10. Keep in mind, however, that the larger cars will usually carry higher rates.

An important conclusion for the underwriter is to be on the alert for new information. Because a certain type of vehicle is "good" today does not mean its successor five years from now will also be good to insure, and vice versa. Costs of vehicles and the way they are built change. And, of course, the potential problems with the vehicle must be weighed in conjunction with the other good and bad points of the risk being considered.

Statistical data on types of autos insured and involved in accidents are collected to some degree by HLDI and some insurers. A number of companies are reflecting their findings in physical damage rating symbols assigned to the various models. Even without (or in addition to) access to information of this formal nature, the underwriter can develop his or her own helpful sources of information on "problem models." Probably the best source, and often available in the same building, is the claims department. Adjusters and appraisers who look at autos on a daily basis and write estimates are in a good position to point out trends or problems with certain types of autos. The underwriter should develop a good rapport with claims personnel so new information is constantly available. Another source of helpful information is a good car magazine available to an underwriting unit or department. With these additional sources of information, a more enlightened decision can be made on whether to insure certain autos, and on what basis as far as deductibles are concerned.

Age of Vehicle. Age of the vehicle is always of interest to the underwriter. Aside from problems with particular types of autos discussed above, new cars are rarely a problem. Once a car is six or

Exhibit 2-10
Relative Injury Claim Frequencies by Size of Claim—Personal Injury Protection Coverages 1977-1979 Models*

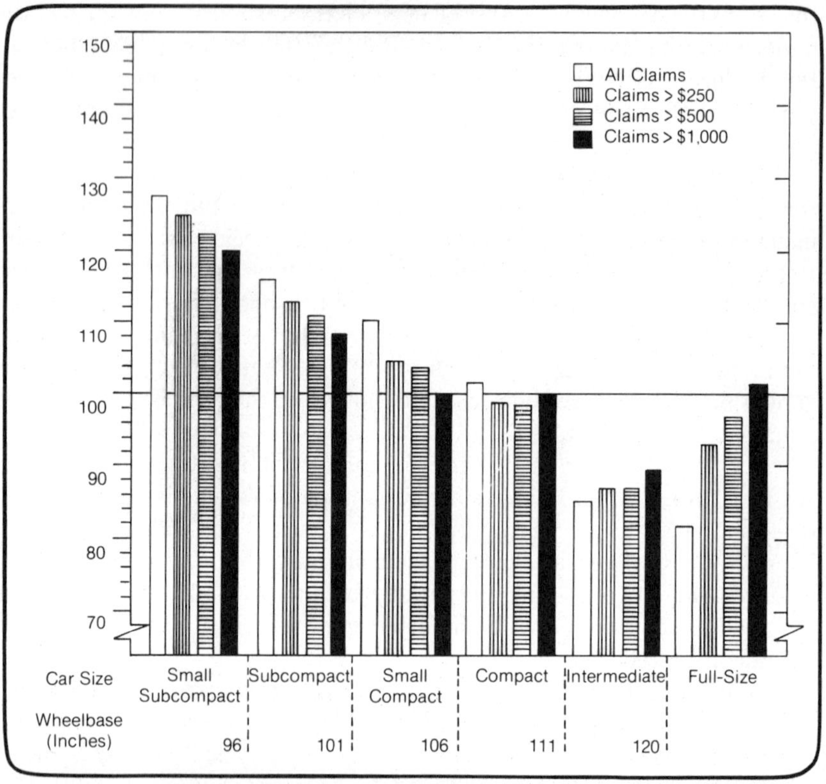

*Reprinted from *The Highway Loss Reduction Status Report*, Vol. 16, No. 7, 13 May 1981, Insurance Institute for Highway Safety, p. 8.

seven years old, however, the underwriter should consider it more carefully.

The underwriter's first concern about an older car is its condition. Are the brakes and tires in good shape or worn out? Is the body solid or rusted out? How many miles are on the car? Has it been inspected? Is the car subjected to long-mileage commuting use? The older the car, the more important these questions become.

Concern with the condition of the car should be matched by interest in the value of the car. By consulting various guides to the value of used cars, the underwriter can get a pretty good idea whether the car's value is $1,000, $200, or whatever. Many underwriters refuse to provide collision coverage for a car more than six or seven years old or comprehensive for a car more than ten years old. Similarly, they may refuse to provide these coverages if the value is less than some predetermined amount. In many cases, this attitude benefits the insured because he or she is not sold coverages which would provide only a very small recovery in the event of loss.

One of the major problems involved with providing comprehensive and collision on older cars is the unavailability of parts. As was indicated under the discussion of type of vehicle, this problem also applies to some new cars as well. Some questions to be asked include the following: Is the car foreign or domestic? Is it still manufactured or has it been discontinued? How popular was it? Are there dealers in the area with parts? Generally, the underwriter will be more willing to insure a ten-year-old Ford or Chevrolet, for example, than a seven-year-old car no longer manufactured. The odds are good that parts can be found for large volume domestic cars, although they may be hard to find for cars which were sold in small volume or which have been discontinued.

No discussion of the age of vehicles is complete without discussing antique and classic cars. As indicated earlier, an antique car is usually considered to be one twenty-five or more years old. Some cars of this vintage are almost worthless while others are better than new. Also, some are used for everyday driving while others are used only for antique car meets or parades.

The restored antique car may be a problem to most underwriters because its value is often hard to determine. In addition, there may be very serious repair and parts problems. Many companies refuse to provide comprehensive and collision coverages on such vehicles. On the other hand, a few companies specialize in providing coverage to this market. The underwriter needs to be aware of the company's attitude on the subject and closely review any vehicle that may fall into the antique category. There may be a willingness to insure it for very infrequent use but reluctance to provide coverage if it is used frequently and exposed to normal traffic hazards. The value of an individual antique car can vary widely and change rapidly. Many companies write coverage on a stated amount basis where the amount of insurance is determined in advance. At the time of loss, the insured will receive the actual cash value up to the limit of liability. The limit of liability may be requested by the insured, and the underwriter may verify the values with an appraisal.

The classic car presents a similar problem. Like the antique, value usually is appreciating rather than depreciating. Again, the problem is value and premium. As normally written, comprehensive and collision premiums decline with age, as the value of a car declines. But if the ten-year-old classic car is worth $2,000 rather than $200, normal rates are inadequate for the potential loss exposure.

The problem is for the underwriter to recognize the classic and decide what to do about it. For example, some consider the 1965-67 Ford Mustangs to be classics and worth a good deal more than their age would dictate, simply because enough people feel this way to create an active market for them. This does not mean that every 1965 Mustang is worth more money, though every owner probably thinks it is. This can also lead to problems in claims settlement. Again, the use of an appraisal and/or the writing of coverage on a stated amount basis might be in order.

Underwriters need to think about how the make, age, and value of the vehicle combine to transform a normal risk into a poor one or one for which premium is not commensurate with loss exposure.

Use of Vehicle. The use of the vehicle can relate to both rating and underwriting considerations. Purely from a rating standpoint, the use of the auto for commuting to work or for business usually means a higher premium reflecting an increased exposure to loss. Some companies rate on the basis of annual mileage with cars driven more than, for example, 10,000 or 15,000 miles a year, subject to higher premiums. Thus, the first job of the underwriter in terms of use is to determine how the vehicle fits into the rating plan the company uses. This gives an idea of the premium it will develop.

An underwriter's concern about use does not stop with rating factors. Assume that a car driven more than fifteen miles to work takes a higher rate. One risk presented to the underwriter might be driven sixteen miles to work; another might be driven fifty miles each way but both would pay the same premium. The latter risk is below average in the class with regard to *use.* This negative factor will be taken into consideration in the overall evaluation of the risk. This evaluation will include the traffic conditions encountered on the fifty-mile drive, the time of day the car is driven, the insured's driving record, the car involved, and many other factors.

Another typical example involves business use of the car, usually by a person in sales work. Some cars used and rated for business are driven only 10,000 miles a year, though 25,000 or 30,000 miles is probably more common. But sometimes the underwriter will encounter a car driven 100,000 miles a year, and consequently the exposure might be substantially in excess of that contemplated by the rate for the applicable class. This is but one facet of the risk, however, and must be combined with other information in making a judgment. Indeed, long mileage coupled with a clean driving record over a period of years might indicate a better than average risk overall.

The underwriter is also concerned if the car is used for commercial purposes, such as taxi or rental car. Such uses are not generally insurable under personal auto policies, but the underwriter must somehow ask or determine if such a use exists. Other uses like racing are important in determining whether the risk is insurable.

Location and Protection of the Vehicle. As with the use of the vehicle, location affects both underwriting and rating. Auto rates generally vary by geographic territory based on the loss experience in the territory. The underwriter must first determine the proper rating territory applicable. Once this is established, the underwriting aspects can be considered.

Location encompasses not only the rating territory but where, specifically, in the territory the vehicle is located. Most rating territories cover extensive areas and the exposures presented are not homogeneous. For example, one insured in a territory may be located on a busy street and exposed to severe traffic hazards. Another may be on a quiet residential street, yet both pay the same premium. The underwriter attempts to evaluate the hazards applicable to each.

In some areas there is a substantial difference between base rates applicable in adjacent territories. The underwriter should be aware of the possibility of a risk from the lower rated territory who because of commuting or business use operates primarily in the higher rated neighboring area. Similarly, when these differences exist there may be a significant incentive for higher rated risks to attempt to benefit from the lower rate by use of a garaging address different from the named insured's home.

From a potential accident viewpoint, the streets driven daily and their characteristics may be important. However, where the car is parked is usually more important to the underwriter, because it is more controllable. A car parked on a busy street is likely to be hit by another vehicle, and many cases will be hit-and-run accidents. Likewise, a car parked on the street may be subject to theft or vandalism. For these reasons, the parking of a car on the street in certain areas would be considered a negative factor with respect to comprehensive or collision and might suggest a higher than normal deductible on these coverages if the risk is acceptable on an overall basis.

On the other hand, a car kept in a garage or even a driveway is less exposed to some types of loss and more acceptable to the underwriter, particularly for physical damage coverages. To evaluate the risk completely, the underwriter should be familiar with the area and its characteristics. Another consideration could be frequent weather problems in an area, such as hail or sandstorm. Here again, the car kept in a garage would be the better risk.

Location could also be important as it relates to the type of auto to be insured. This is particularly so when covering small volume foreign cars, for which parts or dealers are hard to find. As an example, an Alfa Romeo sports car might be routinely acceptable in Westchester County, New York, where parts and repair facilities are available, but questionable in Presidio, Texas, where the nearest dealer may be several hundred miles away.

Sources of Information for Evaluating Hazards

The underwriter has a number of sources available in obtaining information about the applicant or insured. He or she must know not only what they are but when and how to use them. Information costs money, and care must be taken in finding the proper balance between spending time and money and the value of the information obtained.

The Application for Insurance

Types of Information on the Application. Most companies require a signed application from a new applicant for auto insurance. For underwriting purposes, the application is the single most important source of information about the applicant.

Each company develops its own application and the actual questions asked may vary. However, there are some questions common to almost every application and these will be discussed first. Keep in mind that the information on the application must serve two major purposes. The first is to aid in determining if the risk is acceptable to the underwriter, and the second is to determine the premium to be charged.

BASIC INFORMATION ABOUT THE APPLICANT. This includes the name of the applicant, mailing and residence address, and length of time at that location. The same information about previous places of residence may be sought if the current address has been used for fewer than a specified number of years. This information may also include the employer's name and address, occupation, and length of time the applicant has been so employed. Previous employment is also inquired about in many applications.

INFORMATION ABOUT THE AUTOS AND THEIR USE. The year and make of each vehicle, serial number, vehicle identification number (VIN), model, and other details are necessary for rating purposes and are of interest to the underwriter. The "place of garaging" means the usual location of the vehicle while it is not in use, such as a particular address, which determines the proper rating territory. Other questions deal with whether the auto is used for business, to commute to work, or other purposes, and whether or not it is financed. The state in which the auto is registered is important because it usually determines the specific policy form required.

COVERAGES, LIMITS OF LIABILITY, PREMIUM. In this section the applicant checks the specific coverages and limits desired. Most insurers allow the producer to bind liability coverage up to a certain limit, say, $300,000, for an apparently acceptable risk, but require specific underwriting approval for higher limits.

Based on the coverage desired, the producer usually can quote the proper premiums. Premium computation also includes any credits or surcharges resulting from such items as having more than one car insured, driver training, inexperienced driver, chargeable accidents, or any other factors which are a part of the company's rating plan.

INFORMATION ABOUT THE DRIVERS. Especially critical to the underwriter is information about the operators of the vehicles to be insured. This includes the applicant and anyone else expected to be a regular operator of the vehicle(s). Driver's license number and state of issuance and date of birth are needed to secure motor vehicle records. Certain basics, like age, sex, and length of time licensed are usually required for rating. Also, the percentage of miles to be driven by each operator may affect the premium because it determines who is the principal driver of the vehicle. For example, if an eighteen-year-old son drives the car 20 percent of the time and his father 80 percent, the policy would be rated with an occasional youthful male driver. But if the son drove 55 percent of the time, the much higher principal driver rates for youthful operators would apply. Many applicants are well enough in tune with auto insurance rating to know the cost implications of truthful disclosure on this point. The underwriter should be satisfied that other facts are consistent with the indicated percentage of use by youthful drivers.

A common question on applications is whether insurance has been declined, canceled, or nonrenewed by another insurer. In some states, this question can no longer be used, but a question seeking the name and policy number of the previous insurer(s) may be permitted.

An affirmative answer to the question should not result in an automatic turndown. The critical aspect of an affirmative answer is the facts behind the answer. *Why* was the risk declined, canceled, or nonrenewed? The reasons could have little or nothing to do with the quality of the risk. Perhaps a company marketing through independent agents decided to withdraw from an agency and nonrenewed that agency's entire book of business. This can happen for numerous reasons not related at all to the quality of any individual risk in that book, or even to the quality of the overall book. Further, in periods of tight underwriting due to poor loss experience, or when a company's surplus position forces it to limit new business, many otherwise acceptable risks are turned down simply because the insurer is limiting its volume.

The underwriter needs to be aware of what other companies are doing and should look at the applicant in that context. The judgment should be the underwriter's and not a mirror of someone else's decision.

The question concerning a physical disability or handicap is one that needs careful consideration if answered "yes." Some people will indicate a handicap when, in fact, their only problem is that they wear glasses. Other people have hearing problems or cannot use their legs. Each state has provisions for licensing people with handicaps. Generally, the person has to pass a driving test, and the license granted will require specific equipment for the person or the vehicle.

The underwriter needs to know what, if any, restrictions are on the license and whether or not the car is properly equipped. Depending on the type of handicap, further information may be needed about how long the person has been driving with the handicap and the record during that time. In some cases, a medical statement may be requested.

The balance of the questions deal with accidents, traffic violations, or other losses any of the drivers have incurred over a period of time. As previously discussed, these may affect both the underwriting and rating. In most cases, the information required goes back three years, though in some cases it may be longer.

While the questions shown and discussed are typical, many companies ask for additional information. Some ask the producer questions—how long have you known the applicant, does the applicant have other insurance with you, do you recommend the applicant, and the like. Some ask about the character of the neighborhood—commercial, residential, rural, and so on. This information is used along with information on where the car is parked in evaluating potential physical damage hazards. Applications also vary considerably on the coverages offered depending on the state and the filings of the insurer. New questions are added to applications with changing situations.

A sample application is shown in Exhibit 2-11. The reader, of course, must be familiar with the application used in his or her company.

Limitations of Application Information. The information on the application is not always complete or reliable. Several reasons for this problem exist.

First, the question may not be asked clearly or the wording may be ambiguous. Some applications are filled out by the applicant. In other cases, the producer fills it out from conversations with the applicant and then has the applicant sign it. In this latter situation accuracy depends in part on how the producer asked the question and emphasized the importance of accuracy in the answer. There is a considerable difference between asking, "Have you had any accidents in the past three years?" and asking, "You have not had any accidents in the last three years, have you?" The latter type of questioning, particularly if done quickly, downplays the value of the question and favors a negative (though perhaps inaccurate) response. It is important that producers or other company representatives ask the questions clearly and completely so that selection and pricing can be done in an informed and equitable fashion.

A second reason why information may not be complete is lack of knowledge by the applicant or failure to remember. When asked if his son had a traffic ticket, a man may answer "no" simply because the son never told him. This is not an unusual situation and, in a borderline risk, it could make the difference between standard and substandard classification. Similarly, people forget the exact dates of accidents or tickets in some cases. Thus, an accident or violation thought to have occurred more than three years ago may actually have taken place within the three year period. The producer can help here by making an effort to get the person to think about the question.

Over time, an underwriter can develop an awareness of producers involved in submissions with incomplete or inaccurate applications. Sometimes the problem is obvious and tends to repeat itself. In other cases, other information sources lead to the conclusion that more care is required at the producer-applicant contact point. Direct contact with the producer, contact with superiors, or contact with the marketing department is in order when this difficulty arises. The problem may be a matter of better training and/or supervision of people in the producer's office who take and record application information, or it may be more complex and call for action by other levels of authority in the company.

Of course, a third reason for inaccurate information can be outright dishonesty or concealment. The underwriter usually will not find out about this until information is obtained from other sources. However, an alert producer who makes a good effort to obtain full information can help to avoid many of these situations.

Good rapport with producers and their staffs creates a climate in which the underwriter is more likely to get complete and accurate information the first time around. Developing this rapport takes time, but it is valuable and worth the effort it may take to achieve. Further, the producer is well served by providing accurate and complete information for the proper selection and rating of risks. Not only is the producer-underwriter relationship strengthened, but the producer is spared the later work and aggravation of securing extra bits of information that would have been much easier to gather when the application was completed originally. In addition, the producer's profitability (and possible contingent commissions or bonuses) in the

Exhibit 2-11
Automobile Insurance Application

Automobile Insurance Application

NAME: ______________________ TELEPHONE NO: ______________

RESIDENCE ADDRESS: ______________________

PREVIOUS RESIDENCE (if at above less than 2 years): ______________________

EMPLOYER AND ADDRESS: ______________________

POSITION OR OCCUPATION: ______________ BUSINESS TELEPHONE NO: ______________

PREVIOUS OCCUPATION/EMPLOYER (if with present one less than 2 years): ______________________

DESCRIPTION OF AUTOMOBILE TO BE INSURED:

YEAR: ________ MAKE: ________ MODEL: ________ BODYSTYLE: ________ CYLS: ________

IDENTIFICATION NO: ______________ PURCHASED: NEW ____ USED ____ WHEN? ________

AMOUNT PAID: ______________ STATE REGISTERED: ________

PLACE OF GARAGING: ______________ PARKED IN: GARAGE ____ LOT ____ STREET ____ DRIVEWAY ____

ANNUAL MILEAGE: ______________

BUSINESS USE: YES ____ NO ____ COMMUTING: YES ____ NO ____

TYPE OF BUSINESS: ______________ MILES ONE WAY: ____ DAYS PER WEEK: ____

IF CAR FINANCED, GIVE NAME AND ADDRESS OF LOSS PAYEE:

____

COVERAGES	*LIMITS*		*PREMIUM*
BODILY INJURY ________	$ ________		$ ________
PROPERTY DAMAGE ________	$ ________		$ ________
MEDICAL PAYMENTS ________	$ ________		$ ________
UNINSURED MOTORISTS ________	$ ________		$ ________
NO FAULT BENEFITS ________	$ ________		$ ________
COMPREHENSIVE ________	$ ________	Deductible	$ ________
COLLISION ________	$ ________	Deductible	$ ________

OTHER COVERAGES: ____________________

CREDITS/SURCHARGES: ____________________

PREMIUM TO BE PAID IN FULL WITH APPLICATION $ __________

$ __________ WITH APPLICATION, BALANCE IN ____ MONTHLY INSTALLMENTS

DRIVING RECORD INFORMATION

OPERATORS:	1	2	3
NAME:			
RELATIONSHIP TO NAMED INSURED:			
DATE OF BIRTH:			
SEX:			
MARITAL STATUS:			
OPER. LIC. NO./STATE:			
LENGTH OF TIME LICENSED:			
EST. MILES TO BE DRIVEN:			
DISABILITY OR HANDICAP (Explain):			

HAS LICENSE OR REGISTRATION OF ANY OPERATOR BEEN SUSPENDED OR REVOKED IN PAST 3 YEARS? __________

EXPLAIN: ____________________

HAS AUTOMOBILE INSURANCE BEEN REFUSED, CANCELLED, OR NON-RENEWED IN THE PAST THREE YEARS? __________

IF YES, EXPLAIN: ____________________

HAS APPLICANT OR ANY OPERATOR HAD ANY TRAFFIC CITATIONS OR BEEN CONVICTED OR FORFEITED BAIL FOR ANY OFFENSE OTHER THAN PARKING IN THE LAST 3 YEARS? __________

IF YES, EXPLAIN GIVING NAME OF OPERATOR, DATE, PLACE, TYPE AND DISPOSITION OF VIOLATION. __________

HAS ANY APPLICANT OR ANY OPERATOR BEEN INVOLVED IN AN ACCIDENT WHICH RESULTED IN BODILY INJURY TO OR DEATH OF A PERSON OR DAMAGE TO ANY PROPERTY (INCLUDING OWNED PROPERTY) IN THE PAST 3 YEARS? ____________
IF YES, EXPLAIN GIVING FULL DETAILS. ____________

DOES THE VEHICLE TO BE INSURED HAVE ANY BODY DAMAGE OR DETERIORATION, CRACKED OR BROKEN GLASS, BROKEN OR INOPERABLE PARTS WHICH REQUIRE REPAIR OR REPLACEMENT AT THIS TIME? ____________
IF YES, EXPLAIN: ____________

HAS THE VEHICLE BEEN ALTERED OR MODIFIED? ____________
IF YES, EXPLAIN: ____________

APPLICANT'S SIGNATURE

I hereby declare that, to the best of my knowledge and belief, all of the foregoing statements are true and that these statements are offered as an inducement to the company to issue the policy for which I am applying.

I want the policy to be effective at 12:01 A.M. Standard Time on ____________.

In making this application for insurance it is understood that an investigative report may be made whereby information is obtained through personal interviews with third parties, such as family members, business associates, financial sources, friends, neighbors, or others with whom you are acquainted. This inquiry includes information as to your character, general reputation, personal characteristics, and mode of living, whichever may be applicable. You have the right to make a written request within a reasonable period of time for a complete and accurate disclosure of additional information concerning the nature and scope of the investigation.

____
Signature of Applicant

long run should be enhanced by proper selection and rating, which cannot take place in the absence of accurate and complete information.

Official Records

Nature. Recognizing that the application may be incomplete or inaccurate, the underwriter looks for other sources of information. The primary, and usually the only, official records available are the motor vehicle records (MVRs) maintained by most states.

The MVR usually contains information on traffic violations and accidents to the extent they are recorded in the state department of motor vehicle or similar agency. Records will typically go back three years, though this varies by state. The underwriter can usually order MVRs but must ask separately for each driver. Typically, the full name, driver's license number, and date of birth are required, but a few states require additional data such as a social security number. While the MVR can sometimes be ordered directly, many companies order them through an inspection company. There is a charge for obtaining an MVR.

In some areas, local records are also available. It may be possible to obtain local traffic ticket information from a local court or the county courthouse. However, this is the exception rather than the rule.

Limitations. While MVRs are valuable, there are many limitations to them. In a few states they cannot be obtained at all; in many other states, the data is inaccurate or incomplete. The definition of some violations (e.g., reckless driving) is not consistent among various states and even among various areas of one state. The central motor vehicle records are updated by information sent in from all over the state. If a person is found guilty of going through a red light, the information will never show up on an MVR unless the local police or court sends the information to the state motor vehicle department. The speed and efficiency with which this is done varies substantially. Fortunately, many states have compacts with other states under which they share motor vehicle record information. For example, California has compacts with a number of other states under which the latter report all convictions involving a licensed California driver to the California Department of Motor Vehicles. Similarly, for a person who is licensed in another state and requests a California license, a check is made on the driver's record in the former state and the information becomes part of California's Motor Vehicle Record. California provides the same kinds of help to each of the other states with which it has compacts.

Another limitation is that the information available is often very sparse. In some cases, an accident is described simply by a date with no detail. And because most states do not require the reporting of all accidents to the state, the record usually is incomplete.

Problems also arise because of the mobility of the American public. A person with a Texas license now, for example, may have had a license in two other states in the past five years. To obtain the most complete information, it is necessary to find out where the operator has lived in the past few years and the license numbers he or she has had in the various states. This is not always easy to do.

Other difficulties occur because of inaccuracies in names, license numbers, or other factors. Today most motor vehicle records are computerized so that a license number one digit off will usually turn up no record at all.

Even recognizing all these limitations, most underwriters consider the MVR a valuable tool in their review of applications and renewals. Some companies order MVRs on all new applicants, while others do it on a selective basis which may vary by age, other driving information, or area.

The underwriter has to know the relative worth of MVRs in the areas handled. Records in one state may be quite complete, while in another they may be woefully inadequate. The MVR itself costs little, but the underwriter must weigh that and other costs—handling, filing, time in consideration—against the strengths and weaknesses of MVRs in the state(s) of interest to the underwriter. A recent study showed that less than one-third of the serious accidents (over $400 crash damage) reported to insurers are contained on the official state records of the drivers.[7]

Inspection Reports

Nature. Insurance companies have used inspection reports for many years in all lines of business, but use has been particularly frequent in personal auto insurance. Depending upon the nomenclature of the user and provider of these reports, and the nature of the report itself, these may have various labels—consumer information reports, credit reports, classification reports, and so on.

In auto insurance, an inspection report may be ordered in addition to an MVR. The inspection report typically will check on the personal habits and reputation of the applicant or other drivers and how the vehicle is used. This usually involves an inspector for an inspection company going out to the applicant's neighborhood and talking to the applicant, spouse, or neighbors. Questions asked typically involve who drives the car and whether it is used to go to work, for business, or for pleasure. Sometimes information also can be obtained on the physical condition of the vehicle. Whatever information is obtained is reported back to the underwriter in a written report to aid in evaluating the risk.

Exhibit 2-12 is a sample auto inspection report used by the largest national inspection company.

While the cost of such reports varies, it usually is in the range of ten dollars to twenty dollars. Reports of different depths, or with differing emphasis (e.g., financial) can be tailored to the objectives of the underwriter and/or the particulars of a given situation.

Limitations. Inspection reports can be useful, but the underwriter must recognize their limitations. One of the problems is that the inspectors are not always experienced or highly trained and the reports are sometimes of doubtful quality. Also, in many areas, it is difficult to find someone who knows the applicant or anything about him or her. This is especially true in apartment areas or in locales where people do not get to know each other. Where sources are limited, little information can be obtained other than about the general area.

Another problem is the simple fact that many people are reluctant to give out information to a stranger who calls or knocks on the door. The general public's negative attitude to personal investigations often causes the information obtained to be sketchy at best.

While inspection reports may be very helpful in certain situations or for certain purposes, cost, accuracy, and time limitations result in few underwriters ordering reports on all applicants. Many companies feel that their benefits do not outweigh their costs and order reports only in unusual situations. Limitations on the right to cancel business that has been bound makes the time required to secure a report a bigger handicap than was previously the case.

Many companies provide insurance inspection services. Some operate nationally while others are small and operate in one local area. Most underwriters try to use more than one agency as a means of monitoring the comparative quality of reports both in terms of information and timely service. The underwriter needs to constantly review the reports and modify the use of inspection reports accordingly.

Rights of Applicants. For many years applicants had few easily enforceable rights against companies ordered to investigate the person. In some cases, there were inaccuracies or abuses that unfairly damaged a person's reputation. In addition, once the information was sent to a client insurer, it was often difficult to get it corrected.

Much of this problem was solved, or at least alleviated, by the Fair Credit Reporting Act of 1971. Generally, the act requires an insurer to notify an applicant, in advance, that an inspection report may be ordered. Once the report is written and used by the insurer, the applicant has the right to ask the inspection company about the information it obtained. The inspection company has to inform the applicant of its findings. This information can be challenged by the individual who was the subject of the report. The challenge, or the

Exhibit 2-12
Automobile Insurance Report

AUTOMOBILE INSURANCE REPORT

CONFIDENTIAL

ATTENTION OF ____________

____________ **OFFICE**

Acct. No. ____________

Agcy-Br.
Pol. #

RATE: P&C

SIGNIFICANT FEATURES:

M V R	0 - Not Requested By Customer 1 - Attached or Included 2 - Will Follow 3 - Need Further Identification to order- See Remarks

Explanation of MVR Handling on Each Driver:

Automobile #1 **#2**

CLASS

Sources: Time Known ________ Yrs. Previous Reports ________ Yrs. Direct Interview (If so, who?) ________

Police/Traffic Rec. Checked? ________ If known less than 1 year, give former address ________

DRIVERS	Relationship to Insured	Age or Date of Birth	Sex	Marital Status	Occupation (If Insured in Military, See Over)	% Drives Car #1	% Drives Car #2	No. Yrs. Driving	MVR
Insured	Insured								

INSURED:

Speak English Well? ________

Age—sex of children (at home or at school): ________

Name of employer if different from heading: ________

Kind of Business: ________

Time so Employed: ________

Est. Worth $ ________ Est. Income $ ________

IF ANY "YES" ANSWERS—AMPLIFY IN APPROPRIATE PARAGRAPH BELOW OR SECTION ON REVERSE SIDE.

If Car #2 developed, give yr. and make. ____

	CAR #1 NO	CAR #1 YES	CAR #2 NO	CAR #2 YES
1. Is vehicle in poor condition?	☐	☐	☐	☐
2. Any business use of vehicle?	☐	☐	☐	☐
3. Driven to school, work, depot?	☐	☐	☐	☐
If so, est. one way road mileage:	____		____	
# times per week:	____		____	
4. Estimated annual mileage:	____		____	
5. Where is vehicle kept? (Street, Gar., Etc.)	____		____	
6. Any other vehicles in family?	☐	☐		

DO THE FOLLOWING APPLY TO ANY DRIVER	NO	YES	
7. Driver under age 25?	☐	☐	
8. Driving reputation questionable?	☐	☐	
9. Any traffic convictions, revocations, suspensions or criminal record?	☐	☐	
10. Any accidents, fire or theft losses?	☐	☐	
11. Business, financial, or employment reputation questionable?	☐	☐	
12. Personal-Family reputation or associates questionable?	☐	☐	
13. Home or neighborhood environment questionable?	☐	☐	
14. Any driver impaired, physically or mentally?	☐	☐	If Yes, See Over
15. Any driver age 65 or over?	☐	☐	If Yes, See Over
16. Any driver drink to excess? (Boisterousness, intoxication, or regular user)	☐	☐	If Yes, See Over

1. **DRIVERS—USES**: Include all vehicles in family—how used—Cover all drivers, identifying principal operator, driving reputation, etc. If any driver under 25, comment on type of youth (if irresponsible, show off, poor associates, etc., discuss fully); if student, state if high school or college and whether local or out of town. If out of town, give city, state and approximate distance. If any person of driving age does not drive, explain. If questions 1 through 8 answered "Yes," discuss fully.
2. **LOSSES—VIOLATIONS**: If questions 9 or 10 answered "Yes," give details and explain whether developed from outside informants, MVR, Traffic records, etc. Cover information as known to informants—effect on driving reputation, ability and insurability.
3. **PERSONAL—NEIGHBORHOOD**: Describe neighborhood (to reflect grade of risk). Lives with? If retired, former occupation, reason for retirement. If questions 11-13 answered "Yes," or if speaks English poorly, cover fully.
4. **MVR**: If included in report, cover. If further identification needed, be specific as to name and needed identification.

(OVER)

AUTOMOBILE REPORT

COMPLETE ONLY THE SECTION (OR SECTIONS) THAT APPLY.

MILITARY INSURED

Is insured career military person?

Name and location of camp or base?

Does insured make frequent trips to distant points, using this vehicle?

If so, about how far are the points?

How often are trips made?

Does insured lend or rent vehicle to others?

Name of state license on vehicle, if feasible.

DRIVER AGE 65 OR OVER

(Cover any impairment in the "Impaired Driver" section, also.)

Name of driver:

Did you verify age?

Is driver in good physical condition?

Is sight impaired?

Is hearing impaired?

Is driver mentally alert?

IMPAIRED DRIVER (Physical—Mental—Health)

Name of driver:

Nature of impairment (heart condition, poor eyesight, leg or arm injury, epilepsy, diabetes, etc.)

If eye, ear or limb, state whether right or left.

Extent of impairment (one limb shorter than other—how much; if amputated, where—above knee, etc. If hearing impaired, to what extent, etc.;

How long has driver been impaired? ____

Cause of impairment (military service, sickness, accident, existence from birth)

Is impairment improving, remaining same, or getting worse?

Any mechanical aid (artificial arm, claw, hearing aid, etc.)?

Vehicle altered (hand throttle, special brake, etc.)?

DRINK HABITS—ANY DRIVER

Name of driver:

Does he drive after drinking? ____

Describe drinking: when, where, how often, amount of drinking, etc. ____

individual's version of the information, must then be put in the file by the inspection company and passed along to past and future clients who inquire about the same individual.

Insurance companies have set up procedures to comply with the act, and it is important that the underwriter be *completely* familiar with the provisions of the act and the way its mandates are administered by the insurance company. In addition, there may be local or state laws that affect inspections in some areas.

The Producer The producer dealing with the applicant can contribute a great deal to the amount and value of the information available to the underwriter. Even where actual formal underwriting does not take place at the producer level, the producer still is the first person with an opportunity to "underwrite" the risk. In most cases the producer is the only representative of the company to have a personal encounter with the applicant, and the producer therefore may be able to evaluate some of the subjective factors that might not become apparent to the line underwriter. The producer can develop information for the underwriter that goes beyond the scope of the questions appearing on the application. In some cases, the producer may have personal knowledge of the applicant or the applicant's family. In other cases, the producer at least may have met the applicant and be able to offer a crude appraisal of the applicant as an insured. Some applications are handled completely by telephone or mail so little or no personal evaluation is possible.

Once underwriters work with producers, they get to know which are apt to provide complete and accurate information and which are not. Thus, the producer is a very important source of information for the underwriter. But, like other sources, there are limitations the underwriter must recognize.

The producer usually has a heavy sales and service orientation. Remuneration, at least in the short run, is tied to sales either directly or indirectly, so the producer has an incentive to ask the company to write business. A desire to serve and be loyal to clients may cloud the producer's objectivity. Sometimes the producer is simply too close to the risk to be objective in an underwriting sense. This closeness may be based on a personal relationship or on an economic relationship. Perhaps the auto submission is from a person controlling a commercial account already on the producer's books or that the producer would like to write. The applicant may be a center of influence among a large group of prospective clients. Some producers feel they should not spend time on underwriting when others are being paid to perform the underwriting function anyway. They may choose to "leave it to the underwriter to decide," particularly if they represent a number of companies with numerous product lines and feel that they cannot both sell and be well enough informed to function as effective underwriters. Finally, in some cases the producer can do very little underwriting because the risk may be new to the area, have no prior insurance record, or make false statements that the producer cannot detect.

Other Insurers The actual insurance history of an applicant is contained in the records of the applicant's previous insurer(s) and *may* be made available to the underwriter. However, this source may not be readily available. Even if it is available in a physical sense, many insurers are reluctant to share information on former and current insureds and some companies make it a policy not to be a party to requesting it. Thus, information from other insurers simply is not a usable source in many cases.

Where insurers share information, they do so under informal nonbinding reciprocal arrangements, essentially personal in nature, between underwriters in the two companies that involve neither fees nor requirements that information be furnished. The information that may be furnished deals strictly with the loss and/or credit experience while the applicant was insured by the prior company. On the other hand, no release is made of other material, such as information about the personal characteristics of the applicant, which may have been secured from inspection reports or claims personnel, in order to avoid any possible problems with the Fair Credit Reporting Act.

The future of this exchange of information is uncertain. There is concern that some state laws concerning privacy may prohibit or limit this practice. At the same time, other laws are tending to limit the availability or utility of other information, such as inspection reports and MVRs. Furthermore, as limitations are placed on the use of such factors as marital status and sex, it becomes more important to the underwriter that as much accident information as possible is secured. Each underwriter must be aware of the employer's policy on such exchanges of information.

The Applicant One of the best sources of additional information or verification of existing information is the applicant or members of the applicant's household. Some companies conduct direct telephone surveys or inquiries using a specialized survey team trained in how to ask the right questions. They often work in the evening when the chance of the applicant's being home is greatest. In other companies the underwriter conducts his or her own telephone surveys.

Keys to the Need for More Information

It is probably true that the underwriter never has complete information. The task of trying to predict the future conflicts with the need to handle a volume of business. Consequently, the underwriter needs to learn when information is reasonably adequate and when there is a need to know more. Depending on the circumstances, the underwriter may ask the producer to obtain certain additional information from the applicant; or an inspection report may be ordered, a mechanical inspection of the vehicle may be requested, or direct contact with the applicant might be initiated.

Some illustrations of circumstances in which more information may be needed follow. A cancellation or refusal to renew should evoke further inquiry unless the reason has been volunteered and is accepted by the underwriter. Perhaps the application states that there was no prior insurance but the car is two years old, was purchased new, and has been licensed in a state requiring insurance. The facts do not add up and the underwriter must dig deeper. The application may involve two autos and two drivers, both of whom are employed, but indicate "pleasure" use only for both vehicles. It is unusual for a two-car family to leave both cars at home while both drivers are at work, and more information about the means of transportation to work might be required. Or the application might list two cars and only one driver. While this circumstance is not a rarity, it is not the common case. More information might be needed, particularly if the applicant is married.

In deciding what, if anything, is needed, the underwriter has to consider the whole picture. This includes the quality and size of the risk, the cost of obtaining the information, the likely reliability of the information, and what will be done with it when the information arrives. Is the additional information important to the selection decision? Could it make a difference in a decision to accept or reject? A risk of doubtful quality on the surface is unlikely to be acceptable without considerably more information than is normally required for another risk where all the elements are positive. The underwriter decides what is needed and how best to get it based on informed judgment, knowledge of information sources, and experience in evaluating risks.

SUMMARY

Evaluating hazards is perhaps the most difficult but the most challenging underwriting task. In addition to the typical private passenger autos, personal auto underwriters must be familiar with farm vehicles, utility autos, antique and classic cars, motorcycles, and a growing list of recreational vehicles. After determining initial eligibility, the hazards of the risk must be identified and analyzed. The major factors concerning the drivers are driving history and habits, age, sex, marital status, occupation, education, and physical condition. The major factors concerning the vehicle are its age, use, type, location, and protection.

The application for insurance provides the underwriter with most of the information needed for hazard analysis. Official records such as MVRs and inspection reports are often needed to verify and supplement the information on the application. The producer and the applicant are also useful sources of underwriting information.

Chapter Notes

1. *Personal Auto Manual* (New York: Insurance Services Office, 1980), p. GR-1.
2. *The Highway Loss Reduction Status Report,* vol. 15, no. 17, (Washington, DC: Insurance Institute for Highway Safety, 1980), pp. 2, 3.
3. *Insurance Facts,* 1980-81 edition (New York: Insurance Information Institute, 1980), p. 53.
4. *Insurance Facts,* p. 72.
5. *Insurance Facts,* p. 12.
6. *The Highway Loss Reduction Status Report,* vol. 16, no. 7 (Washington, DC: Insurance Institute for Highway Safety, 1981), p. 8.
7. Study by All-Industry Research Advisory Council.

CHAPTER 3

Decision Making and Evaluating Special Situations

ORGANIZING INFORMATION FOR DECISION MAKING

In the previous chapter, the steps taken to evaluate hazards were discussed. An underwriter must determine and evaluate the hazards presented by each applicant, whether the vehicle is a private passenger auto or one of the special types of vehicles to be discussed later in this chapter.

The various underwriting factors (risk characteristics) which are used to identify or measure the hazards were also discussed. Since evaluation requires information, the major sources of information available to the underwriter were described.

The next step in the underwriting process is organizing the information for use in making an underwriting decision. This section discusses the organizing of data, and the following section deals with decision making itself. This chapter is based on two assumptions: (1) the application is for new business or the addition of an insured to an existing policy, and (2) the application is the voluntary market.

Gathering All Necessary Information

UND 61 discussed the subject of "information efficiency." In order to make a good decision, there is a tendency to gather more and more information. The underwriter may feel that more information will make a decision *for* the underwriter and eliminate the need for evaluation and decision making *by* the underwriter. Yet, the securing and analysis of information cost money. A desire for "more information" may conflict with the need to make decisions promptly and keep backlogs to a minimum. Some underwriters find it helpful to have each type of information categorized according to its status as (1) *essential* to the underwriting of a risk, (2) *desirable* to the underwriting of a risk if it can be secured at an acceptable cost and without undue delay, and (3) *available* in the underwriting of a risk but not always worth special effort to obtain. Operating procedures and underwriting guides usually will dictate the types of information regarded as *essential,* but the underwriter's judgment often is involved in understanding the difference between *desirable* and *available* and deciding when additional information deemed to be *desirable* should be obtained. Thus, what ultimately is regarded as "all necessary information" often depends on the judgment of the underwriter in the light of the particular case under consideration. Simple rules cannot be offered in advance.

The application, or "daily," is the underwriter's initial, and basic, working document. It contains essential information which is necessary in underwriting, rating, and issuing the policy.

In some lines of insurance, the application supplies all of the necessary information for a large percentage of the risks submitted and only the unusual case will require further investigation. In auto insurance, however, the motor vehicle record (MVR) is almost always required on all principal operators, and in many cases, on other identifiable operators as well because of the importance of the driving record. Occasionally the producer will have secured MVRs to determine the company, program, or pricing structure in which to place the applicant. In such cases, the MVRs ordinarily accompany the application, thus saving the company both time and money.

Many states permit computer access to their motor vehicle records, which allows insurers, inspection companies, and specialty companies to secure MVRs within twenty-four hours. In these cases, it is preferable to delay the underwriting of the application until the MVR can be secured, rather than to issue the policy and then possibly have to reverse the action because of an unfavorable MVR.

Although the MVR is a vital adjunct to the application, insurers do not always order MVRs on all drivers. An MVR would not be secured on a new driver who does not yet have a driving record, nor on a driver who recently moved to the state. In the latter case, an MVR from the state of prior residence might be requested, or an MVR might be available in the new state if a compact for exchanging motor vehicle information exists between the old and new states. An operator who drives only a small percentage of the time and who presents no cause for concern as to age or other variables might not be checked, especially if all other factors on the application are favorable. If all information shown on the application appears valid and indicates an exceptionally good risk, MVRs might not be ordered on any driver, although for most insurers this would be a rare exception to standard practice. Finally, the motor vehicle records in some states are not completely accurate or are out-of-date, so selective ordering is practiced, with an MVR being ordered only to confirm an admitted record of accidents or citations, or to check a borderline applicant.

As a supplement to the application and MVR, an auto underwriter may order an inspection report. A *full report* may be used if there are suspicions about moral or other hazards, or about the condition of the vehicle.

A *rating report* (also called "uses and drivers" or "classification" report) is used more often. The rating report includes the names of all drivers, the percentage of time each drives each car, and the use to which they put the auto. While basically rating information, some of the data may pertain to underwriting, and rating reports usually are referred to the underwriter in addition to the rater.

Other sources sometimes used by auto underwriters are the producer, the previous insurer, and the applicant. The producer generally has personal contact with the applicant and may be able to provide additional, though subjective, insight.

On selected cases, where questionable circumstances appear and time permits, the underwriter might contact the underwriter of the prior insurer if a reciprocal arrangement exists between the insurers. Information available from this source includes the loss history and, possibly, the reason(s) for cancellation or nonrenewal.

Finally, questions regarding classification may be efficiently and inexpensively answered by the applicants themselves.

Consistency Among Data Sources

Discrepancies among data sources occasionally occur, particularly with respect to accident, driver, and use data. In such cases, the underwriter must settle any questions that arise in order to be able to operate from one set of facts.

The most common discrepancy concerns the driving record. An application might show no accidents or citations, while the MVR on the applicant reveals one or more of these. If the MVR is valid, the applicant either has forgotten an incident, has deliberately misrepresented the facts, or the producer has completed the application on behalf of the applicant and has assumed a favorable driving record. Unless the evidence is such that forgetfulness is a virtually impossible basis for the error on the application, the underwriter should not waste time trying to determine the true reason. The underwriter ordinarily assumes that the MVR is correct, acts accordingly, and notifies the producer of his or her action. Any errors will then be called to the attention of the underwriter who must analyze the rebuttal and take appropriate steps to verify the facts and, if indicated, amend the earlier action.

Discrepancies also can occur in the information on drivers and uses of the vehicle. Again, information from a source other than the application must be compared to information on the application and any discrepancies resolved.

Whether an action should be taken (e.g., declination, cancellation of a risk already bound, or rerating) *before* the producer (or applicant) is contacted is a question having no pat answer. Some insurers check discrepancies with producers prior to taking any action in order to avoid the extra costs that reversing an earlier action would entail and to minimize friction between producers and applicants, many of whom are already clients of the producers in other lines. Other insurers resolve all doubts in favor of the company, take the indicated action, and reverse the action only if the information assumed to be accurate is subsequently disproven. Still others consider the nature of the action and/or the relationship with the producer as important variables. This appears to be the most reasonable approach. A decision to rerate or decline a risk not already bound might be taken before notifying the producer, but if the decision would result in cancellation of a risk already bound, the producer might be notified first. The past performance of one producer might cause an underwriter to check before taking any action, whereas the same consideration might not be extended to another producer with a marginal record or some history of inaccurate completion of applications.

When a risk is already bound, the underwriter must be careful to recognize any time limitation on the right to cancel that might be imposed by state law or insurance department regulation. For example, assume that an incorrect MVR is received due to a mix-up in names. The delay in receiving the correct MVR may preclude the underwriter from exercising the cancellation option. To avoid this situation, prompt decision making is essential, and sometimes the decision must be made without the benefit of the correct MVR.

Inconsistency among data sources is seldom a serious problem to auto underwriters. Most information upon which decisions are made is factual, and when discrepancies are found, they are resolved quickly.

Arranging Data in Useful Form

In the writing of some of the more complex lines of property-liability insurance, some companies use "risk analysis" forms for organizing and measuring risk characteristics. However, such forms are rarely used in the writing of personal auto insurance for two reasons. First, in personal lines, there are generally a smaller number of risk characteristics to consider than in commercial lines. Consequently, the need for a risk or account form diminishes because all of the essential information (application, MVR, outside report) can be reviewed at a glance. Second, the large volume of applications, the similarity of personal lines applicants, and the relatively low unit premium require prompt decision making to avoid backlogs. The use of a risk or account analysis form on routine business would be too costly in time to justify its use, except in special situations.

The amount of information involved in making a decision on an auto application is quite limited compared to most other lines of insurance. This does not mean that auto underwriting is automatic or simple; on the contrary, it can be very challenging and complex. The very fact that only a few data sources are used in the analysis indicates the importance of proper consideration of each item. The auto underwriter does not deal with reams of data on individual risks. When managing a book of business, however, substantial amounts of information will be available such as premium and incurred losses by line, by class, by producer, and so on. Additionally, analysis of losses may suggest a reevaluation of risk characteristics. The use of an analysis form is more useful in this context than in dealing with individual risks.

DECISION MAKING

Before a decision can be made, the underwriter must have taken the steps discussed in the previous pages. First, information needs must be determined. Next, the underwriter needs to know the sources that can be used to secure that information, along with the strengths and limitations of each source. Then the information must be secured and analyzed for completeness and consistency.

The first step in the actual making of the decision is the comparison of the information against the underwriting criteria. Risks may be eligible or ineligible according to the manual rules or special filings of the insurer. Even if eligible, they may be unacceptable. Risk characteristics should be measured against standards and weighed according to importance in the composite risk picture. Finally, alternative courses of action are considered, and the decision is made.

Comparing Information Against Underwriting Criteria

Both eligibility and acceptability are factors to be considered in the underwriting of auto applicants. To do this, the underwriter uses the underwriting guides and manuals which have been provided for that purpose and also his or her own informed judgment.

Underwriting Guides or Manuals Every auto insurer has a list of the types of vehicles which are not eligible for its personal auto insurance program(s). Some applicants will be ineligible, without regard to quality, because of these explicit eligibility rules. A private passenger auto may be found to be used for taxicab or livery purposes, making it ineligible under the company's personal auto program. A pickup truck may be used in the applicant's business—a use which similarly may be prohibited. As soon as the underwriter discovers a fact which places the risk in such a category, rejection is required or consideration under another policy form and/or in another department or affiliate of the company might be initiated. The producer (or the applicant in some cases) should be notified. If history indicates that a producer repeatedly violates eligibility rules, the matter may require the attention of underwriting management or the marketing department.

Virtually every auto insurer also has guidelines for acceptability which may indicate several degrees of acceptability. The most extreme are what may be called "inflexible guidelines." These contain a description of types of risks which the company refuses to insure voluntarily. An example applicable in some companies is any vehicle where the principal operator is under twenty-one years of age and has less than three years of "clean driving experience." A definition of "clean driving experience" may be where the operator's driving record indicates no convictions for traffic violations and no chargeable accidents. "Convictions" generally exclude parking tickets and equipment violations. "Chargeable accidents" might include all accidents except those where the applicant was legally parked, stopped for a traffic control device, received payment from a person who was legally responsible for the accident, or some other specified reason.

Other guidelines might include situations in which the producers are not permitted to bind coverage. In these cases, the application is to be referred to the underwriter for a decision before coverage can become effective. This group would include those types of risks where many applicants would be unacceptable and all would require detailed review before any commitment could be made. These guidelines might encompass an applicant whose driving license has been suspended or revoked during the past five years, one whose driving record cannot be secured promptly, or one whose violations or accidents exceed certain specified maximums over a stated period. Aside from its obvious purpose of permitting full investigation before coverage is in force, this "no binding" approach minimizes producer embarrassment from the cancellation of risks under binder.

The above classifications of guidelines are general in nature. Each insurer decides how they will be used, what they will be called, and what types of applicants or vehicles are included. There is little uniformity in the use, format, or content of such guidelines.

Specific Factors Guidelines such as those just mentioned are broad and impersonal in nature. Some make decisions on a blanket basis for the underwriter and/or producer. Others are precautionary in nature and affect underwriting procedure and the care given by the underwriter to certain types of submissions. The actual standards used in underwriting individual risks and the variables with which they deal are largely inseparable from a company's policies expressed in underwriting guidelines, on one hand, and from the company's classification and rating plans, on the other. However, this text adopts a process approach to underwriting, and that format implies a logical series of steps. Each step must be dealt with independently so that it can be clearly understood. The relationship among the steps and the obvious overlap among the factors dealt with in each step must be kept in mind. Overlaps are unavoidable in describing a process approach to making underwriting decisions. For example, the evaluation of hazards, and the comparison of underwriting information on these hazards against selection criteria, do *not* take place in a pricing vacuum. Risk selection really is "risk selection at a price." Yet, it is cumbersome to look at the whole process before looking at each part as a separate step. Once the problems and case material accompanying this and the next chapter are encountered, there will be ample opportunity to view the process as a whole.

Underwriting decisions are made by weighing the characteristics of each applicant and deciding if the positive considerations outweigh the negative considerations, all in a context that combines not only the individual risk's characteristics but also factors such as the applicable class, the pricing structure, the territory, the company's goals, and the legal and economic environment. The balance of this section deals primarily with only the first of these items—the individual risk's characteristics—and the standards against which these characteristics are compared in evaluating a risk. Along the way, certain relationships between individual risk characteristics and other variables, e.g., rate adequacy and class balance, will be pointed out.

The context of the following discussion is the stage in underwriting an individual risk where all underwriting information has been gathered and a decision soon will be made. The question at hand right now is, "How does the risk look when appraised against the underwriting benchmarks that apply?" The standards most commonly used relate to many hazard factors mentioned in Chapter 2: age, sex, vehicle use, driving record, place of garaging, vehicle condition and type, and miscellaneous factors concerning stability and responsibility. Bearing in mind, of course, that appraisals may differ among underwriters, and realizing that all companies do not use the same standards or attach the same weight to any particular standard, each of these widely used factors will be discussed in a decision making context rather than hazard evaluation context as in Chapter 2. The discussion assumes the existence of no concrete evidence of moral hazard which, should it exist, would negate the need for further underwriting consideration.

Age and Sex. Age and sex as indicators of hazards were dealt with extensively in the previous chapter. But, as indicated there, for most risks age alone is not the sole variable upon which a decision is based. Sex means little except when it is accompanied by certain age ranges, and so sex is combined with age in the discussion. How might company guides and informed underwriting judgment handle age and sex as variables leading to an overall evaluation of the risk? Some examples follow, subject to a critical qualifier. These examples are largely illustrative and *do not* imply the existence of any "standard" approach to the consideration of age and sex in underwriting personal automobile insurance.

1. Unmarried drivers under twenty-one years of age who have good driving records and who own or extensively operate standard family-types of autos and reside with their parents may be acceptable despite the stereotype unfavorable to single young drivers. (Notice the "package" nature of this statement involving as it does, not only age, but driving record, auto type, and place of residence.)
2. Unmarried drivers twenty-one through twenty-four years of age require a close look at the driving experience records. Married female drivers ages twenty-one through twenty-four who are owners or extensive or principal operators are often desirable risks. However, students in this category warrant careful underwriting.
3. Married drivers under twenty-five years of age are generally considered more mature and responsible than their unmarried counterparts, and therefore are less suspect because of age. Married drivers under twenty-one years of age may still be

lacking in maturity, so discretion must be exercised in selecting risks of the younger married group.

4. Risks involving unmarried *student* youthful operators where the autos are garaged away from the parents' home, and not subject to parental control, are usually considered to create a high exposure to loss.
5. A driver training course licensed by the state is recognized as a definite asset in weighing the desirability of a risk with a youthful driving exposure. The applicant should be required to show evidence that he or she has successfully completed the classroom and driving requirements for a driver education course certificate.
6. Youthful operators have positive aspects. On the average, younger people's reflexes are superior to those of older operators, and they tend to recover more rapidly from injuries, which could reduce the amount of medical payments from the insurance company. Students who are unemployed or hold low paying part-time jobs would have low wage losses in states where no-fault laws are in effect. Also, youthful auto insurance clients may make excellent prospects for life, accident and health, and homeowners insurance. (This is significant for companies in all-lines groups. These facts complicate the process the underwriter goes through with an application involving a youthful operator.)
7. The age of the operator, when mentioned in an underwriting context, almost always refers to youthful drivers. However, there is a significant number of licensed and active auto operators who are considered to be in the "senior citizen" group. Elderly drivers normally use their cars less often than other drivers, drive at moderate speeds, and maintain the mechanical condition of their cars at least as well as the average car owner. But it is a fact that, as a category, they have slower reflexes and often have health impairments such as poor eyesight and limited hearing.

This discussion of age presents a good opportunity to show how consideration of a risk involves factors other than the risk itself in isolation. Earlier it was noted that underwriting does not take place in a pricing vacuum. One major underwriting variable in the evaluation of an individual risk is the rating structure used by the insurer.

Auto rates are determined by a variety of factors such as age and sex of the operators and use and location of the vehicle. The classification plan can become quite refined and contain several levels of rates. The differences among rates within a class plan are referred to as *differentials* or *relativities.* Actuaries endeavor to determine accurately the correct differentials among classes, but sometimes the differentials have to be tempered because there is too wide a spread. If this occurs, the spread may be averaged among all involved classes. For example, suppose the unmarried male principal operator class warrants a premium that is four times the base premium, but a state insurance department disapproves such a difference on the basis that it appears to be unfairly discriminatory against young people. Therefore, the differential might be capped at two and one-half instead of four. The result of such a capping is that the unmarried male principal operator class may be inadequately priced, and if a company should write a disproportionate volume of this class, it could adversely affect the underwriting results of the entire book of personal auto business. This will lead to a high degree of selectivity in evaluating risks in this group to offset the inadequate rate level applicable to the group as a whole.

The same type of "smoothing" (narrowing class rate differentials) may occur within other classification factors. For example, it is not uncommon to have one geographical location develop consistently poorer loss ratios than another. Yet, as in the above age class example, there may be a desire or need to smooth out the wide differences so as not to have some rating territories (zones) rated considerably higher than others within a state. It is most important for the underwriter to be acquainted with the factors involved in the development of the rates for any states within the underwriter's jurisdiction. The adequacy of rates for a given class and/or territory is indeed a critical issue in personal auto underwriting and is important in reviewing underwriting results as the section of the chapter on "monitoring" will show.

Use. Use of the vehicle is a key factor in classifying a risk for rating purposes. If the rating plan contains adequate class differentials for different *types* of use (e.g., pleasure only, pleasure and to and from work, etc.), then *for a large number of risks,* there should be a balance among loss exposure, actual losses, and premium income. But when dealing with an individual risk, how might the underwriter react to information on that risk? Mileage is a good example.

When an auto has an unusually high annual mileage (e.g., over 25,000 miles) or a greater than normal distance to and from work (e.g., more than thirty-five miles one way), caution is urged in evaluating the risk. Exposure to loss increases with miles driven. Classification and rating plans recognize this, but class rates are, by definition, rates applicable to the hypothetical "average" risk in the class. The alert underwriter is aware of this and recognizes the possible adverse effects of writing a disproportionate number of high-mileage risks. High mileage alone does not indicate a bad risk, but the underwriter may "program" mileage information as one factor in arriving at a composite picture of the hazards presented by a risk.

Driving Record. The relationship between driving record and accident potential has been well documented and thoroughly discussed earlier in this text. This variable is likely to be the subject of very explicit company guidelines and leaves little room for the underwriter to exercise judgment in comparing driving record information against underwriting criteria. But as previously noted, different degrees of significance can be attached to what "on the record" may appear similar. A "fender-bender" on the way home from the office holiday party on a stormy night *may* be viewed less harshly than an overturn at high speed on a clear day. Apparent patterns, of course, cannot be disregarded, but under certain circumstances, two driving records with similar labels (e.g., one moving traffic violation and one single-car accident), might warrant different kinds of consideration from the underwriter, assuming the ability to verify the facts in each case.

Place of Garaging. The term "place of garaging" means the specific location at which the auto normally is at rest when not in actual use. In personal auto insurance, that location typically would be the residence of the applicant. For many risks, obviously, there is no literal place of garaging because there is no garage in the physical sense. In fact, this absence of a garaging structure is increasing because of the increase in the types of dwelling units without garages—apartments, condominiums, mobile homes, and so on—compared to the traditional single-family house having a garage as an integral part of the structure.

Place of garaging is a basic rate determinant because most classification and rating plans begin with a territorial base rate keyed to place of garaging. Beyond that, however, the underwriter wants to know if the vehicle actually is kept in a garage if the risk is located in areas where vandalism, theft, or hit-and-run collisions can be severe problems. In some areas, it is virtually impossible to develop adequate premium income for comprehensive coverage because of vandalism losses. Ungaraged vehicles normally parked in known areas of frequent vandalism losses are undesirable for comprehensive coverage.

In certain situations, the underwriter should be aware of possible discrepancies between the actual place of garaging and the location cited on the application. Obviously, the company's and underwriter's criteria for acceptability, and their rating practices, are meaningless if the actual location presents hazards substantially different from those of the named location. Multi-car accounts with college students, for example, might present two completely different territorial exposures if the facts were known. One car could be located most of the year in a high crime area with no garaging facilities, and only the car retained at home by the parent(s) might be acceptable for certain coverages or entitled to the favorable rate based on the parent(s)' residence location.

Condition and Type of Auto. The condition of an auto can often be an indication of the applicant's driving habits and attitude toward safety. Autos which are poorly maintained regarding the mechanical operation or overall physical conditon are highly susceptible to accidents. An underwriter cannot achieve a profitable account writing insurance for those who are unwilling to assume the responsibility of proper maintenance.

Sports cars and high-powered standard cars (sometimes referred to as "muscle" cars) call for caution on the part of the underwriter. People who buy these kinds of cars and pay extra money for the purchase and maintenance of high-powered vehicles are very apt to drive them at the higher speeds they are designed to achieve—speeds that may be higher than good judgment would seem to dictate.

The underwriter also considers the length of time that the applicant has owned a sports car or "muscle" car. For two drivers with identical driving records, the underwriter may react positively to the one with that record developed while driving a sports car but negatively to the other who has just acquired a sports car.

Rating plans of many companies provide surcharges for these types of vehicles. These surcharges, however, are no substitute for the exercise of informed judgment by an underwriter.

Physical Impairments. Physical impairments can be a problem if correction of or allowances for the impairment have not been made. A missing limb may be accommodated by adequate modifications of the car, such as hand controls; when this is done, and the applicant has demonstrated a mastery of the vehicle, no underwriting problems remain. A tendency toward blackouts, such as from epilepsy or diabetes, often can be controlled by diet or medication. When there is sufficient evidence of control, usually through confirmation by a doctor, such risks are usually considered to have normal exposures to loss. Some companies may consider some of these risks desirable if any necessary modifications in the vehicle are made since these drivers may tend to drive less than most drivers and may tend to be more careful when driving since they are aware of their handicap.

Previous Insurer. The identity of (or the absence of) a previous insurer may be considered in making the decision. This may sometimes turn up something such as a canceled producer contract which does not reflect upon the insured. If the risk was previously uninsured, a question in the mind of the underwriter could be, "Why does the applicant want insurance now?" The answer may be that the state recently enacted a compulsory insurance law. In that case, many previously uninsured risks would be seeking coverage. Upon reviewing its entire auto book of business, one insurer learned that the frequency of property damage liability losses was significantly higher in the subgroup that had been previously uninsured than in the subgroup that had been continuously insured.

If the applicant identifies the previous insurer, the underwriter may know something more about the risk. For example, some insurers specialize in certain occupational groups (such as military officers or government employees) or substandard risks. If a specialty insurer is listed as the prior insurer, the underwriter may know a little more about the background of the applicant.

Also, some insurers are known for their low rates and they generally attract insureds who simply want the lowest possible price. If the application shows such an insurer, the applicant may turn out to be a short-lived account who will cancel or nonrenew whenever a lower rate is available. This is not to say that such applicants are not good risks, but many underwriters keep tabs on where new business is coming from to keep up to date on the market. Additionally, it is expensive for companies to place business on their books one year and to lose it the next. A renewal generally involves much less expense than a piece of new business.

An auto book of business in a territory or branch office may turn over quite rapidly. Insureds that comprise the "seasoned" book of business move away, change insurers, or change producers, and attrition may be surprisingly high. It is not uncommon for an insurer to write 20 percent to 30 percent of its total premium volume as new business each year. Knowledge of the previous insurer can tell an underwriter where the business is coming from and how the book of business is changing. For example, if the IIA Insurance Company recently raised its rates, a larger than normal number of insureds from that company should be expected. This may not be a problem if the IIA is generally considered to be a good underwriting company. But if the company recently reported substantial underwriting losses, there may be a reunderwriting in effect and the poorer risks may be "weeded out." A larger than normal number of insureds from such a company should tell the underwriter to scrutinize those applications more thoroughly to avoid adverse selection.

Knowledge of the previous insurer may also be a positive sign. An independent agent may wish to reduce the number of companies represented and may be transferring business on renewal from one company to another. If the underwriter receiving this transfer business has analyzed the book of business being transferred and found it acceptable, relatively little reunderwriting may be necessary. In effect, the business being transferred has been "pre-screened" to some extent. Confidence in the producer and in the underwriting standards of the insurer whose business is being transferred are essential.

Miscellaneous Factors. Many other factors are thought to be of significance by some underwriters. These deal largely with signs of financial or emotional stability or with matters, such as occupation, that may be valuable for what they can reveal about the objective factors (auto use, garaging) already discussed. These other factors are too numerous to be cataloged here, but examples may be encountered in the underwriting guides and practices of the underwriter's company.

Regulatory Constraints. Laws and regulations sometimes affect the factors which can be used in underwriting. For example, there is currently a trend to prohibit the consideration of marital status and sex in underwriting. Some states have passed laws on this subject, while others have adopted regulations. One company, Commercial Union, has voluntarily begun using a program in some states which does not use age, sex, or marital status as a rating factor. Other factors being studied are physical impairments, age, and occupation. These factors may be used in rating, in most instances, but often not in risk selection. Where such constraints are present, the factors they deal with must be disregarded or otherwise handled in accordance with the applicable law or regulation.

Both laws and regulations differ by state. Each underwriter must be aware of any limitations on underwriting consideration or action in each state handled.

The Role of Informed Judgment The previous list was not intended to include all factors of concern to auto underwriters. The education, background, and training of the underwriter will lead to concern about subtle factors which, together, indicate a risk which could be underpriced at the classification proposed or which warrants the securing of additional information beyond that routinely available.

No set of underwriting guides will ever replace the judgment of the underwriter. Good judgment, developed through experience and applied with wisdom, must always be an integral part of underwriting.

Weighing Results of the Comparison

In some companies, selection of auto risks has become so standardized that a producer or an underwriting assistant can accept applicants meeting certain predetermined criteria and presenting no cause for concern on others. The difficulty, of course, is in recognizing factors which should concern an underwriter.

If, based upon past experience, the factor or factors presented by an applicant will cause an increase in exposure to loss which is greater than the rate contemplates, the application must be denied or a higher rate must be charged. Conversely, other factors will be found to be no problem, after careful investigation, and the application may be accepted.

In most cases, the risk presents some mixture of pluses and minuses, but with no feature that automatically makes a decision for the underwriter. It is in the handling of this type of risk that effective underwriters earn their salaries. In the underwriting process, the underwriter weighs the findings on each factor. Favorable findings or characteristics are balanced against unfavorable ones. The conclusion will depend upon the answer to a basic question: using all available information, does it appear that the price will be adequate for the exposure?

As an example of the type of weighing which must be given, consider the accident and citation history of the principal operator of an auto. An individual who had a minor accident when weather conditions were snowy and icy would appear to be a better risk than someone who was speeding during good weather conditions and became involved in an accident. The risk who had an accident at 2:00 A.M. could be more suspect than the one who had an accident at 5:00 P.M. These examples incorporate negative issues, but the underwriter must screen the data and decide under what circumstances an applicant with an accident and conviction record can still be considered an acceptable risk.

Judgment will also be required in deciding on the acceptability of an applicant who is newly licensed and has no driving record. Usually new drivers are also youthful, but not in every case. If an older driver is newly licensed, one might become more concerned, since older people frequently do not learn as quickly as their younger counterparts and their reflexes may not be as quick.

If there is an acceptable accident and conviction history and the overall rate level is adequate, then equal weight might be given to the factors of age of operators and use of the vehicle, including mileage. By the time the process is completed, the underwriter will have mentally assigned a "grade" to the applicant. If the grade is well above "passing," then the analysis of any remaining factors would have to produce very negative findings in order to make the applicant unacceptable. If, however, the analysis produced only a marginal passing grade, then the findings on remaining factors that otherwise seem insignificant can become crucial.

Considering Other Factors

At this point, the underwriter will have made a tentative decision concerning the action to be taken based on a composite picture of the hazards presented by the applicant. If the decision is that acceptance is not indicated, there are still two factors that may be considered—the producer and the account.

The Producer Some producers represent more than one company. As a result, the companies represented by the producer may be in competition for the producer's business. Sometimes incentives, such as additional commission, are offered to producers based on the attainment of agreed upon premium volume commitments. This system of incentives may cause a producer to favor one company over another. Many agency agreements provide for additional compensation contingent on a stipulated level of underwriting profit, either on a single line of business, or a total book of business, which could include all lines that a producer places with a particular company. This may result in a producer's protecting potential contingent commissions due from some companies by placing predominantly good business with these companies and placing marginal business with others. For the latter, this process is known as adverse selection. Insurers are constantly endeavoring to avoid being selected against. Chapter 5 will deal in part with monitoring a producer's book of business and sensing this practice. For now, it is sufficient for the underwriter to be aware of the possible problem inherent in multicompany representation by producers.

Regardless of the number of companies represented, the producer will occasionally request the underwriter to accept a borderline applicant. Most companies refer to such requests as *accommodations.* Often this is because the producer feels that there will be a chance of writing other policies if this one is written at the requested rate. Thus, the promise of a homeowners or a commercial account to follow will be the reason used to try to secure auto coverage at the most favorable rates possible. In other cases, the applicant and the producer are personal friends, neighbors, lodge associates, and so on. In still other situations, the producer may have been the producer for the applicant or the family for many years and may feel an obligation to secure the lowest possible rates.

The underwriter may elect to follow the recommendations of the producer if the risk is really just borderline and if the producer has demonstrated an ability to select risks properly. If the producer's book of business has been profitable and substantial, the recommendations should be given weight. The degree of weight given this factor will depend upon the reliability of the producer in addition to profitability, volume, and quality of the risk.

The producer usually is in a position to both see and talk with the applicant, while the underwriter is not. If the producer can verify personal knowledge of the risk and has demonstrated sound underwriting judgment in the past, the producer's recommendations can be given considerable weight in making decisions on borderline cases.

Some underwriters keep a record of business on which the recommendation of the producer, or a request by the producer, was an important factor in accepting an otherwise marginal or unacceptable risk. This information on "accommodations" lets the underwriter or the underwriting manager know the status of one aspect of insurer-producer relations, and it assists in monitoring the underwriting judgment of producers.

The Account A personal auto submission may involve an applicant already insured with the company in another capacity. Most often the applicant is the named insured under a homeowners or other residence contract, but the additional coverages could include personal marine floaters, personal umbrella liability coverage and, in all-lines insurers, life and/or health coverage as well. To what extent, if at all, might or should the auto submission be influenced by the other coverages on the books of the company or group of related companies? In other words, to what extent should the auto submission be considered as part of an account rather than as a totally independent submission?

Each company develops and follows its own rules on account underwriting. Practices may differ because of the lines written, the relationship among the companies of a group (since some policies in the account may be written by companies in the group other than the underwriter's), and the weight given by management to each individual line. Many companies treat each type of contract independently except under the most (for them) unusual circumstances. Therefore, it is difficult to make generalizations on the subject. However, certain acceptable conclusions can be cited. First, consideration of the account as a whole is less common in personal lines than in commercial lines. Second, acceptability of marginal auto business is rarely determined merely by the existence of other personal lines business with the company or group or by the size of the total premium developed by the account including the auto premium. Third, if the auto exposure is marginal and *if* some consideration is given to the account, the balance of the account should be regarded as well above average in order to support acceptance of the auto risk. The desirability of the total account should not be reduced to less than average by the addition of the less desirable exposure. The value of a potentially profitable supporting line (to the risk being considered) is minute when considered in the light of the additional exposure generated by possible auto business.

Considering Alternative Courses of Action

At this point in the underwriting process, the underwriter has identified and obtained the desired information, resolved any inconsistencies among pieces of data, compared the information against company rules or guides and his or her own standards, developed a composite of the hazards presented in the submission, and considered other variables that may have an influence on the ultimate conclusion. The next step is to consider the range of alternatives open to the underwriter in disposing of the submission—acceptance, acceptance subject to modification, or rejection.

Acceptance Unconditional acceptance is completely in order in many cases. Interestingly, the underwriter often will spend more time per submission with cases that end up as acceptable than with cases that result in rejection. This is so because acceptance is not contingent solely on the risk's being acceptable on any one criterion, but on many. In contrast, rejection *may* result from any one of several factors and *can* take place early in the process of hazard evaluation, thus eliminating the need to develop a composite based on consideration of all the variables present. For example, a favorable driving record alone, while an important plus for the applicant, will not itself generate an acceptance, but an extremely poor driving record can eliminate a risk from further consideration. This is consistent with the nature of underwriting as a selection process.

Acceptance Subject to Modification A risk unacceptable if written as requested often may be made acceptable by modifying limits, coverage, deductibles, or pricing. In effect, the underwriter makes a counteroffer to that originally submitted by the applicant. In the process, the underwriter can demonstrate some creativity in making the needs of the insured consistent with the underwriting policies and practices of the company. This may be illustrated by a few examples.

Limits on Liability. Suggesting lower limits on liability coverage is an alternative used by some underwriters. They consider the liability limits to be an item which should be controlled by underwriting. The theory is that high limits (what is considered "high" varies by company) should not be written on persons who present a relatively high potential loss frequency. For example, there may be an applicant who has two vehicles, one of them having a youthful inexperienced licensee as the principal operator. The parents desire high liability limits, but the underwriter does not wish to make such limits available on the youth. In this case, the underwriter can write the policy at basic limits and endorse the policy to provide higher liability limits to the parents' car.

On the other hand, most companies prefer writing separate policies when different limits are to be applied to the two vehicles.

Other companies feel that the rates for high limits of liability are adequate for the exposure. The premium increase for higher limits usually is a percentage increase, which means that the dollar increase is greater for higher rated youthful operators than for the lower rated adults. In these companies, the underwriter may accept any limits desired, because the belief is that after an applicant has been accepted for low limits, the excess limit factors will produce a premium adequate for the higher limits. This matter of high liability limits is another case in which a line underwriter must be guided by the practices of the company.

Coverage Modifications A risk with an undesirable driver in a multidriver household might be written with an exclusion applicable to the undesirable operator in states where this practice is permitted, but care must be exercised to be sure that the implications of the exclusion are understood. An applicant may have an older car of negligible value, and the underwriter may choose not to write physical damage coverages because of potential loss-settlement difficulties. Still, liability and medical payments might be offered if the vehicle has been maintained in good mechanical condition.

Deductibles. A deductible or higher than usual deductible might make acceptable a risk with a history of small vandalism losses.

Higher deductibles might also be used if there has been a history of small comprehensive or collision claims. By making the insured bear a portion, or a larger than usual portion, of any loss, the insured may be motivated to use greater caution in protecting the car. Underwriters should be aware, however, that use of deductibles will have little effect on a major collision loss, or on theft of the car. Although deductibles may reduce the company's exposure to small losses, they should not be used in an attempt to salvage a basically undesirable account.

Nonstandard Pricing. Another possible modification that may be available to the underwriter is nonstandard pricing. This modification is not uniformly available because some states have not permitted companies to file such a plan and, further, some companies have no desire to do so. Nonstandard programs have been instituted to provide coverage through the normal voluntary insurance market for risks that have characteristics that make them more susceptible to loss than the average risk. Nonstandard risks are insurable, but because of their greater susceptibility to loss, the premiums are higher than normal for the class.

Usually the policies used in nonstandard pricing programs are identical in coverage options and limits to those available under the standard programs. At the time nonstandard programs were first introduced, the residual market automobile insurance plans restricted the coverages and limits that were available. Under these circumstances, there was a need for a product that paralleled the coverages and limits available under the standard auto policies (such as the family auto policy), but with an increased premium that gave recognition to the coverage of marginal risks. Since the time nonstandard programs were implemented, the residual market, in most states, has broadened the limits and coverage availability. This action has reduced the need for nonstandard programs, but has not eliminated them.

Rejection If a risk is not acceptable as submitted and cannot be made acceptable through modification of some sort, then it will be rejected (in most states) or accepted and then reinsured in a special statewide facility set up for that purpose (in a few states). This section will first consider the voluntary market, then close with a brief comment about "facilities."

Almost all states still permit insurance companies to decline submissions that the company judges to be unacceptable. However, a distinction must be made between two types of *new* submissions. In many cases, the coverage is effective before the underwriter sees the application. This is caused by the producer's taking the application on, or just before, the expiration date of the prior policy. The producer binds the coverage, so actually the policy is in force before the underwriter has a chance to evaluate the applicant. It is in these cases that the declination in many states must be completed within the specified period of time. This is actually a *cancellation* of a policy and these states prohibit cancellation except for specified reasons (e.g., nonpayment of premium, revocation of driver's license) after the policy has been in force some specified number of days—often thirty or sixty. Of course, in states without such laws or regulations, this type of submission can be treated just like the submission received well in advance of inception date.

In other submissions, the application is received by the underwriter before the proposed effective date of the coverage. This situation occurs when the producer is trying to place an expiration in another company or where the applicant or producer has started the process of replacing an expiring policy well in advance. This practice is desirable from all standpoints. It permits the underwriter to decline to issue the policy; if this can be accomplished before the proposed effective date, no actual cancellation is needed.

A rejection does not mean that a company will never write that particular applicant, or that another company will follow suit. Risks are continually changing, and it may very well be that an applicant who is rejected with good reason may be approved for standard pricing twelve months later in the same company. Additionally, the market for personal auto insurance and insurers' underwriting will change. Each insurer has its own standards for acceptability, and an applicant who is unacceptable in one company may be acceptable in another. An underwriter is always interested in the fact that another company has rejected an applicant because this may indicate that there is a problem, such as in the driving record. However, each applicant should be underwritten on the merits of the case, and not rejected because another company's underwriter declined to write the coverage. Some states actually prohibit such action.

A limited number of states have laws or regulations requiring that all eligible applicants be accepted. In this context, an eligible applicant usually is defined as a resident of the state who owns a motor vehicle registered or principally garaged in the state and has a valid operator's license from the state, and who does not owe any past-due premium for motor vehicle insurance previously provided. If an applicant, eligible according to these criteria, is not acceptable according to the company's normal underwriting criteria, the company must still write the risk at its normal rate, but the risk may be passed on to a *residual market* mechanism set up in the state. Here, rejection is not a permitted alternative, although the writing insurer merely acts as a transfer agent as far as the loss exposure is concerned. Residual market mechanisms of all types will be examined in detail in Chapter 5.

The underwriter knows that rejection might take place well before a point is reached when a formal array of alternatives is set up and fully considered. From the first notice of a new submission, he or she knows that one of the outcomes discussed here will be the result. Rather than set up "considering alternatives" at every step in the underwriting process, this text has followed a general decision-making format in which logic dictates the delaying of a decision until all alternatives are considered. This is the applicable sequence for many submissions and does not conflict with the fact that underwriting information discovered early in analyzing a risk might preclude consideration of any course of action except rejection. In the latter case, the full range of alternatives simply is not available. The *only* possible course of action is rejection once the facts shut off other alternatives.

Making the Decision

Analysis by the underwriter must ultimately lead to a decision on risk acceptability. The preceding steps have pointed in this direction. Indeed, discussion of those steps recognized that decisions might be made along the way because characteristics of the risk eliminate all but one option or because the obviously favorable nature of the risk eliminates the need for a weighing of factors or consideration of other factors. Nevertheless, many submissions go through the entire underwriting decision-making process. These are likely to involve much informed judgment.

The decision actually made will be dictated by the facts and underwriting judgment applied in the context of the particular submission at hand. Thus, no text can deal with actual decisions except in a general fashion (short of using sample cases). Some of the general considerations will be discussed here, however.

Reaction to Recent Experience UND 61 made it clear that a major barrier to making effective decisions can be the recent experience(s) of the underwriter or those with whom the underwriter has contact. This does not mean that experience of the underwriter, or others known to the underwriter, should be ignored. Rather, caution should be exercised in keeping isolated chance events, often those of the recent past, from interfering with an objective outlook in making *current* decisions. On occasion, these events can greatly influence—for better or for worse—the thought processes, and make today's decision solely dependent on past experiences. If the underwriting guides are sound, and the steps in the decision-making process have been followed thoroughly and thoughtfully, the resolution of a current underwriting question should stand on its own. A recent large loss in a particular class of risk should not in itself unduly affect the underwriter's judgment on a new submission in the same class except to the extent that review of the file of the risk suffering the loss teaches the underwriter something that can be generalized to the class as a whole. A barrier to effective decision making occurs when an underwriter permits past personal experience to overwhelm other pertinent information on a risk. Similarly, several large losses from the book of business of a particular producer should not, of themselves, make the producer *persona non grata* with the underwriter.

Scope of Authority Scope of authority refers to the extent to which the underwriter has the power to make decisions without referring to higher authority in the organization. Making a decision on a matter that the underwriter knows, or should know, is beyond his or her authority obviously is a breach of the responsibility running from the underwriter to the employer.

Underwriting authority really extends, to varying degrees, outside the internal company organization to producers. So-called "source underwriting" refers to producer underwriting. Often the producer has authority to bind coverage to meet the applicant's needs as soon as they arise and are made known to the producer.

Some companies appoint managing general agents who have complete underwriting authority subject to underwriting guides as would a branch or regional office. Other companies may delegate a large degree of underwriting authority to profitable producers and monitor the results of the producers' books of business. These companies believe that the producer is in the best position to decide on the acceptability of the risk because he or she talks with the applicant, sees the insured vehicle, and may be better able to determine proper use classification. To provide an incentive to "weed out" the poor risks (and thus forgo the commission on that business), these companies generally provide a *profit-sharing* or *contingency* commission based on the loss ratio and premium volume over a period of time (usually three years). The sum total of these individual risk decisions is of paramount interest to the underwriter who "profiles" the characteristics of the business written by each producer. If these profiles indicate an unbalanced book of business (e.g., too many risks with multiple moving traffic violations), the underwriter would bring this to the producer's attention and suggest a course of action.

Internally, most companies extend full underwriting authority for personal auto underwriting to a local individual. The meaning of "local" depends on a number of factors—size of company, branch, or regional structure, philosophy on decentralizing authority and responsibility, volume of business by territory, and so on. Depending on the company, the individual may be a regional vice president, general manager, casualty manager, or personal lines manager. The person possessing full underwriting authority may be in charge of a territory as large as a city, a state, or several states. In a few companies, and in a number of companies for special situations, underwriting authority may be restricted to the home office.

A typical situation that may require a home office referral is a request for coverage, as new business, for a principal operator who is over seventy years of age. Other requests that may exceed local underwriting authority could be requests for physical damage on antique autos or on expensive foreign autos.

Generally speaking, there is more decentralization of decision-making authority in personal lines than in commercial lines. This is primarily due to the complexities of commercial lines and the high loss potential that can be concentrated in one commercial risk. Large commercial risks often require the assistance of actuarial and engineering personnel who often are located in the home office.

In some companies, an underwriting assistant reviews a private passenger auto application for completeness of information and compatibility with the company's underwriting program. The underwriting assistant probably can make a decision on 60 to 80 percent of the applications. The less flexible the underwriting program, the higher the percentage of decisions at that level because of lessened need for judgment. Those risks on which the underwriting assistant cannot make a decision are referred to a higher level of local underwriting authority. Depending on the company, all or almost all of the items referred can be decided at the higher but still local level. In some companies, underwriting data is coded and fed to a computer, and the computer screens for referral to underwriters. The computer can be programmed to flag certain limits, coverages, driving record points, operator ages, or certain combinations of inputs. Chapter 12 will deal in depth with the role of electronic data processing in personal lines underwriting.

Promptness Promptness in making the decision is important at whatever level it is made. The laws in many states permit rejection of new applicants only during a period of thirty to sixty days, depending upon the state. Once this period is past, the underwriter can only wait for the renewal date and hope for the best. Further, the longer a decision is delayed, the more in jeopardy is the producer's relationship with the client. These factors put a burden on the underwriter to make a decision promptly, especially since the coverage may have been in effect for a week or more before it is referred to underwriting. Delays can occur in the producer's office, in the mails, in the mail department of the company, at the desk of the person who orders an MVR, and even in the underwriting department itself. Adequate information is needed by the underwriter, but care must be taken not to delay the final decision too long while investigation is conducted.

Documentation of the Decision Having made the decision, the final act is to provide adequate documentation. This is crucial in some cases in order to determine who made the decision and why.

When an application is approved by an underwriter, the usual procedure calls for a stamp or initials indicating the approval, along with comments if any are needed. In case of future questions, this practice gives immediate reference to the original underwriter if there is need to explain the course of action which was taken. This practice also permits an underwriter who is later reviewing a file to check the loss history against the original information, which can help to train the underwriter concerning factors that need to be considered.

When an application is referred to the home office or other higher underwriting authority for approval, the local underwriting management will maintain a file documenting this fact. This facilitates later verification of the fact that approval was given and by whom. Analysis might later be made to determine the necessity of such referrals, and documentation is needed for such study.

Some type of notice must be sent to the producer if the applicant is rejected, or if the coverage is accepted on different terms than were requested. It is important that the producer not be left to "invent" reasons for the underwriting decision. The producer must deal with the client and should be provided with clear and logical reasons for the decision. Many insurers provide forms for this purpose, while others suggest the use of letters. A phone call to the producer may be better from a public relations standpoint. This can provide a means of immediate rebuttal or explanation, but it should be accompanied by file documentation identifying the contact and its content. This facilitates later analysis of the types of problems associated with the submissions of particular producers and gives substantiation in case of rebuttal or a resubmission by the producer.

Documentation of the decision is a vital part of underwriting. The task is not complete without it. Knowing what was done, where it was done and by whom, and why the action was taken, is essential to the full discharge of the underwriter's responsibilities.

COLLATERAL COVERAGES IN PERSONAL AUTO INSURANCE

Up to this point, the discussion has been directed primarily toward the basic coverages of the policy—bodily injury and property damage liability, comprehensive, and collision.

Before closing this discussion on the underwriting of private passenger auto insurance, mention also should be made of the collateral coverages which are available. The most common are UM (uninsured motorists coverage), medical payments coverage, auto death, disability, and dismemberment coverage, and towing and labor coverage.

Uninsured Motorists Coverage (UM)

Uninsured motorists coverage is mandatory in many states. In most others, it must be offered by insurance companies but may be rejected by the insured. Little underwriting is possible. If the applicant is acceptable for liability coverage, the uninsured motorists coverage must be written, or at least offered. UM is written only on policies which carry liability coverages. In most states, UM applies only to bodily injury, but a few have included property damage.

These are some territories where the percentage of uninsured motorists is relatively high, meaning the probability that an accident will involve an uninsured motorist also is relatively high. There is nothing that an underwriter can do about this in the mandatory states if the liability coverage is continued. In the states where the coverage may be waived, the company may wish to encourage the waiver, particularly if a supplemental coverage offering medical payments and wage loss protection is available. Implementation of this would involve a company program directed at producers. In few cases would the underwriter be expected to encourage the signing of the rejection form, and in no case should this be a condition required for acceptance because such actions tend to subvert the intention of the legislature in requiring that the coverage be offered.

A coverage similar to UM coverage is *underinsured* motorists coverage. This protects the insured if the negligent third party has liability coverage, but in an inadequate amount to cover the loss to the insured. Many states require the offering of UM limits up to the liability limits carried by the insured. An insured who buys higher limits of UM has indicated a desire to receive that amount if the negligent third party is uninsured. If the third party is insured, but only for minimum amounts, the insured would not be able to collect the limits which were selected. Underinsured motorists coverage pays that difference between the limits carried by the third party and those carried by the insured under the underinsured motorists coverage. Little underwriting can be done under either UM or underinsured motorists coverage.

Medical Payments Coverage

Medical payments coverage provides for most medical expenses resulting from injuries to the insured, the insured's family, and guests, while occupying the covered auto. It also provides protection for the insured and the insured's family if any of them is struck by or is injured while occupying any motor vehicle designed for use mainly on public roads or a trailer of any type. The insured's company pays for such medical expenses regardless of who is at fault. Medical payments limits apply to each person injured in the accident. Limits commonly purchased are $1,000, $2,000, $5,000, and $10,000. A limit of $500 has traditionally been the basic amount available, but this is being phased out because of its inadequacy in view of today's high costs of medical treatment.

Auto medical payments coverage is written only on policies covering liability. If coverage is written for a multi-car household, it should be provided for all vehicles on the policy. This action prevents misunderstandings over the way the coverage applies, and will prevent adverse selection.

Insurers in general regard medical payments coverage as desirable. Little or no underwriting is performed on private passenger auto risks. However, the coverage should be underwritten carefully, if indeed it is available at all, on midget autos, motor scooters, motorcycles, trail bikes, snowmobiles, sport (dune) buggies, and golf carts. Under this coverage, the chance of loss to the operator or passengers occupying these types of vehicles is great. Unless a special high rate is available, the coverage may be unacceptable.

Auto Death, Disability, and Dismemberment Coverage

Auto death, disability, and dismemberment coverage is marketed under various titles by different companies. Many insurers call this coverage option "auto death indemnity and specific disability benefits." It is similar to the accidental-injury coverage written by health insurers, but applies only to accidents sustained by the insureds while occupying or through being struck by an auto. Benefits take the form of a principal sum, periodic payments, or both.

The premium for this coverage is small, but the exposure can be relatively high. Underwriters should be certain that the applicant's physical condition is satisfactory, since an accident could result in substantial lump sum or periodic payments, and it may be difficult to separate an auto accident as a cause from pre-existing physical impairments or deficiencies. Some companies have an age limit, because of the increased probability of disability to elderly persons following an accident. The amount of disability income coverage written should bear a reasonable relationship to the earnings of the applicant—usually no more than 85 percent of the latter—in order to discourage malingering.

Medical payments and auto death, disability, and dismemberment coverages, when combined, give somewhat the same coverages as the first-party benefits in no-fault states (but without any waiver of liability, of course). These coverages generally require little underwriting beyond the safeguards already indicated.

Towing and Labor Coverage

This coverage provides for reimbursement for towing of the insured vehicle because of breakdown of the vehicle, and any labor required at the scene when the insured vehicle becomes disabled, subject to a nominal amount (usually $25). It usually is not available to an insured unless other physical damage coverage (collision or comprehensive) is written on the auto.

Many companies make towing and labor coverage available only for private passenger vehicles. Recreational vehicles are subject to increased frequency of claims due to their being driven in rough and unfamiliar territory. Also, for companies offering substantial limits under this option, average loss severity on recreational vehicles would be high because many breakdowns occur in isolated, barely-accessible areas and, on the larger vehicles, the high cost of the large commercial towing rigs required for servicing.

A key underwriting variable is age of the vehicle. Older vehicles tend to have more breakdowns requiring more use of the coverage. Other than that, little or no underwriting is performed on new applicants.

This coverage is abused by some policyholders. Rather than using it as the emergency coverage it was intended to be, they use it as a maintenance contract. A series of claims because of a dead battery usually means that the insured is using this coverage to get the battery recharged instead of buying a new battery after the first failure. When evidence of this practice is discovered, the underwriter may wish to remove the coverage. Deductible options are not used with this coverage because of the modest policy limit involved. Also, the very small premium for the coverage leaves little room for a credit for a deductible. An entire policy seldom would be canceled or nonrenewed because of towing losses; rather, the coverage is merely removed in these cases. The only exception would be if these claims revealed a vehicle in very poor condition or a policyholder who is careless or presents a moral hazard.

EVALUATING HAZARDS IN SPECIAL SITUATIONS

Most of the efforts of an underwriter of personal auto insurance are directed toward the handling of personal private passenger autos, which make up the bulk of the market. However, there are special situations which require specific attention, and some discussion of these is needed. This section explains the specific underwriting considerations involved in handling personal vehicles other than private passenger autos, policies in mass marketed accounts, and vehicles subject to no-fault laws.

Vehicles Other Than Private Passenger Automobiles

As shown in the early portion of Chapter 2, there are many types of vehicles other than private passenger autos which are handled by the personal lines auto underwriter. These are related to personal use, rather than commercial, so the assignment to the personal lines category is appropriate.

These types of vehicles can be grouped into three classes: farm, recreational, and other, with the latter including trailers, motorcycles, and utility vehicles. The underwriting of each is discussed below.

Farm Vehicles Many types of vehicles may be used on a farm. Some are trucks and should be handled as such. Others are farm equipment, requiring special forms. Still others are private passenger cars which require no special consideration except in classification and rating. Finally, there are those which are of concern here: pickup trucks, vans, and delivery-type vehicles which can be used for either farm or personal use. These vehicles in the latter category are a personal/commercial hybrid, combining characteristics of both types of risk. The owner can use them to go to the store, to visit friends, to take on vacations, and all of the other uses of passenger-type vehicles. However, these vehicles also can be used for light farm work. They can haul animals, a small amount of feed, small pieces of equipment, and can be put to other uses inherent to the operation of a farm or ranch.

Given these factors, a particular vehicle could be personal, commercial, or a mixture of both, depending upon its use. Sometimes the use will be explained on the application, or an indication of related special equipment may indicate the vehicle's use. In other cases, the underwriter must look beyond the use information on the application for help.

The drivers of the vehicle can be a clue to the proper classification. A teenage daughter who uses the vehicle to go to high school will obviously present a personal exposure. The same may be true if the female spouse of the named insured is the principal driver. On the other hand, if the principal operator is the hired foreman on the farm, use can be considered to be for farm purposes. The use ordinarily will be the same if the farmer is the principal operator, and does not have another occupation. Thus, the underwriter often can classify the vehicle by noting the principal operator.

In many areas, particularly those bordering urban centers, farming is a part-time occupation. The "farmer" may use, say, a pickup to commute to and from a full-time job. The underwriter must be alert to this possibility and be sure the risk is properly classified. The lower farm rates are not warranted for a risk of this type.

Based on information such as that referred to above, the underwriter will classify the vehicle either as a personal or a farm vehicle. Rates will be different in most companies for the two classes, and forms are different in many companies. Thus, proper placement is critical to matching exposure to rate and, possibly, policy form.

Many companies establish an automatic dividing line between personal and commercial farm use usually based on gross vehicle weight or load capacity. This practice avoids the difficulties of determining the use of each vehicle, and removes the necessity for frequent checking. A vehicle not exceeding the specific limit would be classified as personal, on the theory that most of its use would be of a personal type. The distinction is more important in rating than in underwriting.

Farm equipment may be insured under an auto liability policy, although it is more often covered under a policy designed for farm risks. This includes such equipment as farm tractors, cultivation equipment, and spray rigs, both on premises and away.

Underwriting will be the same as for personal autos, plus consideration of the use of the vehicle or equipment. The driving record of the principal operator is the most important factor.

Recreational Vehicles The previous chapter briefly described each of the major types of recreational vehicles to aid in distinguishing them from private passenger autos. The discussion that follows concentrates on the distinctive hazards presented by certain of these vehicles. It is important to understand the diverse underwriting considerations that each of them requires. The recreational vehicles to be given attention here are as follows:

- motor homes,
- truck-mounted campers and camper trailers,
- midget autos,
- snowmobiles,
- all terrain vehicles, and
- golf carts.

The house or travel trailer is dealt with briefly in a later section on trailers.

Motor Homes. Motor homes have the same size and handling characteristics as trucks. Therefore they can present problems to drivers not familiar with their operation. These vehicles are vulnerable to damage by fire since cooking is performed aboard them. Coverage may be requested on physical damage and liability on the vehicle itself and on physical damage to household furnishings and other personal effects in the motor home but not permanently attached to it. Coverage on contents usually is restricted to named perils including fire and collision but excluding theft.

Special applications are used by some companies when insuring motor homes. Others may use supplemental forms, or the underwriter will ask the producer additional questions of importance to the risk.

A sample motor home and truck mounted camper application is shown in Exhibit 3-1.

However asked, the questions will cover several categories. One is the familiarity of the applicant with this type of vehicle. If the applicant has never driven anything larger than a sedan, problems might be encountered with a large motor home. However, experience of some insurers is that most new owners are so careful while driving a motor home that their loss record is no worse than on a private passenger auto. Unless substantial driving problems exist, the underwriter seldom will be concerned about this factor.

Another possible concern is with the planned use of the vehicle. Since motor homes represent a sizable financial investment, some owners will lease them to friends, neighbors, or even strangers, in order to recoup some of their expenses. Obviously, such leasing will increase the frequency of use and the related exposure, to say nothing of the problems that can be created by careless or inexperienced lessees. This increase can be balanced by a higher rate for vehicles subject to leasing. Programs of many insurers include separate classes for leased and nonleased motor homes, and may dictate the use of an exclusion applying to leases if the lower rate is used, in an attempt to restrict the exposure to loss.

The equipment of the motor home, and its condition, may be of concern. Since cooking is involved, a fire extinguisher might be required. If the vehicle is more than a year or two old, a mechanic's report certifying the mechanical condition of the vehicle may be required.

Motor homes, in their present numbers, are relatively new. There are no standardized programs or common handling. Many companies use a regular private passenger auto policy form, but some use special forms. Some underwriters require a photograph, while others rely on the description. Some companies insure new vehicles only, while others will write older motor homes but apply special surcharges to older vehicles.

Campers. Camper trailers and truck-mounted campers represent a broad range of exposures. Any type of trailer alters the handling characteristics of an auto, and larger trailers can be cumbersome, thus requiring considerable skill to tow properly and safely. It is essential that the auto be of sufficient size and power to handle the additional weight, drag, and brake requirements. Taillights and brake lights on the trailer should be in good working order. Trailer hitches are safest when attached to the frame of the pulling vehicle.

The statements above are true, but are of little help in the actual underwriting. Charts showing a size-weight relationship, or brake factors, are rare if they exist at all. The underwriter cannot afford to determine if the lights and hitch are in good order because such information can be gathered only from an expensive report. It would be

Exhibit 3-1
Motor Home and Truck Mounted Camper Insurance Policy

Motor Home and Truck Camper Insurance Policy

Named Insured ____________________ Last ____________________ First ____________________ Middle   Phone Number ____________________

Residence Address ____________________ Street ____________________ City ____________________ County ____________________ State ____________________ Zip

Where Garaged?   Same as Above ☐   Other: ____________________

Mortgagee: ____________________ Name ____________________ Address

DESCRIPTION OF VEHICLE

YEAR	LENGTH	HORSEPOWER	MAKE	MODEL	SERIAL NO.	PURCHASE PRICE	DATE PURCH'D	NEW ☐ USED ☐

CAMPER BODY	YEAR	MAKE	MODEL	IDENTIFICATION NO.	CHASSIS MOUNTED ☐ SLIDE-IN ☐	% USE	PURCHASE PRICE	DATE PURCH'D

COVERAGES

BODILY INJURY AND PROPERTY DAMAGE LIABILITY

Limits: (Check box) $15/30/10 ☐ $25/50/15 ☐ $50/100/25 ☐ $100/300/50 ☐

MEDICAL PAYMENTS

Limits: (check box) $500 ☐ $750 ☐ $1,000 ☐ $2,000 ☐

UNINSURED MOTORISTS COVERAGE, LIMITS $10,000/20,000. (See detailed explanation on reverse)

Required by law to be included with liability policies, unless rejected in writing. If desired, include additional premium of $______.

If NOT desired, sign rejection below.

I have read and understand the explanation of uninsured motorists coverage and I hereby specifically reject the coverage.

____________________ Date

____________________ Signature of Insured

READ EXPLANATION ON REVERSE BEFORE SIGNING

PHYSICAL DAMAGE COVERAGES

Coverage	Deductible	Purchase Price or Actual Cash Value
Comprehensive	$ 25	$ __________
Collision	$ 50	$ __________
	$100	$ __________
	$250	$ __________

PERSONAL EFFECTS COVERAGE

	ACV Limit	
Broad Form (Excludes Theft)	$ __________	(Min. Prem. $5.00)
Comprehensive Form (Includes Theft)	$ __________	(Min. Prem. 7.50)

RENTAL ENDORSEMENT SURCHARGE

If insured unit will occasionally be rented to others, add surcharge of 50% of all above premiums except uninsured motorists and personal effects.

AGENT'S ACC'T # __________ Agent's Name __________ TOTAL PREMIUM __________

I hereby declare to the best of my knowledge and belief that all of the statements contained in this application are true and that these statements are offered as an inducement to the company to issue the policy for which I am applying.

____________________ Signature of Applicant

1. Check intended use of vehicle: Private Pleasure ☐, Occasional Rental (not commercial) ☐.

2. DRIVERS NAMES:	% USE	OCCUPATION	BIRTH DATE	SEX	MARRIED		DRIVERS LICENSE NO.	YEARS LICENSED
					YES	NO		

3. Driving records past 3 years for all drivers. (Explain all YES answers below)

Accidents? ☐ YES ☐ NO	Violations? ☐ YES ☐ NO
License suspensions? ☐ YES ☐ NO	Insurance Cancellations? ☐ YES ☐ NO
SR-22 required? ☐ YES ☐ NO	Case Number__________

DRIVING RECORD EXPLANATIONS AND SURCHARGES

(Please Give Driver Name With Explanation)

most unusual for accurate information on these matters to be available to the producer.

As a matter of practice, little initial underwriting is performed on camper trailers. The underwriter may not even know of their existence, unless comprehensive or collision coverages are requested, because liability is covered automatically without additional premium when the trailer is used with a passenger car. In most cases, only after a loss might an underwriter find out about unsafe conditions. At that point, steps can be taken to assure correction, or the policy can be nonrenewed.

When physical damage coverages are requested, the age and value can indicate a substandard piece of equipment. Ordinarily, values are not large and little underwriting is performed.

Truck-mounted campers are handled in the same way. Liability coverage is not affected, and physical damage may be added. A camper body raises the center of gravity, which makes the vehicle more subject to overturning. Again, there is no practical way to measure the exposure. The only real underwriting would be after a loss, if the underwriter learned that the unit was taken in windy areas disregarding wind warnings, or was used on hazardous roads.

Midget Autos. Midget autos (or go-carts) present abnormal bodily injury exposure due to grossly inadequate safety features that offer little protection for the driver. There tends to be inadequate supervision over their use, and often they are treated as toys despite their potential danger. Midget autos are considered just about uninsurable for physical damage or medical payments coverages.

Midget autos do not meet the definition of private passenger auto under most private passenger auto policies. Therefore, they will not be automatically covered as newly acquired or replacement autos. Further, liability is not covered under Section II of homeowners policies, except for injury or damage occurring on the premises, and even this on-premises coverage does not apply if the vehicle is subject to motor vehicle registration. Since these vehicles are capable of injuring people and damaging property, liability insurance should be carried by the owner, even though a financial responsibility law may not apply.

Most companies do not write this coverage, at least not actively. The best market is the specialty insurers. However, many underwriters will accept liability coverage only as an accommodation to policyholders in other lines. In such cases, the only underwriting possible is to be certain that the policyholder is indeed desirable and deserving of special accommodation on this hazardous exposure.

Physical damage coverage is not afforded by the homeowners

policies, and is almost unavailable except perhaps in the specialty market. The same is true for medical payments coverage.

Snowmobiles. These vehicles represent a high degree of exposure to loss for the following reasons:

- inadequate safety features that offer little protection for driver or passengers
- snow hides many unknown hazards such as tree stumps, fence wires, gullies, thin ice on lakes and ponds, and potholes, especially when vehicle is operated during darkness
- often used for racing purposes and driven at high speed
- high theft potential of entire vehicle or its parts
- high possibility of operation by very young operators because many states do not require any licensing to operate

Because of these potential problems, snowmobiles should be underwritten with care. Acceptability standards are often the same as for private passenger autos, particularly with respect to the driving record of the operator or operators. Some companies require that all owned autos must be insured in the company in order to keep informed of any driving problems which arise.

Homemade snowmobiles may be unacceptable because of the problems of unsafe construction and improper equipment. Most commercially built units are acceptable, but an underwriter might find wide ranges of quality among brands. Some types of snowmobiles are driven by propeller, and these may be unacceptable because of the higher speeds generated and the increased chance of injury to the occupant and others.

Individual or family ownership and use of snowmobiles may be acceptable, but vehicles used for racing or held for rental may not. In some geographic areas, units may be used for commercial purposes, such as deliveries. As with autos, these are unacceptable as personal lines risks in many companies.

The exposures to theft and damage to the unit may be minimized by mandatory deductibles. This is a common practice among personal lines underwriters.

It should be noted that the unscheduled personal property coverage of homeowners contracts excludes motorized vehicles unless they pertain to the service of the premises and are not licensed for road use.

A related problem is the trailer which is towed behind an auto for the purpose of transporting a snowmobile. Still another unusual situation is a snowmobile sled, which is a vehicle drawn behind a snowmobile to transport passengers or goods. While unusual exposures may be presented by each of these related units, the underwriter ordinarily is expected to write them if the snowmobile is written. When the applicant owns a trailer or sled, it is logical to expect coverage to parallel the snowmobile protection, and such equipment is usually written in the same policy. Mandatory deductibles on both comprehensive and collision are common.

The policy forms used for snowmobiles and their trailers and sleds ordinarily exclude prearranged speed contests. Some policies exclude injury or loss while the snowmobile is engaged in jumping from embankments or jumps, whether natural or artificial. As in the case of some other recreational vehicles, these forms are generally special policies which are classified as inland marine, although auto-type policies are also used. There is no standardization of forms, coverage, or rating.

Liability is offered on these auto-type policies, including uninsured motorists coverage in conformity with state laws. Medical payments coverage is offered by some insurers, but not all. Whether the snowmobile is required to be registered does not affect the acceptability of the risk. Policy issuance is affected and the necessity to file certificates of insurance and other documents is involved if the snowmobile is subject to motor vehicle registration. Liability coverage is specifically excluded under the comprehensive personal liability policy and the liability portion of the homeowners policies.

Exhibit 3-2 illustrates the types of information needed to underwrite snowmobiles. In the application shown, the applicant selects one of four programs with predetermined "lay-up" periods. This varies among insurers.

All Terrain Vehicles. All terrain vehicles (ATVs) present special underwriting problems because of their primary use off the highway. Use on beaches, deserts, fields, and hilly terrain, especially when coupled with frivolous operator characteristics, means a high exposure to loss. The vehicles frequently are operated by persons with playful driving attitudes and proclivity towards racing. Most sports buggies have high-speed capabilities, severe roll-over potential, and are prone to theft.

Virtually all sport buggies are built from kits or special parts and mounted on an auto chassis, usually one from which the body has been removed because of an accident. These construction characteristics require careful underwriting. It is common to require evidence of good workmanship, proper wiring and brakes, and such safety equipment as seat belts and roll bars. This evidence may be submitted by the producer, or secured by an inspection report.

Customizing is a common practice among builders and owners of

Exhibit 3-2
Snowmobile Insurance Application

Snowmobile Insurance Application

DATE OF APPLICATION ____________

APPLICANT'S NAME	Birth Date / /	Producer No.	PRODUCER'S NAME
ADDRESS *(STREET)*		Prior Policy No.	ADDRESS
CITY, STATE AND ZIP CODE			CITY, STATE AND ZIP CODE

POLICY EFFECTIVE DATE: ____________ 19____ *(POLICY IN FORCE FOR 12 FULL MONTHS WITH COVERAGE IN EFFECT AS SHOWN BELOW)*

☐ PROGRAM I	LIABILITY COLLISION	In effect from September 1 to June 1
	COMPREHENSIVE	Full term *(Includes Fire & Theft)*
☐ PROGRAM II	LIABILITY COLLISION	In effect from September 15 to May 15
	COMPREHENSIVE	Full term *(Includes Fire & Theft)*
☐ PROGRAM III	LIABILITY COLLISION	In effect from October 15 to April 15
	COMPREHENSIVE	Full term *(Includes Fire & Theft)*
☐ PROGRAM IV	LIABILITY COVERAGES ONLY	☐ 9 months—Coverage suspended from June 1 to September 1 ☐ 8 months—Coverage suspended from May 15 to September 15 ☐ 6 months—Coverage suspended from April 15 to October 15

LIENHOLDER: ____________

ADDRESS: ____________

	COVERAGES	LIMITS OF LIABILITY	PREMIUM
SECTION I	PHYSICAL DAMAGE *(ALL RISK)*—ACTUAL CASH VALUE INCLUDING EQUIPMENT LESS $50 DEDUCTIBLE		$
	VEHICLE 1	$	
	VEHICLE 2	$	$
	TRAILER(S)	$	$

SECTION II	LIABILITY—SINGLE LIMIT COVERAGE	$,000. per occurrence	Vehicle 1	$
			Vehicle 2	$
*optional UMC	UNINSURED MOTORIST COVERAGE—*(FAMILY PROTECTION)*	$,000. per person $,000. per accident	Vehicle 1	$
			Vehicle 2	$
	* Follow the Uninsured Motorist Coverage Insurance Statutes of the applicant's state of residence.		TOTAL	$
ENDORSEMENTS:			Less Multi-Unit Discount *(5% of Total to nearest dollar)*	$
			TOTAL POLICY PREMIUM	$

DESCRIPTION OF VEHICLE(S)						
	Year	Manufacturer & Model	Serial No.	H.P.	Month & Year Purchased	Cost
Vehicle 1					/	$
Equipment *(itemize)*						$
Vehicle 2					/	$
Equipment *(itemize)*						$
Trailer 1					/	$
Trailer 2					/	$

UNDERWRITING INFORMATION

1. Is vehicle(s) to be rented, leased or used for racing? ☐ No ☐ Yes, Explain ____________
2. Is any operator physically impaired? ☐ No ☐ Yes, Explain ____________
3. Any accidents or violations in last three (3) years? ☐ No ☐ Yes, Explain ____________

these vehicles. This causes a problem of valuation following a loss, and some underwriters write only a stated value policy.

Photographs of the sport buggy are required by most underwriters, in order to answer the questions concerning both the construction characteristics and customizing described above. Some companies require the photograph with the application from the producer. Others secure one with an inspection report. A sample application for off-the-road vehicles is shown in Exhibit 3-3.

As with snowmobiles, it is customary not to accept those sport buggies which are rented to others. Policy forms, which are not standard, usually exclude prearranged speed contests, and mandatory deductibles are used for both comprehensive and collision. Liability and uninsured motorists coverage are available, but medical payments coverage is not offered by all insurers willing to write these vehicles.

Golf Carts. Liability coverage is afforded on golf carts "while used for golfing purposes" by comprehensive personal liability coverage or Section II of the homeowners policy. Thus, if the only use is on a golf course, the personal liability protection will apply automatically.

If the golf cart is used on the streets, a separate liability policy must be purchased. An auto policy may be issued if the state requires licensing of such vehicles. Otherwise, company programs differ. Some will use an auto policy, while others have special policies for such vehicles.

The physical damage coverages are ordinarily written on the same policy as the liability, if a separate policy is written. However, an inland marine policy is used in some companies. Again, company practices differ. Whether the motorized vehicle exclusion under homeowners policies would apply to a golf cart depends on the nature of the golf cart and the meaning (unclarified) of "motorized vehicles" in homeowners coverage.

Golf carts have limited speed and seating capabilities. However, they are subject to roll-over when used on hilly golf courses, and they present special hazards when operated on public highways or rights of way because of their limited speed capabilities. Except when in use on golf courses, the theft potential may be significant.

Coverage is usually accepted as an accommodation to policyholders in other lines. Premiums are small and exposures can be substantial. The investigation for the other lines ordinarily will supply sufficient information for the underwriting of the golf cart, when supplemented with facts concerning the use of the vehicle. This latter information can be secured from the producer in most cases.

Deductibles usually are required on physical damage coverages because of frequent small losses. Medical payments coverage is not offered by some companies. Others underwrite it carefully because of the high roll-over potential and lack of occupant protection afforded by the vehicle.

Other Vehicles In addition to farm and recreational vehicles, there are other special types of vehicles with which the personal auto underwriter must be familiar.

Trailers. Little underwriting is practiced on trailers used to haul goods. With a few exceptions, liability is automatically covered when used with an insured passenger auto. Physical damage usually is written with little analysis, primarily because values are low. Deductibles are required in most instances, the coverage usually is on a stated amount basis, and insurance must be written for 100 percent of the value of the trailer. Eligibility usually includes all types except those used for commercial purposes.

The second group, travel trailers, includes a greater variety of unit sizes. Some are large and cumbersome, requiring skillful driving to offset restricted visibility, the additional weight that strains braking systems, and the swerving effect that a large trailer can produce on the towing auto. Each company has a size or weight limit beyond which a travel trailer must be written as a mobile home. A representative limit on length is thirty feet. Although the larger of the travel trailers can offer driving problems, most add relatively little in extra hazards. Again, little underwriting is done; if the operator is acceptable for auto coverage, the trailer is accepted. Coverages are the same as for the first group of trailers.

Motorcycles. Age and driving attitude are as important on motorcycle risks as on private passenger auto risks. There are fewer problems if the operator is a careful driver who perhaps has purchased a motorcycle for purposes of economy. On the other hand, there can be major problems if the operator is one who likes to speed through heavy traffic, tackle difficult terrain, or engage in speed contests with another motorcycle.

A clue to the driving attitude is the size and style of the vehicle. Larger motorcycles develop more speed, so many insurers use a limitation on the maximum engine size, such as 500 cc. Style is indicated by such modifications as choppers (extended front forks), custom chrome and paint jobs, and high rise handlebars. Most insurers who write motorcycles only as accommodation lines consider such modified vehicles unacceptable. The size and style are usually secured from the description on the application, but investigation might be needed to verify the facts. Motorcycles used for racing purposes are not acceptable in most companies, with the only market being the specialty insurers.

Exhibit 3-3
Off-the-road Vehicles (Unlicensed) Insurance Application

Off-the-road Vehicles (Unlicensed) Insurance Application

EFFECTIVE DATE ________________ 19___
(POLICY PERIOD: 12 months from 12:01 AM on above date)

APPLICANT'S NAME	BIRTH DATE	PRODUCER'S NAME
ADDRESS	Producer No.	ADDRESS
CITY, STATE	Prior Policy No.	CITY, STATE

DESCRIPTION OF VEHICLE(S)

PLEASE CHECK TYPE OF VEHICLE TO BE INSURED: ☐ MINI BIKE ☐ GOLF CART ☐ TRAIL BIKE ☐ ALL TERRAIN VEHICLE ☐ OTHER ________

	YEAR	MANUFACTURER & MODEL	SERIAL NO.	H.P.	MO. & YR. PURCHASED	COST
Vehicle 1						$
Equipment *(itemize)*						$
Vehicle 2						$
Equipment *(itemize)*						$
Trailer						$

LIENHOLDER: NAME ________________ ADDRESS ________________

UNDERWRITING INFORMATION:

1. Is vehicle(s) to be rented, leased or used for racing? ☐ No ☐ Yes, Explain ________
2. Is any operator physically impaired? ☐ No ☐ Yes, Explain ________

3. Any accidents or violations in last three (3) years? ☐ No ☐ Yes, Explain ____________

4. Names and ages of other operators ____________

PROGRAMS ☐ ANNUAL POLICY ☐ 6 MONTH LAY-UP ☐ 4 MONTH LAY-UP ☐ OTHER ________

Policy is written for a full one year with Liability and Collision suspended from ________ *to* ________ *(where applicable)*

COVERAGES	LIMITS OF LIABILITY		PREMIUMS
PACKAGE PROGRAM			
PHYSICAL DAMAGE	Actual cash value including equipment less $50 deductible		
VEHICLE 1	$		$
VEHICLE 2	$		$
LIABILITY	,000 per occurrence		INCLUDED
PHYSICAL DAMAGE—TRAILER	Actual cash value including equipment less $50 deductible		$
LIABILITY ONLY	,000 per occurrence	VEHICLE 1	$
		VEHICLE 2	$
OPTIONAL COVERAGES		VEHICLE 1	$
		VEHICLE 2	$
________		VEHICLE 1	$
________		VEHICLE 2	$
ENDORSEMENTS		TOTAL	$
		Less Multi-Unit Discount *(5% of Total to nearest dollar)*	$
		TOTAL PREMIUM	$

Exhibit 3-4 illustrates a typical motorcycle insurance application. The importance of describing and arriving at a value for custom parts or accessories is brought out in the application.

When coverage is written, liability and physical damage are ordinarily eligible. Medical payments coverage for the operator and quests is offered with great reluctance or not at all by most companies.

Mopeds. There is little underwriting data available on mopeds. Efforts to gather accident facts on mopeds have been hampered by the lack of registration requirements and dispute on how the moped accidents should be categorized (i.e., with motorcycle or bicycle accidents). Mopeds present hazards in traffic due to their slower speed, lighter weight, and ability to weave in and out of traffic. Also, mopeds present a small, low silhouette that is difficult to see.

Legislation regarding mopeds has been passed in about 80 percent of the states. This legislation is quite varied. Even the legal status of a moped in a state (e.g., it is considered a motorcycle or a motor driven cycle) does not necessarily coincide with that same state's registration and licensing requirements for mopeds. The National Highway Traffic Safety Administration (NHTSA) has recommended that persons operating mopeds have a moped or motorcycle operator's license or at least a moped endorsement to an existing valid license. The NHTSA also recommends that moped registrations be a special class, that there be separate testing of moped operators, and that crash data on mopeds be a category separate from motorcycles and bicycles.

Until such time as there are adequate data on moped experience and underwriting results, underwriters should be very cautious in insuring them. Any evalution should consider them to be similar to motorcycles and possessing many of the same hazards as motorcycles. However, additional hazards exist due to the similarity of a moped to a bicycle with regard to size, speed, and the existence of pedals.

Utility Automobiles. Utility autos may be used for the same purposes as the average family car. When this is the case, the vehicle is eligible for personal auto rates. Those utility autos used for commercial purposes usually are rated and written as commercial lines, regardless of size, unless the commercial use is both infrequent and incidental to personal use.

Problems can arise when there is mixed usage. A jeep may be used as the family car, but also to deliver newspapers over an extensive route or for snowplowing or pushing of other vehicles, for a fee, during emergency periods. A pickup truck may be used on a farm or ranch for business purposes in addition to personal use. A panel truck may be used primarily for the family or for camping, but also can be used for retail or wholesale delivery. The underwriter must secure an accurate description of the use of the vehicle, usually from the application. If the situation is not clear, the underwriter must secure the facts from the producer or an inspection agency. The exposures may be so great that a higher rate is needed.

A study by the Highway Safety Research Institute of the Univerisity of Michigan based on 1977 data revealed some interesting, but alarming, statistics on the on-road crash experience of utility vehicles. Among the findings were:

1. Utility vehicles were involved in fatal crashes 40 percent more often than passenger cars.
2. Utility vehicles crash in rural areas proportionately more often than passenger cars.
3. Utility vehicle drivers who are involved in crashes are younger and more often male than their counterparts in passenger cars.
4. Utility vehicles experience roll-over at a rate that is at least five times higher than that experienced by passenger cars.
5. Driver ejection is more often reported among jeeps than other makes of utility vehicles or passenger cars.
6. Considering all occupants, both the death rate and the rate of serious injury are about twice as high in utility vehicles as compared with passenger cars.[1]

Some of these utility vehicles are equipped for driving over rough terrain and in places not accessible to the family sedan. Jeeps and others may have four-wheel drive which facilitates such use. These vehicles may sustain physical damage that might be reported under comprehensive or collision coverages, such as damage to the undercarriage from a large rock or from sand which gets into the wheel bearings. Extra care must be taken when these coverages are written.

Some vans present the additional problem of expensive customizing. This can include special paint, often multicolored scenes, chrome trim, carpeted interiors, special contoured windows, and others. Many companies have recognized this additional exposure by special handling, such as excluding these customized alterations and offering a buy-back at a higher rate. Whether the rate is increased or not, the underwriter must determine the degree of exposure and be certain that the price is adequate. A complete description of the customizing, including its cost or value, must be secured, either from the producer or an inspection report. One or more photographs are a tremendous aid, and might well be required with all such applications.

Miscellaneous. Underwriters should also be familiar with the characteristics and hazards of amphibious autos and antique autos. Amphibious autos, also called amphicars, are designed for use on land

Exhibit 3-4
Motorcycle Insurance Application

Motorcycle Insurance Application

APPLICANT (NAME INSURED) PLEASE PRINT

(LAST NAME) (FIRST NAME) (MIDDLE INITIAL)

OCCUPATION & EMPLOYER

STREET ADDRESS	CITY	COUNTY	ZIP CODE	POLICY TERM ☐ 12 Months ☐ 6 Months	EFFECTIVE DATE MO.	DAY	YEAR

DESCRIPTION OF MOTORCYCLE YEAR	MAKE	MODEL	SERIAL NUMBER	DISPLACEMENT IN CC'S	PURCHASE PRICE INCLUDING STANDARD FACTORY EQUIPMENT OR ACTUAL $ CASH VALUE ON USED CYCLE	DATE PURCHASED MO.	DAY	YEAR	☐ NEW ☐ USED

Loss Payee Name
Address
City & State Zip

DEALER FROM WHOM CYCLE WAS PURCHASED
Name
Address

DRIVER INFORMATION Complete for principal operator and any other driver

NAME OF PERSON EXACTLY AS SHOWN ON DRIVER'S LICENSE	AGE	DATE OF BIRTH MO. DAY YEAR	MARITAL STATUS	ANY CHARGEABLE MOTORCYCLE ACCIDENTS OR INSURANCE CLAIMS PAST 12 MOS.	HAVE YOU BEEN PRINCIPAL OPERATOR OF A MOTORCYCLE	OPERATOR'S LICENSE NO.
Principal Operator				☐ YES ☐ NO	UNDER 1 YEAR ☐ OVER 1 YEAR ☐	
Other Operators of this motorcycle						
				☐ YES ☐ NO	UNDER 1 YEAR ☐ OVER 1 YEAR ☐	
				☐ YES ☐ NO	UNDER 1 YEAR ☐ OVER 1 YEAR ☐	

When motorcycle has other than standard Factory Equipment, list below Custom Parts or Accessories you wish covered in the package policy and add 15% of their value (round to nearest dollar) in the appropriate section of the premium column.

ITEM	VALUE
______	$ ______
______	$ ______
______	$ ______
______	$ ______
______	$ ______
Total Value	$ ______
	$ ______ x .15
Custom Parts and Accessories Premium	$ ______

Indicate here the coverages desired.

COVERAGES DESIRED	**PREMIUMS**
☐ LIABILITY ONLY	$ ______
☐ PACKAGE POLICY—New & Current Year Models	$ ______
Used Models	$ ______

ADDITIONAL COVERAGES AVAILABLE

☐ Custom Parts & Accessories	$ ______
☐ SR 22 Filing	$ ______
☐ Extended Forks—Add 50% surcharge to each coverage written	$ ______
☐ Total of Applicable Discounts____%	$ ______
TOTAL PREMIUM	$ ______

DATE & TIME OF APPLICATION:______________, 19____. ____ ☐ A.M. ☐ P.M.
PRODUCER ______________________
AGENT LICENSE NO. ______________________

No coverage bound until application received and accepted by General Agent.

I hereby apply to Company for a policy of insurance as set forth above on the basis of the statements contained herein. I agree that such policy shall be null and void if such information is false, or misleading, or would materially affect acceptance of the risk by Company.
PREVIOUS INSURANCE CARRIER

DATE SIGNATURE OF APPLICANT (NAME INSURED) X

As part of our underwriting procedure, a routine inquiry may be made which will provide applicable information concerning character, general reputation, personal characteristics and mode of living. Upon written request, additional information as to the nature and scope of the report, if one is made, will be provided.

as normal private passenger autos, but in addition, are constructed in such a way to permit them to be operated in water. These vehicles often are purchased strictly for pleasure pursuits and frequently are considered as "party" vehicles by their owners.

The maturity shown in driving an auto is usually the only indication available to the underwriter on the attitudes of the amphicar owner. Unless evidence to the contrary exists, a driver acceptable for auto insurance would be acceptable for an amphicar.

Maintenance and mechanical condition may be problems. If the vehicle is not new, the underwriter might request a mechanic's statement of condition. No standardized forms are available for this purpose; a statement from a reputable garage is usually adequate. An inspection report may be ordered if questions remain.

Because of the unusual hazards of amphicars, a marine policy also should be issued to cover the watercraft exposure if the risk meets the underwriting standards for such coverage. Since the marine policy and the auto policy are mutually exclusive, no restrictions exist on writing different limits for the respective policies. The auto policy should be handled in the following manner: (1) normal private passenger auto rating procedures should be used, and (2) coverage should be restricted to apply only while the vehicle is operated on land. Also, an endorsement should be attached which excludes coverage of water hazards. The wording of such an endorsement might provide that the policy does not apply to any amphibious auto or amphibious auto home trailer, including any property contained in or used with any such auto or trailer, while being used on, launched into, or beached from water.

Underwriters on occasion will be presented with risks that are described as antique autos. Special rates are usually used which are substantially lower than the company's regular auto rates. In order to qualify, in addition to the age criterion (twenty-five years old), the antique auto must have "antique" plates and must be maintained solely for use in exhibitions, antique auto club activities, parades, and so on. A company also may require proper garaging. The policy is endorsed to exclude normal street driving, although there is no standard form used by the various insurers.

In evaluating the physical damage exposure, it should be kept in mind that repairs on antique autos are costly and that there is a tendency to inflate the vehicles' values. The availability of replacement parts is important, but an underwriter seldom is in a position to know very much about any particular make or model. A practice followed by many companies is to write physical damage on a stated value basis after ascertaining the value of the vehicle from a dealer or recognized car club. Coverage is written at 100 percent of the value. Deductibles are mandatory in order to avoid the loss settlement problems involved with repairs on small parts which are difficult to secure.

Some companies write physical damage coverage on antique autos under inland marine forms. That subject will be discussed later in this text.

As indicated in Chapter 2, the so-called "classic car" is not necessarily old. Because the value of a classic car is likely to fluctuate over time, some underwriters are less willing to write stated value physical damage coverage on classics than on antiques. The classic is much more likely to be subject to normal road use than the antique and so it is handled in regular fashion on liability coverages.

Mass Marketed Accounts

Background The mass marketing (or mass merchandising) of personal lines insurance is a relatively new concept in providing insurance protection to groups of insureds. Through the mechanism of mass marketing, an insurance company may be able to provide automobile and other personal lines coverages at a premium level of roughly 5 to 15 percent below conventionally marketed products. This reduction in price is made possible by the achievement of expense savings in both the marketing and servicing of the business.

A producer that sells a mass marketed account will receive a lower commission per policy than on conventionally marketed products. However, the high volume potential, the transfer of some policy services over to the company, and the possible access to other lines such as homeowners, present adequate incentive for some agents to aggressively pursue the selling of mass marketed accounts.

An integral part of mass marketing is that the premiums are withheld by the employer from the employee's salary and the employer pays the insurer directly, or the employee gets home billing on an installment plan. The employee gets the benefit of paying for insurance on a monthly basis, but at no additional cost. Additionally, under payroll deduction the insured need not worry about remembering to mail a monthly check—remittance is handled by the employer.

Some feel that in the future the term "employee benefits" will include full or partial employer subsidy of personal auto insurance costs in a way similar to the group life and health benefits that are common today. Should this occur, it is quite likely that mass marketing will undergo dramatic growth. If this is accompanied by automatic eligibility of new employees, as is typical with today's group life and health insurance plans, enormous growth would be almost certain.

In its broadest sense, the concept of mass marketing envisions providing auto, homeowners, personal marine, personal catastrophe, and life products. At the present time, the bulk of mass marketing activity involves the auto line.

Underwriting of Mass Marketing To many individuals, mass marketing implies liberal underwriting programs and permissive acceptability standards. This is erroneous. The adoption of such an underwriting philosophy under any circumstances would prove disastrous unless heavy employer subsidy were available if needed.

The pure premium (loss dollars) portion of the total premium is comparable to the pure premium that would be calculated for the same exposure under a conventionally marketed policy. Achievement of any price advantage under mass merchandising is attributed to reductions in the expense portion of the premium dollar. Therefore, it is apparent that careful selection of employer accounts, and individual risks within accounts, is fundamental to successful mass marketing. While it may be tempting to guarantee writing any employee of a particular employer account, the usual practice is to retain underwriting prerogatives in dealing with each employee. Unless special pricing tools are available, the surrender of underwriting rights would prove to be unwise and unprofitable.

In reviewing a prospective account, careful consideration should be given to (1) the type of individual employee typically hired by the employer, (2) the type of business, industry, or association, and (3) the location of the account. If the average age of the employee is under twenty-five, the underwriter may be confronted with a disproportionate number of youthful operators which the class plan rate differentials did not contemplate. If that group, for example, is less profitable than other classes, overloading a book of business with that group can destroy the balance of the book and the overall adequacy of the rate level. If the business or industry is one with frequent mass layoffs and hirings, the insured group may lack stability, administrative expenses may be higher than anticipated, and adverse selection may be magnified. An undesirable location may mean problems with crime and vandalism losses.

It should be explained to both producers and employers that the purpose of a mass marketing program is to provide convenience and economy to employees in purchasing personal insurance. The purpose of the program is *not* to provide auto insurance to *all* employees at standard rates. As in any typical group, there will be those who present a greater-than-average exposure to loss and who will require nonstandard pricing. And finally, it must be understood that any account may expose a company to an occasional employee who is uninsurable at any price. In these cases, an underwriter should reserve the right to refuse insurance for such individuals.

Some mass marketing plans deny underwriters some of their usual prerogatives in the selection and rejection of risks. When a "guaranteed issue" requirement exists, it is of the utmost importance that each risk be correctly priced as to use class, merit rating plan, and between standard and nonstandard. Proper pricing of each risk on an individual basis is essential if a company is to continue to provide a broad market for the account at rates satisfactory to the company and to insureds under the account. Conversely, underwriting standards for individual risk selection in a mass marketing plan should be no more restrictive than the standards used in the selection of a company's individual business marketed through conventional methods.

The history of mass marketing plans has been one of mixed success. When they were first introduced on a large scale in the 1960s, many people felt that they would attract a large share of the buying public. A few sizable plans were sold, and several insurers devoted much effort to promoting this approach. Unfavorable experience and a lack of solid growth led to withdrawals from the market, however, and the idea has never been as successful as its early advocates predicted.

Part of the problem has been that the majority of plans have been merely payroll deduction plans. Normal rating and selection processes are used. Since the rates are seldom lower than can be secured from some of the large preferred-risk companies, the only real advantage for many prospective insureds is the use of payroll deduction to pay the premiums.

Such programs require a strong sales effort to a large number of people. A sponsor, such as an employer, is needed. The selling of the program to the sponsor, and then to the members of the group, requires considerable effort. Extra expenses for company personnel needed to service the account have been required in many cases. These facts tend to offset one of the theoretical advantages of mass marketing plans—lower rates through reduced expenses, one of which is commissions to producers.

Once a group is signed up and some members join the plan, servicing difficulties may arise because of the many changes inherent in a book of auto insurance policies such as changes in cars, drivers, use, and so on. Also, layoffs and strikes present other problems, and the result often is inaccurate billing.

Another problem is that while no special underwriting is supposed to be practiced, pressures are brought to make exceptions. Managers, foremen, or executives may demand special consideration. The theory of peer group pressure to maintain a good driving record does not operate because rates are not based on the experience of the group.

One of the major problems is that projected premium savings often cannot be maintained. There is little or no reason for loss experience to be better than the average of all insureds. Indeed, it can be worse if enrollment is not sufficient to get and retain an adequate share of the average and above-average risks in each account. Some savings in the expenses of issuing policies and billing for premiums may be achieved by a company because computers can be used. However, the larger auto writers already use computers for issue and billing, so all that the mass marketing company can do is match the expenses. Without an ability to select risks carefully, there is little premium savings, if any, when compared with many large personal lines insurers.

Unless conditions change, the future is not bright for the present type of plan. The real potential for the future lies in the area of what usually is called "true" group marketing. While details may differ, the usual requirements for such programs are employer contribution, no individual risk selection, and a leveling of premiums to covered employees.

Employer contribution is an essential element of a group marketing plan. If all applicants are accepted, and some type of average rate is used, the better risks will realize that they can secure their insurance in a preferred-risk company at lower rates. The poorer risks, in contrast, will rush to join the group. The result will be rates which are constantly moving higher and higher, each increase causing more policyholders to leave because they can secure coverage at lower rates elsewhere. A subsidy by the employer appears to be the only answer. The subsidy may pay the differences between the flat rate charged to every member of the group and the highest rate charged to any one member of the group. This would mean, for most members of the group at least, lower out-of-pocket costs for insureds compared to purchasing coverage independently, and it would encourage enrollment by the better risks and produce a better balanced and more stable book of business from each account.

Another solution is for the employer to pay all of the premiums as an employee benefit. This is entirely possible but would be resisted by most employers, as the cost could be substantial. It is generally felt that employers will not take this step until they are forced into it by the terms of collective bargaining agreements.

Auto insurance, and perhaps other lines as well, may become a subject for collective bargaining between unions and employers at some time in the future. One significant obstacle to this development is the current federal tax law, which considers any contribution by the employer toward employees' automobile insurance costs as taxable income. The tax law is anything but static, however, and may change on this point. If such a change occurs, employer participation probably would start as a subsidy to level the premiums for all employees. The natural evolution would be toward full payment of premiums by employers. Some observers feel that this is an inevitable development, but there is only scattered evidence at this time to indicate that this will happen. If it does, it will have a substantial impact on the marketing, service, and underwriting programs of insurers.

Vehicles Subject to No-Fault Laws

The most talked about subject in the auto insurance industry over recent years has been the concept of no-fault auto insurance. As implemented to date, it represents a modest departure from and addition to the tort system that has been in use as long as the auto itself. The majority of the twenty-four states with "no-fault" laws require first party and liability insurance and restrict in some way, the right of an injured party to sue. The remaining states have no restrictions on lawsuits and vary as to whether the insurance is compulsory.

Hazard Evaluation Under No-Fault Chapter 2 discussed the hazards associated with private passenger auto insurance underwriting. Hazards are identified and evaluated by looking at such factors as driving history, age, marital status, and personal characteristics of the applicant and other identifiable operators. Vehicle characteristics such as type, age, use, and principal location of the vehicle also are reviewed.

No-fault laws do not change the existence of hazards or the need to identify and evaluate them. Further, to this point at least, the existence of no-fault laws has not perceptibly modified underwriting practices. Risks in states which have no-fault laws are underwritten the same, basically, as risks in other states. A number of factors probably contribute to this. No-fault laws do not affect potential accident *frequency,* a major determinant of costs and a very significant underwriting variable. The right of subrogation for an insurer paying no-fault benefits is retained under many of the laws, a fact which tends to make the ultimate allocation of loss costs the same as it would be in the absence of the laws. Even in most states that deny subrogation, the present dollar threshholds (the amount that must be exceeded to allow the claimant to sue under tort) are so low and the other exceptions to the barring of suits are so numerous, that the laws do not affect the application of the fault system enough to make any impression on the differentials in average loss costs among classes.

Nevertheless, no-fault laws and their possible extension raise interesting questions germane to evaluating hazards and underwriting risks. Changes in the *relative desirability* of the various classes may appear, particularly if pure no-fault is ever adopted or if limitations on subrogation and the right to sue are made more rigorous than under present laws. Some illustrations will be used to point up possible changes in direction. The analysis will not be exhaustive but should stimulate the kind of thinking that alert underwriters and underwriting management must do as conditions change. In the interest of conciseness, the discussion will ignore property damage liability and physical damage losses.

First, consider youthful owners or principal operators. They present a higher accident frequency than other classes and are more likely to be at fault in accidents involving others than are middle-aged or elderly drivers. Under no-fault, however, the young as a group possess the following favorable characteristics. Many are single and would not be the basis for the payment of survivors benefits under no-fault. They heal more quickly than older people and may, on the average, generate lower medical expenses per injury than their elders. Wage levels among the young are lower than among the general working population. This fact, coupled with the faster healing time, means average wage loss probably will be lower among the young than among, say, working adults age thirty and older. The young also are less likely to require the payment of replacement services benefits because they are more likely (than people over thirty, for example) to be living with parents and not have the need for services required by a head of household. Might these characteristics place the young in a relatively (to older drivers) less unfavorable, or even favorable, position? The answer simply is not known. Certainly there can be no assumption of any change in accident frequency, and the driving habits of the young will still result in a higher than average frequency of very serious losses involving long-term medical and rehabilitation expenses and wage loss.

At the other extreme of the age scale are elderly drivers. Their healing ability is poor compared to youthful drivers and their need for replacement services high, but many have no, or low, earned income and they are less likely to be involved in serious accidents than the driving population as a whole. For the class as a whole, would the net result of these expectations under no-fault leave the elderly in the same, a less favorable, or a more favorable, position relative to other classes?

Next, consider family structure and income. A family with one auto and four working adults presents a far higher wage loss potential under no-fault than does a family of four with one working adult. Should this aspect of family structure be an underwriting variable in no-fault states? Would a single car risk involving these four working adults be less attractive if all of them regularly rode to and from work in the same auto than if their work locations were separate and three used public transportation to get to and from work? For that matter, up to the point of maximum guaranteed wage loss benefits, might not the level of income of the named insured alone be considered as a factor that helps to measure the potential impact of insureds on loss experience? And should a family of six pay more for no-fault coverage than a family of three, or be regarded as a less attractive risk at the same price, because of the greater medical expense exposure in the larger family?

It remains to be seen if no-fault trends and refinements in loss data permit the development of statistically reliable answers to questions like those raised above. The questions do and will exist, however, and both pricing and selection standards and practices may depend upon the answers.

SUMMARY

Obtaining and organizing information is a crucial step in the personal auto decision-making process. Different sources of information may be inconsistent, and discrepancies must be resolved while attempting to keep the expenses of gathering information to a minimum.

The decision-making process begins with the underwriting guides or manuals of the insurer and proceeds with the weighing of specific factors of the risk including age, sex, driving record, place of garaging, condition and type of auto, previous insurer, and other factors. On a marginal risk, the producer and supporting business may be weighed in the analysis. The majority of submissions will result in simple acceptance or rejection, but others will require a modification of coverage or pricing to be acceptable. This is especially true when underwriting vehicles other than private passenger cars, such as recreational vehicles, motorcycles, antique automobiles, and others.

Recent changes in the personal auto underwriting environment include mass marketed accounts and underwriting vehicles subject to no-fault laws. The lack of sufficient loss and expense data under these situations increases the uncertainty present in the underwriting process.

Chapter Note

1. Richard G. Snyder, Thomas L. McDole, William M. Ladd, and Daniel J. Minahan, *An Overview of the On-Road Crash Experience of Utility Vehicles* (Ann Arbor, MI: The University of Michigan Highway Safety Research Institute, February 1980). Prepared for the Insurance Institute for Highway Safety, Washington, DC.

CHAPTER 4

Classification, Rating, and Underwriting Mid-Term Policy Changes

INTRODUCTION

Personal auto insurance underwriting is done "at a price." This means that the risk being considered is judged in the light of a particular rate classification and premium rate applicable to the risk. The first section of this chapter deals with the classification and rating of personal auto insurance policies.

Once a risk is accepted and its initial underwriting phase completed, it becomes part of a book of business or "portfolio" of risks. However, the underwriting process does not end at that point. Of equal importance to the initial selection of individual risks is the maintenance of their individual quality and the quality of the portfolio as a whole. Opportunity to analyze an individual risk further may be presented by a request for a policy change. The second section of this chapter deals with underwriting policy changes.

CLASSIFICATION AND RATING

Underwriters may feel that the classification and rating of auto risks are not underwriting functions. They may view classifications and rates as being made by company or advisory association actuaries and applied to individual risks by clerical personnel. While this may be true in a functional sense, both classification and rating are such an important part of underwriting that they cannot be overlooked. In most companies, the administration of the classification system is assigned to underwriters rather than to clerical personnel. While judgment is not needed in applying the system to a risk having stated characteristics, considerable judgment may be required to be certain that the characteristics which lead to a particular classification have been properly identified and evaluated. The underwriter must strive to achieve the classification and rate that is commensurate with the exposure presented by each risk.

A misclassified risk means a misrated risk. Misrated risks either are paying more than they should pay, which is an injustice to those policyholders, or less than they should pay, which is an injustice to the company and to other policyholders paying the proper premium. Moreover, errors in classification and rating show up in insurance department audits of pricing practices. An unusual error ratio may attract criticism and could influence consideration of rate filings. Finally, misclassification creates a statistical and actuarial problem wherein misclassified risks become part of a body of premium and loss data for a classification to which they do not belong. Unless the effects are offsetting among all affected classes in the classification plan, both in a given period and over time, both overall rate levels and differentials among classes become distorted. Thus, there is ample basis for stating that one of the most serious responsibilities of the underwriting function is to price each risk according to the classification system under which it is operating.

The Structure of Classification Plans

Classification plans for most companies are based on the following: territory; age, sex, and marital status of operators; and the use of the vehicle. Many plans also include surcharges or credits based on driving record, good scholastic achievement, driver training of youthful operators, number of cars insured, nature of the vehicle, and others.

Territory In the early days of auto insurance, uniform national rates by company were the rule. As the market grew, it became evident that loss experience varied according to the area of operation or geographic location of the insured car. The degree of density of the driving population and traffic patterns and conditions, among other factors, influenced accident frequency and, to a lesser degree, severity. Insureds in the larger cities produced higher loss ratios than insureds in rural areas. As a result, one of the first fine points introduced into auto rating was the practice of isolating geographic areas producing the higher or lower loss ratios and altering the rating structure accordingly.

Within each state, subdivisions may be structured by county; city; areas within a city, township, town, village; or some combination of these divisions. The number of rating territories varies from state to state, and may vary in a given state among companies using different classification plans. In general, the number of territories varies directly with population. One large company has a range of from three territories in Arkansas to fifty in California.

In the process of making or revising rates, the various territories within a state are given a rate or rate modification. This territorial rate serves as the base point for all other rates developed by the classification plan for that territory. A basic goal of territorial classification is to incorporate, within a rating territory, areas having roughly similar characteristics and loss experience. A variety of factors may cause differences in loss experience, and hence rates, from one territory to another. Loss frequency and/or severity can differ because of variations in at least the following factors: population and traffic density, traffic controls, law enforcement, topography, climate, street and highway design and maintenance, wage rates, medical and hospital costs, judicial attitude and conduct, crime rates, claims consciousness, and the availability of legal representation.

The basic rating territories used by many insurance companies are those prepared by the Insurance Services Office (ISO). These are referred to as "bureau" rating territories. ISO receives loss, premium, and exposure unit data from member companies throughout the United States, then compiles and analyzes these results to monitor experience in the territories, recommend changes, and modify the territorial structure from time to time. Some larger companies maintain their own premium and loss data by territory, and some have a sufficient volume of business in their operating areas to develop credible data. The territorial delineations established by ISO and these "independent" companies tend to be similar, but some differences do exist.

Exhibit 4-1 shows an excerpt from the ISO territory pages for Pennsylvania. This style of territorial definition is typical of those used by the industry as a whole.

The ZIP Codes of the Postal Service have been adopted by some companies as a basis for defining rating territories. Rating territories may be structured by grouping together several ZIP Codes. One advantage to this approach is administrative simplicity in collecting data and verifying classification information. However, many rating territories still use streets and the boundaries of governmental units (e.g., city, county, township).

Regardless of the method by which territories are defined, each territory is given a code, and this code is shown in the rate manual for the particular state involved. This same code is used by companies and rating bureaus to allocate premiums, exposure units, and losses to each territory, thus permitting the calculation of loss ratios and pure premiums by territory. Experience for rating territories is generally tabulated on a running three- to five-year basis. Comparison of actual to

Exhibit 4-1
Territory Definitions*

TERRITORY DEFINITIONS

PENNSYLVANIA (State Code 37) — Territorial Schedule and Code

ADAMS COUNTY—(entire County) 23

ALLEGHENY COUNTY—see Beaver Falls, Butler County, McKeesport, Pittsburgh, Pittsburgh Suburban, Washington County and Westmoreland County territories.

ALLENTOWN–BETHLEHEM territory comprises the entire cities of Allentown and Bethlehem and all territory and places lying within the area enclosed by the outside boundaries of the following boroughs and townships in Lehigh County 58

Catasauqua	Fountain Hill	South Whitehall
Coplay	Hanover	Whitehall
Emmaus	Salisbury	

and all territory and places lying within the area enclosed by the outside boundaries of the following boroughs and townships in Northampton County

Bethlehem	Hanover	Hellertown
Freemansburg		

ARMSTRONG COUNTY—(entire County) 49

BEAVER COUNTY (BALANCE)—That portion of Beaver County not included in Beaver Falls territory excluding that part of the borough of Ellwood City which is in the New Castle territory 51

BEAVER FALLS territory comprises the entire city of Beaver Falls and all territory and places lying within the area enclosed by the outside boundaries of the following boroughs and townships in Beaver County 47

Aliquippa	Eastvale	Patterson Heights
Ambridge	Fallston	Potter
Baden	Freedom	

Territorial Schedule and Code

CENTRE COUNTY—(entire County) 53

CHESTER COUNTY (BALANCE)—That portion of Chester County not included in Southern Philadelphia Suburban territory 45

CLARION COUNTY—(entire County) 49

CLEARFIELD COUNTY—(entire County) 49

CLINTON COUNTY—(entire County) 53

COLUMBIA COUNTY—see Northern Columbia County, Pottsville and Southern Columbia County.

CRAWFORD COUNTY—(entire County) 54

CUMBERLAND COUNTY (BALANCE)—That portion of Cumberland County not included in Franklin County or Harrisburg territories 27

DAUPHIN COUNTY—see Harrisburg, Northern Dauphin County and Southern Dauphin County.

DELAWARE COUNTY (BALANCE)—That portion of Delaware County not included in Southern Philadelphia Suburban territory 45

ELK COUNTY—(entire County) 54

ERIE COUNTY (BALANCE)—That portion of Erie County not included in Erie territory 56

ERIE territory comprises the entire city of Erie and all territory and places lying within the area enclosed by the outside boundaries of the following borough and townships in Erie County 09

Greene	Millcreek	Wesleyville
Harborcreek	Summit	

FAYETTE COUNTY—(entire County) 39

FOREST COUNTY—(entire County) 54

Beaver	Harmony	Pulaski
Big Beaver	Homewood	Rochester (borough and township)
Borough	Hopewell	
Bridgewater	Koppel	
Brighton	Monaca	
Center	New Brighton	South Heights
Chippewa	New Galilee	
Conway	North Sewickley	West Mayfield
Daugherty		
East Rochester	Patterson	White

and all territory and places lying within the area enclosed by the outside boundaries of the following borough and townships in Allegheny County

Crescent	Leetsdale	Sewickley (township only)
Leet		

BEDFORD COUNTY—(entire County) 24

BERKS COUNTY (BALANCE)—That portion of Berks County not included in Lancaster County or Reading territories 22

BLAIR COUNTY—(entire County) 57

BRADFORD COUNTY—(entire County) 55

BUCKS COUNTY (BALANCE)—That portion of Bucks County not included in Northern Philadelphia Suburban territory excluding that part of the borough of Telford which is in the Montgomery County territory 43

BUTLER COUNTY (entire County) and all territory and places lying within the area enclosed by the outside boundaries of the following borough and townships in Allegheny County 49

Bradford Woods	Marshall	Richland
Fawn	Pine	West Deer
Franklin		

CAMBRIA COUNTY (BALANCE)—That portion of Cambria County not included in Johnstown territory 52

CAMERON COUNTY—(entire County) 54

CARBON COUNTY—(entire County) 21

FRANKLIN COUNTY—(entire County including that part of the borough of Shippensburg in Cumberland County) 23

FULTON COUNTY—(entire County) 24

GREENE COUNTY—(entire County) 52

HARRISBURG territory comprises the entire city of Harrisburg and all territory and places lying within the area enclosed by the outside boundaries of the following boroughs and townships in Dauphin County 07

Highspire	Middletown	Steelton
Londonderry	Paxtang	Susquehanna
Lower Paxton	Penbrook	Swatara
Lower Swatara	Royalton	

and all territory and places lying within the area enclosed by the outside boundaries of the following boroughs and townships in Cumberland County

Camp Hill	Lower Allen	West Fairview
East Pennsboro	New Cumberland	Wormleysburg
Hampden	Shiremanstown	
Lemoyne		

and all territory and places lying within the area enclosed by the outside boundary of the township of Fairview in York County.

HUNTINGDON COUNTY—(entire County) 53

INDIANA COUNTY—(entire County) 52

JEFFERSON COUNTY—(entire County) 49

JOHNSTOWN territory comprises the entire city of Johnstown and all territory and places lying within the area enclosed by the outside boundaries of the following boroughs and townships in Cambria County 40

Brownstown	Ferndale	Southmont
Conemaugh	Franklin	Stoney Creek
Daisytown	Geistown	Upper Yoder
Dale	Lorain	Westmont
East Conemaugh	Lower Yoder	West Taylor
East Taylor	Middle Taylor	

NOTE: Refer to an atlas or map for places not listed.

* Reprinted with permission from *Personal Auto Manual*, 1976, (New York: Copyright, Insurance Services Office), p. PA-T-1 (effective 1 January 1977).

expected loss ratios provides a guide to changes in rates in each territory.

Ordinarily, the assignment of the proper territorial code to a risk is a routine process of matching garaging location with a particular territorial definition. Earlier chapters of this text illustrated some common problems in this area. The underwriter should always be alert to situations in which the indicated garaging location carries a lower rate than the indicated residence address. Without a satisfactory explanation for the difference, the underwriter must investigate further, perhaps through use of a classification (or rating) report. A common illustration would be a student away from home most of the year who garages a car in a territory rated lower than the home address. Handling practices for this situation differ.

Within a given territory, rates applicable can vary on the basis of a number of other factors described below. The order of discussion is not intended as a procedural guide to the actual classification of specific risks but merely to identify and discuss the factors used in the process.

Age, Sex, and Marital Status of Operators Age, sex, and marital status of the identifiable operator(s) of the vehicle are important elements in risk classification. The three items are grouped under one heading because the rating significance of one item may be dependent upon another.

Youthful operators produce the highest accident frequency of any group of operators segregated on the basis of age. Of the youthful operator group, unmarried male operators generate the poorest results. Thus, within a given territory, this is the highest rated auto insurance risk. Within the youthful operator group generally (which in some states can range from age fourteen to age twenty-nine) there is an inverse correlation between age and accident frequency—the lower the age, the higher the frequency. The same relationship appears to exist between age and convictions. Exhibit 4-2 shows the distribution of convictions by age and sex in California in one year. While these data are for one state and one year, they are indicative of the situation nationally and over time. Males under age twenty show more than twice the conviction rates as the average for male drivers of all ages. Females under age twenty show about 1.6 times the conviction rate of all females.

Historically, classification systems have distinguished at the younger ages between male and female operators. Other things being equal, younger females have generated lower pure premiums than younger males. Recent experience indicates a narrowing of the gap, but most classification plans still result in lower rates for young females than for males of the same ages. However, there are differences among

Exhibit 4-2
Distribution and Rate of Total Convictions by Age and Sex*
(One year record 1974; total sample = 128,209)

Age	Males (n = 68,244)			Females (n = 59,965)		
	Percent conviction free	Percent conviction involved	Conviction rate per 100 drivers	Percent conviction free	Percent conviction involved	Conviction rate per 100 drivers
All ages	79.89	20.11	27.0	91.56	8.44	9.6
Under 20	63.96	36.04	54.9	87.26	12.74	15.4
20 - 24	68.93	31.07	47.6	87.07	12.93	15.5
25 - 29	75.11	24.89	34.0	90.10	9.90	11.6
30 - 34	78.73	21.27	28.3	90.48	9.52	10.7
35 - 39	80.19	19.81	24.9	90.77	9.23	10.4
40 - 44	81.06	18.94	23.7	91.93	9.07	9.0
45 - 49	82.65	17.35	21.6	93.35	6.65	7.3
50 - 54	85.06	14.94	17.9	94.17	5.83	6.4
55 - 59	86.60	13.40	15.9	94.57	5.43	5.9
60 - 64	89.30	10.70	12.1	94.49	5.51	6.0
65 - 69	89.94	10.06	11.5	96.04	3.96	4.2
70 - 74	91.52	8.48	9.6	96.36	3.64	3.8
75 and over	93.35	6.65	7.2	95.82	4.18	4.4

*Reprinted from *The California Driver Fact Book*, State of California, Department of Motor Vehicles, April 1981, Report No. 29 (5th ed.), p. 7.

companies on the relative size of the differential and on the age at which differentials between males and females are no longer used.

There is some limited evidence showing that the accident rate per 100,000 miles driven tends to be *higher* for females than for males. Yet, because females on the average drive far fewer miles than males, the higher accident rate on a mileage basis is more than offset by the reduced exposure from fewer miles driven. Exhibit 4-3 shows the results of one study relating male and female accident rates per 100,000 miles driven to age groups.

Depending on the classification plan adopted or developed by the particular company, youthful operators generally are subdivided into several classifications based on age. Virtually every company uses at least two, and some go so far as to refine youthful drivers into one-year age groupings. Many companies use a four-fold breakdown for male drivers under age thirty: (1) under age twenty; (2) ages twenty and twenty-one; (3) ages twenty-two, twenty-three, and twenty-four; and (4) ages twenty-five through twenty-nine. Companies use different combinations, depending upon their own capabilities, data, and objectives. Obviously, division into more groups decreases the number of risks within each group. While this *may* refine the classification plan and present a more accurate reflection of the exposure by age, a contrary finding would result if the smaller classification developed inadequate data to be credible.

Marital status plays an important role in further refining classifications for both male and female youthful drivers. Most rating plans assign different classes and lower rates to young married operators. The regulations in some states which prohibit discrimination on the basis of sex or marital status are aimed mainly at selection criteria. They do not apply to classification and rating, because statistics support the differentiations applied in the male/female and single/married dichotomies.

Drivers in the age groups between thirty and sixty-five make up the major portion of both the driving population and the book of personal auto business of most insurers. This group is used to set the base rate by territory (i.e., all other rate classifications within a territory are keyed to the rate for this group).

Drivers over sixty-five generally have better results than the other age groups (as discussed in Chapter 2), but experience of individual companies has been mixed. Not long ago most insurers charged more for elderly drivers than for those in the thirty to sixty-five age group. This practice was discredited as a blanket approach by the analysis of increasing amounts of data made possible by a larger over-sixty-five population. So, with many companies, credits were substituted for surcharges. Some companies have found better liability experience for

Exhibit 4-3
Accidents per 100,000 Miles by Age and Sex (N = 10,814)*

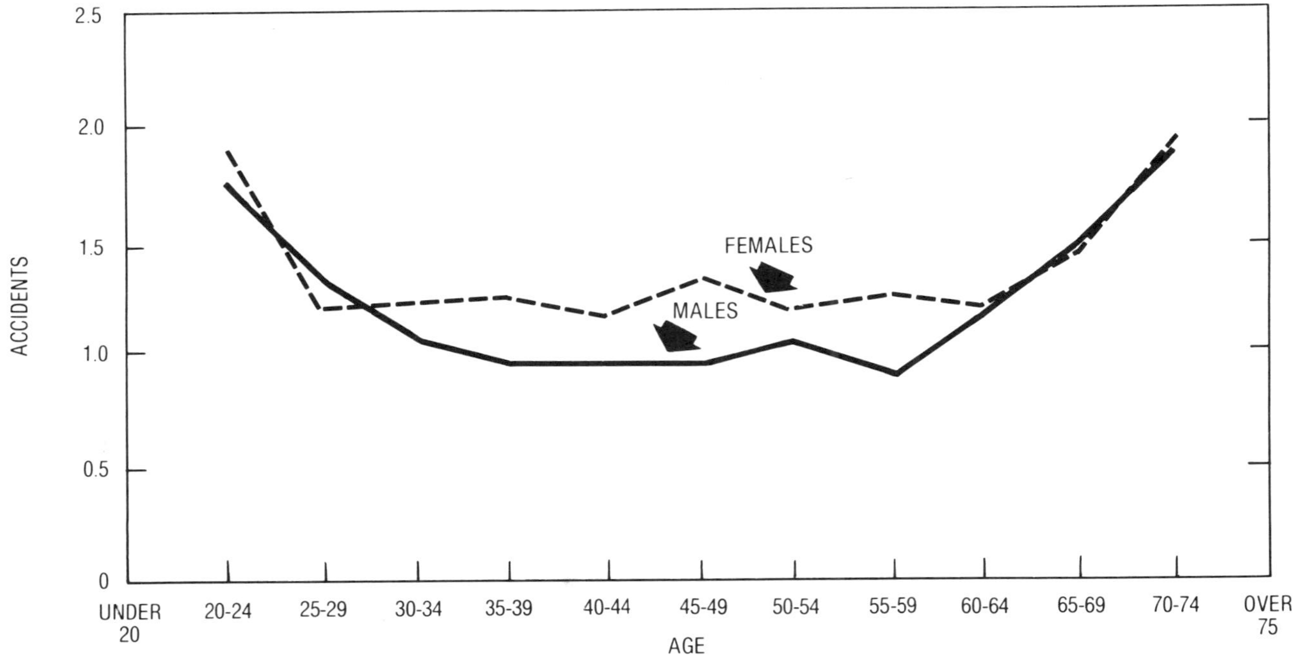

Note: No data for drivers under 20 years of age due to the particular sample which contains drivers with valid license for at least 6 years.

*Reprinted from *The California Driver Fact Book*, State of California, Department of Motor Vehicles, April 1981, Report No. 29 (5th ed.), p. 8.

elderly drivers, but poorer collision experience. There is no uniformity in rating approaches at the present time, but probably a majority of companies give rate credits for drivers over sixty-five.

Use of Vehicles The term "use" includes a number of factors that can affect the classification of a personal auto risk. As with other classification criteria, insurer practices on use as a classification variable are not standardized but are generally comparable.

Use of the vehicle enters the picture even before serving as a rating factor. Personal use must be established if the risk is to be eligible for personal auto classification, rating, and forms. Taxis, buses, auto rental agencies, all types of vehicles used for livery purposes, racing cars, and pickup and panel trucks used in business are all ineligible under most private passenger car rating plans.

For an otherwise eligible vehicle, some business use often is permitted and a separate rate class assigned. Such "combination-use" vehicles would include, for example, cars owned and used in business by salespersons, insurance producers, real estate agents, and employees of a government or governmental agency.

Farm use takes a separate classification with the vast majority of insurers. A discount is given to vehicles which have a farm as the place of principal garaging, are not used in any occupation other than farming, and are not customarily driven to and from work or school.

After eliminating vehicles subject to farm rates and rates applicable because of business use, this leaves nonfarm vehicles used strictly for pleasure or pleasure plus driving to and from work or school. The appropriate questions related to use as a classification variable are: (1) Is the car driven to and from work or school and, if so, what is the one-way mileage to the workplace or school? (2) What is the annual mileage the vehicle is driven?

Almost all insurers secure information on, and classify on the basis of, whether the car is driven to and from work or school. If the car is so used, further refinements often are made on the basis of (usually) the one-way distance to the regular driving destination. Subcategories of "to and from" might read "no more than three miles," "more than three but not more than ten miles," and "more than ten miles." Some insurers use weekly mileage, rather than one-way trip mileage.

In addition to "to and from" information, some insurers classify on the basis of annual mileage driven. Common dividing points are 5,000, 7,500, 10,000, and 15,000 miles per year. An insurer using this factor for classification may apply it to only some of its rate classes.

Information on "use of vehicles" may be misrepresented or may be the subject of a misunderstanding or guesswork. The underwriter should be certain that the use classification is accurate, so far as this can be determined efficiently. If there is no cause for concern, the classification ordinarily will not be checked. Further, if the risk already takes the highest rate available, obviously nothing is to be gained from a rating standpoint by securing additional information. (The information may be important in risk selection, however.)

An example of questionable use information might be a three-car household consisting of a mother, father, and nineteen-year-old son. Assume that one car is assigned to each parent and the third, a sports car, also is assigned to the father as principal operator with the son shown as a user only 5 percent of the time. This information may be accurate, but an underwriter more than likely would check to see if the son might be the principal operator of one of the cars, particularly the sports car.

As another example, consider a one-car family case where the father is shown as working in a factory located in a town some twelve miles away from the family residence. No public transportation is available. The father is the principal driver, but the application shows that he does not drive to and from work. Again, this may be true. Perhaps the father rides with a neighbor who works in the same plant. However, the underwriter should check to determine the facts.

What if the above facts were modified to show that the father does drive to and from work and total annual mileage is shown as being 6,000 miles? If the car is used every day to go to work, the mileage for this purpose alone would be about 6,000 miles. This leaves nothing for pleasure use. Perhaps the insured shares the ride with a neighbor or two, driving only a couple of days each week. However, indications are that the mileage is underestimated, and a verification would appear to be in order.

Many experienced underwriters feel that use information is misrepresented by applicants more often than any other classification or underwriting factor. Underwriters should learn to sense when answers to pricing questions do not match and should check such cases through questioning the applicant or producer, or ordering a classification report.

Other Rating Factors A number of other rating factors are used by insurers. These are applied as credits or surcharges to the rates otherwise developed through the use of the classification plan. Only the more common will be described here. All of these are used to at least some extent, but it is unlikely that any one company uses all of them.

A multiple-car discount is given by most insurers. One common approach is to allow a discount of 10 percent for each car when two or more owned by an insured are covered in the same company. Another approach is to allow a flat (e.g., 20 percent) discount for the second car and none for the first car. Some companies give a discount, sometimes called a "fleet discount," when five or more cars are insured in the same company.

Safe driver insurance plans that allow for lower basic premiums for accident-free driving records and surcharges for accidents are quite common. Many types of these plans are used, but all are designed to reward the drivers who have not had accidents and to charge more for those who have had them. The definitions of the accidents which are counted, and the time period during which they are counted, vary considerably by company and state.

Moving traffic convictions also serve as a rating factor for some companies, expressed in the form of surcharges applied to basic premiums. Most companies writing preferred or standard risks do not surcharge for citations. Instead, they use citations to define their market by making eligibility (i.e., for low or "preferred" rates) contingent upon the absence of citations during a stipulated period, or by using citations as a selection tool only. However, some insurers have programs for increasing the rate because of convictions for moving violations. As with accidents, definitions differ as to which citations are counted and what time period is used. There also are differences on the subject of higher surcharges for major convictions such as driving under the influence of alcohol or drugs.

Driver training credits are allowed by many insurers. The basis for the credit is that a driver (usually a youthful driver) who has completed an approved driver training course will usually be a better driver than those who have not. Minimum hours usually apply, such as thirty hours of classroom education and six hours behind the wheel of a training car. Credits usually are about 20 percent.

Good student discounts are allowed by some insurers. The basis for the credit is the relationship between good grades and study time and personal responsibility. Students who study hard usually do not drive as much as students in general, and good grades tend to indicate that as a group good students are quite responsible. Studies show that good students have better loss experience than students in general. Credits vary by company, but are usually around 20 percent.

Inexperienced drivers are surcharged by some companies. Surcharges may also be imposed for drivers who claim to have experience but whose driving records cannot be verified, such as when the driving has been done in a foreign country. The surcharge is intended to compensate for the lack of an actual driving record as an aid in estimating what may be expected in the future. These surcharges, which are usually a percentage, generally are removed after the driver has been licensed three years and usually apply only to principal operators.

Additional Factors in Rating Physical Damage Coverages Classification and rating of collision and comprehensive coverages use many of the classification criteria and other rating factors discussed above. In addition, the cost and model year of the car, engine size, and some special features are considered.

The basic rating plan for these coverages is to assign a "symbol" to each make and model of car so that rates can reflect the value of the car. Some cars may be so new or unusual as to have no symbol assigned. For these cases, a table relating new car prices to symbol numbers is used to determine a symbol. A complete vehicle description (year, model, body type, number of cylinders, horsepower or cubic centimeters, vehicle identification number, and original cost new) is essential to assure that the symbol used is proper.

For most companies, symbols are now based upon the damageability, repairability, and susceptibility to theft of the particular vehicle. These factors are based upon the actual experience of the company or companies in the past with the specific make, model, and model year of the vehicle. Exhibit 4-4 shows some of the 1981 symbols used by ISO. "Sym" means the symbol which is assigned for rating. The "VIN" (vehicle identification number), as well as the motor cubic inches and horsepower, are given to identify each car as accurately as possible. The signs next to some of the symbols indicate that the symbol was changed from the previously shown symbol due to the ISO's experience with that model and year vehicle (e.g., = means that the symbol for the 1981 four-door Monte Carlo wagon has been decreased by two from 8 to 6 due to ISO's experience).

The model year is also used in rating physical damage coverages. How these years are grouped varies by company. At the time of this writing, ISO was using a separate rate for each year from 1976 to 1983 and one rate for cars of model years 1975 and prior.

Special surcharges are used by some insurers. Fiberglass bodies may be surcharged by a fixed percentage, such as 25 percent, although it probably is more common to use higher deductibles or simply to assign higher symbols to vehicles known to have these bodies (although the latter practice will miss some cars, such as kit-built sports buggies). The basis for the surcharge or special treatment is the damageability and repair costs of these cars.

"Muscle cars," also known as "high-performance cars," were a problem to insurers in the late 1960s and early 1970s. Many companies, unable to identify each one and increase the symbol appropriately, adopted surcharges in the range of 25 to 40 percent based on the ratio

Exhibit 4-4
Symbol and Identification Section—Personal Auto Manual*

1981 SYMBOL AND IDENTIFICATION SECTION—PERSONAL AUTO MANUAL 1981

Model and Body Type	Sym	Sym Code	VIN	ISO IIN
		CHEVROLET		
Chevette				
Hchbk 2 Dr	6	6	1G1AJ0890B	812111
	6	6	1G1AB0890B	812113
	7†	7†	1G1AB08D0B	812114
Hchbk 4 Dr	6	6	1G1AB6890B	812115
	7†	7†	1G1AB68D0B	812116
Citation				
Hchbk 2 Dr	-6	6	1G1AX0850B	812117
	-6	6	1G1AX08X0B	812118
	-6	6	1G1AX08Z0B	812119
Hchbk 4 Dr	=5	5	1G1AX6850B	812121
	=5	5	1G1AX68X0B	812122
	=5	5	1G1AX68Z0B	812123
Camaro				
Spt Cpe	+8	8	1G1AP87K0B	812124
	+8	8	1G1AP87A0B	812125
	+8	8	1G1AP87J0B	812126
	+8	8	1G1AP87H0B	812127
	+10	J	1G1AP87L0B	812128

Model and Body Type	Sym	Sym Code	VIN	ISO IIN
Monte Carlo				
Spt Cpe	8	8	1G1AZ37K0B	812161
	8	8	1G1AZ37A0B	812162
	8	8	1G1AZ3730B	812163
	8	8	1G1AZ37J0B	812164
	8	8	1G1AZ37H0B	812165
Impala				
Cpe	-6	6	1G1AL47K0B	812166
	-6	6	1G1AL47A0B	812167
	-6	6	1G1AL47J0B	812168
	-6	6	1G1AL45H0B	812169
	-7	7	1G1AL47N0B	812291
Sed 4 Dr	=6	6	1G1AL69K0B	812171
	=6	6	1G1AL69A0B	812172
	=6	6	1G1AL69J0B	812173
	=6	6	1G1AL69H0B	812174
	=6	6	1G1AL69N0B	812292
Wagon 4 Dr	=6	6	1G1AL35J0B	812175
	=6	6	1G1AL35H0B	812176
	=6	6	1G1AL35N0B	812177

(†) denotes addition or change.

* Adapted, with permission, from *Personal Auto Manual* (New York: Insurance Services Office), p. 81-7 (July 1981).

of weight to horsepower, or on other factors. The energy crisis in the mid-1970s changed the emphasis in manufacturing from power to economy, and these surcharges have been discontinued by many companies for newer models since few are high powered.

Bumper discounts were given to cars with bumpers meeting the standards of damageability established by governmental agencies in the early 1970s. The hope was that these shock-absorbing bumpers would prevent or reduce damage to other parts of the auto. These discounts, usually about 5 percent, were removed by most companies after a few years' use. The effect of the bumper in reducing accident damage is reflected in the rates via the use of symbols and model years.

The above discussion explains the major types of classification systems used by auto insurance companies. Before leaving the subject, it will be helpful to look at the reasons for classifications and their role in the underwriting process.

Reasons for Classification

Insurance is a device for distributing the financial impact of losses of the few over a large group, with each group member contributing a relatively small amount as a fair share of group losses. A basic operating principle of insurance is that this "fair share" be based on loss potential, and that risks paying the same premium for a certain type of protection be similar in loss potential, or relatively homogeneous. Classification is one method employed to achieve homogeneity. Without it, a driver using a car for pleasure only, in a small town, would pay the same premium as the driver using an auto for pleasure and business nearby in a crowded urban area. These risks are not considered homogeneous enough to be placed in the same group for the purpose of determining that "fair share" referred to above. Yet, if classifications were not used, both of those drivers would pay the same premium. The underwriter knows that the average driver operating for pleasure only, in a rural area, presents a lesser loss potential than the average driver operating for both pleasure and business purposes in a nearby large city. Therefore, the underwriter probably would show a tendency to reject the city driver, feeling that the rate is too low to reflect the loss potential.

A classification system, if properly constructed and administered, can place similar risks in a single rating category. If the city driver is placed in a class of drivers with similar characteristics, and the class is properly priced, the underwriter can accept the risk with the reasonable assumption that the premium will be commensurate with the exposure.

Thus, it can be seen that there are two reasons to use a classification system. The first is to match premium with the exposure to loss presented by the risk. The second is to keep the market open for all types of risks by assuring that the company will receive a premium commensurate with the exposure.

Factors Affecting the Number of Classifications

Fundamentally, no two risks are alike. Carried to its conceptual extreme, the seeking of homogeneity would result in a separate classification for each risk. On the other hand, even casual observation by a person unfamiliar with insurance and loss sharing would support the contention that all persons should not be charged the same price for the protection received in a particular type of insurance, without regard to the exposure presented. The problem, then, is one of "workable" homogeneity—dividing drivers into *relatively* homogeneous groups without creating such a proliferation of classifications that the system becomes too burdensome to operate or so compartmentalized that the data for particular classifications are useless for predictive purposes. A number of considerations and forces influence the resolution of this problem at any given time.

Equity One of the primary reasons for classification is to charge insureds fairly for the insurance protection they buy. This is demonstrated in the historical development of territorial rates. When autos first came on the scene, there was no distinction by territory because there were no data upon which to base a rate differential. As experience developed, it became evident that some geographic locations should pay higher premiums because their loss experience was worse than that in other locations. Thus, rating territories were adopted.

Notice that equity not only isolates risks that should pay *higher* premiums, but it also isolates territories entitled to *lower* premiums. Overall, premium charges are more closely related to loss potential.

The practice of adjusting territorial definitions in order to accomplish greater equity goes on continually. From time to time a company or bureau will separate a portion of an existing rating territory and assign a different code to the risks in that area. Loss experience under the new code is then developed. After a period of time, it may be found that the tentative new territory, which was established on the basis of judgment, actually should have a different rate than the balance of the territory with which it had been rated. Whether the rates in the new territory increase or decrease, greater equity will be achieved.

Competition One of the strongest pressures encouraging classification development and change has been competition among insurers. Perhaps a company might identify a particular group of risks which are better than the others within the classification to which they are all assigned. By separating these risks into a new classification, the company can charge them less and achieve a competitive advantage in the marketplace. In contrast, the newly identified group might be less desirable than others currently falling into the same class, and separating them into a higher-rated class would enable the company to reduce rates on the more desirable of the former class. This reduction makes the company more competitive with respect to the latter group, which includes not only its own insureds but others of the same type currently insured with other companies or newly entering the market. An example of the latter practice was the first adoption of a separate and higher rate for youthful drivers. Companies not adopting the higher rate soon found themselves victimized by adverse selection as their book of business became more heavily populated with youthful drivers. Another example involves the practice of using distance to work as a rating factor. Companies which did not adopt the higher rates for those driving long distances found that they were getting disproportionate amounts of longer-mileage business and were left unable to compete effectively on short-mileage risks.

The effect of competition on classifications is a complex subject. This brief discussion and the examples it contains make clear that an insurer's classification plan is influenced by what other insurers do. The process is a continuous one of action and reaction as companies adjust to new classification practices for competitive reasons. Other types of adjustments (e.g., stricter selection standards) are also possible, of course, as insurers attempt to attune their activities to the realities of a competitive market.

Economy and Ease of Administration Cost is an important consideration in establishing classifications. It is a major reason why differences in classification practices exist among companies. Though companies try to adopt most of the new classifications of their major competitors in order to maintain a profitable position, they often find that a system which fits one operation may not fit others. For example, the computer operation of a particular company may be limited in the number of entries which can be made in the rate class field. If that capacity has been reached when a competitor splits a rate class into two classes, the company may find that it would be very expensive to modify the system in order to adopt the same split. In this case, the costs of changing might more than offset the improved result anticipated from splitting the class. Underwriters seek the most economical classification system, but this must be balanced against the need to remain competitive and to minimize adverse selection.

Some possible classification factors could cost more to administer than they develop in benefits. For instance, assume that a company desired to give a discount to good students, but felt that regular reporting of grades would be necessary to verify that the student maintained good grades. The cost to request and handle the report cards and to administer the program internally might be more than the company would realize from retaining and attracting profitable business involving good students.

Another cost factor influencing the number of classifications is the increased chance of error and misclassification as the number of classes increases. This problem can be demonstrated by considering territory classifications. It is simple to assign one class to a large city, but it becomes more difficult to apply proper classifications when a large number of territories is used. The possibility of error increases with the multiplicity of territories in the city. To the extent that risks are incorrectly assigned to a territory, the business will be underpriced or overpriced.

Credibility The greater the number of classifications, the more difficult it is to achieve statistically credible results in any particular classification and to justify differentials among classifications. Even if cost and administrative ease were not problems, there are limits on the number of classifications because of the need to support the plan's rates and overall structure with credible data. This support is needed to justify rates with insurance departments in most states.

There are probably measurable differences among risks based on the kinds of cars driven, size of motor, body type, driving attitude, experience, occupation, and so on. Each of these factors might help predict loss experience. However, if those features were introduced into a classification system, the matrix of classifications might be so extensive that few classifications would produce enough car-years of exposure to be credible. (A car-year is the experience of insuring one car for one year.) It is "workable" homogeneity that is the necessary goal.

Classification and the Underwriting Function

Choice of Classification Plan The goal of underwriters is to select business which will produce an underwriting profit. Adequate rates are essential in order to reach this goal. However, rate adequacy alone will not produce underwriting profits. A company might use a very adequate rate of $100 for a particular type of risk, but if all major competitors write that type of risk at a rate of $75, the company will write little business in the class. The company might get a chance to write quite a few of those risks that are well below average in the class, but that possibility would not be attractive either. A balance must be struck among adequacy, competitiveness, and economy of administration. This balance is not easy to reach. Sophisticated actuarial techniques and sound judgment by underwriting and marketing management are required.

Many companies adopt "bureau" classifications rather than prepare their own. ISO has a broad enough base to achieve credibility, along with accomplishing the balance among the other factors. At various times in the recent past, as few as 9 and as many as 260 separate rating classes were used within any one territory. These extremes indicate the types of changes which are made to adapt to changing conditions.

Large independent companies use their own classification plans. They are similar to ISO's and to each other in many ways. At the same time, they all differ in some respects. The types of risks at which the sales effort of a company is directed is one determinant of the classification system used. Geographic scope of operations, type of marketing system, and philosophy of management all play a part.

Some states, like South Carolina, mandate a classification plan that must be used by all insurers. The plan in that state is limited to nine classes. Competition in rates in that state is nonexistent because all companies must use the same plan and rates. In the majority of states, where optional classification plans are permitted, each company must make its own decision. Small companies are almost forced to use a rating bureau because their own experience lacks credibility. Larger companies can either be independent or use a rating bureau plan.

In any case, competition encourages some degree of similarity in classifications and rates among insurers. No company can deviate very far from competition and still maintain both a reasonable volume of sales and a normal profit over time if its marketing plan, expenses, and selection standards are roughly the same as those of the insurers with which it is competing.

Underwriting and Rate Making—An Illustration[1]

UND 61 discussed the three methods of rate making: the pure premium method, the loss ratio method, and the judgment method. In many lines of insurance (including auto), all of these methods are used to some degree in the rate-making process. For example, in auto insurance, the pure premium method is used initially to determine the basic rate, the loss ratio method is used to adjust rate levels, and the judgment method is used to compensate for the lack of full credibility of the data.

Knowledge of the auto rate-making process and of the numerical tools of underwriting discussed in UND 61 is helpful to underwriters in two ways. First, it enables underwriters to analyze their existing personal auto book of business in more detail; and, second, it provides information that is useful in revising the insurer's underwriting philosophy or policy.

To illustrate, suppose that data available to a statistical agency or rating bureau show that there are 30,000 insured exposure units in one rating class (e.g., "811210") in a particular territory. Let us further assume that these 30,000 cars produce average annual losses of $3,900,000 including loss adjustment expenses. As a sharing or pooling mechanism, the proportional share (per car share) of the average annual losses in this oversimplified example could be determined by dividing the $3,900,000 by 30,000 or $130 per car. This is a crude estimate of the average *pure premium* which is suitable for this simple illustration—the actual calculation of the average pure premium is much more exact.

If the data are credible, disregarding trend factors and inflation, the pure premium of $130 per car would equal the expected average loss per car, assuming past loss patterns continue in the future.

If it is assumed that the expected loss ratio for this line of business is 65 percent, the allowance for expenses and profit and contingencies is 35 percent (1 – 0.65 = 0.35). Consequently, the manual rate per car may be determined by dividing the pure premium ($130) by the percent (65%) which it bears to the gross premium or manual rate. Thus,

$$0.65x = \$130$$

$$x = \frac{\$130}{0.65}$$

$$x = \$200$$

The manual rate of $200 will be adequate for the insurer only if the combined loss and expense ratio of the insurer does not exceed 100 percent. If the *actual* loss ratio on this class of business is greater than the expected loss ratio of 65 percent, the pure premium of $130 is insufficient to pay for insured losses, and the deficiency must be made up by drawing from policyholders' surplus or reducing expenses.

Assuming a 5 percent provision for profit and contingencies, the expense portion is 30 percent. (Actually, this expense figure varies significantly among insurers and often makes the difference between underwriting profit and underwriting loss.)

Included in the expense portion are commissions, brokerage, advertising, bureau, and association fees, surveys and underwriting reports (outside services), salaries, employee benefit costs, directors' fees, travel expenses, rent, equipment, printing, postage, telephone, taxes, licenses and fees, and real estate expenses and taxes.[2]

Thus, underwriting profit may be derived through a better than average loss ratio (superior risk selection), a better than average expense ratio (superior expense control), or both.

In our hypothetical example, it is realistic to assume that the 30,000 drivers in the class reflect various degrees of underwriting quality. Some are above average, some are average, and some are clearly below average for the class. This is because underwriting quality is a composite of several risk attributes in addition to age, sex, and marital status. These difficult to measure features include vision, reflexes, hearing, emotional stability, maturity, training, parental supervision, associates, occupation, pride in safety, fear of injury, and other subjective factors.[3]

If we assume that these variations in underwriting quality may be measured in terms of pure premium per car, some above average insureds may require a pure premium of only $100, for example, and some below average insureds may require a pure premium of as much as $200. The remaining risks in the class would fall into other pure premium intervals between the extremes.

Frequency Distribution and Curve Frequency distributions were discussed in Chapter 6 of UND 61. In that text, the discussion of frequency distributions was limited to analyzing loss data on a commercial risk and for a fire rate class. Assume that the risk factors affecting underwriting quality could be measured to some extent and quantified—perhaps with the help of a computer. The insureds in the class could be divided into rate intervals of $10 and a frequency distribution such as that in Exhibit 4-5 would result.

To illustrate the underwriting implications of the data, a frequency curve could be plotted as shown in Exhibit 4-6.

The curve is not a *symmetrical* or *normal* curve. Most likely, instances or extremes of bad driving exceed those of good driving. A driver can only be "so good" (i.e., ignoring reserve takedowns, you cannot have a negative pure premium), but from the standpoint of the insurer, the limits of the policy are the only limits as to how bad a driver can be. For this reason, the distribution will tend to be spread out more to the right side of the curve or toward the higher values than to the left. Thus the curve in Exhibit 4-6 is *positively skewed.*

Note that the curve does not go below $85. This is based on the assumption that no driver is perfect and a certain number of unavoidable accidents would be bound to occur among even the best of drivers.[4]

Similarly, the curve does not go above $210 because clearly

Exhibit 4-5

Frequency Distribution of Insureds in a Rating Class, According to Underwriting Quality as Measured by Probable Pure Premium per Car Year†*

Indicated Pure Premium/Car	Number of Insureds
Less than $ 90	400
$ 90– 99	1,100
100– 109	1,600
110– 119	3,200
120– 129	5,500
130– 139	6,100
140– 149	5,200
150– 159	2,400
160– 169	1,700
170– 179	1,200
180– 189	900
190– 199	475
200 and over	225
Total	30,000

†This is for illustrative purposes only. These are purely hypothetical data and might not and need not actually work out to an arithmetic mean of $130.

*Adapted, with permission, from Calvin H. Brainard, *Automobile Insurance* (Homewood, IL: Richard D. Irwin, 1961), p. 466. Corrected for clarity.

unacceptable risks would not be allowed in the insured class but would be protected through some residual market mechanism.

All 30,000 exposure units are included in the area under the curve. Several insurers would participate in insuring this class with the average pure premium of $130 applying to the entire group. If only two companies insured all 30,000 cars, and each insured half, the loss experience of one company might produce an actual pure premium of only $110 while the loss experience of the other might produce an actual pure premium of $150. The average pure premium for the entire group would still be $130 per car.

This points to a major objective of underwriting. If a company writes a true cross-section of a given class of business, its experience will be representative of the experience of the entire class. In statistical terms, the sample (the company's share of risks in a class) should be representative of the universe (all risks in a class) from which it is drawn.[5]

The underwriting objective is to select a sample of risks within a given class that are average (or better-than-average) so that the

Exhibit 4-6
Frequency Curve Fitted to Hypothetical Data of Number of Insured at Different Levels of Underwriting Quality (Pure Premium)*

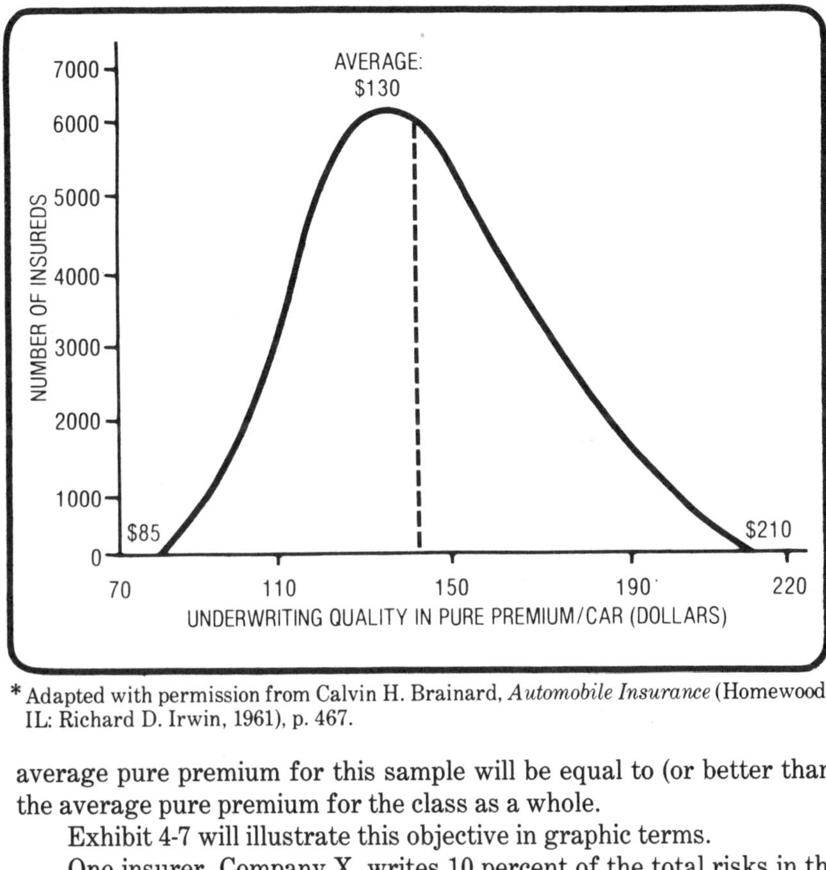

* Adapted with permission from Calvin H. Brainard, *Automobile Insurance* (Homewood, IL: Richard D. Irwin, 1961), p. 467.

average pure premium for this sample will be equal to (or better than) the average pure premium for the class as a whole.

Exhibit 4-7 will illustrate this objective in graphic terms.

One insurer, Company X, writes 10 percent of the total risks in the class, or 3,000 cars. A frequency curve of the *risk characteristics* of Company X's insureds can be compared with the entire class of 30,000 and there are three possible results.

In curve 1, the sample (Company X's share) has the same relative distribution of insureds as the universe from which it was drawn. Thus the pure premium of $130 will be adequate.

In curve 2, the sample has a higher proportion of better than average risks than the universe, and the resulting aggregate losses divided by the number of exposure units produces an average pure premium of $110. Since the pure premium contemplated is $130, an underwriting profit is produced.

In curve 3, the opposite is true and the $130 pure premium will be inadequate.

Exhibit 4-7
Company X Compared with Industry as to Underwriting Quality of Insureds: Three Possibilites*

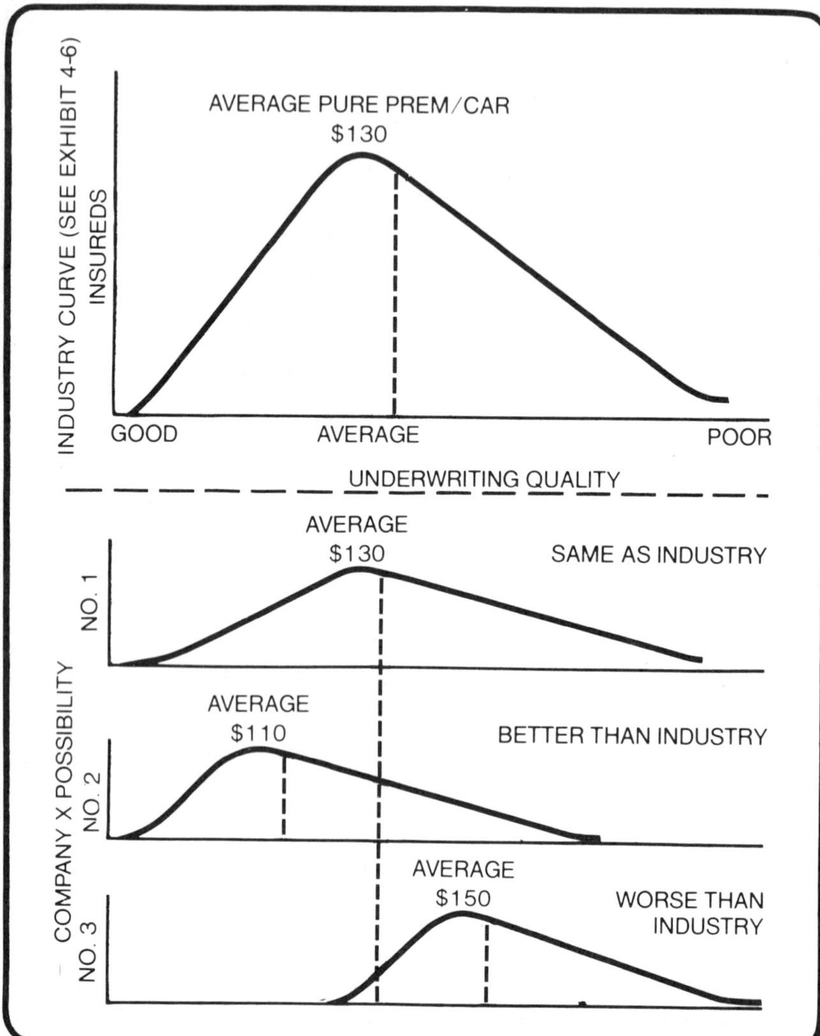

* Adapted with permission from Calvin H. Brainard, *Automobile Insurance* (Homewood, IL: Richard D. Irwin, 1961), p. 469.

Of course, the frequency distributions in the illustrations could be obtained by chance. But it is entirely possible that the distribution in curve 2 was obtained through higher rates, stringent underwriting, and selection of a smaller number of insureds than the distribution in curve

3, which may reflect lower rates and more lenient underwriting, thus attracting a larger number of insureds.

This illustration, though theoretical, attempts to bring together several concepts discussed in the IIA Associate in Underwriting program—the effect of the rate-making process on underwriting, the importance of a classification system, the relationship between underwriting standards and rate adequacy, the use of numerical and graphic tools in analyzing a book of business, and the use of this information as an underwriting management tool.

Classification and Underwriting Practices A disproportionate share of risks in one classification may indicate a problem. Where this occurs, it could mean that the company is overly competitive in that classification. An analysis may be made to try to pinpoint the reason for the heavy population in that particular classification. If the heavy volume results from competitive advantage, but the rate appears to be adequate, there is no problem; one of the goals of the system has been achieved. Or perhaps the change results from changes in selection standards of other insurers for reasons not applicable to the company. If this is the case, perhaps the company needs to reevaluate its standards. On the other hand, it may be found that a major cause is misclassification (e.g., a high percentage of long-mileage risks written at short-mileage rates). If misclassifications continue, underwriting results will be adversely affected. The classification mix should be watched by underwriters and/or underwriting management to detect and correct problems in the administration of classifications, the competitive rate picture, or the selection process.

It is particularly important to monitor the mix of business after a change in classification systems. Beyond the problem of misclassifications that might result from the use of a new system, a change in plan usually will affect the market position of the company for at least some classes. Indeed, that outcome normally would be an objective of the change. The actual outcome after the change may differ from the desired outcome, however. Results of the change can be traced by coding of subgroups in the old class(es) and by analyzing experience in the new class(es) produced by the change.

The most commonly encountered problem in the administration of a classification plan is misclassification, which has already been mentioned but has significance well beyond the illustration above. Evidence from one source suggests that misclassification results in lower than proper rates far more often than it results in higher than proper rates. As an example, Exhibit 4-8 shows the results of a review conducted by one large insurer in one state several years ago. Although the review resulted in a decrease in classification for a few risks (to

Exhibit 4-8
Results of Classification Verification

	Policies		Premium
	Number	Percent of Total Inspected	
Total Inspected	5,989	100.0%	
Class Increased	1,909	31.9	$99,244.00
Class Decreased	112	1.9	4,270.00
Net Increase	1,797	30.0	94,974.00
Average Increase per Policy Inspected			$15.86

which they of course were entitled and which might have helped to retain them at renewal), the net result was a change to higher-rated classifications for 30 percent of the policies checked and an average of $15.86 in additional premium for each policy inspected. This type of result indicates the advantage of inspecting a large volume of risks if misclassification is suspected.

When a book of business is suspected of containing a substantial number of misclassified risks, the underwriter must analyze many files, ordering information to verify the correctness of the classifications. The nature of any indicated corrections will depend upon the reasons for the errors. Perhaps the only problem will be that the rating information has become outdated. It may have been accurate when the policy was written, but subsequent changes in exposure have not been reflected in classification changes. The solution is to secure current information from motor vehicle reports, producers, inspection reports, or from the policyholders themselves.

Sometimes the source of the problem will be that recent changes in the classification system have not been made in existing policies. Such changes should have been made, but may have been overlooked or performed erroneously. A recoding of all involved policies will be needed.

Occasionally a company, branch, or agency will suffer through a period when inaccurate classification occurs with unusual frequency, such as when a new rater did not understand the system. Perhaps a shortage of underwriters or an unexpected volume of business created time pressures that contributed to improper classification. The solution in this case is to identify the risks which were handled during that period and check the classifications used. Often the risks involved can be identified by reviewing policy registers or getting a computer run by policy effective date.

Finally, some producers might be found to have an unusually high percentage of misclassified risks. They may not have understood the rating system or may have deliberately shaded the facts in order to achieve a temporary sales advantage. Whatever the reason, a safe procedure would be to review all of the policies for those producers, verifying the facts and revising classifications as needed.

Proper classification of policies must be applied to existing policies as well as to new writings. Failure to achieve and maintain correct classifications will reduce underwriting profits, since most misclassifications result in premiums being too low. Further, classification data and changes indicated by underwriting results will be distorted. Misclassifications resulting in premiums being too high can cause renewals to decline, leading to a loss in total writings. Reduced sales, in most cases at least, are detrimental to the objectives of the company.

Profitability of an insurance company within the context of this chapter depends both upon proper selection of risks and the accurate application of rating classifications. Underwriters have the essential role in the achievement of both of these objectives.

UNDERWRITING MID-TERM POLICY CHANGES

The underwriting process includes both the initial consideration of new business and the subsequent consideration given to business already on the books. This section of Chapter 4 discusses one phase of the underwriting process as it applies to business already in force—underwriting policy changes during the period of policy coverage.

This subject could be regarded as part of the broader topic of monitoring underwriting decisions, because every request for a policy change provides an opportunity for reviewing a risk already on the books. This text separates the underwriting of policy changes from monitoring because personal auto insurance is a line with a high frequency of mid-term policy changes, and the proper handling of these should be emphasized independently.

Nature of Policy Change Underwriting

The request for a policy change means a request for a change in the scope or terms of the agreement originally entered into between the insured and the company. In effect, a change means a new contract is written even though the actual physical evidence of the change may be nothing more than a sheet of paper pertaining to the change or a revised declarations page reflecting the change.

The underwriting of changes has a major advantage over the underwriting of new applicants. The advantage is that the underwriter now has some experience with the risk. In other words, the composite picture of the risk that was developed in initial underwriting has been broadened to include at least some time on the books of the company. In most cases, this will be a more informative or clearer composite picture than was available previously. The task of underwriting changes in the policy requires consideration of how the proposed change alters this composite picture, including consideration of the new exposure relative to the new rate.

The underwriter generally follows the same process in the underwriting of changes as when underwriting new business, but information gathering is simpler because of the existing supply of readily available information on the risk. Still, an underwriting decision is called for and the same kind of decision-making process should be generally applied even though certain steps may be unnecessary or perfunctory in many situations. More information might be required, such as a current MVR or an inspection report. The producer might be asked to furnish additional information. In some cases, it may be necessary to review the risk *in its entirety* because of the new composite picture that would result if the change were made as requested. To illustrate, a requested change might move the risk into a class or territory that is regarded as underpriced. The underwriter cannot respond automatically, but must now look at the entire risk compared to standards in the *new* class or territory. Coverage changes, such as a higher deductible, might be in order. Within the limits set by any applicable law or regulation, the underwriter may be faced with consideration of the same range of alternatives used in underwriting new business.

Two major considerations not germane to new business underwriting sometimes influence the underwriting of changes. First, most companies regard existing policyholders, in general, as deserving of the benefit of the doubt in borderline situations. Second, state laws or regulations seriously restrict the availability of some underwriting alternatives while a policy is in force. Even where the conditions underlying the contract have changed substantially, such as when the described auto is replaced by one with far less desirable characteristics for the coverages involved, some states interpret their cancellation laws to prohibit termination until renewal date. Some do not permit termination even then except for specified reasons. It is incumbent upon underwriting personnel to be familiar with these restrictions and their impact on the alternatives available in the underwriting of mid-term policy changes.

Not all changes involve an underwriting decision. Reductions in coverage seldom are of concern to an underwriter. There are few underwriting implications to the insured's termination of towing, medical payments, or collision coverages except a loss of premium. Termination of liability coverages may be important to an underwriter because liability protection is so vital under present laws and the underwriter may want to be certain that the policyholder is fully aware of the result of this action. A reduction in liability limits to the minimum required by the state is no problem. The deletion of a loss payee, such as a bank or other lending institution, is not a matter of concern because it merely indicates payment of the loan.

Precisely what gets referred for underwriting consideration, and the practices followed in screening routine changes from those receiving underwriting attention, vary among companies and are explained in underwriting guides.

Common Change Requests

The most common mid-term policy changes which may have underwriting implications, and thus most often get underwriting attention, can be grouped according to whether they (1) change operators, (2) change vehicles, (3) change territory, (4) change limits of liability, or (5) request coverage for excluded property.

Operators A request to add an operator often warrants serious underwriting consideration because the operator is the single most important factor in determining acceptability. The most common type of added operator is the new driver, usually a youthful new driver.

The youthful new driver obviously has had no opportunity to develop a driving record, and so the underwriter is without one important basis for decision making. However, many underwriters look to the driving record of the parents as an indicator of the maturity and responsibility of the youthful new driver. If the parents have been insured under the policy for a few years with good driving records, it may be safe to assume that their child will be trained to drive in a similar fashion. This is not always true, of course, but many underwriters assume it to be true subject to later events proving otherwise. If the youthful new driver is accepted, it is common to mark or otherwise set apart the file for the securing of an MVR a year or so after the addition of the driver. The same practice might be followed after the addition of *any* newly licensed driver, regardless of age.

Driver additions usually have classification and rating implications.

The mechanics of these matters might be handled by computer or by persons other than the underwriter, but their importance is no less than in the underwriting of new business.

Under limited circumstances, a driver *exclusion* rather than addition may be the purpose of a mid-term change. Perhaps the problem rests with only one of the several drivers insured under the policy, and the policyholder may prefer to have that driver excluded rather than have the policy canceled or face nonrenewal in the future.

Driver exclusions are not permitted in some states. In such states the underwriter must refuse a request to delete a driver and proceed on that basis. In contrast, the offer by an underwriter to exclude a driver as an alternative to termination is required in some states if the reason for the desire to terminate is the driving record or status of a particular driver. The applicable section of the Colorado law provides that

> . . . the insurer shall . . . offer to continue or review the insurance but to exclude from coverage by name, the person whose claim experience or driving record would have justified the cancellation or nonrenewal.

Where permitted but not compelled to do so, insurers for the most part agree to use driver exclusions only as a last resort and then only as an accommodation for long-time insureds. The potential problems in their use, for both insurer and insured, are numerous, and the underwriter must be informed on company practice, legal constraints, and the extent to which the exclusion is likely to accomplish the result sought. It does little good, for example, to exclude a driver who is likely to be operating the vehicle, if the state's financial responsibility (or other) law makes the insured responsible to injured third parties in spite of the exclusion.

Territory A change in place of garaging may have underwriting implications. The new territory may be in a high vandalism area and the policy may provide first-dollar comprehensive coverage. The underwriter may feel a deductible is warranted. A change could denote a probable switch in car use, particularly if the change is to a suburban location from a city address. If the insured works in the city, he or she may now have to drive part or all of the way to work instead of using public transportation. In an extreme case, the new distance to and from work may be incompatible with company underwriting criteria. Or the move could be to an area where auto thefts and vandalism are prevalent and where the car must be parked on the street.

In each of these examples, the minimum action required is a review of the need for a change in rate classification and/or territory. However, the underwriter may also need to apply new or higher deductibles, change the coverage limits, remove some coverages, or take some other course of action. The new risk which is presented by the different location may require new underwriting, and all of the options available to an underwriter should be considered if conditions are significantly different from those previously existing.

Vehicle Replacement of a covered vehicle by another similar vehicle is a common occurrence and presents no particular need for attention beyond any appropriate rating changes. However, if a four-door sedan is replaced by a sports car, or an auto by a pickup truck, such a switch could indicate the need for a major classification change. Perhaps a business use is now present, or the change may imply the existence of a new operator who has not been reported to the company. A change to a different type of vehicle requires underwriting review before the change is made. The underwriter must also be on guard for characteristics of the new vehicle which may not be contemplated by the rate. Customized paint decorations, a snow plow on a pickup truck, and a winch on a recreational vehicle illustrate items which could add greatly to loss costs but which are not routine and thus not contemplated by the rate for the exposure. These special features may need to be excluded by endorsement to the policy where such a practice is not interpreted as being in violation of limitations on the right to cancel.

Laws in most states do not permit the declination of a replacement vehicle after the policy has been in force a stipulated number of days, as this would be tantamount to a cancellation contrary to those laws. However, the file could be marked or coded for review prior to renewal if the replacement vehicle is or might not be acceptable in its own right.

Limits of Liability Some companies feel that the acceptability of a risk is not affected by the policy limits and that a risk accepted and on the books at one set of limits is not potentially less desirable if an increase in these limits is requested. Others consider limits as an initial underwriting variable and as a factor for underwriting consideration when a request for higher limits is made at mid-term, at least for certain classes. In the latter case, the question of maximum limits for various classes rarely is left to the line underwriter's discretion. Underwriting guides spell out the breaking points for acceptability. In some cases, these may reflect the terms of reinsurance treaties rather than the underwriting philosophy of the insurer.

Excluded Property Another type of mid-term change deserving of underwriting attention is the so-called "buy-back" of coverage of property that is excluded under the basic policy. Stereo equipment and CB radios are common examples, as are the customized features of vans with some companies. These last are handled in a straightforward way by the additional premium for the buy-back, but sound reproduction equipment (primarily tape decks) and CB radios often are the subject of underwriting concern. Specifically, the underwriter may want to check the area in which the vehicle is used, the use or nonuse of garage facilities, and the record of past theft losses for the particular insured.

SUMMARY

Effective personal auto underwriting depends on proper classification and rating. Classification systems vary among companies but the common factors are territory, age, sex, marital status, and use of the vehicle. Other rating factors may include multi-car discounts, safe driver plans, driver training credits, good student discounts, and charges for inexperience.

The insurance mechanism is based on a pooling of homogeneous risks, and a classification system is one way of achieving homogeneity. The number and types of classes are determined to some extent by competition, economy, ease of administration, credibility, and equity among insureds.

Underwriting policy changes during the policy period gives the underwriter the opportunity to reexamine the risk. The most common changes which have underwriting implications are changes in operators, vehicles, territory, limits of liability, or requests for coverage of excluded property.

Chapter Notes

1. This section is adapted from *Automobile Insurance* by Calvin H. Brainard, Richard D. Irwin, Inc., Homewood, IL, 1961.
2. Brainard, *Automobile Insurance,* p. 452.
3. Brainard, *Automobile Insurance,* p. 465.
4. Brainard, *Automobile Insurance,* p. 467.
5. Brainard, *Automobile Insurance,* p. 468.

Chapter Note

CHAPTER 5

Monitoring and the Underwriting Environment

MONITORING IN PERSONAL AUTO UNDERWRITING

The underwriting decision-making process extends beyond making and implementing decisions to include monitoring—the review of previous decisions. Monitoring is similar to new business underwriting, except that emphasis is given to changes that might affect the desirability of a risk which was once found acceptable. The process is the same—gathering and putting together information, comparing the findings against underwriting criteria, weighing the results of the comparison, considering other factors, identifying and evaluating alternatives, and making a decision.

Chapter 11 of UND 61 dealt with a type of monitoring—measuring the underwriter's performance against standards established for that purpose—that will not be duplicated here. The emphasis there was on the control function of underwriting management's reviewing of the effectiveness of the work of underwriters and the company underwriting process. It essentially was "top down" monitoring. The emphasis here will be on the monitoring activities that do or may go on as part of day-to-day line underwriting effort. This text will use "review and renewal underwriting" as a broad term to encompass these monitoring activities.

A basic division in monitoring activities is one between individual policies and a group of policies or book of business. Individual policies may be reviewed because of claim activity, change request, or change in the risk prior to renewal. Review prior to renewal may be performed routinely on a blanket basis or on an exception basis dictated by company guidelines and/or prior flagging of the file by the underwriter. Groups of policies may be isolated for review, for a variety of reasons, either as of a certain time or as the individual policies in the group near renewal.

Limitations on Review and Renewal Underwriting

Economic Limitations One of the characteristics of the personal lines of insurance described in Chapter 1 of this text is the relatively small premium per policy. This small premium does not provide many dollars for underwriting expenses generally, including the expenses of review and renewal underwriting. No doubt for some risks, the actual expenses incurred—including underwriting and processing time—exceed the expense dollars in the initial premium. These risks may not fully pay their way in terms of expenses until they have been on the books for more than one policy period.

Monitoring costs money. Ideally, each underwriting decision should be reviewed periodically, but realistically, each review increases expenses. If expenses are increased more than losses are decreased, the combined ratio increases and creates upward pressure on rates. Rate increases in a highly competitive line like personal auto could generate adverse selection, a reduction of volume of business, or both.

Contractual Limitations Many limitations on review and renewal underwriting are spelled out in the various policies. Some of these limitations are voluntary—companies incorporate within their contracts limitations more stringent than those the law requires. In other cases, the contracts contain only mandatory limitations.

Voluntary Limitations. While review can take place at whatever time the company or the underwriter sees fit, the ability to take certain actions that might be indicated by the review may be limited. In the late 1960s, many companies voluntarily adopted a restriction on the right to cancel which was incorporated in the policy.

Under this type of cancellation limitation, an underwriter developing unfavorable information of a type other than that listed in the policy can take no action that would affect coverage until the renewal date. Some companies have voluntarily agreed not only to restrict cancellation but to guarantee renewal for a stipulated number of years (such as five years) except under certain designated circumstances not contingent upon loss frequency or severity.

While these voluntary restrictions limit the exercise of cancellation (and perhaps renewal) prerogatives, they do not affect changes in rating classifications. Thus, current information on the risk is still essential for rating purposes even though it may not be of a type providing the basis for cancellation or nonrenewal.

Mandatory Limitations. Insurers in most states are subject to laws or regulations governing cancellation or cancellation and renewal of personal auto policies. In general, these laws (1) allow a limited period, e.g., sixty days, after inception of a policy, during which the insurer can cancel for its own reason(s); (2) severely restrict the reasons for cancellation after this time period, e.g., nonpayment of premium, or suspension or revocation of a driver's license; and (3) require at least a specified number of days, e.g., forty-five, of notice of an intention not to renew or, in a few cases, restrict the right to nonrenew. There are major differences among the laws on what elements of auto policy coverage are subject to these laws. Some laws refer to auto policies without regard to specific coverages; others refer to all the major coverages by designation. Some refer to liability coverages only, one to liability coverages and uninsured motorists, and some to liability, uninsured motorists, and medical payments. Companies usually provide underwriters with a compilation of the various laws and the coverage elements to which they apply. Where a voluntary policy provision is more favorable to the insured than the applicable state law, obviously the policy provision governs the relationship between the parties.

Of major importance in working with these laws is knowing the scope of their application. The requirements concerning continuation are usually quite explicit, but changes dealing with *other than* continuation may not be expressly dealt with and may require the issuance of regulations for clarification. For example, a number of states have interpreted their laws to prohibit alterations of coverage—such as excluding a driver or adding or increasing a deductible—unless requested by the policyholder or unless made at a time when the policy is not subject to the continuation protection of the law. In a state with a renewal guarantee law, this interpretation means that a company-initiated coverage change could not be made even at renewal, at least during the time span during which a policyholder's renewal rights are protected by the law.

The Monitoring Process

Monitoring of decisions on individual risks is a very substantial underwriting activity. In the past, it was routine to re-evaluate risks and take action at virtually any time and for any reason consistent with company guidelines and practices. These interim reviews—whether resulting from policy activity such as claims or policy changes, or from changes in conditions or underwriting standards—are less effective now because of the impossibility of mid-term restriction or cancellation in most states. However, they are still widely used even though the earliest permitted action time may be the renewal date. Files can be marked for nonrenewal or for thorough analysis prior to renewal. Further, in some states mid-term action is permitted on some element(s) of coverage. Identification of the policies to be analyzed depends on the philosophy and practices of the company and its underwriting personnel. If analysis is routine, each policy will receive regular underwriting attention. This practice is rare in personal auto insurance today. In most companies, analysis will be on an *exception* basis wherein files are reviewed only if they fall into certain categories or if the prior judgment of the underwriter led to a marking of the file for consideration at some point in the future. The standards used to denote an exception requiring consideration vary from company to company, from area to area within a company, and from underwriter to underwriter. In general, however, the standards are based on problem classes, actual or potential changes in the risk, or changes in underwriting standards.

Over the years, cost pressures and the advent of automation have dramatically changed the role of the underwriter in handling renewals in most companies. Most risks show no significant change from one policy period to the next. In the absence of a dramatic change in underwriting standards, most renewals and billings can be processed automatically and accurately with the help of computerized systems. Individual underwriting of renewals compromises the cost savings made possible by automation in the large volume, relatively homogeneous, personal auto line. Thus, renewal underwriting by exception has become the norm due in part at least to the processing economies possible through computers.

Computers must be programmed to find the "exceptions" determined by underwriting management to warrant individual attention. Thus, the use of computers to identify exceptions depends on the ability to convert risk characteristics into a logical set of factors that can be identified by a computer program so that the computer can refer the file for individual consideration. The factors used by the computer can be single—policies with sports cars or policies with young teenagers in the household; or multiple—policies with physical damage coverage on cars over a certain age. Or the file referral can be based on a code entered by the underwriter when the risk was originally underwritten or last reviewed. A family risk including a newly licensed driver might be coded for referral after one year so that an MVR can be ordered on the new driver (or the computer can actually process the order for the MVR and refer the file to underwriting).

Automated renewal processing means that a high percentage of renewals are not reviewed for desirability by an underwriter. (However, many companies use prerenewal questionnaires or other sources to secure rating information. Inquiry may be made on all policies or only on those determined by certain criteria. Information gathered most often is processed by raters, subject to certain kinds of data being called to the attention of underwriting.) Reviewing, for example, 20 percent of all renewals obviously results in expense savings compared to reviewing all or most renewals. Because many risks would be renewed "as is" in any case, underwriters are spared the time that would be used for nothing more than processing and moving work, as opposed to analysis and making judgments. On the other hand, automated processing may not be a substitute for the trained eye and intuition of an underwriter, and the expense savings may be partially or wholly offset by higher loss costs. Each company strikes its own balance on the question of sacrificing individual underwriting attention in the interest of expense savings.

While computers have been very helpful in the timely identification of policies deemed most likely to warrant review before renewal, this does not mean that computers are necessary for such a review. Many lines of insurance are reviewed before renewal without any assistance from a computer. No doubt some companies handle personal auto insurance in this way, either reviewing every file or some sample of files before renewal, reviewing every file at least once over a two or three year period, or reviewing on an "as needed" basis according to prior coding by the underwriter at the time of initial acceptance or at the time of policy activity such as a claim. Still, auto insurance has used computers in this process more than any other line.

Routine Sources of Information

The first step in a program to monitor underwriting decisions is to secure information needed in the process. Some of the same sources that were helpful in the initial selection process may be used, but there are differences. One new source available for some risks is claim documents, the use of which will be dealt with in a separate section below.

The application is of lesser value to the underwriter now, but it is helpful in checking basic information and in finding where changes have been made. The application will be supplemented by the entire policy file, which contains details of changes and experience since the policy was issued. Some of the items of importance are claims history; record of premium payments; changes in vehicles, operators, or use; revisions in territory or coverages; and comments from the producer or policyholder. This information from the company's records may need to be supplemented in order to secure a complete picture of the risk. The types of supplemental information that may be needed can be determined from a review of the policy file.

Motor vehicle records (MVRs) are a good source of factual information concerning the driving record outside of information already in the policy file on accidents. When a loss record is being reviewed, there may be an indication that a driver could have been convicted of moving traffic violations. An MVR can confirm or rebut the indication by showing whether there was a license suspension or traffic conviction. When a file is being reviewed before renewal, an MVR can supplement the information in the file. Some companies request MVRs periodically, such as every year, because their rating plans apply surcharges for both accidents and convictions, and verification will contribute to accurate pricing. In these cases, the MVR may also be used by underwriters for evaluating the risk. Other companies secure MVRs at less frequent intervals, perhaps every three years, as a renewal underwriting tool. The practice may be to secure information on all risks, or, more commonly, all with specified characteristics. Both the cost and quality of MVRs vary by state, so judgment must be applied. Even when cost is low, the results may not justify the expense, particularly when the cost of internal handling is considered.

Inspection reports are used when the file indicates a possible problem which can best be clarified by the use of this source—an apparent change in the use of the car, for example. The use of these reports in monitoring is not as frequent as on new writings, because a risk's experience on the books often reduces concern about moral and morale hazards.

Classification reports are used quite frequently by many companies, particularly at renewal. These reports often can produce more in additional revenue than they cost to obtain and use. In states with guaranteed renewal laws, they may be almost the only tool which can be used effectively; even if the policy cannot be nonrenewed, it can be classified and rated correctly.

Classification information often is secured directly from policyholders. Again, this is more common at renewal than at mid-term. Some companies use blanket questionnaires addressed to all policyholders. Others use them only for risks with specific characteristics, such as pleasure use only, or occasional young drivers, where the passage of time is most likely to bring a change to a higher-rated class. Results vary, and practices may be changed periodically. Based solely on cost factors, this may be the most effective source for some companies.

Producers can be a valuable source of information. When a problem develops on a file after a loss or a policy change, the underwriter might ask the producer for more information. However, as important and vital as the producer is to the development of underwriting information, sometimes even that person is unable to be of much help. It is not uncommon today for producers to be geographically separated from many of their insureds. These producers cannot have first-hand knowledge of changes involving clients. Thus, outside reports may be ordered to provide, for example, the current distance driven to work and thus enable the underwriter to correctly classify and rate the policy at renewal. An outside inspection might develop information about a driver who is not currently rated on the policy, prompting the underwriter to go back to the producer to develop and obtain the necessary rating and underwriting information on that driver. Or an outside report may indicate that the policyholder has let the vehicle deteriorate to the point where it presents an excessive exposure relative to the premium. The underwriter may ask the producer to determine if the policyholder intends to improve the condition of the vehicle, if physical damage coverages should be removed, or if the policy should be nonrenewed. These are examples of combining several sources to provide necessary information.

Finally, the knowledge and expertise of the underwriter is valuable. The evaluation of the available information is of prime importance in monitoring the decisions which were made previously. The degree of knowledge, training, ingenuity, and judgment of an underwriter are critical factors in determining the need for information from other sources, and in deciding to confirm or alter the previous decision on the risk.

Claim Information

Claim history is an important source of information in monitoring underwriting decisions. Its importance rests not only on its obvious aspects—type, frequency, and severity of loss—but also on what claim documents can reveal about drivers and car use.

It is not uncommon for accident information to reveal a driver who had not previously been mentioned to the company. Perhaps a teenager has become licensed or the insured has married and the new spouse is a driver. Any time the driver is not listed as an operator, the underwriter should be interested in the driving record of this person and whether he or she will customarily drive the car. The response to such questions may prompt a reclassification and/or a check of the new driver's MVR. If the new driver was licensed only recently it might be advisable to flag the file to check the driving record at some future date.

Quite often an accident or series of accidents will develop the information that the insured is rather free in permitting others to drive the insured auto. This is not a desirable situation for the underwriter since it is virtually impossible to investigate the driving records of all such individuals. Occasionally the "other driver" may be a specific individual, such as a relative or fiancée, who lives nearby and who has frequent access to the car. While these arrangements are not ideal from the company's standpoint, it may be acceptable since a check into the driver's motor vehicle record is possible.

The circumstances of an accident may reveal a use of the car that was unknown to the underwriter. The underwriter should be careful in interpreting such information. Most often it simply means that the use has changed. It may involve only a routine change in classification, such as from pleasure use to driving to and from work, because the insured decided to drive to work where public transportation had been used when the policy was first written. Or it may denote simply a job change. A more serious concern is when the accident uncovers business use that was not revealed in the original application. This could indicate a much heavier exposure than originally contemplated, such as the use of a personal car for delivering prescriptions where the insured owns a drugstore, or a station wagon used to transport persons to and from an airport by an insured who operates a resort. The chances are good that the application would not have been accepted if such use had been known.

Generally, an auto underwriter is more concerned with frequency of loss than dollar amount of loss as an indicator of the underwriting desirability of an insured or applicant. The severity of a loss is strongly affected by chance. If the insured strikes a pedestrian and leaves the claimant with a severely injured arm, the amount of payout is apt to be less if the pedestrian is elderly and retired rather than young and employed. Obviously, the loss of earnings potential will affect the size of the claim, but the insured has no control over the identity or earning power of the claimant. Claim cost is most often beyond the control of the insured. So, while no company is pleased with having to pay enormous sums in settlement of a claim, it is frequency of loss that most concerns the underwriter since frequency, rather than severity, has the greater bearing on the future experience of that particular insured.

The term "frequency" is subject to many interpretations. Some company programs may consider only chargeable accidents in measuring frequency. Others may concern themselves with all accidents, regardless of fault. Certainly the measurement of frequency is affected by no-fault legislation where payment may be required even though the other driver was responsible. Also, the growing adoption of comparative negligence will increase the number of chargeable accidents because many companies count an accident as chargeable even if the insured's negligence was small.

Since the policy provides a variety of coverages, individual claims may be made for a theft, a nonfault accident, an at-fault accident, vandalism, and so on. Does such a mix constitute alarming frequency? Each underwriter must become familiar with the company's position in this regard. However, in most instances frequency is measured in terms of responsibility. If the insured has had two accidents over the past year and the descriptions indicate one or both of them as not due to the insured's negligence, the situation usually is viewed differently than if the insured were responsible in both instances. Likewise, consideration must be given to the number of vehicles insured. However, this consideration normally does not take the form of a proportionate ratio. If company practice accepts two chargeable accidents over a three-year period, it will not usually tolerate four chargeable accidents over the same period if the policy covers two autos. Any family with that many chargeable accidents in such a short span is usually considered a poor risk, regardless of the number of autos insured.

The same reasoning is applied to nonchargeable accidents. Underwriters will rarely encounter a claim in which the insured driver admits complete responsibility for an accident, except in the most obvious circumstances. When an insured is involved in frequent nonchargeable accidents, two plausible interpretations are (1) the auto is used under circumstances involving far higher than average loss probability; or (2) the insured does not adequately practice defensive driving techniques. In either instance, a very close review of the record is warranted, particularly where the accidents appear to result from similar situations such as being "rear-ended."

Most insureds have few incidents requiring claim service, and when they do occur, the information provided is factual and complete. Some, however, look upon insurance as a replacement or substitute for prudent conduct. No amount of underwriting expertise or remedial action can cure the claim conscious insured. Likewise, there is nothing so desirable in an insured as personal care of the auto and natural efforts to avoid situations that might bring damage to property or injury to persons.

Illustrative Review and Renewal Underwriting Procedures on Individual Risks

This text cannot prescribe a program for monitoring individual risks that would fit the philosophy and operating format of all companies. However, a brief description of some illustrative procedures may be helpful.

Continuous Underwriting A number of companies use a monitoring procedure sometimes referred to as "continuous underwriting." This means that *whenever* a file is referred to an underwriter, it is subject to complete review. Whether the file is brought to the underwriter's attention because of an endorsement, a claim, or for any other reason, the file is checked in its entirety and not just on the basis of the transaction or event responsible for the referral.

This "interim" review may run from cursory to exhaustive, depending on the nature and history of the risk. For example, a policy that was issued a few months ago and was not the subject of any particular underwriting concern at that time would be reviewed in only cursory fashion in the event of a vehicle change from one standard car to another. Though the thought process encompasses the file in its entirety, the implementation would be brief. In contrast, consider a policy in force for three years without activity or complete renewal underwriting since issuance. Assume a policy change involves moving from a city territory to a suburban territory and that the current file information indicates employment three miles from the insured's residence and the use of public transportation to get to work. For this risk, the review process might involve new information about occupation and work location, whether the car is now used to go to work, and motor vehicle records. The risk would be reunderwritten and rerated in its entirety even though the ability to take underwriting action might be delayed until the renewal date. The procedure and any action taken should be documented just as would be the case with a new submission.

Renewal Underwriting As indicated previously, practices in the monitoring of renewal business vary among companies. One system—not necessarily typical but certainly representative of programs used by many companies—is illustrated here.

This particular system is totally automated. Computer programming identifies certain situations that are routinely referred to the underwriter 120 days prior to the renewal date by means of a "status print" from the automated system. These situations include: all policies where the MVR is three years old or older; all policies where the outside inspection report is five years old or older; all policies involving a driver age seventy or over; all policies that require recertification of the good student discount; all policies with potential youthful drivers (e.g., the policy was issued seven years ago and there was a ten-year-old child in the family at that time); and all policies where the underwriter, during an interim review or at initial underwriting, set up a request for referral at renewal. For example, if originally there was a young driver who drove a vehicle only occasionally, the underwriter now wants to see if that driver is driving a vehicle on a full-time (principal operator) basis.

In each of these cases the underwriter receives the daily report or file and reviews it for appropriate action. In those cases where the MVR or outside report is over three years and five years old, respectively, a new report is ordered automatically. The date of 120 days prior to renewal is the lead time used because this will allow 60 days to obtain all pertinent underwriting information and to make a decision and still put a "do not renew" transaction into the automated system, if necessary, in compliance with state law. If the policy is not renewed, no renewal declarations page is generated and a nonrenewal notice meeting the state's requirements is automatically printed. This time frame also allows the new data obtained to be put into the system so that the renewal declarations page and billing will reflect any rate changes developed as a result of the new information.

In this particular program, the underwriter requires an "Applicant's Medical Statement" completed by the policyholder in cases where the driver is age seventy or older. If additional information is needed from a physician, there is sufficient time to obtain this. On those cases where recertification for discounts is used, forms are sent out by a service unit and the completed form is returned and reviewed by the underwriting unit.

In addition to the routine referrals discussed above, a secondary data system produces a "Pre-Renewal" worksheet on each risk, by producer. These worksheets are reviewed at the supervisory level of underwriting to designate those policies that should be referred to a territorial underwriter on an "exception" basis. These exceptions are usually based on the number and/or type of claims incurred during the previous year as well as during the four years preceding the last year. For example, a policy with two small comprehensive claims, one in the past year and one four years ago, would not be referred. However, another policy with two comprehensive claims in the last two years would be referred. All policies with bodily injury or PIP claims, or with property damage or collision claims over $300 in the last three years would be referred due to the possibility of a surcharge renewal. Any policies with more than one bodily injury, property damage, or collision loss in the last five years would be referred. Files are then reviewed individually to determine if the policy should be renewed and, if so, on what basis.

Illustrative Review of Underwriting Procedures on a Book of Business

Monitoring a group, or book, of personal auto policies is a

necessary supplement to monitoring individual risks. In fact, with many insurers it is emphasized far more than is individual risk monitoring.

Individual risk decisions are made by the line underwriter based on the underwriting guide and the application of underwriting criteria. Decisions on the reunderwriting of groups of policies may be made at several levels, from line underwriting all the way up through home office staff underwriters. At whatever level made, decisions on monitoring groups of policies often are made jointly or with the assistance of other company departments such as marketing, claims, and actuarial. Because of these facts, the discussion that follows necessarily involves actions that may exceed the authority of most line underwriters. However, line underwriters are involved since (1) the implementation of the monitoring decision will be at the line underwriting level, and (2) line underwriters are expected to make recommendations on monitoring activities to those with authority to make decisions on such matters.

The Process Book of business review and renewal underwriting involves the analysis of a group of contracts identified by the presence of some common denominator. In the examples used below, four of many possible common denominators will be illustrated—rate classification, territory, producer, and type of loss. Other types of policy groupings are certainly possible; their number and characteristics are limited only by the ways in which a company's overall book of personal auto business can be coded, subdivided, and reviewed. The groups actually reviewed by any particular company depend on the nature of the company's ongoing monitoring process (e.g., reviewing each producer's book of business every six months) and the irregular problem-oriented developments that may occur from time to time (e.g., a substantial worsening of the loss ratio in a particular classification).

Analyzing a book of business, *as a book,* involves some considerations not present in reviewing individual risks. Does the book present enough data to be statistically reliable? Might the result or problem be due to external factors, such as rate inadequacy or a catastrophe producing enormous physical damage losses, rather than to the quality of the book of business itself? Might the competitive picture have changed and resulted in adverse selection? Is it too soon for a rate increase or a previous reunderwriting program to be reflected in group results? Are changes in the volume of business written distorting group ratios? Answers to questions like these influence both the making of decisions to conduct reviews and the interpretation of the results of reviews that are made.

Book of business reviews are made whenever routine monitoring rules or apparent problems dictate the need for them. Concentrating on the latter area—apparent problems—monitoring activity is more likely to take place prior to renewal as opposed to at a certain time for a group of policies. In other words, once the block of policies to be subjected to monitoring activity is identified, the activity itself usually takes place as the policies in the block come up for renewal. Thus, although the group is identified as of a certain time, the attention to the policies in the group may be spread over a period of time approximating the normal duration of that type of contract. In most companies, this period is either six months or one year. The reasons for this approach are (1) in most states, any indicated underwriting action cannot be taken until renewal, and (2) the work is spread out into roughly even monthly loads. There are exceptions, of course, particularly where a serious problem situation is suspected and there is a desire to get a precise picture of it quickly to guide future actions.

Regardless of when the work is done, the procedure followed is essentially the same. The reason for the review is established, the policies involved are identified and isolated, the necessary information is gathered, evaluations are made, and actions are taken. In the final analysis, this group review becomes an individual file review because every book includes some desirable business. The only time that an entire book is likely to be nonrenewed is when a producer who owns expirations is terminated and the producer's entire book must be nonrenewed in accordance with the contract between the producer and the company, or when the company is withdrawing from a territory or class of business. In other cases, the individual files within the book are reviewed and appropriate action taken. The review program, then, becomes a special means of identifying problem risks on which underwriting action might be needed, and the file referral is based on the fact that the risk belongs to the group that is being reviewed.

Book of business monitoring techniques can best be illustrated by the use of examples. Four types of group monitoring examples—class, territory, producer, and type of loss—are discussed below. The first two illustrations are presented in a case-type format.

Class The branch office underwriting manager reviewed monthly statistical data from the past three years on the various use classifications of insured vehicles. The use classifications involved were: pleasure only; pleasure plus to and from work less than fifteen miles one way; pleasure plus to and from work more than fifteen miles one way; pleasure and business use; farm use. The manager plotted the data for pleasure use only and found an increase over the three-year period from 22 percent to 42 percent of insured vehicles in that class. This startling increase indicated the possibility of widespread misclassification and prompted a review.

The increase in the pleasure use class, which included autos driven to and from work less than three miles one way, was accompanied by a decline in the percentage of vehicles used to and from work less than fifteen miles one way. Despite a continuing emphasis on proper classification and rating, the information provided by the company's management information system led to a basic assumption that too many auto units were misclassified. Given the nature of the evidence—a sharp increase in lower-rated business—the indication was a substantial loss in premium dollars.

A decision was made to survey a random sample of accounts to check the validity of the assumption. An outside reporting agency was called in, and a special report form was devised. Producers were advised of the activity, and the survey proceeded. As the reports came in, the results were recorded by risk, by producer, and in the aggregate. Policy changes were performed immediately, and any indicated additional or return premium was also recorded.

The completed survey showed that among the risks in the sample, 43 percent should have been, but were not, rated as being used to and from work over three miles one way. In addition, the reports developed information on additional drivers and vehicles. The average additional premium developed for the 200 policies over the current policy period was $15, or a total of $3,000. Out-of-pocket cost per inspection was $2.50 per policy, or a total of $500. Thus, the premium developed more than offset the expenses. Even if administrative costs were added, the additional premium for the current *and* renewal periods would more than cover total costs.

As a result of the findings of this survey, a comprehensive program was established to develop and maintain proper classification information on all risks rated as pleasure use only. This point is critical. A one-time effort may have a broad, but only temporary, effect. The real impact of the monitoring effort will come as underwriters become more aware of the need to properly administer the classification plan so that slippage is minimal and the book of business develops the earned premium commensurate with the exposures involved.

Territory After expanding its scope of operations to include southern California and several states in the far southwest, a regional company noticed a deterioration in its auto physical damage loss ratio. Analysis of results by territory isolated the problem to comprehensive coverage in the new areas in which it was writing. Loss runs for those new areas indicated a peril—wind-driven sand—that the company was unaccustomed to in the areas in which it had been operating for some time. Small losses caused by sand pitting the paint on insured vehicles prompted the corrective action of a mandatory $100 deductible on comprehensive coverage for all new business *and* renewals in most rating territories in the new areas.

Producer Depending on the objectives of the monitoring activity and the capabilities of the data retrieval system, data on risks by producer (and perhaps even by individual producer within an agency) can be isolated and analyzed on a number of bases—loss ratio, rating classification, youthful drivers, high performance or sports cars, types of losses, average premium, and the like. It is common to routinely develop periodic (e.g., quarterly, semi-annual, annual) data by producer on volume, loss ratio, types of business (e.g., auto, homeowners, commercial, etc.) and perhaps other bases.

A great deal of attention is paid to loss ratios, but their significance often is blunted by a lack of credibility in the data on a particular producer. One or two serious losses could keep a producer's book of business unprofitable over several years even though the book, on a risk by risk basis, is of good underwriting quality. Comparisons over several years often are necessary before anything approaching a statistically reliable body of data can be developed.

If the data on a producer indicate a problem with that producer's book of business, the entire book may be isolated for intensive review mid-term or prior to renewal and close attention may be paid to future submissions. Loss runs or loss files may provide useful information. These can sometimes indicate if a particular segment of the producer's business is responsible for the problem, and they may also indicate patterns of discrepancy between application information and information resulting from claims. The company's field representative may have additional insight. He or she may suspect adverse selection due to competition from other companies in the producer's office, or may be aware of poorly trained people working there.

Type of Loss Various types of losses have been the target of book of business reviews, often with considerable success. Examples are all liability losses (to identify negligent operators), all "backing-up" types of losses (to identify operators who are careless or restricted in ability to look behind their cars), and all losses on which a citation was issued (to locate drivers who violate the laws). The only limit to the types of losses which could be reviewed on a group basis is the coding system used by the claim department. Not all of these may be productive, so careful analysis and sampling are needed before a large-scale program is undertaken.

THE PERSONAL AUTO UNDERWRITING ENVIRONMENT

The purpose of this section is to describe the social, economic, and regulatory factors which make up the auto underwriting environment. The impact of this environment on the decisions of underwriting management will also be considered. Making sound underwriting decisions within the context of this complex and changing environment represents one of the most challenging aspects of auto underwriting.

The Social Climate

The late Morris R. Cohen of the City College of New York asked his classes to imagine that a superhuman being appeared on earth and offered to make life incomparably more pleasant and easy in return for the blood sacrifice of 50,000 people a year. Most of Cohen's students were certain that such a request would be rejected, until they were reminded of the auto.[1]

The Economic Importance of the Auto The auto has made life easier, but the sacrificial price has also been paid. Prior to the fifty-five mile per hour speed limit, more Americans were killed and maimed on the highways annually than in the entire Vietnam conflict. Deaths from auto accidents declined after the enactment of the fifty-five mile per hour speed limit, but in recent years such deaths have again begun to increase. Property damage losses have also been enormous, showing a high frequency and severity. The New York Insurance Department estimated that one in four drivers would be involved in a motor vehicle accident each year. Over 56 percent of all drivers would be involved in an accident within three years, 75 percent within five years, and every driver within twenty.[2] The auto hazard is significant for every driver, passenger, pedestrian, and property owner.

The auto has also contributed greatly to the economic growth of the United States. It is the most frequently purchased durable good. The rise and fall of purchases of new cars is inexorably tied to our economic growth. The auto is also directly responsible for a multitude of derivative businesses—from oil companies to fast food restaurants, from drive-in movies to auto insurance companies.

The Necessity of Auto Insurance The importance of the car to our economy and our life-styles combined with the significance of the hazard it presents make auto insurance a virtual necessity. A car represents a large investment. Today, it is difficult to find a new car with a list price under $6,000. And for many people, the car represents the ability to earn a living, as the car is needed to get to and from work or school. Auto insurance is also necessary because of the damage that can be done to others.

The growing necessity for such insurance has led many to believe that it should be compulsory. A statement frequently heard is that auto insurance "should be available to everyone who drives"; often added to this statement is ". . . at a price he can afford."

The Regulatory Factor Regulation is still another environmental factor to be considered. Long before the car became economically feasible to produce, insurance was regulated. The development of autos and the insurance to cover them merely added another line of insurance to regulate. Such regulation is carried out mostly by people in political posts. Of the fifty-two jurisdictions (including Washington, D.C., and Puerto Rico), over half of the regulators are appointed by governors with or without "advice and consent" of the legislature. The others are elected officials, or are appointed by persons, commissions, or governmental bodies other than the chief executive officer of the state. In only one state, Colorado, is it a civil service appointment.

Changes in the profitability of insurers change the mood of regulators. Also, the types of regulations change over a period of time. Many are legislated changes, such as moving from a fault to a no-fault system. Many are interpreted differently or receive different emphasis. An example is the 1974-75 change in the regulators' stress on the "readability" issue back to protecting the solvency of companies. All of these changes in the regulatory process affect the climate in which underwriters must operate.

Auto underwriting would be difficult because of these problems alone. However, in addition, the goals of society are not static. Demands, beliefs, and desires do not remain constant for the individual or society. The underwriting climate is changing constantly.

General Regulation of Auto Insurance

There are several reasons for the existence of regulation in the field of insurance. A primary reason is to assure the solvency of companies, because insurer solvency protects the public. Another reason is to prevent unfair discrimination. Still another is to offset any lack of market competition so that the public will receive all of the benefits of a competitive marketplace.

Implicit in the last reason, the offsetting of a lack of market competition, is an assumption that the line of insurance being regulated lacks one or more of the following elements of a purely competitive system:

1. a large number of sellers—none of which is sufficiently large to affect the price;
2. a large number of buyers—none of which is large enough to obtain a "discount";
3. a uniform product;
4. freedom of entry and exit into the marketplace by companies; and
5. perfect product and price knowledge within the marketplace.

The auto insurance business qualifies for regulation on at least one of these accounts—perfect knowledge. Consumers often do not know what they have purchased when they buy this insurance. They know that their car is "covered," but to a large degree, they do not know the details of the coverage provided. This lack of consumer knowledge about insurance gives insurance regulators a reason to regulate.

The fourth element listed above, freedom of entry and exit into the marketplace by companies, may also apply to the auto insurance business. If "marketplace" is interpreted to mean companies that are sound, there should be freedom for these companies to enter or leave any market—to foster competition and improve the availability of the insurance. This type of freedom does exist and should not be regulated. However, if "marketplace" refers to a freedom of any company to enter the market, or to retire at will, this is not socially justifiable. It would be bad public policy to allow new insurance firms to begin selling auto insurance with inadequate capital, policies incompatible with competitors, inadequate rates, and so on. Neither would it be good public policy to allow firms to retire from the business and leave their current policyholders and claimants without much hope of having losses paid. However, an orderly withdrawal from a marketplace due to continued adverse loss experience should not be denied any company in a free enterprise system.

The figures on the status of state laws and the various involuntary plans in the states used in the succeeding pages are current as of this writing. Laws and regulations change the rules at frequent but irregular intervals. Underwriters are cautioned to secure current information for any state in which they are interested, and to consider this text as information on trends and patterns only.

Rate Regulation Since the days of Public Law 15, the nature of rate regulation has changed. Particularly since the mid-1960s, the changes have become more pronounced. Immediately after passage of the McCarran Act, forty-seven of the then forty-eight states passed a version of the "all-industry rate law." In short, this law required auto insurers to have their rates approved *in advance* of their use. Insurers would submit rates to the various regulators and could not use them until approved. The forty-eighth state, California, took a different position and required that rates could be regulated but did not have to be approved. The trend since 1945 has been toward a California-type system, but there has certainly not been a wholesale adoption of the California law. Exhibit 5-1 shows, in simplified form, the status of rate regulation as of 1981. (This categorization may be somewhat misleading in that some states use different types of laws for different lines of insurance.)

Types of Rate Regulation. Under the California-type "open competition" rate law, no requirements are spelled out other than the basic ones common to all rating laws. Companies may use the rating systems and rate levels they see fit, although they are required to justify rates if necessary and to make rate information available to the insurance department. They must be able to prove that they are using their rating systems as prescribed by the rules promulgated with the rate system.

A second system is the *use and file system.* Rate changes may be put into effect immediately, but the rating plans and rates are to be filed subsequently with the insurance regulator.

Reversing the order, a *file and use system* has become popular since Georgia enacted the first of this type of law in the late 1960s. It is very similar to use and file, except that companies must first file rates with an effective date with the commissioner. After the effective date, the company is free to use its new system of rate levels, unless disapproved before the effective date.

The *all industry* or *prior approval system* is still the most common form of rate regulation. All rating systems and levels must be *filed* with and *approved* by the regulator in advance of their use. There are hybrids of this system. For instance, some laws state that the rates absolutely cannot be used without the commissioner's approval. Others state that if the commissioner has not acted on the approval of rates within a specified time period, thirty days, for example, the rates become effective. Laws of this nature are said to be prior approval with "deemer provisions,"—after the specified time period, the rates are deemed to be approved. Another variety of prior approval is one which states that rates and rating systems have to be approved prior to use only if they are "bureau" rates.

Some states use a *modified prior approval system.* Under it, once rate levels and systems have been approved, changes can be made in rate *levels* without prior approval if there is no effect on the expense portion of the filing. Those changes that affect the relative level of expenses to total premium must be approved prior to use.

An extension of file and use and prior approval laws is the one adopted by North Carolina. Not only are companies required to file

Exhibit 5-1
Type of Rate Regulation by State (As of 1981)

State	Kind of Rating Law
Alabama	Prior Approval*
Alaska	Prior Approval
Arizona	Use and File
Arkansas	File and Use
California	No File
Colorado	No File
Connecticut	File and Use
Delaware	Prior Approval
District of Columbia	Prior Approval**
Florida	Use and File
Georgia	File and Use
Hawaii	Prior Approval
Idaho	No File
Illinois	Use and File
Indiana	File and Use
Iowa	Prior Approval
Kansas	Prior Approval
Kentucky	Prior Approval
Louisiana	Prior Approval*
Maine	Prior Approval
Maryland	Prior Approval
Massachusetts	Prior Approval
Michigan	Prior Approval
Minnesota	File and Use
Mississippi	Prior Approval
Missouri	Use and File
Montana	File and Use
Nebraska	Prior Approval
Nevada	File and Use
New Hampshire	Prior Approval
New Jersey	Prior Approval
New Mexico	Use and File
New York	File and Use***
North Carolina	File and Use
North Dakota	Prior Approval
Ohio	Prior Approval**
Oklahoma	Prior Approval
Oregon	File and Use
Pennsylvania	Prior Approval

Continued on next page

Rhode Island	Prior Approval
South Carolina	Prior Approval
South Dakota	Prior Approval
Tennessee	Prior Approval
Texas	Prior Approval
Utah	Use and File
Vermont	Prior Approval
Virginia	File and Use
Washington	Prior Approval
West Virginia	Prior Approval
Wisconsin	Use and File
Wyoming	Prior Approval

* Certain types of filings are File and Use.
** Casualty filings are File and Use.
*** Filings changing classification or territory are subject to prior approval.

their rates ninety days in advance (subject to the disapproval of the commissioner) but all companies operating in North Carolina must belong to a single rate-making bureau and use their rates exclusively in the state for certain property lines of insurance.

Only slightly different from North Carolina's *mandatory bureau* law are the *state-made rates* laws of Texas and Massachusetts. Companies operating in those two states are required to use the rates developed by a state agency. Deviations may or may not be allowed. In the exhibit, these are shown as prior approval since in essence the changes are "approved" prior to their being used by the companies.

The types of rating laws are easy to differentiate at the extremes, but the prior approval laws may differ subtly. Information on the types of rating laws that exist in each territory and the regulatory philosophy and attitudes used to administer the laws is generally available in each branch or regional office. Only with this knowledge can an underwriter know the degree of flexibility which is available and to what extent rate adjustments can be used to help solve loss ratio problems. If rate relief is not available, underwriting standards must be adjusted to achieve and maintain profits.

Requirements of Rate Laws. In addition to prescribing how and when rate level changes can be made, rate laws also provide for certain administrative practices or procedures that can affect the underwriter. Almost every jurisdiction requires that rates be "adequate, reasonable, and not unfairly discriminatory."

"Adequate" means that the rate levels used, over a period of time and with the current book of business or anticipated book, will produce an income sufficient to cover all losses and expenses, and produce a contribution to surplus (a profit). The insurance code of one state explains adequate by defining inadequate rates:

> No rate shall be held to be inadequate unless: (1) such rate is unreasonably low for the insurance provided, and (2) the continued use of such rate endangers the solvency of the insurer using the same, or unless (3) such rate is unreasonably low for the insurance provided and the use of such rate by the insurer using same has, or if continued will have, the effect of destroying competition or creating a monopoly.[3]

The system of pricing used by insurers often provides for rate adequacy only immediately after a rate increase has gone into effect, though companies are generally permitted to use trend data. Unless projection on such items as "crash parts," jury verdicts, defense costs, and the like is allowed and included in the rate formulation, rates will become quickly inadequate, and underwriting selection standards must be adjusted.

"Reasonable" means that the rates will not be excessive, nor produce "excessive profit" for the insurer. Not all states include the "reasonable" test, but most do include a provision for excessive rates. This area has not created quite the problem that rate adequacy has, but it is an area of underwriting concern. The reasonableness test involves both elements of a rate—the loss portion and the expense portion. If rates were based on individual loss experience in private passenger auto, there would be no "insurance" which implies a pooling of losses. A more important part of reasonableness is the expense portion of the rate. It would be easy to spend money on unnecessary expenses and inflate the rate, passing on to the consumer an insurer's lack of expense control, but rate competition helps prevent that kind of activity. In an open market, an insurer with a high rate level will not attract much business; and the business secured may produce adverse selection.

The final test is that rates be "not unfairly discriminatory." Appropriate discrimination is allowed. Risks with significant hazards that have or will likely generate greater losses than other risks without those hazards should pay more for their insurance. A newly licensed sixteen-year-old should pay more than a twenty-five-year-old with a nine year accident- and violation-free history.

The problems which insurers and underwriters face with these rate tests come principally from the interpretation of the words by regulators, the extent to which each word is enforced, and the balance necessary between these rate requirements on one hand and the need for rate credibility on the other.

Administrative procedures for examining rates also can cause underwriting problems. A file and use law is designed to provide insurers with a means to obtain adequate rates within a short period of time. Yet each file and use law contains provisions that allow the regulator to "disapprove" a rate filing. Usually there must be hearings scheduled and the rate level is allowed to stand for a time, but it can be subsequently disapproved. Of course, this problem does not exist with the prior approval type of law.

A final provision, most common in states with no filing requirement or with file and use laws, is for rate examinations used to test for unfair discrimination. Georgia, under its file and use law, provides for rate examinations each five years, or sooner if requested by the commissioner. The examination process is to audit a sample of policies to determine if the rates filed match those which were charged to insureds. Any significant "discrimination" within or among classes may be revealed by the examination. At that point, the commissioner can use "subsequent disapproval," or other appropriate remedies, to correct the situation.

Forms Regulation Usually the law relative to insurance forms is included in the rating law because the coverage afforded under a form is a major determinant of rate. However, that does not mean that the type of rating law dictates the regulation of forms. For instance, Wisconsin has a use and file rating law, but uses a file and use forms law. North Dakota has a prior approval rating law and a file and use forms law. Pennsylvania uses the prior approval method for both rates and forms.

The importance of these laws was seen in the problems of theft of citizens band radios from cars. Loss frequency was so high that many companies filed endorsements eliminating coverage, just as they had done in the 1960s on stereo tape decks. Such an endorsement would be easier to implement in Wisconsin than in Pennsylvania.

Unless the change is drastic, approval is usually quick. Companies filing for "readable" auto policies can expect their forms to take a longer time for approval. In addition to the usual regulatory checks on coverages, exclusions, and so on, "readable" policies are subject to readability tests that include such items as the number of words in a sentence, number of syllables in a sentence, size of type, amount of "white space," and the like. Readable policies also introduce new language which has not been tested by the courts.

The underwriter should be familiar with the rating and forms laws for each territory handled. They are related, and the ability of a company to get rate relief, or to exclude a coverage, is dependent on both types of laws. The type of rate and forms laws used in a particular state is not the only important element in rate adequacy. States have tried to deal with this problem in many ways—through compulsory insurance, financial responsibility, and residual market laws. In the next section, these laws will be examined in detail.

Underwriting Impact of Other Laws and Practices

Legislation has been enacted in every state to restrict the denial of auto insurance to applicants and to make provision for the insuring of those persons who are denied access to the voluntary market.

Most of the laws discussed in this section are compulsory—either for the insured or the insurance company. The goal of these laws is to allow anyone with a valid driver's license to have access to auto insurance. Laws relating to compulsory insurance and financial responsibility are directed at insureds; those relating to residual market programs, cancellation, and nonrenewal are directed at insurers. They attempt to keep a market open for all drivers.

It must be emphasized that not all residual market insureds are "bad" risks. In many cases, newly licensed drivers for instance, they have just not had a chance to prove that they are good. Others find themselves in the residual market because the private insurance mechanism has not developed the methods to handle unusual situations in the voluntary market.

Rate adequacy is vital in order for any of these laws to work. Where insurers are allowed to charge an adequate rate, none of these laws affects profitability. When laws inhibit rate adequacy, underwriting problems increase.

Laws Restricting Cancellation The auto insurance policy, like other contracts, originally contained a provision that either party could cancel the agreement. The usual provision was that the insurer must give at least five or sometimes ten days' advance written notice. A return of most or all of the unearned premium was, of course, provided.

Social and political pressures have caused the adoption of legislation or regulations in almost every state which supersede the original policy provision regarding cancellation. Insurers are forbidden to cancel policies during the policy period for any reason except nonpayment of premium and revocation of driver's license, and, in some states, misrepresentation, serious health impairment, or other reasons.

Otherwise, the only means available to an insurer who wishes to retire from a risk is to refuse to renew or to continue beyond the expiration date, and even then, the insured must be notified of the decision not to renew at least a specified number of days in advance of the expiration date of the policy. The number of days' notice varies by state, with twenty and thirty being the most common. Additionally, many states restrict the reasons for which insurers may nonrenew auto policies. This is discussed later in this section.

Most states have laws of this type. A number of states also require elaborate procedures and language in the notices of nonrenewal. These deal generally with the size of the print on the notice, the specific words used, and procedures for appeal by the insured and the disposition of the appeal.

Underwriters operating under such cancellation laws must select applicants carefully. If a risk is accepted, the underwriter is powerless to cancel the coverage or to write the risk in a higher rated plan until expiration (and not even then, in some cases).

All of these laws provide for a period of thirty to ninety days (most states use sixty days) within which the underwriter can cancel the coverage. This permits investigation of new applicants; however, it requires the underwriter to decide quickly on the types of information desired, and to make a decision promptly. If action is not taken within this initial time period, the coverage cannot be terminated until it expires at the end of the term. Many companies have a procedure whereby producers can submit an application to the underwriter without binding coverage. Coverage becomes effective only upon approval of the underwriter and, until that time, the application is not subject to the cancellation law.

Some states have gone even further to prohibit a denial of renewal except under specified conditions. Arizona, for example, permits nonrenewal only for nonpayment of premium, misrepresentation, revocation of driver's license during the policy period, permanent disability, or conviction within the preceding thirty-six months of a major violation like reckless driving, leaving the scene of an accident, or drunken driving.

Idaho permits nonrenewal only for such reasons as nonpayment of premium, misrepresentation, submitting a false claim, revocation of driver's license during the preceding three years, history of heart attack, use of alcohol or drugs to excess, conviction within the preceding three years of major violations (as in Arizona), a threat to public safety because of an accident record or defective mechanical condition, or conviction of three or more violations within the preceding three years. Note that a frequency of convictions may result in nonrenewal, but *not* a frequency of accidents.

Underwriters operating under these types of guaranteed-renewal laws must be even more careful in selecting risks. Additional care must be taken when it is realized that, once retained past the discovery period, a risk might remain on the books indefinitely. When restrictions are placed on the underwriting following a claim or the receipt of other types of adverse information, the selection standards at the inception must be tightened. Exceptions should be made very sparingly.

The more extreme the law restricting cancellation or nonrenewal, the more important the underwriting becomes on new applicants. Underwriters must realize that all of the normal underwriting during the life of the policy is concentrated on the selection of new applicants, since later underwriting is prohibited or restricted. Such a law would not, in itself, preclude an insurer from adopting a rate structure with surcharges for risks that develop adverse loss experience but cannot be canceled or nonrenewed.

The trend is toward more stringent laws. These constraints make the underwriter's job more difficult. Some observers believe that the industry is approaching the point where selection will no longer exist. In a few states, that point has already been reached. These laws will be discussed below, following a discusion of certain laws dealing with drivers themselves.

Compulsory Insurance Laws There are two types of laws which impose an insurance-related duty on the driver: compulsory insurance laws which require auto insurance as a requisite to obtaining a driver's license, vehicle registration, or tags; and financial responsibility laws which require proof of financial responsibility after an accident or moving violation.

Exhibit 5-2 lists the twenty-seven states with compulsory insurance laws.

Policing is the key to making a compulsory insurance system work. For instance, in New York, an insurance identification card is required before a license plate is issued. The card must remain in the vehicle at all times. A driver without such a card is subject to fine, suspension, and, in some cases, imprisonment. New York originally had a system whereby the state was notified when insurance was canceled. The Department of Motor Vehicles or state police would investigate cancellation notices received from insurers. If they were able to match a change in vehicle registration with a cancellation notice, no follow-up was required. If there was no matching, the state police or sheriff's office in the insured's jurisdiction would be empowered to remove the license plates if no other insurance was obtained. This type of system obviously required a great deal of paper work and leg work on the part of the state. The process became so cumbersome in New York that a subsequent law relieved the companies of sending a notice of cancellation. Consequently, it is possible for an insured to buy a car, obtain insurance and the ID card, let the policy lapse, and drive without coverage. At the next vehicle registration issue date, the insured would

Exhibit 5-2
States With Compulsory Automobile Liability Insurance as of January 1981*

California	
Colorado	Montana
Connecticut	Nevada
Delaware	New Jersey
Georgia	New York
Hawaii	North Carolina
Idaho	North Dakota
Kansas	Oklahoma
Kentucky	Oregon
Louisiana	Pennsylvania
Maryland	South Carolina
Massachusetts	Utah
Michigan	West Virginia
Minnesota	Wyoming

* Adapted with permission from *Summary of Selected State Laws and Regulations Relating to Automobile Insurance* (New York: American Insurance Association, 1981), pp. 44-60.

obtain insurance again, perhaps making a small down payment on the new policy, and the process would begin again.

The success of compulsory auto insurance laws is directly related to the state's willingness to enforce the law. Failure to comply would mean loss of license (or tag), a fine, and/or a prison term. Some states place drivers in the position of being insurers if they do not comply with the law.

As examples, in California, violation of the compulsory insurance law is an infraction punishable by a fine up to $100. Colorado suspends the license after an at-fault accident and makes the driver personally liable for any no-fault benefits. Noncompliance in Georgia is a misdemeanor punishable by fine and confinement. In Kentucky, "an owner who fails to provide security for liability insurance is subject to a fine, has the duty of an insurer to provide first party benefits, and is subject to subrogation by an insurer providing first party benefits."[4] Minnesota's noncompliance law provides for suspension of owner's registration and operator's license for six to twelve months.

Massachusetts was the first state to require insurance. New York and North Carolina followed in the late 1950s. Most of the twenty most recent states to enact this type of legislation did so primarily because of the introduction of no-fault benefits. Their thinking was that since the driver's own insurance would pay under no-fault, drivers should carry insurance to make certain that benefits were payable.

The underwriting impact of compulsory insurance laws varies, depending upon the individual types of underwriting practiced by companies. The principal underwriting problem when a state adopts a compulsory system is the handling of people who were previously uninsured, but who are now purchasing coverage. For some companies, a move to compulsory insurance would mean no change in underwriting procedures. For instance, if a company would accept a new insured with no previous insurance without a compulsory law, the compulsory law adds little to the underwriting process. Such a company would automatically proceed with an inspection and motor vehicle report for any "no previous insurer" application.

One final aspect of compulsory insurance laws may be important for the underwriter. If the state has such a law, and has adopted an extremely restrictive cancellation/nonrenewal law, new business underwriting must be thorough. The challenge to underwriters is selecting the good risks in a poor class such as youthful operators. If proper selection and monitoring are accomplished, there should be no unusual problems except for the large volume of new business when the law is put into effect.

Financial Responsibility Laws Most states have some kind of financial responsibility law, as shown in Exhibit 5-3. The aim of these laws is to have all drivers prove that they are financially able to meet any legal requirements that may be rendered against them. In states without compulsory insurance laws, this usually means that after a serious motor vehicle accident, conviction for specified moving violations, or judgment because of a motor vehicle accident, such proof must be given to retain a license or registration. The laws are specific as to what constitutes proof of financial responsibility, what minimum limits are required if an insurance policy is used as proof, and so on.

There is no consistency among the state laws as to how long proof of financial responsibility must be maintained. Two or three years is fairly common for all types—motor vehicle accidents, convictions for moving violations, and judgments rendered because of a motor vehicle accident.

A driver or owner is most likely to have to file proof of financial responsibility after a motor vehicle accident. This is because most states require a form to be filed with the state after an accident that develops property damage ranging from minimums of $50 to $500 or more, or where bodily injury is involved. Insurance information is required on the accident form. With the exception of five states, proof of financial responsibility must be filed by both the driver and owner of

Exhibit 5-3

Table Of Limits—Financial Responsibility and Compulsory Insurance Laws*

The table that follows displays the minimum financial responsibility and compulsory limits for all states, the District of Columbia, and the Canadian provinces. (Limits are expressed in thousands.)

	Liability Limits[1]		Liability Limits[1]
Alabama	$10/20/5	New Brunswick	100
Alaska	25/50/10	Newfoundland	75
Alberta	100	New Hampshire	25/50/25
Arizona	15/30/10	New Jersey	15/30/5
Arkansas	25/50/15	New Mexico	15/30/5
British Columbia	100	New York	10/20/5[2]
California	15/30/5	Northwest Territories	50
Colorado	15/30/5	North Carolina	25/50/10
Connecticut	20/40/5	North Dakota	25/50/10
Delaware	10/20/5	Nova Scotia	100
District of Columbia	10/20/5	Ohio	12.5/25/7.5
Florida	10/20/5	Oklahoma	10/20/10
Georgia	10/20/5	Ontario	200
Hawaii	25/Unlimited/10	Oregon	15/30/5
Idaho	10/20/5	Pennsylvania	15/30/5
Illinois	15/30/10	Prince Edward Island	100
Indiana	15/30/10	Quebec	50[3]
Iowa	15/30/10	Rhode Island	25/50/10
Kansas	25/50/10	Saskatchewan	35
Kentucky	10/20/5	South Carolina	15/30/5
Louisiana	5/10/1	South Dakota	15/30/10
Maine	20/40/10	Tennessee	10/20/5
Manitoba	50	Texas	10/20/5
Maryland	20/40/10	Utah	20/40/10[4]
Massachusetts	10/20/5	Vermont	20/40/10
Michigan	20/40/10	Virginia	25/50/10
Minnesota	25/50/10	Washington	25/50/10
Mississippi	10/20/5	West Virginia	20/40/10
Missouri	25/50/10	Wisconsin	15/30/10
Montana	25/50/5	Wyoming	10/20/5
Nebraska	15/30/10	Yukon	75
Nevada	15/30/10		

[1] The first two figures refer to bodily injury liability limits and the third figure to property damage liability for example, 10/20/5 means coverage up to $20,000 for all persons injured in an accident, subject to a limit to $10,000 for one individual and $5,000 coverage for property damage.

[2] 50/100 for wrongful death.

[3] Because Quebec has a complete no-fault system for bodily injury, the minimum limit applies only to property damage within Quebec and combined bodily injury and property damage outside Quebec.

[4] Or, $30,000 combined single limit.

* Adapted from *F. C. & S. Bulletins*, Personal Lines Section (Cincinnati, OH: The National Underwriter Company); Personal Auto; p. Frld-1 (January 1982).

the vehicle involved, in those states with such a provision. It can be seen that after an accident, insurance coverage does become mandatory (or compulsory) if the owner and/or operator wish to continue driving.

In most noncompulsory states, if the driver of a vehicle appears to be at fault, the underwriter may have to file an SR-22 form, proof of financial responsibility, with the state. The SR-22 is a verification that the driver who had an accident or traffic violation and was without insurance at the time, now has insurance coverage. The insurer filing the SR-22 declares that insurance is in effect until it files a notice of termination.

Most states have exemptions from filing of proof of financial responsibility. For instance, Arizona does not require filing of proof of financial responsibility if the operator was released from liability. Oklahoma does not require proof if the vehicle was operated under the direction of the police. There are many other exemptions. Most of these laws and their provisions affect underwriters only when they are requested to file such proof.

Many companies specialize in risks requiring financial responsibility filings. These companies are often referred to as the "nonstandard market." For underwriters in these companies, financial responsibility filings are common. In companies that are allowed nonstandard rating plans or other types of rate flexibility, SR-22 filings may represent a small segment of their daily activity. For auto underwriters in companies writing preferred or standard business, SR-22 filings and associated underwriting are infrequent, occurring only when a producer is seeking a very special accommodation.

The one other time that underwriters specializing in preferred or standard business may become involved in SR-22 filings and the underwriting surrounding such filings is when they are involved in residual market programs. The remainder of this section will address itself to those programs and the underwriting environment surrounding them.

Residual Market Programs The marketing of any product brings with it problems of distribution. In auto insurance, a significant portion of the driving public cannot get coverage through the voluntary distribution system. Yet auto insurance is in some ways quasi-compulsory, so they need the coverage. In order to serve this market, New Hampshire installed an *assigned risk plan* in 1938 and by 1959, all states had such programs, now called *automobile insurance plans.*

The seed for residual markets was planted with the passage of financial responsibility laws. The industry grappled with many possible solutions: state-run plans were a possibility; insurers could pool the experience of this group and share premiums and losses; applicants

Exhibit 5-4
Subsidies Paid on Behalf of Cars Insured in Selected Assigned Risk Plans—1978*

State	Subsidy per Car	Average Actuarial Premium Needed per Car	Subsidy as Percentage of Average Actuarial Premium
New Jersey	$152.21	$386.69	39.4
New York	6.18	380.09	1.6
Pennsylvania	132.55	359.85	36.8
California	36.39	389.65	9.3
Virginia	20.36	246.27	8.3
Louisiana	25.77	245.59	10.5
Michigan	37.71	269.25	14.0
Georgia	3.56	147.14	2.4
Connecticut	42.77	351.30	12.2

* Adapted from *AIPSO Insurance Facts 1980* (New York: Automobile Insurance Plans Service Office, 1980), p. 38.

could be shared; or any number of other possibilities. Originally, the industry settled on the "applicant-sharing" idea, based on an individual company's share of the voluntary market. Due to the minimum limits required under the financial responsibility laws, a fairly uniform exposure would be shared by the companies, and the risk units (insureds) assumed by the companies would be randomly assigned to alleviate the problem of adverse selection. The plans were intended to be self-supporting, but that goal has not been achieved.

Since the early 1970s some states have turned away from the automobile insurance plan applicant-sharing programs to other forms, and each of these is discussed briefly on the following pages. The dominant residual market form is still the automobile insurance plan, with forty-two states and the District of Columbia using variations of it. Florida, Missouri, and Hawaii have gone to a joint underwriting association (JUA) system. Massachusetts, North Carolina, New Hampshire, and South Carolina have gone to the reinsurance facility plan. Maryland has adopted a state insurance plan for its residual market.

Exhibit 5-4 shows the amount of subsidy paid in 1978 on behalf of each car insured under the nine largest assigned risk plans. These states account for about 87 percent of the premiums and about 99 percent of the subsidies of all assigned risk plans or automobile insurance plans (not including reinsurance plans or joint underwriting association) in 1978.

Exhibit 5-5 shows the needed premiums and subsidies for 1978 for the seven states that had reinsurance plans or JUAs in that year.

Exhibit 5-5
Subsidies Paid on Behalf of Cars Insured in Joint Underwriting Associations and Reinsurance Plans—1978*

State	Subsidy per Car	Average Actuarial Premium Needed per Car	Subsidy as Percentage of Average Actuarial Premium
Florida	$ 0	$462.16	0
Hawaii	201.31	512.29	39.3
Massachusetts	146.33	419.27	34.9
Missouri	60.80	540.07	11.26
New Hampshire	77.86	352.10	22.1
North Carolina	36.29	159.45	22.8
South Carolina	46.19	291.32	15.9

* Adapted from data in *AIPSO Insurance Facts 1980* (New York: Automobile Insurance Plans Service Office, 1980), pp. 22-23, 137.

Michigan adopted a JUA effective 1 January 1981 but had an assigned risk plan (automobile insurance plan) in 1978.

There can be no question as to the need for residual market programs in view of the inability to secure adequate rates in some states and the lack of ability to pay on the part of some insureds. Exhibit 5-6 shows the various types of plans in each state and the size of the residual market in each state. As shown in Exhibit 5-6, over 32.4 percent of the private passenger auto market in Massachusetts is written through its reinsurance facility. New Jersey had about 29 percent. At the other extreme, there were twenty states with less than 1 percent penetration.

In spite of residual markets there are a significant number of drivers uninsured. In 1978, only 86.9 percent of registered vehicles were insured (up from 86.5 percent in 1975).[5] Of all vehicles registered in the United States in 1978 about 6.9 percent were insured by the residual market. The remainder of this discussion will center on the different types of residual market plans and their underwriting implications.

Automobile Insurance Plans (Formerly Called Assigned Risk Plans). Automobile insurance plans are the most common type of residual market plans. Each state has its own plan and no two are exactly alike, although there are similarities that can be discussed. Automobile insurance plans are of four basic types.

"Plan A" is a minimum limit of liability plan where each company uses its own rates to determine the price paid by the driver. This plan is in operation only in Puerto Rico.

"Plan B" is used by nine states. It again offers the states' minimum

Exhibit 5-6
Type of Residual Market Program and State Rank by Residual Market Penetration—1980*

	Percent of Penetration	Type of Program†		Percent of Penetration	Type of Program†
1. Utah	.03%	AIP	27. Mississippi	3.12%	AIP
2. Arizona	.08	AIP	28. Dist. of Columbia	3.15	AIP
3. Nebraska	.09	AIP	29. Tennessee	3.93	AIP
4. Colorado	.10	AIP	30. California	3.98	AIP
5. Montana	.11	AIP	31. Michigan	4.02	JUA[1]
6. Nevada	.13	AIP	32. Kansas	4.19	AIP
7. South Dakota	.15	AIP	33. Vermont	4.40	AIP
8. Iowa	.16	AIP	34. Maine	5.02	AIP
9. Oregon	.17	AIP	35. Maryland	5.33	SF
10. Idaho	.18	AIP	36. Alaska	5.68	AIP
11. Indiana	.18	AIP	37. Texas	5.75	AIP
12. Ohio	.18	AIP	38. Georgia	6.65	AIP
13. Wisconsin	.19	AIP	39. Pennsylvania	7.37	AIP
14. Oklahoma	.24	AIP	40. Rhode Island	8.67	AIP
15. Wyoming	.24	AIP	41. Delaware	9.10	AIP
16. New Mexico	.25	AIP	42. Virginia	9.52	AIP
17. North Dakota	.37	AIP	43. Connecticut	10.57	AIP
18. Arkansas	.86	AIP	44. Florida	13.43	JUA
19. Alabama	.93	AIP	45. New York	13.60	AIP
20. Illinois	.99	AIP	46. New Hampshire	15.43	RF
21. Washington	1.43	AIP	47. Louisiana	18.11	AIP
22. Missouri	1.44	JUA	48. N. Carolina	26.49	RF
23. Minnesota	1.52	AIP	49. S. Carolina	27.96	RF
24. West Virginia	1.60	AIP	50. New Jersey	29.38	AIP
25. Kentucky	2.29	AIP	51. Mass.	32.43	RF
26. Hawaii	2.95	JUP			

† AIP—Automobile Insurance Plan
JUA—Joint Underwriting Association
JUP—Joint Underwriting Plan
SF—State Fund
RF—Reinsurance Facility

[1] Effective 1 January 1981

* Adapted from Joseph J. Kopsick, CPCU, *Market Characteristics and Residual Market Population* (Des Plaines, IL: National Association of Independent Insurers, 1981), pp. 12, 13 and *AIPSO Insurance Facts 1980* (New York: Automobile Insurance Plans Service Office, 1980), p. 3.

legal limits of liability, but all companies use the same uniform rates for all participants in the plan.

"Modified Plan B" represents the trend in automobile insurance plans. It includes more coverage than basic liability limits. The insured has the option to increase his or her liability limits above the minimums up to 100/300/50, in some states. Physical damage coverage is also available but limited to private passenger, light commercial, motorcycle, and recreational vehicles. Medical payments insurance is available to private passenger nonfleet risks up to $5,000 per person. Rates are uniform for all companies, and all auto liability insurers participate. "Modified Plan B" is used in eighteen states and the District of Columbia.

"Plan C," used in sixteen states, is basically the same as "Modified Plan B," except that it includes all auto insurers, including those writing only physical damage in the voluntary market.

The distribution system for automobile insurance plans is simple. If an applicant meets the qualifications of the producer's voluntary market(s), the risk is placed with that company. If not, an application is sent to the automobile insurance plan. The plan takes the application and assigns the risk to an insurer. The number of risks assigned to each insurer depends on the company's volume in the voluntary market. Obviously, service may suffer under such an arrangement. The producer may not know the claims procedure for the company to whom the applicant is assigned. Further, all producers receive the same commission rate, usually below that in the voluntary market.

Most automobile insurance plans contain depopulation provisions which are designed to either "keep out" or "take out" of the plan certain types of risks. These types may be youthful drivers, elderly drivers, previously uninsured drivers, or drivers already in the automobile insurance plan. Under the "keep out" program, thirty-nine states give a company credit for each male operator under twenty-five that they write in the voluntary market. Nine states give a credit for each driver over sixty-five that is written voluntarily. Ten states, for a limited time period, have given credits for previously uninsured drivers. Under the "take out" program, five states give credits to companies who will voluntarily insure someone currently in the automobile insurance plan. The "take out, keep out" programs make sense if automobile insurance plans are to be abolished or reduced to a manageable size. They are also intended to provide companies with an incentive to avoid placing good risks that are in a poor class into the automobile insurance plans.

The underwriting implications of an automobile insurance plan are many. Although this business has been unprofitable on an overall basis, the impact varies greatly from state to state depending on the adequacy of rates and the size of the plan. Therefore, underwriters should attempt to minimize their companies' participation in the plans by utilization of "take out, keep out" credits. This would have to be done on a state-by-state basis and would not be possible in every jurisdiction. For instance, if youthful drivers can be underwritten in a state at a profit, and the rating environment allows for rate adjustments, it would be possible to write enough drivers under twenty-five to obtain "keep out" credits in the plan that would meet the obligations of the company. The same could be true for any other category where credit is allowed. Clearly this type of action calls for mature judgment and flexibility. Such a plan would lead to disaster if not properly followed. One auto insurer in a state with adequate rates took advantage of a two-for-one credit for each youthful driver voluntarily insured and "bought" its way out of the plan. The plan subsequently reduced the "keep out" credit to one-for-one, but the company showed a profit on the youthful drivers it wrote voluntarily and was able to avoid the automobile insurance plan in that state. On the other hand, this same company took advantage of one of the temporary "keep out" plans in another state with a rate inadequacy. In a few years, it experienced a deterioration in its voluntary book of business.[6]

Theoretically, if rate adequacy were the only problem, there would be no need for an automobile insurance plan in an open rating state such as California. There are insurers writing substandard business in California who will write any applicant at a price—but not necessarily one which the applicant is prepared to pay. Even though automobile insurance plan premiums are much higher than preferred risk rates, they are lower than those offered by some insurers, and hence many applicants elect to be insured under the plan even though the available coverage is limited.

Many insureds have had problems buying insurance, and are aware of the rating system regarding surcharges. Thus, there is an incentive to "forget" accidents or violations which would increase the premium. Thorough investigation, such as a check of the motor vehicle records, is likely to produce a better loss ratio. For example, one study of automobile insurance plan business found that 55 percent of the risks in the California plan that had accidents or violations were not surcharged, and 26.6 percent of the California risks had five or more incidents and still were not surcharged. The failure to apply surcharges was due to inadequate verification of driving records.

Finally, the underwriter must be careful to examine each auto insurance plan application for one other important reason. The producer submitting the business will usually be unknown to the underwriter, and the underwriter does not know the quality of "first-line" underwriting by the producer on that risk. When the insured needs service, this lack of communication can cause further problems for the insured, the producer, and the company.

Reinsurance Facilities. Every auto residual market program combines a method of providing services with the distribution of the individual risks to the insurers. In the automobile insurance plan, service was provided through all insurers by apportioning all of the applicants to the insurers. Because of excessive losses in some states, coupled with substantial growth in the plans due to an inability of the insurers to obtain adequate rates, alternate methods of handling the markets are being tried. Reinsurance facilities are the most prominent form of alternate handling method. The objectives for the facility are to achieve more equitable pricing, to improve service, and to avoid the stigma of being in the automobile insurance plan. Reinsurance facilities still provide service through all insurers, but losses and premiums are pooled among *all* insurers, rather than each company to whom a risk is assigned retaining the losses and premiums of the risk.

The reinsurance facility, then, more closely approximates a pool after the original cession. Each company can cede no more than a specified percentage of premium (to prevent "dumping" into the facility). The maximum amount ceded depends on the jurisdiction; for example, South Carolina allows only 35 percent of the motor vehicle net direct written premiums of the insurer in that state to be ceded. The reinsurance facility acts as the distribution point for all losses and premiums which are ceded.

Under the reinsurance facility method, all losses are shared by all companies in the proportion of their writings in the state. Thus, if one insured who was ceded in South Carolina developed a $1,000 loss, the loss would not be shared 35 percent by the facility and 65 percent by the insurer, but entirely by the facility with the ceding company's share being its market share of the voluntary market. In practice, the insurer will usually pay the claim and will receive a "credit" for the loss adjustment expenses and claims paid in determining its share of the facility's losses.

The reinsurance facility is important despite the fact that it has been adopted by only four states—North Carolina, South Carolina, Massachusetts, and New Hampshire. Exhibit 5-7 points up the relative importance of these states in residual markets. Notice that these four states, in 1978, had only 7.36 percent of the vehicles registered in the nation. Yet they had 29.88 percent of all participants in the residual market programs. In each of these states, the size of the state's percentage of the national residual market exceeded its percentage of the United States vehicle registrations.

As was noted in Exhibit 5-6, Massachusetts ranks first (in the negative sense) in the percent of penetration of its residual market. South Carolina ranks third, North Carolina fourth, and New Hampshire sixth.

The distribution system under the reinsurance facility has the advantage of allowing the underwriter to make the decision to accept or reject (cede) a risk. Under the automobile insurance plans, the producer sends the application to the plan. Under the reinsurance facility, the

Exhibit 5-7
Reinsurance Facilities
Residual Market Shares by State—1978*

State	Number of Vehicles Registered in State	Percent of National Total	Number of Residual Market Autos	Percent of National Total
Massachusetts	3,166,609	2.75	861,018	11.71
North Carolina	3,240,000	2.82	864,660	11.76
New Hampshire	551,481	0.48	65,244	0.89
South Carolina	1,504,949	1.31	407,111	5.53
Total Reinsurance Facility	8,403,039	7.36	2,198,033	29.88
Total for 50 States	114,998,332		7,356,987	

* Adapted from *AIPSO Insurance Facts 1980* (New York: Automobile Insurance Plans Service Office, 1980), pp. 22-25.

producer accepts the application on the company's form and submits it to the underwriter. The underwriter can examine the risk and decide whether to keep it in the company's voluntary book or cede it to the facility. In most states, the entire policy is ceded. This prevents a company with, for instance, adequate physical damage rates from keeping the physical damage portion of the policy and ceding the unprofitable liability lines only. The advantage of the reinsurance facility is that, in most states, the company decides whether or not to cede. Also, the insureds probably do not know they are in the residual market, and may psychologically feel better toward the insurers. In addition, the producer deals with the same insurer for voluntary and residual business and often does not know if the risk has been ceded.

The disadvantages of the reinsurance facility are similar to those of automobile insurance plans. Quotations by producers must be checked. There is the possibility that "bad" risks will not be underwritten at all. That is, if an application comes in that is obviously going to be ceded, the underwriter may say, "Since we will not be on this risk, why spend money on a credit investigation or a motor vehicle report?" The necessity to properly rate and examine each risk is present in every residual market program.

Joint Underwriting Associations. The joint underwriting association (JUA) method of residual marketing also includes the pooling of experience among all companies as does a reinsurance facility. The method of handling each individual risk differs from both the reinsurance facility and automobile insurance plans. Under the JUA method, a limited number of servicing insurers are designated to handle all residual market risks. The servicing insurer provides these services for an industry pool to which all transactions are submitted. The results of the business in the pool are shared among *all* companies based on each company's share of voluntary market business.

Under a JUA, the insured would go to a producer who would take the application and see if it is eligible under normal underwriting rules. Companies are free to set whatever underwriting standards they wish. If a risk is acceptable to a company, the producer would submit it to the company. If the risk is not acceptable, the application is forwarded to the JUA servicing insurer assigned to the producer. This servicing insurer will handle all premiums, losses, and service necessary for the business of this producer. As an example, Florida has fourteen servicing insurers. These are companies selected because they are of sufficient size to provide proper service to producers and insureds. They would have a good system of statewide claims centers, for example. Every producer would be assigned to only one of the servicing insurers to handle all of the residual business. This allows a servicing insurer to become familiar with the type of business a producer would submit, and still allows it to handle and service all residual market business in the manner that will insure quality service compatible with the servicing insurer's computer and service procedures.

The servicing insurers have much greater control over the operations and results of the JUA than would an individual company in an automobile insurance plan or reinsurance facility. Each application to the JUA is carefully scrutinized, and MVRs are routinely ordered on all new and renewal business. The servicing insurers receive a percentage of the written premium to cover all costs associated with placing the business in the JUA and another percentage of written premium to handle claims. A rate that is proper will usually generate higher written premiums and hence higher servicing fees to the servicing insurers. Unlike the reinsurance plans, rates are based on the experience of the pool and are uniform for all servicing insurers. Like the automobile insurance plans, rates are higher than those in the voluntary market.

Representatives of the servicing insurers serve on the board governing the JUA, but nonservicing insurers have the majority on the board. Consequently, there develops a balance of interest on the part of those companies not servicing the JUA insured, but sharing in the losses that will develop under the plan. This becomes very important in three of four states with JUAs—Florida, Missouri, and Michigan. In these states, the plans are meant to be self-supporting. According to AIPSO (Automobile Insurance Plan Service Office), the Florida JUA had a 109 percent combined ratio for the period 1 October 1973 to 30 September 1976 (the combined ratio is the total of the loss ratio and the expense ratio). Missouri did not fare as well, having a combined ratio of 117 percent from 1 January 1975 to 30 September 1979.[7] Michigan adopted its JUA as of 1 January 1981 and therefore its experience is not available.

Hawaii's JUP (joint underwriting plan) is unique. There is no attempt whatsoever to make the plan self-supporting. The reason is that auto insurance under Hawaii's plan is a welfare benefit for the state's poor. Welfare recipients are not charged for their coverage. They are entirely supported by the voluntary auto insurance market.

Underwriting under a JUA is simplified. Those companies not serving as servicing insurers need only concern themselves with accounting transactions. No underwriting is involved for these companies except to the extent that each company determines the boundaries of its own voluntary programs and the rates for those programs. Business not qualifying is sent by the producer to the JUA.

Servicing insurers, on the other hand, do all of the underwriting. They can train and develop underwriters specifically to handle this type of business.

The Maryland Approach. Maryland has the only state fund program in the United States. Under this concept, applicants not qualifying for the voluntary markets are placed in one company operated by the state government. The Maryland law originally intended for this state fund to be self-supporting. The law specifically provided that tax revenues were not to be used to pay losses. In spite of these stated intentions, the plan is not operating at a profit.

Residual Market Programs—A Summing Up. One key to a successful insurance enterprise is the ability to obtain adequate rates for whatever insurance is sold. In auto insurance, the necessity for rate adequacy is perhaps greatest because of the significant size of premiums developed for the auto insurance lines of business. Due to a number of economic, political, and social factors, adequate rates are difficult to obtain in many jurisdictions.

It falls to the auto insurance industry and the state governments to provide insurance to applicants who are likely to produce losses in excess of their premium contributions. Automobile insurance plans, reinsurance facilities, joint underwriting associations, and the so-called Maryland plan are various attempted solutions to this problem.

All types of involuntary auto plans have increased in importance in recent years. The volume of applications to the residual market plans has swollen dramatically and has been extremely unprofitable over the past few years. This growth of unprofitable business is causing concern among auto insurers. While recognizing that some loss on this business is inevitable, heavy losses will have a serious impact on companies. Policyholders in the voluntary market will be forced to absorb the losses through rate increases.

SUMMARY

Monitoring underwriting decisions is an on-going process. It includes measuring underwriting results as well as review and renewal underwriting. Individual review and renewal underwriting must consider economic limitations as well as voluntary and mandatory limitations on underwriting alternatives. Book of business review follows the same basic process and may analyze the auto book of business according to various bases such as rate class, territory, producer, and type of loss.

The environment surrounding the underwriting of personal auto insurance is both complex and constantly changing. The great economic importance of the auto makes auto insurance a necessity, and this necessity has caused a concomitant need for regulation.

Regulation is necessary to assure the solvency of insurance companies, to prevent unfair discrimination, and to offset any lack of market competition so that the public will receive all of the benefits of a competitive marketplace. The major types of rate regulations are the California rate law, the use and file system, the file and use system, the prior approval system, and the modified prior approval system. In general, rate laws require that rates be "adequate, reasonable, and not unfairly discriminatory." Forms are also regulated, usually in a law included in the rating law, though not necessarily by means of the same system.

Other laws and practices have had a decided effect on the insurance industry. The goal of these laws is to allow anyone with a valid driver's license to have access to auto insurance. The most important of these laws are laws restricting cancellation, compulsory insurance laws, and financial responsibility laws.

The passage of financial responsibility laws encouraged the development of residual market programs for those unable to obtain coverage through the voluntary distribution system. In 1938, New Hampshire installed an assigned risk plan (now called automobile insurance plan), and by 1959, all states had some type of residual market program.

Automobile insurance plans are the most common type of residual market plans. Reinsurance facilities were developed to achieve more equitable pricing, to improve service, and to avoid the stigma of being in the automobile insurance plan. The joint underwriting association

(JUA) method of residual marketing also includes the pooling of experience among all companies as does a reinsurance facility, but under the JUA a limited number of servicing insurers are designated to handle all residual market risks. Hawaii has a joint underwriting plan that is unique—making auto insurance a welfare benefit for the state's poor. Maryland has the only state fund program in the country. Applicants not qualifying for the voluntary market are placed in one company, owned, and operated by the state.

Chapter Notes

1. Karl E. Meyer, *The Pleasures of Archaeology* (New York: Atheneum, 1970), p. 234.
2. State of New York, Insurance Department, *Automobile Insurance . . . For Whose Benefit?* (New York: Insurance Department, State of New York, 1970), p. 3.
3. California Insurance Code, Section 1852.
4. *Summary of Selected State Laws and Regulations Relating to Automobile Insurance* (New York: American Insurance Association, 1980), p. 71.
5. *AIPSO Insurance Facts 1980* (New York: Automobile Insurance Plans Service Office, 1980), pp. 23, 25.
6. Harry C. Niemann III, CPCU, "The Automobile Residual Market: What Are the Facts?" *CPCU Annals,* (June 1975), 28: 85-87.
7. *AIPSO Insurance Facts 1980* (New York: Automobile Insurance Plans Service Office, 1980), pp. 129, 132.

Making Underwriting Decisions: Residence Insurance

CHAPTER 6

Evaluating Hazards

INTRODUCTION

This is the first of four chapters dealing with underwriting residential property risks. In addition to these four chapters, personal inland marine insurance and pleasure boats receive separate treatment in Chapter 10; similarly, the liability portion of residence package policies is dealt with separately in Chapter 11.

THE SCOPE OF RESIDENCE INSURANCE

This portion of Chapter 6 introduces residence insurance underwriting by examining (1) ways in which residences can be described and broadly classified, (2) the significance of the residence insurance market, and (3) some residence loss data.

Types of Residences

Residences can be described and classified by considering a number of factors or variables. An understanding of these is important in risk selection, classification, and rating.

Occupancy Personal residence insurance is focused on (1) the single-family dwelling unit (building and/or contents), (2) small multiple-occupancy dwelling units of (usually) no more than four families (building and/or contents), and (3) contents of persons residing in larger multiple-unit apartment and condominium complexes. Note that some types of structures providing residential facilities—dormitories, nursing homes, boarding houses, hotels and motels, and large apartment buildings—are commercial risks and are outside the scope of this text.

The nature of the occupancy is important in determining eligibility of a risk for the type of policy requested. For example, for most companies, any homeowners form providing coverage of a building structure is available only for one- and two-family dwellings, while a form for tenants is available to cover the personal property of the tenant in multiple-occupancy units of any size.

Location Residential risks are situated in virtually every conceivable location, from totally isolated spots to locations surrounded by thousands of similar units, from major cities of diverse economic strata to equally mixed suburbs and small rural communities.

Location is an important underwriting and rating variable. The location of a risk dictates the availability of police and fire protection, as well as the visibility of the property to neighbors who might report problems requiring police or fire department personnel. Location clearly helps determine susceptibility to a variety of perils such as flood, wave wash, earthquake, hurricanes, brush fires, vandalism, and theft, and may be related to many more.

Each variation in location seems to present its own problems to the underwriter, whose concerns depend in part on the perils covered by the policy being underwritten. Further consideration of this relationship will be provided later in this chapter, and in subsequent chapters, as the underwriting of particular policy forms is discussed.

Protection Class The term "protection" in residence insurance underwriting usually refers to the public protection facilities available to help prevent or extinguish a fire in the area. In most states, a public fire protection class or grade for each city or town is determined by an insurance rating bureau considering such factors as the water supply, fire service communications, fire safety control, and the nature and equipment of the fire department. The lower the number grade (a few states use an alphabetical grading system) assigned, the better the fire protection is considered to be. Most major cities fall in class 2 or 3. Territories or communities carrying the two highest class grades—9 or 10—are usually considered "unprotected," with little or no fire protection. Ungraded communities are assigned class 10.

Protection class is a very important matter in risk selection and rating. Consideration of perils other than fire is not directly affected by the fire protection class involved, but the basic importance of the fire peril to residence coverages means that protection class is fundamental to underwriting these coverages.

Construction Another important factor in the underwriting of residence coverages is the construction classification of the structure involved. Even when insuring only the contents in an apartment, the construction of the building in which the contents are contained must be considered.

There are four basic types of residence construction: frame, masonry (usually brick, concrete block, or stone), fire resistive, and noncombustible. While different areas of the country and different rating organizations show some variation in construction classification systems, these four classes are basic to the systems used.

Briefly defined, a *frame* building is one in which the exterior walls and interior walls, partitions, floors, and roof are of wood or other combustible materials. A *masonry* building is one in which the exterior walls are composed of noncombustible (masonry) materials while the interior walls, partitions, floors, and roof are of wood or other combustible materials. A brick veneer building is a frame structure with the exterior surface either partially or completely covered by a layer of brick. A brick veneer (or masonry veneer) building is not considered to be of masonry construction, but in some states, such a building is rated as masonry. (In some other states, it would be rated as frame, and in still others, there are separate brick veneer or masonry veneer rates.) A *fire resistive* building is one which has masonry, or steel and masonry, walls and partitions, concrete floors, and a tile roof, or similar noncombustible material of a designated thickness or of a specific fire resistance rating.

A *noncombustible* building does not qualify as fire resistive, but all walls and the roof are of metal or steel or similar noncombustible construction. Also, there are no wood supports or wood framing. The latter two types of construction are sometimes encountered by personal lines underwriters when writing contents coverage in apartment houses. Few houses are fire resistive or noncombustible.

The fire rate is dependent in part upon the type of construction. Since almost all policies include fire, this variable is critical to rating. Crime, on the other hand, is seldom affected by the type of construction, but extended coverage rates are lower if the building is classed as wind resistive. Rates for the earthquake peril, in contrast with fire, are lower for frame construction than for masonry, because frame buildings can flex and bend and are less susceptible to earthquake damage than rigid masonry buildings. Other underwriting considerations of the type of construction are discussed in a later section of this chapter.

Nature of the Residence Unit Residential insurance risks span a wide range of types, including the separate single-family home, the rowhouse, the mobile home, and the apartment in a high-rise building. Each of these unit types possesses its own unique characteristics. Some illustrations follow.

A mobile home presents a unique type of residential unit in that it is designed with the capability of being moved in its entirety. Although today's mobile homes often are moved only once or twice, even such limited movement presents the underwriter with a different type of risk. Since they are *mobile,* mobile homes often are placed on temporary foundations and therefore may not be as sturdy in overall construction as a permanent housing unit. At the same time, the underwriter may have difficulty determining the construction quality since the mobile unit may have been built to conform to some outdated state building code.

Farm properties, along with farm residences, also have unique features which may cause problems for an underwriter whose main area of familiarity is single-family dwellings in cities and towns. Barns, sheds, and similar outbuildings used for nonbusiness storage of grain or farm machinery, or for housing livestock, present some unique hazards and require different evaluation procedures by the personal lines underwriter.

Apartment and condominium risks present still different considerations. For example, should ranges, air conditioners, and carpeting be considered as real property and thus insured under the policy of the building owner? Or are they personal property to be included in the tenant's policy? The answer affects insurance to value and insurable interest—both of which must be considered by the underwriter.

Ownership Although the majority of residential dwelling units (or the contents on tenants' risks) are owned by the person residing in the dwelling, this is not a universal situation. Many dwelling units are owned by individuals and rented to other individuals, and many are owned by corporate entities and rented to others. In some situations (condominiums), ownership of the real property involved is held in common by a large group of individuals while the articles inside each unit are owned by one of those individuals.

Regardless of the type of ownership involved, one underwriting function is to make sure that the insured has the required insurable interest in the property before authorizing issuance of a policy. At the same time, the underwriter should realize that a tenant or other nonowner-occupant does not have the same degree of control over the property as does an owner-occupant, nor does the tenant have the same degree of personal involvement in maintaining the property.

The Residential Insurance Market

The residential property insurance market is one of great significance, whether looked at separately or as a segment of the property insurance market generally. In 1979, there were about 79 million (up from 63 million in 1974) occupied housing units in the United States. About 70 percent of these were single-family homes and about 30 percent of the units were multi-family units.[1] This market is spread throughout the United States in roughly the same proportions as population density.

Due to the rapid escalation of building costs and interest rates during the last several years, single-family dwelling starts have experienced slow growth or an actual decrease in some areas. This phenomenon is expected to continue as both costs and interest rates remain high. Meanwhile, condominium and apartment unit construction has been increasing at a more rapid pace than single-family homes (or at least decreasing at a slower rate), particularly in areas of high population density. In some areas, such as southern California, Washington, D.C., and southern Florida, this trend is more pronounced. In 1979, single-unit private housing structure starts accounted for 68 percent of the total private housing structure starts. Two- to four-unit structures were 7 percent and structures with five or more units accounted for 25 percent of the total private housing starts. While on the surface these figures seem to indicate the predominance of the single-unit structure, one need only convert these figures to housing *units* rather than *structures* to get a clearer picture. Multiplying the last two figures conservatively by three and five, respectively, multi-unit construction is easily the predominant type of construction on a basis of units started.[2]

Residence insurance premium volume *on property exposures* comprises a combination of homeowners premiums, farmowners premiums, and premiums on nonpackage dwelling forms. Homeowners premiums alone in 1979 stood at about $8.8 billion, and farmowners recorded volume of $519 million the same year.[3] The nonpackage dwelling forms are not compiled nationally on a basis separate from commercial fire and allied lines premiums.

RESIDENCE INSURANCE PERILS

One of the primary differences among the various residential property insurance contracts is the number and variety of perils insured against. Since a number of perils are common to several different contracts and forms, it would be well to discuss perils generally before discussing the underwriting of particular contracts.

Fire

The peril central to most residence property insurance contracts is fire, which in most cases causes greater dollar losses than any other residence insurance peril. In the nonpackage policies, fire causes a greater dollar loss than *all* other perils combined. In package policies, it causes greater dollar loss than any other single peril, but the presence of theft as a peril covered in these contracts accounts for fire causing less than half the dollar volume of package policy property losses. In personal inland marine floaters, fire runs second to theft as a loss cause.

In 1979, the most recent year for which full statistics are available, there were approximately 2,840 building fires every day. Residential fires accounted for about 70 percent of the total fires in the United States and about 44 percent of the total dollar losses, reflecting the lower values at risk in residential buildings. Total dollar losses from fire were $4.8 billion in 1979. A fire broke out in a residence about every forty-four seconds. There were approximately 5,800 deaths from fire in the United States in 1979.[4]

The causes of fires in residential risks are many. As to general type (nature), the leading categories of fire loss causes in residential dwellings in 1977 and 1978 are shown in Exhibit 6-1. Although not broken down specifically in Exhibit 6-1, traditionally the major causes of fire loss in residences have been related either to carelessness on the part of the resident or some type of mechanical failure or malfunction. In Exhibit 6-1, the heating and cooking categories could include not only defective heating and cooking equipment, but also the misuse of such equipment by the occupants of the home. Smoking is easily related to carelessness on the part of a person in the residence.

One example of how mechanical failure can be ascribed to human failure or incompetence (failure to clean and maintain equipment properly, for example) would be the following Georgia case. An explosion in a frame house awoke neighbors, who called the fire department. Fire fighters found the house virtually destroyed and the flames shooting forty to fifty feet into the air from a propane tank. The owner had previously installed his own propane gas system. He had used galvanized pipe and installed it in the crawl space under the house. Investigation showed that electrolytic corrosion had eaten a hole through the supply line and allowed gas to escape. The accumulated gas was ignited by the pilot light. The resulting explosion and fire caused five deaths.[5]

Another major cause of fire loss in residential occupancies is incendiarism, commonly referred to as arson. Classification is not precise, because many fires are listed as being suspicious in origin. Still,

Exhibit 6-1
Causes of Residential Reported Fires*

	Fires	Deaths	Injuries	Dollar Loss
Heating	20.8%	18.0%	15.8%	21.9%
Cooking	18.7	7.8	18.2	7.6
Incendiary/Suspicious	11.4	10.7	8.8	19.1
Smoking	10.8	32.3	19.7	10.1
Electrical distribution	8.8	9.4	6.9	13.0
Appliances	7.8	3.4	5.6	6.2
Children playing	6.1	8.2	9.2	5.1
Other equipment	4.3	2.3	5.5	5.1
Exposure	3.0	1.3	1.2	4.2
Natural	1.3	.2	.6	1.6
Open flame, torch	4.5	4.7	4.7	4.3
Other heat	2.7	1.7	2.6	1.9

Note: Based on studies in eight states during 1977 and 1978 and in an additional seven states in 1978. Columns of percentages may not total 100 percent because of the effects of rounding.

*Adapted from *Insurance Facts 1980-81* Edition (New York: Insurance Information Institute), p. 44.

the statistics in Exhibit 6-1 show that incendiarism was the third largest cause of loss (up from fourth in 1974). Although it is difficult to prove arson, the startling increase in suspicious and incendiary fires in recent years has shocked the insurance industry.

The human element in fire losses makes the fire peril difficult to evaluate at the underwriting level. However, there are clues that can point to an excessive exposure to fire loss. Poor housekeeping and maintenance of the premises is the easiest to detect; a photograph of the exterior of the structure often reveals cases where there was an obvious absence of either motivation or means (or both) to properly care for property. Substandard construction may be evident from a photograph or from an apparent reluctance to meet the insurance-to-value requirements. Finally, any indications of financial difficulty, such as frequent requests for extensions of time to pay premiums, may be clues to financial problems and moral hazard.

An idea of the relative importance of fire and other perils as causes of *insured* loss can be gained from Exhibit 6-2. The figures include all residential lines in the countrywide book of business of one leading insurer. (The company supplying this information prefers to remain anonymous.)

Exhibit 6-2
Incurred Loss Ratio by Cause of Loss—Homeowners and Tenants Combined

	Incurred Loss Ratio	Percent of Total
Fire and Lightning	22.46%	38.5%
Wind and Hail	7.23	12.4
Theft	14.21	24.3
Water Damage	5.63	9.6
Liability and Medical	4.74	8.1
Other	4.11	7.1
Total	58.38%	100%

Theft

The peril of theft, which is covered under all homeowners contracts, is one of the most frequent causes of loss under these policies. In fact, the high volume of theft losses is blamed for much of the unprofitable posture of the homeowners line in the 1970s. The introduction of many internal limits under the HO-76 program helped to alleviate some of the problem.

Theft coverage tends to be unattractive from an underwriting standpoint because theft is so easily committed in today's mobile world. Electronic equipment, jewelry, and appliances readily available in American homes can be easily stolen and quickly converted to cash or personal use by a thief. Further, the presence of theft as a covered peril leaves insurers subject to moral or morale hazard of an insured. A theft loss is difficult to validate or refute due to the fact that there is no injured third party or no partially destroyed property to examine.

There are factors which increase the probability of a theft loss. A concentration of high-valued contents increases the likelihood that a thief will be attracted to the home. The degree of police protection affects both the likelihood of theft and the chances of apprehension if a theft is committed. Of course, some apartments or condominium complexes have private security services which act as deterrents.

Occupancy affects theft potential. An unoccupied home increases the likelihood of theft. Many underwriters become concerned when asked to insure a residence which is always unoccupied during the day. An isolated location is more susceptible to theft than a location where neighbors are likely to notice and report suspicious activities.

Certain protective measures can be taken by the insured and may, occasionally, be recommended by an underwriter. Burglar alarms are the most obvious such measures. Double-cylinder dead-bolt locks make it more difficult for a burglar to enter or escape. (Dead-bolt locks are not spring-loaded; a double-cylinder lock requires a key to lock or unlock from inside or outside.) Common sense dictates many other theft protection measures—locking all doors and windows not in use, keeping bicycles and other personal property locked in a garage or basement while unattended, and so on.

Homes temporarily unoccupied when the residents are vacationing pose a special problem. Here again such common-sense measures as operating a light on a timer, notifying police and neighbors, hiring someone to keep the grass mowed, and so on, can reduce the likelihood of a loss.

Windstorm and Hail

The windstorm peril covers loss caused by the force of wind and by objects or debris moved or carried by the wind. Thus, if a tree is blown down by the wind and, in falling, damages a home, the resulting damage to the residence may be payable under any of the residential property forms covering perils at least as broad as fire and the extended coverage perils. Some courts have defined windstorm as wind of sufficient velocity to cause damage to property in a reasonable state of repair; others have specified a certain velocity (e.g., twenty-five mph).

There have been a number of spectacular windstorm losses in recent history. One occurred in an area from the Chesapeake Bay to southern New England. From this one windstorm came property losses estimated at $400 million. Wind can and does produce catastrophic losses. Like the "Blizzard of '88," storms with names such as "Hazel," "Camille," "Donna," and "Agnes" cause memories to stir.

The perils of windstorm and hail may be listed separately in named-perils policies, but they are usually considered together. Hail often accompanies a windstorm, and insurers learned long ago that it is better to cover both perils in order to avoid any questions as to whether the damage was caused by one or the other.

In some states, windstorm and hail taken together are the most frequent cause of loss under residence policies, and are second only to fire in the dollar amount of claims paid.

Windstorm and hail coverage provides protection against direct damage to property by either peril. Crucial here—for windstorm, at least—is the word "direct." Generally the courts have held that direct damage by wind results either from the actual force of wind against insured property, or from objects being propelled against the insured property by the wind. Thus, a violent wind could blow some shingles off a house and the resulting damage would be covered. And if the same wind blew someone else's shingles through the insured's living room window, this damage would be covered, too.

In most states, policy provisions dealing with windstorm and hail exclude certain types of property considered to be highly susceptible to windstorm and hail damage. Examples are buildings under construction, awnings, signs, and television antennae. Insurers have excluded such property to protect themselves from insuring high risk items not contemplated in the rate. To insure such highly vulnerable property, in most states an insured must specifically name the items in the policy and pay an extra charge for the specific additional coverage.

All residential property forms covering wind and hail on a named-peril basis contain a condition that limits the extent of windstorm and hail coverage. The interior and contents of an insured building are not covered against the damages resulting from rain, snow, sand, or dust *unless* the direct force of wind or hail first creates an opening in the roof or walls of the building, and the rain, snow, sand, or dust enters through the opening(s). The purpose of this provision is to prevent coverage of losses caused by wind-driven elements entering through normal building openings. For example, damage to furniture caused by rain blowing through an open window is not covered, because an open window is a normal opening. If a window is closed, however, and a windstorm blows the window out, there is coverage.

Although wave wash is excluded in fixed-location property insurance forms, it can be difficult to separate these losses from windstorm losses, because wave wash is usually accompanied by wind of high velocity. Therefore, a dwelling located in an area subject to wave wash is considered a more hazardous risk.

Dwellings in every state are susceptible to windstorm and hail, but some states involve greater exposure than others. The Gulf Coast and parts of the eastern seaboard are subject to hurricanes and tropical storms. Although infrequent, these events cause widespread damage when they move over a land area. The central, south central, and southeastern states are subject to tornadoes more so than other states. While the impact of tornadoes usually is restricted to a narrow path, these storms generate wind speeds capable of demolishing all of the property in that path. Of course, a direct hit by a tornado can result in substantial damage to almost any structure, and there is no means of individual risk underwriting adequate to deal with this possibility. For windstorm and hail in general, both geographic spread of risks and appropriate catastrophe reinsurance are important safeguards in maintaining a profitable book of business over time.

Smoke

As used in extended coverage, the smoke peril was designed primarily to cover sudden "smudge" losses from oil-heating furnaces which, because of improper combustion, sometimes backfire and send clouds of smoke swirling through the building covering walls, floors, and contents with a thin coating of black, oily smudge. During a period of several years' operation, even the best oil burner may deposit a slight smudge throughout the building in which it operates. Such accumulated films of grime are not intended to be covered; hence the words "sudden and accidental" in the policy. Coverage was originally afforded only for smoke discharged by a heating or cooking unit *on the insured premises.* The unit must be connected to a chimney and may not be a fireplace.

Coverage against the peril of smoke has been substantially liberalized under homeowners policies. Sudden and accidental damage by smoke from almost any source is covered, except for agricultural smudging or industrial operations. Smoke damage from a hostile fire has fire as its proximate cause, in which case, of course, it is covered by the fire peril.

Explosion

Explosions are relatively infrequent, but those losses that do occur are likely to be severe. Explosion is not always easy to define, and most courts appear to hold to the idea that "explosion" means what the average person thinks it means. Insurance companies take the position that an explosion, as used in insurance, has four characteristics: (1) it is sudden and violent, (2) it tears objects apart, (3) it generates a loud noise, and (4) fragmentation of the exploding object occurs. In cases of controversy, these four points are applied to determine whether the occurrence was actually an explosion as opposed to a collapse or a rupture.

As limited in extended coverage, the explosion peril contains exclusions intended to eliminate certain kinds of events from the meaning of explosion. They include sonic boom, electric arcing, water hammer, and rupture or bursting of water pipes and of pressure relief devices. These exclusions do not apply under the broader forms or the homeowners policies.

Vandalism or Malicious Mischief

The perils of vandalism or malicious mischief (V or MM) are not included in the extended coverage endorsement. They are included in the broad form, special form, and all homeowners policies.

Most insureds are good risks from the point of view of the vandalism peril. Exceptions are vacant homes, homes under construction, geographically isolated risks (regardless of occupancy), and homes in areas plagued by vandalous acts. It should be noted that coverage is usually suspended after a thirty-day period of vacancy of the insured dwelling. Such a condition is regarded as substantially increasing the likelihood of loss.

Water Damage

The water damage peril is "accidental discharge or overflow of water or steam from within a plumbing, heating or air conditioning system, or from within a household appliance." A separate peril, sometimes combined with the first, is "sudden and accidental tearing apart, cracking, burning or bulging of a steam or hot water heating system, air conditioning system, or an appliance for heating water." Both perils are named in the named-perils homeowners forms except HO-1. Neither involves *exterior* water, such as flood and surface water, which is routinely excluded in all fire and package policies.

A common water damage claim is for damage resulting from a washing machine or a dishwasher. Overflow from such appliances can discharge large quantities of water which ruin floors, carpets, and other floor coverings. Hot water tanks can burst or leak, with similar damage resulting.

Water pipes which form a part of the plumbing system sometimes crack because of electrolysis or rust. Since these pipes usually are hidden in walls, severe damage can result. Under most policies, the cost to repair or replace the plumbing itself is excluded, but the cost of tearing out and replacing parts of the covered building in order to effect repairs *is* covered.

Shower pans can develop leaks which often are undiscovered for months due to the hidden nature and inaccessibility of the structure below the shower. This type of damage is almost inevitable if the pan is not replaced when it starts to deteriorate. Losses of this type which take place over a period of time became so common and costly under homeowners forms that they were excluded within the definition of the covered peril in order to avoid the necessity of substantial increases in premium. The actual exclusion refers to "continuous or repeated seepage or leakage."

A general exclusion added in the years after coverage of this peril was first written was "water which backs up through sewers or drains." This is a fairly common type of loss, sometimes due to poor care and maintenance, and is not covered under any of the forms except in a limited number of states where it must be offered by insurers.

Water damage losses can be separated into three groups. The first includes appliances which malfunction; this can occur any time, and there is no effective means of underwriting against this type of loss. A second group centers on plumbing and heating systems which have been allowed to deteriorate. Because it is unusual to replace pipes and fixtures until they have caused trouble, it is almost inevitable that every dwelling eventually will produce claims from water damage. Older homes are obviously more susceptible to such damage. The third group involves momentary carelessness, such as permitting a bathtub to overflow. The only underwriting for this type of loss is after the fact based on loss history.

Flood

Floods may be caused by exceptionally heavy rainfall, rapidly melting snow and ice, or the overflowing or breaking of a dam or levee. The resulting losses frequently include many lives as well as enormous property damage. To date, a satisfactory method of consistently underwriting against the contingency of such catastrophic loss has not been found within the private insurance sector.

A major difficulty in writing this coverage stems from adverse selection. The demand for flood insurance comes from people living in river basin areas and coastal lowlands. They are quite likely to have a flood loss at some point or another, and they want insurance. The person who lives on a hill or who has property located where no flood is likely to occur will not consider purchasing the coverage. Thus, many flood losses affect a high percentage of total values in an area. Since a way has not yet been found to spread coverage among average risks, flood insurance is attractive only to property owners most likely to suffer a loss.

Homeowners policies exclude damage caused by flood, surface water, waves, tidal water, and overflow of a body of water. Coverage is available through special policies issued by the Federal Insurance Administration through a servicing organization, EDS Federal Corporation. The federal government shares heavily in the aggregate flood exposure and in the cost of insurance of many insureds. Eligibility depends on the community qualifying for participation in the program, primarily by adopting regulations governing land use in flood-prone areas.

Beyond the federal program, flood coverage may be provided by inland marine insurance covering personal property and by some policies covering mobile homes. Inland marine forms are "all-risks" in most cases, with as few exclusions as possible. Since most property covered by personal lines inland marine coverages is of relatively high value and highly mobile, it is likely that policyholders tend to remove such property from an area threatened by flood. This is in contrast to dwellings (which cannot be moved) and household basics such as furniture and appliances (which are impractical to move in a period of emergency).

Mobile homes were originally written on auto policies, since they were merely enlarged trailers. When underwriters began to treat them as dwelling units by using regular dwelling forms, or forms or policies tailored to the mobile home, no attempt was made to exclude the flood peril, which had long been an integral part of auto insurance. As mobile home insurance becomes more of a property line, recognition of the similarity of mobile homes to standard dwelling units may lead to a tendency to exclude flood in mobile-home coverages. In the meantime, underwriters need to be aware of the exposure, and underwrite with caution those mobile homes located in areas susceptible to flooding.

Other Named Perils

Other perils covered in the broader homeowners policies deserve brief mention. These are (1) vehicles, (2) collapse of a building, (3) ice, snow, or sleet damage, (4) freezing of plumbing, heating, and air conditioning systems, (5) sudden and accidental damage from artificially generated electrical current, and (6) glass breakage.

In the extended coverage endorsement and the HO-1, the vehicles peril does not include damage resulting from any vehicle owned or operated by a resident of the residence premises. The coverage is less restrictive in the HO-2 which only excludes loss to a fence, driveway, or walk caused by a vehicle owned or operated by a resident of the residence premises. The HO-3 and HO-5 have no similar exclusions. (Note: this discussion refers only to the dwelling and other buildings coverage. Personal property covers the vehicles peril with no specific exclusions related to it.)

Little underwriting can be done regarding the peril of vehicle damage. However, if there is evidence that property has been damaged by a vehicle, further investigation should be made. If the structure is located in such a position that vehicle damage can be expected—at certain intersections, on a narrow alley, adjacent to a drive-in restaurant—some type of protective device should be required. Perhaps a sturdy post set in concrete would be sufficient, assuming such a measure is legal and economically feasible. On the other hand, if the evidence indicates that the damage is caused by careless driving *by the insured or a tenant,* the only control will be a restrictive form that does not cover that part of the exposure. In these cases, a broad form or HO-2, 3, or 5 should not be written. An alternative is requiring a substantial deductible. Although the peril of damage by vehicles is of small importance in the overall loss picture on dwellings, individual cases can be troublesome and may require careful underwriting.

Collapse of buildings is a peril added in the broader forms. It includes collapse of a part of a building, or of the entire structure. Excluded are awnings, fences, patios, pavement, underground pipes, and the like unless the loss is a direct result of the collapse of a building. The few losses that are encountered as a result of this peril are primarily due to old, deteriorating conditions or substandard construction; both of these conditions should be a warning to the underwriter. All forms stipulate that there is no coverage (except for ensuing fire, explosion, theft, or breakage of glass) for damage resulting from an earth movement.

The weight of ice, snow, or sleet can damage a building and its contents. This peril has been added in the broader forms. Patio roofs and flat-roofed portions of building structures are particularly vulnerable. The exposure is unavoidable in areas subject to heavy snowfalls. Whether or not a loss occurs depends largely on the design and the condition of the structure. A risk in such an area needs special attention to these factors by the underwriter. If there is a potential problem, the only alternative to declination of the application is the offer of a more limited coverage. This peril and the losses it produces are not those best handled by imposing substantial deductibles.

Freezing of a plumbing, heating, or air conditioning system or household appliance is another peril which has been added to broader homeowners forms. Its significance obviously varies among sections of the country. The underwriting is aided by an exclusion of loss "on the residence premises while the dwelling is vacant, unoccupied or being constructed, unless you have used reasonable care to: a. maintain heat in the building; or b. shut off the water supply and drain the system and appliances of water." There is little else an underwriter can do regarding this peril.

Damage from electrical currents comprises a peril which has little potential for effective underwriting. The peril reads: "sudden and accidental damage from artificially generated electrical current." Tubes, transistors, and similar electronic components are excluded property under this peril.

Glass breakage—by any means—is a peril covered in at least limited fashion under the homeowners forms. The only exclusion is loss occurring after more than thirty consecutive days of vacancy. The deductibles commonly used today will control most glass losses. Sometimes an underwriter will encounter a risk with a history of glass losses. If the underwriter deems it necessary, a higher deductible may be applied, or a limited fire and extended coverage form may be used, since it does not cover this peril. Incidentally, a separate residence glass endorsement used to be widely available to cover all glass breakage without the application of any deductible. Because of unfavorable experience and the wisdom of avoiding first-dollar loss protection, the endorsement has been withdrawn in many areas. Where available, it is subject to the same underwriting as the peril of glass breakage under the forms discussed here.

"All-Risks"

"All-risks" coverage on buildings is afforded by the HO-3 and HO-5. The last is "all-risks" on contents also. The actual term is "all risks of physical loss to the property described except . . . ." In practice the vast bulk of loss dollars paid under these "all-risks" forms also would be paid under the homeowners forms using a broad named-perils approach. However, there are two ways in which "all-risks" dwelling coverage expands the protection of other forms. The first is through a lack of qualifying or limiting language pertaining to a peril that is included in named-perils forms; the second is through covering unusual perils not important (or obvious) enough to be put in a named-perils form.

Broader coverage of a peril cited in named-perils forms can be illustrated by the treatment of vehicle damage in the "all-risks" forms. The "all-risks" forms contain no excluded property or situations specific to the peril of vehicle damage except an exclusion under the additional coverage for trees, shrubs, and plants if damaged by a vehicle driven by a resident of the residence premises. Regardless of who owns or operates the vehicle causing damage, under the "all-risks" form the loss is covered except for damage to trees, shrubs, or plants or to property excluded *elsewhere* in the form. Thus, damage to a walkway because of the insured's operation of his or her own vehicle is covered under the "all-risks" forms, but not under the named-perils homeowners form. Another illustration concerns the peril of falling objects, which is named in the broader named-perils forms. In these named-perils forms, there is an exclusion of damage to the interior of a structure unless there is first some damage to the exterior. This exclusion is absent from the "all-risks" forms.

Another benefit of the "all-risks" form—the covering of the "unnamed" perils—is more difficult to describe. The principal difference is that in the event of a loss, the policyholder with a named-perils policy must prove that one of the named perils was the cause of the loss. With an "all-risks" policy, the loss is covered unless the company can prove that it is excluded.

This distinction is of little help in underwriting. However, it is helpful for the underwriter to appreciate the kinds of unusual events that can fall within the scope of "all-risks" coverage. The following actual insured losses would be covered under an "all-risks" dwelling form, but not under a named-perils form:

1. The insured took a hot pan off the stove and set it on the counter, damaging the counter.
2. A bucket of paint was spilled on an oak floor, causing permanent damage.
3. A bottle of bleach was dropped on a linoleum floor, bleaching out the color.
4. A deer entered a home, causing considerable damage before it left.
5. An insured sprayed mosquitoes in the bedroom at night, without turning on the light. In the morning, he learned that the spray can contained red lacquer, not insecticide.[6]

Even these examples, interesting as they are, do not guide an underwriter in the selection of risks. They do point up the value of substantial deductibles in "all-risks" contracts because of increased loss frequency and the large number of covered events that may result from the insured's carelessness. Otherwise, the underwriter need only realize that there are losses of these types that justify a higher premium for "all-risks" than for named-perils coverages.

RESIDENCE INSURANCE RULES AND PRACTICES

Overall Eligibility Criteria

All types of residential policies are subject to rules which specify the type of risks which are eligible for the coverages. In most states these rules are filed with the Department of Insurance. Independent companies file their own rules, while the rating bureau files the rules, along with the rates, for its members and subscribers. Some of the eligibility factors are discussed in the following paragraphs.

Farm Occupancy Generally, program rules and manuals distinguish between nonfarm and farm residential risks, and the latter are written on forms tailored to that class. The definition of "farm" is specified in the rules. Usually a maximum number of acres, such as five, is specified as acceptable for writing the risk under a nonfarm form or program.

Business Occupancy A business is not eligible for a residential policy; a commercial form should be used. Again, there are varying degrees of business occupancy. An appliance repair shop or a woodworking shop on the premises would make the risk ineligible for a residential policy. But most rules permit a small exposure, such as a real estate, insurance, or doctor's office.

Number of Units Single-family dwellings and duplexes are eligible for all types of residential coverages, and three- and four-unit dwellings are eligible for dwelling fire policies, but in most states they are not eligible for homeowners policies. Larger units require commercial forms. Tenants of any habitational type of risk are usually eligible for a residential policy to cover their personal property.

Ownership In most companies, a dwelling which is owned by a corporation is ineligible for a personal residential policy. Such a risk is generally placed in an insurer's commercial book.

Specific Acceptability Criteria

As with auto insurance, not every risk which is eligible by the rules is acceptable to the company. An individual risk may be unacceptable because of factors inherent in the risk itself, whether personal (concerning the occupant) or physical (concerning the property and its use).

Most companies have underwriting guidelines which screen submissions prior to in-depth consideration by an underwriter. These guidelines themselves may rule out further consideration or they may divert the submission from the form or program for which the person applied to something else written by the company. Sometimes these statements are in a positive vein. For example, a manual may state that the company desires to write dwellings which are less than twenty years old, in good repair, and insured to value. It is more common to use negative guides, sometimes as a supplement to the positive statement. An illustrative cross section of company practices might include references to each of the following items. Underwriters, of course, must be familiar with their companies' approaches.

Dwelling Value Many companies consider risks with a dwelling or contents value below a certain specified amount as not acceptable for homeowners coverage. Such minimum dwelling values range from as little as $10,000 to as much as $50,000, depending on the program, form, and underwriting attitude of the company. The rationale for such a requirement is that extremely low-valued dwellings are generally in poor repair or of inferior construction. Alternatively, a low amount of insurance requested may represent low insurance to value and be inconsistent with the underwriting goals of the company. For example, some underwriting guides state that dwellings with an amount of insurance that is less than 80 or 90 percent of replacement cost are unacceptable.

Construction Quality Residences which are constructed of substandard materials or which do not conform to building codes are generally not acceptable. This would apply, for example, to a home with a wood shingle roof in an area where this is unapproved by fire departments, or to homes with inferior plywood siding and constructed prior to a building code.

Age of Dwelling Some companies set a maximum age on dwellings which are acceptable for a homeowners policy or a broad or special form. With some exceptions, old dwellings tend to have outdated and possibly hazardous plumbing, heating, and electrical systems. In addition, physical depreciation or obsolescence of older buildings that are not very well maintained may make an underwriter apprehensive about the prospect of creating a moral hazard by issuing a policy (such as the homeowners) that pays losses to building structures without deduction of depreciation from the full replacement cost of the loss. (However, full replacement cost coverage applies only if the amount of insurance is at least 80 percent of replacement cost at the time of loss.) Even though many companies use an age standard, it is not uniform throughout the industry and exceptions are often granted for modernized, well-maintained dwellings, regardless of their age.

Vacancy A vacant building is generally an unattractive risk due to the possibility of vandalism (often resulting in fire) and the inevitable deterioration due to lack of heat and maintenance. If the vacancy is prolonged by an inability to sell a dwelling, the problem becomes even greater because of the possibility that an owner may decide to "sell" the vacant house to the insurance company via a "fortuitous" fire.

Fire Protection Dwellings located in protection classes 9 and 10, as used in most states, are usually considered to be "unprotected" because they have little or no public fire protection. This greatly increases the chances for total fire losses. Despite higher rates in these areas, some companies consider risks in unprotected areas to be unacceptable unless it is the insured's secondary residence (e.g., a vacation cottage) and it is handled as accommodation business along with a good principal residence. Or, while accepting business in unprotected areas, the company may only write lower limits in recognition of the increased likelihood of a loss being a total loss.

Geographical Location The catastrophe potential of some geographical areas should be a matter of concern to all companies. Reinsurance is generally used to spread the risk and avoid shock losses. However, some companies do not accept risks located in hurricane zones, brush fire areas, or forest fire areas; or they limit their writings to those risks meeting strict qualifications as to location, construction, and the like. Refinements can be made, such as writing all perils except earthquake, in areas of high susceptibility to losses by earth tremors.

Seasonal Occupancy The additional exposures to loss by vandalism, theft, and fire in some areas, prompted some companies to decline to write any dwelling on a homeowners policy if the dwelling is seasonally occupied. This posture is reinforced by the fact that, as a class, seasonally-occupied homes are less well constructed and protected than homes used for permanent occupancy.

HOMEOWNERS PROGRAM FUNDAMENTALS

To this point the chapter has dealt with residence coverages and underwriting principles in a general fashion. Specific forms have been mentioned only to provide background for, and avoid duplication in, material to follow. This chapter now turns to concrete details in discussing the underwriting of Section I—the property portion—of homeowners policies. Underwriting other types of package policies and the dwelling fire forms will be covered in following chapters.

This section is devoted to a very brief overview of some aspects of the homeowners program; the following section deals with evaluating hazards in the underwriting of homeowners policies. Excluded and reserved for later treatment is HO-6, a form designed for owners of condominium units. The HO-8 is only described briefly.

General Nature

There are six varieties of homeowners policies in most states in addition to the form for condominiums. We have referred to them generally as "policies," but technically, each consists of a combination of (1) a policy jacket and declarations page, and (2) one of a series of six policy forms. The basic policy is incomplete, and always requires a form. The forms serve to distinguish one variety of homeowners from another. Where appropriate, one or more endorsements may further "tailor" the coverage already provided by the combination of the jacket and a form.

It is the forms that have numbers and specific labels. While some companies use their own nomenclature, the nationally standardized versions are referred to as form HO-1 (the basic form), form HO-2 (the broad form), form HO-3 (the special form), form HO-4 (the contents broad form), form HO-5 (the comprehensive form) and form HO-8 (actual cash value form). Variations exist in a number of states. Most states have adopted a new, more readable homeowners policy program, HO-76, that both simplified policy language (e.g., by eliminating the verbatim inclusion of the 165 lines of the standard fire policy formerly found on the jacket) and made a number of coverage changes (e.g., applies the same amount of coverage to unscheduled personal property both on and off the premises in all forms except HO-8). Underwriters have no choice but to be acquainted with the particulars of the forms and states with which they are concerned.

Each homeowners form contains two sections: Section I, dealing with property insurance, and Section II, with liability insurance. The latter is the same under all six forms, and will be discussed in Chapter 11 of this text. This chapter is concerned with Section I.

Eligibility

In most companies, eligibility for forms HO-1, 2, 3, 5, and 8 is restricted to owner-occupied one- or two-family dwelling units used exclusively for private residential purposes (although incidental office occupancy is permitted) and involving no more than two boarders per family. Form HO-4, which contains no building coverage, may be written for owner-occupants of buildings that are ineligible for one of the other forms, and for residential tenants.

Deductibles

Most forms are subject to a mandatory deductible clause, which is applicable to all Section I perils. However, it does not apply to additional living expenses.

Originally, the most common deductible was $50 on a diminishing basis. The insurer would pay 111 percent of the loss amount over $50, which caused the deductible to disappear on losses of $500 or more.

Today, flat deductibles are more common. With a $100 deductible, the amount of the loss is determined and the policyholder bears the first $100, with the insurer paying the balance, up to the applicable limits. Thus, the deductible is the same dollar amount regardless of the size of the loss. The $250 and $500 flat deductibles are becoming popular as inflation increases the number of dollars involved in even the smallest losses. Naturally, the premium is lower with a $250 deductible than a $100 deductible.

Some deductibles may be applicable either to all perils or just to theft. Independent filings by various companies include many modifications of deductibles, and in some states the standard deductible is 1 percent of the amount of insurance.

Insurance to Value

Securing an acceptable ratio of insurance to covered values is of paramount importance in achieving a profitable book of homeowners business. If an inadequate amount is initially submitted by a producer and accepted by the underwriter, changing the limit to reflect inflation in later years is unlikely to remedy that problem.

Many insurers prefer to have customers insure to 100 percent of replacement cost under coverage A (except under the HO-8, which was designed in recognition of the fact that insurance to replacement cost was unfair to owners of greatly depreciated homes who would not replace the home "as is"). This affords more complete protection to the policyholder than lesser amounts, and gives the insurer more premium with which to pay losses. Since the limits applicable to other items in Section I are based on the limit applicable to coverage A, an appropriate amount under coverage A benefits the coverage in the entire Section I.

While dwelling coverage equal to full replacement cost is desirable from all viewpoints, most insurers settle for insurance equal to 80 percent of replacement cost as a minimum when writing new business. However, in an era of rapidly rising building costs, 80 percent of value at inception can become inadequate to meet that requirement in a short period of time. The inflation guard endorsement which is described in Chapter 7 helps somewhat with this problem.

The importance of insurance to value must be made clear to personal lines underwriters. This text covers this subject at several points in the next three chapters, since insurance to value is an underwriting factor at various steps in the underwriting decision-making process.

EVALUATING HAZARDS IN RESIDENTIAL POLICY UNDERWRITING

Line underwriters work primarily on individual risks, not on classes or groups. That is, they underwrite one risk at a time. The basic task is to analyze the hazards of each risk presented.

Types of Hazards

Hazards can be grouped into the categories of moral, morale, and physical. (Legal hazard was defined in Chapter 2 and will not be discussed here because it is of lesser importance in property insurance than in liability insurance.) Moral hazard in a residence context can be illustrated by arson, a feigned burglary loss, or claiming that a wallet stolen from the insured's hotel room contained $100 in cash when it actually contained $10. Morale hazard can be illustrated by poor maintenance of home appliances, careless smoking, and failure to safeguard jewelry or other valuables. Physical hazards include the forces of nature and the location, construction, and use of the dwelling. As in auto insurance, moral hazard is almost impossible to detect before the fact although certain circumstances that point to its possible presence can sometimes be discerned. Morale hazards *may* be more subject to detection, but the limitations on the residence insurance underwriter's resources prohibit complete investigation. Physical hazards tend to be more obvious or identifiable through reasoned presumptions by the alert underwriter.

Factors in Identifying or Measuring Hazards

The factors which make up these three types of hazards are the characteristics which determine if a residential property is acceptable for the desired coverage in a given company. It is the underwriter's job to examine each factor of these hazards and determine if it is contemplated by the rate which is to be charged or whether the hazards are such that the risk is unacceptable or acceptable only under different terms. Hazard factors can be separated according to whether they relate primarily to the applicant or to the property and its use.

Concerning the Applicant

Attitude Toward Property. A significant consideration in underwriting homeowners is: "How well does the insured maintain the property?" The exterior appearance of a home will usually indicate a great deal about the occupants and their attitude toward the property. Underwriting results might be improved if all policyholders had the following positive property features: well-trimmed lawn and shrubbery; no peeling paint or rotten wood; roof and gutters in excellent condition; cement walkways or patios free from cracks and heaves; windows intact and clean; and no litter, toys, or tools on the lawn. Positive weight should be given to the insured whose property reflects regular maintenance. This does *not* include the overzealous do-it-yourself owner who attempts work for which he or she is not qualified (particularly on plumbing, heating, and wiring projects). Unfortunately, it is a rare case in which the latter can be identified in advance of losses.

On the other hand, negative weight is given to the opposite property conditions. A cracked window which is not replaced indicates a lack of concern on the part of the occupant. A yard that is littered with old tires, rusty tools, abandoned cars, and so on indicates the owner's lack of interest.

Personal Characteristics and Activities. The fact that insurance policies are personal contracts is fundamental in underwriting homeowners. So many potential losses covered by the contract are largely or partially subject to prevention and causation by the insured that the human, rather than property, aspect of the relationship must be kept uppermost in the underwriter's mind. It is of major importance to determine the personal characteristics of the insured. Irresponsibility, instability, and immaturity may be indicated through an inspection report and an investigation of previous claims, but objective determinations are very difficult to obtain. One can often determine that a person *is* responsible, stable, and mature, but it is very hard to demonstrate that he or she is not!

It is difficult to fully evaluate the character of a person from the information given on the application for insurance. The only facts available from that source bearing upon what could be termed the "human factor" are occupation, loss experience, and marital status. In the vast majority of cases, this data is sufficient. However, where there are indications that a problem may exist, other relevant features should be identified and weighed in making the underwriting decision. For example, claim history may indicate that an unusual exposure is present, which would justify an in-depth review. The appearance of a police record, a history of excessive use of alcoholic beverages or narcotics, questionable associates, and similar characteristics and habits would be viewed with caution by most underwriters.

Unless negative features in other categories warrant a closer examination, the underwriter should be satisfied with the personal aspect of the risk when the occupation and personal data indicate no unusual exposures.

Generally companies regard the fact that an applicant is married as a positive factor (especially in marriages with children). With married couples, the dwelling is less often unoccupied during the day, thus reducing the danger of loss from theft or of a fire going unnoticed until it is out of control. Recent years have seen a marked increase in daytime burglaries. Daytime occupancy helps to reduce such losses.

Increased exposure can also result from a person's leisure activities. Fire loss may accompany hobbies which involve the use of paints, varnishes, or shellacs, such as the refinishing of furniture. The individual who does welding work in the basement or garage is a below-average fire risk. Collecting valuable objects can create an increased exposure to theft when the collection becomes known to the community. Professional thieves are adept at identifying and targeting even the discreet hobbyist with a valuable collection of marketable items. Damage to such objects can also pose an underwriting problem.

While some hobbies can involve negative features, significant weight is not assigned to them unless the exposure is substantial. Like most secondary features, the underwriter will not be aware of the exposure unless the risk has been selected for in-depth treatment, or if it becomes apparent from an investigation or claim.

Claim History. One of the primary principles of underwriting is that a study of the past can help to foretell the future. Many, if not most, decisions on the acceptability of a risk are based on the assumption that the insured's past record will continue into the future. But often this factor requires analysis and interpretation, and should not be followed blindly. The conditions surrounding the risk may be very different from those that existed in the past.

When the claims history of a potential insured is analyzed, the primary concern is with losses that may recur in the future, due either to the characteristics of the insured or the cause of the loss.

If an insured's record is marred by several losses from the same cause, one of two conclusions may be drawn: (1) the insured is not concerned enough with the property to remove the loss cause and prevent future losses from the same source, or (2) the loss cause by its very nature is uncontrollable. For example, if an analysis of an insured's claim history reveals three fire losses over three years due to a malfunctioning oil burner, the underwriter might conclude correctly that this insured did not display enough concern about the property as evidenced by the failure to have the oil burner cleaned or repaired. On the other hand, if the file reveals four wind losses in five years, it may be that no action by the insured—short of moving out of the wind-prone area—could have reduced the hazards.

A risk generally is unacceptable to most companies if there have been several losses due to carelessness, or if the insured has failed to remove causes of loss which are controllable. Furthermore, a risk may be unacceptable if the insured has a history of claims indicating possible dishonesty.

A risk may be acceptable if there have been several losses from the same peril which were not controllable. However, the underwriter cannot ignore the fact that such a claims history is not the usual pattern, and that these claims do cost money regardless of how faultless the insured may be. Steps should be taken to minimize future insured losses from that peril. A high deductible may be in order. The problem peril might be excluded from the contract, either by offering a more restrictive form or policy or actual exclusion of a peril (when permitted) where coverage for it can be secured elsewhere, such as in one of the programs to be discussed in Chapter 9 of this text. Still another possibility is to modify the physical hazards to reduce the chance of loss, such as by requiring the installation of a burglar alarm.

Occupation and Employment Record. Stability and reliability of the insured are important factors to an underwriter. Some types of jobs are more stable than others, while the number of jobs that a person has held during a recent period is an indication of that person's stability. The type of occupation and the employment record may give valuable clues to these factors, which are difficult to measure otherwise.

In looking at the risk as a whole, two factors of interest to the underwriter are (1) the applicant's ability to afford the house and the related upkeep expenditures, and (2) the relationship between what the applicant does for a living and the loss potential of the risk.

Some occupations require considerable travel, which increases the exposure to theft. Other occupations call for a life-style which is not conducive to a stable home life. Still other occupations are notorious for instability and job-jumping.

It is easy to see that the dwelling insurance of an auto mechanic who utilizes a portion of the dwelling to conduct a moonlighting operation of spray-painting autos is a less desirable risk than that of a factory worker who utilizes his or her dwelling for nothing out of the ordinary. Any occupation which utilizes the residence as part of the insured's occupation may create additional hazards.

Most companies have gone further than the elimination of the obviously undesirable hazard and have developed marketing plans for personal residential insurance. To quote from one company's residential program manual:

> ...as a group, the middle income bracket will provide our best insureds. They have enough income to maintain their property, but not enough to travel extensively, to become targets for theft or excessive liability suits, or to afford attractive nuisances (such as swimming pools). The insured whose occupation requires him to travel extensively is going to have an increased exposure to theft, both at home and away from the premises.

Concerning the Property and Its Use

Construction Characteristics. Construction characteristics show wide geographical differences, so it is difficult to make generalizations that are accurate without regard to territory. Obviously, the sound, well-constructed home is desired, but the particulars of what is meant by "well-constructed" must recognize differences in climate and construction practices in various areas of the country. For example, in most parts of the country the underwriter would expect the well-constructed home to have a central heating system, but it would be unrealistic to impose this standard as a general guideline on risks in the nation's southern areas. In those areas many sound housing units are heated solely by space heaters. As long as these are properly maintained and vented to the outside, they ordinarily would not make a risk unacceptable for the homeowners program.

One guide to the quality of a home's construction is the reputation of the contractor who built the home. While helpful, this information often is not available from the applicant, who in many cases has no easy way to identify the builder.

Quality construction requires a roof in good condition made from desirable materials, which might include metal, slate, tile, asbestos, composition shingles, and composition roofing materials. Roofs which would be undesirable from an underwriting standpoint, in most regions, include wooden shingles and boards as well as tar paper.

Underwriters are concerned with the type of roofing materials for two reasons: (1) susceptibility to loss and (2) spread of fire. Some roofs are less likely to burn but may be very susceptible to wind damage. Wood shingle roofs, for example, may help to spread a fire when burning cinders from a fire settle on the roof.

Open foundations present increased fire hazard. In some areas homes with open foundations are either surcharged or are regarded as of questionable construction quality for homeowners coverage.

Plastic or aluminum siding is a building material which can cause underwriting problems. It dents easily and is quite vulnerable to hail damage. Company practices in underwriting risks with these special sidings follow no uniform pattern. In most areas this siding would get no special consideration because of the low frequency of hailstorms. In hail-prone areas, some companies insist on a substantial deductible. The maintenance-free nature of aluminum siding is a positive feature, however.

It might seem that, given a choice, a personal lines underwriter would prefer a masonry building to a frame one, and a fire resistive building to a masonry one. This is not necessarily the case. Although a masonry building is less susceptible to fire damage than a frame building, the rate promulgated for each construction class should reflect this difference. Variation in rate adequacy among classes in some areas may make frame dwellings more desirable than masonry residences.

Assuming adequate rates for each construction class, the underwriter generally is more interested in the quality of construction than in the construction classification itself. Residences constructed of inferior materials or in an unworkmanlike manner, no matter the construction class, are often considered unacceptable risks. Residences which do not meet the standards imposed by building codes on new construction are usually more susceptible to damage from many of the perils insured against in a residence insurance contract.

In many areas of the country, such items as "tar paper" roofing materials, and plywood siding, denote inferior construction features. Such inferior construction features are sometimes found in homes built prior to the advent of modern building codes or in rural areas where building codes are nonexistent or unenforced.

Even modern homes are subject to construction defects. A National Fire Protection Association dwelling fire report cites a case in which "The . . . fire occurred in a *new* split-level house where the flooring behind the fireplace was at a level halfway between the hearth and the upper part of the fireplace. The flooring, which apparently had inadequate clearances, was ignited after the fireplace had been in prolonged use. . . ."[7]

It should be noted that the quality of heating, air conditioning, and electrical systems is usually considered as part of the overall construction quality of a risk. Defects in these systems greatly increase the chance of a fire in a dwelling. Loss records of dwelling fires are replete with such loss causes as "do-it yourself wiring," "electrical fault," "defective chimney," "improper installation of a wood stove," and "defective construction." The quality of construction and the degree of conformance to building codes usually are the deciding features in evaluating the construction characteristics of a residential risk.

Age of Dwelling. Closely related to construction characteristics is the age of the dwelling. Some company underwriting guides use twenty-five years as a benchmark for acceptability. Dwellings more than twenty-five years of age are underwritten with caution, while those more than fifty years old require extreme care. Some of the problems which concern older homes are:

1. Market value may not keep up with the replacement cost. This situation results in the tendency to underinsure and in inadequate premium for the exposure. (The HO-8 responds to this problem.)
2. Plumbing, heating, and electrical systems are outdated and often have been subject to long neglect. Electrical systems become overloaded with modern appliances; furnaces become subject to backfire losses; pipes corrode. Recognizing that a large number of losses occur from malfunctioning of such

systems, underwriters are concerned when faced with risks where age and the possibility of prolonged neglect of systems literally invite losses.

3. Costly and rare (by current standards) building materials often have been used, making partial losses more expensive.

Underwriters should relate the age of the home to the area. The older home may be located in a neighborhood where properties are well maintained. If not, photographs of the home, plus information on the most recent update of the electrical, heating, and plumbing systems are generally required. If the underwriter is satisfied that the negative factors associated with age are not present, then any other negative risk features which combine with age to increase exposure must be examined. Some age problems can be overcome by writing a limited named-perils form of coverage, or by using higher deductibles to eliminate maintenance-type losses.

Protection Type and Quality. An important factor in measuring the hazard is the degree of public fire and police protection available.

From a fire underwriting standpoint, the protection class is very important. Although the rates are higher for the higher-numbered classes, some underwriters feel that the potential for a total loss in an unprotected area is much greater than the rate contemplates. That is, risks in unprotected areas have to be underwritten as potential total losses while those in protected areas will most likely result in partial losses. Accordingly, some underwriting standards will show as acceptable only risks located in classes 1 through 8.

Some areas have little or no public fire protection. Even where some degree of protection is available, most underwriters consider a risk as being "unprotected" unless it is within five miles of a fire station and within 1,000 feet of a fire hydrant. (The actual distances may vary by state, and may even be part of the rating structure in some territories.) The reasoning underlying this position is based on (1) firefighting ability being minimal if the equipment has a long distance to travel, and (2) the need to resort solely to tank trucks when fire hydrants are too far away.

Some homes are located well beyond the limits of a city or town and are quite isolated. When there are no close neighbors, a fire might go unreported until it is completely out of control. Also, such homes usually are at such a distance from the fire department that, even if notified promptly, it may not arrive in time to be effective in reducing the loss.

An underwriter considering acceptance of an isolated or unprotected dwelling would consider several factors in addition to the degree of public fire protection, and the proximity of a dependable water source. The age of the dwelling is a factor, since a newer home usually has electrical and heating systems in better condition than an older home. Since there may be weak or no building codes, construction is also a factor. If the dwelling is isolated, it could help to have a telephone on the premises. This might result in a report of the fire if someone is at home. Smoke detectors would be another favorable factor. These might allow a fire to be discovered quickly.

Another aspect of accessibility is the possible existence of any geographical or physical barriers which may prevent a fire or police department from reaching an isolated "unprotected" risk. Such items as potentially impassable roads (dirt or gravel type) which can be blocked by high spring water or winter snows, or are a distance from a source of water, are all factors which must be examined when evaluating the availability of public protection for a dwelling risk. Such factors are sometimes considered in the rates for unprotected risks.

Location. As previously mentioned, the physical location of the dwelling can be a factor in underwriting homeowners risks. Since fire losses are a major problem, a primary concern is the location from a fire standpoint. The rating classes are an accurate measure of many factors of location, such as the quality of the fire department and the availability of water. However, there are other factors which can cause concern.

A dwelling located in a commercial area may be exposed to a fire from nearby factories, warehouses, or stores; or to heat, smoke, and water damage because of a fire there. A tenant applying for an HO-4 may occupy the third floor of a building housing a metal working shop in the first floor and present an entirely different "exposure" hazard than a tenant in an apartment building. Even dwellings on the fringes of residential and commercial areas may be exposed to losses from gas stations, fast-food restaurants, and vacant stores. These fringe areas can also create increased exposures to vandalism and theft losses.

Some parts of the country are subject to forest fires and brush fires. While the territory subject to abnormal loss may be small, the houses in such areas need special consideration. In some cases many very expensive homes may be in such an area, which may increase the chance of a large loss if one insurer has a number of the homes insured.

Windstorm and hail losses are related to the location of the risk. Most tornado areas are not subject to underwriting by location because it is impossible to pinpoint specific areas of tornado occurrence. On the other hand, the homes exposed most frequently to hurricane winds can be identified with *relative* precision, and care must be taken when considering a risk in such a location.

A dwelling located in an area subject to wave wash is considered a more hazardous risk for two reasons. First, there may be some difficulty in segregating wind damage from wave wash damage. Second, such seaside properties are more heavily exposed to wind than are inland properties. Underwriting information beyond that normally required is in order if such a dwelling is considered. Distance from the water at normal high tide, the existence of sand dunes and seawalls, and the elevation of the building compared with the highest recorded tides or high water mark during past storms are important items of information. Quality of construction and permanence of occupancy are important considerations when considering this (and any other) windstorm exposure, as are any existing precautionary measures against storms, such as storm shutters and sand bags.

Dwellings located in seashore areas that are normally seasonal in nature have great exposure to wind-related losses. They also become isolated in the off-season and therefore are subject to theft losses at a time when police protection has usually been reduced.

Theft and vandalism losses are heavier in certain territories, such as urban core areas. When homeowners policies are written in these locations, the underwriter might require special private protection such as a burglar alarm and double cylinder dead-bolt locks, especially if contents values are high.

The above examples illustrate the part that location plays in underwriting. A risk may be flawless in itself, with high-quality construction, excellent maintenance, and an owner who is above reproach. Still, the house may be in a location which has an unusually high exposure to certain types of losses. The underwriter of homeowners policies must consider the hazards of location on an overall basis.

Sometimes this consideration involves trade-offs, with the location being favorable for some perils in the policy but unfavorable for others. From a fire standpoint, the best risks may be in the large cities where fire protection and building codes are generally the strongest. Yet, many sections of large cities have high frequency rates for theft and vandalism, and these perils are packaged in the policy along with fire. Thus, the question of location presents greater complexity in underwriting homeowners than in underwriting, say, a fire policy with an extended coverage endorsement.

Protective Devices. Although public protection is the primary focus in residential insurance, private protection should not be overlooked. In recent years, private protection devices in the form of smoke detectors, heat detectors, or other household fire warning devices have become popular for residential properties. Even though not always required, the installation of such devices makes a risk more desirable. Such systems have become mandatory in multiple unit housing (apartments and condominiums) in many areas of the country, and some locales are even requiring the installation of such devices in new single-family homes. The Life Safety Code of the National Fire Protection Association provides that, "At least one approved smoke detector powered by the house electric service shall be installed in an approved manner in every dwelling unit. When activated, the detector shall initiate an alarm which is audible in the sleeping rooms." (22-3.2.1)[8] "One estimate . . . is that as many as 3,400 lives could be saved annually if every dwelling unit were provided with . . . two . . . smoke-detectors."[9] In addition to the life safety features of smoke and heat detectors, such devices should be instrumental in reducing property damage losses due to earlier detection and control of fires.

Burglary losses may be reduced with the use of burglar alarms. With American families, it is common for a house to be unoccupied for days or weeks at a time while the entire family enjoys a vacation away from home.

Central station alarms provide the most sophisticated burglar protection. These devices have direct contact with the local police department and will bring police assistance within a matter of minutes. Local alarms are effective in alerting neighbors, if they are present in the immediate area, and will often frighten away the would-be burglar. There are some relatively inexpensive local alarms which provide a defense of the perimeter of the building. The alarms are operated by batteries, and separate units are used for each door and window. They produce a noise which alerts the neighbors and might frighten away the thief.

Sources of Underwriting Information

As was true with personal auto insurance, the underwriter needs information about the risk to (1) determine eligibility; (2) develop a composite picture of the risk; (3) make a decision on acceptability, including any special qualifications and terms; (4) document the decision; and possibly (5) issue a policy. The sources of information in underwriting homeowners policies are familiar by type—the application, inspection report, producer, and other insurers.

The Application for Insurance The producer must complete some type of application (or daily) for every policy. The information contained in the application is the starting point for the underwriter.

Types of Information on the Application. There are two types of material given in the application: facts to be used in the issuance of the policy, and answers to questions concerning underwriting factors.

The first type is included in all applications. In the past, many producers actually issued the policy, and sent a copy (called a "daily report") to the underwriter. Today, fewer producers are doing this since most policies are computer-issued by the insurer. Whatever the format, these facts are intended primarily to facilitate the issuance of the policy and to start an underwriting file. This is not to suggest that data from a "daily report" are unimportant or of little value in underwriting. Indeed, such details as the name of the insured, the property and mailing address, the data on a mortgagee, if any, the rating and valuation data, the property description, the selection of coverages and perils, and the desired limits and deductibles say much about the nature of the risk being written.

The second type of information may not be required by all companies. Some insurers permit the producer to select the risks, at least within guidelines and in certain categories. However, if the insurer intends to underwrite the risk at all, the answers to some questions must be secured. Although there is little uniformity, most applications develop the same general information which can be classified into the following categories:

1. personal,
2. description of property, and
3. insurance information.

A typical application used by a number of companies in conjunction with ACORD is shown in Exhibit 6-3.

Limitations of Application Information. Limitations exist on even the most complete of the applications. The application cannot be so extensive that it anticipates every situation which might arise. Even if this could be done, the form would be too long to be practical. There is a limitation on the number of questions that an underwriter can expect a producer and/or applicant to answer.

Limitations are also present because of the nature of homeowners insurance. The average premium is small, even when compared with auto insurance. This limits the time and effort the producer and company can spend on the placement of the coverage, and thus the amount of information to be placed on the application. In addition, most applicants for homeowners policies are acceptable without the need for modification. This contrasts with auto insurance, where additional factual information is available in the form of MVRs and a higher

Exhibit 6-3
ACORD Homeowner Application*

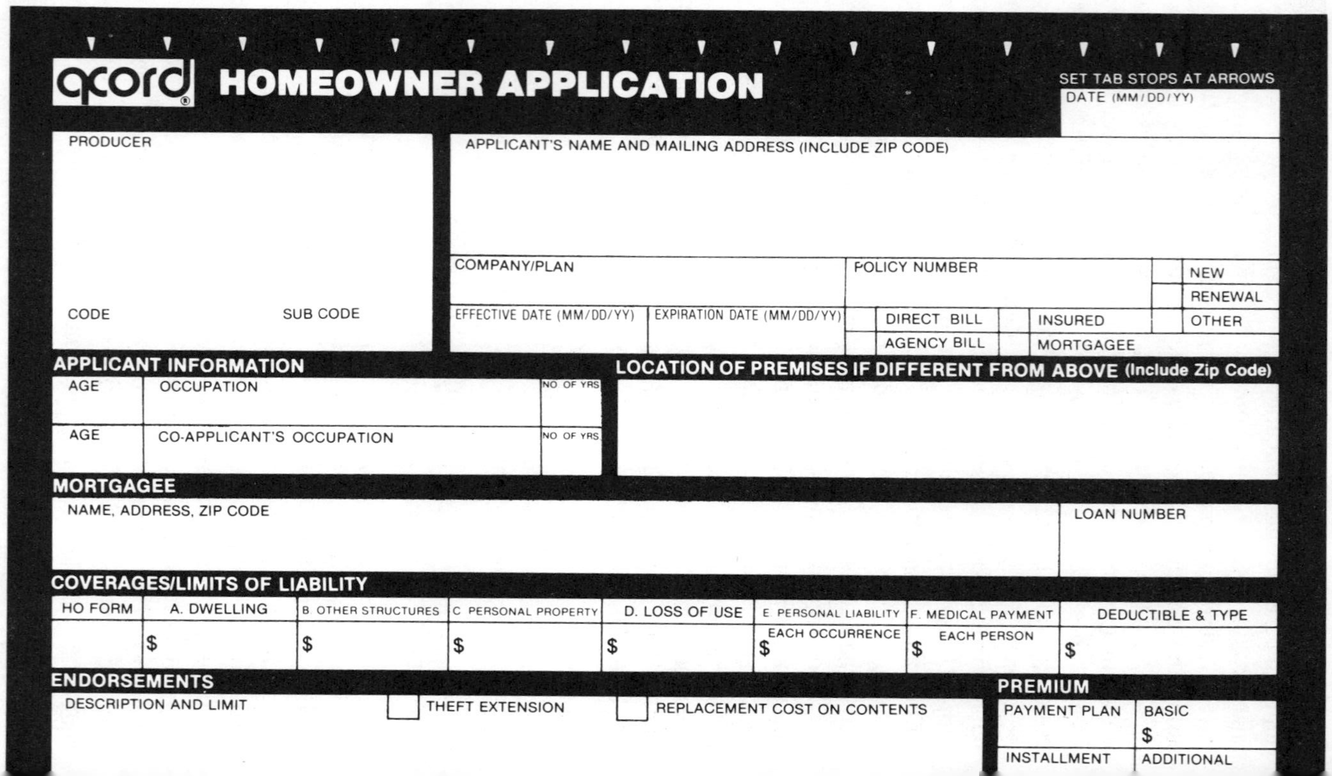
ACORD HOMEOWNER APPLICATION

SET TAB STOPS AT ARROWS

DATE (MM/DD/YY)

PRODUCER	APPLICANT'S NAME AND MAILING ADDRESS (INCLUDE ZIP CODE)				
	COMPANY/PLAN		POLICY NUMBER		NEW / RENEWAL / OTHER
CODE / SUB CODE	EFFECTIVE DATE (MM/DD/YY)	EXPIRATION DATE (MM/DD/YY)	DIRECT BILL / AGENCY BILL	INSURED / MORTGAGEE	

APPLICANT INFORMATION

AGE	OCCUPATION	NO. OF YRS
AGE	CO-APPLICANT'S OCCUPATION	NO. OF YRS

LOCATION OF PREMISES IF DIFFERENT FROM ABOVE (Include Zip Code)

MORTGAGEE

NAME, ADDRESS, ZIP CODE	LOAN NUMBER

COVERAGES/LIMITS OF LIABILITY

HO FORM	A. DWELLING	B. OTHER STRUCTURES	C. PERSONAL PROPERTY	D. LOSS OF USE	E. PERSONAL LIABILITY	F. MEDICAL PAYMENT	DEDUCTIBLE & TYPE
	$	$	$	$	EACH OCCURRENCE $	EACH PERSON $	$

ENDORSEMENTS

DESCRIPTION AND LIMIT ☐ THEFT EXTENSION ☐ REPLACEMENT COST ON CONTENTS

PREMIUM

PAYMENT PLAN	BASIC $
INSTALLMENT	ADDITIONAL

$ | $

RATING/GENERAL INFORMATION

				YEAR BUILT	# FAMILIES	# ROOMS	MARKET VALUE	REPLACEMENT COST			# OF UNITS IN FIRE DIVISION
	FRAME		ALUMINUM SIDING				$	$		TOWN HOUSE	
	MASONRY		FIRE RESISTIVE							ROW HOUSE	
	MASONRY VENEER		OTHER							APARTMENTS	

		PROTECTION CLASS	TERRITORY CODE	PREMIUM GROUP	SPECIAL STATE REQUIREMENTS	DISTANCE TO HYDRANT	DISTANCE TO FIRE STATION			FIRE/EC RATE	# APTS.
	PRIMARY								CLASS RATED		
	SECONDARY					FT.	MI.		SPECIFICALLY RATED		
	SEASONAL										

FIRE DISTRICT/CODE NUMBER	PRIOR CARRIER/POLICY NUMBER/AMT. OF COVERAGE	YEARS KNOWN BY AGENT	ADDITIONAL INFORMATION

EXPLAIN ALL "YES" RESPONSES IN REMARKS	YES	NO	EXPLAIN ALL "YES" RESPONSES IN REMARKS	YES	NO
1. Business conducted on premises?			6. Is wood/coal stove or solar heating used?		
2. Full time residence employees?			7. Any other residence owned, occupied or rented?		
3. Protective devices installed?			8. Any other insurance with company?		
4. Swimming pool on premises?			9. Any insurance declined, cancelled or non-renewed (last 3 yrs.)? Not applicable in Kansas, Ohio, D.C., Illinois or Missouri.		
5. Has wiring, plumbing or heating been updated?					

LOSS HISTORY

DATE (MM/DD/YY)	TYPE	DESCRIPTION OF LOSS	AMOUNT

REMARKS

ATTACHMENTS

	INLAND MARINE APPLICATION
	REPLACEMENT COST ESTIMATE
	PHOTOGRAPH

COMPANY USE

1	2	3	4	5	C	7	8

ACORD 80 (4/81) PLEASE COMPLETE REVERSE SIDE

OPTIONAL ENDORSEMENTS THAT REQUIRE ADDITIONAL INFORMATION

Endorsement	Information Required
HO 40† - Structures Rented to Others— Residence Premises	Identification of Structure • Specify Address if at Secondary Residence Premises Number of Families Limit of Liability •Medical Payments to Others Included or Excluded
HO 41 - Additional Insured - Residence Premises Only	Name of Person(s) or Organization(s) Address Interest •Location of Premises
HO 42 - Office, Professional, Private School or Studio Use- Residence Premises	Occupancy Medical Payments to Others Included or Excluded Dwelling or Described Structure
HO 48 - Other Structures	Identification of Structure Additional Limit of Liability •Specify Address if at Secondary Location
HO 52 - Continuous Renewal Plan Endorsement	Policy terms and effective dates

Endorsement	Information Required
HO 53 - Credit Card and Depositors Forgery *Coverage Endorsement	Limit of Liability Increased to $______
HO 61 - Scheduled Personal *Property Endorsement	Amount of Insurance Description of Items
HO 67 - *Secondary Residence Premises	Attach a completed Homeowners Application
HO 70 - Additional Residence Premises - Rented to Others	Location Number of Families *Medical Payments to Others Included or Excluded
HO 75 - Watercraft Endorsement	Horsepower and Description of Motor Owner (if not Named Insured) Description of Boat Length and Description of Watercraft Rated Speed (miles per hour) Horsepower Navigation Period (each year)
HO 243 - Inflation Guard	Percentage

† Use ISO or Appropriate Company Number
* Applies to Non HO-76 ONLY

FOR COMPANY USE

BINDER/SIGNATURE

INSURANCE BINDER		IF THE "BINDER" BOX TO THE LEFT IS CHECKED, THE FOLLOWING CONDITIONS APPLY:
☐ COVERAGE IS NOT BOUND		This Company binds the kind(s) of insurance stipulated on the reverse side. This insurance is subject to the terms, conditions and limitations of the policy(ies) in current use by the Company.
☐ BINDER		
EFFECTIVE DATE (MM/DD/YY)	EXPIRATION DATE (MM/DD/YY)	This binder may be cancelled by the insured by surrender of this binder or by written notice to the Company stating when cancellation will be effective. This binder may be cancelled by the Company by notice to the Insured in accordance with the policy conditions. This binder is cancelled when replaced by a policy. If this binder is not replaced by a policy, the Company is entitled to charge a premium for the binder according to the Rules and Rates in use by the Company.
TIME	☐ 12:01 A.M. ☐ NOON	

IMPORTANT NOTICE REGARDING THE FAIR CREDIT REPORTING ACT: In making this application for insurance it is understood that as part of our underwriting procedure, an investigative consumer report may be prepared whereby information is obtained through personal interviews with your neighbors, friends, or others with whom you are acquainted. This inquiry includes information as to your character, general reputation, personal characteristics and mode of living. If an investigation is made, you can be assured that it will be handled in the strictest confidence.
If you wish information on the nature and scope of the Customer Report which may be requested, ask your agent for the address of the Company handling your account.

APPLICANT'S STATEMENT: I have read the above application and I declare that to the best of my knowledge and belief all of the foregoing statements are true, and that these statements are offered as an inducement to the Company to issue the policy for which I am applying. (Kansas: This does not constitute a warranty.)

APPLICANT'S SIGNATURE		DATE (MM/DD/YY)	PRODUCER'S SIGNATURE	

ACORD 80 (4/81)

percentage of the risks are surcharged or the coverage is amended in one way or another.

Inspection Reports The underwriter may desire more information than is contained in the application. Sometimes information on the application points to a need for more facts. Other times there will be a combination of factors that demand more investigation. In still other cases, the underwriter will have a "feeling" about a particular risk and desire verification or refutation of this feeling.

Under any of these circumstances, an inspection report is a likely source of the desired information. When the information from the producer is not sufficient for decision making, an inspection report is virtually the only other source available to the underwriter of homeowners policies.

When inspection reports are desired, they are generally ordered from the same companies used for other policies. Several types of reports are available. One type is a comprehensive report which includes a considerable degree of information about the applicant and the property; this type would be requested when the underwriter is concerned about the moral and morale hazards. Another type includes little information about the applicant and, instead, concentrates on the physical aspects of the risk. Still another type is strictly a physical inspection, dealing only with the exterior of the dwelling and the neighboring premises; these are sometimes designated as "drive-by" or "sidewalk" inspections. A typical inspection report is shown in Exhibit 6-4.

Physical inspections may be made by company employees in some cases. Certain insurers with considerable volume of residence insurance employ inspectors in areas of the greatest concentration. In addition, many companies ask their employees who travel in the field, such as special agents or commercial engineers, to inspect an occasional personal risk for a particular purpose. The latter practice is quite expensive in most cases, although costs are hidden. Underwriters use it only in special cases, such as those requiring a decision in a short period of time or those in which inspection by an outside agency is not feasible.

Photographs. Since the physical condition of the building is one of the most important factors in homeowners underwriting, a photograph of the exterior of the dwelling is very helpful. A picture can tell the underwriter more about the construction and condition of the building than a lengthy description. Photographs are available with inspection reports and most of them are secured from this source. However, some companies require the producer to submit a photograph with all applications or on specified types of risks such as dwellings over a particular age.

A significant problem with photographs lies in the fact that the camera angle is all-important. A picture taken from a distance too close to the dwelling will not show the surrounding area. One taken from too great a distance will not disclose such physical problems as a worn roof, or will permit trees or other buildings to interfere with clarity. Because of these difficulties, some underwriters require two photographs taken from opposite corners at a medium distance.

Photographs can help the underwriter check on the relationship between the amount of insurance requested and the replacement value of the dwelling. Further information might be sought in cases where the amount of insurance appears to be far out of line—either too low *or* too high—with the impression of value communicated by the photograph(s).

Fair Credit Reporting Act. As mentioned in connection with auto underwriting, an important factor involved in the request for an inspection report is the effect of the Fair Credit Reporting Act of 1971. This act was passed to provide consumers with some guarantee of the accuracy of data files which are used to confirm or deny them credit or insurance.

The Fair Credit Reporting Act does not prevent an underwriter from canceling or declining coverage on a risk, but it does provide that if such action is based on a report, the consumer must be so informed, and notified of the name and address of the reporting agency.

In the years since the act has become effective, the primary result for the insurance underwriter has been an increase in the paperwork necessary to secure underwriting data on a risk. This in turn has effectively reduced the number of such reports ordered. At the same time, it is felt by some underwriters that such reports tend to be more accurate than before the act, primarily because the consumer now has the right to challenge and change incorrect or incomplete information.

The Producer In addition to providing the information on the daily or the application, the producer is an excellent source to whom the underwriter may address specific questions after the initial risk submission. Such questions may be raised due to the unusual nature of some of the data on the application or daily. At other times, questions may arise when required information does not appear on the application. In such instances, the producer, who often knows the insured, is a natural source of additional information.

Some companies insist that the producer actually inspect the risk and develop firsthand information on which to base an underwriting recommendation. With or without such a requirement, companies place great reliance on the producer's knowledge of the area in which the risk is located, and the values of various types of dwellings in the area.

Exhibit 6-4
Dwelling Property Report—Personal Lines

DWELLING PROPERTY REPORT
PERSONAL LINES

AGCY.-BR.
POL. NO.

ACCT.
DATE
NAME
MAILING ADDRESS

PROPERTY INSPECTED (IF OTHER THAN ABOVE)

AMT. OF COVERAGE: $

PHOTOS
☐ ATTACHED # PHOTOS ____ (IF MORE THAN ONE)
☐ NOT REQUESTED
☐ NOT AVAILABLE (EXPLAIN BELOW)

I PROPERTY OBSERVATION

OTHER:

1. Apprx. Year Built ________
2. Number of Stories: ☐ 1 ☐ 2 ☐ 3 ☐ ________
3. Occupancy: ☐ Single Family ☐ Two Family ☐ ________
4. Predominant Constr. Material:
   - A. Dwg. ☐ Frame ☐ Brick Veneer ☐ Solid Brick or Stone ☐ ________
   - B. Roof ☐ Comp. Shingle ☐ Tar & Gravel ☐ Wood Shingle ☐ ________
   - C. Outbuildings ☐ None ☐ Frame ☐ Masonry ☐ Metal ☐ ________
5. Condition:
   - A. Dwg. ☐ Good ☐ ________
   - B. Roof ☐ Good ☐ ________
   - C. Outbuildings ☐ None ☐ Good ☐ ________
6. Neighborhood:
   - A. Type ☐ Residential ☐ Commercial ☐ Rural ☐ ________
   - B. Status ☐ Improving ☐ Stable ☐

II PROPERTY VALUES

DIAGRAM - SHOW DIMENSIONS

1. GROUND FLOOR SQUARE FOOT AREA

7. PROTECTION:

Approximate Distance in Feet to Nearest Hydrant ____________

Approximate Distance in Miles to Nearest Responding Fire Department ____________

8. HAZARDS NOTED:

- ☐ None
- ☐ Vacant or Seasonal Property
- ☐ Isolated or Hidden
- ☐ Difficult Access for Fire Department
- ☐ Dead Trees or Limbs
- ☐ Combustible Brush or Debris
- ☐ Open Foundation
- ☐ Adjacent Property Hazard
- ☐ Flooding or High Water
- ☐ Other ____________

REMARKS — RECOMMENDATIONS FOR IMPROVEMENT — POSSIBLE PREVIOUS CARRIER

____

____

____

____

____

____

____

____

Quality Grade	______
Base Cost	______
Garage/Carport	+ ______
Baths (extra)	+ ______
Fireplace(s)	+ ______
Porch	+ ______
Basement: ☐ Finished ☐ Unfinished	+ ______
Central Air Cond.	+ ______
Adjusted Base Cost	= ______
Area Index	× ______
2. ESTIMATED REPLACEMENT COST EXCLUDING LAND	= ☐
3. ESTIMATED MARKET VALUE EXCLUDING LAND	= ☐

FIELD REP. ____________ B. O. ____________

III **PROPERTY AMPLIFIED**

Interview? ☐ No ☐ Yes ____________ (Who?) Other Source - Time Known ____________

OCCUPANT ____________ ☐ Owner ☐ Renter ☐ Lessee

1. Approximate age ____________
2. Marital status ____________
3. Employer ____________
4. Occupation/Job Title ____________
5. Occupation - Spouse ____________
6. How long this address? ____________
7. Ages children: At Home ____________
   Away (Schools, etc.) ____________
8. Ages other relatives Living in Household ____________
9. Anyone in household smoke? NO ☐ YES ☐

10. Type heating unit: ____________
11. Type fuel: ____________
12. Central Air Conditioning? NO ☐ YES ☐
13. House Purchased ☐ New ☐ Resale
14. Approximate Date Purchased ____________
15. Approximate Price Paid (Including land) $ ____________

ANY MAJOR REPAIR, REMODELING OR ADDITION? (Structural, Electrical, Plumbing, etc.) NO ☐ YES ☐

TYPE?	WHEN?	BY WHOM (LICENSED CONTRACTOR, NON-PROFESSIONAL)?

ANY PREVIOUS PROPERTY LOSSES OR DAMAGE? ☐ None

CAUSE:	INSURED	NEIGHBORHOOD
Fire, Lightning, Smoke, Explosion OR Wind, Rain, Hail, Snow, Ice, Freezing	☐	☐
Glass Breakage, Vandalism, Electrical OR Water Back-up, Leakage, Plumbing, Heating	☐	☐

REMARKS ____________

IV	NO	YES		NO	YES
1. Dwelling normally unoccupied during day?			9. Items of unusual value?		
2. Business conducted from premises?			10. Swimming pool or other recreational facilities?		
3. Any full time or part time domestic employees?			11. Boats or recreational vehicles?		
4. Any roomers or boarders?			12. Liability hazards (attractive nuisances, etc.)?		
5. Frequent or extended famiiy travel?			13. Any theft or liability claims?		
6. Maintain other residence?					
7. Property fenced?			14. ANY SPECIAL LIGHTING, SECURITY MEASURES OR PROTECTIVE EQUIPMENT?		
8. Any animals owned?					

REMARKS—Recommendations DETAILS OF "YES" ANSWERS

V **PERSONAL CHARACTERISTICS**

INSURED____________ years known sources______

Reference Information
☐ Yes______ years
☐ No

NARRATIVE REMARKS:

7. Cover present and former employment/business connections, general business reputation, and general stability.
8. PERSONAL: Describe life style, associates and reputation.
9. FINANCIAL: Cover in detail present & past financial standing, reputation for living within means and any factors that might affect earning capacity.

Other Insurers The records of the previous insurer are sometimes made available to the underwriter, giving access to this valuable information. The reporting of experience usually is gained through a telephone call or a written inquiry from the present underwriter to the underwriter of the previous insurer.

SUMMARY

Residences can be classified by considering a number of factors, such as occupancy, location, protection class, construction, nature of residence unit, and ownership.

A great variety of perils are insured against by different residence property insurance contracts. Fire, windstorm and hail, smoke, explosion, vandalism or malicious mischief, water damage, and flood are the major perils of concern to underwriters. Other perils named in various contracts are damage by vehicles; collapse of buildings; ice, snow, or sleet damage; freezing of plumbing, heating, and air conditioning systems; short circuits; and glass breakage.

All types of residence policies are subject to rules which specify the types of risks eligible for coverage. Farm occupancy, business occupancy, number of dwelling units, and ownership may all affect eligibility. Further, not all eligible risks are acceptable for residence insurance in all companies. Standards for dwelling value, construction quality, age of dwelling, vacancy, fire protection, geographical location, and seasonal occupancy all may be taken into consideration when a risk is presented for coverage.

The homeowners program in particular has six basic forms used in most states: HO-1 (basic form), HO-2 (broad form), HO-3 (special form), HO-4 (contents broad form), HO-5 (comprehensive form), and HO-8 (actual cash value form). In addition, the HO-6 is designed for owners of condominium risks. Eligibility is usually restricted to owner-occupied, one- or two-family dwellings used exclusively for private residential purposes (although incidental office occupancy is permitted) and involving no more than two boarders per family. Deductibles are common, and satisfactory insurance to value is usually required.

Factors in the identification and measurement of hazards are the applicant's attitudes towards property, personal characteristics and activities, claim history, and occupational and employment record. Construction characteristics, age of dwelling, protection type and quality, location, and the existence of protective devices are important factors concerning the property and its use. Sources of information for the underwriter include the application, inspection reports, photographs, and the producer.

Chapter Notes

1. Bureau of the Census, Washington, D.C.
2. *Economic Report of the President,* Transmitted to Congress January 1981, Washington, D.C.
3. *Insurance Facts, 1980-81 Edition* (New York: Insurance Information Institute), p. 12.
4. *Insurance Facts, 1980-81 Edition* (New York: Insurance Information Institute), p. 42.
5. "A Study of One- and Two-Family Dwelling Fires," Publication NFPA FR 75-1 (Boston: National Fire Protection Association, 1975), p. 18.
6. *F.C. & S. Bulletins,* Management and Sales Section, (Cincinnati, OH: The National Underwriter Company), Fire and Allied, pp. Arl-1 to Arl-4.
7. "A Study of One- and Two-Family Dwelling Fires," p. 12
8. James K. Lathrop, ed. *NFPA Life Safety Code Handbook,* 2nd ed. (Quincy, MA: National Fire Protection Association, 1981), p. 612.
9. "Standard for the Installation, Maintenance and Use of Household Fire Warning Equipment," Publication NFPA 74, Life Safety Code (Boston: National Fire Protection Association, 1973).

CHAPTER 7

Decision Making, Classification, Rating, and Underwriting Endorsements and Other Residential Package Policies

INTRODUCTION

This chapter completes the discussion of the underwriting decision-making process for homeowners policies, and then turns to a brief treatment of classification and rating of these policies. The underwriting of common homeowners endorsements is then considered, and the chapter concludes with the underwriting of package policies for owners of mobile homes and condominium units.

ORGANIZING INFORMATION FOR DECISION MAKING

Once the company underwriter receives the application (or policy declarations in the case of a producer-issued policy), a decision must be made to accept, accept with modification(s), or reject. Before a decision can be made, all information necessary to the decision must be in hand. The underwriter must determine whether it is possible to make a sound decision based on the information already available, or whether more information must first be obtained.

In some cases, by the time the underwriter receives the submission, a homeowners policy has already been issued by the producer or coverage has been bound. In other cases, the underwriter is requested to furnish a policy at once, so the insured can provide the mortgagee with a policy when the home purchase is consummated. Under such circumstances, if there are no obvious problems with the risk, a tentative decision may be made to accept, subject to a favorable inspection report. Such a tentative decision should not alter the final decision, but merely defers it until the information-gathering process can be completed.

Gathering All Necessary Information

The key to a sound underwriting decision is information. The more *usable* information the underwriter has about the risk and the more wisely this information is used, the better able the underwriter is to base a decision on facts, rather than intuition.

Kinds of Information Ideally, the underwriter would like to have all pertinent information about both the applicant and the dwelling. As a practical matter, some kinds of information, particularly about the applicant, are often either unavailable or prohibitively expensive to obtain. Nevertheless, the underwriter must have certain basic information regarding the dwelling and the applicant.

The Dwelling. Information on the dwelling should be sufficient to disclose above-normal degrees of hazard with respect to construction, occupancy (use), protection, exposure, age, location, maintenance, and internal systems such as heating and plumbing. These categories obviously are not mutually exclusive. Age may denote possible problems with internal systems, location may be a key to exposures, and so on. Also needed is information on the dwelling's value in order to determine (1) an acceptable amount of insurance relative to value, and (2) possible discrepancies between market value and replacement cost.

The Applicant. Compared to information on the dwelling, complete information on the applicant (and family, perhaps) is relatively difficult to obtain. Information on occupation, marital status, age, and length of time in the area is ordinarily available. So, too, is information on the applicant's and others' insurable interest in the property. In contrast, information on many factors related to possible moral and morale hazards—financial condition, drug abuse, criminal activities—often are difficult to obtain even though worthy of great weight in forming a composite picture of the risk.

Information on some aspects of employment or life-style, such as frequent travel, which may create unusually high probabilities of loss from certain perils like theft and vandalism, may be easier to secure, but the cost may be high.

Sufficient Information How much information is enough? Obviously, the application must contain information required to classify and rate the risk, to issue the policy, and to maintain statistical data. In addition to the application (or policy declarations), the underwriting file may also contain other current or expired policies of the insured carried by the company, a photo (if submitted by the producer), and possibly an outside report.

The amount of information needed depends on the circumstances of the individual case. At one extreme, an underwriter might be able to make a decision based primarily on knowledge of the producer. If the particular producer has had 100 acceptable homeowners risks out of the last 100 submissions, the underwriter might assume that application number 101 probably is acceptable, and the risk *might* be accepted with only a cursory review based on minimum information. At the other extreme, it is possible that an unusual risk would require nothing short of an inspection of the house by a field representative or inspector and an interview with the applicant to develop a satisfactory amount of information, although this procedure is very costly to the insurer.

Despite the lack of precision in deciding how much information is enough, certain guidelines can be followed by the underwriter. First, the application should be complete. If application information fails to indicate the distance to the nearest hydrant for a dwelling in a city of fire protection class 2, the missing information may be needed for rating even if it is not crucial to the decision on acceptability. However, missing information on previous losses or on dwelling age prevents the underwriter from making an informed decision.

Underwriters can and should work with producers to encourage them to submit only fully completed applications. When a question is left blank, the underwriter's curiosity should be aroused. A missing answer may be innocuous—for example, investigation of a nonresponse on previous losses may merely disclose no previous losses. On the other hand, the risk could have a loss history so poor that further consideration of the submission is not warranted.

Second, even when the application is complete, it cannot be properly evaluated unless the responses are presented in understandable form. Consider an application with the following notation: "Additional real estate, lot #369, N.E. corner of Rolling Hills Subdivision." Based on such a notation, the underwriter cannot tell whether the "additional real estate" is a piece of vacant investment property (and possible attractive nuisance), a duplex rented to others, a seasonal residence, or something else. More information is needed both to underwrite and rate the risk.

Third, the underwriter must be satisfied that the home is properly insured to value. To determine this, it is necessary to establish an approximate replacement cost. Many homeowners applications require an indication of replacement cost, but the information furnished by the producer may be based on anything from an uneducated guess to an appraisal using a simplified technique furnished by an insurance company or appraisal firm. Therefore, it may be necessary to employ an inspection service, which may furnish a more accurate estimate of replacement cost.

Finally, it may be necessary to get more information (e.g., an inspection report or an appraisal) if the risk falls into a category where company underwriting rules require an inspection report, as is often the case with an older or very high-valued home. It may also be that the initial data contains information which indicates possible problems with the account, or information which the underwriter might doubt. In such cases, it would be wise to postpone a decision until more information is obtained.

Consistency Among Data Sources

In addition to the need for complete information, there must be consistency (i.e., the information in a single source, or referred to in more than one source, should not be contradictory). If the information is consistent, the underwriter is ready to begin forming a composite picture of the risk. If it is not consistent, the difference(s) must be resolved so that the underwriter can work with one set of information. Resolution may involve a simple decision by the underwriter, or may trigger a need for still more information from the applicant, the producer, or some other source.

Examples can best point out the importance of checking for consistency. The distance from a fire department should be consistent with the fire protection class shown on the application. If the application indicates a $150,000 house, but the applicant is single and in a type of job that typically pays $10,000-$15,000 annually, further investigation is indicated. If the application and/or photo indicate a small house and an area inconsistent with the amount of insurance requested, more information may be needed. An application may show no previous losses, but the claim file for the applicant's auto policy in your company shows a recent total fire loss to the auto because of a fire in a detached garage on the property. In the absence of other information, the underwriter must rely on the claims file as an accurate source. While this reliance might not dictate a particular underwriting decision, it certainly should create a questioning attitude on the accuracy of other information on the application.

DECISION MAKING

Information is the raw material for making underwriting decisions, but it is of no value unless used in a way that leads to the making of the right decision. The first step in the use of underwriting information is comparing it against underwriting criteria.

Comparing Information Against Underwriting Criteria

Once information needs are met, the underwriter must consider the nature of the information against standards for eligibility and acceptability. These standards may be explicit as found in underwriting guides and manuals. Some authorities refer to these as "objective" underwriting criteria. In contrast, the standards may be those of the underwriter based on knowledge of similar risks, the producer, and the competitive picture. These enter the realm of underwriting judgment and might be referred to as "subjective" underwriting criteria.

Underwriting Guides or Manuals For most risks, the rating manual used by the underwriter serves to identify those applicants that are eligible to be considered further as prospective homeowners accounts. (Chapter 6 briefly discussed homeowners eligibility.) Within a particular state, little inter-company variation is found on this point. Beyond this point, however, the individual company's underwriting guide narrows the field by isolating some types of otherwise *eligible* risks that are regarded as *undesirable* by the company's underwriting management.

As is true with personal auto, many underwriting decisions affecting homeowners risks actually are made in advance at the company home office by the development of underwriting policy. Policy as expressed in the guides reduces the number of cases in which local underwriting judgment is exercised (but not the importance of that judgment), and serves to direct the marketing efforts of producers toward risks the company is likely to accept.

Underwriting guides vary from company to company. An excerpt from an underwriting guide is reproduced in Exhibit 7-1. This is *illustrative* only and is not intended as a demonstration of what a guide should contain. Each underwriter *must* be familiar with the guide covering his or her own territory.

It is common for the underwriter to have some leeway to accept some risks not meeting guide standards, although this flexibility usually is prescribed by stated boundaries or the need to appeal to higher authority. In a limited number of cases, creative underwriting

Exhibit 7-1
Excerpts from Alpha Insurance Company's Underwriting Guide

SCOPE	All underwriting personnel handling homeowners business.
DEFINITION	The term "homeowners" as used in this program consists of ISO form HO-1, 2, 3 and 4 (Tenants), and 6 (condominium owners). HO-8 is considered in a separate section.
PURPOSE	To provide a consistent underwriting program for all homeowners business.
PROGRAM	This program is designed for the better part of the average and all of the preferred risks within the homeowners spectrum.
POLICY	All rules contained in this manual must be followed. They may not be amended to accommodate local or regional conditions. Any modifications or amendments to this program will be made by the appropriate home office department.
Eligibility	The eligibility rules are set forth in the Homeowners Manual. Although the eligibility is broad, it must be realized that neither the Homeowners Policy nor the premiums were designed to cover all varieties of risk. If presented with an ineligible risk that is otherwise desirable, consider underwriting it by using alternative forms of coverage.
Vacant/ Unoccupied Property	Any vacant or unoccupied risk must be referred to home office with details on supporting business, producer, etc. Vacant and unoccupied dwellings or apartments are not desirable risks in most instances, especially for Homeowners coverage. This is because the lack of prompt owner or occupant awareness of fire, water damage, burglary or similar incident is likely to promote what may have been an inconsequential loss into a substantial or near total loss.
Insurance to Value	Older Homes, Unusual Construction. Do not write risks if the Actual Cash Value (ACV) is less than 60 percent of the replacement cost. There are a number of items to consider in evaluating a risk of this nature. Older homes (built prior to 1945), homes of unusual construction or design and homes with ornate features can produce higher average losses even from minor occurrences. Restoring or repairing parquet flooring, ornate banisters, odd sized windows, unusual staircases, etc., generally require special handling and therefore costs more than the repair of normal construction. Dwellings in this category are more susceptible to losses from the old plumbing, electrical, and heating systems, especially if they have never been modernized.

through coverage changes may bring a marginal risk into substantial compliance with guide standards and result in the risk being judged acceptable.

Individually Applied Standards If a risk is eligible and meets the standards of the underwriting guide, the underwriter must then develop a composite picture of the risk through evaluating its characteristics and the circumstances under which it has been submitted. The format adopted here to discuss this step is different from that used in the Chapter 3 discussion of "Specific Factors." Here the discussion is based on a series of pertinent questions that serve to put into focus the quality of the individual risk. There will be less emphasis here on specific hazard factors than in Chapter 3, but the goal—measuring the presence or absence of factors bearing on the acceptability of the risk—is the same. This alternative question-based model is simply another approach to achieving that goal.

To make an appropriate underwriting analysis, the homeowners underwriter will try to know or determine the answers to these questions:

1. Where did the business come from, and why?
2. What is it and where is it?
3. Will it be satisfactorily insured to value?

Where Did the Business Come From, and Why? Seldom does the underwriter know exactly why a given application has been submitted. But inferences can be made, based on the underwriter's knowledge of the producer, the previous insurer, and the company's relative position in the marketplace.

THE PRODUCER. Knowledge of the producer is important to the underwriting decision. For the new underwriter, or the underwriter with a new territory or a new producer, this knowledge must be acquired by experience.

The underwriter should have a feel for the producer's ability to "field-underwrite." Some producers are familiar with company underwriting standards, and practice good front-line selection. Others tend to send applications on every account they encounter and wait for the underwriter to tell them if it is not acceptable. Some producers are motivated solely by sales and commissions; others are motivated by a desire to develop and maintain a good book of profitable business. If a producer has a contingency (profit sharing) contract under which the contingent commission varies with the profitability of the business which has been written, that may be additional motivation to good selectivity by the producer.

When an independent agent is involved, the underwriter should know which other homeowners insurers are represented, and how the "right" company for each risk is chosen. Some favor the company with the lowest price; others choose the company with the best service, the company with the easiest application, or the company with the friendliest underwriter. Some place homeowners business with the company that writes the auto insurance; others are not in the habit of account-selling. Some producers favor one company for nearly all of their homeowners business; others try to spread it around on an equitable basis. If the producer spreads the business around, the underwriter should have an idea how the producer decides which account to put with which company. It could be that the better accounts go to a competitor who is more selective.

The underwriter should also be concerned with the company's marketing attitude toward each producer. The nature and number of applications received can be better understood if the underwriter is aware that the producer is being pushed for more production, or that he or she has been restricted from writing a large number of new homeowners policies.

Consideration of the producer obviously is not started from scratch with each submission. Over time, however, the underwriter develops a profile of each producer with whom he or she deals. These profiles are not static and must be modified as later experience and conditions dictate. The underwriter should know the situation well enough to make informed judgments about the source of business.

THE PREVIOUS INSURER. The name of the previous insurer may give a clue to the desirability of the risk. If the previous insurer is a low-priced company, the underwriter might wonder why the account changed to a higher-priced market. It is possible that the insurer refused to renew. The reason for the action, if it can be determined, would be helpful underwriting information.

THE MARKETPLACE. No underwriting department sits in isolation. Underwriters in all companies are working toward the same goal of a profitable book of business. Their rates and market attitudes have a daily impact on one another's performance. Perhaps the previous insurer recently raised rates, with the result that many customers are seeking another insurer. If so, were the rates raised due to severe underwriting losses, which may indicate that the prospect is part of an unprofitable book of business discarded by another underwriter?

The underwriter servicing independent agents should also note whether the previous insurer is a company represented by the same producer. If so, it would be logical to consider why the producer has switched the account. Some applications ask if the risk is new to the producer's office and if the answer is "no," the reason for the transfer must be stated.

The underwriter should develop an awareness of subtle changes in the flow of business. Many underwriters keep new business counts by week or month, and by producer. Often, a monthly production report or billing or account statement may be used for the same information. Any change in the pattern has a cause.

Sometimes the change can be traced to the competition's actions in modifying rates, commissions, or underwriting standards. Information on other companies' activities is not difficult to secure. Producers themselves often will volunteer this information in the hopes of being provided an alternative market. The marketing or production department, if there is one, may develop information. Local and regional newspapers often carry news releases of companies' filings. Trade magazines and journals devote considerable space to reporting on companies' activities.

Different policy forms may have different profit pictures at various times. For example, if the tenant's homeowners policy is unprofitable in one geographical area, competitors may tend to restrict their writings there, and this may be a clue to potential problems. On the other hand, other insurers may be acting on the basis of incomplete or outdated information, and an insurer whose figures are credible and up to date may be able to secure a competitive advantage.

What Is It and Where Is It? Answering this question involves analysis of the hazards presented by the individual risk. The types of factors of interest to most underwriters were listed and discussed in Chapter 6. The underwriter needs to ask, "How does this risk compare with the kind of business my company writes, or the kind of business we want to write? Are there hazards not discussed in the underwriting guide which substantially increase the exposure? Are there features of this risk which are better than average for the class? Or is the risk average for the class?"

A necessary prerequisite to consideration of the individual risk's characteristics is knowledge of the coverage provided by homeowners policies in general and the form applied for in particular. Armed with coverage knowledge and insight into the producer and market conditions, the underwriter can set out to evaluate the characteristics of the applicant and the dwelling that are germane to the final decision. What are the underwriting implications of the dwelling's age, location, construction, use, protection class, condition, and surrounding exposures? What are the underwriting implications of the applicant's occupation, job history, family status, attitude toward the property, and loss record? Does the applicant appear to be personally stable and in reasonably sound financial condition? Is there more than one mortgage on the property? Has the applicant stretched earning capacity to a dangerous point? Is there an additional residence premises? If so, what and where is it and how often is it occupied and, in turn, how often is the *principal* residence left unoccupied? Does the loss record or other information indicate that the risk is a target risk for certain perils such as theft or vandalism?

In measuring the risk's characteristics against underwriting standards, the underwriter must be careful not to let personal biases influence the appraisal. People have their own set of values and personal experiences that can distort their appraisal of the nature and significance of items of information. The underwriter who abhors guns and personally advocates very strict controls on the distribution and licensing of guns may subconsciously react negatively to an applicant who is a gun collector, while another underwriter who is an avid hunter may not give that fact a second thought. Neither would be underwriting with objectivity. The actual exposure is the same. The risk may be acceptable, or it may present a far above average exposure to loss when the hobby is viewed in the light of other factors. However, the decision should not rest on the *personal* biases of the underwriter. The making of informed judgments presumes unbiased information and its unbiased application to the underwriting question at hand, not decision making based on prejudices.

Will It Be Satisfactorily Insured to Value? Most homeowners policies contain a replacement cost provision that requires an amount of insurance equal to at least 80 percent of the replacement cost of the dwelling at the time of loss if losses are to be settled without deduction for depreciation. If the amount of insurance is less than 80 percent of the replacement cost, the policy pays the larger of the actual cash value or the percentage of replacement cost that the amount of insurance bears to the 80 percent figure, but not less than the actual cash value. (This provision applies only to the dwelling and appurtenant structures, and not to the unscheduled personal property.) Thus, the term "value" in homeowners underwriting efforts to secure "insurance to value" means replacement cost rather than actual cash value.

Applicants generally do not understand this replacement cost provision. They do not realize that if they have insured their home for at least 80 percent of its replacement cost, they will receive "new for old" in the event of a loss. If the insurance at the time of the loss is less than 80 percent of replacement cost, there will be a deduction for depreciation. Likewise, the average layperson does not recognize the distinction between insurable value and market value. The replacement cost of a home may be considerably more than what it could be sold for.

Yet, market value is often the figure that is considered when a prospect applies for insurance.

Most companies set homeowners underwriting standards for insurance to value. One company might require that all dwellings be insured for at least 90 percent of replacement cost. Another company might refuse to accept any home unless it is insured for at least 80 percent of replacement cost. Many companies feel that the applicable deduction for depreciation in adjusting losses is not adequate to offset the reduction in premium of a seriously underinsured risk. Whether the company underwriting standards are firm or flexible, it behooves the underwriter to develop a book of business which is insured to value within the parameters set by company guidelines. Further, if underwriting standards cause the insured to carry more insurance than would otherwise be carried, the protection of the insured is enhanced.

Many homeowners tend to resist insuring to value. They do not like to feel they are buying more insurance than they need. They are not usually encouraged by the mortgagee to increase their insurance, because the amount outstanding on the mortgage continues to decrease and, despite underinsurance, the mortgagee's interest is protected. Also, homeowners often recognize that the chance for a total loss is relatively small. They believe they are well-protected if they have purchased insurance to cover the "expected" loss.

OLDER HOMES. Older homes pose a difficult insurance-to-value dilemma. As homes age, they depreciate. Yet, the replacement cost of an older home usually increases due to inflation and possibly obsolete building styles that would be expensive to reproduce today. When a home has depreciated to the point where the actual cash value is a great deal less than the replacement cost, it may be neither feasible nor desirable to insure for even 70 or 80 percent of the replacement cost, and since the rates are predicated on insurance to value, many companies refuse to insure old homes under the more common homeowners forms or any policy with replacement cost coverage.

These homes are often quite ornate and large. The home shown in Exhibit 7-2 was built in the early 1900s. The market value is about $40-50,000, yet replacement cost based on a construction cost table per square foot for that quality of construction would probably approach $100,000. To insure to replacement cost might tend to create a moral hazard while insuring to market value would generate a premium that is too small relative to the loss exposure. The problem is enhanced if the house is located in a declining neighborhood.

A house of this type could cause many problems in case of a loss. To replace the ornate wood and gingerbread on the outside, or perhaps a mahogany staircase inside the house, could involve exorbitant costs.

Exhibit 7-2
Older Home

HOMEOWNERS FORM HO-8. In response to the aforementioned problem regarding some older homes where the replacement cost far exceeds the market value or actual cash value and insuring to replacement cost would be prohibitively expensive, a modified version of the HO-1 was introduced. This form deletes the replacement cost condition associated with the other forms of the homeowners program and replaces it with a provision to settle losses on an actual cash value basis. ISO has designated this form as the HO-8.[1]

> The modifications of Form HO-8 and of Homeowners rules in conjunction with it are in four areas: actual cash value settlements are promised in lieu of replacement cost, Theft coveage is restricted, certain broadened coverage agreements of the simplified language forms are rescinded, and other Property coverage options are closed.
>
> **Actual Cash Value**
>
> The lengthy Replacement Cost condition commonly associated with Homeowners coverage is eliminated from Form HO-8. Instead, there is a simple statement that property losses are settled at actual cash value, limited to the amount required to repair or replace the property.

"Actual cash value" is generally taken to mean the cost of repairs or replacement minus whatever amount represents an improvement to the property over its condition at the time of loss. A roof, being an easily separable item, is frequently used as an example. If a roof with a life expectancy of 20 years is destroyed in its tenth year, the owner has lost the last 10 years in the life of the roof. If, when the roof is restored, a new 20-year cycle is begun, the owner has 10 years more roof life than before the loss. The owner must contribute to the cost of restoration to account for the improvement which the new 20-year roof has over the old roof with its life expectancy of 10 years.

However, the agreement respecting actual cash value settlements in Form HO-8 incorporates a significant departure from comparable provision in older Property forms. Traditionally, the maximum payable under actual cash value is specified as being the cost of repairing or replacing the insured property with material of like kind and quality. The agreement in Form HO-8 expresses its maximum as the cost of repairing or replacing the insured property. It does not specify that the restoration needs to be on the basis of like kind and quality. Thus, for example, if interior surfaces of plaster are damaged or destroyed, the "actual cash value" is limited to the cost of repairing or replacing them, but not necessarily the cost of replastering. Since modern methods call for the use of drywall in lieu of plaster, the cost of replacing the plaster walls may be limited to the cost of using drywall.

Since there is no Replacement Cost condition, there is also no compulsion for the insured to purchase coverage in amounts beyond the minimum required for Homeowners eligibility (the same as for Form HO-1). Partial losses are paid in full, up to the limit of the coverage and subject to the actual cash value considerations just discussed. Naturally, the insured should be encouraged to purchase as much protection as is economically feasible in face of the always present potential for a total loss.

Theft Coverage Restrictions

The Theft coverage of Form HO-8 is restricted to occurrences on the residence premises and the maximum recovery in any one occurrence is $1,000.

The separate $1,000 limits applicable to silverware and to guns in the other forms of the simplified language series are, of course, not required in Form HO-8.

In some territories, Theft coverage rates are also based on application of a special deductible of $250 under this form. The deductible, as specified by Insurance Services Office, is applied to the loss and not, as under Special Theft Deductible endorsement HO-177, to the limit. Thus, the insured with a $1,500 loss recovers the policy's limit of $1,000; the insured with a $1,200 loss recovers $950; and recovery on a loss of $750 amounts to $500.

Note that this Theft deductible, like any other deductible under the arrangement of the simplified language forms, must be indicated on the Declarations page.

The limit (and the deductible) applies to all coverage and under the peril, whether the loss involves personal property, structural items, or a combination of these.

Coverage Restrictions

The introduction of the Homeowners 76 series of forms was marked by several instances of broadening of Homeowners protection. But three of these broadened features are rescinded under the terms of Form HO-8. The coverage reverts in these instances to the provisions of older forms. And one restriction not contemplated in the older forms is added.

The full limit of Coverage C is applied only to unscheduled personal property on the residence premises—rather than covering on a worldwide basis. Coverage of property away from the residence premises is limited to 10% of the Coverage C amount, or to $1,000 if that happens to be greater.

Unscheduled personal property away from the residence premises is covered only if it is owned or used by an insured. The customary option for an insured to elect coverage for property owned by guests or by residence employees while these people might be staying with the insured at another residence is not included in the Coverage C agreement of Form HO-8. The option for covering property of others on the residence premises remains, however.

Any recovery for the expense of removal of debris of covered property is included in the limit applying to the coverage item. The other forms of the simplified language series go on to provide an additional five percent of the otherwise applicable limit if that limit were to become exhausted by a covered loss. Form HO-8 does not. To illustrate, under Form HO-1 of the Homeowners 76 series with $25,000 insurance under Coverage A and a building and debris removal loss of $26,000, the Coverage A limit automatically increases to $26,250. Under Form HO-8, the limit remains as written: $25,000.

The maximum recovery for insured loss on any tree, shrub or plant is $250, in lieu of the $500 limit provided in the other forms of the simplified language series.

Coverage Options

The only options available to an insured with Form HO-8 are those of Section II—Liability portion of the Homeowners program. Property coverage has to be as contained in the form. Increases in amounts of various coverages or coverage for various additional property exposures is not permitted. And, since there is no provision for increasing Coverage C to account for property pertaining to an incidental school, office or studio in the insured dwelling, there is also no requirement that the Liability coverage be amended to account for the exposure.

Premium

> The premium for use of Form HO-8 is considerably higher than for Form HO-1. In the lower ranges of coverage amounts—$15,000 to $30,000—the additional premium for Form HO-8 over Form HO-1 amounts to approximately 50%. The difference narrows as larger amounts are applied under Form HO-8, but a sizeable gap remains even in the higher range of coverage amounts.

UNDERINSURANCE ON THE CONTENTS. The value of contents may offer special problems. Under HO-1, 2, 3, and 5, the amount of coverage on unscheduled personal property is an amount determined by applying a percentage (usually 50) to the dwelling amount. Under HO-4, the principal sum itself applies to unscheduled personal property.

Nothing in the policy penalizes the policyholder underinsured on contents unless, of course, the loss exceeds the policy limits. People tend to underestimate the value of their personal property, and they also tend to underinsure in order to save premium dollars. To get an idea of the value of contents owned by a prospect, the underwriter should consider such factors as the age and occupation of the prospect, the size of the family, the number of rooms or size of the dwelling unit, the value of the dwelling, and the price or rent level of the neighborhood.

Underinsurance on contents creates the same kind of rate inadequacy problem as does underinsurance on dwellings. In those forms covering both dwelling and contents, most companies will permit a reduction in the standard amount of contents coverage at a slight premium credit. There are circumstances under which the reduction may be clearly in order, e.g., newlyweds just beginning to furnish a house, but the underwriter may want to evaluate the circumstances before freely granting such a reduction in other cases.

OVERINSURANCE. A home is overinsured when the policy limit exceeds the replacement cost or the market value (if market value is lower than replacement cost). Since the latter situation—if the difference is substantial—often is handled by limiting the coverage to an actual cash value policy form, the following discussion will deal with replacement cost as a standard for overinsurance.

Overinsurance is less common than underinsurance. Also, overinsurance does not result in inadequate premiums, as with underinsurance. But overinsurance may present a more serious loss exposure due to the potential moral or morale hazard.

Mortgagees typically require insurance for at least the amount of the mortgage. When the home is purchased, the purchase price usually includes the value of the land, as well as the value of the building and appurtenant structures. When the down payment is low or the value of the land is high, the amount of the mortgage may exceed the replacement cost of the building alone. Mortgagees frequently will not permit insurance coverage lower than the outstanding loan.

In other cases, the home may be overinsured because the insured thinks the home is worth more than it really is. In these cases, the underwriter has a duty to the insured to suggest that the home may be overinsured. It is neither fair nor conducive to amicable loss settlements to accept the premium for a $50,000 policy if the insured could collect only $40,000 in a total loss.

Some states have *valued policy laws,* which generally require that the entire amount of insurance be paid in the event of a total loss regardless of the value of the property. (These laws usually apply to real property only.) The underwriter who works in a state with a valued policy law has one more reason to carefully analyze insurance to value because the standard for valuing losses spelled out in the policy is overridden by the statute mandating payment of the policy limit in total losses.

In extreme cases, a request for an amount of insurance that would result in overinsurance may indicate the presence of moral hazard. In general, underwriters do not knowingly accept a risk that is overinsured beyond a level sufficient to allow for increases in replacement cost during the policy term. If the amount of insurance requested looks unduly large, before accepting the risk on any terms (even a reduced amount of insurance) the underwriter may want to look into those factors that could indicate the presence of moral hazard—past losses, mortgage payment records, financial status of any business interest of the applicant, and the possible need to divide assets because of a marital breakup—as well as check carefully on the producer's knowledge of the applicant.

DETERMINING REPLACEMENT COST. How does the underwriter determine the replacement cost of a home? The amount shown on the application may or may not be accurate, depending on the method used to determine value and the intent of the person making the determination. Many outside reports provide a figure based on the investigator's drive-by estimate of current replacement cost. In addition, there is a trend in the industry for companies to provide simplified appraisal methods with which a producer can easily develop an estimate of replacement cost. Some companies have even made such an appraisal mandatory on certain classes of business. The number and types of methods used to determine insurable value depend on company goals and standards, the underwriter, and the credibility of the producer or outside inspection service. Exhibit 7-3 illustrates one way of calculating replacement cost using the construction cost index available through appraisal companies.

The underwriter must always be careful when discussing insurance to value. No simple method of determining value provides more than a sound estimate. If the underwriter suggests increased limits, care must be taken not to imply a guarantee that the home is insured for full value. It is a good practice to document all conversations or correspondence regarding insurance to value to protect the company in the event of a claim.

Weighing the Results of the Comparison

Many homeowners submissions contain a combination of both good news and bad news. When this is true, the underwriter must weigh the good news against the bad news to determine whether the risk is on balance acceptable, borderline, or unacceptable.

If a risk clearly meets all underwriting standards, and is satisfactorily insured to value, it is easy to make the correct underwriting decision. If the risk fails to meet minimum standards, and cannot be made acceptable, once again the correct decision is obvious.

Many risks will fall somewhere between these two extremes. The difficulty of making the correct underwriting decision on these risks is compounded by the many coverages of the homeowners package. A risk may have little or no loss potential in some areas of coverage but higher than average loss potential in others. For example, the risk may have no appurtenant structures (in which case appurtenant structures coverage is superfluous), but may have unusual construction, the repair of which could increase the period during which additional living expenses would be paid. The underwriter must determine whether these two factors balance each other by evaluating all of the factors concerning the risk and applying informed judgment.

Consideration of Other Factors

It is possible that a risk under consideration presents such a degree of conflicting aspects that the underwriter could justify either a decision to accept or a decision to reject. When this is true, the underwriter will consider other factors apart from the risk itself, such as producer accommodation and supporting business.

Producer Accommodation The importance of knowing producers as a source of information on new business was explained earlier in this chapter. When a risk is borderline, the underwriter may be pressured by the producer to accept the risk as an accommodation. The first factor to consider is the volume and profitability of the producer over the past few years. The profit (or lack thereof) on

Exhibit 7-3
Calculating Replacement Cost*

Your Homeowners or Fire policy could rebuild your house . . . but only if the house is insured to value! Follow the simple 5-step procedure, then use the attached postage-paid card to order proper replacement insurance.

Step 1: UNIT COUNT

List the unit-count of your house, referring to the chart below. Enter the number "1" for each Table A "unit" your house has; enter the number "½" for each Table B half "unit" your house has. Modify as you deem necessary. For example, an exterior wall that is 50% brick, 50% frame should count ½ unit.

Table A – Enter "1" for each "unit" listed below.	
	Kitchen
	Dining Room
	Living Room
	Bedroom(s)
	Bathroom(s) (3 or more fixtures)
	Den or Study
	Family or Recreation Room
	Utility Room
	Finished Basement
	Finished Attic
	Two-Car Garage (attached)
	Brick Stone Exterior Walls
	Central Air Conditioning
Table B – Enter "½" for each half "unit" listed below.	
	Half Bath (2 or less fixtures)
	One-Car Garage (attached)
	Dinette Breakfast Nook
	Unfinished Basement
	Unfinished Attic
	Enclosed Porch Breezeway
	Fireplace
	Total Unit Count (Table A + B)

Step 2: CONSTRUCTION CLASS

Read the following class descriptions and check the one that most nearly applies to your house.

☐ **Class I**

- Plain design
- Stock-type plans
- Little or no ornamentation
- Tract-type, built for speculation
- Low cost is primary consideration
- Materials and workmanship just meet building codes
- Usually dining area part of living room or kitchen
- No special-purpose rooms (recreation, den, pantry, etc.)
- Most older houses are not in this class

☐ **Class III**

- Individual design
- Built from modified or designer plans
- Contracted by a specific buyer
- Average to above-average quality materials and workmanship
- Meets or exceeds building codes
- Dining room and foyer common
- Den or family room

Class II

Standard design
Built from standard or designer plans
Some ornamentation added to attract buyers
Built for speculation or contracted
Average quality materials and workmanship
Meets or exceeds building codes
Dining area or dining room
Den or family room common
May have foyer

Class IV

One-of-a-kind design
Built from prepared architect plans and written specifications
Contracted by a specific buyer
Above-average quality materials and workmanship
Exceeds building codes
Unique floor plan
Large rooms
Dining room and large foyer
Den or family room and other special-purpose rooms

Step 3: BASE COST

Locate the appropriate Construction Class (from Step 2) column.

Find the Base Cost in the selected Construction Class column across from the calculated Unit Count (from Step 1). If necessary, you may interpolate the Base Cost between the two classes.

UNIT COUNT	CONSTRUCTION CLASS			
	I	II	III	IV
4	10,000	–	–	–
4½	11,500	–	–	–
5	12,400	15,700	19,800	23,600
5½	13,800	17,500	22,100	26,400
6	↓	↓	↓	↓
6½				
7				
7½				
8				
8½				
9				
9½				
10				
10½				
11				
11½				
12				
12½	–			
13	–			
13½	–			
14	–			
14½	–			
15	–			
15½	–			
16	–			
16½	–			
17	–			

Step 4: LOCATION FACTOR

[From separate table.]

Step 5: REPLACEMENT COST

Multiply the Base Cost (from Step 3) times your Location Factor from Step 4 listed on the back. These factors are listed by the first three digits of your zip code.

$	Base Cost
X	Location Factor
= $	Replacement Cost

residence insurance lines would indicate how well the producer underwrites this class of business. The second factor to consider is the mix of business—personal versus commercial, and homeowners versus auto. A marginal risk from a profitable producer with a good spread of business deserves a second look.

An accommodation for a profitable producer (or a new producer with a potential for profit) enhances the company's position and should result in an increased flow of higher quality business. If the decision is to accommodate, follow-up steps must be taken to assure the increased flow of quality business. The producer has less incentive to remember the obligation than does the underwriter. Therefore, when an accommodation is made, the underwriter should:

1. log the facts in an "accommodation diary";
2. immediately confirm the accommodation by written memo, specifying all particulars; and
3. follow up each accommodation for "payment" on not less than a quarterly basis.[2]

A log of producer accommodations will reveal how often these exceptions have been made.

Supporting Business If a company writes more than one policy for a given insured, some account underwriting may be necessary. The insured may be the president of a major manufacturing concern insured by the company. The personal home may be a high-valued mansion, which might be undesirable from the underwriter's standpoint because of the high concentration of values. Under normal circumstances, this account should be rejected, but if the insured is upset by such a declination, the company could lose a profitable commercial account.

The underwriter might also want to consider other personal lines placed with the company by the prospect. Does the prospect consider this company to be "my insurance company," as evidenced by a long-standing relationship with the company? Has the company carried a profitable auto policy on the same insured for the past ten years, and also a personal umbrella and a personal articles floater? Or is the applicant a traveling salesperson with an unsatisfactory theft exposure who has already had several recent auto losses with the company? A long-standing satisfactory relationship or a number of collateral lines might be positive factors encouraging the acceptance of an otherwise borderline homeowners risk.

On the other hand, the insured may have an auto policy with the company which appears to be turning into a problem. This might lead to a choice to reject a homeowners application which would otherwise be marginally acceptable.

If it looks as if the auto policy may be nonrenewed, putting the homeowners on the books means that it too might be transferred to some other insurer in the near future. This would be counterproductive because the expense allowance in the initial (and possibly only) premium might not be large enough to cover the direct and indirect costs of putting the homeowners business on the books.

Occasionally, "politics" will even enter the picture. The prospect may be the producer, or a relative or employee of the producer. The prospect may be an employee of the underwriter's company. He or she may be a friend of the underwriting manager, or a local politician for whom a declination might have an adverse impact on the company. These factors cannot be ignored. But they do not make a bad risk good! When exceptions are made on risks of this type, the file should be thoroughly documented so that in the future others will know why the risk was accepted.

Considering Alternative Courses of Action

The best decision cannot be made unless the best alternative course of action is among those being considered. A creative part of underwriting involves investigating all the feasible alternatives: acceptance, acceptance subject to modification, and rejection.

Acceptance The course of action most frequently taken in homeowners underwriting is to accept the business as submitted. Most risks meet standard underwriting guidelines. If it is decided to accept a risk, little more needs to be done than to issue or process the policy and document the decision.

Acceptance Subject to Modification If a risk is not acceptable as submitted, but can be modified to make it acceptable, the underwriter should propose the necessary change(s). The company cannot make a profit on rejected business which could have been accepted if the underwriter had considered all alternatives. The underwriter might propose a modification for one of several purposes.

The risk may not qualify as submitted. For example, assume the underwriting guide prohibits the underwriter from issuing policies when the limit of coverage on the dwelling is less than $20,000, and the underwriter has received an application on a small home of a retired couple which is in good condition with a requested limit of $18,000. Further assume that the underwriter has determined that at $18,000 the home would be insured to about 80 percent of replacement cost. Under these circumstances, the underwriter might suggest that the limit be raised to the minimum level of $20,000.

For another risk, the proposed modification might reduce the insured exposure to an acceptable level. This might take the form of a modification of coverage (e.g., a higher deductible) or a modification of the risk itself (e.g., installation of an alarm system). Following are a few examples of the many possible coverage modifications:

1. A modification of coverage or limits to meet manual or underwriting guide requirements (for example, insuring the previously mentioned home for $20,000).
2. A larger deductible on all perils. This might be particularly appropriate for the high-valued home or the risk with a history of small losses. It might also be appropriate in a neighborhood where minor vandalism problems are common, or for an older home to eliminate maintenance claims such as wind-damaged roofing.
3. Larger theft deductibles. This modification might be desirable in high-crime areas, particularly for a tenant's policy, or for a residence which is unoccupied during the day. A risk quite acceptable for fire may be unacceptable for theft. For example, assume a risk has been submitted and everything meets with the underwriter's approval except that a son's bicycle has been stolen four times in the last three years from the lawn or from the school yard. Aside from these, there are no losses. What can the underwriter do to handle this particular situation? One approach is the application of a $250 theft-only deductible with no change in the deductible applying to the other perils. This provides the coverage the insured needs except for eliminating what history indicates will be a certain loss in the future.
4. Insurance to value. The underwriter may offer to accept coverage only if the policy limit is increased or decreased to bring the limit in line with the replacement cost of the home.
5. Exclude part of the exposure. In some states, it is permissible to exclude certain property that otherwise would be covered by the homeowners (e.g., a garage in poor condition), and thus make the risk acceptable.
6. Write a narrower form. The applicant may be offered an HO-1 instead of the requested HO-2 or 3. This option is particularly useful where the loss history or dwelling age points to a definite problem with the risk's plumbing or heating system, or where construction and location (and perhaps irregular occupancy) indicate problems with freezing or the weight of ice and snow.
7. Alter the price. Some companies maintain both a "preferred" and a "standard" homeowners program, with the latter taking higher rates than the former.

In addition to modifications within the homeowners spectrum, the underwriter may decline to issue a homeowners, but be willing to write another type of dwelling form. If the theft peril is a problem, if the dwelling value is too low, or if replacement cost greatly exceeds market value, a fire and extended coverage dwelling and contents policy or an HO-8 may be offered.

Rejection If other courses of action are not feasible, the underwriter must make a prompt declination. This will require a prompt notification to the producer, and may also require direct notice to the insured and to the mortgagee if a policy or binder has already been issued. Where possible, the producer should be notified before the applicant. Notice must be made within the cancellation period specified by state law, if one is applicable, or by policy conditions. If too much time has elapsed and the policy cannot be canceled, the next best alternative is to mark the account for nonrenewal (if this is allowed by law) and, if possible, modify the coverage to limit the exposure.

It is good procedure to document an underwriting file with the reason for the declination. It is possible that the producer or the insured may challenge the declination, sometimes even by going to the state insurance commissioner or through some public or private consumer affairs agency. The underwriter or a supervisor may be forced to reexamine the file and reevaluate the underwriting decision. A well-documented declination will be of value if the file is reopened, or if the risk is resubmitted later.

Care must be taken on the matter of *releasing* information as to why a declination was made. Some reasons for rejection contain the seeds of possible legal difficulties such as libel or slander actions. The privacy and the reputation of the applicant must not be jeopardized. Sometimes, the insurer is required to make available to the applicant the reason(s) for rejection. Any applicable laws (e.g., Fair Credit Reporting Act) must be followed to the letter.

Making the Decision

The underwriter must be able to make a prompt decision based on facts and informed judgment, and to stand by that decision. Not all decisions will have the desired outcomes. Some good accounts will have losses, and some bad accounts will not. Some accounts which appeared to be good accounts may turn out to be undesirable in the long run. Underwriters are not expected to be perfect, but they are expected to make sound decisions.

The same precautions mentioned in Chapter 3 apply here as well. In brief form, these are (1) remain as objective as possible by not overreacting to recent chance events; (2) respect the underwriting authority granted; (3) be prompt in making the decision; and (4) document the decision adequately.

HOMEOWNERS CLASSIFICATION AND RATING

Homeowners premiums are said to be "indivisible." This means that the package, including the Section II liability and medical payments coverage, is treated as a unit in developing premiums and applying premium charts to individual risks. No separate calculation or identifiable portion of the premium is attributable to the dwelling as opposed to unscheduled personal property, or to the property coverage as opposed to the liability coverage, or to the fire peril as opposed to the theft peril. However, rating bureaus and some companies separate loss experience in various ways for their own purposes. An example of this was cited in the previous chapter where percentages of losses and loss payments for various perils under dwelling packages for one insurer were shown. Still the data are treated as a unit for comparing actual with expected losses, developing premium modifications, and pricing the coverage for the buyer.

The term "premium" rather than "rate" is used in this discussion because the homeowners pricing process produces what the insured will be charged for the package rather than a price for unit of exposure (such as $.52 per $100 of coverage on the dwelling). This basic premium charge may be increased or reduced by charges or credits produced by certain endorsements or by the election of optional limits (e.g., increasing the standard Section II liability limit of $25,000) as permitted by program rules.

Homeowners Rating Characteristics

Homeowners policies are class-rated, with a few exceptions. Occasionally, a single-family dwelling of fire resistive or unusual construction is specifically rated. Tenant or condominium policies in fire resistive apartments or buildings with commercial occupancy may be based on specific rates. But, generally, it would be impractical for insurance companies or bureaus to rate each dwelling individually.

Homeowners premiums are developed by rating bureaus and, in some cases, by individual companies. It would be incorrect to say the bureaus "make" the rates. Actually, the rating bureau in or covering each state accumulates statistical data based on homeowners experience in each territory and publishes rates based on that data. Many companies use these bureau rates. However, where rating laws permit, insurers may deviate from the bureau rates, and the bureau rates serve only as a point of departure. Also, some insurers develop their own rates on an independent basis, computing the premiums in approximately the same manner used by a bureau.

Homeowners premium generally is lower than the aggregate premium for the same coverages purchased separately. Originally this was due largely to the economies of issuing one policy instead of several, and this is still an important factor today. However, other factors are also at work. Most persons who own homes of any substantial value have purchased a homeowners policy, leaving rented dwellings, low-value dwellings, and poorly maintained dwellings as a large part of the fire and extended coverage market. These dwellings historically have had a higher loss ratio than higher-valued, owner-occupied homes. Persons who own their homes have a greater interest in maintaining the property well, and better-maintained homes have fewer losses. Low-value dwellings are more likely to be of poor construction quality and isolated from effective fire protection. Another factor is that there is now less adverse selection in homeowners business. For example, people who had an abnormal exposure to theft were ones most likely to buy theft policies, but now this peril is packaged in homeowners policies and a better spread is achieved. Still another factor is better insurance to value, particularly on personal property, which is automatically covered in an amount equal to 50 percent of the dwelling amount on homeowners policies.

Credits are granted in some rate manuals for fire, smoke, or burglar alarm systems. Recognition is given only for those systems which are approved by the rating bureau or company and are properly maintained. Each manual and company underwriting guide must be consulted in order to determine the types for which credit is given, and under what circumstances.

Preferred Programs Many companies have more than one set of premiums available within a given state. Preferred homeowners programs sold at lower premiums usually are intended for newer homes which meet other strict eligibility criteria. The discounted premium may be written through subsidiary companies in a group, or by the parent or another company writing a standard rated program. Where a preferred program is available, the underwriter has an additional responsibility to classify and rate the risk in the proper program.

Whether a company uses preferred rates or standard rates, the underwriter should be aware of the company's competition. The types of risks which are written will depend, to some degree, on the relative rate level used by the company. Companies try to secure rates which are adequate but competitive; they must not price themselves out of the market but must consider the effect of increases in rates on renewals. The right balance is sometimes difficult to maintain.

Classification Factors

Several factors are used to determine the premiums for a homeowners risk. The discussion assumes a form providing dwelling coverage, unless otherwise noted.

Territory Territorial grouping is basic to homeowners rating. In some states the entire state is one rating territory, while in others the state is subdivided into two or more territories. Each territory is a relatively homogeneous economic or geographical area. For example, one widely used territorial breakdown divides Michigan into two territories: Territory 02, Wayne County (which includes Detroit), and Territory 01 (the balance of the state). Wayne County is basically an urban area. It has a higher crime rate than the rest of the state and a larger percentage of older homes. For these reasons, the premiums in Wayne County are higher than those in the balance of the state. Territorial breakdowns in other states may be due largely to different exposures to windstorm, hail, or other perils. In some states, premiums are lower in metropolitan areas primarily because of superior fire protection and generally better construction.

Construction For the purpose of homeowners classification, the most common types of construction are brick and frame. Definitions of the types for rating purposes are given in the manuals, and are somewhat different among the states. Brick is commonly defined to require walls of masonry construction—brick, stone, or concrete block. Frame construction depends on the combustibility of supports. Specific rules on aluminum siding over frame walls apply in some states. It is common to class a dwelling as "frame" if at least one-third of its wall area is of frame construction.

In some areas, the premium is increased for an "unapproved roof," which includes roofs consisting in whole or in part of wooden shingles, boards, or tar paper. Roofs of this type are more hazardous because they are more easily ignited by flying brands from a neighboring house fire, trash fire, or forest fire.

Occupancy The number of family units occupying the dwelling *may* affect rating. Generally, the premiums in the manual are for one- and two-family dwellings, there being no additional charge for a two-family house. Additional premium is generated when, by endorsement, the definition of residence premises is changed to "three and four" rather than "one and two" family dwelling. Not all states permit writing homeowners on three- and four-family dwellings.

Protection This refers to the protection class which is assigned to the community or area in which the dwelling is located indicating the quality of public fire protection available. Most companies use classes assigned by a rating bureau, but a few have adopted their own versions. In some areas, private fire protection companies operate, usually on a subscription basis, and credit may be allowed for them, or the applicable protection class for rating purposes may be lowered. Ordinarily, however, protection class reflects only the fire protection offered by a city, county, forestry department, or other public entity evaluated along with water supply, police department, construction laws, and the like.

In some states, rating consideration is also given to the distance from the nearest fire hydrant. As distance from a hydrant increases, so does the time necessary for a fire department to set up and get a stream of water on the fire. Also, the water pressure at the nozzle of a firehose is decreased by frictional losses through a long hose, which further reduces firefighting ability.

The Importance of Proper Classification and Rating

The ease of rating homeowners insurance does not diminish the importance of proper classification and rating. Statistical data are used to develop future rule and rate changes and influence underwriting standards. Rate changes based on the data developed by misclassified or misrated policies could have an effect (either positive or negative, but unjustified in both cases) on a company's competitive or profit picture in a given territory.

In addition, underwriters must be careful that policies are correctly classified and rated because unfair rating discrimination is illegal. The insurance company may not charge a significantly different rate for two risks with approximately the same loss producing characteristics. The underwriter who intentionally or unintentionally violates the classification and rating system filed with the state may get the company into serious trouble in the event of an Insurance Department audit or a complaint. Improper classification as a sales tool must never be allowed.

UNDERWRITING HOMEOWNERS PROPERTY ENDORSEMENTS

The homeowners program provides for a number of endorsements that may be used to modify the coverage found in the basic homeowners forms. This section deals with the underwriting of some of the more common endorsements affecting Section I—the property section—

of homeowners policies. To be discussed under this heading are the inflation guard endorsement, the theft coverage extension endorsement, the scheduled personal property endorsement, endorsements for covering secondary residences, and endorsements which provide increased or reduced limits on specific coverages.

The endorsements to be described in this section may be used to amend a policy when it is initially issued, or they may be used to modify in-force coverage of an existing homeowners. Underwriting mid-term changes in homeowners insurance differs little from the same step in personal auto insurance. However, mid-term changes in a homeowners are less likely to affect the desirability of a risk as a whole than are auto changes. Additionally, the mid-term changes on the homeowners are much less frequent than are auto changes. As a result, the depth of underwriting consideration given to homeowners changes is, on the average, less than that given to auto changes.

Inflation Guard

The replacement cost of most homes continues to increase due to inflation. Insurance to value at inception does not solve that continuing problem. The home that was properly insured at the inception of the policy may be significantly underinsured by the end of the policy period. This problem could be overcome with overinsurance in anticipation of inflation, but at best, that solution is uneconomical for the insured.

Coverage The inflation guard endorsement automatically increases all Section I (property) limits by a percentage (usually 1 percent), on a noncumulative basis (i.e., the percentage is applied to the policy limit at inception regardless of when during the year the limit is increased), every three months during the policy period. Consequently, the other limits which are stated as a percentage of Section I also increase. (Different percentage increases are available in some territories.) Thus, if the dwelling was originally insured on an HO-2 for $30,000, the amount of coverage on the dwelling at the end of three months would be $30,300. At the end of six months, the dwelling would be covered for $30,600, appurtenant structures for $3,060, unscheduled personal property for $15,300, and additional living expenses for $6,120.

The inflation guard endorsement is available on HO-1, 2, 3, and 5. Usually it is not available on HO-4 (tenants), HO-6 (condominium), or HO-8 policies although some companies are offering it on the first two. Some independent companies have prepared their own inflation guard endorsements, often providing that adjustments will be made according to an index rather than a fixed percentage. For example, the Consumer Price Index might be used as a fair measure of the fluctuation in the

Exhibit 7-4
Inflation Guard Endorsement

INFLATION GUARD ENDORSEMENT HO-184

(Forms HO-1, HO-2, HO-3 or HO-5—Coverages A, B, C and D-Section I)

In consideration of an additional premium, it is agreed that the Limits of Liability specified in the Declarations of this policy for Coverages A, B, C and D shall be increased by 1% of such specified limits at the end of each period of 3 months after the effective date. If the policy is continued by extension certificate, the Limits of Liability during this extension term shall be as specified in the extension certificate increased by 1% of such limits specified at the end of each period of 3 months after the effective date of such certificate.

value of household contents, and one of several construction cost indexes might be used to measure dwelling value. Although the details differ, the intent and handling are similar. A flat percentage-type endorsement is reproduced in Exhibit 7-4.

Underwriting The inflation guard endorsement is *not* a substitute for insurance to value, and should not be used as such. It is only as good as the base which it increases. The purpose of the inflation guard endorsement is to reduce the effect of inflation during the policy period on a home which is insured to value at the inception date. If the home is underinsured at the outset, the endorsement serves only to reduce the amount of underinsurance that would otherwise occur during the policy period.

Use of the inflation guard is encouraged by virtually all insurers. Some require the endorsement on all homeowners policies; in fact, some insurers have filed deviations which automatically include inflation guard. Seldom is there a reason to decline this coverage. However, the underwriter might conceivably choose to discourage or deny the use of it when the dwelling appears to be overinsured, either due to a high mortgage or to a difference of opinion regarding valuation.

Theft Coverage Extension Endorsement

Coverage Without the theft extension endorsement, theft of property from an unattended auto or boat is not covered unless the vehicle is locked *and* there are visible signs of forcible entry. It is easy to break into a car without leaving "visible signs," such as with a coat hanger.

By eliminating certain exclusions, the theft extension endorsement provides coverage for theft of personal property from an unattended

Exhibit 7-5
Theft Coverage Extension

THEFT COVERAGE EXTENSION **HO-46**

(Form HO-2, HO-3 or HO-4 Only—Section I)

In consideration of an additional premium, the following items c.(2) and c.(3) under the Theft Exclusions applicable to property away from the described premises of the Perils Insured Against, are deleted:

"(2) property while unattended in or on any motor vehicle or trailer, other than a public conveyance, unless the loss is the result of forcible entry into such vehicle while all doors, windows or other openings thereof are closed and locked, provided there are visible marks of forcible entry upon the exterior of such vehicle or the loss is the result of the theft of such vehicle which is not recovered within 30 days, but property shall not be considered unattended when the Insured is required to surrender the keys of such vehicle to a bailee;

(3) property while unattended in or on private watercraft unless the loss is the direct result of forcible entry into a securely locked compartment and provided there are visible marks of forcible entry upon the exterior of such compartment."

This endorsement must be attached to Change Endorsement when issued after the policy is written.

auto or boat, whether locked or unlocked, even when there are no visible signs of forcible entry. With most insurers the endorsement may not be used with the HO-1 policy. It is not needed under the HO-5 because the coverage is already there. A representative theft coverage extension endorsement is shown in Exhibit 7-5.

Underwriting Under most circumstances, exposure is minimal because "normal" losses fall within the deductible. However, the underwriter should consider the seriousness of the exposure. Examples of risks for which this endorsement might be declined are those located in high-crime areas, those where the vehicle is parked outside at night, and those which have had a number of previous losses of this type. Traveling salespersons are considered poor risks for the theft extension endorsement, as are others who travel a great deal, particularly if they own expensive cameras or golf equipment. Finally, the underwriter should watch for the morale hazard, trying to avoid writing those persons who may want the coverage as a substitute for proper safeguarding (e.g., locking cars) of personal property. A loss history, if available, is of some help in identifying above-average morale hazard.

Scheduled Personal Property Endorsement

Coverage The scheduled personal property endorsement (essentially the same as a personal articles floater) is an inland marine form available as an endorsement to the homeowners policy. The endorsement provides "all-risks" coverage on scheduled items.

This endorsement is used because it provides coverage for items where coverage is limited in amount under the homeowners (jewelry, furs, stamps, coin collections, and so on) or because it provides broader coverage than the named-perils personal property coverage of the HO-1, HO-2, HO-3, HO-4, or HO-6. For example, although musical instruments are not excluded or subject to an internal limit under any of the homeowners forms, the amateur violinist may choose to schedule a violin in order to have coverage against breakage, water damage, and so on, with no deductible. And, if the instrument has value as a collector's item, possibly it should be insured as "fine arts," with the insurance written on a valued basis. In case of loss, the insured could collect the amount scheduled rather than the actual cash value.

Underwriting Underwriting the personal articles floater will be discussed in detail in Chapter 10. In this chapter only the underwriting relationship of the scheduled personal property endorsement to the homeowners will be discussed.

The unscheduled personal property coverage in homeowners policies *excludes* "property which is separately described and specifically insured in whole or in part by this or any other insurance." Any item which is scheduled is no longer covered by the basic homeowners, even if it is inadequately covered in the policy or endorsement where it is scheduled.

The homeowners policies provide broad coverage for the typical American household at rates commensurate with the typical exposure. The presence of one or several high-valued items of personal property may increase the exposure beyond that contemplated. To get a premium for the extra exposure, the underwriter may choose to schedule certain items if their existence is revealed by, for instance, a remark or response on the application. Consider a photographer with $5,000 of camera equipment. Although the camera equipment is automatically covered under the homeowners, it represents in this case far more than is found in the average house and it is attractive to burglars. The underwriter may require that some or all of the camera equipment be scheduled to get the additional premium the exposure demands. By the same token, the applicant may desire to schedule the property to secure coverage against such perils as breakage and water damage.

In other cases, a request for this endorsement may indicate that the risk is less desirable as a whole for homeowners insurance. If there is an extensive collection of high-valued jewelry, furs, or other attractive items, the home could be a target risk. This could be the case if the scheduled items are not in proportion to the value of unscheduled personal property. For example, $30,000 of scheduled coverage on a homeowners policy with $20,000 of unscheduled personal property coverage would be considered a potential problem by many underwriters. In these cases, the underwriter should make a thorough check of the security precautions taken by the applicant, including the use of safes, locks, and burglar alarms.

Secondary Residences

Coverage If the HO-1, 2, 3, or 5 insured is the owner-occupant of a secondary residence, coverage may be provided by endorsement. If the basic policy is an HO-2, HO-3, or HO-4, and the insured is a tenant at the secondary location, coverage may also be provided by endorsement. (Tenants coverage is not available by endorsement for the secondary residence of an HO-1 insured because the tenants coverage provides broader named perils coverage than the HO-1 policy.) Usually a separate homeowners policy is required if the secondary residence is in a different state than the primary residence. If both residences are in the same state, either an endorsement or a separate policy may be used. These rules apply in most states, but there are a few local variances.

Underwriting Secondary residences are underwritten much the same as primary residences. However, several additional points must be considered. Because the insured cannot normally occupy two residences at the same time, there may be far higher than average exposure to loss at the secondary location for most of the year. And, if the secondary residence is in a remote location, hazards may be increased because of the time that may elapse between a loss and discovery of the loss. A winter burglary at an isolated lakeshore cottage may not be discovered until weeks or months later. Seasonally occupied property often presents a high theft and vandalism exposure and, in certain areas, potential problems with freezing and collapse from the weight of ice and snow.

From a claims standpoint, due to the overlap of some coverages, it is desirable that both residences be insured in the same company with essentially the same coverage. However, from an underwriting standpoint, it may often be desirable to insure only the primary residence in the homeowners program. The secondary residence can then be insured under a dwelling fire policy or perhaps even by another insurer.

The underwriter who considers only the primary residence has not done a good job of underwriting. The secondary residence should be acceptable on its own merits. However, many underwriters will accept a marginal secondary residence with nominal values when it is written as an endorsement to a desirable homeowners policy on the primary residence.

Increased or Reduced Limits on Specific Coverages

Coverage Several endorsements are available to increase certain limited property coverages of the basic policy. As an example, the coverage on jewelry and furs is limited to an aggregate of $500 in any one loss by theft. This may be increased to $1,000 for an additional premium in most states. Recently, some companies have experimented with offering higher amounts of coverage, either continuing the named-perils coverage or on an "all-risks" basis.

Another example is the coverage on money and securities. The basic limits are $100 and $500, respectively. These limits may be increased by endorsement for an added charge.

Automatic coverage is provided, as a percentage of the dwelling amount, on the nondwelling items in Section I. Under HO-1, 2, 3, and 5, appurtenant private structures are limited to 10 percent of Coverage A (dwelling amount), unscheduled personal property is 50 percent, and additional living expense is 10 percent (HO-1) or 20 percent (HO-2, 3, and 5). Each of these may be increased. In addition, coverage on unscheduled personal property may be reduced to an amount not less than 40 percent of the dwelling amount under most forms.

Underwriting The underwriter normally will want to know why the modification is requested, since most policyholders' needs are met with the standard coverages of the basic policy. The insured may require higher limits on appurtenant structures because of a large garage, a stable, or an elaborately equipped swimming pool.

When asked for a substantial increase in coverage C (unscheduled personal property), the underwriter should ascertain if the increase is warranted. Is there an unusually high value of contents relative to the apparent home value? Does the occupation of the applicant indicate a higher income and thus a reason for more personal property than might otherwise be expected? Has there been a recent inheritance? Are valuable antiques among the property? If the high values are due to specific items, the underwriter may wish to consider whether a scheduled personal property endorsement would be more appropriate.

If the request for higher limits of coverage is reasonable, and the additional exposures present no unusual increase in hazards, coverage is usually granted without additional underwriting. However, requests for decreasing coverage on unscheduled personal property may be viewed with a bit more skepticism. Even though the premium reduction is small, many underwriters feel that there is not a corresponding decrease in exposure because the preponderance of personal property losses, particularly from theft, are small, and still covered in full by the reduced amount. Nevertheless, there are circumstances under which the standard amount simply produces more coverage than the insured has in contents values. The value of contents may be below 40 percent of the amount of insurance on the dwelling. In addition, there may be definite clues to the propriety of allowing a reduction in coverage. Examples include (1) risks with a number of items scheduled and thus removed completely from the basic coverage of the homeowners; (2) newlyweds or former apartment dwellers recently moved into a large house; and (3) coverage on a newly purchased second residence likely to have very modest personal property values for a time.

UNDERWRITING OTHER RESIDENTIAL PACKAGE POLICIES

Since the advent of the homeowners, several other package policies providing residential insurance have been developed. All have certain structural similarities to the homeowners (e.g., both property and liability coverages packaged together), but each has distinctive elements reflecting the market it serves. This section of Chapter 7 deals with two of these specialized residential packages—for mobile-home owners and condominium unit owners. A third—for farmowners—will be discussed in the next chapter.

Mobile-Home Owners

Distinctive Features of Mobile-Home Units Mobile homes should be distinguished from recreational vehicles such as motor homes, camping trailers, and travel trailers. Unlike mobile homes, these recreational vehicles are portable structures designed as temporary living accommodations for recreation, camping, and travel. They can be towed, hauled, or driven by the owner from one site to the next.

Mobile homes are much larger structures, designed for permanent living at a specific location. For insurance purposes, most companies consider a home trailer larger than thirty feet to be a mobile home. Mobile homes are constructed to be towed on their own chassis, set up with or without permanent foundation, and connected to utilities. They can consist of one or more units that are folded, collapsed, or telescoped when towed, and expanded later for additional living area. Sometimes more than one unit is involved, and the units are towed separately and joined at the site; these are called "double-wides."

Mobile homes have been efficiently designed so that space is used to maximum advantage. Also, the home must remain towable within state highway regulations. However, once towed to the site, mobile homes will usually remain in parks specifically designed for them, or on private property.

Mobile homes are complete homes. They include living rooms, kitchens, bathrooms, as many as three bedrooms, appliances, and furniture as well. All they need to make them complete is a space where they can be connected to phone, sewer, and utility lines.

Mobile home living experienced dramatic growth during World War II because of the shortage of conventional housing in that period. At that time they were produced as rapidly as possible, and were often crowded together in "trailer courts" which sprang up on vacant land in readily available, but often relatively poor, locations. Where these early mobile homes often were characterized by cheap construction and transient occupants, newer mobile homes are constructed according to higher standards and in the main are occupied as permanent residences.

Mobile homes have become popular in recent years because of their low cost. Most are mass-produced and can be constructed for substantially less than a conventional dwelling of similar size. In addition to the purchase price, the owner who does not own the land must pay to rent space in a mobile-home park.

Mobile homes often are sold complete with furniture and appliances. However, once they are situated in a "permanent" location, owners frequently add exterior accessories such as awnings, carports, cabanas, porches, steps, skirting, fencing, and utility sheds.

From an insurance standpoint, the mobile-home owner shares most of the same exposures as the conventional homeowner. However, several features of the mobile home create increased exposures that require special coverage.

Mobile homes are by definition somewhat mobile. They can be moved from one site to another, almost always by a firm who specializes in transporting them. Obviously, the conventional homeowners policy does not cover a home in transit. An entire mobile home can even be stolen, another characteristic lacking in the conventional home. A fire in a mobile home can spread rapidly. Total losses frequently occur within fifteen minutes of the time a fire is started. This is due partly to the compact nature of mobile homes, and partly to the combustibility of the plastics, other synthetics, and wood paneling in their construction.

Mobile homes are also highly susceptible to wind damage because they are light in weight and are not secured to the ground as tightly as a conventional home. Another problem is hail, which can severely damage the thin aluminum skin on most mobile homes by denting and chipping it.

Distinctive Policy Features Until recently most insurance companies avoided the mobile-home market. Specialty markets were the primary writers of mobile-home insurance. However, in recent years other insurers have come to recognize the growing market for mobile homes, the better construction techniques being used, and the favorable loss experience of the specialty markets. As a result, several major insurance bureaus have developed policies and rating plans specifically tailored to the mobile-home owners market. Additionally, many companies have retained or developed independent programs.

There are variations among the coverage programs offered in the different markets. The underwriter who is involved with mobile-home owners business should undertake a study of the specific policies involved. To illustrate typical distinctive features of the mobile-home owners policies, the mobile-home form developed by Insurance Services Office (ISO) will be a point of reference in this text. This form closely resembles an HO-2, but has several distinctive features.

Coverage on the mobile home itself is on an actual cash value basis. Replacement cost coverage seldom is written because mobile homes depreciate more quickly than conventional dwellings. However, the popularity of this coverage on homeowners policies has caused some demand for the protection. A few companies are experimenting with offering it as an option, usually for a flat charge.

The insurance coverage on the mobile home includes appliances, furniture, and accessories which were original equipment, (or their replacements), steps, and oil or gas drums or tanks. Nonstandard items such as awnings, shelters, cabanas, porches, carports, water pumps, air conditioners, or other additions or structures are not included unless coverage is specifically added for those items, at an additional premium. The items must be listed and described.

Additional living expense coverage is included with a limit per day for up to a maximum number of days. Emergency removal expense is a supplementary coverage which is automatically included. This provides reimbursement for reasonable expenses up to a limit if it is necessary to move the entire mobile home because it is exposed to danger by an insured peril, such as a fire in a neighboring mobile home.

Collision coverage is available as an endorsement to cover the mobile home and its contents against collision damage while being transported from one site to another. Coverage usually applies for thirty days from the date of the endorsement.

Because the mobile home is portable, there is exclusion of loss due to conversion, embezzlement, or secretion by any person in possession of the mobile home under a bailment lease, conditional sale, purchase agreement, mortgage or other encumbrance. The effect of this exclusion is to eliminate coverage of the mortgagee if the mobile-home owner should abscond with the entire mobile home. An endorsement, the "mobile-home vendors single interest endorsement," is available which protects only the vendor's or lienholder's interest for loss by collision, conversion, embezzlement, or secretion. Thus, the lienholder's interest can be protected if the owner should leave with the mobile home, or if the owner should transport the mobile home without first obtaining collision coverage.

Special Underwriting Considerations Under the ISO Mobile-Home Policy Program, the policy is class-rated. Rates are based on the price of the mobile home when new, the age of the unit, the public fire protection, the territory, whether the mobile home is a year-round or seasonal residence, and the "tie down status." There are three categories of "tie down status": "without tie downs," "with chassis tie downs," and "with full tie downs." With chassis tie downs, the frame of the mobile home is bolted to anchors sunk into the ground or into a concrete slab or foundation. "Full tie downs" add cables over the top of the mobile home. As might be expected, the lowest rate is for mobile homes with full tie downs, and the highest rate is for mobile homes without tie downs. In order to use the rating class for chassis tie downs or full tie downs, all mobile homes within thirty feet must be secured with at least the same type of tie down, because otherwise a wind causing no direct damage to the insured mobile home could blow a neighboring mobile home into it, causing substantial damage. Tie downs are especially important in coastal areas or inland areas known to have heavy windstorms.

In addition to the tie downs, mobile-home underwriters are concerned with several factors which do not affect the conventional dwelling or have additional nuances compared to their use in underwriting conventional dwellings.

The Mobile-Home Park. If the mobile home is situated in a park, the underwriter will be concerned about the quality of the park. The quality can be determined by such factors as the degree of crowding of lots, the condition of the streets, and the maintenance of the common grounds. Underwriters should determine the quality of the park from the producer, from an inspection report, or from visits by company personnel to the area.

Construction. The quality of construction of mobile homes has improved substantially over the past ten to fifteen years. Compliance with current standards is certified by use of the seal of the Mobile Home Manufacturers' Association and the Trailer Coach Association. When the seal of these associations is attached to a mobile home, it indicates compliance with heating, electrical, and plumbing standards in effect at the time of manufacture. In spite of these improvements, mobile homes are still more flimsy than conventional houses, are more susceptible to damage by wind and hail, and are far more likely to have a total loss from fire than conventional houses.

Age and Value. Newer mobile homes are much more desirable than older units because construction quality and standards continue to improve. Age is also an important consideration because the life span of a mobile home is shorter than that of the conventional dwelling.

The value of mobile homes and the rate of depreciation vary by location. Therefore, the dealer's invoice should be checked and local dealers might be questioned about values. Prices may also be developed from publications which give the values for mobile homes. One of these is the *Mobile/Manufactured Blue Book* published by National Market Reports, Inc., of Chicago, Illinois. These directories cover both new and used models and should help in determining values.

Collision Endorsement. If this coverage is requested, the underwriter will want assurances that the home will be moved in a safe manner. The degree of expertise of the mobile home transporter must be considered by securing the name of the mover and checking its reputation.

Concentration Hazard. The underwriter should also be concerned if a number of mobile homes are insured by the company within the same mobile home park. A single windstorm could cause a severe loss if the mobile homes blow into one another. Some companies restrict the total amount of business they insure in a single park.

Flood Exposure. Some mobile-home policies (not ISO forms) cover against flood damage. This is a carry-over from the days when mobile homes were considered as trailers and were written on auto policies. Where this coverage exists, it must be underwritten carefully by giving consideration to the location from the standpoint of potential flood damage. Some mobile-home parks have been built on low land adjacent to rivers. Zoning laws might prohibit the building of permanent buildings in such locations due to the flood hazard. Substantial losses could result if a number of insured mobile homes were located in a park flooded by a river. If a risk presents an undue flood exposure, the underwriter might be able to delete the peril. Otherwise, the risk might warrant declination.

Vendors Single Interest Endorsement (VSI) This coverage may be added to a mobile-home policy to cover only the interest of the mortgagee against loss by collision or by embezzlement, conversion, or secretion of the mobile home while it is in the possession of the purchaser. It also covers the expense of repossessing and returning the mobile home. If VSI coverage is requested, the underwriter will want to carefully consider the moral hazard. If the insured should leave the present site without notification to the company or the mortgagee, the company could be required to pay the outstanding amount of the mortgage. A mobile home on a permanent foundation is more desirable for this coverage, because it is much more difficult to move than one which is not on a permanent foundation. Also, since some mortgagees do not request this endorsement unless they are concerned about the insured, there may be an element of adverse selection.

Condominium Package

Distinctive Features of Condominium Units *Condominium* is a Latin word meaning joint ownership or control. It denotes individual ownership with unrestricted right of disposal of one or more units in a multi-unit project. The land and all other common parts of the unit are held in common with owners of the other units.[3] A residential condominium may be in a high-rise building, a low-rise building, or even a group of attached or detached single-family homes. To oversimplify a bit, condominium unit owners are like the tenants of an apartment, except they own (rather than rent) their apartment units, and are part-owners of all of the buildings which comprise the condominium.

The easiest way to understand condominiums is to compare the condominium with other forms of home ownership.

Owner-occupied Dwellings. The owner-occupant acquires title to a piece of land by a deed which states that any and all improvements on the land, including buildings, are conveyed with the land.[4]

Row Houses. Row houses may have common walls, but the individual units are separate entities. They are eligible for regular homeowners policies.

Apartments. The apartment tenant resides in a building owned by a landlord who may or may not be a resident. The building may also be occupied by other tenants who usually have lease agreements with the landlord. Any fixture added by the tenant generally becomes the property of the landlord.[5]

Cooperative Apartment Buildings. The situation is basically the same as in an apartment. Although the tenants have a corporate interest in the building because they own stock in the cooperative, they are still tenants and lease their apartments from the corporation.[6]

Townhouses. Although townhouses are often confused with condominiums, there is no necessary relation between the two. Townhouse owners are the same as the owners of dwellings. However, they may have some special problems because of agreements relating to common walls or common use of the land for various purposes by all of the townhouse owners.[7]

Planned Urban Developments (PUDs). PUDs differ from condominiums in that the individual owner in a PUD has a fee simple title to the land on which the unit stands. Thus PUDs are either detached dwellings, multiple unit townhouses, or multi-unit one-story projects. In the PUD the individual owner does not usually own an undivided share in the common area, but rather a nonprofit corporation owns the common area. This protects the individual owner from individual liability from actionable injuries occurring in the common area.[8]

Condominiums. The purchase of a condominium unit involves a completely different kind of ownership. The person who buys such a unit owns a space which can be described in various ways in the declarations or agreements relating to the property. In some states, the purchaser buys to the middle of the walls, ceiling, and floors of the unit. In others, the space may be described differently in the deed, according to the enabling act in force in that state. The owner may own to the outside of the wall and therefore own the plumbing, electrical, and other utilities in the walls. A condominum owner also acquires a proportionate interest in the "common elements" of the building: the ground surrounding it, the stairs and hallways, the roof, the boilers, and all the other things necessary to the functioning of the building. A statute is required in order for the condominium association to exist, because its basic concepts are at odds with what is required for the conveyance of property under common law.[9]

Insurance on condominiums is a difficult subject because of the different entities involved. Both the association and the unit owner have property interests and liability exposures.

The association will usually purchase a commercial multi-peril policy to cover its interests. Coverage on the unit owner's interest is discussed in this chapter. It is often difficult to determine exactly where the line is drawn between the association's and the unit owner's responsibilities. Because of the variation among state laws and master deeds or declarations, it would be dangerous to make generalizations. If the association is properly insured and if the unit owners are properly insured, it is hoped that all insurable losses will be covered by the insurance programs of either or both entities.

Distinctive Policy Features The condominium unit owners package will be referred to here as HO-6, the ISO designation for the

Exhibit 7-6
Comparison of Coverages and Limits

A comparison of coverages and limits on a $100,000 home or an apartment or condominium with $50,000 of contents

Coverage	HO-2	HO-3	HO-4	HO-6
A. Building	$100,000 Broad Named Perils	$100,000 "All-Risks"	N/A	N/A
B. Appurtenant Structures	$10,000 Broad Named Perils	$10,000 "All-Risks"	N/A	(Optional) Broad Named Perils
C. Unscheduled Personal Property	$50,000 Broad Named Perils	$50,000 Broad Named Perils	$50,000 Broad Named Perils	$50,000 Broad Named Perils
D. Additional Living Expense	$20,000 Broad Named Perils	$20,000 "All-Risks"	$10,000 Broad Named Perils	$20,000 Broad Named Perils ("All-Risks" optional)
Additions and Alterations	Included as building	Included as building	Included under coverage C up to $5,000	$1,000 (may be increased) Broad Named Perils ("All-Risks" optional)

form. The HO-6 closely resembles the HO-4 (tenant's policy). Although coverage is a little broader, rates used for the basic policy in most territories are the same as rates used for the HO-4.

The basic HO-6 policy is essentially an HO-4 which has been modified to meet special needs of condominium unit owners. The policy may be modified by endorsements to add coverage for appurtenant structures and a few other important exposures. These characteristics will be explained in the following paragraphs.

To understand how the HO-6 relates to the other homeowners forms, refer to Exhibit 7-6. This chart compares the coverages and limits of the HO-2, 3, 4, and 6, assuming a $100,000 home or an apartment or condominium with $50,000 of contents.

All four forms provide broad form coverage on unscheduled personal property, coverage C. Additional living expense coverage is also provided automatically in all forms. In the HO-2 and HO-3, coverage is 20 percent of the dwelling limit. In the HO-4, coverage is 20 percent of the unscheduled personal property limit. The HO-6 includes coverage equivalent to that of the HO-2 by automatically providing additional living expense for 40 percent of the contents limit.

Additions and alterations are not separately insured by the owner of a conventional dwelling. Any additions become part of the building and are insured as such. Additions and alterations made by the tenant are usually minor and are automatically covered under coverage C up to 10 percent of the coverage C limit. However, the condominium unit owner may need coverage for additions and alterations, so $1,000, as an additional amount of coverage, is provided for broad named perils. The $1,000 limit may be increased by endorsement.

Coverage for additional living expense and additions and alterations, under the HO-6, may be endorsed to provide "all-risks" protection. When this is done, the condominium unit owner has essentially the same coverage for these coverage elements as is found in an HO-3. Another option adds coverage for appurtenant structures, such as a carport or storage shed.

Two additional endorsements are available which respond to the unique needs of the condominium unit owner. Condominium owners sometimes rent their condominiums to other parties. (In fact, some people purchase condominiums as an investment for the sole purpose of renting them.) The basic HO-6 permits occasional rental to others, but a "rental to others" option permits unlimited rental and amends the additional living expense coverage to pay for loss of rent when the premises are rented.

One more option is of prime importance. If the condominium association should fail to purchase adequate insurance for itself, there might be an uninsured or underinsured loss. If that happens, the association will recoup the loss by assessing all of the individual unit owners. Loss assessment coverage may be purchased to indemnify the unit owners in such a situation. An uninsured loss, or an inadequately insured loss, might occur if the association's liability limits are inadequate to pay a claim, if their property insurance limits are inadequate to prevent a coinsurance penalty, if their property insurance limits are inadequate to pay for a large loss, of if they suffer a loss from an uninsured peril. The loss assessment coverage will indemnify the insured for such an assessment due to a liability loss or to a property loss within the scope of the HO-6 perils.

To reduce the problem of overlapping coverage, the HO-6 states that coverage is excess over the amount recoverable from other insurance in the name of the condominium association covering the same property.

Special Underwriting Considerations To some people, condominiums combine the advantages of home ownership with the advantages of apartment living. Others feel that the disadvantages of both styles are combined in a condominium.

In some communities, condominiums are the lowest-cost type of new housing available. It is possible to sell a condominium unit for less than a detached residence because there is a savings in the use of common walls, and because fewer square feet of land are required for each unit. In some cases, these low-cost condominiums are sold with a minimum down payment to persons who can barely afford to own a residence. A condominium complex may suffer from poor maintenance and from other hazards associated in general with minimal investment in property by occupants.

Other condominium complexes run to the opposite extreme. Because it is possible for the association to own and maintain a swimming pool, golf course, tennis court, club house, and other amenities, some condominium complexes have become virtual resorts. Such high-valued condominiums share the exposures associated with high-valued dwellings, or apartments with high contents values.

Many apartment buildings are being converted to condominiums. These may be less desirable than newly constructed condominium complexes. Often the promoter will face-lift an old apartment enough to sell the units at a profit to low-income condominium purchasers (often the persons who previously rented the unit) who cannot then afford to repair the hidden defects that have not been corrected. Loss adjustment may also be more difficult in the converted building because common areas are less clearly differentiated than in buildings constructed as condominiums.

Insurance to value is an important consideration with condominiums. It is difficult to determine the value of contents, since appraisal is virtually impossible, and there is no coinsurance requirement in the policy. Yet, underinsurance leaves the underwriter with an inadequate premium for the exposure. Generally speaking, contents values should run higher with condominiums than with apartments. Because condominium owners are a less transient group than apartment dwellers, they are apt to acquire more personal property. Condominiums may also average more people per household, which is another reason for higher contents values. The underwriter should also verify that additions and alterations are insured to value. In many condominiums, all cabinets, plumbing fixtures, and even the paint on the walls will be considered as additions and alterations.

The optional loss assessment coverage requires particular consideration by the underwriter. If substantial amounts of loss assessment coverage are requested, the underwriter should verify that the association has a sound insurance program on common property and on the association's liability. This information in many cases can be secured from the applicant or the condominium management, through the producer. The association should provide the unit owner with a certificate of insurance. Ideally, the liability policy should have sufficient limits, and all property should be insured to full replacement cost for at least the broad form perils. There should not be a large deductible on the association policy. A deficiency in any of these areas increases the potential for loss under the loss assessment coverage.

The unit owners rental to others option must also be written with care. In many cases, the underwriter may determine that the rental exposure exceeds that contemplated by normal HO-6 rates.

The underwriter must also consider the possibility of an undesirable concentration of values. If the producer solicits most of the unit owners in a large complex, the company may be exposed to a catastrophic loss in a single fire. In this case, company capacity must be considered. It may be necessary to arrange for reinsurance, or even to decline good business, in order to remain within company capacity.

SUMMARY

The information needed for a sound homeowners underwriting decision must be carefully gathered, organized, checked for consistency, and compared against underwriting criteria. If a risk is eligible for a policy, the underwriter must evaluate it, perhaps using the following questions: (1) Where did the business come from, and why? (2) What is it and where is it? and (3) Will it be satisfactorily insured to value? The results of the comparison and evaluation must then be weighed. If the risk is still neither clearly acceptable nor unacceptable, other factors such as the reputation of the producer, the existence of other policies from the same account, and the relationship of the applicant to both the producer and the underwriter might be investigated. Then the decision to accept, accept with modifications, or reject can be made.

When a risk is accepted for a homeowners policy, it must also be classified and rated. Preferred or standard rates may be used, and the underwriter must always be aware of the competition. In determining the premium, the underwriter examines the territory, construction, occupancy, protection, and exposure of the dwelling. The importance of rating the risk correctly cannot be overemphasized, as improper rating is both economically unwise and even illegal.

Policy changes in homeowners accounts provide the underwriter with an opportunity to monitor the risks. Some of the more common endorsements affecting the property portion of homeowners policies are the inflation guard, theft coverage extension, scheduled personal property, coverage on secondary residences, and increased or reduced limits on specific coverages.

The underwriting of other residential package policies involves some special considerations. Packages for mobile homes must reflect that such homes are portable, are often situated in thickly settled parks, and are less substantial than conventional homes. Other factors are the existence and type of tie downs, the quality of the mobile-home park, the need for a collision endorsement, the concentration hazard, and the vendors single interest endorsement (VSI).

Condominiums involve a special kind of ownership. Units in a condominium dwelling are owned individually while other areas of the building are owned in common. The association of unit owners must have insurance coverage on some areas, while individual owners must have coverage on privately owned areas. As a result, the underwriter must take extra precautions when considering such risks, and should especially be aware of condominiums of either very high or very low value, insurance to value, concentration of values, and the number of people per household. Distinctive policy features include loss assessment coverage and "rental to others" coverage.

Chapter Notes

1. This section is adapted from *FC&S Bulletins* Personal Lines Section, (Cincinnati OH: The National Underwriter Company, April 1978), Dwellings pp. Hod-1 to Hod-4.
2. J. J. Launie, J. Finley Lee, and Norman A. Baglini, *Principles of Property and Liability Underwriting,* 2nd ed. (Malvern, PA: Insurance Institute of America, 1977), p. 498.
3. Anthony D. Grezzo, *Condominiums,* (2300-00202) (Washington, DC: United States Government Printing Office, September 1972).
4. Norman A. Miller, *Condominiums and Insurance Property Loss Considerations* (Chicago: Property Loss Research Bureau, 1973).
5. Ibid.
6. Ibid.
7. Ibid.
8. *The Home-Association Handbook,* Technical Bulletin 50, (Washington, DC: Urban Land Institute, 1964), p. 10.
9. Miller.

CHAPTER 8

Farms, Ranches, Dwelling Fire, and Monitoring Decisions

INTRODUCTION

The first section of Chapter 8 deals with underwriting the farm and ranch package. Following that is a discussion of the underwriting of residential property risks under the so-called "dwelling fire" forms—the basic dwelling and contents form, the broad form, and the special form. The chapter concludes with a section on monitoring underwriting decisions in residence property insurance in general.

UNDERWRITING FARM AND RANCH PROPERTIES

The Nature of Farm and Ranch Risks

In colonial days, the family-owned and operated farm was the norm. Today, such family farms still exist, but their number and the dollar amount of production from them continue to decrease. Due to increasing values of land and equipment and the need for sophisticated processes and automated production, the farmer has had to become a production planner, a scientist, and a business expert. With land selling in the Midwest for $2,000 or more an acre and combines and tractors costing thousands of dollars, a family farm supporting, for example, a father and son and their families may easily have a total value of over $1 million. While this is still technically a family farm, it is also a commercial enterprise, very capital intensive, and often as complex to insure as light manufacturing and mechanical contracting risks. This complexity increases when the subject is the corporate farm, usually managed by an employee of a farm management corporation.

At the same time, almost all farms contain some of the elements of personal risks. The family farm may have one or two (or more) dwelling buildings, private garage(s), and household contents. These exposures also exist for the corporate manager living on the farm premises.

In this chapter, farms and ranches will be combined for discussion and any reference to "farms" includes ranches.

Farmowners-Ranchowners Package Policy Program

Farm and ranch risks may purchase a package policy that resembles the homeowners but is flexible enough to meet the unique needs of this class.

The following discussion is based on the farmowners-ranchowners program of the Insurance Services Office. This program is widely used and most independently filed programs are very similar. The designation "FR" will be used to refer to this program and the forms used in it.

General Nature The FR program combines both property and liability insurance in the same policy. The residential (as opposed to farming) property exposures all involve the same percentage amounts as the homeowners program (e.g., unscheduled personal property is covered for 50 percent of the amount on the dwelling). However, there is no built-in coverage item dealing with appurtenant structures in the FR due to their increased presence and values on a farm. These must be insured on a scheduled basis through an endorsement. Another difference between FR and homeowners is that additional living expense coverage in the FR program is uniformly 10 percent of coverage A (dwelling amount) and does not vary from 10 to 20 percent, as it does in the homeowners program.

Subject to these differences, FR forms 1, 2, and 4 correspond to the HO-1, 2, and 4. An FR-3, corresponding to HO-3, is also used in a few states, but there is no FR program counterpart to HO-5, 6, or 8. All policies contain Section II coverage that is either the equivalent of separate farmers comprehensive personal liability coverage (the FCPL will be discussed in Chapter 11 of this text), or the equivalent of a standard general liability coverage part. This chapter focuses on Section I, the property insurance element of the FR program.

Distinctive Coverage Features and Options Section I of the FR program may, or in some cases must, include coverage of certain farm (as opposed to residential) property. The complete list of coverage "items" under Section I is as follows:

Coverage A. Dwelling
Coverage B. Unscheduled Personal Property (Household)
Coverage C. Additional Living Expense
Coverage D. Farm Personal Property (Scheduled)
Coverage E. Farm Personal Property (Blanket)—$25,000 minimum amount
Coverage F. Barns, Buildings, Structures, and Additional Dwellings (Scheduled)

Coverage of farm property (coverages D, E, and F) is accomplished through the use of forms FR-6, 7, or 8, respectively. A $100 deductible applies to Section I. Higher deductibles are available.

FR-6. Form FR-6 covers "farm personal property" on a *scheduled* basis against fire, lightning, removal, the extended coverage perils, vandalism or malicious mischief, theft, collision, and electrocution of livestock. "Farm personal property," which must be distinguished from the household-related items under coverage B, includes all property used or produced in the business of farming except for real estate or autos. This would include equipment, livestock, farm produce, poultry, supplies, farming machinery, and other similar items *except* autos, trucks, land, and buildings.

Coverage under FR-6 (coverage D under Section I) requires that each separate class of property be listed separately and an amount shown for each. There is provision on the form for thirty-eight items and a total amount. Some examples of different items are:

- Item Number 1—Grain
- Item Number 4—Hay in Open Stacks
- Item Number 5—Machinery, Vehicles and Equipment
- Item Number 6—Borrowed Farm Machinery, Vehicles and Equipment
- Item Number 19—Dairy Cattle
- Item Number 23—Swine
- Item Number 38—Portable Buildings and Portable Structures

Certain extensions are a part of the form. The named insured may apply (but not as additional insurance) up to 10 percent of the limit of liability for grain, hay in open stacks, and hay in buildings. Similarly, 25 percent of the limit of liability may be applied for machinery, vehicles, and equipment. In both cases, such property must be within 100 miles of the premises. Principally, the exceptions to this coverage would be while the property is in the custody of commom carriers, elevators, sales agents, and so on. Specifically insured machinery is also covered within 100 miles, and replacement machinery is automatically covered for thirty days for amounts up to an excess of $15,000 over the amount specified.

The major exclusions are:

1. loss caused by enforcement of building codes;
2. loss caused by or resulting from various forms of earth movement unless fire or explosion ensue and then the company is liable only for such ensuing loss;
3. loss caused by
   - flood, or
   - backup of sewers or drains, or
   - surface water

   unless fire or explosion ensue and then the company is liable only for such ensuing loss;
4. loss caused by or resulting from power failure; or
5. loss to outdoor radio and television equipment.

FR-7. Form FR-7 (coverage E of Section I) covers farm personal property on a *blanket* basis against the same perils listed in FR-6. The only extension consists of the option to apply 10 percent of the blanket amount against loss by fire and unharvested grain, grain harvested but kept in the open, or hay, straw, and fodder in the open. FR-7 has an 80 percent coinsurance clause as a basic part of the form and a deductible may be applied to this form as with FR-6. Exclusions are similar under both forms. Additional interests may be similarly covered, and extra expense coverage is available.

The blanket feature is simple, requires less attention during the policy term by both insured and producer, and covers the various items without the need to report new or replacement livestock or implements. It also covers without regard to the values on each of the classes of livestock, implements, equipment, machinery, or grain, provided the total amount at time of loss meets the coinsurance requirement. These features make the blanket form appealing. When properly written and updated, it is a valuable tool to the insured, producer, and underwriter.

On the other hand, the use of the blanket form in a period of rapidly rising values brings special concerns which must be carefully considered by the underwriter.

1. It may be difficult at time of loss for the claims adjuster to ascertain compliance with the coinsurance requirement, because the various items covered under one amount may be separated geographically by many miles and taking an inventory may be difficult and impractical.
2. Unless frequent updating and reevaluation are done, values will rise much faster than the amount of insurance. This will tend to

result in premium inadequacy and increase the chance of the insured's being a coinsurer in the event of loss.

3. The blanket form presumes a constancy of values which does not in fact exist. For example, the fact that corn converted to pork increases in value may cause an inadequacy of both coverage and premium. The peak season or reporting form should be used if values fluctuate frequently.

FR-8. In the FR program there is no automatic extension of coverage to appurtenant private structures as there is under homeowners. This is because farm and ranch risks present a much greater probability of substantial values in structures other than the dwelling. Every building on a farm or ranch must be described and separately insured if coverage is desired. In the FR program this is done with FR-8 (which corresponds to coverage F of Section I).

FR-8 provides space for scheduling thirty structures of various types. In addition, fences, outdoor radio and television equipment, private power and light poles (including outdoor wiring and attachments), and windmills, towers, and tank or pump houses (including pumping machinery and equipment while contained therein or attached) may be covered for a specific amount by scheduling them in the form.

The description of covered property is similar to that of other forms covering structures. For example, if a particular structure is scheduled, the form automatically includes coverage of attached sheds and permanent fixtures (except silos, which must be scheduled). Improvements and betterments in insured structures are covered, as are building materials and supplies on the premises which are intended to be used in construction.

Perils insured against are the same as for the two personal property forms (FR-6 and FR-7) except that theft, collision, and electrocution of livestock are not applicable to the exposure and hence are not covered. A deductible may be applied. Extra expense coverage is available, additional interests may be named, and replacement cost coverage is available for buildings (as described later), structures, barns, and additional dwellings covered under FR-8. Coverage provided without the replacement cost endorsement is on an actual cash value basis. The exclusions under the FR-8 are similar to those on the FR-6 and FR-7.

Optional Coverages Some of the major additional coverages available for use with the FR program include:

1. optional $250 theft deductible applying to loss by theft of property covered under coverages B, D, and E of the policy. This endorsement can be used with the FR-1, 2, 3, 4, 6, and 7;
2. accidental shooting and drowning of livestock, except poultry;

3. extra expense coverage for an insured to continue normal farm operations which have been interrupted as a result of damage to or destruction of property covered under coverage D, E, or F;
4. specific items of glass may be covered on a scheduled basis only;
5. credit card and depositors forgery coverage for loss resulting from unauthorized use of a lost or stolen credit card, forgery or alteration of checks or drafts, or loss due to acceptance of counterfeit paper currency;
6. earthquake coverage;
7. sound receiving and transmitting equipment;
8. inflation guard endorsement;
9. increased limits of liability on a number of the coverages; and
10. replacement cost coverage for Coverage F.

Eligibility and Required Coverages An FR policy must include both Section I and Section II mandatory coverages. The manual lists those risks that are not eligible for Section I coverages as:

1. farms which are not occupied by the insured unless
    a. tenant operated under the insured's supervision, or
    b. operated under contract management;
2. farms which are vacant or unoccupied;
3. buildings and contents used for custom and/or commercial purposes such as (but not limited to) (a) crop drying, grain grinding, seed grain drying and alfalfa or hay chopping for others (except incidental operations); (b) sales barns, barns used for dancing purposes; and (c) greenhouses;
4. mobile homes or their contents (except under coverage D or F).

Additionally, to be eligible for the FCPL, the dwelling must be designed and used for family residential purposes and permitted incidental occupancies. There may be no more than two families or more than two roomers or boaders per family. Farms owned or operated by a corporation can be covered only if financially controlled by one individual or by one individual with other family members residing on the same farm premises. Farms where the principal business is raising, boarding, or using horses for riding, racing, or show are ineligible, as are farms where the principal purpose is to supply commodities for manufacturing or processing by the insured for sale to others.

Exhibit 8-1 shows the mandatory and optional coverages under Section I as outlined in the manual. Note the division between owner occupants, owner nonoccupants, and tenants. These are the three classes of individuals which would be eligible for the FR program.

Exhibit 8-1
Mandatory or Optional Coverage—Farmowners-Ranchowners Program*

Coverage	Owner Occupant	Owner Non-Occupant	Tenant
A—Dwelling	Mandatory	Mandatory	—
B—Unscheduled Personal Property (Household)	Mandatory (50% of Coverage A)		Mandatory
C—Additional Living Expense	Mandatory (10% of Coverage A)	Mandatory (10% of Coverage A)	Mandatory (10% of Coverage B)
D—Farm Personal Property (Scheduled)	Optional	Optional	Optional
E—Farm Personal Property (Optional) (Blanket) $25,000—Minimum Amount	$25,000	$25,000	$25,000
F—Barns, Buildings, Structures and Additional Dwellings (Scheduled)	Optional	$10,000	Optional

*Reprinted, with permission, from *Commercial Lines Manual* (New York: Copyright Insurance Services Office, 1979), p. FR-7 (3rd Edition 8-80).

Minimum Amounts The minimum amounts of insurance required by most companies in most states are:

Coverage A—Dwelling: $20,000 for a superior dwelling, down to $12,000 for the lowest acceptable class.
Coverage B—Unscheduled Personal Property: 50 percent of coverage A. Where there is no coverage A, $6,000 to $4,000, depending on the quality of the dwelling.
Coverage C—Additional Living Expense: 10 percent of coverage A (or B on tenant policies).
Coverage E—Farm Personal Property—Blanket: $25,000.
Coverage F—Barns, Buildings, Structures and Additional Dwellings: $15,000 to $10,000, depending on quality.

Classification and Rating Rating FR policies involves premium determination for the dwelling and related coverages and separate consideration to any of coverages D, E, and F that are insured.

Dwelling and Related Coverage. The premium for coverages A, B, and C of Section I and for Section II is indivisible (like the homeowners premium). However, a new dimension—dwelling type—is involved. Dwellings are classified into three types—1, 2, and 3. The types refer to the construction characteristics and the state of repair of the dwelling, and the numbers denote quality, with "1" the highest quality and "3" the poorest. For example, characteristics of a type 1 dwelling include superior construction and excellent repair, a modern heating system which meets certain specifications, a continuous enclosed foundation, a modern interior plumbing system, and a modern electrical system.

A type 2 dwelling must be of standard construction and maintenance characteristics and have either a modern heating system as described in type 1 or space type heaters with thermostats, and all other requirements of type 1.

A type 3 dwelling is one not meeting the requirements for type 1 and type 2.[1]

The premium is then taken from tables based on factors such as protection class, location in state, form (FR-1, 2, or 3), amount of insurance, type of dwelling, and a construction factor. When coverage is written without coverage B for an owner-nonoccupant, a flat percentage reduction is applied to the basic premium.

Tenant risks are rated similarly. Amounts of insurance on unscheduled personal property combined with dwelling type, construction, location, and protection class produce a premium for coverages B and C and Section II.

Farm Coverages. Farm coverages take rates per $100 of insurance. Rates for barns, silos, trailer homes, dwellings and contents, hay, machinery, vehicles and equipment, livestock, windmills, blanket personal property, and several other property items are included in the manual. Other property is rated according to the applicable farm, fire, and allied lines section of the Commercial Lines Manual.

As with dwellings under coverage A, buildings under coverage F are classified as to type.

Type 1 buildings must have superior characteristics and be in excellent repair. They must not be over one-story high (a story may be defined as a usable level); the foundation must be continuous and of masonry or concrete; the floor must be incombustible; the building must be fully enclosed; and there can be no hay storage.

Type 2 buildings must have better than average characteristics and maintenance. They must have a foundation similar to that required for type 1, except that pole barns are eligible. (Pole barns are inexpensively built structures, framed on poles or posts driven a minimum of four feet below ground level.) Buildings must be fully enclosed, but open sheds and hay storage are permitted. Type 3 buildings are those not meeting standards for types 1 or 2, except for certain structures. Private greenhouses; buildings used or constructed for crop drying, grain grinding, seed grain cleaning and drying, or alfalfa or hay chopping; and portable buildings and structures and fences are also type 3.

Silos are classified as type 1 if they are all steel reinforced concrete with integral roof, foundation, and walls, and unload from the bottom. Type 2 silos are all masonry silos not qualifying as type 1. (They might not be eligible for type 1 classification because they unload from other than the bottom). Type 3 silos are all frame including frame ironclad.

Underwriting FR Policies

Underwriting package farm policies requires careful evaluation of the composite risk picture since some of the items covered are likely to be less desirable than others. A farm will rarely have either all new or all old dwellings, buildings, and equipment. Instead, underwriters may encounter dwellings, buildings, and equipment that are reasonably well maintained, but one or two items—such as obsolescent buildings—that are less desirable than the rest of the risk. They must then decide if the whole risk is acceptable at the premium developed, or if it is unacceptable, or if most of it as submitted is acceptable and the less desirable exposures can be handled by excluding items, using deductibles, or requiring more premium.

The risk may be an excellent risk for one peril insured, such as fire, but be highly susceptible to wind and hail damage because of its location. Or, if no particular weather hazard is present, it may present an unusual theft or vandalism exposure.

The attitude of the prospective insured toward covered property and how the insured will be likely to care for such property are important underwriting variables. Questions that should be raised in connection with these include:

1. Is the farm a profitable operation?
2. Is it progressive and up-to-date?
3. Is the insured active in the business? Does he or she supervise it closely? The retired farmer may be deserving, but if he or she lives in town and rents the farm to a tenant to operate, the exposure is different than if the farm were operated by the owner.
4. Is the machinery well maintained and replaced at reasonable intervals?
5. Are the buildings in good repair? Unrepaired buildings indicate, at best, morale hazard in addition to physical hazard. Does a lack of repairs indicate a lack of funds for maintenance? The careful underwriter will require photographs, diagrams, and

complete information on heating, wiring, and other pertinent information in underwriting farm buildings.

6. What is the reputation of the insured in the community for competence, honesty, and credit standing?
7. How well does the underwriter know the producer, and how well does the producer know the insured?
8. Are there any past losses of a suspicious nature?
9. How many lien and/or mortgage holders are listed on the application? Is the applicant overextended financially?

Underwriting of an FR package policy is similar to that of a homeowners policy. Similar types of information must be secured, similar sources are used, and most of the same alternatives are available. An additional step is needed, however, because of the commercial aspects of a farm. The underwriter must be familiar with the types of farming in the area, and must be able to determine if an applicant appears to have a profitable and stable operation. Additional information must be secured, in many cases, to answer the questions listed above.

Single-Line Farm Coverages

Farm and ranch packages have been on the market for many years and have been advertised, promoted, and sold on a broad scale to most eligible buyers. Fire and allied lines coverage (not part of a package) tends to be requested primarily on residual business—business that does not qualify for one reason or another for a package. There may be exceptions to this generalization. For example, a tenant occupant of a farm dwelling may be of excellent character and a respected and careful farmer and caretaker of property, but would not be eligible for FR coverage on the dwelling. If the terms of the lease give the tenant responsibility for insuring the dwelling, it would have to be covered under a farm property form. Still, a basic question the underwriter asks on such a submission is, "Why is this not on a package form? Is it too old? Of too little value? Does it present unusual hazards? What is the state of repair? Is adverse selection at work? Is the premium adequate for the exposure?"

Except for certain perils (e.g., theft, collision, electrocution of livestock), the hazards to be considered are the same as those for a package. But with the bulk of the average and above-average business already under packages, care is required in evaluating the nonpackage fire and allied lines submission.

Valuation Problems in Farm and Ranch Underwriting

Insurance-to-value problems are no less severe in underwriting farm and ranch risks than in residence coverages generally. In addition, the nature of the operations of many of these risks creates subtleties in valuation that do not affect nonfarm situations.

Implement and building prices have changed very rapidly. It is not unusual for an implement to have a higher value now than at the time of purchase two or three years ago. On the other hand, due to changes in farming methods, some buildings and implements have declined in value. For example, in most areas, hay is now rolled into large bales and left in the field, instead of being stored in barns. This has not only relocated a part of the fire risk from the farm to the field, but it has made the barn formerly used for storage largely obsolete and of greatly decreased value.

In a similar fashion, hog farming has changed. Where not too long ago a farmer raised twenty hogs with a building and a pig pen, there now exists a pork factory with a highly specialized building. The hog is put into this building almost at birth, and fed and watered automatically with computer measured amounts of food.

Increase in values in the normal course of production is routine to the agriculture business. For example, corn used as seed has a high value, but when converted to a corn crop it has a constantly changing value as it grows, ultimately reaching a market value when fully grown and harvested. At this time, it may be dried by a drier the farmer keeps for such a purpose (which itself will increase the value of the corn); it may be stored, thus maintaining or increasing the value at risk on the premises; or it may go into feed used by a farmer for hogs.

Possible Underwriting Responses to Valuation Problems To cope with these valuation problems, the underwriter may wish to consider the following actions, which have been effectively used by underwriters of farm properties. These should be viewed as general guidelines to be evaluated in the light of the risk being considered. In some cases, these courses of action will need to be modified to reflect the specific characteristics of the risk, applicable regulatory provisions, and company policy.

1. Insist on an adequate percentage of insurance to value at policy inception. In addition, it is necessary to have a clear understanding with the producer and policyholder of the valuation base (e.g., replacement cost or actual cash value), and attempt to maintain this agreed-upon percentage of insurance to what most often is rising value. To safely accomplish these objectives, the underwriter might do the following:

- Insist on insurance to 80 percent or higher of replacement cost for buildings, actual cash value for equipment, and market value for farm products.
- Determine the age of the building and whether insuring it for replacement cost would introduce a moral hazard. This can be determined not only by questions on the application but by requiring the producer to submit photographs of each building.
- Determine the size of each building and the physical relationship of buildings to each other. A diagram to reasonably accurate scale is of great value in assessing the risk.
- Determine the usage and condition of each building. Would the horse barn be rebuilt if it were destroyed by fire? What type of wiring exists? How are the buildings maintained? Are they in need of painting, or does it appear the farm is well managed and profitable?
- Determine if equipment (e.g., a tractor), is the same type the farmer would buy today. If so, is it insured for today's value with provision for annual review?
- Require a periodic inventory of farm property.

2. If possible, use a maximum policy term of one year. This practice provides several benefits. Rates can be changed annually, if needed, and requiring annual renewal information helps in maintaining insurance to value.
3. Require specific insurance on high value equipment items. Combines today may cost $100,000 and should be insured for full value at policy inception. The value of used equipment can often be found in various guidebooks published for that purpose.
4. Tailor the policy to reflect fluctuating values. For example, a peak season endorsement increasing the amount of insurance on grain for a period of from, say, September through January, will serve the policyholder better by covering the peak value season of harvest and storage, and will result in premium commensurate with the exposure. The insured pays only for the increased amount of insurance for the time it is needed. Exhibit 8-2 shows a copy of the peak season endorsement used with FR-6.
5. Watch for overinsurance on older buildings and equipment. In contrast to the problem of maintenance of insurance to value on newer buildings and equipment, the valuation problem with older or obsolescent buildings and equipment is one of overinsurance and the possible moral or morale hazards that

Exhibit 8-2
Peak Season Endorsement*

PEAK SEASON ENDORSEMENT
(FORM FR 00 06 ONLY)
COVERAGE D—SCHEDULED FARM PERSONAL PROPERTY

In consideration of an additional premium and subject to all of the conditions of this policy applicable to Coverage D—Scheduled Farm Personal Property, the limit of liability applicable to each numbered item of Form FR-6 which is listed in the following Schedule, is increased for only the period of time and not exceeding the limit of liability specified below.

SCHEDULE

Item No.	Increase in Limit of Liability	Period of Time		Limit of Liability	Annual Rate	Additional Premium
		From	To			

This endorsement must be attached to Change Endorsement when issued after the policy is written.

may result. If a fifteen-year-old combine is to be insured, does it match the rest of the farm in vintage and use? If it does, should the entire farm be considered a good risk? If it does not—if the rest of the equipment is more modern and valuable—how is this particular combine used? Has the equipment been altered to increase its value?

6. Watch for underinsurance on products that increase in value during the season. A dairy farm will have a rather constant level of values from year to year, except for inflation, depreciation, and the change caused by normal upgrading and replacement of equipment. On the other hand, a hog farm will have a constant increase in the value of the product—the hog—as the season progresses. Some insurance forms use one amount of insurance for the combination of grain and livestock on the theory that as the grain is fed to the hogs, the increase in value of the hogs will match the decrease in value of the grain. This is deceptive thinking. If the grain is worth the same when converted to pork, what incentive would the farmer have to raise hogs? It is only because of the expectation of increased value (and return when sold) that the farmer goes to the time and expense of feeding the grain to the hogs to be sold as pork. This value added must be contemplated in the policy programming.

   There are several methods to handle this problem of increasing values. One is to write the policy for the maximum amount expected to be at risk during the policy year and to review it annually for adequacy. A second method is the use of the peak season endorsement previously mentioned. For the larger farm with modern equipment and high values, a reporting form might be considered. This form requires the farmer to report inventory on a periodic (usually monthly or quarterly) basis. Insurance follows values, the insured pays only for what is needed, and premium is commensurate with the exposure.

In summary, valuation problems are intertwined with underwriting approach and philosophy in general. Rarely will a farm be found that does not have one or two old buildings among its modern, up-to-date farrowing pens and pole barns. A twenty-year-old tractor may also be found among the new generation of modern, high-value equipment. The existence of these should not deter the farm underwriter from successfully insuring the entire risk. Evaluate the risk, tailor the coverage by using deductibles and excluding the obviously unused buildings and equipment if necessary, and be careful not to overinsure the older items or underinsure the newer ones. A profitable book of business depends in large part on the underwriter's ability to find alternative methods to profitably insure most farms.

UNDERWRITING DWELLING FIRE POLICIES

By dwelling fire forms, this text means those types of forms that antedated the homeowners and other residence package programs but continue in use today. Specifically, these are the basic dwelling and contents form, the dwelling building(s) and contents broad form, and the dwelling building(s) special form. Where needed, the terms "basic," "broad," and "special" will be used to refer to these forms. All are written by attachment to the standard fire policy.

The Nature of the Market for Nonpackage Policies

The reasons for the use of dwelling fire forms for residential risks include the following: eligibility, the underwriter's choice, the insured's choice, and builders' risks.

Eligibility Dwelling fire policies are used for residences which do not meet the eligibility requirements for a package policy. The dwelling fire forms have only a few basic eligibility requirements: the building (or contents) to be insured must be (or be in) a residence, and the residence must have no more than a specified number of dwelling units. For building, or building and contents coverage, the maximum is four units in most companies. For contents only, many companies permit the subject contents to be in any residential structure having up to twenty dwelling units, while others allow the writing of household contents in a dwelling unit located in a building of any size and description, such as an apartment over a retail store.

Package policies impose additional eligibility requirements: the dwelling must usually be owner-occupied, and it must meet certain minimum value requirements. Consequently, the dwelling fire forms are normally the only choice available for:

1. residences rented to others,
2. vacant dwellings (such as homes for sale), and
3. dwellings or personal property which fall below the minimum values for a package policy.

Condominiums rented to others may be insured under the HO-6, but as noted in the previous chapter, this is not always the most desirable way to handle the exposure.

Dwelling fire forms may also be used for multiple-family buildings (apartments), boardinghouses, nurses' residences, motels, and similar residential risks. Since most operations falling into these categories are usually considered commercial lines business, they will not be discussed in this personal lines text.

Residences Rented to Others. Properties falling into this category include a wide range of risks such as mansions and homes in exclusive neighborhoods, new duplexes or single-family homes, and 100-year-old property in deteriorated areas. Physically, these dwellings range from extremely attractive to very rundown.

Vacant or Unoccupied Dwellings. Because homeowners rules limit new business eligibility to owner-occupied dwellings, vacant or unoccupied homes usually are written on dwelling fire forms. The home may be for sale, or it may have been sold but not yet occupied by the new owner.

Almost every residence is vacant at one time or another. A vacant home is unoccupied and furniture and other contents have been removed from the premises. This may present the underwriter with a greater exposure to vandalism, fire, and water damage than a residence that is merely unoccupied. Values encountered in this group run the full range from huge to nominal. Seasonal resort property, suburban homes, and central city residences may fall into this grouping. Some homes will be vacant for a period of days while a sale is negotiated; others will be vacant as long as a year, or more.

Low-value Property. This category includes not only low-value buildings, but also low-value contents. Homeowners policies in most states have a minimum of $15,000 on dwellings ($10,000 if seasonal) and $7,500 on contents. Many companies use even higher minimum amounts of insurance for eligibility.

In contrast, dwelling fire policies are available for as low an amount as $1,000 on contents, with annual rates as low as $3 for $1,000 of contents coverage in some territories. Of course, minimum premiums are used (often about $25 regardless of term—one year or three years) in order to cover the cost of handling, and many companies have established minimum amounts for eligibility.

Low-value homes may be small, fairly new homes built in communities with a low construction cost; they may be small prefabricated cottages on recreational or seasonal property; or they may be homes with a deteriorated value due to age, location, or condition. In some communities this will include entire complexes of low-value homes mass-produced after World War II.

Contents values may be small for the student renting an apartment, for a financially troubled family, for newlyweds, or for anyone renting a furnished apartment or home.

The Underwriter's Choice Many risks which do not meet the underwriting criteria set by a company for a package policy are still insurable under a dwelling fire form. In some cases, the producer recognizes the problems and submits an application (or policy) for a dwelling form. In other cases, a package policy is requested and the *underwriter* makes the counteroffer of a dwelling fire form.

This may be the underwriter's choice for several reasons:

1. The dwelling forms provide less coverage with regard to perils and may, in a given case, eliminate coverage for those perils which are unacceptable.
2. The rate level is higher, so the premium may be more commensurate with the higher exposure level.
3. The dwelling forms do not anticipate insurance to replacement cost value to the same extent as do most of the homeowners forms.
4. The risk, though technically eligible, does not meet the company's acceptability rules for a homeowners policy. These rules might relate to age, size, value, insurance to value, or other variables.

Less Coverage. Unlike the homeowners, the dwelling forms do not provide theft coverage or liability coverage. Extended coverage and vandalism are optional in the basic form. Even with these added perils, the basic form does not cover water damage. In cases where the risk is acceptable except for an undesirable peril or perils, one of the dwelling forms may be used. As an example, the theft exposure might be too great for acceptability under a homeowners policy. The underwriter may offer broad form coverage, which gives almost the same coverage to property as the HO-2 or HO-4, except for theft.

Higher Rate Level. With the bulk of the risks in the average to preferred range already under package policy coverage, the balance of residential risks develop less favorable loss experience resulting in a higher rate than that "built into" the indivisible homeowners premium for those same perils. Thus, a policy covering only fire and extended coverage would, on the average, carry a higher rate per $100 of coverage than would be charged for those same perils under, for example, an HO-1 *if* the HO-1 premium were developed in that fashion.

Less desirable homes require this higher rate to compensate for the added hazards of risks in that group. In order to match hazards with rate level, the underwriter will want to get the losses for the less desirable risks into the nonpackage statistics where there is a higher rate level to support the losses. If experience is poor for these less desirable risks, the losses will not affect the loss ratio for homeowners business.

Insurance to Value. This text has emphasized the importance of insurance to value for package policies. It was noted that the homeowners forms contemplate insurance to a high percentage of replacement cost of the dwelling, and the rates are set accordingly. It was also noted that it is not always possible to get insurance to value, and that for many older homes with severe depreciation or obsolescence it may not even be feasible. In addition to the HO-8, the dwelling forms, particularly the basic form, provide a good alternative when insurance to value is a problem.

Acceptability Rules. Most companies have established rules or guides for acceptability of package policies. One common example deals with age of the dwelling. Another is size, with perhaps 1,000 square feet of living area being a minimum. Still another is value, with $20,000 being used as a minimum by some companies. While exceptions may be made, most risks not meeting these underwriting rules are offered dwelling fire forms.

The Insured's Choice The dwelling fire forms are used for residences for which the insured desires coverage at a minimal premium. In some cases, the dwelling form is used to provide "just the basics," as cheaply as possible. The insured may be a couple on a fixed income who always carried "just fire insurance" on their home, or someone with a home mortgage partly paid off who carries only enough insurance to satisfy the mortgagee's requirement. Or, the insured may be a lender who is primarily interested in covering its interest for fire and extended coverage. It should be noted that as fire rates increase relative to homeowners rates, the fire premiums may be higher than the homeowners premium for the same limits even in view of the more limited coverage. The homeowners policy underwriting carries an insurance-to-value concern which may allow the insured to select lower limits under the dwelling fire policy.

Builders' Risk A homeowners policy may be used to insure the owner and future occupant of a home under construction, but not the contractor building a home for resale. "Permanent-type" dwelling fire forms can also be used, and in addition, may be used to insure the builder or other owner who will not occupy the home. In either case, the home is insured as though it were a completed building with full rates being charged.

A better approach in most instances is to use a dwelling form with a builders' risk endorsement. The builders' risk completed value endorsement (the form most commonly used) and rating recognize that the home value is near zero when the construction begins, and that the full value is reached only when construction is complete. By using a discount, a premium is developed which reflects the average values at risk. This is a sound approach, particularly for homes for which construction extends over some period of time.

Distinctive Considerations

Rating Unlike the indivisible homeowners premium in which one package premium covers the entire policy, there is a divisible premium for dwelling forms. The dwelling and the contents have different rates, and there is a separate rate for the peril of fire, for the extended coverage perils, for vandalism, and for the broad and special forms, if applicable.

Building fire rates in each state are based on the type of construction, the protection class, the number of living units, and whether the building is owner-occupied. The contents rate is based on construction type, protection class, and number of living units.

Rating bureaus publish class rates for the dwelling forms. However, fire-resistive homes, or a dwelling which is not occupied solely as a residence (such as an apartment above a tavern), may be specifically rated. Extended coverage and vandalism rates are higher if the building is seasonal or vacant.

In dealing with dwelling fire policies, it is important to note that the definitions of various types of construction may be different from the definitions used in homeowners rating. In some states, a home of brick veneer construction is considered "brick" in the homeowners program, but is rated as "frame" in the dwelling policy program manual.

Underwriting Most of the property underwriting considerations already discussed under package policies are also applicable to nonpackage policies. However, there are additional considerations which relate to the nature of the risks for which dwelling fire forms are used. Some companies have a detailed questionnaire used with dwelling fire policies or applications, completed by the producer, to provide additional information needed to make a decision on this class of business.

Some companies require that a photograph accompany each dwelling fire application. This requires producers to drive to each home and take the pictures, and sometimes they discover unexpected hazards. Poor maintenance and exterior housekeeping, roofing in need of repair, and other adverse situations can be discovered from photographs but are seldom revealed by applications. Pictures may also help in gaining an idea as to building value, or at least support or refute the amount of insurance requested relative to indicated value of the dwelling.

In the age of the computer, many homeowners policies are

machine-issued. On the other hand, many companies do not use computers for the lower volume of dwelling fire policies. Some of these policies are issued manually in the producer's office, due in part to tradition, although the volume is decreasing steadily. The underwriter faced with a producer-issued policy on an undesirable risk has to cancel the policy rather than decline it.

When insurance is written on both dwelling and contents, the insured may choose any limit for contents. This is unlike the homeowners where coverage is automatically set at a fixed percentage of the dwelling amount, subject to some modification. If the contents amount on a dwelling form for an owner-occupant is significantly less than that percentage of the building amount, the underwriter might suspect that contents are not insured to value and further investigation should be made.

Beyond these general underwriting considerations, other factors must be considered, depending on the reason the dwelling form was chosen as discussed above.

Eligibility. Dwellings that are ineligible for homeowners are usually written on a dwelling form. That, in itself, does not increase or decrease the desirability of the risk. Therefore, each risk must be judged on its own merits, without prejudice.

In addition to the criteria discussed in previous chapters, the underwriter must also consider hazards related to the specific factors which make the risk ineligible for a package program.

RESIDENCES RENTED TO OTHERS. To the landlord, a building may be nothing more than an investment, and he or she may want maximum return on a minimum investment—which implies minimum upkeep. Underwriters must remember they are insuring the *person*, although the property is the subject of insurance.

Hazards may be increased by the attitude of the tenant(s). The combination of owner-tenant attitudes toward rental property makes it imperative that the underwriter analyze the moral and morale hazards as well as the physical hazard.

The underwriter should also consider the nature of the insured's investment in rental property. The individual of comfortable but modest means who owns a small duplex in his or her own neighborhood has a different relationship with the investment property than the individual who owns ten homes in the center of town and lives some distance away. Although it is dangerous to generalize, the first owner quite possibly maintains the property as well as his or her own home; the absentee landlord may do nothing more than collect the rent and provide as little maintenance as possible.

Pride of ownership or, conversely, lack of maintenance, can usually be judged based on an outside report. Just a photograph will give some indication, although a black and white picture of one side of a building may make it look much better than it really is.

Additional evaluation is necessary for newly purchased rental property. Usually the new owner will tell the producer (who will tell the underwriter) that the insured plans to renovate the home and eliminate the problems that developed during previous ownership. The renovation may be accomplished, it may be delayed despite good intentions, or it may never materialize. If the risk is in marginal physical condition, and improvements are promised, the underwriter must follow up to assure that the risk is upgraded in a reasonable period of time.

In recent years there have been serious arson problems involving rental property. Some owners have found it cheaper to pay a fee to a "torch" for a guaranteed sale (to the insurance company) than to pay a commission to a real estate broker *if* the broker should find a buyer. Most such "sales" are successful, because arson is hard to prove. Even if it can be shown that the fire was intentional, it is usually impossible to prove that the owner planned the loss.

An alert and informed underwriter will be aware of communities where suspicious fires have been common, and will be doubly careful in those areas. Any history of fire losses to other rental property owned by the insured may be a danger sign. The financial condition of the insured and the marketability of the property should also be considered.

One major difference between insurance on the tenant and insurance on the owner is the size of the loss. Therefore, the same underwriting standards apply to both types of insurance. It would certainly be unwise to insure the building if one were unwilling to insure the contents. Thus, the underwriter considering a rental building should determine whether he or she would insure the tenants.

VACANT AND UNOCCUPIED BUILDINGS. Some hazards are reduced when a dwelling is vacant. Loss caused by occupants' smoking, cooking, and use of electrical appliances is virtually eliminated. However, this is more than offset by the increased probability of vandalism and the fact that, on the average, losses remain undiscovered for longer periods of time in these buildings than in occupied buildings. Intruders may enter a vacant home and may spend an evening, a night, or several weeks without being detected, causing extensive damage.

Loss caused by other perils may also go undetected for some time. A fire may not be discovered until it is out of control. A leaky water pipe may not be discovered until the basement overflows. The heating system in a vacant home may malfunction during winter weather, causing overheating or freezing of water pipes.

In evaluating a vacant home, the underwriter should consider first the reason the home is vacant and the probable duration of the vacancy. Secondly, the underwriter should consider the location, particularly as it relates to the likelihood of vandalism. An isolated dwelling, or one in an area with a high vandalism exposure, is potentially more dangerous than one in the center of a small rural community.

Lastly, the underwriter should consider whether the home is checked frequently. The owner, a relative, or a neighbor may check the home daily; or it may not be checked at all except by routine police patrol, if available.

There is a substantial rate increase, usually around $1 per $100 of insurance, for vandalism coverage on a vacant home. This added rate helps to offset the increased hazard. Still, the underwriter must judge whether the increased loss potential is greater than the increased premium.

LOW-VALUE BUILDING AND/OR CONTENTS POLICIES. The package programs require certain minimum amounts of insurance. Few homes which fall below these minimums are top quality risks. Many low-value dwellings have a low value because they are badly deteriorated. The replacement cost may be four times the market value, but it would be impractical and undesirable to insure for that amount.

Other dwellings may have a very low value because they are very small homes. Consider the small retirement cottage in an area with low labor costs, or the resort cottage. These homes may be desirable risks and should be evaluated on the same basis as the homeowners risk.

The requested limit may be low because the market value has deteriorated due to a lack of housing demand in a certain area. Insurance to replacement cost, or even to actual cash value, might be unrealistic both for the applicant and the insurer. The premium could be quite small; yet the risk may be physically attractive.

A low-value contents policy may be requested by the individual who has very little personal property. Again, there may be no undesirable hazards. But there is a strong chance that insurance to value is lacking.

The underwriter needs to recognize the small amount of premium involved in a low-value dwelling or contents fire policy. After acquisition costs are paid, there are not a lot of dollars left to pay for underwriting information that might be desirable. Often, it may be wise to decline a low-value dwelling policy because it just is not practical to handle. But in some cases, there will be other considerations such as the producer or the account.

The Underwriter's Choice. When a homeowners application has been submitted, the underwriter sometimes decides that the risk is acceptable subject to modifications. A common modification is to write the risk on a dwelling fire form rather than on a homeowners.

If the dwelling form is chosen because it provides less coverage, underwriting may present little problem. For example, if there has been a history of theft losses in an otherwise desirable risk, the dwelling form may be chosen because it does not provide theft coverage. However, when a package policy is not acceptable because the risk is not desirable, the underwriter needs to determine whether the risk is so undesirable that it must be rejected, or whether it is insurable on a dwelling form. Although "degrees of desirability" could be discussed at some length, it is unnecessary. Once a package application has been thoroughly analyzed, the underwriter has determined to what degree the risk is or is not desirable.

Sometimes the basis for suggesting a modification is the relationship of insurance to value. In some cases the insured refuses to purchase adequate limits. In other cases, when a home has depreciated to the point where the actual cash value and/or the market value is a great deal less than the replacement cost (the so-called "white elephant"), insurance to replacement cost value is not feasible, and may even create a moral hazard. The basic dwelling and contents form provides coverage on an actual cash value basis, so insurance to replacement cost need not be a concern.

There is no coinsurance clause in the dwelling forms in use in most states, at least for private dwellings. The insured will *not* be penalized for a partial loss within policy limits if the insurance is substantially less than the actual cash value. He or she will be paid actual cash value up to the policy limit (or more on building losses in the broad and special forms if the conditions of the replacement cost extension are met). Yet, because most losses are small losses, the company deserves a premium commensurate with the exposure. The underwriter should be satisfied that the dwelling and/or contents limits are within the guidelines for the program and form involved.

The dwelling forms are one modification that may be used when a package policy is requested; another is rejection. Coverage is almost always available somewhere else, either in a "substandard" market that specializes in below-average business with above-average rates, or in the FAIR plan. FAIR plans will be discussed in the following chapter.

The Insured's Choice. When an owner-occupied home which appears to be eligible for a package program is submitted on a dwelling form, the underwriter might become curious. Most insureds and producers will request the broader coverage of the homeowners if they feel the risk is acceptable.

It may be that the client wants only minimum coverage to satisfy the mortgagee. This could be because the insured has too little money to afford the few extra dollars that the package would cost (assuming the package is more expensive). This could indicate morale hazard, because the client may have a difficult time maintaining a home. When insurance is chosen solely to satisfy the mortgagee, there is a strong possibility of underinsurance. (Of course, the home might be overinsured if it has just been purchased with a small down payment, and the mortgage includes the cost of the land.)

Finally, some owners of desirable homes choose to buy separate policies because they feel that their occupancy offers too low an exposure to theft to make it worthwhile to buy a homeowners policy, or they choose not to insure the theft exposure. Such applicants would be acceptable for dwelling fire forms.

Builders' Risks. A dwelling which is under construction may be insured in any of three different ways—with a builders' risk endorsement to a dwelling form, a dwelling form, or in some cases, a homeowners policy.

THE BUILDERS' RISK ENDORSEMENT. The most common builders' risk endorsement is the completed value form, which may be used with any of the dwelling fire forms to cover a home from the time construction begins until the time construction is completed. Because of the method of premium calculation (explained below), this form should not be used if construction has already begun. Coverage ceases and must be replaced with "permanent" insurance once construction is completed or the home is occupied (depending upon the particulars of the form in use).

Under this form, the normal rate that would apply to the building upon completion is applied to the projected completed value of the home exclusive of land. The premium developed is then discounted to 55 percent (some states use 50 percent) of its total and this discounted figure is the charge to the insured. The discount recognizes that the full completed value is not at risk during the period of construction and that the *average* amount at risk will be about mid-way between zero and the completed value, or half the completed value. The extra 5 percent allows a small cushion in case the actual average amount at risk is more than 50 percent of completed value.

Builders' risk coverage must be replaced with "permanent" insurance once the dwelling is complete. Were it not for this rule, the company would be writing insurance after completion at a 45 percent discount. In some states the completed value builders' risk endorsement covers dwellings for a specified period of time after completion (often thirty days), but in most territories the form says that coverage ceases as soon as the building is occupied. If the owners of a completed dwelling have not replaced the builders' risk insurance with "permanent" insurance under a homeowners or dwelling fire policy, they may be uninsured. This is one advantage of using "permanent" insurance from the start.

Builders' risk policies are always canceled on a pro-rata basis, and the unearned premium is refunded. It would not be fair to impose a short-rate penalty for a policy which is usually needed for less than a year and which cancels itself as soon as the home is completed and/or occupied.

Builders' risk coverage using the completed value endorsement must be made effective as soon as construction begins if the reduced rate is to be justified. If the premium is predicated on the assumption that the average amount at risk will be about half the completed value, the premium will not be adequate for the exposure if the average amount at risk during the policy term is, say, two-thirds of completed value. This would be the case if the building were one-third completed when the coverage became effective. In this situation, the premium would be smaller since the length of the policy period would be shorter. The premium would not be the same as it would have been if the policy were effective when construction began.

When a builders' risk form is written, the underwriter should be satisfied that construction will progress at a normal rate. Some underwriters set a diary to check on progress and possible completion. This can minimize unknown changes in hazard, such as might occur if the insured runs out of money and construction stops prior to completion. It can also help the insured avoid occupying a home without realizing that coverage has ceased.

An accurate completed value is also essential. Matching premium with exposure depends upon the proper value base.

If faced with a late request for coverage, there are two options open to the underwriter: to "back-date" the coverage to correspond with the date construction began (assuming there have been no losses), or to offer a form of "permanent" insurance rather than the builders' risk. The latter is usually the preferred choice, as is explained below.

DWELLING FORM. This is the only fire form available if construction has already begun. The underwriter would accept most applicants under this form, because the problems of the builders' risk form are not present. In fact, there is some rate redundancy, since not all of the values are exposed to loss during the construction period, yet the full premium is charged. The underwriter should require the same insurance to completed value as will be required after completion in order to avoid the cost of handling periodic increases in the amount of insurance. In general, a submission of this sort is acceptable if it would be acceptable were construction completed.

HOMEOWNERS POLICY. This may be the simplest means to handle dwellings under construction, particularly if the construction period will be short and the risk will be attractive as a homeowners account upon completion. However, not all companies or states permit the writing of a homeowners policy on a dwelling which is not completed, and thus not occupied. Where permitted, it avoids the problems of the builders' risk form and, since most owners of homes prefer a homeowners policy, it avoids the handling costs in rewriting on a homeowners policy later. Again, the risk is acceptable during construction if it would be acceptable under the same terms were the home completed and occupied.

GENERAL CONSIDERATIONS. Certain factors warrant consideration regardless of the approach used in insuring a residence under construction. The underwriter needs to evaluate the hazards unique to the construction process. At first glance, the hazards seem to be reduced. There are no occupants to start fires by their negligence, and during much of the construction there may be no plumbing, heating, or electricity to cause problems. But there are other factors which increase the hazard.

Like vacant properties, homes under construction are particularly attractive to vandals, thieves, and neighborhood children. The vandalism rate of the neighborhood should be considered, as well as the protection available. The home may be readily visible by neighbors, protected by guards, or frequently patrolled by police. Or no one may look at it for days at a time. Further, even in a community with good fire protection, such as class 3 or 4, hydrants may not yet be installed in a developing subdivision.

The exposure is increased by the activities of construction workers. Many builders' risk fires have been started by plumbers carelessly using a torch to "sweat" a pipe. Inadequate electrical cords rigged inside the home may cause losses. Temporary heating equipment used to protect workers in cold weather may cause problems. Theft of fixtures already installed may be a problem if the special form is used.

It is not feasible to evaluate all these items in underwriting the builders' risk on a single building, but the underwriter should be aware of such factors. If the contractor is an established firm with a good record in home construction, the underwriter can regard the hazards inherent in the construction activity as being at an acceptable level.

Also to be considered is the length of construction. If the owner is building the home during evenings and weekends, the lengthy construction period may increase the exposure. On the other hand, a prefabricated home built within two weeks is hardly a builders' risk; the exposure is that of a completed dwelling.

MONITORING IN RESIDENCE INSURANCE UNDERWRITING

The monitoring phase in the residence insurance (homeowners, farms, ranches, and dwelling fire) underwriting process has much in common with its counterpart in personal auto underwriting. The ability to monitor is severely constrained by the small average unit premium, even more so than in auto insurance. Although not as widespread as in auto, cancellation restrictions and nonrenewal notice requirements imposed by the states are increasingly common. Policies may be reviewed individually or as part of a book of business. Individual policy review may result from claims, changes in the risk, endorsements, or renewal consideration. Renewal underwriting may be routine or on an exception basis. Book of business review may be part of an ongoing program or problem-oriented, and the overall portfolio of residence business can be stratified for this purpose in a variety of ways, as was true with auto.

On the other hand, there are differences between the two lines. Residence insurance is more stable than auto in the sense that mid-term changes are far less frequent in the former. There is less endorsement underwriting activity *during the policy term* in the residence coverages than in auto, and thus fewer "built-in" opportunities to review files. Changes in the risk are less common in residence coverages; they offer no counterpart to the driver, use, and vehicle changes so common in auto. Loss frequency is generally lower in the residence coverages, so experience with the risk is, on the average during comparable periods, not as helpful as an aid in reviewing decisions made previously as it is in auto. Finally, the problem of maintaining insurance to value, which is an integral part of monitoring in residence insurance, has no counterpart in auto insurance.

The Monitoring Process

In review or renewal underwriting, emphasis is given to changes that might affect the desirability of a previously acceptable risk. The possible changes are not restricted to changes in the risk, but could include changes in underwriting standards of coverage. Underwriting of residences frequently changes as companies compete for position with rate, program, and underwriting changes. What was formerly borderline business may warrant a different decision under present underwriting criteria and/or marketing strategy.

Isolating Risks to Be Reviewed Choosing the risks to be reviewed depends, as in auto, on the philosophy and practices of the company and its underwriting personnel. Renewals are rarely reunderwritten on a routine basis except perhaps with respect to insurance to value, which will be discussed later under a separate section. It is more common to reunderwrite renewals on an exception basis where developments, while the policy is in force, point to a need for reconsideration prior to renewal. In addition, some particular classes might be of such concern that risks in those classes are checked closely prior to renewal.

A monitoring program might call for the automatic referral to underwriting of risks in the following groups:

1. High Potential Frequency or Severity. This referral list might include very high-value dwelling policies, low-value dwellings or contents policies, and all nonowner-occupied dwelling fire policies.
2. Significant Change in the Risk. Underwriting might review all policies on which there has been claim activity meeting specified criteria as to frequency, severity, or type. This group might also include all farmowners contracts to check whether the farm personal property schedule and the scheduled coverage on barns and other structures are up-to-date. Dwellings may have aged to the point where certain additional information is needed or where the risk no longer qualifies for the form currently in effect.

   A loss does not necessarily mean that the hazards have changed, but loss information certainly changes the set of data used in evaluating hazards and forming a composite picture of the risk. Standards for referral usually are explicit. For example, any risk with two or more losses over the past three years, exclusive of catastrophes, might be referred.

   Sometimes *failure* to change will be an important factor. Perhaps a rental property was accepted with a promise that the property would be renovated. The underwriter will want to verify whether the work has been done; if it has not, the policy probably should be nonrenewed.
3. Changes in Standards, Programs, or Coverages. This list would include any classes affected by a change in the underwriting guide, the manual, forms, or any action taken because of a book of business reunderwriting program. For example, a high loss

ratio on condominium business might prompt a review program to check insurance to value. Recent windstorm problems might change mobile-home standards to require full tie-downs or change underwriting standards on dwelling risks in certain areas. A new policy may broaden (or restrict) coverage.

The goal of the referral criteria is to isolate those contracts on which the probability of underwriting action is relatively high. Even if all renewal business is referred to underwriting, risks falling outside the scope of some set of criteria similar to the illustrations above typically would get only a cursory review.

Gathering Information Once the risk warranting review is isolated, the information necessary for the task must be gathered. Available information may include loss data and perhaps a report to the underwriting department by an adjuster.

As with auto, frequency and type of loss(es) are more important than severity. Late reports may be available that were not yet received at the time of a previous evaluation. Policy changes made since the last review may alter the underwriter's impression of the risk. For example, the addition of several expensive scheduled items to a homeowners policy may indicate a higher theft exposure than was initially recognized. File information, including correspondence, or information on other policies held by the insured, may shed additional light on the risk.

Additional information beyond that available internally may be requested for the review. The producer may be asked for more information, or a new outside report may be ordered. Some companies use renewal questionnaires sent directly to the insured.

Using Information With the needed information in hand, the underwriter examines it using the same procedure as with new business but focusing on changes and current underwriting standards. The basic nature of the risk probably will be essentially the same unless there has been a structural addition, a mobile home has been moved, or contents are in a new location. Little underwriting action on basic nature of the risk is necessary unless the risk is in a group that is being reunderwritten because of a deterioration in results in a particular area, or with a certain type of structure.

The most likely sources of change are those mentioned above—losses, other policy activity, failure of a risk to upgrade, or new underwriting standards, or a change in coverages provided. The risk is again appraised and a new composite picture formed. Other factors, if present, are considered, (e.g., if "supporting business" was a factor in the previous decision, is it still a factor?).

Considering Alternative Courses of Action The underwriter can (1) cancel or nonrenew; (2) continue the coverage on its current basis; or (3) continue only with restricting modifications (e.g., increased deductible) or coverage enlargements (e.g., increased limits). Any decision to continue can be accompanied by an effort to upgrade the account if the circumstances warrant. For example, the form could be broadened, a package might be suggested in lieu of a dwelling fire policy, and endorsements (e.g., theft extension) might be suggested.

Under normal circumstances, most policies will be renewed with limits upgraded to maintain insurance to value. In some cases it will be appropriate to renew "as is." If a modification is proposed, the producer and the customer should be given ample time before renewal to consider the modification. If the decision is to discontinue coverage, notice must be given to the policyholder and to the mortgagee with no less lead time than that required by law or contract, whichever is the more liberal to the insured. If a renewal is inadvertently mailed or adequate notice of nonrenewal is not given, the monitoring effort will have been useless in most states. Whatever decision is made, it should be documented for the benefit of those who will work with the file in the future.

Insurance to Value

Insurance to value was heavily stressed in the sections on new business underwriting, and it is no less a consideration with renewals. If new business is insured to value, and if values increase but limits do not, eventually policyholders become underinsured and the premium level is no longer adequate. Continuation of this practice will inevitably result in an increased loss ratio, all other things being equal.

Many do not realize the severity of the problem. On 3 April 1974, a tornado caused approximately $60 million damage to residences in Xenia, Ohio. A "post mortem" study showed 46 percent of the dwellings had been insured to less than replacement cost. The average home was insured to only 77 percent of replacement cost, but 83 percent of the companies surveyed reported that they "required" insurance to at least 80 percent of replacement cost, and 16 percent of the companies "required" 90 percent or 100 percent insurance to value. The average Xenia homeowner was out of pocket $7,000.[2] The companies were short, too. They were not receiving the premium levels they should have been with insurance to value.

Theoretically, the insurance-to-value requirement of the replacement cost extension would have been applied where applicable and would have reduced the insured losses to a level more nearly commensurate with the premium. But the study showed: "There was very little evidence that adjusters applied the coinsurance penalty. On the contrary, . . . application of depreciation was insignificant and overpayment was the rule rather than the exception on underinsured property."[3] A more recent study by Equifax showed that 58 percent of American homes were not insured to full replacement cost and about 33 percent failed to insure to 80 percent of replacement cost.[4]

The value of personal property rises, too. Contents of apartments and condominiums and farm personal property increase in value. Both building limits and contents limits need to be continually upgraded.

One large company undertook a special project to bring all homeowners policies in force up to 100 percent of replacement cost in one part of a western state. Underwriters selected sixty-nine policies which appeared to be underinsured. An inspection company checked each of these risks, actually calculating the size and value. The recommended amount of coverage for each policy was then sent to the appropriate producer, who had been previously encouraged by the company to secure approval of the insureds. All sixty-nine policies were increased as recommended. The average amount of insurance was raised from $58,891 to $71,855, an increase of 22 percent.

Based on an estimated average annual premium of $325 at the old amount, the average increase amounted to $72 per policy, or $5,000 for the sixty-nine policies. The price for the inspections was about $5 per report, for a total cost of $345. This was a one-time charge, and the benefits to the insured and the company of higher insurance to value will continue for years.

Another way of upgrading values is by means of the computer. Some companies have data processing systems that can accept raw appraisal data on new business. At renewal, the computer issues a renewal policy with limits increased to reflect the current replacement cost, based on many factors: construction type, location, square foot area, number of bathrooms, and so on. This is probably the most efficient way of maintaining insurance to value on renewal. With such a system, renewal upgrading is done on a routine basis by computer, and the underwriter need only be concerned with other changes on a routine or exception basis.

The previous chapter pointed out that overinsurance may occur when the insurance limit reflects a new mortgage that includes the value of the land. In such a case, the computer can be instructed, "Do not change limits until replacement cost exceeds building limit."

Considerations in Reviewing a Book of Business

Regardless of the approach taken to new business underwriting—individual attention to every new risk, preliminary screening by clerk or computer with actual underwriting by exception only, extending substantial authority to producers with "underwriting" being largely the management of portfolios of business—it is essential to review group results, and to analyze risks in a group as particular needs arise. The principles of monitoring a book of business in residence insurance are no different from those discussed under auto insurance. The reason for the review determines the nature of the book isolated for review. Information is gathered and analyzed, evaluations are made, and actions are taken. The nature of the alternatives considered, and the implementation of the chosen course(s) of action, depend upon the purpose and findings of the review. These can range from encouraging more production, easing underwriting standards, or reducing rates, to tightening underwriting guides and standards, terminating or restricting producers, or reunderwriting all individual risks in the group. These lists are not exhaustive, obviously, and may not represent practical alternatives in every case encountered in a competitive and highly regulated business.

Monitoring books of business in residence insurance does offer some differences from auto, however. Residence insurance results are more likely to be influenced by the perils of nature, particularly windstorm, than is the case with auto. Thus, in some areas, residence insurance experience is likely to be quite volatile from period to period. Short-run results may have to be tempered by viewing them in the context of severe weather disturbances that, while predictable in the long run, can seriously distort the apparent quality of a book of business. In addition, some corrective actions may require a longer period of time as compared to auto to make a difference because of the longer policy periods in the residence insurance field.

In book of business monitoring generally—auto, residence, or other lines—the entire process takes place within a context of both internal and external factors that often influence the process. Temporary problems or situations in a company may affect the bottom line of a book of business. Personnel shortages, inexperienced staff, processing lags, volume changes that distort loss ratios, and the like are part of the information set that must be incorporated into the interpretation of results. So, too, are external factors like changes in competitors' positions, rate adequacy, class rate differentials, the regulatory climate and changes, and the potential effect of changes in one line (e.g., auto), on the ability of the company to retain its desired volume and mix of business in another line (e.g., homeowners). For example, even though producers and underwriters are effective, they cannot "cure" a problem of generally inadequate rate levels. If a company is getting an increased book of business in a problem class, is it the nature and location of its producer plant that is responsible or is it a tightened market among competitors? Or are both factors at work? Sometimes the decision is a judgment call, but the important point is that the judgment should be as informed as possible and not based solely on "the numbers." Otherwise, the range of alternative actions considered may be too small and not include the alternative that would deal with the heart of the problem.

SUMMARY

The nature of farming in the United States has changed drastically since the time of the American Revolution. Far fewer people are actually engaged in farming, and farms themselves are becoming large, highly automated, and industrialized businesses. However, most farms still contain elements of personal risks and the farmowners-ranchowners (FR) package policy was designed to cover the common loss exposures of most farms.

The FR program combines both property and liability coverages, as does the homeowners. With a few differences, the residential (as opposed to farming) property exposures correspond to those for homeowners.

Classification and rating of FR policies involve premium determination for the dwelling and related coverages. Underwriting FR policies is complicated by the fact that in a package policy many items are covered and some of these are likely to be less desirable than others. Also, due to the commercial nature of many farms and ranches, the underwriter must ascertain if the risk is a sound business venture. Occasionally an underwriter will have a request for a single line of coverage, and care is required in evaluating these nonpackage submissions.

Insurance to value is also a problem with farm and ranch risks. To combat this, the underwriter should consider the following: (1) adequate insurance to value at inception, (2) shorter policy terms, (3) special insurance on high-value equipment, (4) tailoring the policy to reflect fluctuating values, (5) the possibility of overinsurance on old buildings and equipment, and (6) the possibility of underinsurance on products that increase in value during the season.

Dwelling fire forms are those that antedated the homeowners and other residence package programs but continue in use today. Specifically, these are the basic dwelling and contents form, the dwelling building(s) and contents broad form, and the dwelling building(s) special form. The reasons for the use of these forms instead of package policies may include the following:

1. eligibility (e.g., residences rented to others),

2. the underwriter's choice (e.g., failure to meet package underwriting criteria),
3. the insured's choice (e.g., the desire for coverage at lowest cost), or
4. builders' risks (e.g., insuring the future occupant of a home under construction).

Special underwriting considerations stem from the reasons the nonpackage form was chosen in the first place. For instance, there are special hazards inherent in risks rented to others and in vacant and low-value buildings which must be carefully investigated by the underwriter. A dwelling under construction may be covered in one of three ways—by adding a builders' risk endorsement to a dwelling form, by a dwelling fire form, or by a homeowners policy, depending upon the circumstances of the risk.

Monitoring in residence insurance is similar to personal auto monitoring. However, residence insurance is more stable than auto in that mid-term changes are less frequent, changes in the risk are less frequent, and loss frequency is generally lower in residence. However, the problem of insurance to value, important in residence, has no counterpart in auto.

In the monitoring process, the following steps may be taken by the underwriter. First, the risks to be reviewed must be isolated, perhaps due to high potential loss frequency or severity, significant changes in the risk, or changes in underwriting standards. Second, information concerning the risk must be gathered. Third, the risk must be examined in the light of new information. Only then can the alternatives be considered: (1) cancel or nonrenew, (2) continue coverage on its current basis, or (3) continue only with restricting modifications or coverage enlargements. Insurance to value must be carefully monitored on renewal business. In reviewing a book of business, it is essential to review group results and to analyze risks in a group as particular needs arise. All of the possible factors must be considered in order to choose the correct course of action.

Chapter Notes

1. Rule 8.A. *Commercial Lines Manual* (New York: Insurance Services Office, 1979), pp. FR-2 (1st Edition 7-78), 3 (2nd Edition 1-79).
2. "Insurance Copes with Catastrophe: The Xenia Tornado," *CPCU Annals,* June 1976, p. 142.
3. "Insurance Copes with Catastrophe: The Xenia Tornado."
4. "Study Reports Most Homeowners Underinsured," *The Weekly Underwriter,* 6 March 1982, p. 20.

CHAPTER 9

The Underwriting Environment

THE SOCIAL CLIMATE SURROUNDING RESIDENCE INSURANCE

Some of the same types of social and political pressure facing auto insurance are also having an impact on residence insurance. While there are no laws specifically requiring people to carry residence insurance, real property involving buildings is usually financed, and a lender or mortgagee often requires that there be insurance to protect its interest. Thus, a person who cannot secure insurance on property which is financed may be prevented from purchasing that property.

Even if no lending requirement exists, there is still a real need for residence insurance. For many, a home and/or household personal property represents all or most of their tangible assets. Such people can ill afford losing these items because of a fire or other insurable peril.

Further, some residential areas, especially in large cities, have become badly deteriorated and subject to vandalism, theft, and multiple-property fire losses with the result that insurance companies have become very cautious in their writings there. Property in these areas is sometimes poorly maintained, absentee ownership is widespread, and multiple-occupancy is common, making losses more difficult to settle. All of these factors have led to a somewhat limited voluntary insurance market in many of these areas.

The combination of a need for insurance and a restricted market has invited legislative attention. Pressures are increasing steadily toward requiring that property insurance be available at "affordable" rates for residents of these areas. Although these pressures began (and largely remain) directed towards the "essential coverages," such as fire, extended coverage, and vandalism, practices in several states indicate that the trend may be to include crime coverages and homeowners policies.

GENERAL REGULATION OF RESIDENCE INSURANCE

The regulation of residence insurance has much in common with the regulation of personal auto insurance. The same insurance commissioners regulate both lines. The types of rate regulatory laws are the same for both: open competition, use-and-file, file-and-use, prior approval, and state-made rates. However, in some states, different types of laws apply to each line. For example, a few states require prior approval of auto rates but permit file-and-use on residences.

State laws generally have the same requirements for all rates—they must be adequate, not excessive, and not unfairly discriminatory. The interpretation of these terms and the application of the laws vary by state and by commissioner. Auto rates appear to be somewhat more politically sensitive than are residence rates, which tend to require change less frequently. Still, many feel that the permitted amount of the increase in premium often is limited by factors unrelated to loss experience and actuarial considerations and that residence underwriters in some states are handicapped by a difficulty in securing necessary rate increases.

Policy forms are also regulated in much the same fashion for residences as for autos. Most state insurance laws provide for the use of a standard fire policy in contracts covering the peril of fire at fixed locations, and some of these laws require a standard fire policy to be a part of homeowners and other residence packages as well. Nonstandard forms and endorsements are required to be filed for approval in most states. Because of the relationship between rates and forms, the expected ability to secure approval of revised forms or amendatory endorsements, such as limitations when new problems arise, is important to the underwriting function. The citizens band radio problem which adversely affected auto insurance also caused difficulties for underwriters of homeowners policies, and restrictive endorsements were prepared and filed when the extent of the problem became evident. In both lines, losses were controlled more effectively in states that permitted quick use of the amended forms.

Laws restricting underwriting action historically have been less common in residence insurance than in auto. However, many states have enacted restrictions on mid-term cancellations and requirements for advance notice of nonrenewal. Nonrenewal is permitted in all states, but a few limit the reasons for nonrenewal.

RESIDENCE INSURANCE AND THE CATASTROPHE EXPOSURE

Because all property underwriters need to be concerned with the possibility of catastrophic losses, virtually every company limits its vulnerability to these losses through the purchase of reinsurance. Large losses can arise from many perils and may involve one risk or a combination of risks.

Single Risks

Commercial property underwriters are more concerned with large single risks than are personal lines underwriters. Commercial buildings and contents may involve many millions of dollars of exposure at one location, so underwriters are constantly faced with the necessity of securing facultative reinsurance or using existing reinsurance treaties.

Residence underwriters recently have become more involved with large single risks—and hence with reinsurance. One reason is the rapid increase in construction costs. As recently as the late 1960s, a dwelling with a replacement cost of more than $100,000 was uncommon in most areas. Today, replacement costs in the $100,000 category are fairly common in many areas, and dwellings in the range of $250,000 to $500,000 are not as rare as they once were.

Another reason residence underwriters are handling larger amounts of insurance is the greater emphasis on insurance to value. Until the mid-1950s, a common minimum rule was insurance equal to 50 percent of actual cash value. The introduction of replacement cost coverage at that time raised the desired minimum amount of insurance for risks eligible for forms with that coverage to 80 percent, or sometimes to 90 or 100 percent, of the replacement cost. At the same time, many underwriters adopted a minimum amount of insurance of 70 to 75 percent of actual cash value on fire and extended coverage dwelling policies.

Still another reason for large values in single-dwelling risks is an increase in contents coverage. One goal of the homeowners program was to increase insurance to value on personal property by automatically relating the amount of that coverage to the amount on the dwelling. For those risks affected, this move alone probably doubled the average amount of insurance on contents. Greater emphasis was also given to insurance to value in residence policies written on an actual cash value basis.

When an underwriter considers the possibility of a large loss on a single risk, the total building and contents coverage at one location must be included. Extensions of coverage that provide additional amounts of insurance must be added if they are also exposed to a single loss. Thus, a total loss on a home insured for $100,000 under a homeowners policy might also involve $50,000 on personal property, $10,000 on an appurtenant structure, $20,000 on additional living expense, and, in some states, $5,000 on debris removal. The total at this one location could be $185,000, without adding any options such as coverage of scheduled items.

Residence insurance underwriters must know the *line limits* (the amounts the insurer may retain internally) of the insurer on individual risks, and the action to be taken on applications that exceed the limits. Obviously, reducing the amount of insurance usually is not a desirable alternative because of insurance-to-value objectives.

If the requested amount of insurance exceeds the line limits, one of two courses of action may be taken. First, the producer may place part of the risk with another insurer so that the risk is shared. Second, the underwriter may use treaty reinsurance or may obtain facultative reinsurance for the amount of insurance that exceeds the line limits.[1]

Reinsurance programs dealing with individual residential risks vary enormously. Some small companies may retain only $10,000 of the property exposure per risk, others $25,000, $50,000, $100,000, or $250,000. Some large companies do not use reinsurance on residential property coverages at all except perhaps for the occasional need for facultative coverage on a very large risk. Many factors may influence a decision on retention limits—size of company, surplus position, recent experience, management attitudes, location, and protection characteristics of individual risks, to cite some.

Multiple Risks

Residence underwriters are more concerned, generally, with the single-event, multiple-loss exposure presented by a group of risks than with large individual risks. Every state presents some types of catastrophe exposures, although there are substantial differences by peril.

Fire The chances of a fire wiping out most or a substantial portion of a city, as happened in Chicago in 1871, are slight today. Fire-resistive construction, firefighting equipment, and water supplies make the probability of such a fire very remote unless caused by another peril, such as earthquake or riot.

However, catastrophes from fire are not impossible, or even unlikely, in some areas. Forest fires can destroy small communities and vacation resorts. Brush fires in the hills of Southern California can destroy millions of dollars of residence property. In the Bel Air fire (November 1961), over 500 buildings were destroyed or severely damaged. This was the largest number of buildings so affected in a single fire on the North American continent since 1923. The insured loss was estimated at $24 million.[2]

In such areas, underwriters need to limit aggregate exposure to an amount determined by management to be the tolerable per-loss maximum.

Tornado Every state is subject to tornado damage, but the midwestern and southern states are particularly vulnerable. Spring and early summer are the worst months. A typical tornado will cause destruction within a narrow path and for a short distance. However, some have extended for hundreds of miles, causing millions of dollars in damage. There is little an underwriter can do to avoid large losses other than to avoid a concentration of risks within a small area, such as a housing tract or mobile-home park. If coverage is to be written in problem states, almost the only protection is adequate excess (catastrophe) reinsurance.

Hurricane Portions of states along the narrow strip close to the Gulf of Mexico or Atlantic Ocean are subject to hurricane damage. Because the bulk of hurricane-related damage is limited to a short distance from the water, usually about fifty miles, underwriting programs can successfully limit the exposure. Estimates must be made as to the length of the section expected to be damaged. Ordinarily, the storm moves directly inland over a path less than 100 miles wide, but occasionally a hurricane will move along a coast, damaging property for a distance of hundreds of miles. The usual underwriting practice is to maintain records on the dollars of coverage exposed in each area to determine the maximum amount which can be lost in one storm, and to limit writings when the tolerable limit is reached. Here again, if a company provides a market of any consequence in hurricane-prone areas, excess reinsurance is the best protection against shock loss.

In order to broaden the market in coastal areas, some states have established *beach* plans which require the industry to provide coverage. Every company writing the applicable lines in the state must share in the losses in these plans. Therefore, loss payments on beach plan business must be included in the calculation of a company's possible aggregate loss in a single event. This practice leads to further restrictions of the market, and thus more need for the plan, but it is essential to an accurate appraisal of maximum loss in one event. The operation of these plans is explained later in this chapter.

Flood One of the worst types of property catastrophes is flood. Compounding the insurance problem is the fact that, for the most part, only those property owners who are seriously exposed to flood have any interest in flood insurance. This presents the potential for adverse selection at its worst.

Most property policies exclude flood, rising water, and surface water. Coverage is available in limited amounts through a plan of the federal government. This plan is discussed later in this chapter.

Earthquake No part of the country seems to be immune from the possibility of a major earthquake, although some areas are more susceptible than others. This peril usually is associated with the far west but, interestingly, some of our worst quakes over the past two centuries have occurred east of the Rocky Mountains. Since 1900, however, most tremors have occurred in a narrow band along the Pacific coast, with California and Alaska suffering the greatest damage.

Those insurers who write a large volume of earthquake coverage must periodically check the total exposure in each area. Estimates of probable maximum loss must be made by area. If the probable maximum loss is too large in the eyes of the insurer, writings may need to be restricted, or more excess (catastrophe) reinsurance purchased. Progress in earthquake predictions may reach a point where adverse selection, already felt to be something of a problem in this line, will magnify greatly and create an unmanageable catastrophe exposure for the private insurance sector.

Riot Until the mid-1960s, residence underwriting almost ignored the perils of "riot, riot attending a strike, and civil commotion." These perils are included in every version of the extended coverage endorsement, and, of course, in the broader forms also. It is probably safe to say that the rate included a miniscule loading, if any, for these perils.

The urban riots beginning in 1965 shattered that complacency. Watts, Detroit, Newark, and other cities were shaken by disorder which involved the burning and mob destruction of many homes and businesses. Suddenly the catastrophe exposure from riots became a matter of great concern to every property underwriter who had written policies in the larger cities. This concern was heightened even more when the excess reinsurance market restricted the availability of riot coverage in catastrophe reinsurance contracts.

Because of the unpredictable character of the losses, and the tremendous loss potential involved, underwriters moved quickly to take two corrective steps. One was to limit exposures in the areas that appeared to have a substantial potential for riot losses. The other step was to seek more reinsurance. These steps were instrumental in the development of the FAIR (Fair Access to Insurance Requirements) plans and the federal riot reinsurance program, which are explained in the next section.

RESIDENCE INSURANCE AND GOVERNMENTAL PROGRAMS

Difficulty in obtaining insurance is no longer a private matter. The inability of any substantial segment of our society to obtain adequate insurance coverage has prompted governments at all major levels to take an active interest in solving the availability problem.

The federal government has been instrumental in establishing three of the four plans that affect residential risks and which are discussed below: FAIR plans, flood insurance, and crime insurance. States have had a part in each of these except flood insurance. The fourth type of plan—beach plans or windstorm plans—have been established in a limited number of states under state sponsorship. There are numerous special programs of limited scope (e.g., mine subsidence in Pennsylvania), but these will not be covered here.

FAIR Plans

Background and Structure Over a period of about five years, beginning with 1965, property losses from riots and civil disorders skyrocketed to an amount in excess of $300 million.[3] These enormous losses greatly compounded a problem that had existed in some locations for several years—the availability of fire and extended coverage insurance on some properties in inner-city areas. The tumult of the late 1960s also turned college campus areas into very sensitive locations. Many schools found renewals difficult, rates sharply increased, and enormous increases in deductibles.

In 1968 President Lyndon B. Johnson appointed the National Advisory Panel on Insurance in Riot-Affected Areas (known as the Hughes Panel) to investigate property insurance costs and availability and to formulate possible solutions to these problems. Its recommendations are incorporated in the Urban Property Protection and Reinsurance Act of 1968, part of an omnibus housing bill, effective 1 August 1968. This act is intended to relieve the restricted market for property insurance in certain urban areas with severe riot potential, and it increased the availability of coverage through encouraging a combined effort of private insurers and state and federal governments.

The act also established a nineteen-member Advisory Board to formulate general policies to be administered by the Federal Insurance Administrator under the direction of the Department of Housing and Urban Development (HUD). Currently, the program (including the National Insurance Development Fund used to finance riot reinsurance) is administered by the Federal Insurance Administration, a part of the Federal Emergency Management Agency. The Advisory Board comprises representatives from the federal government, private insurance, state insurance authorities, and several segments of the business community.

A factor in the restriction on writing in riot-prone areas was the exclusion of riot losses placed in some catastrophe reinsurance treaties after the disorder of the 1960s. With no reinsurance and the possibility of large losses by riots, insurers became increasingly reluctant to write or renew policies in these areas. The federal government stepped into this vacuum by offering to insurers reinsurance for losses caused by riot or civil unrest.

In order for insurers operating in a state to be eligible to purchase federal riot reinsurance, participation in a FAIR plan, established under state auspices but meeting minimum federal standards, is required. As of early 1982, twenty-six states had plans in operation as did Puerto Rico and the District of Columbia. Interestingly, failure of twelve states to comply with an amendment in 1978 requiring that the FAIR plan rates for standard insureds be no higher than rates in the voluntary market for standard insureds, has resulted in the plans of these states no longer meeting the federal requirements. Thus, riot reinsurance availability is tied to FAIR plan participation. The goal of FAIR plans is to enlarge the market for basic property insurance in a way that will be equitable among insurers writing that coverage in a state. The desirability of these dual objectives—broadening the market and protecting against shock losses from riot and civil unrest—led to rapid development of FAIR plans.

Although FAIR plan experience has proven to be unprofitable, the riot reinsurance program has been quite profitable for the federal government. Exhibit 9-1 shows the incurred-to-earned loss ratio for the FAIR plans from 1971 to 1979. The ratio peaked at almost 130 percent in 1975 and bottomed out in 1972 at about 70 percent. Even at its best, the plan business was unprofitable.

Exhibit 9-2 shows the experience of the riot reinsurance program for the decade ending in 1978. As shown by the exhibit, the plan has been profitable.

There are two sets of coverages that are of importance when considering FAIR plans and the riot reinsurance which companies can purchase. The first coverages are those that must be offered by the

Exhibit 9-1
FAIR Plan Incurred-To-Earned Loss Ratio 1971 Through the First Quarter of 1979*

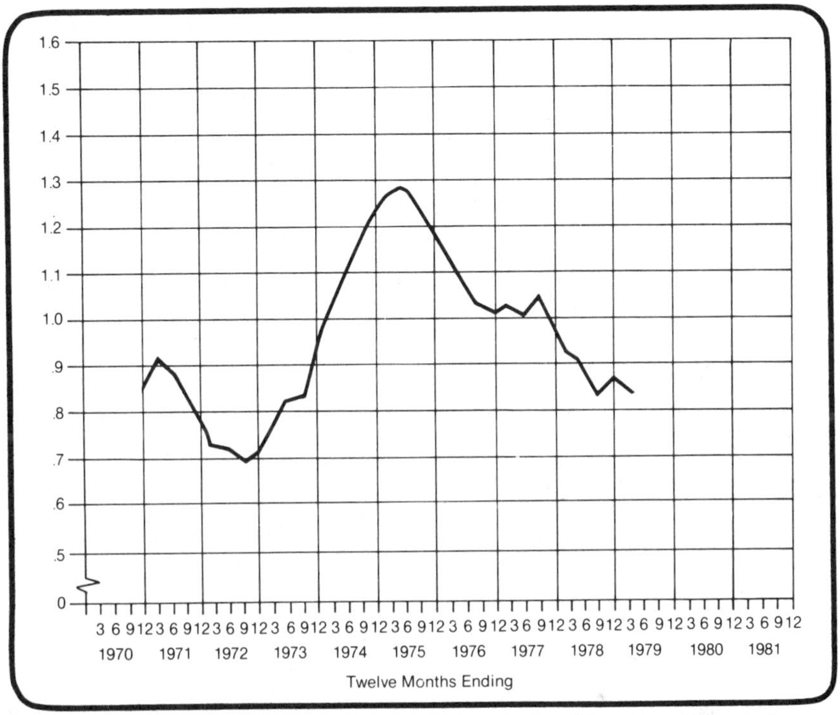

*Reprinted with permission from the National Association of Insurance Commissioners, *Proceedings 1980*, Vol. I, p. 780.

FAIR plan as one of the requirements of being "approved" by the Federal Insurance Administrator. These coverages are fire, extended coverage, vandalism, and malicious mischief. Separate from these are the "mandatory" coverages for insurers wishing to participate in the riot reinsurance of the federal government. If an insurer participates in this program of reinsurance, the following coverages must be included under the reinsurance contract (if the coverages are offered by the insurer in the state): fire and extended coverage, vandalism and malicious mischief, other allied lines of fire insurance, burglary and theft, and those portions of multiple-peril policies covering similar perils to those mentioned previously as mandatory. In addition, certain other perils are optional to the insurer. These include inland marine, glass, boiler and machinery, ocean marine, and aircraft physical damage.

There is a continuous pressure for the list of mandatory coverages under the FAIR plans to be extended. In some states, this has been

Exhibit 9-2
Federal Riot Reinsurance Premiums and Losses 1968-1978 (in thousands of dollars)*

Fiscal Year	Contract Year	Paid or Payable Reinsurance Premiums	Paid Losses	Administrative Expenses (1)	Studies and Surveys	Investment Income Earned (1)	Status of Program Funds
1969	1968-69	$35,333	$ 2,861	$ 245		$ 1,097	
1970	1969-70	22,338	3,187	355		3,397	
1971	1970-71	10,947	2,834	454	51	4,469	
1972	1971-72	6,225	1,379	365		4,367	
1973	1972-73	2,168	449	349		4,699	
1974	1973-74	2,258	355	377		5,606	
1975	1974-75	1,146	927	286		5,943	
1976	1975-76	997	377	354		7,489	
1977	1976-77	1,148	—	305 (3)		5,932	
1978	1977-78	1,169 (2)	1,082	313 (3)		5,062	
		$83,729	$13,451	$3,403	$51	$48,061	$114,885

(1) Administrative Expenses and Investment Income Earned are on a fiscal year basis
(2) The 1977-78 contract year reinsurance premiums include $21,000 of unallocated premium. The reinsurance premium adjustments for the 17 month term of this contract will add over $400,000 after the adjustments are completed pursuant to the contract.
(3) Includes $200,000 allocated for FIA technical support.

* Adapted, with permission, from National Association of Insurance Commissioners, *Proceedings 1979*, Vol. II, p. 798.

done voluntarily. Some of the voluntarily provided coverages include crime insurance, homeowners insurance, sprinkler leakage coverage, earthquake coverage, and time element coverage.

Operation FAIR plans are not meant to replace normal channels of securing insurance, nor do they guarantee that insurance will be available for an uninsurable property. The purpose is to make basic property insurance available to all homeowners and businessowners.

FAIR plans involve three principal elements:

1. procedures for inspecting property,
2. a facility in each state for placing coverage with participating insurers, and
3. a joint reinsurance association for equitable distribution of losses.

A person with an interest in real property or in tangible personal property located in an urban area typically applies to an insurance placement facility. The facility is composed of all property insurers operating in the state. It can take the form of a joint reinsurance association administered by a few servicing insurers or it can have its own staff to write and service the business. In both cases, all expenses, losses, and premiums are shared proportionately by all members based on the total writings of each for the coverages provided by the plan.

The facility is entitled to inspect the property. The insured is entitled to review the inspection report and may request a copy from the facility. The report contains a photograph of the risk and underwriting and rating information—the construction, occupancy, protection, and exposure. The facility must then decide whether the risk is acceptable (at either standard or surcharged rates), unacceptable, or conditionally acceptable subject to improvements. Any required improvements must be verified by reinspection before a risk can be judged acceptable. However, the act does stipulate that factors such as neighborhood or area location or any environmental hazard beyond the control of the property owner are not reasons for declining a risk.

This point is at the heart of the FAIR plan program. Environmental hazards beyond the control of the property owner can be illustrated by neighborhood vandalism, a tendency toward arson in the area, deteriorated adjacent buildings, and similar hazards. Normal underwriting procedures may not permit the voluntary writing of risks exposed to severe environmental hazards. FAIR plans cannot take this factor into consideration in determining acceptability.

Not every FAIR plan has continued the practice of inspecting every dwelling risk. Some have found that the cost of inspection is greater than the increased premium from the surcharges permitted.

Because a policy or binder is issued upon receipt of a premium (it may be a deposit or estimated premium) with the application, regardless of improvements which might have been made, the applicant is served as well under either system. The intent of the procedure is to guarantee protection while keeping the net cost of the FAIR plan as low as possible. No risk can be declined without an inspection and an explicit statement of the reason(s) for the declination. Cancellation privileges are very limited. When notice of cancellation is given, the reason must be sent in writing to the insured.

Federal Flood Insurance

The difficulties in writing insurance against the flood peril for fixed location properties were discussed earlier in this text. The National Flood Insurance Act of 1968 (Title XIII of the Housing and Urban Development Act of 1968) established a program of flood insurance involving both federal subsidies to property owners and federal reinsurance for the private insurers participating in the program through membership in the National Flood Insurers Association (NFIA), a pool of insurers whose membership exceeded 100 insurers at one time.

Operation Before coverage under the program can be purchased by property owners in a particular community, that community must be designated as an eligible community by the FIA. In general, approval for participation requires that appropriate officials in the community demonstrate a need for the coverage, furnish information on flood hazards, and commit the community to land use and flood damage control measures to minimize future losses from flood. In particular, areas having so-called "special" flood hazards are to be identified. These areas must be made subject to very stringent future land use limitations as a condition of qualifying for the program.

The flood insurance program has undergone some changes since its inception in 1968. In 1973, the maximum coverage limits were increased, and many property owners were forced to purchase the coverage. In 1977, the limits were again increased. Also at this time, changes were made which would hopefully increase participation in the program. For example, communities which had special flood-prone areas (defined as an area having at least a 1 percent annual chance of flooding) had to participate in the flood insurance program or be denied financial assistance from any federal officer or agency. Additionally, persons who were trying to obtain mortgages on homes in these areas from a federally regulated or insured financial institution had to purchase flood insurance. The law was later amended to permit such loans if the community was not a participating community, as well as to permit disaster assistance if the disaster was a nonflood-related natural disaster. However, a provision states that one year after the date flood insurance becomes available in a community, property owners will not be eligible for any federal disaster assistance for any losses they could have insured.

Perhaps the most important change to the underwriter was the abolishment of the private insurer-federal government partnership at the end of 1977. The abolishment was primarily due to a projected savings of $14 to $15 million. Prior to its being abolished, the Federal Insurance Administration (a division of the Department of Housing and Urban Development) had contracted with the National Flood Insurers Association. The contract called for the NFIA to administer the flood insurance program. There were two rates established—the actuarial rate (varying with the exposure) and the chargeable rate (a rate established to help meet the objective of making flood insurance available where necessary at reasonable rates). If NFIA charged the chargeable rate to a person, NFIA was reimbursed by the FIA for the difference between the chargeable and the actuarial rate.

As mentioned, at the end of 1977 this arrangement was abolished, and beginning in 1978, by the authority granted to HUD under the 1968 Act, national flood insurance became a program in which the Federal Emergency Management Agency (FEMA), of which FIA is a division, purchases administrative services only from a private contractor. The insurer now is the National Flood Insurance Fund, which is run by the FIA. The firm providing the administrative services is EDS Federal Corporation. The marketing of flood insurance continues to be through local producers, as it was under the FIA-NFIA arrangement.

Once a community qualifies, the FIA maps out the eligible areas within the community. Property owners within these areas can secure insurance through the "emergency" program, which applies flat federally subsidized rates (chargeable rate) on a uniform national basis varying only according to type and value of the structure involved. These rates are determined by the FIA. Once the FIA establishes actuarial rates (i.e., risk related and presumably actuarially self-supporting without federal subsidy) for a community, the community becomes eligible for the "regular" program. Or, if actuarial rates have already been developed for the territory that includes the newly qualifying community, the community is eligible for the "regular" program immediately.

If a community qualifies for only the emergency program (pending the development of actuarial rates which FIA must promulgate), buyers can secure only limited amounts of coverage at subsidized, or so-called "chargeable" rates. If, or when, the community qualifies for the "regular" program, the amounts of insurance available increase, but the additional layer of coverage carries "actuarial" and not "chargeable" (subsidized) rates. Under the emergency program, *new* construction in the designated "special" flood hazard areas is not eligible at all. Under the regular program, this type of risk is eligible, but *all* the coverage (not just the amounts in excess of the emergency program limits) is written at the applicable actuarial rate.

Key Program Features

Eligible Structures. The flood program originally was restricted to one- to four-family dwellings and structures occupied primarily by small business concerns, with the criteria determining "small" spelled out in the act. Currently, however, almost all walled and roofed structures that are principally above ground and affixed to a permanent site are eligible.

The Peril. A covered event can result from (1) the overflow of inland or tidal waters, (2) the unusual and rapid accumulation or runoff of surface waters, (3) mud from any source, or (4) erosion from abnormal water levels. When any of these events invades land areas that are normally dry and inflict a condition (which is both general and temporary) of partial or complete inundation or impact, the event is covered. Thus, flood insurance aims to cover the traditionally uninsurable exposure to natural forces that may cause widespread damage verging on or being a catastrophe. There is no intention to cover as flood the ordinary water damage that results from burst plumbing, sewer backup, and the like, to which all structures, regardless of location, are subject. The intent is to cover water damage that results from a condition general to the area. Flood insurance also pays for reasonable expenses for removal and temporary storage (up to forty-five days) of insured contents to protect them against loss when flood is imminent.

Deductible. The coverage contains a mandatory deductible that applies separately to building and personal property items. The deductible is equal to $200.

Waiting Period. Except for the first thirty days following initial eligibility of an area for flood insurance, the purchasing of coverage on a new home as a condition for a loan, and adding additional coverage to an existing policy (for all of which insurance can be made effective immediately), there is a waiting period of five days before coverage can commence. This is to dissuade property owners from purchasing coverage under the prompting of imminent flood conditions.

Coinsurance. Coinsurance is not used in the program.

Covered Property. Definitions of covered property parallel those in standard dwelling and commercial property fire forms.

Valuation. Family residences insured to 80 percent of replacement cost or available limit (whichever is less) have losses to the structure settled on a replacement cost basis. Otherwise, settlement is on an actual cash value basis.

Current Status. Participation in the program began very slowly. By 1972, only 27,000 policies had been issued. The year 1977 saw flood policies in force exceed the million mark for the first time. Exhibit 9-3 shows the program growth from inception until 1977. In the middle of 1980, the program had over 1.8 million policyholders in approximately 20,000 communities, with approximately $80 billion of insurance in force.

Contributions by policyholders have not come close to supporting the program, but federal subsidies and reinsurance kept the program in the black insofar as the NFIA participants were concerned. Federal subsidies have been reduced since the program's inception.

Federal Crime Insurance

Background and Structure Title VI of the Housing and Urban Development Act of 1970 established the Federal Crime Insurance Program. Administration of the program is in the hands of the Federal Insurance Administration. In this program, the federal government is directly in the insurance business rather than acting as a motivator, reinsurer, or source of subsidy in activities involving private insurers. Congress decided on this approach after considering several alternatives, including a federal reinsurance program and mandating the addition of crime perils to those available from FAIR plans.

The approach taken by the act was to encourage resolution of problems in availability and affordability at the state level through some residual market programs. If there were no satisfactory actions at the state level by a specified deadline, the act authorized the Secretary of HUD to make insurance directly available "at affordable rates" in any state in which a need existed.

Little was done at the state level except in California, where the FAIR plan was broadened to include crime coverages, and in Michigan and New Jersey.[4] Subsequently, HUD through its Federal Insurance Administration implemented the Federal Crime Insurance Program and as of December 1981 the Federal Insurance Administration was issuing policies in twenty-six states, the District of Columbia, Puerto Rico, and the Virgin Islands. Policies are issued and serviced by servicing companies under contract with FIA and are selected by competitive

Exhibit 9-3
National Flood Insurance Program Growth 1969-1977*

Date	Eligible Communities	Policies in Force	Coverage in Force (Billions)	Paid Claims (Millions)	No. of Claims
Dec. 31, 1969	4	16	—	—	—
June 30, 1970	158	5,500	$ .089	—	—
June 30, 1971	637	75,684	1.2	$ .252	—
June 30, 1972	1,174	95,123	1.5	2.5	1,905
June 30, 1973	3,054	272,448	4.6	15.0	7,067
June 30, 1974	5,775	385,478	8.5	36.6	14,457
June 30, 1975	13,191	539,888	13.7	26.3	10,927
June 30, 1976	14,502	793,779	22.8	81.4	21,032
June 30, 1977	16,786	1,123,575	33.6	60.0	11,819
Dec. 31, 1977	17,368	1,199,749	37.1	51.7†	9,245†

†6 month period only

Note: Because the premiums collected from policyholders are subsidized and because such subsidies vary between the amount of business written in each of the Regular and Emergency Programs, aggregate "premium" figures would be misleading and, thus, are inappropriate for inclusion in this exhibit.

* Adapted, with permission, from Samuel H. Weese and J. Wesley Ooms, "The National Flood Insurance Program—Did The Insurance Industry Drop Out?" *CPCU Journal*, Vol. 31 (December 1978), p. 204.

bidding. Licensed agents and brokers act as intermediaries in the sale of the insurance, although application can be made directly to the servicing company or the FIA. However, premiums are credited to and losses are paid from the National Insurance Development Fund (the same fund used with the riot reinsurance program). Marketing, determining eligibility, and servicing are the only functions performed by the private sector.

Operation Residence crime coverage under the program is available to any individual property owner who:

1. agrees to allow inspection of the premises;
2. agrees to report all covered events to the authorities, even if no claim is to be filed (e.g., because of the deductible); and
3. has and agrees to maintain the protective devices required by HUD.[5]

Current requirements for protective devices on residential properties are limited to locks. All exterior doors, other than sliding doors, must have a dead bolt or self-locking dead latch lock that cannot be opened by prying or turning a knob. All sliding doors and windows opening to porches, platforms, and other accessible locations must have locks, with no particular type(s) specified. Premises without the appropriate locking devices are uninsurable in the program.

Once in force, coverage cannot be terminated or nonrenewed because of loss history. Coverage can be terminated because of failure to maintain the necessary protective devices, nonpayment of premium, fraud or misrepresentation on the application, renewal statement, or in connection with a claim, use of premises for illegal purposes, substantial failure to comply with program regulations, and willful or repeated failure to report losses to the authorities. The problem regarding the protective devices is more common with commercial risks where the requirements are more demanding and expensive.

Residential risks can secure a minimum of $1,000 and a maximum of $10,000 of coverage. A separate policy is required for each location, and a deductible of the greater of $50 or 5 percent of the loss applies per claim. There are limits of $100 on money, $500 on securities, and $500 on jewelry, including watches, furs, antiques, fine arts, necklaces, bracelets, rings, gems, and coin and stamp collections.

The policy covers burglary and robbery (as defined in the contract) and damage to premises caused by an actual or attempted burglary or robbery.

The FIA has three uniform national rate classes used in rating residential risks. Areas are ranked as low, average, or high-crime areas and one schedule of rates applies within each area and to all areas similarly ranked. Rates are graded down as the amount of insurance increases. In 1981, rates in the high crime areas ranged from forty to eighty dollars.

Current Status The FIA intends for the crime program to be self supporting, but to date it has not come close to that goal. Premiums and losses of the program have been placed in the National Insurance Development Fund as mentioned earlier. A former FIA administrator, Gloria M. Jimenez, recently reported that as of October 1980, premiums had equaled about $50 million and losses and expenses had been about $143 million. The difference has been taken from the fund. Much of the money taken has been that placed in the fund for riot reinsurance. Ms. Jimenez reported that she had tried to fund the program through appropriation, but had no success.[6]

Beach (Windstorm) Plans

Background and Structure Beginning in the late 1960s and early 1970s, states along the Gulf of Mexico and the Atlantic Ocean established plans, known as beach or windstorm plans, to provide windstorm coverage for coastal properties. The purpose was to assure an adequate market for the coverage as well as a fair method of distributing responsibility among insurers. As of mid-1981, seven states had established beach plans. In addition, Georgia provides some coverage for beach areas as an extension of its FAIR plan. Exhibit 9-4 shows the policies issued and insurance in force as of 1979.

These plans are alternately referred to as "beach" or "windstorm" plans because (1) the "problem" properties are those in or adjacent to coastal areas, and (2) the major "problem" peril is windstorm. No plan is statewide insofar as residential risks are concerned—eligibility is restricted to certain areas. Some plans involve a syndicate of insurers (Alabama, Florida, North Carolina, South Carolina, and Texas) with its own organization while others use the servicing carrier concept (Louisiana and Mississippi). Whatsoever the structure, insurers participate in the fortunes of the plan according to a stated proportion of statewide writings in fire and allied lines, homeowners, commercial multiple peril, and (in Florida) mobile-home dwelling business written under auto policies.

Operation In Mississippi and North Carolina, the coverage available is standard fire and extended coverage. In Alabama and Louisiana vandalism and malicious mischief coverage is also available. Only windstorm and hail coverages are available in Florida and South Carolina. In Texas, windstorm, hurricane, and hail coverages are

Exhibit 9-4
Policies Issued and Insurance in Force in Beach Plans 1979*

State	Policies Issued New	Policies Issued Renewal	Insurance in force (000 omitted)
Alabama	329	1,870	$ 61,000
Florida	7,067	19,981	1,910,662
Louisiana	7,563	†	222,876
Mississippi	1,329	5,593	141,227
North Carolina	270	711	243,545
South Carolina	720	2,730	228,428
Texas	46,093	†	1,816,410
Totals	63,371	30,885	$4,624,148

† included with new

* Adapted from *Insurance Facts: 1980-81 Edition* (New York: Insurance Information Institute, 1980), p. 34.

available. In these states, fire and other perils are written on separate policies through normal channels.

Most real and personal property in designated areas of these states may be covered. One uniform exception is autos. In three states, farm property is not eligible (Alabama, North Carolina, South Carolina). Manufacturing property is ineligible in North and South Carolina. Mobile homes are eligible without qualification only in two states, excluded in one, and eligible only if secured to the ground in four others. Louisiana's plan does not write structures built over water. Each plan specifies certain conditions as rendering a property uninsurable. Found in all or most plans as acceptable bases for denying coverage are (1) property that is vacant or open to trespass; (2) unrepaired previously damaged property; (3) property subject to poor housekeeping or overcrowding and storage of rubbish and flammable material; (4) property which is in some way in violation of the law or public policy; and (5) newly constructed property not in accordance with the appropriate building code.

Amounts of insurance up to $500,000 on residences are available in South Carolina, up to $200,000 on residences in Florida, Mississippi, and Texas, and up to $100,000 in the other states. Standard rates set by the rating bureau serving the state are used in most cases, but there are a few localized exceptions.

Plans vary as to when coverage can become effective. Some bind upon receipt of premium; others as long as twenty days after receipt of premium. All plans safeguard against short-term adverse selection by refusing to accept applications when potential storm damage is imminent. The plans use U.S. Weather Bureau designations of weather disturbances within stipulated boundaries of longitude and latitude as the basis for placing a freeze on new applications.

Current Status The combined liability for these pools has been increasing and is now over $4 billion. Experience has been good in most states. Most areas have been spared major catastrophes during recent years.

Underwriters know that this exposure is characterized by an infrequent, but potentially catastrophic, loss pattern. Windstorm coverage in beach areas must make substantial profits in the good years in order to balance the inevitable poor years. If a major storm damages an area only once every ten years, the plan will report a large profit for nine of those years although the total experience for the ten-year period may be a substantial loss.

The experience of a single year—indeed, the experience of a single storm—could convert cumulative underwriting results for a decade from favorable to unfavorable. Yet, in their short history, some of these plans have been under pressure to reduce rates because their operations have been "profitable."

Hurricane Frederic and its devastating attack on the state of Alabama shows how "one bad year" can affect the results of a beach plan. Out of a total exposure of almost $70 million, losses from Frederic which were covered by the plan amounted to about $30 million. Based upon the premiums for 1979 (the year in which Frederic struck), the final loss ratio for that year for the plan will be in the neighborhood of 3,348 percent. For the seven years it was in operation prior to Frederic, the Alabama plan had an underwriting profit of $1,379,000. Frederic will cost the plan $30 million. If the plan returns to the same rate of profitability as it had prior to Frederic, it will take 154 years to recover from the effects of this one storm. Since the losses are shared among the insurers in the state (with the exception of those who have "written" themselves out of the plan by voluntarily insuring property in the beach areas), the effect on any one insurer should be minimized. However, one insurer (the tenth largest in the state) added nearly 15 points to its combined loss and expense ratio as a result of payments under the beach plan.[7]

A property underwriter can have similar fluctuations on a regular book of business. A company may write a volume of business in an exposed area in order to get a credit for voluntary writings. This practice, which reduces the company's participation in the beach plan, is encouraged in all plans. On those risks, the underwriter should expect large profits in the good years in order to offset the losses of the bad years.

Implications for the Underwriting Function

Property underwriters—including residence underwriters—need to be aware of the existence of these government-related or sponsored plans. Underwriting decisions may be affected by them in many instances.

What should an underwriter do when faced with a borderline risk which could be written in one of these plans? Should the application be denied and the risk be referred to the plan, or should the underwriter attempt to write it in the normal market?

The answer depends in part upon the peril(s) of principal concern. Virtually no flood coverage for dwellings or their contents is written in the normal market beyond that provided by some inland marine coverages on personal property. Thus, the residence insurance underwriter would have the answer in advance on the flood question, except with mobile homes in those companies writing contracts covering the flood peril on that class of property. However, other perils which have accounted for the plans' formation may offer less obvious solutions. Fire, vandalism, crime, and windstorm in a number of areas can be written either in the normal market or in one of the described plans. The following discussion offers an approach which underwriters might follow when faced with risks having problems with these perils. Company rules must be followed, obviously, and the comments that follow are not a substitute for those guides.

The first impulse of many underwriters is to decline the borderline application. This may be based on the premise that the plan is established to take care of problem risks and, since each company has only a relatively small share of the plan (or none with crime insurance), any one risk placed there cannot hurt any company very much.

This type of thinking should be evaluated in light of the purpose and role of each company and the insurance industry. An insurance company cannot grow, or even survive, if it does not write business. In a general sense, one of the duties of an underwriter is to accept business that has a reasonable chance of being profitable. Further, every application to a plan tends to reinforce the need for the plan and, in the eyes of some at least, raise questions as to the utility of the private insurance mechanism. If a sizable share of the business in any line that is commercially insurable on a broad scale is written through a plan, this may lead to a questioning attitude about the need for, and wisdom of, private insurers handling the business on any scale. Thus, continued growth in these plans, while perhaps expedient in the short run, may be a factor in the shrinkage of the role of the private sector in the long run.

The opposite extreme is to accept all risks to keep them out of the plan. This is not a viable alternative, even if the personal philosophy of an individual underwriter might hold that all persons have a right to protection in the company of their choice at a rate which is affordable to them. If rules, rates, and guides have been soundly formulated, risks that clearly are not acceptable under the guidelines of an insurer will cause a deterioration in the company's ability to provide a market in the long run if they are written.

Actually, this course will cause even more problems for the public than the first alternative. Losses will exceed expectations, and the company must either raise rates or restrict its market. If it raises rates, coverage becomes less affordable for many. If the company restricts its writings, availability is reduced. Either way, neither the public nor the insurer is served well.

A reasonable approach for an underwriter is to try to find a means of writing the business in a way expected to produce a profit. There are many techniques that can be used. Special rating plans or surcharges may be available in some cases. If the problem is with vandalism, a fire and extended coverage policy can be written, or possibly the peril can be covered but the deductible increased. If the problem is with small theft losses, a larger deductible can be proposed. If burglary is a potential problem, a recommendation can be made for adequate locks and other protective devices. If the problem is windstorm on a mobile home, an approved tie-down device may make the risk acceptable.

Not all applications can be accepted with modifications, of course. However, in general, the underwriter should try to find a means of fitting the risk into dimensions acceptable to the company. Declination and forcing a risk into a residual market plan should be a last resort—one used only when no other reasonable course of action is available.

UNDERWRITING RESIDENCE INSURANCE IN A CHANGING ENVIRONMENT

Residence insurance underwriters work in a continually changing environment. Factors beyond the control of the individual underwriter, the underwriting department, and the company have a definite impact on underwriting, and these forces underscore the need for alertness and adaptability. This section of Chapter 9 discusses how these factors affect the underwriting environment.

Insurance-to-Value Problems

This text has already addressed the subject of properly relating the amount of insurance to the value of covered property exposed to loss. Insurance to value is so important to a profitable book of residence insurance business, however, that it warrants further discussion, particularly in view of economic conditions in the recent past and projections for the near future. Securing and maintaining appropriate insurance to value is difficult even in an economy with stable prices. In an economy with substantial upward drifts in price levels, the difficulty is compounded.

Insurance-to-value goals may be difficult to achieve for several reasons. Experience indicates that applicants tend to underestimate values, particularly on personal property. Many applicants are truly uninformed on the replacement cost or actual cash value of their homes. They may relate insurance amounts to original cost of the home to them, to market value as determined by sales of comparable property in the area, to the mortgage amount, or to some other measure (or to guesswork) that may be a poor guide to valuation for insurance purposes. Appraisals for that purpose may be well-advised and are frequently used by commercial risks, but most homeowners probably would be unwilling to bear the expense. Further, even if a homeowner knew what replacement cost meant and fully understood the intricacies of replacement cost coverage in homeowners policies, he or she might still resist purchasing coverage equal to full replacement cost. Producers may hesitate to insist on better insurance to value. They may feel that an underinsured account is better than no account at all or they may lack knowledge of source underwriting practices and account servicing. The small average premium on residence policies places an expense constraint on the ability of the underwriter to use competent professional appraisal services to determine values. Finally, a home adequately insured to value at inception may be 10 to 15 percent underinsured by the end of a policy year in some areas due to the increases in labor and material costs that have characterized our economy in recent years.

In dealing with insurance to value, the underwriter may find the following generalizations useful:

1. There is no substitute for insurance to value at inception. Whatever the policy standard of valuation—actual cash value or replacement cost—a risk underinsured at inception will have an unrealistically low base on which later efforts (e.g., inflation guard or index-based endorsements, flat amount or percentage increases at renewal) have to work in an inflationary economy.

2. Replacement cost (or actual cash value, for that matter) on a recently built home may not be measured well by the price at which the builder or developer sold the home to the insured, even exclusive of the price for land, excavation, grading, and foundations. In the construction of a housing development, the cost per building unit plus the developer's profit may be substantially less than the replacement cost of one unit in the development. Sometimes the developer can take advantage of large-scale production methods and quantity buying of components and produce a house (again exclusive of the items above) at a unit cost of, say, 75 percent of what it would cost to replace an individual house a short time later. In such an instance, insurance for the purchase price minus the land, excavation, and so on, would produce an understatement of replacement cost for the individual dwelling.
3. Underwriters are performing a service to the applicant or insured by insisting on insurance to an appropriate percentage of insurance to value. (What is "appropriate" depends on company guides, e.g., 80 percent to replacement cost as a minimum, and 90 to 100 percent as highly desirable in homeowners.) Protection is in accord with the potential loss and, in the broadened dwelling forms and residence packages, potential disputes are minimized.
4. Underwriters are performing a disservice to those insureds with appropriate insurance to value if insureds with a less than desirable level of insurance to value are accepted or renewed. The former are subsidizing the latter. While insureds with low insurance to value may have a problem with a replacement cost recovery on a building loss (in contracts with that feature), the replacement cost extension does not affect personal property losses. In addition, it may be difficult or quite time consuming, particularly on small losses, for an adjuster to apply the insurance-to-value requirement in the replacement cost extension. Thus, a number of losses may be paid on a full replacement cost basis where a literal application of the provision would produce a lesser result.
5. Producers' estimates are just that—estimates—though some may be made with the help of reasonably reliable calculation aids. While no doubt most producers recognize the importance of insurance to value to the company, the client, and themselves, it is realistic to recognize that sometimes they work under conflicting pressures or with second-hand information, or both. Unless a producer has a known record of obtaining and

maintaining insurance to value, the underwriter is well advised to be independently curious on the question of insurance to value. At the minimum, the underwriter can have some familiarity with construction cost per square foot for various types of construction in the area and can make his or her own rough calculation if dimensions and/or area are shown on the application or inspection report.

6. General purpose indexes (e.g., the consumer price index) might not appropriately measure changes in the cost components that impact directly on dwelling insurance to value ratios. Over the past decade, increases in construction costs have exceeded increases in broader indexes. Inflation in the near future is unpredictable both for construction costs in particular and overall costs in general. In spite of the unpredictability of both, efforts to secure and maintain insurance to value should be keyed to the more relevant changes in construction costs rather than to changes in a broader spectrum of costs.
7. In a contrary vein, the particulars of a mortgage transaction may tend to encourage insurance to replacement cost on new homes. Sometimes a down payment of as little as 10 percent is required, and the land alone may be worth more than that. Nevertheless, the lender requires insurance for the full amount of the mortgage. For example, a new home may sell for $100,000, with the land value being $20,000. A 10 percent down payment equals $10,000, so the loan is $90,000. The replacement cost of the home is probably around $80,000 ($100,000 – $20,000), so coverage exceeds the replacement cost at the time of purchase. This factor often tends to offset the fact that tract-built homes can be constructed at a cost which is lower than the cost of a home built by a contractor who may be summoned to rebuild just one home after a fire.

Underwriters employ a variety of methods to secure and maintain proper insurance to value, as mentioned here and earlier in this text. The specific methods used by an insurer will depend upon a number of factors—marketing philosophy and practices, approach to underwriting renewals, the particular area in which the risk is located, the extent of computer processing used, and others. Whatever methods are employed, underwriters must be alert to the need for securing and maintaining proper insurance to value as one of the most effective means of achieving satisfactory underwriting results in residence insurance.

Altered Importance of Certain Perils

Chapter 1 introduced the notion that the underwriting of personal lines takes place in the midst of changes in the nature and importance of insured perils. This is particularly so in residence insurance, especially in the residence packages with their broader range of covered perils.

Fire has been and no doubt will continue to be a major producer of losses, both in frequency and severity, under residence contracts. Yet, progress is being made through strengthened building codes and increased use of detection devices.

Water damage losses have been increasing in frequency. Plumbing problems, wind-driven rain, and freezing of systems have been major contributors to this increased frequency. In older homes the problem can often be traced to deteriorated galvanized (instead of copper) piping and poor insulation against freezing. If what appears to be a cycle of more severe winter weather continues, freezing losses will continue to mount. In addition to the problem generally, more severe winters mean more power failures due to storms and more problems with poorly protected seasonal property.

New homes present a somewhat different set of problems because of greatly increased use of water-using fixtures and appliances—multiple baths, dishwashers, and garbage disposals. Poor materials and workmanship can cause major losses. For example, piping placed in holes drilled through "green" lumber can be pressured and come apart as the lumber dries out or the house settles. Homes with radiant heat (pipes imbedded in cement floors) have been troublesome. While the water damage peril does not cover damage to the system itself, it does cover the costs of getting at the system. When the problem appears to be a major one, many insureds today prefer to simply disconnect the system and install baseboard hot water heat.

"All-risks" dwelling coverages are vulnerable to seepage and moisture losses. For example, poorly installed or maintained rain gutters can result in water from gutters backing up over the flashing, getting under roof shingles, and running down walls. Damage can also result from moisture freezing under shingles, particularly wood shingles, or being driven by wind through improperly sealed openings.

Potential water damage losses often are difficult to foresee in the individual risk situation. Many of the potential problems are hidden or prohibitively expensive to detect. For many risks, the loss record is the only solid underwriting information that might be available on an economically feasible basis.

Theft is a peril covered in all the residence packages, and it has been growing in importance and perplexity for underwriters since the earliest of those contracts was developed. The proportion of losses attributable to theft under these contracts has increased substantially over time to the point where the advantages of including theft in a package (better spread and insurance to value) may be mixed blessings at best. The increase in two-wage-earner family units, the increase in leisure time and vacations, and the increase in second homes all mean more inviting targets for thieves.

Control of theft loss potential is a serious concern to underwriters. The granting of premium credits for approved alarm systems is increasing, although statistical correlation of credits and reduced losses must await the accumulation of more experience. Special theft deductibles are growing in use, particularly on large risks and tenant risks. Some companies give a premium discount if the insured participates in a property-marking program. Police departments and civic groups in many areas make available a special marking tool for etching an identifying mark or number on hard surfaced personal property such as cameras, TVs, and radios to deter thieves.

Losses from the theft peril are largely reflective of fundamental conditions and changes in our society. Most living units are not armed fortresses, and law enforcement personnel have necessarily limited ability to deter and solve thefts. Yet, theft is widely insured and the protection seems increasingly needed. Handling it on a basis satisfactory to both insurers and insureds is one major challenge presented by the residence insurance underwriting environment. The "inside" limits on theft of jewelry, silver, and so on have helped to at least assure that if the loss occurs it will either be limited (by the inside limits) or a more adequate premium is charged (through scheduling).

Increase in Tenant Population

Apartment living has been on the increase for several years. This fact has underwriting implications, particularly when viewed in conjunction with shifts in household size and formation, and geographic population shifts.

Insurance to value is difficult to determine on a tenant risk. Inspection is out of the question because of prohibitive cost. Aggregate personal property values probably are less accurately estimated than real property values. Cost indexes are inapplicable, and there is no dwelling principal sum to which the personal property coverage is keyed. Some clues such as marital status, household size, number of rooms, occupation, the presence or absence of a schedule of property, and length of time at the address can be helpful in evaluating insurance to value, but the task can be difficult and is subject to error.

Compounding the problem is the small average unit premium and hence very modest number of dollars in the expense loading for tenant risks. Further, tenants are more likely to be transients and on the books for shorter periods than the average risk involving a dwelling structure. Recouping the heavy initial outlays and costs of underwriting time through the expense loading in renewal premiums is difficult.

Many newer apartment complexes are structured to appeal to the increase in leisure time and offer a wide range of recreational facilities and activities. This contributes to frequent periods of brief unoccupancy and an increased theft exposure. On the other hand, many apartment complexes use guards and closed-circuit TV systems to monitor people entering and leaving, but these are of little use in spread-out "garden" apartment complexes with multiple buildings and easy access to the perimeter and buildings of the complex.

Inflation and Rate Lags

In a period of rapidly increasing prices, rate level changes tend to lag behind changes in the prices of the goods and services that loss payments provide or represent. If rate makers were able and permitted to accurately anticipate price changes when rates are set, the problem would disappear. But neither actuarial tools nor the regulatory climate in which they are used allow for this.

One result of the high inflation rates of the 1970s and early 1980s has been the virtual abandonment of the three-year prepaid policy in residence coverages. If three-year policies are written, they are subject to annual premium adjustment. This permits quicker implementation of a rate change over a book of business. Changes can be made at the next annual anniversary date.

In addition, attempts are being made to more promptly report and analyze premium and loss data. This will reduce the impact of outdated figures and increase the impact of more current data on the rate revision process.

Role of Mass Marketing in Distribution

The concept of mass marketing or mass merchandising in property and liability insurance was discussed in Chapter 3. It was explained that insurers may be able to offer personal lines insurance at reduced rates because of savings in expenses. Payroll deductions are an integral part of the process, and underwriting is essentially on an individual risk basis.

The broad principle of mass marketing encompasses all types of personal insurance. However, most programs are limited to auto.

Residential coverages could be included, but for several reasons, this is seldom the case. A major problem is mortgagee requirements. Mortgagees who collect and escrow the premium money and pay the premium as part of the mortgage payments when due are not easily accommodated under the payroll deduction approach to premium payment of a mass-marketing plan.

Another reason residential policies have not been common in mass-marketing programs is that residence premiums usually are not as great a burden as auto premiums. Large premiums cause people to seek easier means of making payments, and the larger auto premiums make monthly payments and payroll deductions attractive.

Still another reason for the limited use of residence coverages in mass-marketing plans is that most people do not see the availability and affordability of these coverages to be the problem that auto coverages often are. Rightly or not, auto mass-marketing plans are seen by some as being a solution to the availability and affordability problems.

Whatever the reasons, residence coverages have not been sold widely through mass-marketing plans. If or when the plans become more widespread for auto, there will be increased pressure to add the next largest line, homeowners.

Second-Stage Packages

Homeowners insurance purchased jointly with one or more other coverages, such as auto or life, make up a marketing idea known as second-stage or combination packages. These package programs were designed to capture a larger share of the insurance market, because they would be less expensive for the insured as well as more convenient since there is one policy, one premium, and a convenient payment plan. For instance, some companies offer an auto-homeowners package; others offer a homeowners combined with life and accident and health; and still at least one other combines auto, homeowners, and umbrella liability coverage.

There are some drawbacks to insurance packages. One of these is the merit-rating system used for auto-homeowners combinations. It is a system whereby individual risk loss experience is used in determining rates. This can work in the favor of a "preferred" risk who has had no losses or accidents. However, a claim in either area raises the rates on the whole package under some package plans. What many producers have done in this case is to withdraw the insured from the package program at renewal time and replace the risk (each part separately) with one or more companies on separate policies.

Some packages guarantee that the policy is renewable for five years. This is good for most insureds, but, of course, rate adjustments will be made as needed with each renewal period during the five years.

If an insured has a good merit rating, package rates may be less expensive than separate rates, but in most cases the combination is merely the sum of the two premiums.

Replacement Cost Valuation Basis on Unscheduled Personal Property

Many companies have begun to offer a replacement cost endorsement on coverage C (unscheduled personal property) in homeowners contracts. This endorsement allows replacement or repair of an item at current costs without deduction for depreciation. If the item is not replaced or repaired, the valuation basis for settling the loss reverts to actual cash value.

Several qualifications and restrictions are common to most endorsements providing this coverage. They stipulate that the replacement cost of any single item is limited to the amount it would cost to replace the item with new property of like kind and quality. The endorsement typically does not apply to rare and antique items, which are usually handled on a valued basis. There are also restrictions against coverage on stored or unused property and property not maintained in workable condition. Some companies extend this replacement cost coverage to the Section II supplementary coverage of damage to the property of others.

One company's endorsement provides that the company's liability for loss of or damage to any one item will not exceed the smallest of:

1. replacement cost at the time of a loss;
2. 400 percent of actual cash value at the time of loss;
3. full cost of repair;
4. any special limits of liability described in the policy; and
5. the limit of liability for coverage C.

Although most companies offering this endorsement have no special eligibility requirements, they do, in general, require that coverage C be increased from 50 percent of coverage A to a substantially higher amount—70 to 80 percent—depending on the company. This reflects the higher dollar loss potential of the replacement cost valuation basis.

Coverage may apply to primary or primary and secondary locations. Each location is rated separately, but the single minimum premium applies per policy. A deductible of $100 or more is desirable.

Exhibit 9-5 shows the replacement cost endorsement used by ISO.

Exhibit 9-5
Personal Property Replacement Cost Endorsement*

PERSONAL PROPERTY REPLACEMENT COST

SECTION I

For an additional premium, subsection a. and b. of Condition 3 Loss Settlement are deleted and replaced by the following:

- **a.** Personal Property at replacement cost.
- **b.** Awnings, carpeting, domestic appliances, outdoor antennas and outdoor equipment, whether or not attached to buildings, at replacement cost.
- **c.** Structures that are not buildings at actual cash value at the time of loss but not exceeding the amount to repair or replace.

Paragraph (c) in Condition 3. becomes paragraph (d).

1. PROPERTY NOT ELIGIBLE

Property listed below is not eligible for replacement cost settlement. Any loss shall be settled at actual cash value at time of loss but not exceeding the amount necessary to repair or replace.

- **a.** antiques, fine arts, paintings and similar articles of rarity or antiquity which cannot be replaced.
- **b.** memorabilia, souvenirs, collectors items and similar articles whose age or history contribute to its value.
- **c.** articles not maintained in good or workable condition.
- **d.** articles that are outdated or obsolete and are stored or not being used.

2. REPLACEMENT COST

- **a.** We will pay not more than the smallest of the following amounts:
  - **1.** Replacement cost at time of loss without reduction for depreciation;
  - **2.** the full cost of repair at time of loss;
  - **3.** 400% of the actual cash value at time of loss;
  - **4.** the limit of liability applying to Coverage C; or
  - **5.** any special limits of liability stated in this policy
- **b.** When the replacement cost for the entire loss under this endorsement exceeds $500, we will pay no more than the actual cash value for the loss or damage until the actual repair or replacement is completed.
- **c.** You may make a claim for loss on an actual cash value basis and then make claim within 180 days after the loss for any additional liability in accordance with this endorsement.

All other provisions of this policy apply.

HO-290 (Ed. 5-80)

* Adapted, with permission, from Insurance Services Office, New York.

Construction Methods and Materials

Manufactured Housing One of the major developments in housing has been the introduction of manufactured houses. These include precut, panelized, prefabricated, and modular homes. (Another type, the mobile home, has already received attention.) A brief description of each of these may help the underwriter to understand some of the problems they represent for the residential insurance business.

With precut homes, the factory delivers precut, premarked pieces to the building site, with detailed instruction sheets for assembly. Producers of the precut homes usually market through local dealerships, and the local representative will erect the shell if requested.

Panelized units are used extensively for primary and secondary homes as well as for condominiums and apartments. Whole wall, floor, and roof sections are premade at a factory or lumber yard. Such a home is not a do-it-yourself project since connecting the panels requires knowledge and equipment which amateurs normally do not possess.

Prefabricated homes are made in sections with plumbing, electrical, and other internal systems installed.

Modular homes are even more complete than prefabs when they arrive at the site. Highway laws restrict the size of these units to, for example, no more than fourteen feet in width and sixty-four feet in length. Once at the site, several units may be combined horizontally and/or vertically.

Whereas manufactured housing once represented inexpensive, poorly constructed, or transient housing, the picture has changed considerably. Today's home construction market situation, with spiraling costs for materials and labor and often costly delays, have made manufactured housing more attractive economically to some homeowners. The quality of construction by the most reputable factories is equal to on-site construction, and the variety of designs available today has done much to erase the earlier stigma of "boxes for houses." Also, the speed with which they can be built makes them ideal as second homes.

One of the major problems with the prefabricated and modular units is obsolescence. If a manufacturer goes out of business—a relatively common occurrence in this field in recent years—the homeowner is left without service and tailored replacement parts when something wears out or is damaged. Replacement in kind becomes a major problem, and sometimes necessitates large scale repairs where only small damage is done because of unavailability of proper replacement materials. Where the residence policy covers such a loss, claims are greater than expected.

The underwriting criteria for manufactured homes are generally the same as for conventionally built dwellings. Construction quality in general is good for the reputable veteran manufacturers. Location, occupancy, and protection are sometimes negative factors because many are second homes characterized by long periods of unoccupancy and located in rural or undeveloped areas with little fire protection. Concern may be in order about snow and wind loads—depending on the unit, its location and use, and the form involved. A large expanse of fairly flat or slightly pitched roof (which is characteristic of some modulars and prefabs) may be subject to collapse. Roofs improperly pitched or overhung may lead to dampness and water damage. An underwriter must be familiar with climatic hazards in the area, how these homes are anchored, and how strong they are.

To the authors' knowledge, no studies or figures are available relating specifically to losses on this type of housing. The comments above merely underline routine underwriting considerations that may have particular importance when reviewing these homes.

Solar Energy At present there are a number of houses around the country using solar energy for heating, cooling, and, to a lesser extent, the generation of electricity. Solar heating is not a new idea, but its cost has put it out of reach for the average home. However, rising costs for fossil fuels and concern about their availability have combined with improvements in solar heating technology to make harnessing the sun's energy a more affordable and attractive alternative than it once was. As of 1980, approximately 6 percent of our energy needs are supplied by solar sources (about twice that from nuclear energy).[8]

In general, the energy derived from solar energy units will be used to provide either space heating or water heating, with space heating being the more important use. The radiation from the sun is absorbed by a collector of some type, stored, and then distributed to the place where it is needed. The transfer can be with or without some type of medium (e.g., water). Controls can be automatic or manual, and generally there is a backup heating system.

Solar heating systems are generally classified as *active* or *passive.* Active systems can be further subdivided into liquid (water usually) or air systems. In an active system, some type of pipe or fan is used to carry the heat from the collectors to the place where it is needed. Passive systems on the other hand will use the walls of the house or a separate stationary wall as both the storage device and medium through which the heat is distributed. The passive house will use some type of wall opening or flap to move the heat to the places desired. The passive systems may also involve the use of large containers of water either on the roof or against a wall on the southern exposure. The large

Exhibit 9-6
Solar Energy Systems*

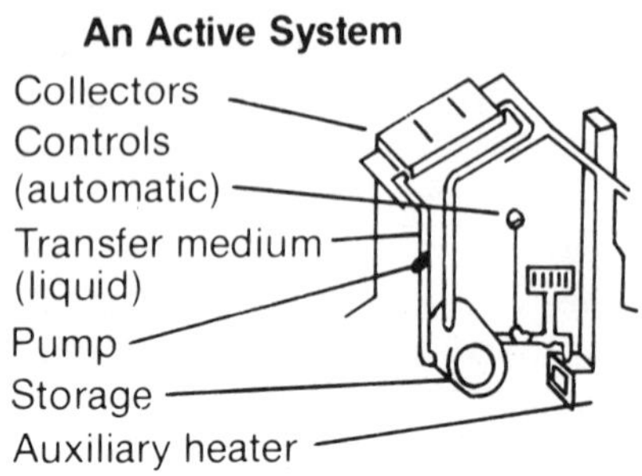

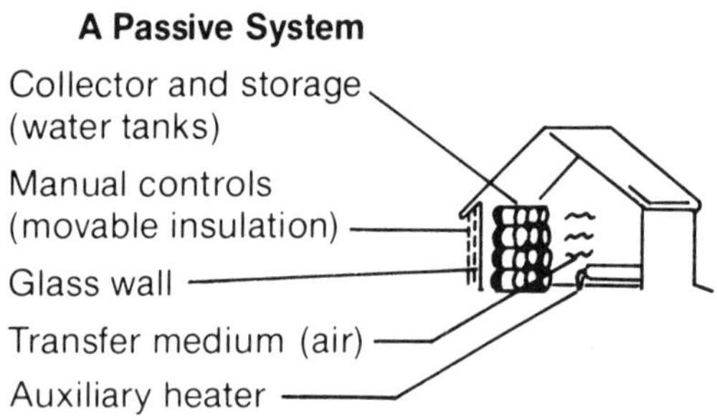

* Adapted from U.S. Department of Energy.

containers can be used both for heating and cooling. Exhibit 9-6 shows both an active and a passive system, in general.

Active systems are the type used more often in the older or established homes since a passive system may require extensive remodeling of an existing home. Most persons who consider adding some type of active system to an existing home do so at a time when they are contemplating updating their current system. The current tax law is very favorable (through the use of tax credits) with respect to the construction of solar energy systems. One of the first considerations the person must have under either system with a new or existing house, is that the house must have a good southern exposure to be able to take full advantage of the sunlight.

As mentioned, passive systems are usually limited to new home construction. The main use of passive systems is space heating. When designing a passive solar home, the location, siting, north-south

Exhibit 9-7
Siting and Alignment of House for Solar Energy Collection*

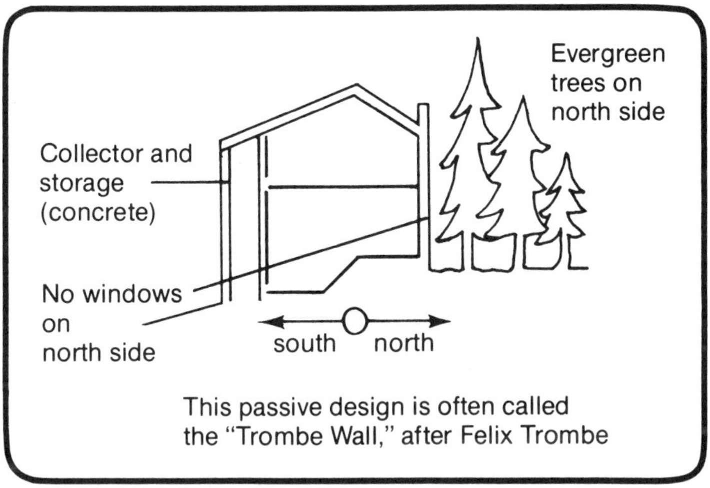

* Adapted from U.S. Department of Energy.

orientation, landscaping, and quality of construction are very important. Exhibit 9-7 shows how a passive solar home should be situated.

To install an active solar system in an existing home requires some modifications, the extent to which depends on the type of system and the condition of the house. There may be need for additional insulation, weatherstripping, and storm doors and windows. Since the solar collectors are usually placed on the roof (they can also be placed on a wall or in the back yard), there may be need to add piping and ductwork to the existing heating system. The storage tanks can be placed in the basement, underground, or outside the house. The basement is the most popular location.

In essence, to heat the solar home at night, the heat generated during the day and stored during the day is called upon. In addition to the pipes running from the collectors to the storage area, there is need for more pipes or ductwork (in the case of a hot air system) to move the heat from the storage area to the living areas. Most systems are designed to provide anywhere from 50 to 75 percent of the heating needs of the home. Successive cloudy or very cold days may require that the auxiliary heat be used.

Insuring the Solar Heated Home. Generally, insurers do not differentiate either by rate or by policy between the solar heated home and the conventionally heated home. The one difference may result from the increased values present in the solar heated home (represented by the cost of the solar heating equipment). Many underwriters view the solar system as just another heating system and look for it to be properly constructed and installed just as they would want a conventional heater to be properly constructed and installed. The primary consideration for the underwriter is probably who did the installation of the system and how qualified they are in the area. Except for the solar collectors, many of the exposures of the solar heated home are the same as any other home (pipes, ducts, and so on). If a professional contractor experienced in solar systems installed the insured's system, the underwriter probably has little worry. However, if the insured installed the system himself or herself, the underwriter may want to investigate a little further.

In spite of the fact that the systems are fairly freely written, there are some additional considerations of the solar system of which the underwriter must be aware. Broken glass is one concern. The solar collectors are often made of glass and are subject to breakage, as are windows. However, the collector panels are often more exposed than most windows, making them susceptible to hail and vandalism damage. Some type of protective screening that would not interfere with the solar collectors may be used.

Because many of the collectors' panels are located on the roof, there is an increased chance that the weight of the water in the collectors, may cause the roof to collapse. This should not be the case in well constructed homes but should be considered in older homes. Closely related to this is the fact that since the panels are installed on the roof, there is a chance that if the panels were improperly installed, water may collect under the panels and cause damage to the roof.

As with any plumbing system, there is a chance that the pipes used in the system may freeze and burst, causing water damage. The location of pipes at the top of the home may increase the normal exposure here. One possible solution is to use antifreeze in the water-filled pipes if it will not interfere with the operation of the system. Improper installation of the pipes may cause this exposure to be increased since water damage may occur from leaks in the system rather than from freezing.

Explosion of some part of the solar system is a possibility if the pressure relief devices fail to operate. The result may be some property damage from the explosion but mostly damage from the water released by the explosion.

A final consideration is the possibility of increased living expenses if the solar system is damaged. Replacement parts and repair may not be as quickly available as they would for a conventional heating system. If the heat does not work, the family will have to move out, possibly for a lengthy period, until the system can be repaired.

Experience under solar heated homes has not been sufficient to draw any definite conclusions. Companies and underwriters should continue to monitor business with solar systems to see whether they are creating any special hazards.

Alternative Heating Methods. As the prices of gas, electricity, and heating oil rise, persons are looking for other methods to heat their homes. Solar heating is one example. Other examples that are popular at this time are kerosene heaters and wood-burning stoves. When used and installed properly, each of these should present no insurmountable problems. However, underwriters are quickly learning that many of the units are not installed or used properly.

Kerosene heaters are made to be used in well-ventilated rooms and should use only the highest grade of kerosene available. They should be used away from any flammable materials and should be extinguished before persons retire for the night. Many of the newer and better models are equipped with automatic shut-off valves that extinguish the flame if the unit is tipped.

Wood-burning stoves are becoming quite popular in the colder portions of the nation. With this increased use, however, one can seldom open a newspaper without reading another report of a fire from an improperly installed stove. The improper installation is not limited to persons with lower incomes. Persons with homes worth over $150,000 will spend $800 on a stove and yet will try to cut corners and save the extra $50 that it would have cost to have the unit properly installed by a person who is qualified to do the installation. Wood stoves produce tremendous heat, and it is quite important that the stove be located far enough away from flammable materials and flooring. Most manufacturers give the recommended safe distances for the installation, and in addition, some communities have ordinances regarding the installation of wood stoves.

There is little an underwriter can do with regard to either of these exposures. At the present time, there are no policy provisions that prohibit their use. What insurers can do, and are doing, is to try to inform their insureds about the proper use of each device. Flyers are being enclosed in many renewal billings. Some companies are making special mailings to their insureds. Insurers can also work with local authorities to see that effective ordinances are passed regarding the installation and use of such devices. As with solar systems, underwriters should keep alert to any patterns that might be developing with regard to losses from these devices and make recommendations to management as to corrective action that might be taken.

Housing Unit Location

Despite efforts to reverse the trend, recent years have seen increasing deterioration of many of the nation's cities. High taxes, high crime rates, noise and air pollution, and business relocations have caused many people to seek better and safer housing in the areas surrounding large cities. The result has been an increase in dwelling units—single-family dwellings, apartment complexes, and condominiums—in suburban areas. The traditional suburban circle has expanded. Many commute twenty-five to fifty miles each way to jobs in the city. Commuting has become more feasible because of the growth of limited-access highways, commuter buses, car pools, parking lots, and even employer-provided transportation. For many, the long commute is worth the benefits of suburban living. In addition, many suburban counties have succeeded in enlarging their commercial-industrial base, resulting in more jobs being available in those locations.

Cities are making efforts to stem and reverse this flow. Erosion of the urban tax base has prompted many cities to try to attract a larger and more varied population back into city limits, not just for shopping, cultural activities, or sporting events, but to live. Groups and individuals have received federal funds for refurbishing projects. Private capital is involved in the renovation of many old buildings for occupancy or rentals. Wholesale abandonment and demolition were common just a few years ago, but soaring construction costs for new buildings have caused many enterprising people to take another look at the possibilities offered by existing structures. Improvement of conditions in the inner city and the influx of a more affluent group of apartment and home dwellers may ultimately result in fewer risks being placed in FAIR plans, although other factors have an important bearing on that issue.

The flight to suburbia is not without its underwriting concerns. One of these is the lack of fire protection. Most suburbs close to cities have matured and provide fairly good fire and police protection. However, more distant suburbs are not as developed, and their municipal services are not as extensive. Most have only volunteer fire departments with modest equipment. They often have mild (or nonexistent) zoning laws which allow the building of large homes, huge apartment complexes, and even housing developments without hydrants. Sometimes adequate water simply is not available. Many of the homes have private wells rather than public water. Apartment and condominium complexes with enormous insurable values are sometimes built with virtually no functional public protection available. Single-family dwellings in the more distant suburbs tend to be large, and losses follow suit. Some homes are built for the view or the owner's solitude and are almost inaccessible to fire equipment.

The theft peril takes on different dimensions in the suburbs. Suburbs close to a city may have as many burglaries as the nearby city, but police protection may not be as good. In suburbs, generally, alarm systems may be connected to a station many miles away and response time may be so great as to render the alarm virtually useless, particularly in a large but lightly populated area where the police have a large territory to cover. Also, in some smaller suburban communities, local police protection is nonexistent (with state police used) or consists of one or a few part-time officers.

The growth in suburban living, the upgrading of many urban areas, and the changes in the mix of hazards as a result, reflect the constancy of change in the underwriting environment. Good underwriting decisions require an awareness of that environment.

SUMMARY

The increasing need for residence insurance, coupled with the growing restriction of the market in some areas, has created a growing demand for making residence insurance available at "affordable" prices.

Catastrophe exposures are of great concern to residence underwriters. The recent increase in large single risks underscores this concern. However, residence underwriters are more concerned with the single-event, multiple-loss exposure presented by a group of risks. Fire, tornado, hurricane, flood, earthquake, and riot are the chief perils considered in this respect.

Government on the federal and state levels has had to take an active interest in solving the availability problem. FAIR plans were established to enlarge the market for basic property insurance in an equitable way. The National Flood Insurance Act of 1968 founded a program of flood insurance involving federal subsidies to property owners. Title VI of the Housing and Urban Development Act of 1970 established the Federal Crime Insurance Program in which the federal government is directly in the insurance business. Some states have formed plans to provide coverage to risks located near the ocean or the gulf. Underwriters must be aware of the existence of these government-related plans, as many of their decisions may be affected by them.

The changing environment causes many problems for underwriters. The necessity for insurance to value, the altered importance of certain perils, the increase in the tenant population, the problem of inflation and rate lags, the techniques of mass marketing, replacement cost valuation basis on unscheduled personal property, new construction methods and materials, and the flight from the inner city to the suburbs all continue to challenge the contemporary underwriter. The necessity for remaining alert and adaptable to these changing conditions has never been greater.

Chapter Notes

1. For a discussion of facultative and treaty reinsurance, see Chapter 5 of J. J. Launie, J. Finley Lee, and Norman A. Baglini, *Principles of Property and Liability Underwriting,* 2nd ed. (Malvern, PA: Insurance Institute of America, 1977).
2. Robert B. Holtom, "Fire Insurance in Brush Areas," *The CPCU Annals* (Spring 1963), p. 21.
3. Robert I. Mehr and Emerson Cammack, *Principles of Insurance,* 7th ed. (Homewood, IL: Richard D. Irwin, Inc., 1980), p. 259.
4. Robert Riegel, Jerome S. Miller, and C. Arthur Williams, Jr., *Insurance Principles and Practices: Property and Liability,* 6th ed. (Englewood Cliffs, NJ: Prentice-Hall, Inc., 1976), p. 599.
5. "Federal Crime Insurance," *F.C.&S. Bulletins,* Casualty and Surety Section (Cincinnati: National Underwriter Company, November 1975), p. Cdf-1.
6. "Reinsurance Pool Funds Crime Losses," *The Journal of Commerce* (2 March 1981), pp. 1, 14.
7. "Frederic Put Alabama Beach Plan to a Tough Test," *Best's Insurance Management Reports,* Property/Casualty, 3 December 1979 (Oldwick, NJ: A.M. Best Company, 1979).
8. "Switching on the Sun," *Journal of American Insurance,* Summer 1980, p. 1. The remainder of this section is taken from this and related articles in the same issue.

Underwriting Other Personal Lines

CHAPTER 10

Personal Inland Marine and Pleasure Boat Insurance

INTRODUCTION[1]

The term "marine insurance" broadly refers to insurance on property which is *in transit.* Marine insurance is defined in a document of several pages known as the Nation-Wide Marine Definition. Although, in practice, underwriters have made a distinction between "wet" or ocean marine and inland marine insurance, no such distinction is made in the Nation-Wide Marine Definition itself.

This Definition is necessary because of the very heterogeneous nature of the line. A brief review of the conditions that prevailed before the adoption of the Definition will demonstrate the necessity.

In the early days of marine insurance, marine cargo policies simply covered property from port to port. When merchants and manufacturers began to move inland from seaport cities, marine cargo policies were extended to cover from warehouse to warehouse. Later, insurance became necessary for purely inland transportation risks (such as truck cargo) and marine underwriters were asked to provide it. Although the protection needed for pure inland transit risks had little or no relationship to ocean marine insurance, the marine underwriters were experienced in providing broad coverage of transportation. It was at this point that marine underwriters began to extend their operations to another area of insurance—and this was the beginning of inland marine insurance as it exists today.

Finding themselves in a growing business, the marine underwriters began to enter into related—and sometimes even unrelated—fields of insurance. They responded to the need for insurance on property in transit via all kinds of land conveyances, and later by air. With the increased affluence of the American people, there came a demand for insurance on jewelry, furs, and other valuable property—and the response by marine underwriters was to issue "all-risks" type floater insurance. They began to include in one policy coverages against many perils that were not previously available even under a combination of policies, and they introduced the *floating* feature to cover property wherever located.

In these early days, there were no rule books for inland marine insurance. The only limitations on a marine underwriter's activities were his or her own judgment and imagination. New policies and forms were being developed rapidly, and competition for the so-called inland marine business was keen. Some underwriters, in their quest for business, included storage of goods under their transportation policies and thus crossed the line separating marine insurance from fire and casualty lines. The fire underwriters did not develop broader forms of their own because they were closely regulated. The result was utter confusion. Hence, an edict from the Superintendent of the New York Insurance Department was sent to the insurance companies directing them to self-regulate, or face imposition of statutory restrictions. This ultimatum led to the adoption of the Nation-Wide Marine Definition in 1933. Later amended in 1953 and 1976, it has the force of law in the great majority of states. Obviously then, a good working knowledge of the Nation-Wide Marine Definition is a prerequisite to understanding what inland marine insurance is all about.

Realizing that questions of risk eligibility under the Definition would arise from time to time, the originators of the document provided for the Committee on Interpretation of the Nation-Wide Marine Definition, which continues to function today.

Although the Definition performed its function well over the years, it was generally conceded in the early 1970s that there was a need for updating it to enable inland marine underwriters to better respond to current (at that time) insurance requirements. This brought about the 1976 revisions. Electronic data processing policies, combination builders' risk-installation floaters, and difference in conditions policies are a few examples of coverages which were recognized as Marine under the revised Definition. Moreover, for clarity, the 1976 revision was organized to make a clearer distinction between commercial lines and personal lines floaters.

In 1980, inland marine insurers country-wide recorded an underwriting loss of \$1.05 million—the first deficit in 14 years. Premium volume rose 75 percent from \$1.26 billion at the end of 1975 to \$2.20 billion in 1980.[2] These favorable results over the years can probably be attributed, in part, to rates that are more responsive to current conditions. Most companies write only annual policies. Moreover, due to the fact that a substantial percentage of inland marine insurance is written on a scheduled basis, the problem of insurance to value during inflationary periods can be more easily controlled.

The need for the usual broad coverages provided by personal inland marine policies can be easily understood when the provisions and exclusions of other policy types are examined. The dwelling fire insurance policy, for example, is extremely limited in the coverage needed to properly protect valuable personal articles. Usually, insurance applies, for the most part, at a particular location and does not "float" with the property other than in a limited way for up to 10 percent of the amount applicable to household and personal property. In many jurisdictions, a deductible applies. The various homeowners policies are also limited in the protection provided for certain types of personal property. For example, personal property usually situated at any residence of the insured other than the residence premises (as defined) is subject to a maximum of 10 percent of coverage C or $1,000, whichever is greater—and such an amount may not be sufficient to cover certain types of valuable articles. Moreover, the special limits of liability on certain property restrict coverage. Three of the eight restrictions are (1) $1,000 on the loss of guns or silverware by theft, (2) $500 in the aggregate for loss of jewelry, watches, precious and semiprecious stones, and furs by theft, and (3) $500 in the aggregate on watercraft, including trailers (whether licensed or not), furnishings, equipment, and outboard motors. All the foregoing deficiencies or gaps in coverage can be filled by an inland marine policy, often with no deductible or with deductibles frequently less than the amounts stipulated in the various dwelling or package policies.

Major Policy Types

Personal inland marine insurance policies may be classified as (1) scheduled, (2) blanket, and (3) combination. Examples of the scheduled class include the furs, jewelry, silverware, camera, musical instrument, and fine arts forms. Blanket forms include the personal effects and wedding presents floaters. Other policies may be written either on a scheduled or blanket basis, or both. These would include the personal property floater, and policies covering stamps, coins, and valuable papers.

Personal (as well as commercial) inland marine policies may also be classed as "filed" or "nonfiled." If the rates, rules, and forms of a particular class have become standardized and generally filed by rating bureaus on behalf of the insurance companies with the various state insurance departments, they would be considered filed. A nonfiled class would be one that is not standardized and is simply drawn up and rated in accordance with the underwriting practices of an individual insurance company. Most of the popular personal inland marine lines are filed. They include jewelry, furs, camera, fine arts, and several other forms. Examples of some nonfiled lines are: antique autos, binoculars, and artificial limbs.

Common Characteristics

Some of the common characteristics of personal line inland marine policies are:

1. The "all-risks" coverage feature. The majority of inland marine forms are of the "all-risks" type.
2. The floating feature. Many of the forms provide worldwide protection, such as the jewelry floater. Other forms, such as the fine arts floater, apply only within the United States and Canada. On the nonfiled classes, underwriters may restrict their insurance to even more confined geographical limits, depending on the needs of an insured and the types of property covered. Boats, for example, are usually covered only while in the particular territory stipulated in the policy, and are rated accordingly.

General Underwriting Considerations

Underwriters place great importance on proper investigation of moral hazard (dishonesty), as well as morale hazard (carelessness), prior to acceptance of a risk. Although moral and morale hazards are probably the most important underwriting considerations in any kind of property and liability insurance, they must be *thoroughly* investigated when the perils of burglary, theft, and mysterious disappearance are covered. A dishonest person could readily "arrange" to collect from the insurance company for a burglary, theft, or mysterious disappearance. Thus, an underwriter's first task is to determine that an applicant for insurance is basically honest. More often than not, sufficient character information may be obtained from the producer. If the producer cannot give an unqualified recommendation of the applicant, detailed information can usually be obtained through a consumer investigation.

After checking the applicant's acceptability from a personal standpoint, an underwriter must also be satisfied that the risk otherwise measures up to standards. Careful underwriting requires answers to the following general questions:

1. What is the applicant's occupation, reputation, and financial condition?
2. Has the applicant had any losses in the last five years?
3. Has the applicant carried similar insurance of the type requested? If so, was the other company willing to renew?
4. Where is the property kept when not being used or worn?
5. Is the applicant's home (assuming the property to be insured is kept at home when not being used) left unattended for unusually long periods of time? Is it located in a high-crime area?
6. What precautions are taken by the insured to protect the property (at home and when traveling)?

The answer to the first question will tell the underwriter the source of the applicant's income, whether the income justifies the ownership of the property insured, and whether or not the insured's character constitutes a potential moral or morale hazard. The second question is extremely important, as history tends to repeat itself, especially insofar as loss frequency is concerned. The third question will reveal the applicant's standing with the previous insurance company—whether or not he or she was considered an acceptable risk. The answer to the fourth question has to do with physical hazard, including both burglary and fire. The answers to the fifth and sixth questions help to further assess the theft exposure. The ACORD (Agency-Company Operations Research and Development) personal inland marine application is shown in Exhibit 10-1.

UNDERWRITING SCHEDULED INLAND MARINE INSURANCE

Scheduled inland marine insurance may be written under separate policies of the types described in this section. When written this way, a "floater" for the specific property insured is attached to a declarations page and to a personal inland marine floater policy which serves as a "jacket."[3] The same coverage for one or more classes of scheduled personal property may also be provided under a personal articles floater or as an endorsement to a homeowners policy (see Chapter 7). Whichever method is used, coverage and underwriting considerations are essentially the same. Generally speaking, underwriting scheduled inland marine insurance is less complicated than underwriting blanket insurance. When asked to cover a schedule (list) of property with an amount of insurance applying to each item insured, the underwriter knows exactly what is to be covered and for what amounts.

In most cases, the amount of insurance set opposite each article or

Exhibit 10-1
ACORD Personal Inland Marine Application

ACORD **PERSONAL INLAND MARINE APPLICATION**

SET TAB STOPS AT ARROWS

DATE

PRODUCER

APPLICANT

MAILING ADDRESS (INCLUDE ZIP CODE)

COMPANY | POLICY NUMBER | ☐ NEW ☐ RENEWAL

CODE	SUB-CODE	EFFECTIVE DATE	EXPIRATION DATE	BILLING PLAN	PAYMENT PLAN
				☐ AGENCY ☐ DIRECT BILL	

APPLICANT & LOCATION INFORMATION

AGE	MARITAL STATUS	OCCUPATION	SPOUSE'S OCCUPATION	OTHER

LOCATION OF PROPERTY (IF DIFFERENT FROM ABOVE) ☐ ADDITIONAL LOCATION	DWELLING TYPE(S)	CONSTRUCTION TYPE(S)	# FAMILIES (IN EACH)

COVERAGES

#	PROPERTY	AMOUNT OF INS.	RATE	PREMIUM	#	PROPERTY	AMOUNT OF INS.	RATE	PREMIUM
1	JEWELRY				8	COINS			
2	FURS				9	GOLFER'S EQUIPMENT			
3	FINE ARTS				10				
4	CAMERAS				11				
5	MUSICAL INSTRUMENTS				12				
6	SILVERWARE				13				
7	STAMPS				14				

☐ UNATTENDED CAR COVERAGE (Stamps/Coins) ☐ NON-MOBILE ORGAN COVERAGE ☐ BREAKAGE COVERAGE (*ON SCHEDULE)
☐ BROAD FORM PAIR & SET COVERAGE ☐ SAFE CREDIT (IDENTIFY PROPERTY, SAFE CLASS ETC)

TOTAL $

ADDITIONAL RATING INFORMATION

GENERAL INFORMATION

#	EXPLAIN ALL "YES" RESPONSES IN REMARKS	Yes	No	#	EXPLAIN ALL "YES" RESPONSES IN REMARKS.	Yes	No
1	Any protective devices/systems in use?	☐	☐	6	Any coverage declined/cancelled/non renewed? (Last 3 yrs.)	☐	☐
2	Will any property be exhibited?	☐	☐	7	Any other insurance with this company?	☐	☐
3	Will any special restriction/endorsements apply?	☐	☐	8	Did any loss occur during the last 3 years?	☐	☐
4	Will any type of deductible apply?	☐	☐	PRIOR INSURER & POLICY NUMBER			
5	Is any property used professionally/commercially?	☐	☐				

REMARKS:

SCHEDULE OF PROPERTY

#	PROVIDE A DETAILED DESCRIPTION OF EACH ITEM, FROM WHOM PURCHASED ETC. IF ADDITIONAL SPACE IS REQUIRED, USE THE SCHEDULE ON THE REVERSE SIDE. BE SURE TO ATTACH ALL REQUIRED APPRAISALS/BILLS	PURCHASE/ APPRAISAL DATE	AMOUNT OF INSURANCE
1			

ACORD 81 (7/80) PLEASE COMPLETE REVERSE SIDE

Continued on next page

SCHEDULE OF PROPERTY (CONTINUED)

#	DESCRIPTION	PURCHASE/ APPRAISAL DATE	AMOUNT OF INSURANCE

BINDER/SIGNATURE

INSURANCE BINDER		IF THE "BINDER" BOX TO THE LEFT IS CHECKED, THE FOLLOWING CONDITIONS APPLY:
☐ COVERAGE IS NOT BOUND ☐ BINDER		This Company binds the kind(s) of insurance stipulated on the reverse side. This insurance is subject to the terms, conditions and limitations of the policy(ies) in current use by the Company.
EFFECTIVE DATE	EXPIRATION DATE	This binder may be cancelled by the Insured by surrender of this binder or by written notice to the Company stating when cancellation will be effective. This binder may be cancelled by the Company by notice to the Insured in accordance with the policy conditions. This binder is cancelled when replaced by a policy. If this binder is not replaced by a policy, the Company is entitled to charge a premium for the binder according to the Rules and Rates in use by the Company.
TIME ______ M	☐ 12:01 A.M. ☐ NOON	

IMPORTANT NOTICE REGARDING THE FAIR CREDIT REPORTING ACT: In making this application for insurance it is understood that as part of our underwriting procedure, an investigative consumer report may be prepared whereby information is obtained through personal interviews with your neighbors, friends, or others with whom you are acquainted. This inquiry includes information as to your character, general reputation, personal characteristics and mode of living. If an investigation is made, you can be assured that it will be handled in the strictist confidence.

If you wish information on the nature and scope of the Customer Report which may be requested, ask your agent for the address of the Company handling your account.

APPLICANT'S STATEMENT: I have read the above application and I declare that to the best of my knowledge and belief all of the foregoing statements are true; and that these statements are offered as an inducement to the Company to issue the policy for which I am applying. (Kansas: This does not constitute a warranty.)

APPLICANT'S SIGNATURE		PRODUCER'S SIGNATURE	

FOR COMPANY USE

item is the limit of liability in event of loss of, or damage to, that particular item. Unless otherwise indicated, the insurance company is liable for no more than the *actual cash value* of the damaged or destroyed item, despite the fact that it might be less than the amount of insurance that applies to the particular item(s) scheduled in the policy. Hence, the underwriter is reasonably well protected against those who might be tempted to "lose" overinsured property. The policy terms may, however, state that the amount of insurance is agreed to be the *value* of an item for insurance purposes. Fine arts is the class generally insured on a "valued" basis because the item cannot be reproduced or replaced and the "value" must be agreed upon when the policy is issued. When this is done, care must be exercised to make sure that the values placed opposite each scheduled item are properly substantiated. It should be pointed out, however, that even in those cases when an insurance company is liable for no more than the actual cash value, the amount of insurance should be as close as possible to that amount. Otherwise, misunderstandings may arise when a loss occurs if the company settles a loss according to the policy terms but for less than the stipulated amount of insurance on a scheduled item.

The floater jacket contains a loss to a pair, set, or parts clause which states that in the event of loss or damage to an item which is part of a pair or set, the insurer agrees, at its option, either to (1) repair or replace any part to restore the pair or set to its *value* before the loss; or (2) pay the difference between the actual cash value of the property before and after the loss. Thus, consideration is given to the importance of the item to the pair or set, but the loss of the item is not construed to mean the total loss of the pair or set. If the loss is to a part of the covered property which consists of several parts, the insurer agrees only to pay for the value of the part lost or damaged. The pair or set portion of the clause in the fine arts floater differs somewhat and is discussed later.

Jewelry and Fur Floaters

The jewelry and fur floater covers scheduled furs and jewelry owned by or in the custody and control of the insured or any member of the insured's family of the same household.

"Scheduled" means that each item to be insured must be fully described in the policy with an amount of insurance applying to each article. Engagement rings may be insured in the names of the two parties who have an interest in the ring, irrespective of domicile.

The insurance covers "all-risks" of loss or damage to the insured property while located anywhere in the world subject to the usual exclusions of war, nuclear incident, wear and tear, gradual deterioration, insects, vermin, or inherent vice. Inherent vice means a quality or property within an object that results in the object's tending to destroy itself. For example, fur coats may deteriorate in time whether used or not. Some of the perils that would be insured against with the "all-risks" coverage for jewelry and furs are windstorm, tornado, theft, explosion, water damage (including flood), earthquake, tears, stains and burns, breakage, misplacement, or disappearance.

Among the personal inland marine classes, jewelry ranks highest in premium volume. Premium volume for the five year period 1976-1980 was nearly $1 billion. The loss ratio (incurred losses to earned premiums) for 1976-1979 was 46.75 percent, but jumped to 72.4 percent in 1980 due primarily to the fluctuations in the value of gold and silver.[4] Because of the large premium volume, careful treatment of jewelry business is important.

Next to bullion, jewelry is perhaps the easiest class of personal property to convert into money. That being the case, it is a target for thieves, and it should be given the highest degree of care by the insured. All of the questions previously listed in this chapter as general underwriting considerations should be answered to the satisfaction of the underwriter. Particular emphasis should be placed on where the jewelry is kept (and how safe it is) when not in use; whether or not applicants are careful and honest; and how often it is used or worn. When requested to insure a modestly valued engagement ring or other items of nominal worth, an underwriter usually does not and, indeed, cannot afford to conduct a detailed study of all the underwriting facts of a risk submission. On the other hand, providing insurance on high-valued items should be based on full and satisfactory character and exposure information.

Substantiations of values should be required in all cases. A previous policy in another company is not satisfactory evidence of value. The establishment of values before a loss greatly reduces adjustment problems, and reduces the chance of ill feelings. Although the best substantiation is usually the purchase price, that information is often not available on old or inherited jewelry. When it is necessary to have jewelry appraised to determine its quality and value—as well as to secure accurate descriptions for use in writing the policy—the services of an experienced and competent jewelry appraiser should be used. Usually, there are certain jewelry firms in almost any given area that have proved themselves over the years to be competent and dependable appraisers.

When insuring jewelry, the importance of securing detailed descriptions cannot be overemphasized. Without proper description, it is difficult to identify the property insured, and next to impossible to settle a claim equitably if a loss should occur. Property cannot be properly replaced, nor can the actual cash value be determined, if it is not accurately described.

Although common sense dictates that proper descriptions of insured jewelry are necessary, it is not uncommon to see policies with items of jewelry described along the following lines:

	Amount of Insurance
One lady's solitaire diamond ring	$4,500

A more acceptable description would be:

	Amount of Insurance
One lady's solitaire diamond ring with brilliant cut diamond of excellent clarity weighing 1.55 carats; 14 karat yellow gold, tiffany setting	$4,500

If an underwriter is asked to provide a valued policy (one whereby the company agrees at issuance that it will consider the amount set opposite each item as the value in the event of total loss), verification of value should be most carefully scrutinized and policies issued only for insureds of the highest caliber (i.e., people whose honesty and integrity can be vouched for without question).

It is important for personal line underwriters to be certain applications for "all-risks" jewelry or fur floaters emanate from producers who know and can recommend their clients as honest and careful people. Indeed, good underwriters make it a practice to satisfy themselves that the producers who place jewelry insurance with them can be depended upon to accurately supply them with all the underwriting facts needed to make a decision regarding the acceptance of a jewelry submission.

Although desirable, applications are not always used in practice. Some producers prefer to use a letter to give the underwriter all the information required. The use of applications assures that all important questions will be answered and important information will not be overlooked by the producer. An appraisal form is shown in Exhibit 10-2, although most appraisers of jewelry or furs use their own forms; in fact, many of them prefer to use ordinary letters to describe and show the value of the property they have appraised.

Although furs are attractive to thieves, they are not as easy to steal as jewelry and, therefore, the rates are lower. Nevertheless, careful underwriting along the lines of jewelry insurance is called for on risks involving substantial values.

Most owners of furs place the furs in storage during the off season. When furs are stored, the owner must place a value on them, and the charge for storage is based upon the declared value. If the furs are insured under a fur floater, there is, of course, coverage while they are

Exhibit 10-2
Appraisal of Jewelry or Furs

APPRAISAL OF JEWELRY OR FURS

Property of ______________________________

Address ______________________________

IMPORTANT

List each article separately. Give detailed description including the number of stones and weight or standard gauge measurements.

Item No.	Article	Description	Valuation
1.			
2.			
3.			
4.			
5.			
6.			
7.			
8.			
9.			
10.			
11.			
12.			
13.			

None of the above articles is imperfect or in need of repair except as follows: (Give details)

I hereby certify that the above named person has submitted the above listed articles for appraisal and that the values indicated are in accordance with my best knowledge and belief.

Date ______________ ______________ Jeweler Furrier

Address ______________________________

in storage. Therefore, when declaring the value for storage purposes, the minimum amount may be declared with a consequent saving on storage costs.

Cameras and Related Equipment

Unlike jewelry and furs, cameras have serial numbers, model numbers, dates of manufacture, and other pertinent identification information which aid police in recovery attempts. Similarly, thieves cannot "melt down" cameras as they can jewelry or silverware. Also, there is an active market for used cameras and equipment, so it is not difficult to establish values in event of loss. Unfortunately, this active market also makes it easier for stolen cameras to be sold.

Because of its nature and use, camera equipment is usually not kept in a safe. Nevertheless, it is valuable equipment, and carelessness results in losses. Underwriters should try to confine their acceptances to people who are expected to take good care of their equipment and not leave it in the back seat of an unlocked car or other visible and accessible place to tempt thieves. If a producer knows the applicant, he or she is in a better position than the underwriter to know whether or not carelessness or other morale hazard exists.

Camera floaters provide world-wide "all-risks" coverage subject to the same exclusions found in the jewelry and fur floater. The rates provided in the manual are based on personal use of the equipment, but there is no policy exclusion of cameras used professionally.

Musical Instruments and Equipment

Musical instrument floaters are designed to cover musical instruments and articles of equipment pertaining thereto, owned or in the custody or control of the insured and members of the insured's family of the same household.

The "broad form" musical instruments floater provides world-wide coverage against "all-risks" of loss or damage to the scheduled musical instruments and articles of equipment pertaining thereto. The policy contains the usual exclusions relating to wear and tear, gradual deterioration, insects, vermin, or inherent vice, war, and nuclear incident.

A "limited form" musical instrument floater providing world-wide coverage against loss or damage to the scheduled musical instruments and articles of equipment pertaining thereto is available. This is a specified perils policy and insures against loss or damage caused by the perils of fire, lightning, cyclone, tornado, flood, theft, and accident to conveyances. In addition to the usual exclusions, the form also excludes loss or damage to the insured property while left unattended in or on any auto unless in the custody of a common carrier. Rates for the limited form are usually 10 percent less than those for the broad form policy.

Musical instruments for nonprofessional musicians can be treated from an underwriting standpoint much like cameras and related equipment. Generally, musical instruments are larger than cameras and not quite as subject to theft or mysterious disappearance losses. This reduced exposure to loss is reflected in the rates which are significantly less than the noncommercial camera rates. The musical instruments floater contains a condition that the musical instruments will not be played for pay unless the policy is endorsed. The underwriter can thus be assured an additional premium is paid. This is because instruments played professionally are subject to substantially greater exposure to loss or damage than those owned by nonprofessionals. Professional musicians often have high valued instruments, which should be appraised to confirm the insured value. The transit and theft exposures are significant with professional musicians.

Silverware

The silverware floater has become a more important class from the standpoint of premium volume since the HO-76 program was introduced, limiting the coverage available on silverware. (The HO-76 program is in use in forty-five states as of March 1982.) Experience for the 1976-1980 period resulted in a 63.02 percent loss ratio with a premium volume of $12.2 million.[5] The ease with which silverware can be melted down and sold makes it very attractive to thieves.

The silverware floater may be written on a scheduled or blanket basis. The "all-risks" coverage, like that applicable to the other classes considered up to this point, is subject only to the war, nuclear incident, wear and tear, gradual deterioration, insects, vermin, or inherent vice exclusions. There is a stipulation in the form that pens, pencils, flasks, smoking implements or accessories, or articles of personal adornment are not considered to be silverware, and hence, not covered. Silverware does include silver-plated ware, goldware, gold-plated ware, and pewter-ware.

Fine Arts

The terms jewelry, furs, and musical instruments are self-explanatory, but the term "fine arts" leaves room for interpretation. That being the case, the ISO rules applicable to fine arts insurance as filed with the various state insurance departments define it as follows:

> Private collections of paintings, etchings, pictures, tapestries, art glass windows, and other bona fide works of art (such as valuable rugs, statuary, marbles, bronzes, antique funiture, rare books, antique silver, manuscripts, porcelains, rare glass and bric-a-brac) of rarity, historical value or artistic merit.

The filed fine arts rules, rates, and forms apply only to private collections. Hence, the term "private collections" had to be defined. For purposes of the insurance, the following definition is used:

> Property owned by any individuals, firms, corporations, or associations that are not dealers, auction rooms, museums, art galleries, or art institutions ordinarily open to the public.

In addition,

> the term "private collection" shall not be deemed to include property in the custody of dealers, auction rooms, museums, art galleries or art institutions ordinarily open to the public when insured in the name of such dealers, auction rooms, museums, art galleries or art institutions.

To clarify the above definition of private collections, the fine arts rules further state that hotel risks and university, college, and school risks shall be treated as private collections. Additionally, private collection includes public schools, state universities, and the like, if written in the name of the state or political subdivision thereof, or the authority having jurisdiction over such schools or universities.

The standard fine arts policy, unlike most other personal inland marine floaters, is a *valued contract* (i.e., the amount of insurance set opposite the respective articles covered is agreed to be the value of such articles). The important advantage of this feature is that values on the insured property are established prior to loss, thus facilitating claim adjustment. It means that underwriters must be careful to be as sure as possible the amount of insurance placed on each item is properly substantiated. In every area, there are certain competent appraisers of fine arts, including antiques and other valuables. The insurer's claim department or independent adjusters may have knowledge of such specialists who can assist in determining values. Some faculty members of art schools are considered expert appraisers.

In addition to the war, nuclear incident, and wear and tear, gradual deterioration, insects, vermin, or inherent vice exclusions, the "all-risks" coverage of the fine arts floater is subject to the following exclusions:

1. Damage caused by any repairing, restoration or retouching process;
2. Breakage of art glass windows, statuary, marble, glassware, bric-a-brac, porcelains and similar fragile articles unless caused

by fire, lightning, aircraft, theft, windstorm, earthquake, flood, explosion, malicious damage, collision, derailment or overturn of conveyance;
3. Loss to property on exhibition at fair grounds or premises of national or international expositions unless the premises are specifically covered by the policy.

The breakage exclusion may be deleted with respect to all or any part of the fine arts schedule for an additional premium determined by applying breakage rates to the aggregate value of the articles on which breakage coverage is desired.

Another feature of the fine arts floater is the amended "pair or set" clause which requires the insurer to pay, in event of the loss of any article(s) constituting a part of a set, the full amount of value of such set as shown in the schedule. The insured must agree, however, to surrender the remaining article(s) of the set to the insurer. This condition eliminates adjustment difficulties in determining a fair value for any part(s) of a set. Note that this is exactly opposite from the pair or set clause in the other floaters.

Generally, personal fine arts insurance has been profitable over the years, despite the fact that the premium for this "all-risks" coverage is, in many instances, less than the premium for fire and extended coverage. The reason is probably that the property covered is well taken care of, and the handling of it is minimal (e.g., paintings hanging on the wall are not subject to the same abuse as many other kinds of property). Moreover, since fine arts insurance is written on a scheduled basis, underwriters are aware of exactly what is insured. Thus, underwriters will not be called on to pay a loss for something they did not realize they were insuring—possibly some type of property they might not have wanted to insure in the first place. Also, scheduling is conducive to insurance to value as people are more aware of values of property that is listed and described. Whatever the reason, the loss experience on fine arts insurance justifies the relatively low rates for the insurance.

Underwriters of fine arts floaters should be especially interested in answers to the following questions:

- How were values determined?
- What protection is available against fire and theft (e.g., smoke detectors, fire alarms, burglar alarms)?
- Is property located in buildings that are unoccupied for long periods throughout the year?
- Is property shipped out for exhibition frequently?
- Is the transit exposure such that the low fine arts rates are not adequate?

Stamp and Coin Collections

Although one "all-risks" form insures both stamp and coin collections, the property is quite different and the rates reflect that difference. Although stamps are attractive to thieves, coins (which often do not even require conversion to money) are even more so. Hence, the rate for insurance on coins is substantially higher than the rates that apply to stamps.

Like the silverware floater, stamp and coin collection floaters can be issued on a blanket or scheduled basis, subject, however, to a limit not exceeding $1,000 on unscheduled coins or other numismatic property and subject to a limit of $250 on any one unscheduled stamp, coin, or other individual article or any one pair, strip, block, series, sheet, cover, frame, card, or the like. The limitation enables underwriters to better control the risks they assume. Many underwriters require that a list of property be supplied to them whether or not it is scheduled in the policy. This procedure is essential on large collections to facilitate proper adjustments in event of loss. In such cases, it is also good underwriting practice to make sure that policyholders catalogue their collections and keep their records in fireproof safes or safe deposit vaults away from the locations where their collections are kept. To encourage proper safekeeping, a 10 percent credit in the premium is allowed if the insured agrees (via a clause added to the policy by endorsement) to keep not less than 75 percent of the value of the property in a fireproof safe or vault with a combination lock when the stamps or coins are not in use or on exhibition.

In addition to the war, nuclear incident, and wear and tear, gradual deterioration, insects, vermin, or inherent vice exclusions, the worldwide "all-risks" coverage provided by the stamp and coin floaters does not insure against:

1. fading, creasing, denting, scratching, tearing, thinning, transfer of colors, inherent defect, dampness, extremes of temperature, gradual depreciation, or any damage from handling or being worked upon;
2. disappearance of individual stamps, coins or other articles unless the item is described and scheduled with a specific amount of insurance, or if the item is mounted in a volume and the page to which it is attached is also lost;
3. loss of property in the custody of transportation companies, nor shipments by mail other than registered mail;
4. theft from any unattended auto unless being shipped as registered mail;

5. loss to property which is not an actual part of a stamp or coin collection.

Although the unattended auto clause may be deleted for an additional premium, a prudent underwriter should be cautious whenever such a request is received. In addition, when substantial values are to be covered, answers to the following questions will help to assess the risk of loss:

- Does the applicant make it a practice to send out stamps or coins on approval when selling a part of the collection?
- Does the applicant travel with the insured property extensively?
- Is the property taken outside the country?
- Does the applicant maintain an accurate, up-to-date inventory of the stamps and coins in the collection?
- Does the applicant participate in exhibitions?
- Is the property kept under lock and key or is it in open display?

BLANKET INLAND MARINE FLOATERS

The broader scope of blanket insurance makes it inherently more of a problem to handle from an underwriting standpoint than specifically scheduled property coverage. Even if the policy insures a specific type of property (e.g., the silverware floater) on a blanket basis, the underwriter may be insuring more than was intended. And if the policy applies to various kinds of property (e.g., the personal property floater), the underwriter can be even more "in the dark."

Scheduling property helps to achieve insurance to value, but blanket coverage does not. The scheduling of property makes it unnecessary to incorporate various property exclusions, which necessarily form a part of a blanket form. Otherwise, inland marine underwriters would be called upon to pay for losses to property they did not anticipate insuring or, possibly, property that the Nation-Wide Marine Definition would not permit them to insure. Thus, although the insuring clauses of both scheduled and blanket policies are similar in that they both insure against "all risks of physical loss to the property described except," the blanket policies must contain more exclusions than the scheduled floaters.

In addition to the problem of delineating the extent of the coverage through special conditions or property exclusions, as well as the problem of insurance to value, there is also an inherent *small loss problem* peculiar to blanket insurance. It results from the variety and kind of property covered, some of which is bound to be lost or damaged due to its nature or use. For example, the personal property floater insures almost all kinds of household personal property owned, used, or worn by the insured, including dishes and glassware that are used every day of the year. Some of such fragile property is almost certain to get broken during the year; hence, a breakage exclusion is absolutely necessary if coverage under the policy is to apply to fortuitous losses only. Clothing is another example. Small items of clothing will inevitably disappear mysteriously from time to time. If mysterious disappearance is covered by a blanket policy, the problem of small losses may be substantially reduced through the application of a deductible.

The Personal Property Floater

Prior to the introduction of the homeowners policies in the early 1950s, the personal property floater (PPF) was one of the most important personal inland marine lines in terms of premium volume. As the homeowners policies were accepted, the popularity of the PPF fell to the point where it is no longer an important line of business for most companies. However, people who own valuable property that warrants "all-risks" coverage are still interested in the policy. Because of the existence of other coverages (e.g., homeowners, contents replacement cost endorsement, and valuable items policy), the PPF is being withdrawn by some companies.

Subject to certain limitations and exclusions, the PPF covers all personal property owned, used, or worn by the person in whose name the policy is issued and members of the insured's family of the same household. At the option of the insured, the policy covers unscheduled personal property of guests or servants while on the premises of the residences of the insured. The ISO form contains thirteen categories of unscheduled personal property as shown in Exhibit 10-3.

In addition to personal property, the policy also covers loss or damage caused by theft or attempted theft to real property at the insured's residence which is not specifically excluded. For example, in the event of damage to doors or windows of an insured's dwelling by burglars, the damage would be covered. The policy further covers loss or damage by vandalism or malicious mischief to the interior of residences of the insured. Coverage for both is for an amount not exceeding $2,500.

The policy also covers the actual loss of or damage to improvements, alterations, or additions made by the insured to buildings occupied as residences by, but not owned by, the insured, or to premises occupied by the insured in condominiums. The limit for such coverage is shown on the policy.

Exhibit 10-3
ISO Personal Property Floater

IPF 17 01

PERSONAL PROPERTY FLOATER

"Your residence" means the residence stated in the Declarations or in the policy.

AMOUNTS OF INSURANCE—UNSCHEDULED PROPERTY AT YOUR RESIDENCE

(a) The amount of insurance shown below for each numbered category is the total amount of insurance for each occurrence for all property in that numbered category

Categories of Property	Amount of Insurance
(1) Silverware, goldware and pewterware (including in each case flatware and hollowware)	
(2) Clothing (yours, your spouse's and other members of your family living with you)	
(3) Rugs (including all floor coverings) and draperies	
(4) Musical instruments (including pianos and organs); electronic equipment and accessories (including television sets, radios, records and tape players and recorders, records and tapes)	
(5) Paintings, etchings, pictures, sculptures, tapestries and other objects of art	
(6) China and glassware (including bric-a-brac)	
(7) Cameras and photographic equipment and supplies	
(8) Guns; golf, hunting, fishing, bowling and other sports equipment and supplies	
(9) Major appliances such as refrigerators, washing machines, dryers, ranges, mixers and trash compactors	
(10) Bedding (including blankets, comforters, covers, pillows, mattresses and springs); linens (including dining room and bedroom)	
(11) Furniture such as chairs, tables, sofas, desks, beds, chests, lamps, mirrors and clocks	
(12) All other personal property (including books, wines, liquors, foodstuffs, garden, lawn and other tools and equipment, trunks, traveling bags, children's playthings, miscellaneous articles in basement and attic) and professional books, instruments and equipment while actually in your residence	
(13) Building additions and alterations.	
Total Amount Of Insurance—Unscheduled Property At Your Residence.	$

Coverage is world-wide, but there is one important exclusion to the property covered and that applies to property regularly situated throughout the year at other than the principal residence of the insured. Such property is excluded unless specifically endorsed onto the policy. In essence, a separate policy is issued for the other location(s).

There are also limitations on amount of insurance on certain classes of property. The limit on any one loss of unscheduled jewelry, watches, fur, precious or semi-precious stones or gems is $500 unless coverage under Item (c) (unscheduled personal jewelry, watches, and furs) applies. Thus, high valued jewelry or furs should be scheduled if an insured is to be properly protected. There are also limits on money, numismatic property, precious metals and bullion ($100), as well as on notes, securities, philatelic property, documents, and so on ($500). These may be increased to $500 and $1,000 respectively for an additional premium.

The policy contains seven categories of excluded perils, including the three typical exclusions. Certain types of property are also excluded. Among the items of property excluded are (1) animals, fish, and birds; (2) autos, aircraft, boats, trailers, campers, motorcycles, and other motorized vehicles designed for transportation or recreational purposes (although their equipment is covered while removed therefrom and on the premises of the residences of the insured); (3) owned property pertaining to a business, profession, or occupation (except professional books, instruments, and equipment if shown as insured) while at the residence premises; and (4) as mentioned, property regularly situated throughout the year elsewhere than at the residence premises. It should be noted that these items are not generally considered usual and ordinary household personal property, and insurance is easily obtained to specifically cover them when needed. The main function of property exclusions in a personal property floater is to confine coverage to property of typical households.

The description of the personal property floater contained in these pages was simply intended to cover the highlights of the policy. The form itself and the rules contained in bureau or company manuals should be referred to for details of coverage, forms, and the many options.

Unlike most other personal inland marine floater policies, fixed-location coverage is most prominent under the PPF. Hence, contents fire rates are used as a base for policy rates, plus loadings which depend on territory. Rates for scheduled items are the same as when separately insured.

Underwriting the Personal Property Floater Although physical hazard cannot be treated lightly when underwriting personal property risks, the most important factors to consider are moral and morale hazard because the PPF is so broad in coverage.

Obviously, the best approach to profitable PPF underwriting is to get *all* the facts needed to assess the loss potential. Completion of a detailed application signed by the applicant is a most important first step.

After obtaining a completed and signed application, prudent underwriters will verify the information if there is any question regarding its accuracy. Accurate loss history must be obtained, as well as the applicant's experience, if any, with the previous insurer. Some of the points that cannot be ascertained from an application include the attitude, character, and habits of the applicant and the applicant's family. Most underwriters try to provide insurance only to honest and reasonably careful people. Usually, character information should be obtained from producers or through consumer investigative reports.

Insurance to Value Profitable underwriting of blanket insurance for individuals—in fact, profitable underwriting of just about any kind of property insurance—requires a continuous effort to obtain insurance to value due to the large number of small losses. Underwriters should stay on the alert and be sensitive to signs of underinsurance. A method of encouraging insurance to value by means of an abbreviated inventory guide is contained in most applications for PPF insurance. Unlike many other kinds of personal inland marine insurance, underwriters of the PPF usually require completed applications, and conscientious completion of the small inventory section will go far towards making an insured aware of the values he or she has, and encourage insurance to value.

The Personal Effects Floater

Personal effects floaters are used to insure individually owned personal effects such as are usually carried by tourists and travelers. The property must belong to and be used or worn by the insured, the insured's spouse and their unmarried children permanently residing with them. Like all other "all-risks" insurance, the extent of the coverage afforded by the personal effects floater must be determined by referring to the exclusions. Some of the items of property excluded are autos, motorcycles, household furniture, property specifically or otherwise insured, money, accounts, deeds, passports, notes, securities, tickets, animals, physicians' instruments, contact lenses, and artificial teeth and limbs. Also excluded are personal effects while on the domicile of the insured; personal effects in storage except incidental to transportation; and property in custody of students while in fraternity or sorority houses, dormitories, or on the premises of educational institutions, except for fire only. The loss of jewelry or furs is limited to 10 percent of the policy amount subject to a limit of $100 for any one such article. Ordinary breakage is excluded along with war, nuclear incident, wear and tear, gradual deterioration, insects, vermin, or inherent vice, and any damage from being worked upon. There is also an exclusion and limitation pertaining to theft from an unattended auto.

The above description only paraphrases the coverage, and should not be considered complete. A personal effects policy form should be referred to for a detailed study of the conditions, limitations, and exclusions, some of which can be deleted for additional premium. For example, it is common practice to delete the unattended auto clause in its entirety. The limitation pertaining to property in the custody of students may also be deleted, as may the domicile exclusion in most states.

More often than not, personal effects floaters are short-term contracts, ordered for people who are getting ready to leave on a trip. Under the circumstances, there is insufficient time to underwrite such risks in the same manner as other "all-risks" insurance. Moreover, the relatively small average premium for personal effects policies makes thorough underwriting impractical. Under the circumstances, underwriters must rely almost entirely on their producers to submit risks of good quality. Questions that should be asked of the producer to determine the acceptability of a personal effects risk would be:

1. What is the occupation of the applicant?
2. Do you know the applicant personally and can you recommend him or her without qualification?
3. Has any company refused to issue or re-issue similar insurance?
4. Has the insured sustained any losses that would be covered by a personal effects floater? (Get details about all losses sustained.)
5. What is the insured's destination?
6. What means of travel will be used?
7. Is the amount of insurance requested close to the actual values that will be at risk?
8. Does the applicant have any other insurance with the company or with the producer?

Answers to the above questions should bring to light any physical, moral, or morale hazards that may exist. Occupation, for example, is important. If a person is an entertainer or engages in some other occupation that involves traveling much of the time, there is a greater chance of loss by crime than if that person were a teacher. Obviously, the applicant should be known and well-recommended by the producer if answers to all the other questions are to be meaningful. Past loss history is important and pertinent information to obtain in underwriting almost any kind of property insurance. Means of travel and destination will tell something about the physical hazard(s) that the applicant can be expected to encounter.

The question often arises regarding the need for a personal effects floater if the applicant already has a homeowners policy. The answer is simply that most homeowners policies provide only named perils coverage on personal property. Loss from disappearance or misdelivery (a relatively frequent occurrence) would usually not be covered by homeowners insurance, whereas coverage would prevail under a personal effects floater. Also, homeowners policies are sometimes issued subject to fairly high deductibles; but the personal effects floater may be written for full coverage or, optionally, subject to a twenty-five dollar deductible clause. For a small premium, personal effects policies can close some of the gaps of homeowners coverage.

Wedding Presents Floater

The wedding presents floater is an "all-risks" policy that can be written for a term that must expire no later than ninety days after the wedding date. Its purpose is to provide temporary insurance on valuable wedding presents until the couple can get more permanent coverage.

The policy contains variations of the typical exclusions previously discussed, although like the other blanket policies considered in this chapter, there is no "infidelity" exclusion. "Breakage" and "marring and scratching" exclusions apply to fragile items. Certain types of property are excluded (i.e., realty, animals, autos, motorcycles, aircraft, bicycles, boats, money, notes, and similar property).

The wedding presents floater has been a consistently profitable class, but premium volume has been small. Apparently, there is a minimum of moral or morale hazard. Moreover, by the time the property is put to use, other more permanent insurance has been obtained. Burglary and mysterious disappearance are the important causes of loss, and underwriters should be satisfied that the property will be kept at locations where it will be reasonably safe (i.e., dwellings or buildings of good construction not subject to abnormal crime hazards and which are otherwise acceptable risks for fire and theft insurance).

Trip Transit Insurance

Although trip transit insurance is generally studied in conjunction with commercial forms of transportation floaters, it is also a class of insurance that is obtained to cover personal property of individuals. It simply covers one shipment (e.g., furniture and other household goods while being shipped by movers, usually to a new residence).

The usual perils covered by a trip transit policy include fire, upset, overturn, or collision of a conveyance, and flood. Theft and other perils may be added by endorsement. "All-risks" coverage is available, although prudent underwriting would call for a deductible to apply to ordinary breakage, marring, or scratching—such damage to at least a small degree being almost inevitable.

The bill of lading issued by a common carrier serves as a receipt from the carrier for the goods being transported. Additionally, it serves as the contract of carriage between the shipper and the carrier, setting forth the obligations and responsibilities of each party.

The "Uniform Straight Bill of Lading" contains a clause to the effect that "the agreed or declared value of the property is stated by the shipper not to exceed _______ per _______." This statement may be left blank (in which case there is no release of the carrier's liability) or it may be filled in, thereby releasing the carrier of part of its liability.

Over a period of time, the terminology used by underwriters has led to some confusion. Underwriters call a bill of lading in which there is no release of the carrier's liability a "straight" bill of lading or just a bill of lading. Those bills of lading in which there *is* a release of the carrier's liability have been called "released" bills of lading. The confusion arises from the fact that in both cases, the underwriter is referring to a variation of the same document (a Uniform Straight Bill of Lading). The term "straight" is technically used to distinguish the straight bill of lading from an "order" bill of lading—the primary difference being that the "straight" bill of lading is nonnegotiable and the "order" bill of lading is negotiable. The confusion in terminology should not overshadow the underwriting significance of these distinctive terms.

Rates vary between companies and depend on the perils covered, and the method and distance shipped. For example, a basic named peril policy to cover a 1,000 mile furniture shipment by public truck made under a usual "released" bill of lading might warrant a rate in the neighborhood of $1.00 per $100 of insurance. To provide theft cover, an additional $.25 might be added. "All-risks" cover would generate a total rate of, perhaps, $1.50 per $100 of insurance. Underwriters may also take into consideration the competence and reputation of the trucking company when rating risks.

Some of the questions asked by the underwriter are:

1. How is the shipment to be made (e.g., public trucker, railroad, owned or rented truck)?
2. If by public trucker, what is the trucker's experience, financial status, and reputation? (This is even more important since the passage of the Motor Carrier Act of 1980 makes it easier for new carriers to enter the motor truck field and has increased competition.)
3. If theft coverage is requested, what protective methods and devices will be used?

Furniture is usually shipped under a "released" bill of lading. Consequently, the underwriter's subrogation rights are greatly reduced. If the same shipment were to be made by rail, the rate charged could be as much as 50 percent less than the rate for a public truck shipment because rail shipments are generally less hazardous. On the other hand, if the insured uses a personally owned or hired truck, the underwriter would want to know whether the driver is capable of handling a heavy vehicle. If acceptable, the rate would probably be 15 percent to 20 percent higher than the public truck shipment in view of the absence of any subrogation rights.

It should be understood that the rating and underwriting of nonfiled classes of business are interrelated. If the underwriter feels that a risk is more hazardous than normal, the rate should be increased. Of course, if it is felt that the exposure is too great, the risk may have to be declined. This should be done only after making sure that there is not some way that the shipment can be made in a manner safe enough to qualify for coverage.

Distinguishing Among Floaters

Many people who are otherwise well-versed in property and liability insurance underwriting have difficulty distinguishing among the personal property floater, the personal effects floater, and the personal articles floater. Some even use the terms interchangeably. Following are brief descriptions of all three:

1. *The personal property floater* is an "all-risks" policy that covers personal property owned, used, or worn by the insured and members of the insured's family of the same household in all situations except as excluded. The policy covers property on a blanket basis, as well as twelve categories of more specific items of value (e.g., silverware, clothing, cameras, guns, etc.) that an insured may prefer to schedule.

2. *The personal effects floater* is also an "all-risks" contract but much more restricted in its scope than the personal property floater. Its purpose is merely to cover *personal effects such as are usually carried by travelers* and which are owned, used, or worn by the insureds and their unmarried children residing together. It is not the intent of the policy to cover furniture or other property which travelers do not carry with them.
3. *The personal articles floater* is simply a combination policy to cover various classes of valuable property under one policy instead of several individual policies. Prior to its existence, the rules filed with the state insurance departments did not provide for insuring more than one class under the same policy. The personal articles floater, however, may insure jewelry, furs, fine arts, cameras, musical instruments, silverware, and other property. Coverage is no different from that provided under individual policies and, in addition to the advantage of having just one policy rather than several, only one minimum premium is required (i.e., the minimum applicable to the class that requires the highest minimum premium as provided for in the rules).

PLEASURE BOAT INSURANCE

Following World War II, pleasure boating started to become one of America's favorite pastimes. In previous years, it was mostly the affluent who could afford to own and operate pleasure boats, but today families of all income groups have taken an interest in boating, and the result has been a booming pleasure boat industry. The growth of boating has also resulted in a concurrent growth in the volume of pleasure boat insurance to the extent that it has become an important segment of the inland marine insurance business. For the 1976-1980 period, the industrywide premium volume of outboard boat, canoes and rowboats, and outboard motors class business amounted to $449 million. This class is the second largest personal inland marine class. The inboard and other classes are much smaller (e.g., according to ISO data only, about $83 million versus $29 million). Coverage for pleasure boat insurance is not standardized. Many of the statements made in this section are made upon what many insurers who write the business are doing. There are no "standard" forms.

Underwriters generally segregate pleasure boats into the following classes:

1. outboard motorboats,
2. inboard/outboard motorboats,

3. inboard motorboats, and
4. sailboats.

Each one of the above classes contains subcategories that, to some extent, may be arbitrary. There is a great diversity in the way underwriters treat pleasure boat insurance, and it is one area of insurance where innovation and individuality prevail. Rating is an example. Some underwriters of inboard boats have one set of rates for "runabouts" (the smaller types of boats which are usually capable of relatively high speeds) and another set for cabin cruisers, which are slower. Some allow rate credits for insureds who have Power Squadron training; others do not. The Power Squadron is a national organization composed of people who are interested in pleasure boating. It offers courses in boating safety, maintenance, navigation, and related courses. Some companies grant credits for low-powered boat risks; others do not differentiate.

Traditionally, *outboard* motorboat insurance has been treated as inland marine insurance. *Inboard* craft, on the other hand, have generally been handled by ocean marine underwriters. Undoubtedly, the reason is that outboards are, by comparison, smaller than inboards and they do not venture out into the seas to the same extent. They are usually used closer to shore and generally not for long voyages. Although both are subject to many similar perils, inboards are usually heavier and require at least a modicum of boating experience depending, of course, on size and power, as well as other factors. Often, a person will start out with an outboard and later purchase an inboard. In any event, it is generally conceded that inboard underwriting requires a broader knowledge of boats and the hazards to which they are subjected than outboard underwriting. This should not be interpreted to mean that outboards should not be carefully underwritten. Quite the contrary. Indiscriminate underwriting of outboards can indeed be costly to insurers, and there is no question at all that sound standards of risk acceptance are prerequisites to profitable underwriting of the class.

Outboard Motorboats

Most outboard policies are written on an "all-risks" basis. They cover the *actual cash value* of the insured property at the time of loss subject to the limit(s) of liability of each insured item. The amount of insurance is broken down to apply to three or four classes of property as shown in Exhibit 10-4.

Policy Exclusions As in every "all-risks" policy, the exclusions must be studied to determine the extent of the coverage. Typical

Exhibit 10-4
Classes of Outboard Motorboat Insurance

Items	Limit of Liability
Item 1 Outboard motorboat, including its equipment (except motors) permanently attached. MANUFACTURER LENGTH MODEL NO. SERIAL NO. YEAR	$________
Item 2 Outboard motor(s), including equipment pertaining thereto consisting of electric starting equipment and controls. MANUFACTURER HORSEPOWER MODEL NO. SERIAL NO. YEAR	$________
Item 3 Outboard motorboat equipment as described in Items 1 or 2 above consisting of anchors, life preservers, portable fuel containers, fire extinguishers, lines seat cushions, horns, batteries, pumps, boat covers, flags, oars and oar locks, and similar mobile equipment.	$________
Item 4 Boat trailer used and designed for carrying the outboard motorboat described in Item 1. MANUFACTURER SERIAL NO. YEAR	$________

exclusions found in boat policies, in addition to the standard war and nuclear incident clauses, are:

1. loss or damage caused by wear, tear, gradual deterioration, inherent vice, latent defect, mechanical breakdown or faulty manufacture, corrosion, rust, dampness of atmosphere, freezing or extremes of temperature;
2. loss or damage caused by repairing, adjusting, servicing, or maintenance operation, unless fire ensues and then only for the loss or damage by such ensuing fire; and
3. loss or damage caused by infidelity of the insured's employees or persons to whom the insured property may be entrusted.

The wear and tear and the repair and adjustment exclusions are inserted to confine coverage to losses of a fortuitous nature and to reduce the likelihood of providing coverage for maintenance type claims.

Special Conditions Most outboard motorboat policies contain special conditions that nullify coverage if the insured property is:

1. used as a public or livery conveyance for carrying passengers for compensation;
2. rented by the insured to others;
3. used in any illicit or prohibited trade or transportation; or
4. while operated in any official race or speed test.

To be meaningful, rates must be determined by grouping a large number of homogeneous exposure units. These above exposures create a much greater exposure than anticipated. If underwriters were to cover livery or rented boats in the same group as those used for only personal recreation purposes, the greater exposure of such risks to loss would adversely affect the loss experience of the group (and the insurer) and require higher rates. The same reasoning applies to boats operated in any official race or speed test. Special condition (3) applying to any illicit or prohibited trade or transportation is, to a great extent, redundant inasmuch as insurance contracts which are against public policy are not enforceable.

Other special conditions of coverage often found in outboard motorboat policies are:

1. A full (100 percent) coinsurance clause applicable to miscellaneous items of boat equipment, such as boat covers, oar locks, fire extinguishers, batteries, and the like. (Most losses being partial, some insureds would take a chance and insure only a part of their miscellaneous equipment. The coinsurance clause would penalize them for maintaining only partial insurance, thus encouraging insurance to value on miscellaneous boat equipment.)
2. A clause stating that no recovery for a total loss shall be made unless the expense of recovering and repairing the property insured shall exceed the amount of insurance. (This clause is included to forestall disagreement in event an insured refuses to accept an adjustment based on the cost to repair by asserting that the boat will not be satisfactory when repaired. That is, the insured cannot insist upon payment of a total loss if the cost to recover and repair the boat is less than the amount of insurance.)
3. A so-called "repair clause" that the insured will accept repairs of plywood, plastic, fiberglass, and molded hull boats (when

repairable) in accordance with manufacturer's specifications or accepted repair practices, and that there shall be no abandonment of the insured property to the insurance company. (This clause is included for much the same reason as the preceding clause—to make it clear that reasonable repairs will be accepted.)

4. A substitute acquisition clause (for the convenience and protection of the insured) to provide coverage on newly acquired property similar to the property described in the policy purchased for replacement. This clause usually applies for thirty days from date of acquisition.

Deductibles Although many underwriters still issue outboard motorboat policies with a $25 deductible applying to all losses, higher deductibles are becoming more popular. Some underwriters allow a credit of 10 percent off the $25 deductible rate if the deductible is increased to $50. A 25 percent credit may be granted for a deductible of $100. Whether or not an insured would accept a higher deductible would depend on the actual dollar amount of the deductible credit. Obviously, a 10 percent credit based on a premium of $35 would not constitute much of an incentive. But a 10 percent credit from a $400 premium might be worthwhile. A deductible primarily is used as an underwriting tool in cases where there has been a history of small losses or where underwriting information indicates the potential for frequent small losses.

Liability Coverage Most outboard boat owners have a homeowners policy or a separate comprehensive personal liability (CPL) policy (personal insurance coverages policy with a CPL coverage form, in some states) to protect them from liability claims arising out of owned or occupied premises and personal activities. However, the liability provided by these excludes liability coverage on outboards of more than twenty-five horsepower or inboards or inboards-outboards of more than fifty horsepower. Sailing vessels twenty-six feet or longer are also excluded. Within limits, if the boat is larger than these described, the policy can be endorsed to provide coverage. Liability coverage may also be obtained by endorsement to the outboard motorboat policy available through some but not all underwriters.

Underwriting Outboards Like auto insurance, the underwriting of outboards depends heavily on the operator. The most important factors to consider are training (e.g., Power Squadron) and experience. An operator should have a reasonable working knowledge of boating safety and be familiar with the waters that will be navigated. People who are new to boating present a higher probability of loss due to their inexperience in operating and maintaining boats, and unfamiliarity with the hazards of boating. Some new boat owners lose their enthusiasm shortly after acquiring a boat, leading to lack of proper attention to maintenance (morale hazard). If a boat is owned by more than one individual, the loss potential may be increased due usually to greater use and the possibility that each individual owner will assume that another owner has maintaned the equipment properly.

Some boats are kept at the residences of insureds and others are moored. Usually, the theft hazard is greater for moored boats, and underwriters should familiarize themselves with the mooring places subject to a high incidence of theft. Boats that are transported long distances may present an abnormal transportation exposure.

Waters in which boats are used have an important bearing on loss experience. Some waters are dangerous for small craft, and some of the man-made lakes have a tree stump problem whenever water gets low.

Age of operator(s) is important. Youth has its advantages but one of them is usually not prudence. Boats operated by children not supervised by adults should be underwritten with care.

The small boat/high horsepower combination has been an important factor behind many losses. Insurance on high horsepower motors alone is generally not acceptable to underwriters because the motors may be used on any kind of boat. Some of the boats used may not be sturdy enough to accommodate the power.

Occupation is another factor to consider, and will provide a clue as to the insured's financial ability to own and maintain a boat.

Finally, the past loss experience of an applicant may reveal what can be expected in the future.

General Information Exhibit 10-5 is a typical outboard motor and motorboat application. The questions asked should bring out the underwriting information required by most outboard motorboat underwriters.

The rates (per $100) for outboard motorboats include rate differentials due to training, experience, deductibles, and waters navigated. It should be noted that there are two important categories: fresh and salt water. Obviously, saltwater risks are considered somewhat more hazardous for small boats than for those operated in freshwater lakes and rivers. The higher rates for salt water use reflect the increased hazards of the ocean and bays.

Inboard Motorboats, Inboard/Outboards, and Sailboats (Yachts)

Pleasure craft larger than the outboards previously discussed are generally written under "yacht" policies, which are a form of ocean

Exhibit 10-5
Personal Watercraft Application

ACORD WATERCRAFT APPLICATION

SET TAB STOPS AT ARROWS

DATE

PRODUCER		APPLICANT			
		MAILING ADDRESS (INCLUDE ZIP CODE)			
		COMPANY/PLAN		POLICY NUMBER	☐ NEW ☐ RENEWAL
		EFFECTIVE DATE	EXPIRATION DATE	BILLING PLAN	PAYMENT PLAN
CODE	SUB-CODE			☐ AGENCY ☐ DIRECT BILL	

COVERAGES

COVERAGE	#	LIMIT	PREMIUM
HULL	1		
	2		
OUTBOARD MOTOR	1		
	2		
PORTABLE ACCESSORIES	1		
	2		
TRAILER			
LIABILITY (OR PROTECTION & INDEMNITY)			
MEDICAL PAYMENTS			
OTHER			
DEDUCTIBLES (BOAT #, TYPE, AMOUNT)		CREDIT	TOTAL $

OTHER COVERAGES AND ENDORSEMENTS TO APPLY

DESCRIBE ALL CREDITS TO APPLY TO EACH BOAT

BOAT 1

POWER ☐ INBOARD ☐ WATERJET ☐ OUTBOARD ☐ SAIL ☐ INBOARD/OUTDRIVE ☐			TYPE OF HULL ☐ CABIN CRUISER ☐ HOUSEBOAT ☐ OPEN COCKPIT ☐ ☐ SAILBOAT			HULL MATERIAL ☐ FIBERGLASS ☐ METAL ☐ WOOD	FUEL TANK ☐ FIBERGLASS ☐ METAL
YEAR	MANUFACTURER/MODEL				REGISTRATION NUMBER	HULL IDENTIFICATION NUMBER	
LENGTH	MAXIMUM SPEED	DATE PURCHASED	COST NEW $	PRESENT VALUE $	NAME OF BOAT		
BERTH/STORAGE LOCATION				LAY-UP PERIOD ☐ DRY ☐ AFLOAT	WATERS NAVIGATED		

BOAT 2

POWER ☐ INBOARD ☐ WATERJET ☐ OUTBOARD ☐ SAIL ☐ INBOARD/OUTDRIVE ☐			TYPE OF HULL ☐ CABIN CRUISER ☐ HOUSEBOAT ☐ OPEN COCKPIT ☐ ☐ SAILBOAT			HULL MATERIAL ☐ FIBERGLASS ☐ METAL ☐ WOOD	FUEL TANK ☐ FIBERGLASS ☐ METAL
YEAR	MANUFACTURER/MODEL				REGISTRATION NUMBER	HULL IDENTIFICATION NUMBER	
LENGTH	MAXIMUM SPEED	DATE PURCHASED	COST NEW $	PRESENT VALUE $	NAME OF BOAT		
BERTH/STORAGE LOCATION				LAY-UP PERIOD ☐ DRY ☐ AFLOAT	WATERS NAVIGATED		

ENGINE/OUTBOARD MOTOR 1

YEAR	MANUFACTURER/MODEL				SERIAL NUMBER	FOR BOAT #
H.P.	☐ GASOLINE ☐ DIESEL	DATE PURCHASED	COST NEW $	PRESENT VALUE $	OTHER	

ENGINE/OUTBOARD MOTOR 2

YEAR	MANUFACTURER/MODEL				SERIAL NUMBER	FOR BOAT #
H.P.	☐ GASOLINE ☐ DIESEL	DATE PURCHASED	COST NEW $	PRESENT VALUE $	OTHER	

ACORD 82 (10/79) PLEASE COMPLETE REVERSE SIDE

continued on next page

EQUIPMENT

#	TYPE	1	MAKE, MODEL, SERIAL NUMBER, VALUE, ETC.	2	#	MAKE, MODEL, SERIAL NUMBER, VALUE, ETC.
1	BILGE PUMPS	☐		☐	1	
2	COOKING STOVE	☐		☐	2	
3	FUME DETECTOR	☐		☐	3	
4	CO_2/HALON SYSTEM	☐		☐	4	
5	FIRE EXTINGUISHERS	☐		☐	5	
6	DEPTH SOUNDER	☐		☐	6	
7	RADAR	☐		☐	7	
8	RADIO DIRECTION FINDER	☐		☐	8	
9	SHIP TO SHORE RADIO	☐		☐	9	
10	ANTI-THEFT DEVICES	☐		☐	10	
11		☐		☐	11	
12		☐		☐	12	

TRAILER

YEAR	MANUFACTURER/MODEL	SERIAL NUMBER	# AXLES	CAPACITY

OPERATORS

#	NAME	DATE OF BIRTH	AUTO DRIVERS' LICENSE NUMBER	STATE	OPERATORS EXPERIENCE (USE OPERATOR #'S)
1					(PRIOR BOATS, YEARS, POWER SQUADRON, U.S.C.G.A.)
2					
3					
4					

LIENHOLDERS

BOAT 1	NAME & ADDRESS	LOAN #
BOAT 2	NAME & ADDRESS	LOAN #

GENERAL INFORMATION

#	EXPLAIN ALL "YES" RESPONSES IN REMARKS	YES	NO	#	EXPLAIN ALL "YES" RESPONSES IN REMARKS	YES	NO
1	Is the boat chartered to others?	☐	☐	6	Was any drivers license suspended/revoked? (Last 3 years)	☐	☐
2	Is the boat used commercially or for business purposes?	☐	☐	7	Did any loss occur during the last 3 years?	☐	☐
3	Is the boat used for racing?	☐	☐	8	Is there any other insurance with this company?	☐	☐
4	Is the boat used for water skiing?	☐	☐	9	Was any coverage declined, cancelled or non-renewed during the last 5 years?	☐	☐
5	Does the applicant employ a paid crew?	☐	☐				

REMARKS

BINDER/SIGNATURE

INSURANCE BINDER		IF THE "BINDER" BOX TO THE LEFT IS CHECKED, THE FOLLOWING CONDITIONS APPLY:
☐ COVERAGE IS NOT BOUND ☐ BINDER		This Company binds the kind(s) of insurance stipulated on the reverse side. This insurance is subject to the terms, conditions and limitations of the policy(ies) in current use by the Company.
EFFECTIVE DATE	EXPIRATION DATE	This binder may be cancelled by the Insured by surrender of this binder or by written notice to the Company stating when cancellation will be effective. This binder may be cancelled by the Company by notice to the Insured in accordance with the policy conditions. This binder is cancelled when replaced by a policy. If this binder is not replaced by a policy, the Company is entitled to charge a premium for the binder according to the Rules and Rates in use by the Company.
TIME ______ M	☐ 12:01 A.M. ☐ NOON	

IMPORTANT NOTICE REGARDING THE FAIR CREDIT REPORTING ACT: In making this application for insurance it is understood that as part of our underwriting procedure, an investigative consumer report may be prepared whereby information is obtained through personal interviews with your neighbors, friends, or others with whom you are acquainted. This inquiry includes information as to your character, general reputation, personal characteristics and mode of living. If an investigation is made, you can be assured that it will be handled in the strictist confidence.
If you wish information on the nature and scope of the Customer Report which may be requested, ask your agent for the address of the Company handling your account.

APPLICANT'S STATEMENT: I have read the above application and I declare that to the best of my knowledge and belief all of the foregoing statements are true, and that these statements are offered as an inducement to the Company to issue the policy for which I am applying. (Kansas This does not constitute a warranty.)

APPLICANT'S SIGNATURE		PRODUCER'S SIGNATURE	

FOR COMPANY USE

ACORD 82 (10/79)

marine insurance. The term "yacht," in this text, refers to inboard motorboats, inboard/outboards, and sailboats collectively.

A question frequently asked by those not familiar with power boating is, "What is the difference between an outboard and an inboard/outboard motorboat?" The answer must take into consideration their similarities—both are manufactured and sold to include the motor, power train, and propeller as a unit. Also, in steering, the propeller provides directional control for both types. The main, and important difference, is that the outboard motor is on top of the drive train which is vertically connected to the propeller underneath it. The motor may simply be attached to the transom (back) of a boat, requiring a minimum of installation work. The inboard/outboard unit is a horizontal combination with the engine just fore of the propeller. Instead of the entire unit being placed on the back of the transom, the engine itself is located in front of the transom at the rear extreme of the boat, and the power train extends through the transom to the propeller which, like an outboard, provides directional control. Thus, control is similar to an outboard, but there are greater hazards incident to inboard craft such as motor leaks, fire, and explosion. Exhibit 10-6 illustrates these two types of boats along with many others with which the underwriter should be familiar.

It is probably safe to state that small sailboats, up to about eighteen feet in length, are more frequently covered under outboard motorboat forms than are the inboard/outboard. However, the larger sailboats, many of which have small auxiliary inboard engines, are generally written as yachts. A key underwriting factor in sailboats is the existence and extent of racing, which is associated more with sailboats than with other boats.

Yacht Insurance Until the 1960s, most yacht policies employed the old English terminology of the Lloyd's contract adopted in 1779. There was a reluctance to go to modern wording as the old terms had been thoroughly tested and interpreted in the courts. But due to the great popularity of boating, the majority of marine insurance underwriting companies eventually introduced policies with more modern wording which now predominate in the market.

Today, "all-risks" forms prevail and, although many companies have given their yacht policies unique titles, competition has resulted in the coverage becoming quite similar (i.e., about as broad as possible).

The four basic coverages provided by most yacht policies are (1) *hull insurance* (to cover the vessel itself); (2) *protection and indemnity* (to cover the legal liability of the yacht owner); (3) *longshoremen's and harbor workers' compensation* (to provide the yacht owner with the insurance necessary to comply with the federal

Exhibit 10-6
Know Your Boats*

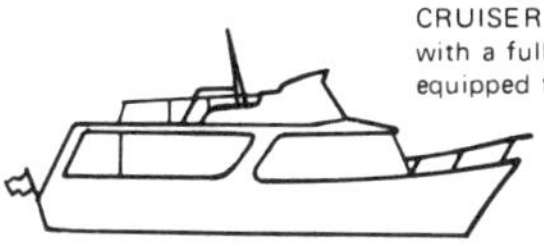

CRUISER – a power boat with a fully enclosed cabin equipped for living aboard.

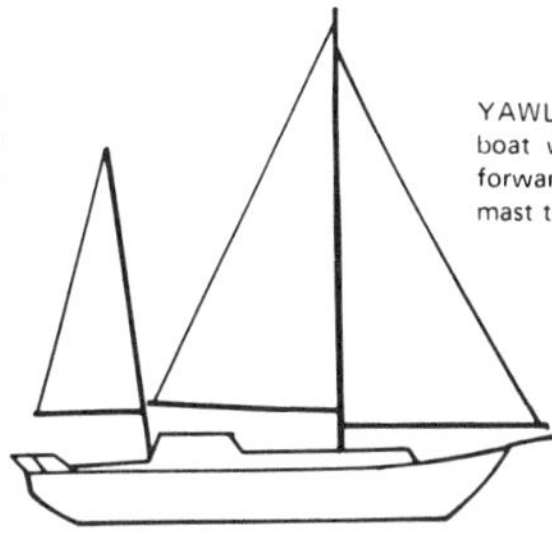

YAWL – a two-masted boat with the tallest mast forward and the shorter mast to the rear.

AUXILIARY – a sailing yacht principally propelled by means of sails, but equipped with an inboard engine to provide supplemental power.

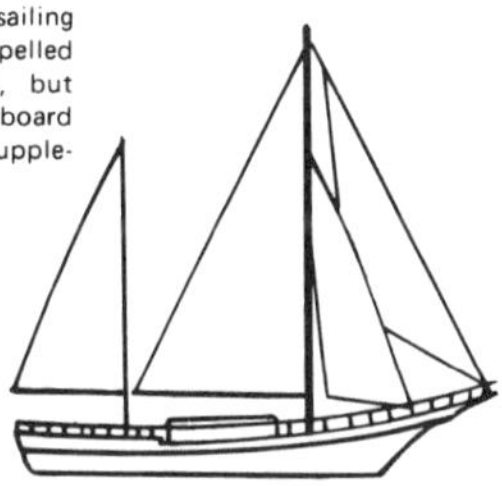

OUTBOARD – a boat equipped with a detachable motor fixed to the stern.

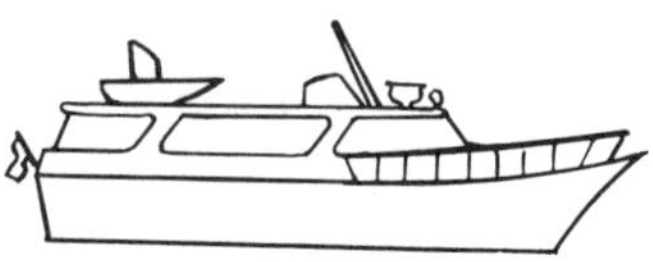

TENDER (Dinghy) – a small boat carried aboard a larger vessel, often used for transporting passengers to and from shore.

CUTTER – a single masted sailboat with the mast placed nearer the center than that of a sloop. It has a single mainsail and usually two headsails.

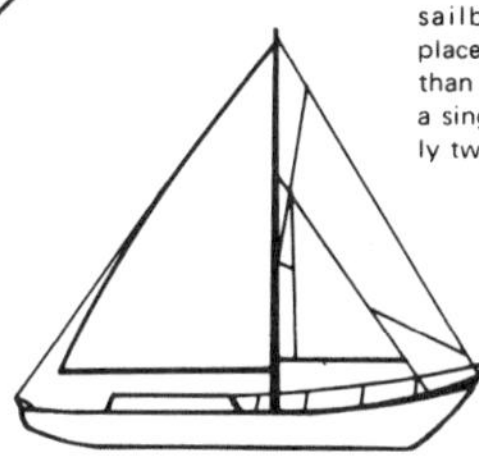

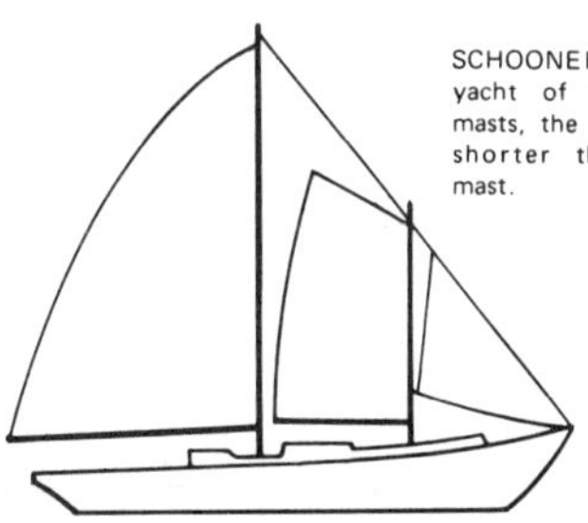

SCHOONER – a sailing yacht of two or more masts, the foremast being shorter than the main mast.

RUNABOUT – a smaller motorboat with an open cockpit.

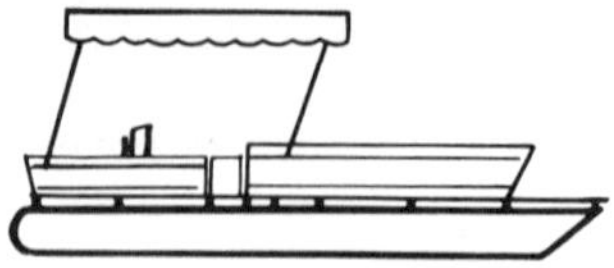

PONTOON BOAT — a flat deck placed on pontoons (portable floats), primarily used on inland lakes and waterways.

CATAMARAN — a boat with twin hulls side by side, usually sail powered.

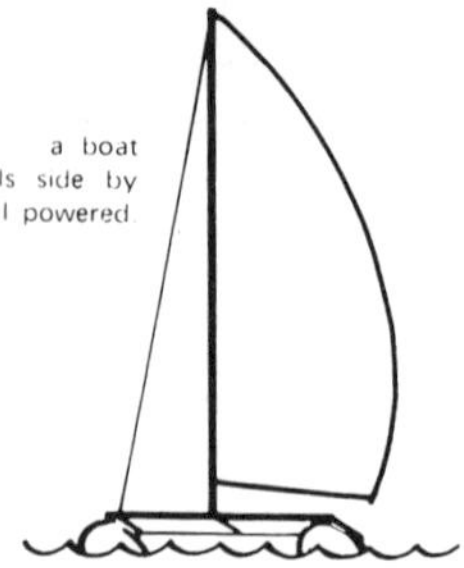

CATBOAT — a sailing boat with one mast well forward and only one sail.

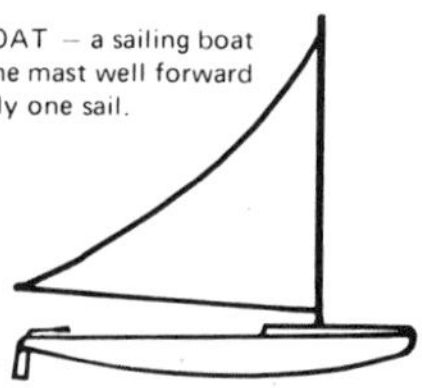

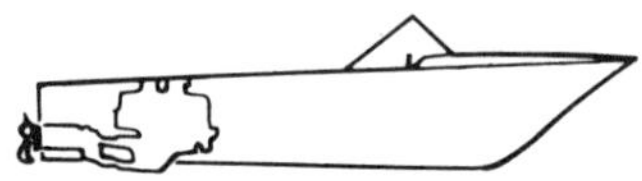

JETBOAT — an outdrive boat powered by an inboard engine, and equipped with a jet pump to propel the boat. The hull is totally free of any underwater propeller or protrusions.

SLOOP — a single masted sailboat with two sails (a jib and a mainsail rigged fore and aft respectively).

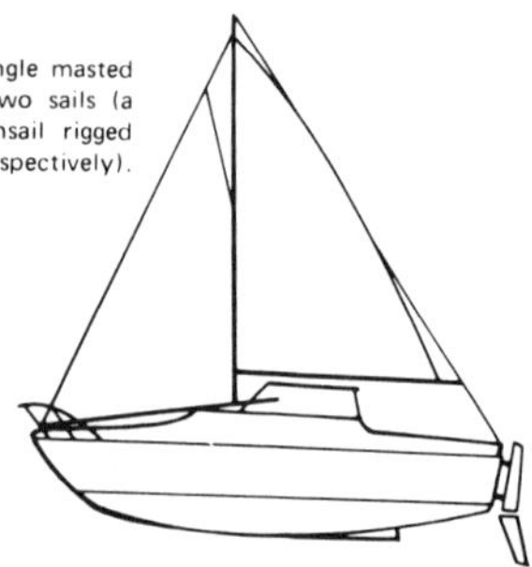

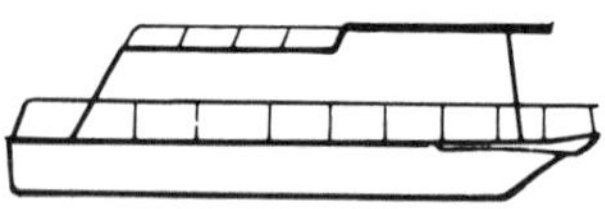

HOUSEBOAT — a power boat fitted for use as a dwelling or for leisure cruising, with a super-structure much like a house, and usually flatbottomed.

MOTOR SAILER — a combination of a powerboat and sailboat, with more power than an auxiliary, but with a mast or masts and complement of sails.

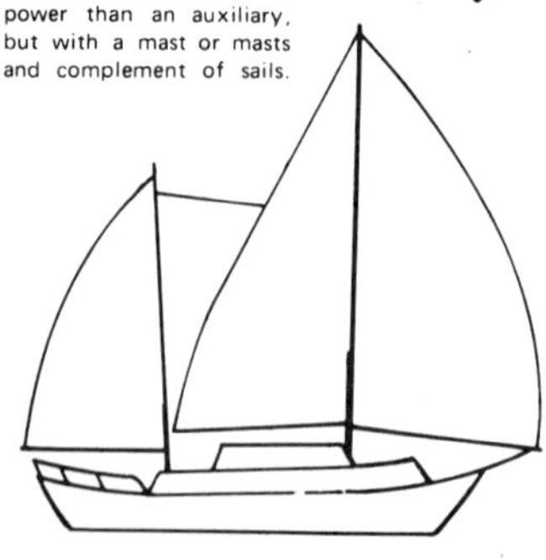

INBOARD-OUTBOARD (also called outdrive, stern drive) — Engine to the rear, but inboard, with the drive portion outside the stern.

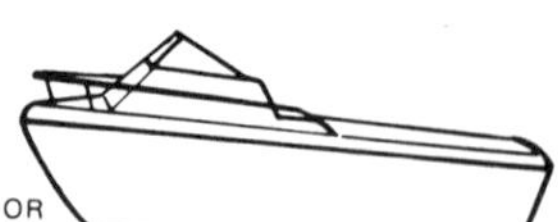

SPORT FISHERMAN OR CUDDY CABIN — an open power boat with a small cabin forward.

*Reprinted with permission from Aetna Life & Casualty, Casualty & Surety Division, "Marketing Report—Special Boating Issue," April 1972, pp. 24-25.

statutes, if applicable); and (4) *medical payments* (similar to that provided by auto insurance). Coverage for trailers is sometimes considered the fifth coverage.

Hull Insurance. Hull coverage includes the basic craft and its equipment consisting of spars, sails, machinery, and small boats (tenders). It should be understood that equipment of the yacht is covered but the term "equipment" does not include ordinary personal property, clothing, and the like that would not constitute normal yacht equipment.

EXCLUSIONS. As in other "all-risks" contracts, the exclusions must be examined to determine the extent of the coverage. The following exclusions generally apply to the hull coverage:

1. loss due to wear, tear, gradual deterioration, marine life, rust, corrosion,
2. mysterious disappearance of equipment,
3. damage caused by ice or freezing while the craft is afloat,
4. war, and
5. wrongful conversion or infidelity of persons to whom the insured property is entrusted except marinas, marine repairers, carriers for hire, master or crew.

All coverage under the policy is excluded if the vehicle is used in an official speed contest (except for sailing vessels). Another exclusion that is applied when insuring faster boats is the machinery damage exclusion. Although contact with submerged objects and debris does little, if any, damage to a craft operated at low speed, it can cause severe damage to boats operated at high speed. For that reason, underwriters exclude damage to rudder, propeller, shaft or machinery unless the damage is caused by burning, collision with another vessel, or sinking resulting from a covered peril. Underwriters may sometimes assume coverage for a substantial premium increase, subject to the policy deductible.

SPECIAL CLAUSES. Some special clauses typical to yacht hull coverage are:

1. Sue and Labor Clause. This places an obligation on the insured, in event of loss, to act as if he or she had no insurance at all (i.e., to use all lawful and reasonable means to recover or safeguard the property from further damage). Such "sue and labor" expenses incurred by the insured are covered by the policy as additional insurance over and above the amount of insurance on the yacht itself.
2. New for Old Clause. Partial losses for all but sails and canvas are fully covered (after applying any franchise or deductible

clause). When repairs are made, there is no depreciation, and payment is made on the basis of new for old. This creates a problem on older boats, as most losses are partial and it is equally expensive to replace a spar, for example, on an old yacht as on a new one. The problem has been alleviated to some extent by way of higher rates for old boats. However, the increased rates are often not considered sufficient to cover the other risks incident to insuring older boats, and many underwriters have an arbitrary age limit on boats they will insure. Others, if they are to accept an old boat, will load their rate substantially.

3. Navigation Limits—Navigation Period. Yacht policies limit cruising to certain designated areas. Common limits on the east coast are from Eastport, Maine, to Cedar Keys, Florida. Other common limits are the Great Lakes including the St. Lawrence River not above Quebec, and the Chesapeake Bay. Loss experience varies in the different areas as do rates to reflect the experience.

   Policies usually show the lay-up period for insured vessels which in northern climates might extend from November 1 to May 1. Obviously, perils of the seas are more severe during the winter months in northern climates and, unless there are extenuating circumstances, underwriters are understandably reluctant to substantially lengthen the navigation period.
4. Lay-Up Returns. Although insurance policies for smaller yachts do not provide for return premium if the vessel is laid up and out of commission (due to the expense of processing small return premiums), policies for larger yachts, say those valued at $10,000 or more, usually stipulate that return premiums for lay-up periods of fifteen consecutive days will be granted.
5. Running Down Clause. Traditionally, yacht policies provide a form of property damage liability insurance under a clause called the running down (or collision) clause. It forms a part of the hull insurance and applies only to liability for damage to another vessel and its freight and cargo, including loss of use of the damaged craft. The liability is usually limited to the amount of insurance on the hull. There is no bodily injury liability cover under the running down clause.
6. Valued Policy. Like most marine policies on vessels, yacht policies are usually valued contracts. Both the agreed value and the amount of insurance are shown in the policy and, in event of total loss or damage, the insurer is liable for the amount of insurance which is the agreed value.

7. Private Pleasure Only. The yacht policy warrants that the insured vessel will be used for private pleasure purposes only; that it will not be hired out without prior permission of the company by endorsement. Violation of any part of the private pleasure clause will terminate all coverages, as it should be kept in mind that the underwriter originally issued a policy based on the stated use of the yacht, as well as its ownership and condition. Violation of the clause could change the entire complexion of the risk and turn a good one into a poor one.
8. Continuation Clause. This clause protects the yacht owner in the event his or her policy expires while the insured craft is at sea by extending the expiration date until arrival at port of destination. This extension applies provided notice is given to the company and additional premium is paid as required.

Protection and Indemnity. Protection and indemnity insurance covers the insured's liability for loss of life, illness, and bodily injury (and limited collision coverage) arising from his or her interest in the insured yacht. The insured is protected whether the injured person is a guest on board, a member of the crew, or a member of the general public.

Under maritime law, a yacht owner's liability to the captain or a member of the crew for personal injury sustained by them while in the performance of their yacht duties is for "maintenance and cure." The yacht owner is obligated to provide "maintenance and cure" whether the injuries were sustained accidentally or due to the owner's negligence. The claimant could, however, disregard the right to receive "maintenance and cure" and bring a damage suit against the yacht owner if it could be proved that the injuries sustained were due to the owner's gross negligence. With respect to other persons such as guests or members of the general public, the owner's liability is limited only to those injuries which are due to negligence.

In addition to paying for injuries for which the insured is responsible, the policy covers litigation expenses when the liability of the insured is contested.

Protection and indemnity insurance supplements the "running down" or "collision" clause and covers the insured's liability for damage to all other types of property of others by reason of the insured's interest in the yacht as follows:

1. Loss or damage to any property interest whatsoever but only for the excess of such loss or damage that is not otherwise covered by the running down or collision clause in the hull section of the policy.

2. Any attempted or actual raising, removal, or destruction of the wreck of the insured yacht or property thereon, or any neglect or failure to raise, remove, or destroy the wreck, including the reasonable expenses in marking the wreck.

Those insured under the protection and indemnity section of the policy and the collision clause of the hull section include, in addition to the named insured, any person, firm, corporation, or other legal entity who may be operating the insured yacht with the prior permission of the named insured. This does not include a paid master or paid crew member or person, firm, agent, or employees operating a shipyard, boat repair yard, marina, yacht club, sales agency, boat service station, or similar organization.

A single limit of liability applies to bodily injury and property damage. If the insured has a protection and indemnity limit of $50,000, this means that $50,000 would be available for protection against either bodily injury or property damage claims or both.

United States Longshoremen's and Harbor Workers' Compensation Act Insurance. When the protection and indemnity insurance is carried, insurance covering the yacht owner's liability under the United States Longshoremen's and Harbor Workers' Compensation Act is automatically included.

This insurance applies to employees (other than the captain and the crew) and provides compensation for longshoremen and harbor workers when they are not subject to the state workers' compensation law. This insurance will apply principally to chauffeurs, butlers, maids, and other employees who, if injured aboard the yacht while it is upon navigable waters of the United States or in any drydock, might be construed as coming under the Longshoremen's and Harbor Workers' Compensation Act, provided it was held at the time of the accident and they were engaged in maritime employment.

Medical Payments. Medical payments coverage applies to each person, including the insured and members of the family who sustain accidental bodily injury while in or upon, boarding or leaving the insured yacht while waterborne. All necessary expenses for medical, surgical, ambulance, hospital, and professional nursing treatment, as well as funeral expenses (in case of death resulting from such injuries) would be covered if incurred within one year of the accident.

Underwriting Yacht Insurance There are no standard rates, rules, or forms for yacht insurance. However, competition keeps rates in line. If a company's experience calls for a rate increase, the amount of the increase must be determined in light of what its competitors are doing. Otherwise, an increase in a company's rate level could drastically affect its premium volume. Yacht owners often get together to discuss boating, and one of the things they talk about is insurance. It does not take long for the word to get around if one company's premium is not competitive with the rest of the industry. By the same token, a company that wants to "scoop the market" may do so—often to its sorrow when an adverse loss ratio develops—by writing business at rates that are too low.

What must a company do to keep this line profitable? The answer lies in either continuously adequate rates, stringent underwriting, or both. The particular action a company must take involves a thorough analysis of its losses including where they are occurring, causes, severity, and frequency. For example, if a company is experiencing a frequency of small losses, it may consider an increase in deductibles. If a preponderance of losses occurs in a particular territory, corrective action may be necessary only in that territory.

Like all other property and liability insurance, yacht underwriters must consider moral, morale, and physical hazards in determining risk acceptance. It is axiomatic that underwriters of any kind of insurance cannot win where moral hazard prevails. There is no substitute for an honest insured, and every effort should be made by underwriters to confine their writings to that type of person. Morale hazard—carelessness, indifference to loss—must also be ruled out. For example, an insured who neglects the boat and does not pay proper attention to maintenance will probably be a poor operator. If the insured has been involved in several boating accidents, his or her capability bears scrutiny by the underwriters. Due to the expense associated with boating, some people may not be able to afford to maintain their yachts properly. Certainly, a risk involving an owner of a forty-foot yacht with only a moderate income should be investigated thoroughly.

Physical hazards involve not only the condition of the yacht itself, but also where and how it is used. Underwriters should be concerned about the location of mooring—how well the boat is protected against theft, heavy weather, or other hazards while moored. The waters in which the vessel is used should also be considered. A particular yacht may be a perfectly good risk if used on relatively placid waters but not if operated for longer cruises in the ocean. Underwriters should satisfy themselves that there is no abnormal exposure with respect to how a yacht is used. Extensive business entertaining, for example, would affect the desirability of a risk.

Due to the serious fire and explosion hazards incident to boating, the type of power plant in a yacht has an important bearing on its desirability for insurance. The most hazardous, and also the most common, is the gasoline engine. Less hazardous and, therefore, less costly to insure is the vessel powered by a diesel engine. The least hazardous yacht to insure, from a fire and explosion standpoint, is the sailboat without power. On the other hand, such a sailboat might well be a higher risk due to its greater susceptibility to stranding. To minimize the fire hazard in a power boat, fixed fire extinguishing systems may be installed. In some policies, such systems are required under the hull coverage. Yachts should have safe electrical systems, safe fuel systems, and safe galleys to keep the fire hazard at a minimum.

Although most losses happen while yachts are being operated, many serious losses occur during lay-up season in boatyards. Underwriters should be familiar with the locations at which the yachts they insure are laid up and stored. They should not be subjected to any abnormal fire, vandalism, or theft hazards.

The speed of a boat affects its desirability for insurance. Even though the machinery damage exclusion is incorporated, fast boats are hazardous and they should be underwritten accordingly. For example, small fast runabouts used for water skiing are extremely hazardous.

To summarize, yacht underwriting is similar to other kinds of underwriting in that it involves collecting pertinent data to judge a risk's acceptability, although there are more underwriting variables to consider than is the case with many other kinds of insurance. Ownership, condition of the yacht, type, value, where used, how used, where stored, and speed must be considered and a judgment made from such information regarding underwriting acceptability, rate, size of deductible, and the imposition of any necessary policy restrictions.

Inspection and Engineering Service The premium for many of the smaller personal inland marine risks cannot justify the expense of inspections. However, that is not the situation in yacht insurance. Hence, underwriters frequently require inspections of risks they are requested to insure before they agree to issue a policy. Although inspections are often waived with respect to new yachts of certain manufacturers, most underwriters will order an inspection if there is any question about risk acceptability. Such inspections not only benefit the company as a tool of risk selection; they also provide a valuable service for the yacht owner who may, without the aid of an inspection, be unaware of serious safety hazards that may exist. Experienced marine surveyors generally are used.

Some of the deficiencies an inspector looks for in evaluating a yacht for insurance are:

1. dry rot in wooden hulls
2. cracks in structural members
3. safety hazards that could cause fire or explosion. Installation of the following may be recommended:

- flame arresters and drip pans for carburetors
- insulation of exhaust pipes
- proper means of ventilation
- the proper type and number of fire extinguishers
- an acceptable galley stove to replace one that is hazardous
- safe and properly designed fuel tanks, including proper fills and vents for tanks

As in all types of underwriting, both the insured and the insurer are better off whenever a poor risk can be made into a good one. Compliance with recommendations made by inspectors can often accomplish this goal. Another point to keep in mind is that an alternative (whenever feasible) to certain requested coverages is much better than a declination. For example, an underwriter may be requested to issue an "all-risks" policy on a yacht that does not warrant such broad coverage. He or she may, however, be willing to accept the risk on a more restricted form. If this can be worked out, the underwriter has salvaged a risk for the producer and company, and hopefully, has provided reasonable protection for the applicant.

SUMMARY

The term "marine insurance" broadly refers to insurance on property in transit. Due to the heterogeneous nature of the line, the Nation-Wide Marine Definition was formulated in 1933 and a Committee on Interpretation was founded. Revisions have twice been made to the Definition.

Personal inland marine insurance policies may be classified as (1) scheduled (furs, jewelry, silver, and so on); (2) blanket (personal effects, personal articles, and so on); and (3) combination (personal property floaters, stamps, coins, valuable papers, and so on). Some common characteristics of these policies are the "all-risks" coverage feature and the floating feature. Crime and fire are the major causes of loss in personal inland marine insurance. Some general underwriting considerations are the applicant's occupation, reputation, financial condition, loss history, and protection of the property to be covered.

The underwriting of scheduled inland marine insurance is generally simpler than the underwriting of blanket insurance because the underwriter knows exactly what property is to be covered. The major classes of scheduled inland marine insurance are (1) jewelry and furs, (2) cameras and related equipment, (3) fine arts, (4) stamps and coins, and (5) miscellaneous property floaters. In addition to the standard exclusions for war and nuclear incident, other typical exclusions are for wear and tear, insects, vermin, or inherent vice; and damage to property due to processing (unless caused by fire or explosion).

The broader scope of blanket inland marine insurance floaters causes problems for the underwriter. It is difficult to delineate the extent of the coverage, insurance to value is hard to achieve, and there is an inherent small loss problem.

The need for pleasure boat insurance has increased dramatically since World War II. Pleasure boats are usually separated into the following categories: (1) outboard motorboats, (2) inboard/outboard motorboats, (3) inboard motorboats, and (4) sailboats. The last three categories are often collectively referred to as yachts.

Some underwriting considerations for outboard motorboats are the boating knowledge of the operator, the mooring conditions, the waters in which the boats are operated, and the size (horsepower) of the motor.

Inboard and inboard/outboard motorboats and sailboats are generally covered by yacht insurance policies. The four basic coverages provided by most yacht policies are (1) hull insurance, (2) protection and indemnity, (3) longshoremen's and harbor workers' compensation, and (4) medical payments. While the premium for many of the smaller personal inland marine risks does not justify the cost of inspection reports, the higher premiums involved in yacht insurance make such inspections possible.

Chapter Notes

1. This chapter relies heavily on *A Practical Approach to Inland Marine Insurance* by James D. Youd, CPCU (Boston: The Standard Publishing Company, 1974).
2. *Inland Marine Insurance, 1976-1980* (New York: Inland Marine Underwriters Association, December 1981), p. 3.
3. This discussion of floaters is based on the ISO "Inland Marine Floater Policy—Personal Lines" (March 1977 edition).
4. *Inland Marine Insurance, 1976-1980,* p. 6.
5. *Inland Marine Insurance, 1976-1980,* p. 6.

CHAPTER 11

Personal Liability Insurance

INTRODUCTION

The comprehensive liability concept, providing insurance coverage for all the usual activities of an individual or a family on a broad basis, has proven to be practical, affordable, and successful in its operation. This liability approach requires that coverage be limited by exclusion rather than by the insuring agreements, and it is similar to insuring property on an "all-risks" basis.

The comprehensive personal liability policy (CPL), of course, was a change from the previous concept of providing coverage for specified or designated activities. Prior to the development of the CPL, a separate policy was used to cover each separate liability exposure. One policy would cover the exposure of owning or renting a residence, another policy would be used to cover the exposure of owning animals, still another policy would be used to cover the exposure from specified sports activities, such as a golfer's liability policy, and so on. Because these policies were purchased only when there was a very real, and generally very hazardous exposure, there was adverse selection against the insurance companies. It was necessary to charge a relatively high premium on most of these policies because the small number of policies sold had to cover substantial fixed expenses.

By contrast, the packaging of all these insurance coverages into the CPL, with its indivisible premium, allowed a much lower combined premium. It diminished the adverse selection and provided for expense savings by eliminating the costs of issuing separate policies. The premium is based on a class rate, and little recognition is given to the wide variations in exposures among individual risks.

In 1981, the ISO began to file on a state-by-state basis the personal insurance coverages policy program. The personal insurance coverages policy (PIC) includes a policy jacket and declarations page to which a coverage form is attached. This policy and the coverage forms replace the previously used comprehensive personal liability policy, residential theft policy, and the residence glass policy. The language and format of each of the old policies was modified for readability but the coverages were not changed. Thus, under the new program, the comprehensive personal liability policy does not technically exist but has been replaced by a personal insurance coverages policy with a comprehensive personal liability coverage form. Since the coverage did not change however, people still refer to the coverage as a comprehensive personal liability policy. To avoid confusion and for ease of reference, this text will use the term comprehensive personal liability policy (CPL) to refer to the new personal insurance coverages policy with a comprehensive personal liability coverage form.

The comprehensive personal liability policy is designed for the average individual and his or her family. It covers liability which does not arise out of the insured's business or profession, or out of the use of an auto, airplane, or large watercraft. The policy applies to the premises where the insured maintains a residence, and to the non-business activities of the named insured and members of the household.

When CPL coverage was first developed, it was written as a separate policy. Through the years, the coverage was gradually made available in endorsement form for attachment to other policies such as comprehensive general liability and fire policies. As the homeowners policies and other similar package policy forms were developed, the CPL coverage became an integral part of the total package. Because of the packaging of this coverage with other coverages developing much higher premium, the underwriting of comprehensive personal liability often has been given little attention. Theoretically, there should be no difference in underwriting CPL coverage whether it is written in a separate policy or as part of a package policy. When it is made a part of a package policy, it still has essentially the same insuring agreements, exclusions, and conditions that are applicable when written as a separate policy, and the underwriting considerations should be the same. These underwriting considerations will be discussed in detail later in this chapter.

The CPL combines coverage for "tort" liability, "no-fault," and, in some cases, "statutory" coverage. The "tort" liability coverage is provided on an "occurrence" basis for all sums which the insured shall become *legally* liable. All bodily injury or property damage resulting from any one accident or from continuous or repeated exposure to substantially the same general conditions is considered to be the result of one occurrence. The "no-fault" coverage applies to medical payments and is provided on an *accident* basis, without regard to fault. This is to enable the insured to discharge what might be termed a moral obligation. The "statutory" coverage is granted in those few states that allow, or require, that statutory workers' compensation coverage for all employees, other than in a business, be provided by the comprehensive personal liability policy or comprehensive personal liability coverage (Section II) in the homeowners policy. Several states, however, require domestic employees to be covered under workers' compensation, but such coverage is provided by a workers' compensation policy.

UNDERWRITING PERSONAL LIABILITY

Coverage Features

The comprehensive personal liability policy may be issued to an individual or a husband and wife who own or reside in a private dwelling, a condominium unit, or a mobile home or trailer home, or who reside in an apartment.

The CPL is not available in connection with farms or business property other than incidental business occupancies such as an office or a private school or professional studio (for music, dance, or other instructional purposes).

There are three coverages included in the CPL: (1) personal liability, (2) personal medical payments, and (3) damage to property of others.

Personal Liability The personal liability portion of the policy protects the insured against loss as a result of bodily injury liability to members of the public or residence employees (except when workers' compensation insurance is carried or is required) and property damage liability caused by an occurrence.

The personal liability coverage is written for a single limit which is the company's maximum liability per occurrence for damages due to bodily injury or property damage liability, or both combined. The minimum single limit of the CPL policy is $25,000. (In March 1982, ISO announced a new homeowners/plus program which will raise the minimum liability limits under the homeowners, and thus presumably the CPL, to $100,000. The new program will be filed slowly beginning in July 1982 in order to receive feedback on its acceptance. It is possible the name will be changed prior to complete implementation.[1]) This limit applies whether one or several persons are injured by a single occurrence. For example, if judgments awarded against an insured for one accident were $18,000 to a guest, $5,000 to another guest, and $2,000 to a third guest, a $25,000 single limit policy would cover the judgments.

In addition to the limit of liability, most policies further agree to pay all expenses incurred by the company and all costs taxed against the insured in any suit or claim; premiums on any bonds; expenses incurred by the insured for first-aid required by the time of the accident; and up to $50 per day for all reasonable expenses, including loss of earnings or wages (but not loss of other income), incurred by the insured at the request of the company.

The CPL covers the person named in the policy, and all resident relatives. (Children of the insured who are away at school or college are considered as residing with the insured, and are therefore covered.) In addition, any person other than a relative under the age of twenty-one who is in the care of the named insured or a resident relative is also covered. Any person or organization that is legally responsible for the use or possession of animals or watercraft (covered in the policy) belonging to the named insured or the other two groups of insured mentioned is insured under the policy with respect to the animal or watercraft. For example, a neighbor may take care of the insured's dog while the insured is on vacation. The neighbor would be protected if the dog caused injury or damage while in his or her care. Likewise, a friend who borrows an insured's boat would be protected in case of an injury or accident. If the person or organization has such custody in the course of any business or without permission of the owner, they are not insured. With respect to the operation of any vehicle covered by the policy, an employee of the named insured or person included in the other two groups of insureds is covered.

The policy covers each location where the insured or spouse maintains a residence and which is shown in the declarations, as well as newly acquired premises to be used as a residence. Business property and farms are *not* covered by the CPL. In connection with residence premises, coverage is extended to cemetery plots and burial vaults; temporary residences and premises occasionally rented to any insured, such as a motel, hotel, or a rented seasonal dwelling; vacant land (except farm land); and land upon which a one- or two-family dwelling is being constructed as a residence for any insured.

Property on which any business is conducted is considered to be business property, and is therefore not covered. This also includes property rented to others and property held for rental to others by any insured. (However, if the named insured occasionally rents his or her own residence to others as a residence, the residence is not considered as business property.) If the insured occupies part of a one- or two-family dwelling for residence purposes and rents a portion of the building to others, the portion rented out is not considered business property unless the rental is for the accommodation of more than two roomers or boarders.

One important exclusion of most liability policies relates to damage to property of others that is rented to, occupied or used by, or in the care of the insured. This exclusion is modified in the CPL. The policy protects the insured for his or her legal liability in such situations if the property damage is a result of fire, explosion, or smoke. This coverage is commonly referred to as "fire legal liability." It is particularly important to any insured who rents a dwelling. If a tenant causes fire damage to the premises, the landlord generally looks to the tenant for recovery. Even if the landlord carries fire insurance, his or her insurance company will seek recovery from the tenant through the subrogation clause of the fire policy. The same situation would be true if the insured caused damage to a motel or hotel room which he or she was renting.

There are occasions when the insured assumes the liability of others under a lease or other type of agreement. Most CPL policies provide coverage for liability of others assumed by the insured under any *written* agreement relating to the premises.

Personal Medical Payments Payment, up to the limit per person, is made for reasonable expenses incurred within three years from the date of an accident causing bodily injury (as defined) for necessary medical, surgical, X-ray, and dental services. This includes ambulance, hospital, prosthetic devices, professional nursing, or funeral services for each person who sustains bodily injury, sickness, or death in an accident. There is no coverage for the named insured or regular residents of the household other than residence employees (with an exception to be noted later). Coverage applies when a person is injured while on the insured location with the permission of an insured, or while elsewhere if the injury or disease arises out of a condition of the insured location or the ways immediately adjoining. Coverage also applies if damage is caused by the activities of an insured (e.g., the insured injures a friend while playing golf; the insured's child injures a friend; and so on); by the activities of a residence employee arising out of duties of his or her employment by an insured; or by an animal owned by and in the care of an insured. The basic medical payments limit in the comprehensive personal liability policy is $500 per person. This is raised to $1,000 under the new homeowners/plus policy.

Personal medical payments coverage is applicable to injuries suffered by residence employees of an insured while at the insured location except when covered by workers' compensation. It also covers if elsewhere sustained and not arising out of or in the course of their employment. Servants may be injured by falls, cuts, and burns in the course of their duties. Outside employees, whether casual or regular, are sometimes seriously injured while working about the lawn, putting up or taking down screens or storm windows, cleaning debris out of gutters, or house painting. The personal medical payments coverage applies regardless of negligence on the part of the insured. Medical, surgical, hospital, nursing, and funeral expenses are paid, all within the per-person limit.

Damage to Property of Others While the previously described personal liability coverage protects the insured who is *legally liable* for property damage, the damage to the property of others coverage does *not* require that the insured be liable.

The protection afforded is similar to personal medical payments in that payments are made regardless of legal liability. It is intended primarily for cases where the insured has a moral obligation to pay for damage caused by him or her to property of others. An illustration would be in a case of an insured who borrows his neighbor's lawnmower and accidentally damages it while cutting his own lawn. This type of loss is covered under the damage to property of others portion of the policy. Damage must be caused by an *insured* and is subject to several other restricting clauses. This means that damage caused by animals is not covered under this insuring agreement but the insured's liability for the damage would be covered by the liability insuring agreement.

The limit of coverage under damage to property of others is $250 per occurrence in both the comprehensive personal liability policy and the comprehensive personal liability coverage of the homeowners policy. This limit may not be increased.

Occurrence Versus Accident

The CPL policy covers liability for injury, disease, or death, and damage to property of others caused by an occurrence. As mentioned earlier in this chapter, the term "occurrence" is broader than the term "caused by accident." When coverage is on a "caused by accident" basis, the loss must be caused by a single sudden and easily identifiable event. "Occurrence" basis includes the above plus a continuous or repeated exposure to conditions which result in bodily injury, sickness, death, or damage to property. On an "occurrence" basis, the cause of a single loss could occur over the entire period of policy coverage. For example, if an insured burned trash in his backyard, and over a period of several months, the smoke damaged the paint on his neighbor's house, the resultant damage would have been caused by an "occurrence."

Personal liability and damage to property of others coverages are on an "occurrence" basis, but medical payments coverage is on a "caused by accident" basis.

Residence Premises Exposures

All property owners, or tenants in control of property, have certain obligations in relation to injury caused to people who come on the land. Traditionally, the common law has divided this obligation, or degree of care owed to people using the property, into three major categories, which are (1) invitees, (2) licensees, and (3) trespassers.

Invitee The *highest* degree of care is owed to the invitee. While distinctions between an invitee and licensee are often not clear-cut, generally an invitee includes a person who is on the premises for the benefit of the owner or lessee. Probably the best example is an individual who goes into a store or other business establishment. He or she is considered an invitee and, as such, should expect that the premises are safe to enter. An example of an invitee for a personal risk would be someone who is asked on the premises for the benefit of the owner, such as someone called in to perform a service. Others could include mail carriers, deliverers, meter readers, and some government employees, such as inspectors or officers, who have a legal right to come onto the premises.

The status of invitees can be important to dwellings which contain incidental office occupancies. The basic comprehensive personal liability policy can be endorsed to cover an incidental office, private or professional school, or studio. The access of the public to the premises increases the possibility of injuries. This factor must be considered when evaluating a homeowners or CPL application with an incidental business exposure.

Licensee A licensee is a person who enters the premises for his or her own benefit, but with the permission, express or implied, of the owner. Included in this group are door-to-door sellers. However, the most confusing part of this category is that it generally includes social guests. While the guests are "invited" by the owner, they are generally considered as being owed only the degree of care due a licensee.

The law generally requires only a *minimum* degree of care to be taken on behalf of licensees. The owner does have to warn the licensee of dangers not apt to be seen (for example, a rotted step that might collapse when the licensee stepped on it) and must refrain from conduct which would expose the licensee to harm.

Trespasser A person on the premises who does not fall into either of the other classes, that is, is not there with the permission or at the invitation of the owner, is a trespasser. The owner of the premises owes the trespasser the lowest degree of care. In premises liability situations, few homeowners recognize that any duty exists. Many people think that they can do anything to a prowler, potential burglar, or other trespasser. This ignorance of *their common law duty* can easily lead to liability claims.

Little investigation is possible to determine the exposure to either licensees or trespassers. However, information may come to the underwriter that an applicant or insured has set traps or otherwise established active defenses against burglars or other intruders. Members of the public, and even some producers, are proud of such activities although they may be illegal. The underwriter must weigh the benefit of a lower theft exposure with an increased liability exposure.

Current Trends As indicated above, the likelihood of recovering from a property owner traditionally depended on which of the three categories he or she belonged to—invitee, licensee, or trespasser. A more recent trend in some states is to ignore these distinctions and to make judgments based on ordinary negligence standards. In other words, the owner would be held to that degree of care that a reasonable person should exercise in similar circumstances. Obviously, expansion of this concept could have an effect on underwriting.

The Attractive Nuisance Doctrine An attractive nuisance is an artificial or unusual condition which can be expected to attract children. Examples are swimming pools, swing sets, play houses, and so on. The attractive nuisance doctrine is particularly important in residence liability underwriting, since this condition often exists in typical residential premises. While legal application of this doctrine varies from state to state, the effect of the attractive nuisance doctrine where it exists is to change the legal status of certain trespassers to invitees, thereby raising the standard of care which is owed by the owner of the attractive nuisance. The doctrine holds that the owner of an attractive nuisance has the duty of reasonable care to assure that young children will not be lured by this enticing or unusual object, to their detriment. Factors to consider in underwriting the attractive nuisance are discussed later in this chapter.

Factors in Identifying or Measuring Hazards

The CPL is a personal liability policy—therefore, to an underwriter, a critical factor is the personal habits and activities of the insured. In addition to the named insured, the personal activities of relatives who reside in the household also must be considered.

Occupation The occupation and employment record of the applicant are important for two reasons. The first reason is to determine stability, responsibility, and the other similar factors which affect desirability for other lines; ordinarily this is handled in conjunction with underwriting other coverages. The second reason is to determine possible business exposures on the premises (such as a private school).

Attitude Toward Premises Housekeeping and maintenance of the premises are key indicators of potential losses. Fortunately, these are also critical in underwriting the property portions of homeowners policies, so the two types of exposures can be handled together. Generally, a condition which would result in rejection of a property line will also cause rejection of the liability, even if submitted as a separate policy.

Claim History Another indicator of possible future losses is the history of claims. This is as true of personal liability as it is of auto liability or property lines. For this reason, applications ordinarily request information on all losses during the past several years.

If losses have occurred, the same type of alternatives are presented to the underwriter as on other lines. Depending upon the type of loss, an exposure may be excluded, the application may be rejected, or the coverage may be written as requested. Deductibles are rarely used on personal liability lines.

Personal Activities A major exposure under the CPL is the personal activities of the insured and members of the household, along with special hazard characteristics of a personal nature. Sports liability is one such area of major concern.

Golf. While former President Gerald Ford may have been the best-known golfer to strike someone with a driven golf ball, he certainly was not the only golfer to achieve this feat. Generally, the homeowners application does not ask if the owner or members of the household play golf, nor is it possible to determine the skill of any golfers that may be in the household. This hazard is one that is contemplated in the rate and there is little that an underwriter can do about it.

Golf cart liability is covered both on and off premises under the basic CPL policy. Off-premises coverage is limited to golfing purposes only. Many companies write a separate recreational vehicle policy which covers both liability and physical damage to the vehicle.

Watercraft. The basic CPL in most states excludes off-premises liability coverage for inboard or inboard/outboard (outdrive) boats of more than fifty horsepower, sailboats which are twenty-six feet or more in length, and outboards, singly or in combination of more than twenty-five horsepower. The primary purpose of the horsepower limitation is to avoid the waterskiing exposure and the liability exposure of large watercraft which are not contemplated in the basic rate. Although many states require an observer to be located in every waterskiing boat along with the operator, small, fast boats typically traverse the water in a bow-up attitude which obstructs vision ahead of the boat. The head of a skier or swimmer in the water is very small and hard to locate at high speeds, and the possibility of spotting such a person is even more unlikely if the water surface is disturbed by high winds or multiple boat wakes. If a person is struck by the propeller of a boat, severe injuries or death can occur.

The limitation on sailboats to twenty-six feet is also related to the fact that boats over that size have reduced maneuverability and require greater expertise to operate safely. One can fend off a twenty-foot sailboat approaching an obstacle such as a dock or another boat at slow speeds. Attempting the same feat with a sailboat that is twice as long may result in serious injury.

To some degree, the sailboat's potential for both property damage and personal injury can be equated with its size and therefore its mass. There is one exception. In recent years there has been a rapid growth in the popularity of small, fast catamarans (see Exhibit 10-7). These boats, fourteen to twenty feet in length, are extremely light and have no auxiliary power. In congested waters, or in any waters where the operator is unskilled or careless, catamarans can cause both bodily injury and property damage.

Other Sports Liability. Snowmobile liability is covered automatically under the basic comprehensive personal liability policy only while on premises. This would include some limited use in cases where the insured had a large lot or owned unimproved land. It also includes the "attractive nuisance" hazard of the parked snowmobile with respect to very young children who might be injured while playing on the parked vehicle. Most policies permit endorsement of snowmobile liability, usually for a flat rate per snowmobile, although many companies prefer to write a separate recreational vehicle policy. Liability exposures of snowmobiles include upset and overturn with injury to passengers; striking skiers, pedestrians, wires, or fences; and the danger of falling through the ice on frozen lakes and rivers. Ideally, loss history and a motor vehicle report on the operators would be useful for underwriting this exposure. A person with a poor auto driving record is unlikely to be a safe snowmobile operator. Once again, cost and data gathering limitations may preclude the use of this source of information.

Ice boats, although limited in number, present potential bodily injury liability hazards. Ice boats are capable of speeds well in excess of sixty miles an hour. Collisions at these speeds could result in serious injury. An ice boat of less than twenty-six feet in length would automatically be covered under the ISO comprehensive personal liability coverage as a sailboat.

Another sport which frequently results in bodily injury is hunting. In some cases, the cold weather in which hunting occurs is countered with alcohol. Guns and alcohol make a poor mixture.

Firearms. The increase in crime has led to more and more individuals keeping firearms in the home for protection. Most people who maintain firearms for hunting or target shooting are well versed in gun safety and know how to safely keep and store firearms. There are notable exceptions, but the record of gun club members is generally quite good. It is another thing entirely if a person who, knowing little or nothing about firearms, decides to buy a gun for self-protection. Such a person may leave a loaded weapon in a place where children can readily reach it.

Personal Injury An extension of coverage which is not yet very common is personal injury. This is injury arising out of false arrest, malicious prosecution, libel, slander, defamation of character, invasion of privacy, wrongful eviction or wrongful entry, and similar torts. Personal injury protection is not offered by all companies.

Business Pursuits The basic CPL excludes coverage for business pursuits. To constitute a business pursuit, ordinarily there must be two elements present:

1. Continuity—a customary, continuous engagement in a certain activity *or* pursuit of a stated occupation.
2. Profit motive—a means of livelihood, gainful employment, means of earning a living, procuring subsistence, or profit.

The CPL is designed for *personal,* not commercial or business exposures. However, certain business pursuits may be added by endorsement, such as sales personnel and office employees who are not self-employed.

Teacher's Liability and Corporal Punishment Like business pursuits, teacher's liability can be added by endorsement and can be extended to include coverage for corporal punishment. Under some rating plans, athletic, laboratory, manual training, and physical training teachers are placed in one rating group, and all other teachers in a second group. The first group contains those types of teaching activities more likely to generate a loss. For instance, either athletic or physical training teachers might have supervision of swimming as part of their normal activities.

Corporal punishment is a continuing problem in elementary and secondary schools. If the teacher does strike a child, the parents may bring an action against both the teacher and the board of education. State laws vary with regard to liability of teachers for disciplinary acts.

Premises Exposures In addition to evaluating the insured and his or her activities, the underwriter must also look at the hazards arising out of the premises and related exposures. Since the comprehensive personal liability coverage is most often written along with the homeowners policy, the basic source of underwriting information is the homeowners application. It contains so few questions regarding the comprehensive personal liability exposure that it is difficult to determine from the application if any attractive nuisances exist.

CPL losses tend to be low in frequency, but high in severity. This is the most difficult type of loss situation to control, because the low frequency makes predictability virtually impossible except on the basis of a very large class or book of business. This is coupled with the fact that the policy is usually sold as a package, but even when it is sold alone, it commands a relatively low premium. The expense factor of this low premium does not permit extensive investigation and inspection of the individual premises. The result is that the underwriter of this type of business is faced with a highly unpredictable loss situation which must be underwritten on the basis of scanty information.

Animals. The increase in burglaries and other serious crimes has led more and more homeowners to purchase large dogs for protection. While vicious dogs may reduce residence burglary losses, they are often undiscriminating in selecting victims, leading to an increase in comprehensive personal liability losses. A dog bite on the face of a youngster can lead to permanent disfigurement and a policy limit settlement. It is difficult to determine the temperament of a person's dog, since the owner usually is quite biased on the subject.

Information on dog bites usually comes to light during the policy term as a result of a claim. While it is unlikely that an applicant or insured will reveal information on previous dog bite claims, the underwriter may want to consider the following on new business if a previous dog bite has occurred:

1. Was the attack provoked?
2. Does the animal have vicious tendencies?
3. What is the total number of previous losses and circumstances?
4. How serious were previous claims?

Some states are enacting legislation making dog bites a matter of absolute liability. Under this type of statute, the underwriter will have to carefully review the circumstances surrounding the previous loss. If, after careful review, the circumstances indicate that the dog does not have vicious tendencies, that the attack was provoked, and that the applicant has exercised due diligence in controlling the dog, the risk is generally acceptable.

Horses are another type of pet which might cause injuries, and thus a resulting liability payment. While little underwriting can be done, concern should be present if a horse is frequently loaned to other persons, and if it has exhibited dangerous characteristics.

Other pets may cause problems, also. Where possible, full information must be secured. This is particularly important when wild animals are kept because the law usually imposes strict liability on the owners, regardless of fault.

Attractive Nuisances. The swimming pool is probably the most common type of attractive nuisance. Playhouses and backyard gyms including swings, slides, and climbing bars are also common. When the underwriter becomes aware that such hazards exist, the first underwriting consideration is the physical conditions at the premises. Many city ordinances require that swimming pools be fenced with suitable material to a height of at least six feet, and have self-closing gates. If a playhouse or backyard gym is present, what is its physical condition? Is it well-built or is it slapped together out of packing crates by two ten-year-old engineers?

An even more important underwriting consideration is the morale hazard. A six-foot fence topped with barbed wire is not a barrier to the neighbors' two-year-old toddler if the gate is always left open and is easily accessible. A well-built backyard gym may be dangerous if the homeowners are seldom home and let the entire neighborhood utilize it without supervision. Most applications ask no questions relating specifically to this point. However, the producer's overall evaluation of the insured should relate to this as well as to every other aspect of morale hazard.

Often the only way the underwriter becomes aware of such hazards is when the claim is filed. While physical inspection of the premises would have indicated the existence of a playhouse, for instance, cost considerations usually preclude physical inspections for a separate comprehensive personal liability policy. The underwriter may ask the producer for information indicating their presence.

Incidental Office Occupancy. If the insured maintains an incidental office, a professional or private school, or studio occupancy in his or her dwelling or in a separate structure on the premises, the liability exposure may be covered by endorsement.

An incidental office, professional or private school, or studio is usually acceptable if the premises are occupied principally for dwelling purposes, and if there is no other business conducted on the premises. Most occupancies are acceptable provided these criteria are met. Caution should be used when underwriting nursery school and day-care occupancies, when there is an indication that the applicant or members of the household are engaged in other than part-time babysitting on the insured premises, and in situations, regardless of the number of children involved, where there are activities such as swimming instruction, riding instruction, and so forth.

Any exposure involving an inordinate number of business visitors each day should be carefully underwritten. This includes studio occupancies such as gymnastics, exercises, aerobics, and other related activities. In determining if the number of visitors is acceptable, the following factors should be considered: (1) the age and/or sex of the business visitors (court awards may be higher when minors or young women are injured); (2) the income and social status of the insured as well as the neighborhood and/or dwelling in which the office or studio is located (a third party is more apt to sue a wealthy and/or prominent individual); and (3) the general upkeep of the premises. Because of the increased number of individuals coming onto the premises, it is essential that the insured exercise extreme caution and care in maintaining the premises. Sidewalks, driveways, and other approaches should be clear of obstacles such as low-hanging branches, or ice and snow.

Residence Construction. Most comprehensive personal liability policies provide coverage for a new residence in the course of construction that will be used as a residence by the insured. This coverage applies if the insured is acting as his or her own general contractor, or if the entire work is being undertaken by independent contractors.

A building site can provide an attractive nuisance hazard by enticing youngsters to play in the uncompleted structure after the workers have left. The coverage in the contract does not include workers' compensation for the individuals employed in the construction of the new residence, except for residence employees.

Dwellings Rented to Others. Liability coverage may be extended to residential premises that are generally one- to four-family dwellings owned by an insured and rented to others. Most companies decline to write a CPL for any risk where there is an indication that the insured is buying for resale, operating a motel, boarding house, or tourist court, or renting a multiple-occupancy building on a short-term (less than thirty days) or seasonal basis.

If the insured requests coverage on more than three rental properties, the underwriter may want to consider the following before reaching a decision on the acceptability of additional exposures:

1. What is the total number of rentals and what portion of the insured's total income does net income from rental properties represent?
2. What is the insured's intent (resale, income supplement, etc.)?
3. Who handles the rental of the properties and takes care of properties during vacancy (insured, friend, rental agency, family member)?
4. Have the properties been occupied continuously?
5. Are all properties located in the same town or same geographical area?

In general, rental properties are acceptable when occupied and cared for on a regular basis.

The above factors in identifying and evaluating hazards are not exhaustive. They are merely representative of the exposures that are most common in underwriting personal liability.

Sources of Information

Questions included in every application for a homeowners policy or separate CPL develop the information necessary to complete the declarations page. Some companies use more detailed applications or a supplemental application with questions directed toward the liability exposure. These questions ask about any business pursuits on the premises, any full-time residence employees, and any watercraft which are excluded by the policy but for which coverage is desired. They also concern any other residence premises, other than business or farm properties, because coverage would extend to them and a proper rate must be charged.

In spite of these questions many liability exposures are never revealed to the underwriter, at least not until a loss occurs. A careful survey by the producer might reveal a dangerous playhouse, but the cost of individual inspections and loss control activities by the company is prohibitive. When there are indications of unusual exposures, the underwriter uses the usual sources to secure more detail. The producer, the applicant, other files, and inspection reports are all possible sources.

The low cost of this coverage allows little expenditure of time or money to check potential hazards. Most investigation is carried out in conjunction with other lines, particularly on the homeowners policy. On the other hand, an underwriter cannot overlook the potential exposure to loss of $25,000 or more, and must secure adequate information on which to make a decision.

Decision Making

The alternatives are more limited on comprehensive personal liability than on most personal lines policies. Deductibles are not used, and seldom are limits of liability reduced.

On homeowners policies, the underwriting decision of the balance of the policy ordinarily controls the liability section, almost as an afterthought.

Some tailoring of the contract is possible. A dangerous dog or other animal may be excluded. However, applicants understandably want coverage for all exposures, and especially for those which are most serious, so an exclusion may cause the loss of the entire policy. If the exposure is too severe, of course, the underwriter must insist upon the exclusion, or may reject the application altogether.

It is in the monitoring of policies in force that much of the underwriting of CPL coverages takes place. On a new submission, the underwriter seldom learns of a dangerous dog or problem children, although it is the producer's responsibility to inform the underwriter if such conditions exist. After the policy has been in force for a time, a loss may be reported. The insured's dog has bitten the meter reader, or a child has thrown stones through the window of the house next door. At this point, the underwriter must make a decision. If it appears likely that more claims will occur, the dog can be excluded, but little underwriting action can be taken regarding the child. Often the choice is between nonrenewal or simply accepting the exposure. This illustrates another advantage to the insured of package policies: the underwriter might cancel or nonrenew a small CPL policy, but would give more consideration to the entire picture if a sizable homeowners policy is involved.

UNDERWRITING FARMER'S COMPREHENSIVE PERSONAL LIABILITY INSURANCE

Farmer's comprehensive personal liability (FCPL) insurance is a combination of comprehensive personal liability insurance and the business liability protection needed for farm premises, operations, and products. The preceding discussion of personal liability applies to the FCPL as well, so this section will focus on the differences.

Policy provisions, eligibility rules, rating rules, and optional coverages are quite standard. The program developed by the Insurance Services Office and used by most companies is the one explained in this section. Details may differ with some independent companies, but these differences are minor. The rules for the FCPL are included under the farmowners-ranchowners (FR) program discussion in the ISO commercial lines manual.

The FCPL may be written as a separate policy, or as an endorsement to another policy. This coverage is also included as part of the farmowners package policy, which was described in Chapter 8. Coverage is virtually identical under all of these forms.

Named Insured

The different circumstances involving ownership of a farm require flexibility in rating and coverage. The coverage can be written for an individual who operates a farm and lives on a farm; the owner and operator of a farm who lives elsewhere; the owner who does not operate the farm but rents it to others; and for joint ownership or partnership operation of the farm. A corporation may not be insured as a named insured under the FCPL unless financially controlled by one individual.

When the farm is owned by an individual, the policy differs under the various categories mentioned only with respect to the rating of the policy. The coverage for a joint ownership, or partnership, may be tailored to fit the coverage the partnership wants to buy. The coverage may be written:

1. to provide coverage for the partnership only with respect to the farm premises, with coverage for the individual partner restricted to activities arising out of the ownership, maintenance, or use of farm premises; or
2. to cover the farm operation for the partnership and the individual personal liability of one or more of the individual partners.

When a policy is written to provide coverage for the personal activities of individual partners—whether or not they reside on the farm premises—charges must be made for the individual residences of the partners.

Like the comprehensive personal liability policy, the policy must be issued to cover all of the owned residence and farm premises, but the policy may be extended to provide other coverages on an optional basis.

Commercial Exposures

There are three types of commercial exposures on a farm which are covered by this policy. They concern the farm operations on the premises, products liability, and the unique problems connected with custom farming.

Premises and Operations Since the intent is to cover farms and farming operations, the FCPL includes premises which the named insured owns, rents, or *operates as a farm*. Farming is an exception to the business pursuits exclusion and is therefore covered under the FCPL, whereas it would be excluded under the CPL.

The liability portion of the FR policy does not define farming. It only includes farming through the above mentioned business pursuits exception which reads "the policy does not apply . . . arising out of business pursuits . . . except activities therein which are ordinarily incident to . . . farming." One other method of writing this coverage states that "farming" includes the operation of roadside stands maintained principally for the sale of the insured's farm products. This classification is not necessary in the first case since the stands would be included as incidental to farming.

The policy cannot be written where the principal purpose of the farm is to supply commodities for manufacturing or processing by the insured for sale to others. Examples include creameries and dairies (but not dairy farms), farms operating freezing or dehydrating plants, and poultry factories. Also, the coverage cannot be written for farms whose principal business is raising or using horses for riding, racing, or show purposes.

It is the intent of the FCPL to extend personal liability coverage to include the business operation of a "farm" and incidental business activities relating to the operation of a farm. In extending the coverage to apply to farming operations, the policy fails to define what constitutes the term "business," because a definition might be too limiting if new processes or practices are developed.

As a result, certain incidental business type activities have been construed to be covered under the farmer's comprehensive personal liability policy as not falling within the accepted definition that "business" is the insured's "trade, profession, or occupation." In certain sections of the country, it is not uncommon for a farmer to have producing oil wells on his farm. This is, technically, not the insured's business and any occurrence resulting from the production of the oil has been held to be within coverage of the FCPL policy. In other sections of the country, it is customary for a farmer to allow individuals and companies to lease hunting rights during certain seasons of the year. It also follows that this is not "business" use of the premises within the accepted general definition and is, therefore, covered under the policy.

The underwriter should be aware that coverage exists for these exposures which are not normally considered to be farming. Inspection reports, claim reports, and information on applications and from producers should uncover these facts. When the underwriter learns that any such exposures do exist on an applicant's farm, he or she must secure complete information about the operation, and decide if the risk can be handled at the specified rate. If not, the exposure must be excluded, or the application declined.

Products The policy provides protection for the insured's liability arising out of farm products at no additional charge. Coverage is afforded by the absence of an exclusion, and contains no provision for adjustment of premium because of increased volume or varied products. There is the usual exclusion of property damage to products manufactured, sold, handled, or distributed by the insured or work performed by or for the insured arising out of such products or work or any part thereof.

Custom Farming Custom farming is defined as any farming operation not incidental to the insured's other farming activities performed by the insured for others at a charge under contract or agreement. The basic policy includes custom farming that is *incidental* to the insured's other farming activities. Note that this is an underwriting rule and not a policy exclusion. Unless endorsed, the policy covers custom farming regardless of extent.

Since a custom farming operation may well involve the use of heavy and expensive machinery such as combines and similar equipment by the insured's own farm employees for others, this type of operation may greatly increase the employers' liability hazard.

Since custom farming is included within the basic coverage with no additional charge, it is important that the underwriter monitor the amount of custom farming involved in a particular risk. When the amount of custom farming is more than incidental to the farmer's operation, an additional premium should be charged on an audit basis, determined by gross receipts. Since the term "incidental" is a judgmental one, careful monitoring is necessary to assure that the underwriter obtains appropriate premium for the exposure.

Important Options

There are a number of options available under the FCPL. The

forms which are most important are discussed in the following paragraphs.

Employers' Liability In the comprehensive personal liability policy, the only covered employers' liability exposure is for residence employees. In the farmer's comprehensive personal liability policy, farm employees may be covered in addition to residence employees. However, the basic policy does *not* automatically provide coverage for farm employees, such as those who plow, plant, and pick the produce, or are otherwise employed by the insured in the operation of the farm. This can include everyone from a foreman to a day laborer. These employees must be added in the declarations or by endorsement, and an appropriate charge made for them.

The following points summarize the treatment of employers' liability under most FCPL policies:

1. Employers' liability and medical payments coverage is included in the basic premium for domestic employees—not farm employees—at the farm or elsewhere. If there are more than two full-time employees, an additional charge is required (again an underwriting rule and not a policy exclusion).
2. Employers' liability and medical payments coverage on farm employees is optional in those states where workers' compensation is not required. The policy excludes liability for farm and residence employees if the insured has a workers' compensation policy or if the insured is required to provide workers' compensation benefits.

Animal Collision There is an optional coverage dealing with farm animals, other than dogs, killed by collision with a vehicle not owned or operated by the insured or his or her employees. The collision must occur when the animal is upon a public highway, but may not occur during transport of the animal. There is a maximum limit of $300 per animal.

A small premium charge is made for this coverage. Loss frequency is expected to be low. The underwriter should determine the loss history, if that is feasible, since poor fencing and proximity to major highways can easily generate an unacceptable situation.

Extended Medical Payments The manual rules make it possible to grant higher medical payments limits than contemplated by the basic rate. Further, medical payments might be extended to cover an insured and member of his or her household if they are injured while engaged in work which is necessary or incidental to farming operations conducted on the premises.

No coverage is granted for any person under ten years old or over seventy years old, nor to employees of of the insured, and no coverage is extended to accidents which do not relate to the insured's farming operations. Essentially, the underwriter should view this as accident insurance for the insured and his or her family. There is little that could happen to these persons which, with a little stretch of the imagination, would not be deemed to arise out of farm operations.

Dwellings Rented to Others The policy can be extended to cover individual one- or two-family dwellings rented to others by an endorsement which amends the definition of "insured premises" to include the designated dwelling. Unlike the coverage for newly acquired *owned* dwellings, there is no automatic coverage for newly-acquired one- or two-family *rented* dwellings, because the definition of "insured premises" is amended only with respect to those which are designated in the policy. It is the responsibility of the insured to notify the company when a new rented dwelling is acquired.

Classification and Rating

The FCPL rating approach is similar to that of the CPL in requiring that charges be made for each farm premises and each residence premises of the insured.

If the insured lives on a nonfarm premises, the liability charge is made for the farm just as if the insured lived there, and other residence premises are classified and charged as additional residence premises maintained by the named insured or spouse.

If the insured lives on nonfarm premises and does not operate the farm but rents it to others, the charge for the nonfarm premises is made as if the insured were buying a CPL policy with the charge for the farm made under the optional coverage of "farm premises rented to others."

With respect to joint ownership or partnership operation of a farm, an initial charge is always made for the farm premises. Additional charges for the personal liability of various joint owners or partners will vary depending upon the coverage selected by the owners.

Special Underwriting Considerations

In addition to the usual investigation into the character of the insured, certain specific considerations are peculiar to the FCPL coverage. The definition of "farm" includes all residences and buildings on the premises. It is customary in many sections of the country to provide dwellings for farm laborers as an inducement to working on the farm. An underwriting factor to consider is the number and condition of such tenant dwellings on the premises. The dwellings in which the farm laborers live should be examined to determine the general sanitation and facilities for proper water, lights, and heat. The bodily injury exposure from fire resulting from improper wiring, and improper maintenance of premises, must be considered. It should be determined if hunting is permitted on the farm premises or if there are incidental "business" operations on the farm in addition to the regular farming operations.

The underwriting manual of many insurers contains restrictions against the writing of farms whose principal business is raising and using horses for racing purposes. The policy itself does not contain such an exclusion. Many farmers and stock owners raise quarter horses as a hobby, and these quarter horses are often raced at various tracks.

Some farms exist for the purpose of raising Shetland ponies for sale, and on the farms there are various show rings used to display and sell the ponies. Often, bleachers or grandstands will be set up for spectators, which presents an abnormal exposure for a farm. The same situation exists with respect to exhibit of cattle, both on the premises and away.

The underwriter would be wise to examine the general condition of the farm premises—the fences, buildings, residences, and so on. If coverage is afforded for farm employees, the underwriter should determine whether the insured pays a reasonable wage, the degree of supervision of the employees, and the condition and safety of equipment with which employees will be involved.

The same exposures are present in relation to the dwelling as under a CPL. Thus, the same considerations must be given. Of course, the personal exposures, like hunting and sports, are present in every risk except for farms operated by corporations.

Custom farming can result in increased exposure to loss. The underwriter should know the geographical area covered by the operation, and might accept only those traveling short distances and not involved in hazardous operations. Since the handling of the equipment is critical, a preferred risk ordinarily would be one where the owner either operates the equipment or directly supervises the operation and employs only experienced workers.

Special liability exposures may exist on farms where the public has access to the land. Examples are those where customers may pick their own fruit, farmers who permit picnicking on the property, and those who provide hayrides or other recreation for the public. Any unusual exposures must be checked carefully.

UNDERWRITING PERSONAL EXCESS (UMBRELLA) LIABILITY INSURANCE

The personal excess liability policy, or "umbrella policy" as it is commonly called, is designed to provide high limits of insurance ($1 million or more) for both professional people who have a malpractice or errors and omissions exposure, and also for others who need catastrophe liability protection as part of their personal insurance program.

Umbrella insurance, as known today, was first marketed in the United States in the 1940s by Lloyd's of London. In the early 1960s, American insurance companies began developing their own policies and marketing programs. Although coverage is not standard, most personal umbrella policies are very similar. The coverage provided by the personal umbrella is broad and is designed to cover an individual and his or her family for personal liability, auto liability, aircraft and watercraft liability in excess of required primary limits, and to include some coverages not insured in primary policies subject to a retention (deductible) of usually $250.

The retention does not apply to losses for which the insured has underlying (primary) coverage, such as an auto liability policy. For losses covered by the umbrella policy and *not* covered by any underlying policy (such as personal injury), the insured "retains" the first $250 (usually) of the loss.

Personal excess liability is a classic example of a low frequency, high severity loss exposure. Predictability is impossible on any individual risk and extremely difficult on a book of business, due to the relatively small number of exposure units. Loss reserves on individual cases are generally large, and very large IBNR (incurred but not reported) loss reserves are typical of this class of business. Thus, a large number of policies must be written to pay for just one large loss.

The underwriting of personal umbrella generally follows the pattern used by the company for other lines, particularly personal auto. So much of the exposure is based on the auto that the umbrella could be considered as being a high-liability limit auto policy; viewed in this way, the applicant must first qualify for acceptance for auto liability coverage.

At the same time, the underwriter cannot ignore the chances of loss presented by the other coverages. Some of these, such as personal injury and contractual liability, have a potential for very large losses. Persons who might be called public figures are the most susceptible to losses for personal injury, and are among those most likely to request such a policy.

The same sources of information are used as in other lines,

including the application, MVRs, inspection reports, and other policy files. A copy of the ACORD personal umbrella application is shown in Exhibit 11-1. Although most companies do not require that the underlying policies be written in the same company, it is common for at least some of them to be so written; in such cases, the other policy files are essential sources of information. If the underlying coverage is written by another insurer, the underwriter must be certain of the stability of that company. Some insurers require that the underlying insurer have a certain rating by Best's or higher (e.g., B^+ or higher). Outside inspection reports may be used more often on umbrella policies than on most other lines because of the importance of such factors as financial condition, public exposure, and personal habits. Any hint of possible problems must be clarified as completely as possible, because the potential of a large loss is so great.

Frequency of loss is seldom a factor. However, a series of losses under the auto policy, for example, may indicate a situation which could lead to an umbrella loss. The underwriter must establish a monitoring system which will result in prompt referral of such losses. Where such reports are received, a careful analysis is required to see if any underwriting action is needed.

Adverse selection is a serious problem in this line. Generally, the applicants for this coverage are those with an above-average likelihood of being sued, and those having substantial net worth. These factors can cause an increased chance of loss and higher than average loss severity.

Class selection is practiced by the use of auto acceptability as a general rule, supplemented by special umbrella underwriting rules. Individual risk underwriting is the key to a successful result. Applicants should be analyzed carefully, and any doubtful factors must be investigated thoroughly.

WORKERS' COMPENSATION INSURANCE IN A PERSONAL LINES CONTEXT

A new development in personal lines insurance is the trend toward providing workers' compensation benefits to domestic employees through the comprehensive personal liability policy or Section II of a homeowners policy.

General Nature of Workers' Compensation Laws

The principle of workers' compensation laws is that an injured employee receives benefits regardless of fault. In return, the workers' compensation benefits are a sole remedy for the employee; suits against the employer are prohibited (exceptions are being made to this last rule, however).

The basic intent of these laws is to guarantee that employees be protected against loss of wages and medical expenses from injuries sustained in the course of, and arising out of, their employment, regardless of their own carelessness or that of a fellow worker. Beyond this common principle, the provisions differ among the states. Most states exclude some types of employees, and the benefits vary widely.

Since this coverage depends upon an employer-employee relationship, workers' compensation is a commercial type of insurance. Its principal treatment is contained in UND 63, where more details of laws and coverages are given. However, householders may also have employees. Some of these employment situations are of interest to personal lines underwriters.

Domestic, Farm, and Casual Employment

Some workers' compensation laws state that all domestic employees are entitled to workers' compensation protection while others specify certain domestic employees that are to be protected. Included in this group are full-time inservants, such as maids, cooks, valets, and babysitters. Also included are full-time outservants, such as gardeners and caretakers. There is sometimes an earnings or hours worked requirement for these workers to be covered by the law.

Farm employees can fall into two categories. Those who perform domestic types of work, as described above, are covered under the same provisions as in nonfarm homes. The same number of hours are required. Outservants, under this category, are limited to domestic types of work, not farm employment. The other category is those who perform farm types of labor, working with the animals, crops, or whatever the farm work includes. These farm employees are the same as other business employees and are usually covered for workers' compensation benefits regardless of the number of hours worked.

Casual employment refers to nonbusiness, occasional work, not of a domestic type. This can include waxing the employer's car away from the employer's premises, repairing the employer's boat, helping to clear land at the employer's mountain cabin, and similar employment. Most state workers' compensation laws exclude these workers unless their employment exceeds both a time and money threshold, such as a task which requires more than twenty consecutive days and pays $300 of total wages in three months.

In all of these cases, individual state laws specify the extent of the coverage and the eligibility requirements. When questions arise,

Exhibit 11-1
Personal Umbrella Application

acord® **PERSONAL UMBRELLA APPLICATION**

SET TAB STOPS AT ARROWS

PRODUCER	APPLICANT			DATE
	MAILING ADDRESS (INCLUDE ZIP CODE)			
	COMPANY		POLICY NUMBER	☐NEW ☐RENEWAL
	EFFECTIVE DATE	EXPIRATION DATE	BILLING PLAN	PAYMENT PLAN
CODE / SUB-CODE			☐AGENCY ☐DIRECT BILL	

UMBRELLA INFORMATION

COVERAGES		PREMIUMS		CALCULATIONS
POLICY AMOUNT	RETENTION	BASIC	$	
$ MILLION	$	RESIDENCES	$	
		AUTOMOBILES	$	
OPTIONAL COVERAGES TO APPLY		RECREATIONAL VEH.	$	
		WATERCRAFT	$	
		OTHER		
		TOTAL	$	

PRIMARY POLICY INFORMATION

TYPE OF POLICY	COMPANY/POLICY NUMBER	POLICY PERIOD	LIMITS OF LIABILITY	
			BODILY INJURY	PROPERTY DAM.
AUTOMOBILE				
PERSONAL LIABILITY				

WATERCRAFT				
RECREATIONAL VEHICLES				

REAL ESTATE

LIST ALL OWNED, LEASED OR OCCUPIED RESIDENCES, BUILDINGS, FARMS, VACANT LAND ETC.

#	LOCATION	DESCRIPTION	YR. BUILT	OCCUPANCY
1				
2				
3				

AUTOMOBILES

LIST ALL AUTOS OWNED, LEASED OR FURNISHED FOR REG. USE

#	YEAR	MAKE & MODEL
1		
2		
3		

RECREATIONAL VEHICLES

LIST MOTORCYCLES, SNOWMOBILES, DUNEBUGGIES, MINIBIKES ETC.

#	YEAR	TYPE, MAKE & MODEL
1		
2		
3		

WATERCRAFT

LIST ALL WATERCRAFT OWNED, LEASED, CHARTERED OR FURNISHED FOR REGULAR USE.

#	YEAR	TYPE, MANUFACTURER, MODEL	LGTH.	H. P.	MAX. SPEED.	☐ COST NEW ☐ CUR. VAL.	WATERS NAVIGATED
1			FT.			$	
2			FT.			$	

ACORD 83 (10/79) COMPLETE REVERSE SIDE

Continued on next page

OPERATOR INFORMATION

SET TAB STOPS AT ARROWS

LIST ALL MEMBERS OF HOUSEHOLD AND ALL OPERATORS OF VEHICLES/WATERCRAFT AS REQUIRED BY COMPANY

#	NAME	DATE OF BIRTH	DRIVERS LICENSE NUMBER	STATE	VEHICLE, CRAFT, % USE, ETC.
1					
2					
3					
4					
5					
6					

EMPLOYMENT

OCCUPATION	EMPLOYER NAME & ADDRESS
SPOUSE'S OCCUPATION	EMPLOYER NAME & ADDRESS (IF NOT EMPLOYED, SO INDICATE)

PRIOR EXPERIENCE

HAS ANY LOSS OCCURRED ON ANY PRIMARY OR EXCESS POLICY, EXCEEDING $5,000., DURING THE LAST 5 YEARS? ☐ NO ☐ YES (EXPLAIN)	PRIOR CARRIER & POLICY NO.?

GENERAL INFORMATION

#	EXPLAIN ALL "YES" RESPONSES IN REMARKS	Yes	No	#	EXPLAIN ALL "YES" RESPONSES IN REMARKS	Yes	No
1	Any Aircraft Owned, Leased, Chartered or Furnished for Reg. Use?	☐	☐	8	Do you employ any Residence Employees?	☐	☐
2	Any Driver Convicted For Any Traffic Violations? (Last 3 Years)	☐	☐	9	Any Non-owned Property exceeding $1,000 in Value, in your care custody or control?	☐	☐
3	Any Driver With Mental/Physical Impairments?	☐	☐				

5	Any Real Estate, Vehciles, Watercraft, Aircraft, Owned, Hired, Leased or Regularly used, not covered by Primary Policies?	☐	☐		Primary Policies?	☐	☐
				11	Does any Primary Policy have reduced limits of Liability or eliminate Coverage for specific exposures?	☐	☐
6	Do you engage in any type of Farming Operation?	☐	☐				
7	Do you hold any Non-remunerative Positions?	☐	☐	12	Was any Coverage Declined, Cancelled, Nonrenewed? (Last 5 Years)	☐	☐

REMARKS:

BINDER/SIGNATURE

INSURANCE BINDER		CONDITIONS:
☐COVERAGE IS NOT BOUND ☐BINDER		This Company binds the kind(s) of insurance stipulated on the reverse side. This insurance is subject to the terms, conditions and limitations of the policy(ies) in current use by the Company.
EFFECTIVE DATE	EXPIRATION DATE	This binder may be cancelled by the Insured by surrender of this binder or by written notice to the Company stating when cancellation will be effective. This binder may be cancelled by the Company by notice to the Insured in accordance with the policy conditions. This binder is cancelled when replaced by a policy. If this binder is not replaced by a policy, the Company is entitled to charge a premium for the binder according to the Rules and Rates in use by the Company.
TIME ___ M	☐12:01 A.M. ☐NOON	

IMPORTANT NOTICE REGARDING THE FAIR CREDIT REPORTING ACT: In making this application for insurance it is understood that as part of our underwriting procedure, an investigative consumer report may be prepared whereby information is obtained through personal interviews with your neighbors, friends, or others with whom you are acquainted. This inquiry includes information as to your character, general reputation, personal characteristics and mode of living. If an investigation is made, you can be assured that it will be handled in the strictist confidence.
If you wish information on the nature and scope of the Customer Report which may be requested, ask your agent for the address of the Company handling your account.

APPLICANT'S STATEMENT: I have read the above application and I declare that to the best of my knowledge and belief all of the foregoing statements are true; and that these statements are offered as an inducement to the Company to issue the policy for which I am applying. (Kansas: This does not constitute a warranty.)

APPLICANT'S SIGNATURE		PRODUCER'S SIGNATURE	

FOR COMPANY USE

ACORD 83 (10/79)

underwriters must determine the provisions of the applicable law. All of these coverages are written as regular workers' compensation policies, ordinarily handled by commercial lines underwriters.

Comprehensive personal liability policies exclude bodily injury losses to any person, including a residence employee, if the insured has a policy providing workers' compensation benefits for the injury or if the insured is required to provide workers' compensation benefits.

However, employers' liability is included under CPL to handle those employment situations where the state law does not require the carrying of workers' compensation coverage, but where the injured person is an employee. For example, if an occasional babysitter or cleaning person is injured on the job, the liability and medical payments portion of the CPL will apply. These coverages are subject to the policy limits, of course. The usual common law defenses are available to the employer and to the insurer.

Recent Trends

The National Commission on State Workmen's Compensation Laws recommended in the early 1970s that benefits be extended to domestic employees. The goal is to broaden the scope of this coverage to more workers.

One group of employees which is not protected by traditional workers' compensation laws is domestic workers who work for more than one employer. An example is a cleaning person who works one day every other week for a household, and for other households the other days. Another example is a babysitter who works each evening at different homes. These people may be full-time workers but do not qualify for workers' compensation benefits under many state laws.

One approach is to cover these domestic workers, and perhaps occasional domestic workers as well, as an added coverage in conjunction with CPL. One advantage of this approach is that both coverages are related to a residence. Another is that most homeowners carry CPL insurance, either on a separate policy or under a homeowners or farmowners policy. Still another is that the premium for most households will be so low that it is unrealistic to write a separate policy; unlike a $200 or so premium on a regular workers' compensation policy, the annual premium for occasional domestic workers is in the neighborhood of $5, so it is most efficient to endorse the coverage on another policy.

The first state to move in this direction was New Hampshire, which adopted legislation effective 1 January 1976 adding workers' compensation to CPL policies. California was the next state to adopt this approach, effective 1 January 1977. Other states have followed. In New

Jersey, for example, many people were not carrying workers' compensation insurance, even though they were liable for the benefits, because it was not required. This situation was corrected in 1980 when by law, every homeowners and CPL policy was amended to include workers' compensation at a five dollar annual minimum surcharge.

In most of these states, the workers' compensation experience is required to be kept separate from other coverages. For statistical purposes, this is not part of CPL or homeowners, but is a separate coverage, added to these policies.

Since workers' compensation coverage is part of the policy in some states, the underwriting alternatives are limited. If an extreme workers' compensation exposure exists, the underwriter does not have the alternative of declining or canceling that coverage. If an adequate premium cannot be secured, the entire policy must be evaluated. Either the balance of the policy will support the added exposure, or it will not, and then the entire policy must be terminated.

From a workers' compensation standpoint, it is difficult for underwriters to secure much information on the desirability of a risk. More commonly, problems develop on policies in force, requiring reevaluation after the policy has been written. Because of this, the underwriter must establish a monitoring system which will permit a constant evaluation of the risks. As with other lines, a good monitoring system is necessary to maintain profitability.

It should be expected that the trend to extend the various workers' compensation laws to include all, or practically all, employees will continue. This is one of the "essential recommendations" of the National Commission on State Workmen's Compensation Laws, and the states seem to be trying to comply with these "essential recommendations" as rapidly as is practical. This is creating some unusual problems for insurance companies. Some companies writing homeowners policies or comprehensive personal liability coverages are not licensed to write workers' compensation coverage. If licensed, many are not staffed with experienced personnel to handle workers' compensation claims.

In underwriting the employers' liability exposure, the considerations should be essentially the same as when providing the full workers' compensation exposures. The major difference is that the determination of the amount of loss settlement with employers' liability is handled as common law liability and is subject to the policy limits of liability. Workers' compensation is handled as statutory liability with benefits as specified in the particular state's workers' compensation law, but with no policy limit applying. Another difference is that in employers' liability claim situations the injured party or claimant must prove some negligence on the part of the employer, whereas the workers' compensation benefit payment does not require proof of such negligence or even that any negligence is involved.

For example, assume that a policyholder has hired a cleaning person to wash the kitchen walls. The employer has instructed that only a stepladder, which is supplied, be used. The employee disregards this instruction and stands on a chair to reach one corner. The chair breaks, and the employee falls, breaking an arm. Under common law, the employer would usually not be liable; medical payments would be provided under CPL, but not liability for lost wages, pain and suffering, or medical benefits above the amount of the CPL policy. Under workers' compensation, if applicable, broad medical payments coverage would be available, plus loss of wages.

With respect to safety hazards, there is very little the underwriter can actually look for in this area. The premiums are generally too little to allow for engineering service on these accounts. Probably, the underwriter's primary concern should be the general attitude of the insured towards safety. Although this is very difficult to measure, it can often be estimated from reports on other lines of coverage such as auto insurance, the fire portion of the homeowners policy, and so on. The greatest loss exposure from the workers' compensation portion of the policy will probably arise from part-time yard workers, although there may be some frequency of back claims caused by lifting.

SUMMARY

A practical, affordable, and successful liability concept is contained in the comprehensive personal liability policy (CPL), which provides broad insurance coverage for all of the general activities of an individual or a family.

There are three coverages included in all CPL policies: personal liability, personal medical payments, and damage to property of others. The personal liability portion protects the insured against loss as a result of bodily injury to members of the public or to residence employees, and damage to the property of others caused by an occurrence. Medical coverage includes payment, up to the limit per person, for reasonable expenses incurred within three years from the date of an accident for necessary medical services. The CPL also generally includes coverage for damage to property of others caused by an insured, regardless of his or her legal liability for such damage. CPL coverage also extends to property owners and their obligation under common law to invitees, licensees, and trespassers.

The CPL is a personal liability policy—therefore, an underwriter must take into consideration the personal habits and activities of the insured, and any relatives who reside in the insured's household. Factors to consider are occupation and employment history, the insured's attitude toward his or her premises, claim history, personal activities, and sports liability.

Sports liability can be a factor if the insured is a golfer, operates watercraft or snowmobiles, or is an inexperienced hunter, for example. The existence of pets may be another factor to consider—for instance, a potentially vicious dog.

CPL losses tend to be low in frequency, but high in severity. This is difficult for the underwriter, who is faced with a highly unpredictable loss situation that must be underwritten on the basis of often scanty information. The attractive nuisance factor is an example, as is the morale hazard.

FCPL insurance is a combination of CPL insurance and the business liability protection needed for farm premises, operations, and products. FCPL may be written as a separate policy, or as an endorsement on another policy, or as part of a package policy.

The personal excess liability policy, or "umbrella policy," is designed to provide high limits of insurance for both professional or nonprofessional people who require this coverage. The underwriting of personal umbrella generally follows the pattern used for other lines, particularly personal auto.

Workers' compensation insurance is a new development in personal lines insurance because of the trend toward protection of domestic employees through the CPL. In all such cases, individual state laws specify the extent of the coverage and the eligibility requirements.

Chapter Note

1. "ISO to Introduce New HO Policies," *National Underwriter,* Property & Casualty Insurance Edition, 5 March 1982, p. 66.

Additional Subjects in Personal Lines Underwriting

CHAPTER 12

Electronic Data Processing[1]

INTRODUCTION

Insurance companies are under extreme pressure from regulators, competitors, and the public to make quick decisions based on current, accurate information. The increasing use of electronic data processing systems (EDP) has made this requirement far easier to meet. EDP systems can improve policyholders' service by reducing policy preparation time, increasing the accuracy of billing, and providing the data for timely management reports. While both computer equipment (hardware) and operating programs (software) involve a considerable dollar outlay, the services they provide can be well worth the cost.

In some companies, data are gathered for each producer every month on policy count, new and renewal business volume by line, and loss and expense dollars. These data are then aggregated by territory, state, and region to provide a companywide total. The EDP system has the capability not only of assisting in routine processing of business, but also of making reports available to management on the current status of a book of business on either an aggregated or disaggregated basis. The ability to identify problems by line of business or by territory, or even by individual producer, enables management to make timely responses to changing conditions.

Components of a Management Information System/Data Based System[2]

A *data base* is an orderly collection of business facts stored to meet information requirements. The ideal data base would contain all

Exhibit 12-1
A Data-Base Approach*

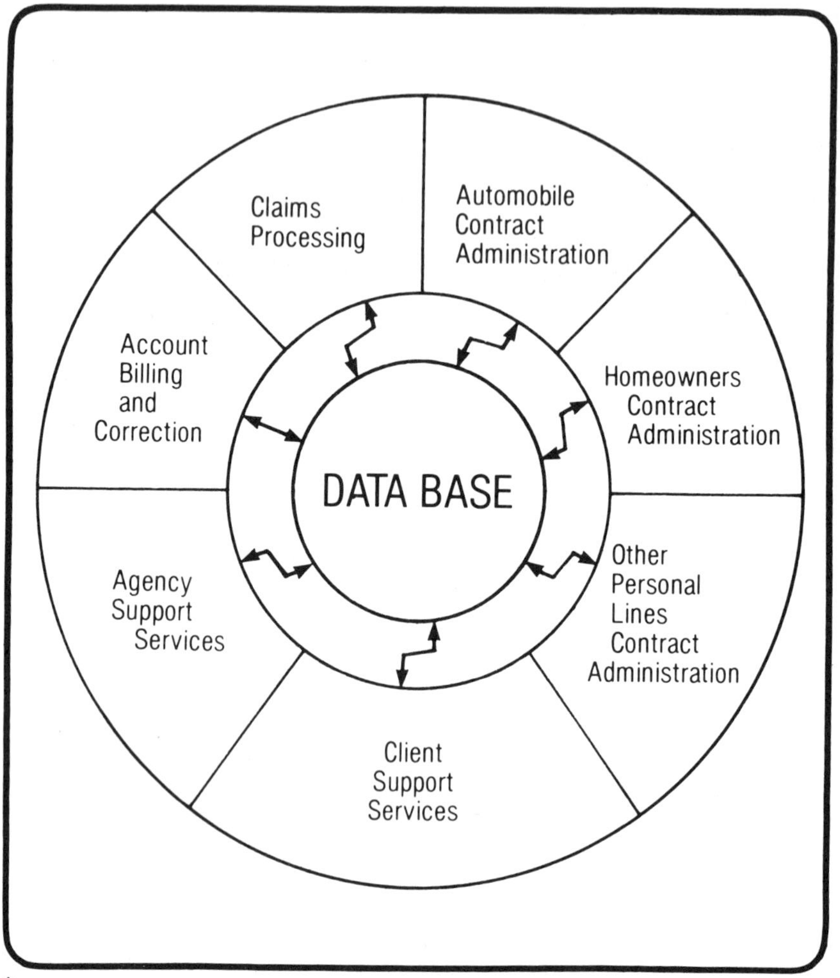

*Reprinted with permission from *Property/Liability Personal Lines Insurance: DB/DC Information Systems Design Concepts*, 2nd ed. (Armonk, NY: IBM Corporation, 1974), p. 25.

essential information required in the process of conducting a business. This data base would contain past, current, and forecast information which would be stored in a logical manner and available for retrieval as needed. Exhibit 12-1 reflects the manner in which the file information would be assembled within the computer under a data-base approach. The data base should be constructed in a *nonredundant* and *interrelated* manner so data items can meet different needs. Nonredundant means that individual data elements, such as policy numbers, appear only once (or at least less frequently than in normal file organizations) in the data base. Interrelated means that the files are constructed with an ordered and planned relationship which allows data items to be tied together, even though they may not necessarily be in the same physical file. If an insured has an auto and a homeowners policy with the company, the two files should be interrelated so that underwriting information can be "tied together." The data base should be designed to meet the needs of the marketing, claims, premium audit, loss control, and accounting departments as well as the underwriting department.

An effectively designed insurance management information system would ensure maximum use of information resources. Such a business information system should provide the following potential advantages:

- It would allow management to condition its experience and judgment with the pertinent information within the system in order to establish sound long-range objectives and operating plans.
- It would also allow management to readily deduce the significant elements of present performance and apply this information to strategic and tactical plans for the future.
- It would ensure that all plans and decisions are based upon the same timely, accurate, and consistent data.

DATA AND ITS PROCESSING

The information which is received or created by an insurance company is used for many different purposes. The following discussion shows, in a general way, how data are processed and used by some companies, particularly in the personal lines auto business.

Data and Data Sources

The initial data are used for underwriting, rating, recording of certain statistical information, and production of the actual policy. The same data are used to develop such items as premium notices, agency commission entries, and claims statistical information when a loss occurs. The sample matrix in Exhibit 12-2 shows insurance activities or functions and some of the operating data involved.

In this sample matrix, types of information are shown on the horizontal lines, and the functions which are performed on the vertical lines. The *X's* indicate the functions for which the data are used. For example, the policyholder's name, the second item of information, is used in the issuance of the policy, billing of the premium, verification of

Exhibit 12-2
Insurance Information Matrix*

	New Policy Risk Analysis	Premium Calculation	Policy Issue	Endorsement Underwriting/Issue	Client Billing	Agency Reconciliation	Agency Recording	Verification of Coverage	Claim Recording	Claim Payment	Renewal Underwriting/Issue
Client Number	X		X	X	X	X	X	X		X	X
Name			X		X			X		X	
Address	X	X	X	X	X			X		X	X
Policy Number	X		X	X	X	X	X	X		X	X
Line of Business	X	X		X	X	X	X		X		X
Coverage/Limits	X	X	X	X			X	X	X		X
Deductible	X	X	X	X			X	X	X		X
Risk/Exposure	X	X	X	X			X	X			X
Policy Dates	X	X	X	X	X	X	X	X	X		X
Rate Data	X	X		X							X
Premium Amounts	X	X	X	X	X	X	X				X
Claim Number								X	X	X	X
Claimant Number								X	X	X	X
Claimant N/A								X		X	
Reserve Amount								X	X	X	X
Agent Number	X		X	X	X	X	X			X	X
Commission Percent	X			X	X	X	X				X
Due Dates					X	X					
Amount Due					X	X					
Loss Summaries	X			X							X

*Reprinted with permission from *Property/Liability Personal Lines Insurance: DB/DC Information Systems Design Concepts*, IBM Corporation, 2nd Ed., October 1974, p. 33.

the coverage when a claim is presented, and the drawing of the check or draft in payment of a claim.

As indicated above, most data are acquired from the original application or coding sheets. Additionally, data are derived and created internally in order to provide information in a manner different from that on the application, such as by statistical codes. Further, as claims develop, another group of data will be put into the computer to reflect the claims activity. Internal to the computer, other data will be created as claims information is paired with policy information. There is a great volume of this type of internal generation of data, limited only by the defined needs of the company or the limitations of the computer system.

Steps in the Processing of Data

Once received in a service office of a company, the information on the application is keyed into the computer either directly from the application itself or from additional input coding sheets completed by personnel within the service office. Before the advent of EDP systems, this was done by means of a paper and pencil bookkeeping system, which later became an "accounting system" using key-driven machines (adding machines, calculators, and so on). Following that was punch card accounting, and finally the full computer-supported "data processing system" to process "information" (data).

No matter what device is used, the procedures to process data remain basically the same: (1) the entering of the source data or input, (2) the orderly, planned processing within the system, and (3) the end result or output from the system, such as the policy being issued, or commission being recorded to the proper producer. Processing is carried out in a pre-established sequence of instructions that are followed automatically by the computer:

- Read
- Sort
- Classify
- Calculate
- Edit
- Select
- Write

Each data processing system is designed to perform a specific number and type of operation. It is directed to perform each operation by an instruction which defines the basic operation to be performed and identifies the data, device, or mechanism needed to carry out the operation. The entire series of instructions required to complete a given procedure is known as a *program.*

For example, the computer may have the operation of multiplication built into its circuits in much the same way the ability to add is built into a simple adding machine. Just as an adding machine is directed by depressing keys, the computer must be directed to perform multiplication. Once so directed, the computer must be instructed "where" in its memory storage it can find the factors to be multiplied. Further, the comparatively simple operation of multiplication implies other activity that must precede and follow the calculation. The "factors to be multiplied" had to be put into the computer, or the computer had to have obtained them from already available records. In addition, once the calculation is performed, instructions would dictate what is to be done with the product (retain in storage or print out).

An entire procedure is composed of individual steps grouped in a sequence that direct the computer to produce a desired result. Thus, a complex problem must first be reduced to a series of basic machine operations before it can be solved. Each of these operations is coded as one instruction or a series of instructions, in a form that can be interpreted by the computer, and is placed in the main storage unit as a portion of a stored program.

The possible variations of stored programs provide the data processing system with almost unlimited flexibility. A computer can be applied to many different procedures simply by "reading in" or "loading" the proper program into storage.

Examples in Underwriting

Inspection Reporting Activity By placing into the data processing system the name of the inspection company from which an inspection was ordered, a coded reason for the ordering of the report, the data ordered, and the policy number (which would then make all other data regarding that policy number available), the system could:

1. be used as a suspense file to alert the underwriter if the requested report is not received, and
2. produce data by producer, by inspection company, or by underwriter as to the frequency of reports and reason ordered.

Underwriting Terminations When an underwriter terminates a policy, a coded reason for termination could be inputted which would permit the computer (with proper programming) to compile certain known policy information and create output indicating such things as:

1. the amount of business terminated by an underwriter, where it was terminated, and why;
2. comparison with inspection reporting information to determine what inspection companies were involved with termination, and the resulting percentage compared to number ordered; and
3. timeliness of initial underwriting terminations.

Inception Year Analysis Since the computer has all pertinent policy and claims information, a company is able to track the development of all business placed with that company during a given calendar year. By using an input coding system, the computer can develop underwriting experience by risk characteristic on an inception year basis. The data from the application, MVR, and inspection report are coded to identify a number of risk characteristics, such as "licensed less than one year." An inception year report then relates earned premium to incurred losses by risk characteristic. Thus, underwriters can compare claim frequency on any group of new business written in a given year with the claim frequency of any other group that has been coded by risk characteristic. This information may be analyzed by territory, by state, by regional office, and on a companywide basis. It is useful in modifying the underwriting guide to reflect current conditions and as an indicator of rate adequacy. Risk characteristic codes may include such factors as:

- number of accidents in a specific period of time
- type of accidents
- number of violations in a specific period of time
- type of violation
- license revocation
- combinations of the above which include the interaction of these characteristics

This allows management to analyze the degree to which certain underwriting management decisions influenced the final loss ratio of that year of business.

Claim Frequency and Severity Reports Underwriting managers benefit greatly from timely computer reports that help to analyze past underwriting decisions. Exhibit 12-3 illustrates a type of underwriting management report that separates personal auto loss experience by type of coverage.

The loss ratio for the current year is compared to the two preceding years to show if a trend is developing. The reported claim frequency per 100 cars brings out some important facts to consider in the decision-making process. For example, the claim frequency on medical payments was about 0.07 per 100 cars for the first preceding

Exhibit 12-3
Personal Auto Underwriting Experience

PERSONAL AUTO
IIA INSURANCE COMPANY — PERIOD ENDING 12-31-X1
UNDERWRITING EXPERIENCE, REPORTED CLAIM FREQUENCY & AVERAGE PAID CLAIM

UNDERWRITING EXPERIENCE

CAUSE OF LOSS	EARNED PREMIUM	INCURRED LOSS & ADJ. EXP.	I.L.A.E.† RATIO CURRENT YEAR	FIRST PRECED.	SECOND PRECED.
BI	2,260,411	1,090,456	48.2	66.1	69.3
PD	1,372,009	776,804	56.6	79.4	65.5
MED PAY	178,647	5,384–	CR	CR	CR
PIP	617,604	245,173	39.7	94.9	89.6
COMP	692,647	429,890	62.1	65.9	65.2
COLL	1,231,194	759,536	61.7	93.0	68.2
TOTAL	6,352,512	3,296,475	51.9	78.7	64.6

REPORTED CLAIM FREQUENCY/PER 100 CARS

	EXPOSURE UNITS OR PAID CLAIMS	CURRENT YEAR	FIRST PRECED.	SECOND PRECED.	CURRENT YEAR/FIRST PRECED. AMOUNT	CURRENT YEAR/FIRST PRECED. PERCENT	CURRENT YEAR/SECOND PRECED. AMOUNT	CURRENT YEAR/SECOND PRECED. PERCENT
BI	27,331	1.70	2.06	1.57	.36–	17.48–	.13	8.28
PD	27,324	6.72	8.38	6.83	1.66–	19.81–	.11–	1.61–
MED PAY	16,112	.02	.07	.12	.05–	71.43–	.10–	83.33–
PIP	26,591	1.93	2.48	2.40	.55–	22.18–	.47–	19.58–
COMP	24,898	9.79	9.83	8.59	.04–	.41–	1.20	13.97
COLL	19,398	7.36	8.97	7.22	1.61–	17.95–	.14	1.94

AVERAGE PAID CLAIM

	EXPOSURE UNITS OR PAID CLAIMS	CURRENT YEAR	FIRST PRECED.	SECOND PRECED.	CURRENT YEAR/FIRST PRECED. AMOUNT	CURRENT YEAR/FIRST PRECED. PERCENT	CURRENT YEAR/SECOND PRECED. AMOUNT	CURRENT YEAR/SECOND PRECED. PERCENT
BI	515	2,891	2,369	3,443	522	22.03	552–	16.03–
PD	1,940	417	375	320	42	11.20	97	30.31
MED PAY	4	357–	212–	219	145–	68.40	576–	263.01–
PIP	442	654	719	667	65–	9.04–	13–	1.95–
COMP	2,994	140	138	125	2	1.45	15	12.00
COLL	1,602	486	511	417	25–	4.89–	69	16.55

year. The claim frequency on comprehensive losses during the same period was 9.37 per 100 cars. Of course, this must be adjusted for the lack of full credibility on this book of business.

Exhibit 12-4 presents the same type of underwriting management information on homeowners business.

Reported claim frequencies per 100 houses and average paid claims are computed by *cause of loss.* Although the peril of fire had the highest claim severity by far, fire losses were less frequent than theft or liability losses. Analysis of recent loss experience should be made available to line underwriters to assist in new business selection and in monitoring.

PRINCIPLES OF ELECTRONIC DATA PROCESSING

System Components and Structure

By stretching logic a little, today's large scale computers can be compared to a high speed network of railroad facilities. The units of information in the computer are comparable to the cars, and programmers who organize and regulate the flow of information in the system are comparable to the people who run the railroad.

The tracks are computer wires; the switches are electronic devices in the central processing unit; the sidings are terminals that permit one to get in and out of the system easily; the railroad yards are storage devices of various types that let us "park" information when not in use; our maximum speed limit is the speed of light (186,000 miles per second or about a foot every billionth of a second).

The general organization of such a system is shown in Exhibit 12-5. As can be seen from the chart, the primary ingredient at the beginning and end of a data processing system is people.

Hardware The term *hardware* refers to physical machines. This includes the computer itself. The *central processing unit* (CPU) is the heart of the computer system. It is sometimes called the mainframe or processor. It is here that all control and calculation functions take place. Input and output devices are also considered hardware. All input and output devices are connected to the CPU by cable. The CPU delegates the reading and writing of data to the input and output machines. In addition to these machines, there are supporting devices which are attached to these machines and perform various "housekeeping" functions for the primary devices already mentioned.

Exhibit 12-4
Homeowners Underwriting Experience

HOMEOWNERS
IIA INSURANCE COMPANY — PERIOD ENDING 12-31-X1
UNDERWRITING EXPERIENCE, REPORTED CLAIM FREQUENCY & AVERAGE PAID CLAIM

UNDERWRITING EXPERIENCE

CAUSE OF LOSS	EARNED PREMIUM	INCURRED LOSS & ADJ. EXP.	I.L.A.E. RATIO CURRENT YEAR	I.L.A.E. RATIO FIRST PRECED.	I.L.A.E. RATIO SECOND PRECED.
TOTAL	3,053,088	1,303,107	42.7	49.7	67.2

REPORTED CLAIM FREQUENCY/PER 100 HOUSES

	EXPOSURE UNITS OR PAID CLAIMS	CURRENT YEAR	FIRST PRECED.	SECOND PRECED.	CURRENT YEAR/FIRST PRECED. AMOUNT	CURRENT YEAR/FIRST PRECED. PERCENT	CURRENT YEAR/SECOND PRECED. AMOUNT	CURRENT YEAR/SECOND PRECED. PERCENT
FIRE	28,948	.94	1.31	1.39	.37–	28.24	.45–	32.37–
W & H†	28,948	.59	.67	.66	.08–	11.94–	.07–	10.61–
WAT DAM††	28,948	.67	.76	.74	.09–	11.84–	.07–	9.46–
THEFT	28,948	2.87	3.78	3.90	.91–	24.07–	1.03–	26.41–
VAND	28,948	.13	.18	.24	.05–	27.78–	.11–	45.83–
MYS DIS	28,948	.00	.00	.01	.00	.00	.01–	100.00–
ALL OTHER	28,948	.89	1.55	1.20	.66–	42.58–	.31–	25.83–
LIAB & MP	28,948	1.43	1.70	1.61	.27–	15.88–	.18–	11.18–
C C	28,948	.00	.00	.00	.00	.00	.00	.00

AVERAGE PAID CLAIM

	EXPOSURE UNITS OR PAID CLAIMS	CURRENT YEAR	FIRST PRECED.	SECOND PRECED.	CURRENT YEAR/FIRST PRECED. AMOUNT	CURRENT YEAR/FIRST PRECED. PERCENT	CURRENT YEAR/SECOND PRECED. AMOUNT	CURRENT YEAR/SECOND PRECED. PERCENT
FIRE	256	2,134	1,253	1,829	881	70.31	305	16.68
W & H	164	332	332	394		.00	62–	15.74–
WAT DAM	157	448	440	446	8	1.62	2	.45
THEFT	759	503	411	364	92	22.38	139	38.19
VAND	36	271	364	203	93–	25.55–	68	33.50
MYS DIS				354		.00	354–	100.00–
ALL OTHER	252	247	285	263	38–	13.33–	16–	6.08–
LIAB & MP	352	662	457	451	205	44.86	211	46.78
C C						.00		.00

†WIND AND HAIL
††WATER DAMAGE

Exhibit 12-5
Computer System*

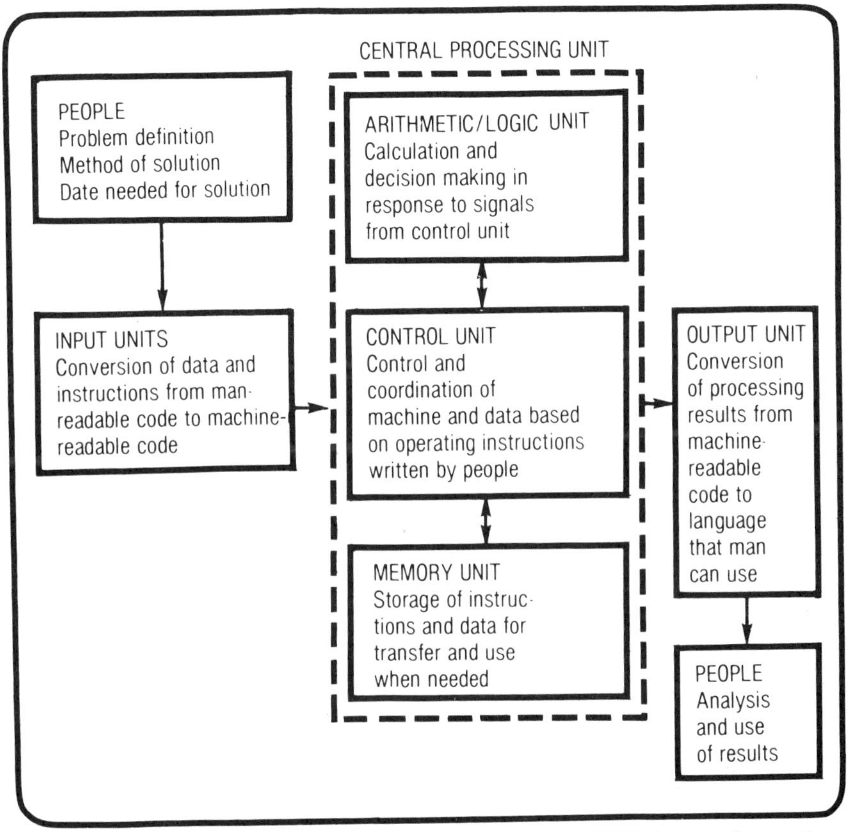

*Reprinted with permission from *More About Computers*, IBM Corporation, p. 8.

The Central Processing Unit (CPU).[3]

HUB OF ALL ACTIVITY. The CPU is the hub of all activity in the computer system. All calculations are performed by the CPU, and no machine in the system operates except under the control of the CPU. Input devices are used to read data. Output devices are used to write data. It is the central processing unit, however, which actually processes (performs calculations and controls) data.

THREE UNITS. The CPU itself consists of three units—the primary storage or memory unit, the arithmetic/logic unit, and the control unit. Each unit is responsible for different functions.

Primary Storage. The primary storage unit of the CPU, as its name implies, stores data. Specifically, it stores data that is of immediate importance to the job being run. *Primary storage* differs from other computer storage (e.g., magnetic disk) in that it resides in the CPU and contains only data pertinent to the program currently being run.

An analogy may be helpful. An underwriter analyzes insurance applications to distinguish acceptable from unacceptable submissions. The underwriter, however, does not keep all of the insurance policies written by the company on the desk. Instead, the underwriter selects only those applications or policies with which it will be necessary to work on that day (or perhaps that morning, or even that hour). Underwriters work this way because desk space is limited and because underwriters do not need every file at one time. For similar reasons, the primary storage of the CPU is used only for data currently needed. Other terms for this storage include *main memory* or *core.* Main memory must be distinguished from *auxiliary memory* or *auxiliary storage,* terms referring to *media.* The term core comes from the fact that historically computer storage in many computers consisted of a magnetic core.

Arithmetic/Logic Unit. Before a calculation is made, data is transferred from primary storage to the *arithmetic/logic unit (ALU).* After a calculation is completed, the answer is transferred to primary storage. If this sounds like some sort of "musical data" game in which the CPU spends a great deal of time moving data back and forth from one section to another, remember that the computer is very limited in its functions (it can add, subtract, multiply, divide, and compare numbers). Everything must take place according to an ordered sequence. The speed at which the computer operates more than makes up for the seemingly cumbersome and rigid internal sequence it must follow.

Control Unit. If the CPU is the heart of the computer system, then the *control unit* is the heart of the central processing unit. It controls the activities of the CPU and, therefore, of the computer system as a whole. The control unit receives and interprets program instructions from primary storage. Based on the instruction, the control unit will issue commands to the appropriate part of the computer system.

STORAGE STRUCTURE. The primary storage unit of the CPU is divided into four areas: *program storage, input storage, output storage,* and *working storage.*

Program storage is where the computer stores the instructions of the program it is currently executing. The program must be represented in the same manner (binary codes) as data. (Binary numbers are discussed later.) Input storage is the place where data is stored immediately after it is read into the system by an input device. Output storage is where the data is stored immediately before it is to be written by an output device. Working storage is where data that is partially processed is stored. The relative size of these four areas can be altered and controlled by the programmer.

ADDRESSING STRUCTURE. *Addressing* informs the computer where each of the four major storage areas starts and stops. Regardless of the medium used for storage in the computer, each unit of storage medium—that is, each individual magnetic core or each individual semiconductor circuit—represents a *bit.* Bits are combined to form a *byte.* Bytes are combined to form a *word.* Some computer manufacturers use other terms but these are standard in the insurance industry.

Each word, byte, and even bit, can be located by its address, its location within the computer. Locating a bit, byte, or word is similar to sorting mail for post office boxes. All the boxes look the same. The way to tell them apart is by counting the rows and columns or by the identifying number of each. Of course, this does not mean that every bit in the computer has a number painted on it. But the computer "counts" bits starting from the first one until it gets to the bit it needs. If this sounds time consuming and inefficient, remember that today's computers operate internally in time measured in nanoseconds (one thousandth of a millionth of a second; in other words, a billionth of a second). This tremendous speed overcomes an otherwise inefficient process.

The central processing unit, then, is the center of activity in the computer system. From its control unit, all functions of the system are directed. In its arithmetic/logic unit, all calculations and logic comparisons are performed. Its primary storage unit holds all data currently being utilized, in magnetic core, semiconductor, or another medium. Data is located within primary storage in major storage subdivisions. Individual pieces of information, that is, bits of data, are located within the CPU by the addressing procedure.

Software A stored program is the set of instructions that tell a computer which steps to take and in which order to take them. It also tells the computer which data to read, and, at the proper time, which data to write. The term *software* includes all the programs used to run the computer. These instructional programs can be divided into two categories. Programs used to perform operations necessary to the basic operation of the computer are called *system software.* Programs applying to specific problems being processed in the computer are called *application software.*

In an insurance company, all those programs dealing with insurance matters and company matters would be considered application software. System software would include those programs dealing with the operation of the computer itself and which would be scarcely known beyond the confines of the data processing department. Both kinds of software have increased greatly in prominence over the past few years. There are many reasons for this, not the least of which is the steadily decreasing cost of hardware per unit of storage. In this environment the question becomes, "How much software can we develop to take advantage of lower hardware costs?"

Historically, the capacity of the hardware increased dramatically while the capacity of the software remained relatively limited. As more and more programs were written and data storage capacity grew, new and more efficient methods of hardware operation were developed.

Progress in the software area was slower. If more programs were needed, more programmers were hired. There were no radical improvements in the efficiency of programming. This is slowly changing. Still, software is often the bottleneck in the systems development process. Because of this, more attention is being given to software and, specifically, to the methods employed in its development. Software is now produced and offered for sale by a confusing array of organizations. An insurance company has the opportunity to purchase a payroll system or an auto rating system, rather than employ its own staff to produce and maintain these programs.

The Computer's Language

Electronic devices respond, of course, to electrical signals. To make these signals represent information, a code is used, much like any spoken or written language. The language of the computer is based on a code of high frequency electrical pulses, or bits, generated and timed by an electronic clock in the computer.

The computer's pulse language can be represented by the binary digits *one* and *zero.* The one represents a pulse, or bit, and the zero represents no pulse, or no bit. Using these two symbols, many different information codes can be developed, and many, in fact, are used in various parts of a computer or for different kinds of information-handling problems. However, the code used in most of today's computers is based on the binary number system.

Binary Numbers

The binary number system is different from the conventional

Exhibit 12-6
Decimal and Binary Systems*

Decimal	Binary	Decimal	Binary
0	00000	9	01001
1	00001	10	01010
2	00010	11	01011
3	00011	12	01100
4	00100	13	01101
5	00101	14	01110
6	00110	15	01111
7	00111	16	10000
8	01000	17	10001

*Reprinted with permission from *More About Computers,* IBM Corporation, p. 11.

decimal system in only one respect—the number of symbols on which it is based. The two symbols can be manipulated in much the same way as can the ten decimal symbols.

For example, in a decimal number, the first column on the right represents units, and zero to nine can be symbolized there. To handle numbers larger than nine, columns are added to the left using the same ten symbols. The value of a symbol increases ten times each time it is moved one place to the left.

In a binary number system, the first right-hand column still represents units, but the value increases only *twice* each time a symbol is moved one place to the left. Exhibit 12-6 shows how to count to seventeen in the two systems.

The two binary symbols can be coded by computer designers and programmers to represent any number, alphabetic character, punctuation mark, or special symbol.

In the Binary Coded Decimal (BCD) system, for example, letters of the alphabet are represented by placing zeros and ones in front of the binary symbols for numbers one through nine. One such code is shown in Exhibit 12-7. With some refinements, similar codes based on the same basic principles are used in today's computers.

The computer can be made to convert quickly from one code to another, so the user of the machine can use a form of English, French, decimals, or even graphic symbols drawn on an electronic display tube to communicate with the machine and get information out of it.

Exhibit 12-7
Binary Coded Decimal System*

A	110001	J	100001	S	010010
B	110010	K	100010	T	010011
C	110011	L	100011	U	010100
D	110100	M	100100	V	010101
E	110101	N	100101	W	010110
F	110110	O	100110	X	010111
G	110111	P	100111	Y	011000
H	111000	Q	101000	Z	011001
I	111001	R	101001		

*Reprinted with permission from *More About Computers,* IBM Corporation, p. 11.

Input and Storage

Punch Cards and Paper Tape Punch cards were once an important way to store information or instructions outside the computer and to enter this data into the machine. Today, they are much less important due to numerous other more efficient input and storage devices. Punch card readers convert the code of holes in the cards to electrical impulses that are sent into the *central processing unit* or CPU (the unit of a computing system that contains the circuits that calculate and perform logic decisions based on a man-made program of operating instructions).

Punch paper tape works in a similar way, but the coding is different and the punches are stored in a continuous roll of paper. Paper tape readers convert the hole-code to electrical impulses that can be used in the computer.

Magnetic Tape The general public commonly comes in contact with magnetic information every day in the form of bank checks. The printed account numbers on most checks contain magnetic particles that can be sensed by machine. But most people seldom see the forms of magnetic storage.

Today, computer data often is stored magnetically on reels of plastic tape in the form of binary digits or bits of information. This kind of magnetic storage is easy to use, is relatively inexpensive, and permits high-speed operation.

Magnetic tape is made by depositing a layer of magnetic material on plastic tape and magnetizing this tape in a code of ones and zeros. For example, a magnetized spot on the tape can represent a one, and another spot either magnetized in the opposite direction or not magnetized at all can represent a zero. With this method of representing data, information can be packed quite closely together and retrieved at the rate of several hundred thousand bits per second.

Magnetic tapes can be kept indefinitely, if desired, and take little storage space, or they can be erased and used again for recording new information. They are used to send information into computers, to record output, and to store intermediate results of computation.

Information can be recorded on magnetic tape only serially, in the sequence it is received, and it can be retrieved only in the same way. If a needed record is at the end of the tape, the entire tape must be run to find it. Disc storage solves that problem.

Magnetic Disc Magnetic disc storage has become a major method of storing large amounts of information and making it available to a central processing unit any time it is needed.

In magnetic disc storage, information is stored in code on a layer of magnetic material which is deposited on flat discs resembling stereo records. When a particular piece of information is needed for processing or as output to the user, the system does not have to screen through all the information on a disc sequentially—it can locate and retrieve the needed data directly.

Stacked storage discs are available in preassembled disc packs that can be interchanged to suit the job. These give the user access to large quantities of stored data and programs which can be selected as needed for active use during a computer run. With disc packs, the CPU has access to several hundred million characters of information. Information can be transferred from the disc to main storage at rates of more than 800,000 characters per second.

Magnetic disc storage is especially useful in handling claims records and underwriting files where it is necessary to find a random record quickly, change it to reflect new information, and then return the updated record to its previous location on the disc.

Processing of Data

The distinction between batch processing and online processing is very important in determining how data should be processed. This section will elaborate on each and explain how these two different modes of processing coexist in many computer installations.

Batch Processing In the batch processing mode, data are converted into some computer readable form, gathered into batches, and then taken physically or telecommunicated periodically to the computer for processing. This "period" could be every hour, every day, or every week; most often, it is every day or overnight. Turnaround time is quite slow when compared with online processing, but for many purposes batch processing works quite well. Most important is that it makes efficient use of the computer's time: computers work most efficiently on large volumes of similar data.

Batch processing was the most common form of processing in the second "generation" and during the early part of the third "generation" of computers (about 1958 to mid-1960s). As time went on and computer speeds and capacities increased, managers questioned whether the efficiency of the computer was more important than the efficiency of the people using it. For example, overnight processing dictated that any error made by someone in the punched card would not be detected until the computer could edit it. It is common practice for keypunchers to check one another's work by repunching the same cards. This is called *verifying.* This process catches some of the errors before the data enters the computer for processing. Because errors detected by computer edit were not returned to the person making them until the following morning, worker efficiency was sacrificed. A keypuncher could make one mistake and, because the computer would not catch it until that night, might go on making the same mistake on subsequent cards punched that day. It is psychologically better to detect errors and correct them as soon as possible.

During the early 1960s, many companies were computerizing new functions such as inventory control, billing, and order follow-up. The computer produced monthly reports and the like in a clearly satisfactory manner, but did not provide fast access to data that was completely current. The parts warehouse with computerized inventory could have a listing of all items in stock, but it would only be as current as the last batch run. The accounts receivable report of an insurance producer was similarly out of date on most working days. The computer system was not as good as the old manual system in this respect. With batch processing, the ability to go "directly to the file" was limited.

Online Processing It would be inaccurate to say that online processing chooses human efficiency over computer efficiency. Instead, online processing offers a more desirable balance between the two. The term online signifies a direct, current link with the computer. This implies the presence of a computer terminal. This terminal may be a teletype machine, cathode ray tube (CRT), or other device. Ordinary touch-tone telephones can be used as terminals with the buttons providing the means for transmitting data to the computer. Obviously, telephones are slow and limited in flexibility when compared with other terminal devices.

To say that one is online with the computer does not specify the functions the terminal is able to perform. The systems design can provide a highly limited capability, such as policyholder data verification. On the other hand, remote terminals can be given full capability to retrieve, add, and change any data in a policyholder file.

Online processing was a boon to many computer users, including programmers. They can maintain their programs by using a terminal located near their desks. Other users, too, are eager to take advantage of the potential provided by online terminals. A terminal allows remote use of at least a portion of the organization's computer. It also allows rental of a terminal and purchase of service from a vendor's computer (timesharing).

Real-time processing is a specific type of online processing through which the user not only has direct access to the computer and its files, but can also modify or use those files immediately and directly. Real-time processing exists when information is processed in time to be used in a business transaction. A familiar example is the airline reservation computer. Space availability is checked, space committed, and the ticket issued while the customer waits at the ticket counter. Only a portion of online processing is real-time processing.

When online processing became a practical reality for many companies in the third and fourth computer generations, did they abandon batch processing? No, because adopting the online mode did not require abandoning batch processing. Many applications are still processed most efficiently in the batch mode.

Hybrid Processing Hybrid processing combines features of batch and online processing. A keypuncher may operate a CRT terminal for data input, an element of online processing. The computer holds the data on some auxiliary storage device (that is, tape or disk) until a sufficient number have accumulated, and then processes the data, thus providing an element of batch processing.

Output Unit

Output devices record or write information from the computer on cards, paper tape, and magnetic tape; print information on paper; generate signals from transmission over teleprocessing networks; and produce graphic displays, microfilm images, and other specialized forms. The number and types of input/output devices connected directly to the computer depend on the design of the system and its application.

Computer Programming Languages

One of the earlier and most widely used language translations was *Fortran* (acronym for formula translation), developed by a group of people from several organizations after three years of work that involved the writing of 25,000 lines of detailed machine instructions.

Fortran is based on the language of algebra plus a few rules of grammar and syntax imposed by the computer. It was developed primarily for engineers and scientists familiar with math who were the ones using most of the computers then in operation.

Fortran was not adequate, however, to handle problems like payroll or billing. Computers began to be used extensively in business in the late fifties and early sixties, and in 1960, *Cobol* (common business oriented language) was developed to meet these special business needs.

Cobol was the result of cooperation between the federal government and users and manufacturers of computers. It facilitates the expression of business problems in language very similar to business English. To find the value of present stock on hand in an inventory, for example, a Cobol statement might look like this (with the asterisk meaning "multiply"):

```
COMPUTE STOCK - VALUE =
UNIT PRICE*(STOCK-ON-HAND+RECEIPTS–SHIPMENTS).
```

The translation program (the compiler) stored in the computer would convert this sentence into the sequence of machine language instruction needed to guide the computer through the calculation.

The basic Cobol vocabulary consists of 250 key words which can be expanded without limit by specifying *names* for data and for the storage location of instructions. In the example above, the word compute is the only key word; all of the other words are names.

Another programming language that has gained wide acceptance is *A Programming Language* (APL). Based on symbols for mathematical and logical functions, APL is concise, easy to learn, and requires a minimum number of characters to define complex operations. It is useful in a wide variety of applications, ranging from the analysis and solution of problems in mathematics to financial analysis, text editing, forecasting, and computer-assisted instruction.

To give the programmer more help, a general-purpose language called *Programming Language/I* (PL/I) was developed. The "I" in PL/I is pronounced "one." The result of a cooperative effort of IBM and user groups, this language can be used efficiently for either business or technically oriented programs.

PL/I was designed to take full advantage of the greater versatility of today's computers and to make programming easier for beginners and experts alike. It is a modular language, so the programmer does not have to use the entire language; a subset fitting specific needs may be used. By using small subsets, beginning programmers can start using the language quickly.

THE COMPUTER PEOPLE

Everyone has become a "computer person" to some extent. That is, everyone has had to adapt to the computer in business. (Personal life has not been immune to this change, but those considerations are beyond the scope of this discussion.) People now request "input" rather than the opinions of others. People now use a "systems approach"—rather than common sense—to solve problems.

People who use computers are called *users.* The term's meaning varies, however, depending on who is using it. For example, for workers in the data processing department, all the other departments in the company are user departments, and all the other employees are users. From the point of view of the computer operator, however, everyone else is a user—including programmers. Adding to the confusion, computer vendors (that is, computer manufacturers) consider all their customers, including the operators, as users. To understand the specific meaning of the term, therefore, it is necessary to show it in context. This chapter uses the relatively common term *end user* to apply to all users other than the data processing department. In other words, the term end user is reserved for those people for whom a specific computer use is intended.

There has been a large growth in the number of people working in the field of computers. There has been an impressive division of labor, too. The first uses of computers in business were usually rather simple batch-processing tasks. For example, one of the most common uses of early business computers was to replace old accounting machines that had been used to produce monthly billings. At that time, there was little need for a large staff of computer programmers, systems analysts, operators, managers, and others. But as computer power grew, more and more people were required. And as computer sophistication grew, more and more division of labor was needed. One of the first areas where this occurred was in programming. With the earliest computers, programmers actually operated the machines. After writing a program, programmers would process it on the computer and then review the results. Soon it was realized that programmers could be more productive if all they did was write programs. Someone slightly less skilled could be hired to operate the computer. As the next section will show, the *computer operator's* job has also gone through several divisions.

A better understanding of the people who manage computers is important if one is to derive the full benefits of computer equipment. The very first step toward such an understanding is to shed all stereotypes or preconceived views of computer people. Computer programmers are as varied in personality as are insurance underwriters, producers, or company presidents. The challenges that they face, though sometimes different in nature, lead to many of the same feelings of success, failure, pleasure, frustration, triumph, and tragedy that all others know as part of working life.

Operations

The term *operations* refers to the department charged with the responsibility of physical maintenance, operation, and security of the computer itself. In many companies this department has been given the title *data center*. Other similar titles are common. While an underwriting department is always called the underwriting department, data processing groups may have different, though fortunately similar, titles. The staff will be referred to by a number of names: data processing, information processing, or computer staff.

Development Operations began as a data processing department. As the equipment evolved, the position of *operator* was considered less desirable than some of the other jobs in data processing. This was appropriate in the days prior to advanced operating systems, data communications, multiprogramming, and other features requiring significant operator activity. Picture an operator at that early time. An operator might be asked to run, for instance, the monthly customer billings. Under the previous manual system, that process might take ninety-five person-hours. The computer might take four hours for the same job. From a business perspective, this meant a dramatic increase in productivity. But from the point of view of an operator, it meant that once the data had been loaded into the computer (through cards or some other means), it was four hours before the computer could do anything else. College students often held these positions because they could study during the long operating runs and therefore accepted a relatively low salary.

Change came with the advent of multiprogramming, under the control of sophisticated operating systems. In addition to the four-hour job, the operator could simultaneously process other jobs on the computer. In fact, before too long, additional operators were needed to keep up with the loading of punched cards and magnetic tape, and, of course, with the very frequent task of loading the printer with paper. Unfortunately, many people retain the now anachronistic image of an operator as a person with little training in technical data processing whose primary function is the mounting and dismounting of tapes on tape drives. This image grows even less accurate with each passing year. Operations work today requires as much—or more—technical training than many programming positions.

Positions Only the major positions in an operations center will be discussed here.

Operator. The basic position of *operator* still exists today. Most large-scale systems have the computer in operation for more than the standard work day. Spreading the computer's work over two or three shifts enables a company to purchase a smaller computer than would be needed if all the computer work had to be done during the regular eight-hour day. Often there is a *lead operator,* also called a *shift supervisor,* for each shift. This person directs the activities of the other operators. The work operators do can be divided into five categories: (1) compilations and assemblies; (2) testing; (3) production runs; (4) problem solving; and (5) miscellaneous activities.

COMPILATIONS AND ASSEMBLIES. After programs are written, or modified in any way, they must be assembled or compiled. Assemblers translate an assembler program into machine language. The computer can process machine language while the compiler performs the same sort of translation on high level (procedure-oriented such as PL/I) languages. This process of assembly or compilation usually consists of physically loading a deck of punched cards into the computer's card reader and removing the printed result (called a *compilation listing* or a *program listing*) from the computer's printer. Many installations now use terminals to perform this function. In these cases, the programmer either loads the card deck into a remote card reader terminal (often called *RJE* for Remote Job Entry) or, instead of using punched cards, directly types the program instructions into an online terminal. This saves the operator time and increases the programmer's productivity.

TESTING. Programs must be tested. These tests are run by the operator. If programmers were perfect and never made mistakes in their written directions for running tests, this function would be a relatively simple matter. Unforeseen problems, however, often occur. Since programmers no longer run programs, they must write directions for someone else—the operator—to follow, increasing the chance of error.

PRODUCTION RUNS. Once sufficient tests have been run on a program to pronounce it free from known error, it is placed in production status. Production runs are recurrent data processing jobs:

the day in, day out, jobs performed for end users. End users may not fully realize how much other work is performed by the computer in order to enable production work. Yet a little thought will lead to a realization that without compilations and testing, production work is impossible. More specifically, the only way to change or correct a program is to re-compile or re-assemble it.

PROBLEM SOLVING. The monthly accounts for producers are to be produced on the third shift tonight. You are the operator. It is 2 A.M. and the program has failed to run to completion (commonly called a program blow: "The accounts program blew!"). Quick! What do you do? The different things that can "go wrong" are much too large in scope and in number to chronicle here. Suffice it to say that problem solving takes up a large portion of the operator's day (or night).

MISCELLANEOUS ACTIVITIES. Preventive maintenance of mechanical equipment, running "diagnostic" programs on the computer to check basic hardware and software functions to be sure that they are operating properly (diagnostics can be used according to a schedule in order to pinpoint problem areas before larger problems develop or they can also be used in problem solving situations where the major problem has already occurred), and operation of the computer console are some of the miscellaneous activities performed by operators.

Scheduler. In most large-scale installations, one or more persons is responsible for scheduling. This was probably one of the operator's functions in early installations. With increased activity, though, it is inefficient for the operator to stop every time someone walks in with a new program or job. The scheduler receives requests from users, establishes a schedule, and communicates the schedule to operators. Problems are reported back to the scheduler who then resolves the problems with end users.

Tape Librarian. Magnetic tape provides great storage capacity at low cost (compared to the cost of disk and other auxiliary storage media). For this reason, data kept for historical purposes is typically stored on magnetic tape. Legal requirements often underlie data retention policies. Insurance companies have obvious needs for occasional access to historical documents. Tape librarians do for computer tapes what other librarians do for books: they oversee the storage of tapes and aid in searches for tapes.

Systems and Programming

Once the early programmer's functions had been divided into those of programmer and operator, the stage was set for the next division between programming and systems analysis. Further divisions have taken place, but this discussion is restricted to the areas of major importance.

Systems Analysts The *systems analyst* is the data processing employee charged with the responsibility of specifying the size, scope, and characteristics of programs and systems of programs. Although this is perhaps an adequate description of responsibility, it does not go very far toward telling one what the systems analyst does. Primary activities of a systems analyst include information gathering, design, specification, and follow-through.

The systems analyst interacts with end users in devising programs to meet their needs but it is unlikely to do the detailed programming. Most systems analysts interview end users to obtain information. The danger with this approach is that it relies heavily on the user's ability to communicate what he or she needs and the analyst's ability to interpret what the user is saying. Each has limited knowledge of the other's field.

Once sufficient information has been gathered, the systems analyst begins with the design of the program or system. Systems analysts rarely design individual programs. They usually design a system and then programs within that system's context. Once the system design has been determined, the systems analyst gives the programmer documents that describe or specify what the system must do and the manner in which it must be done. These are called the specifications and usually take the form of flowcharts, decision tables, or print layouts.

Probably the most time-consuming of all the activities of the systems analyst is the follow-through. Follow-through includes many things: answering the questions of the programmer; assisting in or even directing the implementation of a new system; answering the questions of users and resolving errors (bugs) in the new system; and any related tasks. The systems analyst is often a jack-of-all-trades, spending as much time maintaining and improving old systems as designing new ones.

Programmers We have been discussing *programmers* in this chapter as if their work were all the same. This is true in the sense that all of them work with the detail code, or instructions, of programs. In another sense, however, programmers can be identified by the types of programs they work on. Here again we find division of labor.

Applications Programming vis-a-vis Systems Programming. The distinction made between applications software and systems software also applies to applications programming and systems programming.

An *applications programmer* works on business problems. In the case of an insurance agency, the applications programmer works on programs related to the agency's business, such as accounts receivable, accounts current, policyholder files, and related programs. Applications programmers normally use procedure-oriented languages, although they are by no means restricted to these. The languages for a given program depend on the language selection criteria and, at least to some degree, on the personal preference of the programmer.

Systems programmers primarily work with operating systems software. This being the case, most of their work is done in symbolic language. There is a trend, however, toward the use of some higher level languages in systems software. One of the prime reasons for this is that systems programmers are scarce. As computer systems grow more complex, systems programmers require more training. And as new systems proliferate, trained systems programmers can become "obsolete." Writing systems software in higher level languages qualifies many others to enter the field of systems programming.

Development Programming vis-a-vis Maintenance Programming. Some *shops* (the buzzword for data processing departments) organize programmers into development and maintenance staffs. Development programming is concerned with programs that are being written for the first time—either applications programs or systems programs. Systems software is for the most part written by the computer manufacturer or a firm that specializes in it. In contrast, applications programming offers many opportunities for development work and is generally thought to offer greater recognition and reward. Paradoxically, though, the more development programming that is done, the greater the amount of maintenance programming that will be required in the future.

Maintenance programming includes correcting, improving, and sometimes even overhauling existing programs and systems. Although it suffers from lower status, it is of crucial importance. It may be tolerable to fall several days behind in development (that new report for the claims department). It may not be acceptable to report delays in maintenance (correct the program that prints the claims drafts for policyholders).

Current Trends The distinctions between systems analysis and programming outlined above are valid from a conceptual point of view. In terms of specific job descriptions, however, the picture becomes increasingly blurred with time.

Historically, systems analysts were programmers who had been promoted. Gradually, recognition grew that the two jobs came about because they required different skills. Consequently, some organizations offered a career path for programmers that did not necessitate a switch to systems analysis.

Still, in terms of status, systems analysis was considered preferable to development programming, much as development programming was preferable to maintenance programming. To combat this tendency, some companies combined the two positions to create the position of *programmer analyst.*

Many companies chose to alter the structure even more dramatically by going to a *project management* approach. With this approach, programmers and analysts are assigned to a specific major project and remain members of that project's group for its duration. Project management does not replace the traditional structure but usually exists in addition to it. Many software projects are of sufficient complexity and duration to warrant project management.

Structured Programming. Edward Yourdon, one of the leading exponents of *structured programming,* gives the following explanation:

> . . . the notion of structured programming is a philosophy of writing programs according to a set of rigid rules in order to decrease testing problems, increase productivity, and increase the readability of the resulting program.[4]

This concept is probably the most talked about one in programming circles today. It means imposition of a standard logic on program design. If it achieves its promised productivity, structured programming will have a significant impact on computer work.

User-Oriented Languages. RPG is a procedure-oriented language. It was designed to allow those with little or no programming or other computer experience to learn programming, particularly of simple report programs, in a relatively short period of time. Some manufacturers and vendors have carried the concept further and produced languages called *report writers.* These languages are designed so that an end user can define parameters and the report writer will then create a program that will produce the desired report. Similar languages are being used in some online systems where a report is requested through a cathode ray tube. These are often called *query languages.* Both report writers and query languages may constitute a new type of language, *user-oriented language.* This would mark a next major step in the development of software, the previous ones being machine, symbolic, and procedure-oriented languages.

User-oriented languages offer two major benefits. First, they allow users to produce their own programs. This bypasses the programmer and thereby saves time. Second, the programmer is freed from time-consuming chores. Report programs usually do not challenge the programmer. Thus, programmers and users are both happy to see the introduction of a report writer in the organization.

Query languages are still somewhat primitive. Some of them are more "user-oriented" than others. User expectations are often unmet.

It is anticipated that they will improve until most of the intended benefits are realized.

ELECTRONIC DATA PROCESSING AND THE LINE UNDERWRITING FUNCTION

There is little doubt that computers and electronic data processing have had a great impact on the insurance industry. Many insurer functions such as billing, policy issuance, accounts payable, producer's commission statements, and statistical reporting are mechanized and the results have been expense savings, improved accuracy, and faster processing.

The use of the computer in the risk selection process has been limited primarily to personal lines. This section discusses some of these computer uses based on the experience of three insurers. The reader is reminded that the descriptions that follow reflect the experiences of only three insurers and are not based on the accumulated experience of the insurance industry.

Underwriting Individual Risks

Companies have used various techniques to "screen" business as it comes to the company from the producer. These uses isolate applications with no significant characteristics and process them completely outside the underwriting department. This means that such policies would be issued automatically by the system with no underwriting intervention.

Most of the work to date along the lines of computer screening has been in personal lines auto. This is the line which has the greatest volume of risks, a large number of factors which can be identified as having an impact on results, and thus the greatest potential for savings. Therefore, most of the following discussion will be concerned with personal auto insurance.

The most common procedure for screening new applications involves having clerical personnel code the pertinent application information into a form suitable for input into the computer. These people may be trained to recognize those risks which are clearly ineligible under the rules of the company and would be referred to underwriting immediately. All other applications are processed into the computer.

There are two primary screening methods being used. Under the *referral by exception* method, the computer is programmed to refer to underwriting all applicants having one or more characteristics which have been determined by underwriters to be factors which might affect acceptability. When the computer encounters one of these factors, the file is referred to underwriting.

Under the *referral by total point count* method, each characteristic which can be identified and programmed into the computer is assigned a weight or value. Referral to underwriting is keyed to the number of points generated by an application. This procedure is effective in monitoring policies in force and handling renewals, as well as in screening new applications.

Referral by Exception In this method, the computer is programmed to accept all applicants except those having characteristics which require a referral to the underwriter. The following list is representative of the personal auto underwriting tests which have been utilized by companies. It is important to note that failure on any *one* of these tests refers the application to the underwriter.

1. Name. If the application is in the name of one individual or husband and wife, it would pass the computer's test. However, if it is other than an individual or husband and wife, the system would refer the business to the underwriter. In addition, if the name insured includes several individuals (other than husband or wife), it would also be referred to the underwriter.
2. Residence Address. If the address indicated it was in a city with a street address, or a rural address, the computer would pass the application. Any other cases such as "post office box," "hotel," etc., would cause the application to be referred to the underwriter.
3. Mailing Address. If the mailing address is the same as the residence, the application would pass. However, if it was any other address, the file would be reviewed by the underwriter.
4. Years with Present Employer. If self-employed or with present employer one year or more, it would pass. All others would be subject to underwriters' review.
5. Coverage. The test would be constructed to detect ineligible or obviously erroneous combinations of coverage, such as applications involving medical payments coverage where liability and property damage coverage had not been requested. This test can be designed to refer to underwriting cases involving limits higher than the company will automatically write in certain classes.
6. Autos in Household. If the company insured all the autos in the household, the underwriting test would pass. If, however, there were other vehicles in the household *not* insured by the company, the underwriting department would review.

7. Physical Defects. Any impaired driver would be reviewed, but an indication of no impairment would pass.
8. Prior Accidents. Any prior losses would cause an underwriting review.
9. Prior Violations. No moving violations would pass the test; however, a certain number of violations in a given period of time would cause an underwriting review. Any request for a financial responsibility filing would also cause a review.
10. Type of Vehicle. High-performance cars, sports cars, and so on would be cause for referral.
11. Residence Stability. Individuals who have resided at their current address for several years would pass the test, but all others would be referred to an underwriter.

The above list could, at the discretion of the particular company, include any number of characteristics unique to the type of business which that company would be writing. Obviously, the longer the list, the greater the number of risks referred to underwriting and the less the computer is aiding the underwriter by screening.

Referral by Total Point Count The referral by total point count method is useful in new business selection and monitoring a book of business. It seeks to predict loss frequency by assigning points or weights to key risk characteristics.

Using a technique called "discriminant analysis," the computer "discriminates" among applicants on the basis of established criteria. Each characteristic is assigned a point value, some being weighted more heavily than others. By combining the values of all characteristics, a total score for each risk is determined.

The first critical step in establishing a discriminant analysis program is in identifying the factors to be used and assigning a point value to each. This step should involve the underwriters who will need to handle a group of policies under the system. A survey of a large number of both accepted and rejected applications is necessary in order to assure that the identification and weighting of characteristics are as precise as is reasonably possible. A hypothetical system of point values which might be assigned by a particular company is shown in Exhibit 12-8.

The next step in establishing a discriminant analysis system is the establishment of a level for referral to an underwriter. If the level is too low, a large number of risks will be referred to an underwriter, which virtually renders the system worthless. On the other hand, a high level will cause a number of borderline risks to be accepted or retained, which will eventually have an adverse effect on underwriting results. The level at the start of a program should be established only after a

Exhibit 12-8
Hypothetical Illustration of Point Values Used in Discriminant Analysis

Factors	Point Value
Age of Principal Operator	
18 and below	50
19-21	30
22-25	20
26-29	10
30-65	0
66 and over	10
Age of Vehicle	
0-5 years	0
6-10 years	10
11 and over	20
Type of Residence	
Private dwelling	0
Mobile home	5
Rooming house	25
Months at Address	
2 and below	20
3-6	10
7 and over	0
Years on Present Job	
1 and less	20
over 1	0
Jobs in Past 10 Years	
1	0
2-5	15
6 and over	25
Accidents in Past 3 Years	
None	0
1	20
2	35
3 and more	60
Major Citations in Past 3 Years	
None	0
1	60
2 and more	90
Minor Citations in Past 3 Years	
None	0
1	20
2	30
3	40
4 and more	50

survey of a large number of actual cases is tested against various possible levels. In general the level should be established rather low at the start and raised as statistical studies may indicate.

Using these value points, the company might set the computer to refer to underwriting all applicants having a total value of fifty or more. Note that a policy having two accidents or three minor citations in the past three years would not be referred to an underwriter unless there were other adverse factors. On the other hand, a risk with three or more accidents or one major citation in the past three years would be referred.

Many refinements and changes might be desired. For example, three points could be deducted for each year that the insured had been with the company. Points could be added for the number of times the policy had been canceled for nonpayment and then reinstated. The only limitations are the ability of underwriters to identify factors which might be relevant, and the capacity of the computer.

The program of the computer applies the point values to each factor and computes the total. If the total is below the established referral limit, the policy is issued without referral. If the total point count is above the referral limit, the computer prints out some type of referral to underwriting, and no further activity takes place except as performed by an underwriter.

Every change in a policy will cause the computer to recalculate the points and to refer the policy when the stated level is reached. Some of these entries will be made within days after the new application is entered. For example, a company might order motor vehicle records on every new piece of business. For that matter, the computer could be instructed to order an MVR for risks which are otherwise acceptable but which reach a lower level, such as twenty in the above example. When the MVR is received, and accidents or citations are entered, the point count is calculated again. Referral depends on the new level. In like manner, every change in the policy, during its entire life, can be programmed to cause a new figuring of the points. Alternatively, this could be delayed until renewal time and then the calculation would be performed; this might be a better solution in a state which prohibits mid-term cancellations. One major type of entry for policies in force is a record of every loss. Minor losses, such as towing or small glass claims, need not cause a referral, unless other factors are so borderline that the low points for such a loss, perhaps five in the above case, would push the risk over the referral level.

It is obvious that the data which are placed into the computer must be as accurate as possible. This is a particular problem with loss data. Every effort must be made to be certain that the codes which identify the type and cause of loss are administered as carefully as possible. A system of this type is effective only if the information upon which it depends is accurate.

It should be emphasized at this point that the computer is not making underwriting decisions. It is doing what underwriters have told it to do. Applications will be accepted only if they meet the criteria established by the underwriters. All others are referred to an underwriter for decisions. The computer is helping the underwriter locate those files which need attention and the computer is doing a lot of the detail work which underwriters formerly needed to do. Thus, underwriters have more time to analyze the problem cases and to assist management in identifying and solving larger problems.

Computer Evaluation Computer evaluation has a direct effect on the role of the underwriter. For the first time, the effect that most risk characteristics have on loss frequency can be analyzed statistically. The art of risk selection becomes more precise, the traditional approach to gathering as much information as possible about a risk is conditioned to what is significant, and the entire underwriting process can be directed toward areas needing expertise.

Much of the routine file review of all classes of business can be eliminated, as the computer supplements risk selection and frees the underwriter for review of marginal classes of business reflecting frequency potential in excess of what current pricing contemplates.

Situations will occur periodically where any mechanical system will evaluate risks that, based on risk characteristics, will conflict with an underwriter's decision as to acceptability. However, this need not be a dilemma if the past results of these characteristics are available and can be evaluated properly in terms of their usefulness in predicting frequency. Underwriters should always remain as the "court of last resort" for any decision on risks for which acceptability is in question. Marginal risks need review by underwriters skilled in analysis of the ultimate profit potential for a risk. Computer screening of risks that offer less frequency potential for their class gives the underwriter more time to evaluate the more complex risks needing attention.

Changes in Workflow Workflow throughout the underwriting department is somewhat altered with the use of computers for the referral of auto business. Auto applications can now be screened for application completion and proper rating, yet not be referred to an underwriter unless the score of the computer's calculation reflects a need for an underwriter's review. A considerable amount of business can be rated, issued, and sent to the customer without underwriter review. All business that is computer accepted, however, can be spot-checked at a later date when requested by the underwriting department.

Any computer system designed to aid in risk selection should also include the capability to collect and store the risk characteristics of each application and develop reports in whatever format is needed by the underwriter. This information system can provide statistical data by producer, class of business, or any other criteria selected. Underwriters will have a tremendous analytical tool for use in market research and pricing. This is all available on a timely basis and gives greater opportunity for managing the book of business.

Effects on Underwriting Guidelines Under most existing systems, producers are guided by certain general corporate standards of acceptability for various classes of auto business. Past company experience has indicated that similar characteristics (e.g., accidents, traffic violations, age) have had an effect on frequencies recorded in a company's statistical records. Therefore, certain general standards for acceptability are given producers as field underwriting guides for acceptable business to be written.

These guidelines are used by companies to limit the writing of an excessive amount of business containing unacceptable risk characteristics. Certain risk characteristics such as past accidents and traffic violations can be shown as producing frequencies that are unacceptable for a particular pricing class. However, there are other risk characteristics which may have a significant effect on future loss frequency. If these could be identified and measured, they could be used as a base for guiding underwriters in establishing rules for acceptability. These rules would then be helpful to producers in their efforts to select risks which would be acceptable to underwriters.

Guidelines given to the producers are not only designed to restrict writing certain classes of business in any significant volume, but also to aid the producer in properly selecting the correct pricing market for a prospective customer and reduce the chance of a customer being refused insurance protection; a situation which the customer, producer, company, and insurance regulator seek to reduce.

Other Computer Control Activities

Chapter 5 discussed the monitoring of a book of business by territory, by class, by producer, and by type of loss. Through the use of the computer, many additional control activities can be implemented. The following represents some of these computer control activities that have been or are being used.

Quality Index Number A profile of the risk characteristics of the new business written can be captured and reported to underwriting managers by territory or by producer. A *quality index number* can be produced which reflects the mix of business, such as youthful operators versus adult-rated business, and any other risk characteristics, such as traffic violations or driving experience. If a producer's quality index number is deteriorating, corrective action may be taken.

Vehicle Identification Number Use of the full vehicle identification number (VIN) for autos to cause the computer to automatically create the vehicle description on declaration pages and also create the insurance rating symbol for the vehicle is a valuable help. This approach eliminates the human error factor associated with having people "look up" the current symbol in a manual. In addition, the computer locates, within certain parameters, those VINs which are incorrect and will not issue the policy until they are corrected. In various surveys it has been estimated that there is an 8 percent to 10 percent error associated with manual verification of rating symbols. Not only does this technique of VIN utilization provide a better rating approach, but also the company is capable of profiling its business on the basis of make and type of vehicle being insured. As mentioned earlier, such statistics are now being used to price physical damage coverages.

Zip Codes Another aid is the use of zip codes as a help in rating both autos and homeowners. From an underwriting standpoint, the elimination of the time spent to confirm the correctness of the rating territory and the increased accuracy of rating the application have been of great help. From a data processing standpoint, the rating modules can be created around the address of the applicant and the maintenance problems of accuracy are diminished considerably, since most people are cognizant of the need for accurate zip codes.

City Codes Where zip coding cannot be used for accomplishing this type of rating accuracy, companies can use the city name to create a computer table equating the city name to the proper rating territory. All of these things take time to implement, but can save thousands of dollars in people-time and rating inaccuracies.

Immediate Access By placing into the computer all pertinent information from the application, and having the information immediately available from the computer via a cathode-ray tube (CRT), the underwriting function can operate essentially in a "paperless" environment. The immediate availability of policy information for purposes of file review, telephone calls, and profiles, provides a significant advantage to underwriters. The ability to have immediate claim coverage confirmation is also a significant asset for the company and its dealings with policyholders and claimants. Further, policyholders benefit due to more accurate billing and policy status information as well as the increased ease with which policy changes are made.

With all policy information in the system, the company can create any number of screens on the CRT reflecting combinations of information useful for such purposes as billing questions, coverage questions, and accident experience rate modification.

Alpha Search File A number of companies have included in their systems design an alpha search file that identifies the policy number by named insured. This approach can also be utilized to input information regarding individuals for whom the company may desire not to provide future insurance because of adverse information or adverse claim experience. This approach also allows the underwriter to check each new business application to see if (1) current coverage is being provided, (2) coverage was provided at some time in the past and the underwriter should review the record, or (3) there are names of individuals or members of household whom the underwriting department had previously determined they did not want to insure. This alpha search file approach is also ideal for checking a book of business against listings for license suspension or revocation, or listings in local newspapers regarding recent citations or court actions.

Cancellation and Noncontinuation Information The computer can record the reasons for cancellation and noncontinuation and the final disposition of the file. Often, an underwriter receives a call immediately after the individual receives a notice of termination. The computer makes the reasons available immediately because the underwriter does not have to search through a paper file in order to provide an answer.

Combined Auto/Homeowners Files Having available all the information regarding the entire risk being insured is particularly advantageous to an underwriter. Frequently an underwriter is not aware of risk characteristics pertinent to one or the other line of insurance. The computer can combine both files for immediate access, and at less expense.

Third Party Notifications The computer can also be used to send notifications to lienholders or mortgagees. The mechanization of this process assists greatly in reducing the possibility of error.

Joggers Systems may also have an automatic technique built into them to refer to the underwriter cases timed for future action, such as notification that a "youthful" driver will attain driving age in the state in which the vehicle is principally garaged or a file which has been set up for nonrenewal. The fact that driving age may vary by state can be handled by a table within the computer for referral at the right time.

Another example occurs in facility type states where there may be cause for future review of the policies. This may involve a policy that was borderline but was retained by the company awaiting verification of a driving record to determine whether future cession to a facility would be in order. Another possibility would be the follow-up involved if the underwriter decided additional MVRs would be in order on future anniversary dates.

Merit Rating Many companies have a type of merit rating surcharge for accidents and/or traffic violations. To have the system internally adjust the premium based upon addition, deletion or aging of accidents or traffic violations is valuable. Again, this type of mechanization assists in the accuracy of the application of rates, plus the timeliness of such application of rates. It is not unusual for an underwriting department to have a backlog of claims to review, and billing dates could be missed for which additional premiums might be charged had the information been in the computer for rating purposes.

Claims Referrals A number of companies have used a system by which claims meeting certain criteria are referred to the underwriting department. A typical set of criteria prompting a referral are:

- five comprehensive losses in last thirty-six months
- five noncomprehensive losses in last thirty-six months
- three noncomprehensive losses in last twenty-four months
- two noncomprehensive losses in last twelve months
- an indicator to refer the claim file to the underwriter after the next loss

A further approach in claims processing in underwriting would be to input risk review "watch" codes to monitor claims on an individual policy basis, such as:

- caution letter concerning claims record sent to policyholder
- trend in bodily injury losses
- trend in comprehensive losses
- general trend in claim frequency

For example, if the third watch code is entered, the computer automatically would generate a current claims summary after the next comprehensive loss. There are some shortcomings to this type of referral system since it does not take into account length of years between claims or possibly the chargeability of the accident, but it is a device by which companies can more selectively refer the claim files to the underwriting department after the first loss or several small losses have occurred.

It should be noted that a number of companies do not in fact feel the claim referral formula approach is the answer to their everyday underwriting activity. They tend to believe that whenever a chargeable loss occurs, or several nonchargeable losses have occurred, the individual underwriter needs to review the entire risk for continued acceptance. Athough this is the longer, and more expensive way, it often proves the better solution in controlling a book of business.

MVR and Inspection Ordering It is becoming increasingly prevalent—although still in only a few states—that a company's computer can communicate directly with the state motor vehicle record computer and/or inspection company computers. There is a good deal of activity on the part of inspection companies to further this technique, since this would be of direct benefit to the acquisition of additional business from the companies for those who cannot go directly to the state. The degree to which the computer can directly assist the underwriting function in obtaining necessary information (even before the underwriter has seen the application) can be highly beneficial. Thus, an underwriter could make the decision before any policies are issued, avoiding situations where a policyholder receives a policy one day and a termination notice the next. Also, this avoids the time lag involved with the old methods whereby a company remains on a risk longer than necessary.

Other Computer Processing It is particularly advantageous to the underwriting function that any type of rating criteria used by the system to create premiums be entirely mechanized. In this way, information taken directly from the application prompts the premium computation as opposed to coding techniques which were originally used in the early days of data processing. Such things as updating driver classifications when policyholders or insureds become a certain age or claims charged against the policy have aged a number of years consistent with the rating formula, are extremely significant to proper control of a book of business from both the standpoint of accuracy as well as nondiscrimination in rate application.

ELECTRONIC DATA PROCESSING AND THE FUTURE

Insurance companies are heavy users of computers today, and the trend is toward increased use.

With huge sums being spent on computers, it is not surprising that companies are searching for additional ways to use them. Although accounting and statistical duties have represented most of the uses in the past, there are tremendous possibilities for savings by converting other duties to the computers. The underwriting process is one which is being studied.

Mechanization of Homeowners and Other Residence Lines

A few companies have used computers in homeowners insurance to refer only the questionable risks to underwriters. The objective factors of age and construction of the dwelling and the degree of fire protection have been the chief factors used. Attempts to refer risks on the basis of such stability factors as length of time in the area or on the job have not been used, because residence insurance underwriters generally focus on other factors. Another reason may be that residence insurance has not been as volatile in loss results as auto, so fewer factors are used to select risks.

Any attempt to predict the loss becomes difficult when dealing with windstorms, earthquakes, and other catastrophe losses. These perils account for a sizable portion of the loss dollars, but are difficult to predict with respect to the individual policyholder.

Because of the heavy use of objective data, residence insurance seems to be well suited to computers. Undoubtedly there will be more efforts in the future to program the computers to refer problem risks, such as those with aging dwellings or high loss frequencies.

Changes in Techniques

As the use of computers increases, adjustments will have to be made in management decision-making techniques. Some of the more obvious ones are the following:

1. In order to achieve the best results with computers, the people who use them must train themselves to think clearly and with precision. If the computer can produce more detailed and comprehensive information, underwriters will be able to improve their decision-making capabilities.
2. The computer does provide information more rapidly, but to make such information more useful, parameters must be established concerning which items can be resolved automatically and which items would need the personal attention of knowledgeable underwriters.
3. The computer makes information available more abundantly, but excessive data and reports could create a very expensive "paper jungle." What constitutes necessary information must be determined.

4. The computer's real value is as a competitive marketing aid and as a source of information for monitoring. Its implementation for these purposes will require complete cooperation among the different functional departments.
5. The computer has introduced still another communications problem within the business environment in its capacity as a "quasi-decision maker," and the people making use of computers must make certain that the information produced is understood by all who need it.
6. Still another area is in the creation of auditing and sampling activities done by, for example, home office underwriting staffs to monitor the quality of business being accepted in branch offices. With all pertinent details of individual risks in the computer, and available on an on-line basis, the home office staff does not have to rely totally on field audits.

The increasing use of electronic data processing methods by the personal lines underwriting function has created many possibilities for improved efficiency and service to policyholders. The ingenuity of the people involved with the use of such systems will undoubtedly open up even more opportunities for improvement in the future.

SUMMARY

Pressures from regulators, competitors, and the public have contributed to the increasing use of electronic data processing (EDP) systems in the insurance industry. These systems have enabled companies to mechanize operations previously handled manually, improving efficiency and accuracy of service to policyholders and aiding underwriting personnel in establishing sound objectives and making decisions.

The major component of a management information system is the *data base,* a collection of facts stored in a nonredundant, interrelated manner to most effectively meet a variety of information needs. The initial data used in the system are obtained from the application or coding sheet. After input, the computer can provide many different types of information, such as inspection reporting activity, underwriting termination analysis, and inception year analysis.

The major components of an EDP system are as follows:

1. Input Units. Input and storage are handled by the use of punch cards, magnetic tape, and magnetic discs on which information is initially recorded.

2. Central Processing Unit (CPU). This unit has three sections—arithmetic/logic, control, and memory. These sections control the operation of the computer and the movement of information, specify operations to be performed, and handle the calculations and logical operations.
3. Output Unit. Output devices record or write information on cards, paper tape, and magnetic tape, and produce information in a number of other ways.

The language of the computer is based on a code of electrical pulses and utilizes the binary number system. The earliest computer language was Fortran, and Cobol, PL/I, and APL were later developed to meet business needs and to make programming easier.

The use of EDP and computers has had a great impact on the insurance industry, handling such activities as billing, policy issuance, accounts payable, producer's commission statements, and statistical reporting. Heretofore, however, there has been limited use of the computer for risk selection. Efforts are being made in this last area, and computers are now being used in some companies for the screening of new applicants, using either the "referral by exception" method or the "referral by total point count" method which incorporates the discriminant analysis technique.

Beyond the screening of risks, computers are now being used for evaluation of a book of business. This allows the actual effect of specific risk characteristics on loss frequency to be proven statistically. Computers also alter the workflow of the underwriting department and help in the formulation of more realistic underwriting guidelines. In the underwriting of a book of business, the computer can organize masses of data around many different points of concern.

Companies are constantly searching for new ways to utilize the expensive, versatile machines which are being used more and more in the insurance industry. Investigation is in force on the impact of risk characteristics on pricing statistics and the possible uses of computers in homeowners and other residence lines.

Chapter Notes

1. Portions of this chapter are adapted from Michael D. Gantt and James Gatza, *Computers in Insurance* (Malvern, PA: American Institute for Property and Liability Underwriters, 1980).
2. The first three sections of this chapter rely heavily on the following texts:
    - *Property/Liability Personal Lines Insurance: DB/DC Information Systems Design Concepts,* 2nd ed., IBM Corporation, October 1974.
    - *More About Computers,* IBM Corporation.
    - *Introduction to IBM Data Processing Systems,* Student Text, 4th ed., IBM Corporation.
3. Elias M. Awad, *Introduction to Computers in Business* (Englewood Cliffs, NJ: Prentice-Hall, Inc., 1977), pp. 115-119.
4. Edward Yourdon, *Techniques of Program Structure and Design* (Englewood Cliffs, NJ: Prentice-Hall, Inc., 1975) p. 144.

CHAPTER 13

Account Underwriting and Producer Relations

INTRODUCTION

Thus far, this text has concentrated on the underwriting of individual lines of business, with occasional mention of the need to consider the entire account. However, personal lines underwriters need to know not only how to handle individual lines, but also how to handle personal lines *accounts*. They need to be able to monitor the performance of each policy, each line of business, each account, and each producer's book of business in order to be fully able to control their own books of business. The first part of Chapter 13 discusses the personal lines account, including account selling, account underwriting, and personal package policies. The second part of the chapter concentrates on producer relations.

PERSONAL LINES ACCOUNTS

Accounts

An account is defined as the set of insurance coverages held by a single insured.[1] A typical set of personal insurance coverages might include the following:

1. *Auto insurance*—two cars, insured for liability, comprehensive, collision, medical payments, uninsured motorists, and towing and labor.

2. *Homeowners insurance*—dwelling, appurtenant structures, contents, additional living expense, comprehensive personal liability, medical payments, and damage to property of others.
3. *Jewelry floater*—several expensive items of jewelry and family heirlooms.
4. *Yacht policy*—thirty-foot inboard/outboard and trailer, insured for physical damage, medical payments, and liability.
5. *Personal umbrella policy*—excess liability superimposed on auto, homeowners, and yacht policies.
6. *Individual life insurance*—varying forms, for various amounts, on husband, wife, and children.
7. *Group medical insurance*—provided through employer.
8. *Group disability insurance*—provided through employer.
9. *Accident insurance*—purchased for school-age children under a group accident policy.
10. *Credit life and disability insurance*—in connection with various loans and charge accounts.

The underwriter who is reviewing an auto or homeowners policy is examining only part of the entire "account."

In this chapter, the terms *account, account underwriting, account buying,* and *account selling* refer to insurance normally purchased on an *individual* basis. Group insurance (numbers 7 through 10 shown in the preceding list) cannot be sold directly to the individual by the company or producer, but individual life or accident and health insurance (not purchased through an employer or other group) may be an important part of the account. This chapter will not deal with life and health insurance since it is invariably handled by a different underwriting department than that which handles property and liability coverages.

Account Selling

In account selling, one producer or underwriter endeavors to write all of the insurance for a particular insured, rather than only part of the account. This increases premium size and provides the producer with an opportunity to minimize overlaps and gaps in coverage which might otherwise occur.[2] The ultimate goal of account selling is the elimination of one-policy "accounts," unless the one policy is the entire account. (A one-policy account might be that provided for a teenager living with parents who purchases a car. Auto insurance may be the teenager's only insurance need, and the teenager's auto policy might be termed an account. However, many producers and underwriters would consider this part of the parents' account.)

Account buying, which is purchasing all insurance from one producer, does not come naturally to many insurance buyers. Since insurance requirements develop at different times, people are likely to fill those requirements from various sources. Many people obtain their first insurance policy when their parents purchase a small life insurance policy for them. When they buy their first car, they purchase auto insurance, sometimes from the producer who serviced their parents, sometimes from another source. When they purchase a home, or perhaps when they move to an apartment, they seek to insure other property. At that time, the real estate agent or mortgagee may steer them toward a different producer. Because the auto policy and the homeowners policy were purchased at different times, from different producers, to meet different needs, with different expiration dates, people frequently do not even associate one with the other. Yet, insurance professionals should recognize that the various insurance policies in an individual's portfolio are interrelated. It is often advantageous to the insured, producer, and underwriter to have all coverages in the same company.

When all coverages are handled by one producer, he or she can see to it that coverage is coordinated. Separate outboard boat liability coverage may be unnecessary if that coverage is included in the homeowners policy. Liability limits on underlying policies may be coordinated with the requirements of the umbrella policy. When a producer properly controls an account, the insured can have a coordinated insurance program rather than a handful of policies.

There are also benefits to the insured if all coverages are with the same company, since some claims involve coverage under more than one policy. This might be the case, for example, if a car burns and personal property inside the car is also destroyed. Usually one adjuster can handle both claims, if all coverage is with one company. Any question as to which policy covers what damaged item is then irrelevant to the insured, unless different deductibles are involved. The insured will not have to wait for two different companies to determine which has the coverage or what share will be paid by each of the companies.

In addition to better client service, account selling has two major benefits from the producer's point of view: increased volume and reduced competition.

Increased Volume In order to increase premium volume, the producer must continue to write new policies while retaining many of those already written. There are two sources of additional premium: existing customers and new customers. Of the two, existing customers are generally more accessible.

Many producers maintain customer profiles using forms like that

Exhibit 13-1
Account-Profile

ACCOUNT PROFILE

ACCOUNT ______________ RESIDENCE ______________
PRODUCER ______________ BUSINESS ______________
PRODUCER CODE ______________ EXT ______________

INSURED ______________ OTHER ______________
ADDRESS ______________ CITY, STATE ______________ ZIP ______________
BUSINESS ______________ EMPLOYER ______________
BIRTHDATE ______________ SOCIAL SECURITY ______________ D.L. ______________
SPECIAL HANDLING INSTRUCTIONS: INCOME: 0-10 ______
10-15 ______
15-25 ______
25 + ______

IMPORTANT MEMBERS: NAME	D.O.B.	SOCIAL SECURITY	OCCUPATION	D.L.

COVERAGE	HAVE	INTERESTED	X-DATE	PREMIUM	REMARKS
AUTOMOBILE				$	
HOMEOWNERS				$	
FIRE				$	
LIFE				$	
HEALTH				$	
COMMERCIAL				$	
COMMERCIAL				$	
SPECIALTIES				$	
				$	
				$	
				$	

CLAIMS HISTORY:

POLICY NUMBER	REPORTED	COMPANY	PAID	AMOUNT	DESCRIPTION
				$	
				$	
**				$	
				$	
				$	
				$	
				$	
				$	
				$	
				$	

**FILE TO BE REVIEWED BY MANAGEMENT: ____________ DATE ____________

COMMENTS: CROSS FILE ____________

ACCOUNT NUMBER ____________

REMEMBER X—DATES REFERRED BY ____________

shown in Exhibit 13-1.[3] Elaborate color-coding systems are sometimes used to identify at a glance which coverages have been written for each customer. Computers may be used to develop customer profiles and to develop lists of existing customers who may be prospects for additional coverage.

Reduced Competition Whenever there is more than one producer servicing an account, the chances of losing the business increase. The auto producer takes the chance that the homeowners producer will successfully solicit the auto business.

In addition, there is the possibility that the "other" producer will be first to approach the insured with a new coverage. If this occurs, the entire account may be lost.

Producer Attitudes Toward Account Selling Increased premium volume, reduced competition, and minimized coverage overlaps and gaps may be accomplished through account selling. Though rewarding, account selling requires extra sales effort. If there are different anniversary and expiration dates on different lines within an account, it is necessary to get the expiration date ("x-date") of the line(s) not currently written and to contact the insured at an appropriate time before the x-date with a request to write the rest of the account.

Not all producers are interested in account selling. Some agencies reach a saturation point. Growth would be possible, but it would require hiring and training additional personnel, additional office space, and additional payroll expenses until the new personnel were fully trained. Agencies in this stage of development may not show much growth, but this stability may be of value in an underwriter's overall book of business.

Much of the aggressive producer's effort is devoted to writing new business. In many cases, the producer can only succeed in writing one line of business for a new customer. Perhaps he or she can fill one requirement that is not met by the present insurer, or can offer a lower price for one line of coverage. Under such circumstances, it is not likely that the producer would encourage the prospect to keep all the policies together with another producer. Rather, part of the account will be written and the rest will be solicited later.

The way in which business is solicited depends largely on whether it is written as an account or a single policy. Many customers choose an insurer only on the basis of price—a practice encouraged by some producers. If the producer sells the auto business solely on price, it is difficult at that point to request the homeowners business if the premium is higher than the premium on the insured's existing policy. In fact, it is difficult to retain the auto business if the company raises rates, because the producer has told the insured that it is advisable to change insurers to get a lower price.

Some producers may refuse to do anything but account sell. They may refuse even to prepare a quotation unless they can quote on the entire account. Even then, they may stress coverage and service, and minimize the importance of price. This sales approach may not be very effective when a customer is primarily concerned with price.

Company Attitudes Toward Account Selling Company attitudes toward account selling vary, but the concept is widely supported. Marketing programs are often geared to account selling. During sales campaigns, producers are encouraged to solicit existing policyholders for umbrella business or for boat insurance.

But, if a company experiences difficulties with a particular line of business (for example, if auto experience deteriorates), they may cease to solicit new auto policies while continuing to solicit new homeowners business. Thus the same company that encouraged account selling may ask producers to continue writing homeowners, but to place the auto policies elsewhere.

There are many advantages to account buying and account selling, from the standpoint of insured, producer, and underwriter. There are also disadvantages, depending on the attitude of the buyer and the producer, the nature of the risk, and the willingness of the underwriter to accept and service the entire account.

Account Underwriting

Account underwriting refers to the concept that the profitability of a particular insured's business should be determined on an overall basis.[4] All other things being equal, business handled as an account may receive better treatment than a single policy. A request for additional coverage or unusual coverage might be met with little resistance if the files indicate that the insured has been loyal (and profitable) over a period of years. A request for a personal umbrella, for example, might be processed without hesitation for a known account, whereas an unknown applicant would be investigated quite thoroughly before the policy was issued.

If an insured has an unusual need, such as a trip transit policy covering a single move of household furniture, the producer and underwriter will try to write the policy as an accommodation for a valued account. An unknown customer might be rejected if the same request were made.

A borderline risk does not become a good risk because it is part of an account. However, the insured can benefit when all exposures are weighed on an account basis. Producers benefit when they are better able to serve their customers and increase their commission per client.

Generally, the company will also benefit from account selling and account underwriting. More information will be in the file when more than one policy is written, which will improve the underwriter's composite picture of the risk. One outside report may provide information usable on two or more policies. An underwriter who has tentatively decided to nonrenew an auto policy which has experienced three towing claims and one broken windshield during the past two years might take into consideration that the homeowners and the boat policy have been loss free. The auto experience could indicate a "claims-consciousness" problem, but the absence of homeowners and boat claims reduces this likelihood. While the auto policy by itself may be borderline, the entire account may be desirable.

In some EDP systems, information duplicated on several policies, such as the named insured and the address, may be stored in the computer memory only once, reducing processing costs on multiple policy accounts.

Making Underwriting Decisions on Accounts To make the correct underwriting decision on any policy, the underwriter should compare information against underwriting criteria, weigh the results of the comparison, and then consider other factors. Before making an underwriting decision on any line of coverage, the underwriter should consider its impact on the entire account.

First, the underwriter must know whether the exposure being analyzed is a single policy or part of an account. The application may provide this information, or procedures may call for the underwriter to receive the entire file on all accounts.

Second, the underwriter should know the company's attitude toward account underwriting. If the underwriting guide dictates that each policy must stand on its own merit, collateral business only provides additional information. And even when collateral business may not justify acceptance of a submission that would otherwise be rejected, the quality of the collateral business may affect the underwriter's subjective evaluation of the submission.

It is easy to make a decision to accept an account with no adverse exposures. It is nearly as easy to reject an account with many adverse exposures. The decision becomes more difficult when part of the account meets all criteria, but another part does not. In such a case, the underwriter must weigh the account's strengths against its weaknesses, identify the alternatives, and select the best alternative.

When a marginal submission is received, its merits and demerits must be measured or weighed against the merits and demerits of each policy in the account. To do this, an underwriter may ask questions such as:

1. What are the respective *limits of liability?* An HO-1 with a limit on the dwelling of $15,000 is hardly expected to balance a youthful driver with a marginal driving record who requests limits of $100,000/$300,000 bodily injury and $25,000 property damage. Conversely, the $15,000 homeowners may support a request for hull coverage on a sailboat valued at $800 that would be unacceptable as a single account.
2. What are the respective *premiums?* As an incentive to write a substandard auto policy, underwriters are frequently offered the applicant's homeowners policy when it expires. The annual homeowners premium of $80 is not expected to outweigh the negative risk characteristics of the auto policy carrying a surcharged premium of $650.
3. What are the respective *frequencies of loss?* An insured or producer is often successful in using supporting business to place or retain a policy with a high loss frequency. The premium on the supporting business may be sufficient to offset a series of vandalism and theft claims under a homeowners policy, for example. The potential cumulative loss in this situation, however, must be carefully considered in underwriting the account.
4. What are the respective *severities of loss?* Even a loss-free account consisting of an auto policy, a homeowners policy, and personal umbrella may not be sufficient to balance the potential loss severity presented in a $10,000 fine arts floater on an antique Sevres vase. The high probability of a total loss must be carefully weighed against the probable severity of the supporting lines of business.

Despite a request to write all coverages for an account, one alternative may be to accept part of the account and reject another portion. Depending on the circumstances, an underwriter might offer to write the homeowners and reject the auto, or vice versa, or might accept both auto and homeowners while rejecting a jewelry floater.

Other alternatives include a counteroffer to write limited coverage on property, or a nonstandard (surcharged) pricing program for the auto policy. On an unprotected seasonal dwelling, the underwriter may offer to "share the line" with other insurers and write, for example, 25 percent of the amount of insurance. Rejection is appropriate only after all reasonable alternatives have been considered. This is always true but is especially important in account underwriting. The underwriter's counteroffer of some sort of acceptable coverage is a demonstration of positive underwriting.

The decision-making process applied to accounts is not really different from that applied to individual lines of coverage. The chief differences involved when considering several policies are there are more factors to weigh, and there may be a wider range of possible alternatives from which to choose.

There is more premium in an account than in a single policy. Since more exposures are involved, there is a broader spread of exposures. Increased premium and broadened spread of exposures are goals for which many companies constantly strive, and thus underwriters more often than not find it desirable to expand their book of business by encouraging producers to account sell. Account selling leads to account underwriting, which can contribute to the successful attainment of underwriting objectives.

Second-Stage Package Policies Today, many insurance policies contain coverages that were originally handled by several single-line policies. Also, several companies have developed package policies which combine the auto and homeowners coverages, and sometimes other personal lines coverages (such as marine floaters and umbrellas) into a single policy. There is a great deal of variation in packages currently being underwritten. Some contain extra coverages not found in conventional forms; some are blended so that it is impossible to tell where auto coverage ceases and residence coverage begins. Some have a common deductible or a common limit of coverage on all property.

Combination policies, in many cases, are priced lower than individual policies. A slightly lower price can be justified if acquisition expenses and underwriting expenses are reduced. In addition, with highly selective underwriting, prices can be lowered because of lower anticipated losses.

To some extent the combination policy is a marketing device. The producer can make many sound arguments to persuade a customer to put all coverages together. The price is itself a strong argument. Also, the coordinated benefits of an account policy can eliminate gaps and overlaps in coverage.

Some companies have been reluctant to handle second-stage package policies. Underwriting decision making is complicated further if the underwriter must reject the entire account when the auto is unacceptable and the residence is acceptable, or vice versa. A rate increase because of poor experience with residences may cause a loss of accounts, which is more serious than a loss of only one line of business.

Second-stage package policies may be the way of the future, or they may be a passing fad. They present an attractive concept by covering all or most property and liability (and sometimes life) insurance needs with one policy. They offer interesting marketing opportunities, and the possibility of reducing company expenses.

Second-stage package policies also offer underwriting challenges. As with account underwriting involving several policies, there are more factors to consider than with a single policy. There is also a better spread of exposures. Because more coverages are provided by a package policy, one adverse exposure may have less impact when weighed against an entire account. It may be that, with a broader spread of exposure, second-stage package policies are less likely to suffer from adverse selection. Again, this potential is attractive to underwriters.

The future of the second-stage package policy remains uncertain. Depending on the results of those now offering such programs, such programs may proliferate or they may phase out.

PRODUCER RELATIONS

Producer Functions

To be successful, producers must have a feeling of responsibility for their client's welfare. In addition, they must have:

- knowledge of coverage and the insurance business,
- time and facilities to provide necessary services,
- good contacts with their insurance markets so as to obtain prompt and favorable action for their clients,
- fair and prompt claim service, and
- the ability to command the respect and cooperation of clients, competitors, underwriters, claim adjusters, marketing representatives, and others.

These qualities are necessary for producers to successfully perform their four chief functions of:

1. sales,
2. retention,
3. servicing accounts, and
4. field underwriting.

Sales Without insurance sales, the producer earns no commission; unless insurance is sold, the company has no business to underwrite. Aggressive selling is essential to the new producer who must build a book of business sufficient to support the agency. As the agency grows, and service activity increases, sales activity often decreases. Yet new business production remains important even when an agency has stabilized. New accounts are needed to make up for the normal attrition occasioned by deaths, people moving out of the area, and those policyholders who, for one reason or another, will place their business with another producer. The impact of this attrition, which is greatly influenced by the market conditions at any given time, has been estimated at anywhere from 15 percent to 30 percent of a producer's annual volume of personal lines business.

New business sales result from actively seeking contact with persons likely to become customers. The producer must initiate the contact, either by telephone, direct solicitation, or direct mail with telephone follow-up. Often it is necessary, as a first step, to obtain the expiration date of present coverage, and contact the prospect forty-five to sixty days before the "x-date." And, once their prospects have agreed to make the purchase, the producers must complete detailed applications, collect the premium, submit the applications to the company, wait for the policies, and deliver them before the sale is actually completed.

Retention The commission structure in property and liability insurance is different from that employed in life insurance, recognizing differences in producer activity. Life insurance producers collect a large commission for new business, and a very small commission when future premiums are paid since life insurance involves very little servicing, once written. Some property-liability insurers pay the same commission for both new and renewal business; for others the commission is reduced for renewals, but is still greater than the renewal commission for life insurance.

Personal lines are highly competitive, and many customers show little loyalty. To minimize attrition, the producer must provide good service, and must keep in touch with customers by remaining attentive to their changing needs and to changing products. If renewal premiums are not paid promptly, the producer may need to contact customers to discover if there are any problems which might cause them to purchase insurance elsewhere.

Servicing Accounts The producer may initiate service or respond to requests for service. The best producers, those who control their accounts, do both. Because the average policyholder's exposure to loss is constantly changing, the producer should provide customers with ongoing counsel on the changing environment and its impact on insurance needs. This would include such recommendations as increasing liability limits, increasing property limits, and deleting coverages no longer needed, such as collision coverage on a car that is severely depreciated.

Service may be requested at any time during the policy period.

Questions need to be answered. The customer may ask, "Am I covered if I rent a trailer?" or "Does my policy cover my daughter if she drives a friend's car?" Such questions need to be answered promptly and correctly.

Policy changes must be handled, and the volume of policy changes involved, particularly with auto policies, is enormous. Endorsements or revised declarations must be checked to ascertain that the company made the change requested, and finally, they must be delivered to the insured. For agency-billed policies, the change must be processed through the accounting system, and additional premium collected, or return premium refunded.

In order to initiate policy changes and handle billing problems, the producer must be keenly aware of individual company practices. Direct-billing systems are ostensibly designed to reduce producer involvement in the billing and collection process. They do reduce producer involvement in routine transactions, but the producer usually becomes involved if there is a billing problem.

Service is vital whenever there is a claim. The producer or clerk handling claims must give assurances that the claim will be handled promptly and fairly. Of course, if there is no coverage, that must be tactfully explained.

The producer's involvement in claim service may involve only referring the insured to the company claim telephone number, or it may involve completing the report and issuing an agency claim draft in full payment of the claim.

Field Underwriting Underwriting begins in the producer's office. Company underwriters sometimes fail to realize how many unacceptable risks they do not see because these are declined by the producer.

Most producers attempt to produce profitable business. If they persistently sell to customers who develop a high loss frequency, they will eventually lose their markets. Insurance companies cannot, in the long run, afford to retain producers who do not practice sound risk selection. However, very few producers can perform the complete task of underwriting, particularly when their commissions are based on quantity rather than quality. Producers can be expected to refuse applicants who are obviously ineligible or who are in prohibited classifications. Borderline and doubtful risks are more often sent to the underwriter for a decision.

Good field underwriting requires more than a general awareness of each company's underwriting philosophy. The producer must be aware of the reasons for underwriting policies, so that they can be explained to policyholders. For example, some companies require a medical statement of auto operators who have reached a certain age. The purpose is solely to determine whether there are any conditions which would seriously impair the insured's ability to properly operate a motor vehicle. If this concept is not properly communicated to an aging policyholder, the impression might easily be given that the insurance company was trying to find a way to discontinue coverage. The producer must be able to convince the policyholder that this underwriting practice is consistently applied to protect the company and the general public.

Many companies use profit-sharing programs (or contingency commissions) to provide an additional incentive to producers who develop profitable business. Under a profit-sharing (contingency) contract, the producer receives a share of the profits the company makes on the producer's book of business, often according to a fixed formula. Since profit-sharing develops an incentive to produce higher-quality business, many feel its emphasis should be increased. They believe more underwriting authority should be given to producers, and their compensation system should be revised, with reduced emphasis on commissions and increased emphasis on profit sharing. Proponents of this philosophy feel that, if producers are compensated more for quality and less for quantity, they will exercise even more selective field underwriting.

While there is merit in that idea, it has not always worked as intended under existing profit-sharing programs. Producers with a book of profitable business try, to varying degrees, to maintain its quality to earn the contingency payment. But when experience deteriorates due to shock losses or inadequate rates, the profit-sharing checks disappear. With no short-term prospect of returning to profitability, the producer may become less quality conscious, and experience may deteriorate further.

Underwriters as Marketing Personnel

In all of the major producer functions—sales, retention, service, and field underwriting—there is a strong need for the underwriter's involvement. This is not necessarily a duplication of effort. The more aware the underwriter is of the producer's role and specific needs, the better the underwriter can address them and encourage a strong working relationship.

As one means of strengthening the relationship between producer and underwriter, some companies have combined the underwriting and marketing functions of personal lines. This is done by making personal lines marketing one of the responsibilities of the underwriting department.

It is hoped that this type of field organization will, among other things:

- help to centralize responsibility for production and underwriting results;
- encourage joint planning between the producer and company;
- make the underwriter more aware of conditions in the marketplace; and
- reduce the number of communicators, and therefore improve communications between the producer and the company.

When marketing and underwriting functions are combined, the underwriter may be better able to underwrite *producers* rather than *individual accounts.* If combined with a workable producer remuneration system which rewards producers for profits as well as for volume, it may be found that most individual account underwriting is done at the producer (or agency) level. Most of the principles taught in this text may be applied by agency personnel as well as company personnel.

Many companies are headed in that direction. Others, taking a more conservative stance, hold that the underwriter must be free to make sound underwriting judgments and should therefore not be responsible for production.

Common Interests and Goals

Because underwriters have varying degrees of responsibility for production, and producers practice varying degrees of underwriting, it follows that the two functions share many similarities.

The income that supports both producers and underwriters is generated when a producer makes a sale. To provide an incentive for sales, producers are rewarded for sales volume. Because of this system of rewards for performance, producers attempt to emphasize new business sales, account selling, and upgrading and renewal of existing accounts. Because no commission is generated by a sale that is not consummated, producers tend to concentrate their efforts on accounts that will produce business acceptable to their underwriters.

Producers are also rewarded for good underwriting results. Profit-sharing agreements, where applicable, increase the producer's income if results are favorable. Other, more subtle rewards also exist, such as increased willingness by underwriters to make exceptions for producers who have been profitable. Negative results lead to negative rewards, such as reduced willingness by underwriters to grant exceptions. Continued poor performance can result in termination of a producer's contract. Therefore, although producers' short-term rewards (commissions) are based on volume, long-term rewards are based on volume combined with profits.

Underwriters' performance evaluations are often based on their success in reaching profit goals, but frequently they are also given volume goals to meet. Although overly restrictive underwriting may aid short-term profitability, it is also necessary to maintain or increase volume to meet long-term objectives. While underwriters' short-term rewards are based on profits, long-term rewards are based on profits combined with volume.

It can be seen that the objective of both producers and underwriters in the long run is to produce an increasing volume of profitable business. The different emphases of production and underwriting creates a system of checks and balances. Because producers are more directly rewarded for volume, they tend to be a little more aggressive than underwriters. Underwriters tend to be a bit more cautious, lest their results be impaired by an unwise decision.

Establishing Producer Relations

Personal lines underwriters are both underwriters of individual risks and managers of a book of business. In many cases the latter function is more important than the former. Since "good" producers consistently submit good business, one goal of the personal lines underwriter is to develop all "good" producers. If that goal can be achieved, there will be less need to underwrite individual risks. It will be necessary, however, to be sure the producers maintain their level of performance.

To be an effective manager of a book of business, the underwriter must establish good producer relations from the beginning. At this point, the underwriter and the producer should agree on mutual goals and objectives. Then the underwriter should monitor results to determine whether goals are met. Through tactful discussion with the producer, results should be reviewed and new goals set for the future. Corrective action by the underwriter, in the form of a reunderwriting program, may be necessary if results have been unsatisfactory.

At the initial meeting between underwriter and producer, the following points should be kept in mind:

1. There must develop a feeling of partnership. In order that mutual respect be forthcoming, both producer and underwriter must agree on ways to achieve their common objectives.
2. The producer should be made aware of and generally accept underwriting policies and procedures, and must be given a clear presentation of the company's underwriting philosophy and the

classes and types of business it finds acceptable. The underwriter must understand that every rejected application is a potential source of irritation to the producer, office staff, and applicant. A large number of rejected applications should indicate the need for further discussion between the producer and the underwriter concerning underwriting guidelines. Also, the underwriter should be aware that every company processes business a little differently, and notable differences should be discussed.

3. The expectations of both the producer and underwriter should be established. The underwriter should be prepared to identify what he or she expects from the producer and what could be expected in return.
4. A course of action should be agreed upon, and the underwriter and producer should decide how to measure the effectiveness of these actions. This is the point at which both parties should identify their financial objectives and how such things as the accuracy of underwriting data will be tested and the frequency of testing. Discussions at this point should include the size and nature of growth and loss ratios anticipated, together with any qualifications that might apply on new business and renewal business. For example, companies withdrawing from certain geographic areas and/or major service or processing problems might cause temporary limitations on new business.

Once mutual goals and objectives have been established, the process is one of monitoring results to determine whether goals have been met and to establish goals for the future.

Monitoring Producer Effectiveness

Results are monitored in various ways at various times. There is an informal ongoing monitoring process in which the underwriter continuously evaluates each producer based on daily contacts. In many companies there is a more formal review when monthly or quarterly statistical reports are made available, or when research must be done for other reasons. Then there is the annual review, at which time producer results are formally analyzed.

The formal annual review will be discussed here. Various elements of the formal review may be used for less formal evaluations. Of course, the same approach will be helpful to an underwriter newly assigned to a group of producers.

Gathering and Organizing Information The amount of information available and the format for organizing it are different in different situations, since each company has its own type of computer system and filing system. Although the format may vary, there are several general categories of useful information:

1. objective statistical data,
2. agency files,
3. information available from the claim department, and
4. information available by direct contact with the producer.

A discussion of each of these categories will be useful in determining the great amount of information available to examine producer results.

Objective Statistical Data. Exactly what data is available depends on each company's management information system. Likewise, interpretation of statistical data should be done with a knowledge of how the data are compiled. For example, the underwriter should know if quarterly reports include incurred but not reported (IBNR) losses or contain only reported incurred losses for that quarter. (At any given time there is a certain volume of losses which can be estimated and which have not been reported. To maintain the overall integrity of the data, these IBNRs are allocated on an equitable basis among all producers. Before attempting an in-depth analysis of a computer printout, an underwriter should be armed with a guide to its interpretation. Various types of data may be available on each producer such as:

1. Number of policies in force by line of business. This is a static figure, and indicates how many policies of each type the producer has on the books at one time. Compared with previous policy counts, the underwriter can determine whether the number of policies is increasing or decreasing and what lines are affected. This figure thus provides a measure of production and conservation activities.
2. Number of new business policies for the previous year by line of business. Caution is required in analyzing these figures, because policies that have lapsed and been rewritten may count as new business. New business policies are a measure of current production activity. A comparison with new business policy counts for previous years can indicate whether production emphasis is increasing or decreasing. Comparison of new business production between various lines of business shows in what areas production efforts were concentrated.
3. Dollars of new business premium by line of business. Here again, the underwriter must understand the statistical base. A comparison with other figures may be misleading if only the initial premium is counted in this figure, on quarterly-billed business.

4. Dollars of written premium for the previous year by line of business. This figure represents the total or aggregate of all premium transactions recorded on the books of the insurer (whether paid, unpaid, or financed), less cancellations, reductions, experience credits, retrospective returns, and discounts. In effect, it equals premium billed during the year.
5. Dollars of earned premium for the previous year by line of business. Since one-twelfth of an annual policy premium is earned each month, this amount represents the amount of insurance premium actually used up by customers of the producer during the reporting period. During periods of growth, earned premium will be less than written premium. When volume is decreasing, the converse is true.
6. Dollars of incurred losses by line of business. This figure includes all losses "incurred" during the reporting year, including losses which have not been paid but for which a reserve has been set aside. It also includes adjustments in reserves for losses incurred during previous reporting periods. Depending on the accounting system, it may include loss adjustment expenses, and an allowance for IBNR losses.
7. Loss ratio by line of business. Here the underwriter must note whether the loss ratio is the ratio of incurred losses to earned premium, paid losses to written premium, or some other measure. The underwriter should also be aware of the permissible loss ratio for each line of business.
8. Loss ratio by line of business for the past five years. By combining five years' experience, this figure is much more credible than a one-year loss ratio because it is based on a larger set of data. Yet this figure should be analyzed only in conjunction with other data, such as the current year's loss ratio, and with the realization that the data still might not be credible. If the five-year average is favorable and the current ratio is unfavorable, an undesirable trend may be developing or the producer may have had an unlucky year. If the five-year average is unfavorable and the current year is favorable, this may reflect either an improvement in agency underwriting or a lucky year.
9. Dollars of commission by line of business. This figure represents the producer's gross income received from the company in the past year. Out of this commission, the producer has to pay taxes, staff salaries, and all overhead and office expenses.
10. Other statistical information may be available in just about any form that can be handled by computer, such as a breakdown of

the number of auto policies sold by each agency in each rating category.

In analyzing each producer's statistical information, it is also useful to have available statistical information on the underwriter's office and the company as a whole, to determine whether each producer is doing better or worse than "par."

Files on Each Agency. Each underwriting office may have one or more files containing materials pertinent to each producer. These files may contain the following types of information:

1. information regarding the original agency appointment;
2. the agency contract;
3. correspondence or memorandums dealing with unusual events (such as a change of ownership);
4. correspondence establishing goals for the agency;
5. letters of declination, or letters accepting marginal risks;
6. records of producer's timeliness of payments to the company on producer-billed business; and
7. records on company-billed business which has lapsed for nonpayment.

Claims Department Information. Information may be available from the claims department, such as the following:

1. correspondence regarding claims;
2. comments on producer's use of draft authority, if the producer is permitted to pay certain claims;
3. confidential reports on questionable risks;
4. narrative descriptions of specific losses;
5. subjective impressions of each producer's clientele; and
6. subjective impressions of each producer's professionalism in claims handling.

Information Gathered from Direct Contact with the Producer. Despite the voluminous statistical information available in the underwriting office and the amount of objective and subjective data available in correspondence, other files, and through conversations with the claims department, it is necessary to obtain additional information by direct contact with the producer. Without direct contact, the underwriter's impression cannot be complete, and the evaluation may be inaccurate. A desk underwriter may have to rely on a marketing representative's description of agency operations. But it is preferable to make a first-hand visit, particularly when other information indicates impending problems.

A first-hand visit provides information on the agency layout and location, which greatly affects the agency's public image and potential clientele. There are big differences among a booth in a department store, an office on the thirty-second floor of a skyscraper, and an office nestled in the corner of an auto body shop. The agency located in a modern shopping center may have a greater potential of attracting desirable personal lines customers than the agency in a deteriorating trailer on a used car lot. A location with lots of pedestrian traffic may attract more walk-in business than a location away from street level.

Within the agency, allocation of responsibilities among personnel is important. In some situations the producer personally handles commercial accounts but delegates personal lines work to less experienced personnel.

Analysis of Producer Performance Producer results should be analyzed to see whether they are in line with company goals and objectives, and with the goals and objectives established for that particular producer. Company goals and producer goals may vary, and the relative emphasis among different categories to be analyzed may vary. Although not all-encompassing, there are four points that can be considered in every analysis of personal lines producer results:

1. spread of business,
2. extent of new business activity,
3. volume perpetuation, and
4. loss experience.

Spread of Business. Under normal circumstances, a certain "mix" of business is desirable. Most personal lines companies would prefer a balanced book of auto and homeowners business, with some miscellaneous lines.

Where there is more than one auto program, or more than one homeowners program, a mix is usually desirable. If a given producer's spread of risk is much narrower than the norm, it may indicate that the company is being used only for one line rather than all lines. The result may be adverse selection.

For example, one company may find a given producer with a relatively low proportion of homeowners to auto business. Further investigation might show that another company with a discounted residence insurance program is getting the bulk of this producer's homeowners business. Because the company is getting only those residences rejected by the company with the discounted premiums, adverse selection may result.

The mix between personal lines and commercial lines business is also important, particularly if personal lines insurance is incidental to a commercially oriented insurance agency.

Extent of New Business Activity. In analyzing new business activity, the underwriter should consider both volume and mix. A certain volume of new business production is needed to overcome attrition. With no new business production, the producer's volume will shrink. A significant new business volume, with reasonable attrition, is needed for growth.

The spread of business on the books indicates the results of past production. The mix of new business production indicates present emphasis. Current production may indicate that the producer is trying to improve the overall mix due to previously established goals. Or, the results may indicate that the producer is not using the company at all for certain lines of business, in which case the reason needs to be determined. The producer may have found the company is no longer competitive in a certain line of business due to a rate increase.

It is also necessary to consider whether the company is getting its proportional share of new business for the size of the agency. If the agency has recently taken on another company, they may be honoring a commitment to the new company to build volume.

Volume Perpetuation. An analysis of new business production, attrition, and mix of business should provide an indication of the agency's growth. Although companies would like to see all agencies grow, they must realistically admit that many reach a saturation point and may even begin to reduce volume. An intentional volume reduction may be beneficial if part of an agency reunderwriting program. Many producers have discovered that they could make greater profits with fewer accounts by weeding out those that are less desirable.

Loss Experience. In looking at the producer's loss ratio, several factors need to be considered. First, it is necessary to ask whether a high loss ratio is caused by a frequency or a severity problem. One or two shock losses may represent nothing more than one or more fortuitous losses. But they may also represent a book of business prone to shock losses, and some judgment is required to determine which is more probable.

Loss frequency is a greater danger sign. If a producer is unprofitable over a reasonable period of time and there have been no shock losses, there is either a very low agency volume or a poor book of business which requires reunderwriting. There may be outside circumstances at work, such as an inadequate rate structure, or an unusually severe winter leading to a plethora of fender-bender claims.

If there is one line of business which is particularly unprofitable, the underwriter might ask whether there is undue production emphasis by this producer on an unprofitable line of business.

An examination of specific loss files, particularly on high severity claims, might be in order to determine whether there are any trends.

An evaluation of loss ratio must be made in the light of agency volume. A small amount of personal lines business can be made unprofitable if one Cadillac is stolen. When several million dollars of business is involved, the loss ratio is much more meaningful as an indicator of underwriting results.

Identification and Development of Alternative Courses of Action Seldom, if ever, are a producer's results so good that they cannot be improved. Whenever a producer is profitable, companies tend to look for a greater volume with little reduction in profitability. If a producer is unprofitable, the underwriter might anticipate a reduced volume of business sufficient to achieve profitability.

Reunderwriting first involves identifying the problem. A planned reduction in all personal lines business is not the answer to an unprofitable book of homeowners. If homeowners alone are the problem, homeowners alone need to be reunderwritten.

Also, if one class of business has been found unprofitable, it is necessary to determine what characteristics are common to the undesirable segment of that class. If residences are the problem, is it the old homes, the unprotected homes, or the homes in one neighborhood that seem to cause problems? Are the problems isolated to physical hazards, or are there certain moral and morale hazards characteristic of the producer's clientele? Are risks properly classified and rated? Has the premium level deteriorated due to inadequate rates, or due to inadequate insurance to value?

These questions and dozens like them, based on information throughout this text, may provide the key to identifying the problems in a producer's book of business. Once identified, the "weeding" process can begin, and must be continued until all insureds in the problem class have been reanalyzed. If the problem is with a book of three-year residence policies that cannot be canceled at anniversary, the reunderwriting process may take three years.

Under most circumstances, the producer should be kept advised of any reunderwriting program if producer and underwriter are to work as a team. In fact, the producer should often be asked for advice. Given the chance, producers will often take thc initiative in correcting their problems to preserve a long-term favorable relationship with their companies.

Implementing the Decision After the best alternative has been chosen, it must be implemented as soon as possible. In addition, the selected course of action must be monitored to determine whether the

Exhibit 13-2
AGENCY A—1981 Results

Line of Business	New Bus. Items	Gross Written Premium	Net Earned Premium	Net Loss Incurred	Loss Ratio
Standard Auto	8	$ 22.468	$ 21.337	$ 9.033	42.3%
Preferred Auto	15	42.159	42.041	18.185	43.3
Nonstandard Auto	0	0	353	3.338	944.9
Subtotal Auto	23	64.627	63.732	30.555	47.9
Homeowners	2	8.897	9.827	1.531	15.6
Fire, EC & Allied	1	1.065	888	0	0
Inland Marine	0	675	838	152	18.1
Ocean Marine	0	0	0	0	0
Umbrella	0	132	118	0	0
Liab. & Burglary	0	−159	78	0	0
Total Personal Lines	26	75.237	75.480	32.239	42.7
Total Agency	31	$123.804	$125.005	$44.912	35.9%

desired results are being obtained. It is this final step which makes all underwriting decision making a continuing process.

CASE STUDIES IN MONITORING PRODUCER RESULTS

It has been repeatedly emphasized that statistics alone do not provide enough information on which to analyze a book of business. Agency files, loss records, claim information, and information based on first-hand producer contact also need to be weighed before arriving at a decision to take corrective action.

The case studies that follow are designed to provide some insight into the process of analyzing statistical reports. From the facts reflected in the statistics, inferences can be drawn which should be supported by other data before they can be used as a basis for an underwriting decision.

The figures shown in the case studies in Exhibits 13-2, 13-3, and 13-4 are actual figures taken directly from computer printouts on three different producers in the same metropolitan area. The listings for "Total Agency" reflect the total of personal lines and commercial lines results for each producer.

Agency A is a profitable agency with emphasis on personal lines. Approximately 60 percent of this agency's (gross written premium)

Exhibit 13-3
AGENCY B—1981 Results

Line of Business	New Bus. Items	Gross Written Premium	Net Earned Premium	Net Loss Incurred	Loss Ratio
Standard Auto	0	$ 22,203	$ 27,542	$ 76,546	277.9%
Preferred Auto	0	18,556	20,380	4,341	21.3
Nonstandard Auto	0	721	1,949	4,309	221.0
Subtotal Auto	0	41,480	49,871	85,187	170.8
Homeowners	40	23,333	18,884	2,383	12.6
Fire, EC & Allied	0	1,589	1,889	50	2.7
Inland Marine	4	3,112	2,790	0	0
Ocean Marine	3	1,532	1,409	360	25.5
Umbrella	1	292	570	0	0
Total Personal Lines	48	71,338	75,413	87,980	116.7
Total Agency	192	$320,851	$227,473	$158,092	57.0%

volume is in personal lines, and twenty-six out of thirty-one policies sold in 1981 were personal lines policies.

None of the personal lines business has created obvious loss problems. Although the nonstandard auto loss ratio is 944.9 percent, that is based on an earned premium of only $353. It is likely that this agency has one nonstandard auto policy on the books, and that policy has had a loss.

The negative figure under liability and burglary reflects a policy that was canceled during the year, with $159 of premium returned.

Despite the fact that this producer has been profitable, there are some areas for concern. Almost all new business has been auto policies, with only two homeowners and one residential fire policy. It would appear that the agency is favoring another company with homeowners business, or is not account selling. Although homeowners business would appear highly profitable based on the loss ratio, there is really not enough homeowners volume to absorb even a moderate loss.

The lack of new business production and the low premium volume in marine and umbrella lines indicate that this producer is not account selling or upgrading existing accounts.

Corrective action would include an investigation to determine why the company is not receiving more homeowners business from this producer, and an attempt to develop more homeowners and other personal lines business.

Agency B has about the same personal lines (gross written premium) volume as Agency A, but the total agency volume is almost

Exhibit 13-4
AGENCY C—1981 Results

Line of Business	New Bus. Items	Gross Written Premium	Net Earned Premium	Net Loss Incurred	Loss Ratio
Standard Auto	6	$ 34,113	$ 41,713	$ 52,961	127.0%
Preferred Auto	5	92,754	109,905	158,739	144.4
Nonstandard Auto	0	763	1,198	−189	−15.8
Subtotal Auto	11	127,601	153,050	203,568	133.0
Homeowners	53	30,169	31,252	35,609	113.9
Fire, EC & Allied	27	6,105	5,192	3,758	72.4
Inland Marine	21	1,250	860	2,065	240.0
Liab. & Burglary	0	0	1	0	0
Total Personal Lines	112	165,125	190,355	245,000	128.7
Total Agency	134	$197,127	$221,984	$292,298	131.7%

three times as large. Personal lines play a much smaller role in Agency B than in Agency A.

Although the total agency loss ratio appears favorable, personal lines have been unprofitable, on the whole.

There is a striking contrast between Agency A's and Agency B's emphasis on new business production. While Agency A wrote almost entirely auto policies, Agency B has written no new auto policies. Instead, they have written forty new homeowners and some marine policies.

It was suggested that Agency A should increase its emphasis in lines other than auto insurance. Therefore, it might appear desirable to encourage Agency B to increase auto production. However, such a recommendation might be disastrous. Agency B's book of auto business has been unprofitable. Other lines of business have been profitable. A closer look at the figures indicates that noticeable efforts have been made to reduce auto volume while increasing volume in other lines. This can be noted from a comparison of written premiums and earned premiums for each line of business. The larger earned premium in auto lines indicates a shrinking premium volume. The larger written premium in other lines indicates an increasing volume.

In short, it appears that the producer or underwriter has already implemented a program to correct problems. If the program of corrective action is continued, and if auto renewals are reunderwritten carefully, the agency may be made profitable.

Agency C has more than twice the personal lines (gross written premium) volume of Agencies A and B. Obviously, this agency has some rather severe loss ratio problems. But before examining the losses, several other figures are of interest.

A low volume of new auto business has been produced in 1981, due to underwriting restrictions or agency reasons. The emphasis on homeowners and other lines may represent a shift in production emphasis, as the gross written premiums do not seem consistent with a past emphasis in these lines.

The number of new dwelling fire policies is noteworthy. It might be desirable to review the composition of this segment of Agency C's business to determine whether it is business rejected from the homeowners program. With only $5,192 of earned premium in that line it is difficult to judge for sure, but there are indications this line might be unprofitable in the long run.

The large number of inland marine policies is worthy of notice. It may indicate a good job of account selling, or it may indicate a concentration of undesirable exposures. Again, there are early indications that this line of business may cause problems.

The negative losses and negative loss ratio in the nonstandard auto line indicate a reserve take-down, or a case closed for less than the amount reserved. The $189 had been charged as an incurred loss in a previous accounting year.

On balance, Agency C requires close attention by the underwriter. Almost every line of business has been unprofitable. Although production emphasis has decreased in auto lines, the area with the greatest dollar losses, there are indications that the new business in other lines may be undesirable.

Before establishing a program of corrective action, more information would be necessary, but it appears a strong underwriting posture might be in order. After gaining insight from other sources, it might be necessary to reunderwrite all business on renewal and to set very high standards for all new business from this agency.

SUMMARY

Personal lines policyholders typically own a number of insurance policies. Although each policy may be handled by producers and underwriters as an isolated piece of business, there are many benefits to be derived from account selling and account underwriting. A producer who practices account selling can increase agency volume and do a more thorough job of servicing customers. An underwriter who treats insureds as accounts rather than policies has more information on which to draw, and is able to weigh more factors in arriving at an account underwriting decision. The personal package policies now offered by many insurers present a modern vehicle for account selling and account underwriting.

Although producers and underwriters share common goals, their points of view may differ due to their varying functions. Producer responsibilities include insurance sales, retaining existing accounts, providing policyholder service, and field underwriting.

While producers are field underwriters, underwriters are also marketing personnel. In addition to analyzing individual risks, underwriters must analyze the producers who produce the individual policies. In many organizations, responsibilities are shifting so that the bulk of the individual risk underwriting is done at the producer's level. Underwriters are then primarily responsible for monitoring producer results, with less effort spent analyzing individual applications. No matter how the responsibilities or functions are distributed, both producers and underwriters share the long-term goal of producing a good book of profitable business.

To effectively monitor producer effectiveness, a working relationship needs to be established. This is highly important when producer and underwriter first begin working together. Mutual goals and objectives must be agreed to, and underwriting policies and procedures should be made clear.

To determine whether goals and objectives have been met, the underwriter must periodically gather information, analyze the results, and take corrective action if necessary. This process must be repeated at appropriate intervals if desirable results are to be maintained.

Information is available from a variety of sources. Statistical print outs are a primary source. Each underwriter must be able to interpret the statistics provided to him or her. In addition to statistics, various agency files, claim reports, and other information must be analyzed. Much of the necessary information can be gained only by first-hand contact with the producer.

Some points to consider in analyzing agency results include the spread of business, the extent of new business activity, volume perpetuation, and loss experience.

Corrective action may take many forms, depending on the situation. Seldom are both production and profit so good that they cannot be improved. Of course, it does little good to identify goals for improvement unless such goals are communicated to the producer, and producer and underwriter work as a team to achieve the new goals.

Chapter Notes

1. J. J. Launie, J. Finley Lee, and Norman A. Baglini, *Principles of Property and Liability Underwriting,* 2nd ed. (Malvern, PA: Insurance Institute of America, 1977), p. 4. (This chapter builds on concepts discussed in Chapter 12 of *Principles of Property and Liability Underwriting.*)
2. Launie, Lee, and Baglini, Chapter 12.
3. George Nordhaus and Stephen Brown, *Marketing Property and Casualty Insurance* (Santa Monica, CA: Insurance Marketing Services, Inc., of California, 1976), p. 70.
4. Launie, Lee, and Baglini, p. 4.

Bibliography

AIPSO Insurance Facts 1980. New York: Automobile Insurance Plans Service Office, 1980.

Automobile Insurance... For Whose Benefit? New York Insurance Department, 1970.

Awad, Elias M. *Introduction to Computers on Business.* Englewood Cliffs, NJ: Prentice-Hall, Inc., 1977.

Brainard, Calvin H. *Automobile Insurance.* Homewood, IL: Richard D. Irwin, Inc., 1961.

California Insurance Code, Section 1852.

Economic Report of the President. Transmitted to Congress January 1981, Washington, DC.

F.C. & S. Bulletins, Management and Sales Section. Cincinnati, OH: The National Underwriter Company.

F.C. & S. Bulletins, Personal Lines Section, Dwellings. Cincinnati, OH: The National Underwriter Company, April 1978.

"Federal Crime Insurance." *F.C. & S. Bulletins,* Casualty and Surety Section, February 1973.

"Frederic Put Alabama Beach Plan to a Tough Test." *Best's Insurance Management Reports,* Property/Casualty. Oldwick, NJ: A.M. Best Company, 3 December 1979.

Gantt, Michael D. and Gatza, James. *Computers in Insurance.* Malvern, PA: American Institute for Property and Liability Underwriters, 1980.

Grezzo, Anthony D. *Condominiums* (2300-00202). Washington, DC: United States Government Printing Office, September 1972.

The Highway Loss Reduction Status Report, vol. 16, no. 7. Washington, DC: Insurance Institute for Highway Safety, 1980, 1981.

Holtom, Robert B. "Fire Insurance in Brush Areas." *CPCU Annals,* Spring 1963.

The Home-Association Handbook, Technical Bulletin 50. Washington, DC: Urban Land Institute, 1964.

Inland Marine Insurance 1976-1980. New York: Inland Marine Underwriter Association, December 1981.

"Insurance Copes with Catastrophe: The Xenia Tornado." *CPCU Annals,* June, 1976.

Insurance Facts, 1980-81 Edition. New York: Insurance Information Institute, 1981.

Introduction to IBM Data Processing Systems, Student Text, 4th ed. IBM Corporation.

"ISO to Introduce New HO Policies." *The National Underwriter,* Property & Casualty Insurance Edition, 5 March 1982.

Lathrop, James K., ed. *NFPA Life Safety Code Handbook,* 2nd ed. Quincy, MA: National Fire Protection Association, 1981.

Launie, J.J.; Lee, J. Finley; and Baglini, Norman A. *Principles of Property and Liability Underwriting,* 2nd ed. Malvern, PA: Insurance Institute of America, 1977.

Mehr, Robert I. and Cammack, Emerson. *Principles of Insurance,* 7th ed. Homewood, IL: Richard D. Irwin, Inc., 1980.

Meyer, Karl E. *The Pleasures of Archeology.* New York: Atheneum, 1970.

Miller, Norman A. *Condominiums and Insurance Property Loss Consideration, 1973.* Chicago: Property Loss Research Bureau, 1973.

More About Computers. IBM Corporation.

Niemann, Harry C., III. "The Automobile Residual Market: What Are The Facts?" *CPCU Annals,* June 1975.

Nordhaus, George and Brown, Stephen. *Marketing Property and Casualty Insurance.* Santa Monica, CA: Insurance Marketing Services, Inc., of California, 1976.

Personal Auto Manual. New York: Insurance Services Office, 1980.

Property/Liability Personal Lines Insurance: DB/DC Information Systems Design Concepts, 2nd ed. IBM Corporation, October 1974.

Public Attitude Monitor, 1980, Attitudes of the Public toward Automobile Insurance. All Industry Research Advisory Council, March 1981.

"Reinsurance Pool Funds Crime Losses." *The Journal of Commerce,* 2 March 1981.

Rule 8.A. *Commercial Lines Manual.* New York: Insurance Services Office, 1979.

Snyder, Richard G.; McDole, Thomas L.; Ladd, William M.; and Minahan, Daniel J. *An Overview of the On-Road Crash Experience of Utility Vehicles.* Ann Arbor, MI: The University of Michigan Highway Safety Research Institute, February 1980.

"Standard for the Installation, Maintenance and Use of Household Fire Warning Equipment." Publication NFPA 74, Life Safety Code. Boston: National Fire Protection Association, 1973.

"A Study of One- and Two-Family Dwelling Fires." Publication NFPA FR 75-1. Boston: National Fire Protection Association, 1975.

Summary of Selected State Laws and Regulations Relating to Automobile Insurance. New York: American Insurance Association, 1976.

"Switching on the Sun." *Journal of American Insurance,* Summer 1980.

Youd, James D. *A Practical Approach to Inland Marine Insurance.* Boston: The Standard Publishing Company, 1974.

Yourdon, Edward. *Techniques of Program Structure and Design.* Englewood Cliffs, NJ: Prentice-Hall, Inc., 1975.

Zellers, Duane D. "Regulation of Cancellations and Nonrenewals." *CPCU Annals,* June 1973.

Index

A

B

C

D

E

F

G

H

I

J

K

L

M

N

O

P

Q

R

S

T

U

V

W

Y

Z